QUILTWORKS
across
CANADA

Eleven
Contemporary Workshops

GAIL P. HUNT

Quiltworks Across Canada: Eleven Contemporary Workshops©
© 1996 by Gail P. Hunt

Pacific Quiltworks, Ltd.
4740 Mountain Highway
North Vancouver, British Columbia
V7K 2Z9 Canada

Canadian Cataloguing in Publication Data

Hunt, Gail P. (Gail Patricia), 1953-
  Quiltworks across Canada

  Includes index.
ISBN 0-9680423-0-9

  1. Quilting--Canada. 2. Quiltmakers--Canada. I. Title.
TT835.H86 1996   746.46   C96-910449-9

Some notes about this book:

With respect to imperial vs. metric weights and measures: In Canada, at the time of printing, quilters buy fabric by the metre, but use inches and fractions from olden days in all our measurements and sewing. All instructions reflect this inconsistency, and include conversions where appropriate. In the cases where "yardage" is quoted in metric, the bracketed amount refers to yards. References to distances may be in miles or kilometres (a kilometre is .62 of a mile).

When a term is *italicized*, it is either a foreign word, or its meaning is explained in the glossary at the back of the book.

Canadian Living Magazine has graciously granted the author permission to include Lois Wilby-Hooper's quilt photograph and workshop, both titled "*Canadian Seasons*".

Photography: Gail Hunt, except in cases where photo credits are noted with the photograph

Illustrations: Gail Hunt and Carol Galloway

Cover design: Kelly Brooks

Copy editor: Dona Sturmanis, The Word is Out

Design and layout: Vancouver Desktop Publishing Centre Ltd.

Printed in Hong Kong by Kings Time Industries, Ltd.

To my parents Dick and Ruth Hunt
who taught me the value of good organization and hard work.
Your unconditional love sustains me through all life's challenges.

ACKNOWLEDGEMENTS

To begin, I must begin at the beginning.

For help in locating "my" quilters for the book, I thank Beth Barrett-Bowles, Sherrie Davidson, Pam Godderis, Ann Bird, Agnes Ryckman, Deborrah Sherman, Linda Kallos, and Carol Pettigrew.

To the past and present boards of the *Canadian Quilters' Association/Association canadienne de la courtepointe*, thank you for your moral support of this project.

For **so very much** I appreciate the quilters featured in this book: Wendy, Laurrie, Susan, Carol, Win, Adaire, Lois, Janet, Iris, Sherry, Pat, Judy and Alice. To only scratch the surface, you agreed to participate in this project, to open up your private lives to my insistent scrutiny, to comply with all my niggling requests, perhaps to prepare a photo-ready workshop at a time when you were too busy, really, and to handle the consequences of my mistakes with grace and generosity. Not only all that, but you and your families welcomed up to seven warm bodies to your hearth and home, and made us feel like treasured friends. Thank you, quilters. Thank you, families of quilters.

Some quilting friends agreed to try out the instructional properties of the workshops. For this valuable assistance, I thank Annette Blair, Beverly Sayyari (many times), Marjory Potter, Renate Doerfert, Diane Hutchison, Monica Bennett, Joan Darker, Leila Robertson, and my first quilting teacher, Dolores Bell.

To the hundreds of quilters who completed survey forms, came to see slide shows about the project, and preordered the book: your encouragement has kept me positive and brought this project to fruition. Special thanks to the many guild program convenors who have invited me to speak about this passion.

A number of quilting guilds and individuals, as well as a foundation, generously gave me grants plus good wishes to help with this ambitious project. **From the bottom of my heart, I thank my own Fraser Valley Quilters' Guild in Surrey, British Columbia, The Textile Arts Guild of Richmond, British Columbia, Thelma Lloyd and Viola Bowdish of T.A.G.O.R., my parents Dick and Ruth Hunt of Maple Ridge, British Columbia, the Manitoba Prairie Quilters, Winnipeg, Manitoba, the Waterloo County Quilters Guild, Kitchener-Waterloo, Ontario, Grace Selvage of Buckhorn, Ontario, the Beaconsfield Quilters' Guild, Beaconsfield, Quebec — twice! (once in cahoots with Win Burry), and the Sheila Hugh MacKay Foundation Inc., of Rothesay, New Brunswick.** Your faith in me and in this project has sustained my spirit.

Dozens of people gave this neophyte free advice, which I truly appreciated. A few authors and publishers went out of your way to give me your valuable time and advice: Valerie Hearder, Larry Goldstein, Joyce Becker, Gord Mallory and Beverly Johnson. Thank you.

To my fearless editor, Dona Sturmanis, you deleted and slashed but left my self-concept intact. And to the world's most patient typesetter, Patty Osborne: you deserve to go do a novel now! Readers Sid Midtdal and Caroline Garby helped in the early stages, and Cindy Kuzma, Nancy Cameron Armstrong and Fay Potter found most of my typos (the remaining ones are my fault.)

Finally, I owe a huge debt of gratitude to my own dear family: to my children, Brendan Baker, Rafferty Baker, Liam Baker, and Tess Baker: who behaved yourselves for 22,604 kilometres, addressed and stuffed envelopes, and sometimes give me peace and quiet to write. To my partner, Doug Baker: **very large thanks** for supporting another of my im/com-pulsions, and with such good humour, too. Even though you aren't a quilter, you have lots of other good qualities to make up for it.

C O N T E N T S

INTRODUCTION: THE TRIP STORY

Ah, a romantic notion: Spend 24 hours a day for 69 days together with the whole family, including four kids and the golden retriever, driving across this broad country doing research for a book about Canadian quiltmakers. Whatever possessed me?

"Another one of Mom's schemes to keep us away from T.V.? Some idea that we might pick up some (argghh) education? A survival program to toughen us up?" No to all of the above. Simply a naive national pride, a belief that in the area of interest I'm passionate about (quilting), we have our fair share of heroines (mostly unsung). There are quiltmakers out there working quietly, expertly, diligently, making artistic statements for private or public benefit. I believe these Canadian quiltmakers deserve recognition, so I decided to write a book about a select few of them.

By asking quilters all across the country "Who is doing interesting work in your region?" I narrowed my choice to one quiltmaker from each province who was willing to participate in the project. It was no easy task confirming the willing or qualified quiltmakers. In several provinces, there was a great excess of excellent candidates (many of whom are featured in Appendix #8, *A Directory of Canadian Quilting Professionals*), so it was a real struggle to choose only one. In a couple of provinces, there appeared to be no quiltmaking teachers who worked in a contemporary style. One of my chosen quiltmakers had the audacity to move to another province and another of my favourites turned out to be an American, which disqualified both of them. These problems were eventually sorted out, however, and 11 quiltmakers were booked for photography sessions. (Also included is a First Nations representative, and the author. Then in 1996, just as the book was nearly going to press, I had the good fortune to visit Canada's two territories: The Northwest Territories and Yukon. Those lucky events allowed me to add another chapter on "Quilters From Canada's North" to complete the Canadian geographical picture).

Because my favourite kinds of quilt books to read are practical ones that teach me something, as well as having a human interest angle and a strong aesthetic component, I asked most of the featured quilters to produce a workshop to be photographed for the book. This book is designed to be beautiful to look at, as well as to be a practical how-to guide for a smorgasbord of contemporary quilting techniques. It is not designed to teach basic quiltmaking skills, as there are many excellent reference books for basic quiltmaking (see Appendix #4: *Sources*). Rather, it's about extras, some fun frills and explorations.

So, my homework done, I started dropping hints to my husband, Doug Baker, who doesn't like surprises. By the time I began writing letters to the prospective quiltmakers in January 1993, I pretty much had Doug convinced that it was his own idea to take out a new mortgage, ask his law practice partners for a leave of absence, and expose ourselves to the culture of Canada, to the high adventure of a road trip. I scheduled our summer visits and convinced the family that this would be something they would love to do. We bribed our children, Brendan, Rafferty, Liam and Tess (aged 13,10,7, and 5, respectively) with rash promises, to convince them that they were going to have a great time stuffed into a 48-square-foot space together all day and night. We promised them visits to the Hockey Hall of Fame in Toronto, to the Baseball Hall of Fame in Cooperstown, New York, to the Fortress at Louisberg on Cape Breton Island, Nova Scotia. We promised them money. And for our daughter, Tess, we promised we'd never let her out of our sight. She was the easiest and cheapest to bribe, by far.

British Columbia quilter **Wendy Lewington Coulter** agreed to be my first subject, so we could iron out the details in my system before we set out on our cross-Canada trip. Wendy makes striking appliqué quilts with human figures. These, combined with her social messages, drew me magnetically to her work in 1989. After a glorious morning taking portrait shots in West Vancouver's oceanside Lighthouse Park, I photographed her workshops "Drawing for the Terrified" and "Machine-Appliquéd Portrait."

By late June 1993, our trip preparations were complete, and Astrid the Astro van pulled Norman the Nomad trailer out from our homeside curb in North Vancouver, British Columbia. Over the Canadian Rockies we chugged, to Edmonton, Alberta, where we sagged into **Laurrie Sobie**'s driveway and turned her world upside down for a couple of days of frenzied photography, interviewing and touristing.

We proceeded across the golden prairie into Saskatchewan accompanied continually by the Canadian Broadcasting Corporation (CBC) public radio, which made us feel at home wherever we were. By the time we met up in Saskatoon with fibre artist **Susan Andrews Grace**, Doug was beginning to change his opinion about quiltmakers. He now finds them (and their families) to be interesting, intelligent people who can talk about many subjects besides quilts!

Susan's quilted works are the most unusual featured in the book, as she does mostly installation pieces for gallery exhibitions. We photographed her workshop on Shibori dyeing, an ancient Japanese form of controlled pattern dyeing.

Then we drove to Nepewa, Manitoba, where Doug discovered his own focus for being on this cross-country trip. He saw Canadian novelist Margaret Laurence's gravestone. For the rest of our journey, the staffs of local tourist information centres were sent into a frenzy to find famous peoples' graves in their towns.

We all had a super time visiting with Manitoba quilter **Carol Galloway** and her family in Winnipeg. Carol is exceptionally well-organized. She had her lengthy workshop all mapped out and samples prepared at different stages, plus dinners all cooked and in the freezer, **and** the house clean. (This is not normal behaviour for quilters, and she will undoubtedly have to undergo years of psychotherapy to improve her condition!)

After a three-day-long drive across Ontario to **Win Burry**'s summer home on the Muskoka Lakes, we were gratefully refreshed by swimming. Win is one of the finest quilters I have had the pleasure to meet. She only makes quilts for her family, at a rate of about one per year. She prefers not to teach workshops, however, so her chapter includes a discussion of her sources of inspiration — many of which come from nature and First Nations spirituality.

In the culturally-rich French-speaking province of Quebec, we met quiltmaker **Adaire Schlatter**. Her expert broad-based work has a refreshing contemporary look. An ardent gardener, Adaire especially shines with floral appliqué, and her workshop concentrates on this inventive technique, using real flowers as patterns.

We said *au revoir* to *la belle Québec*, and hello to fair New Brunswick, where we met **Lois Wilby-Hooper**. Lois's lovely scrap quilt and workshop, Canadian Seasons, was featured in *Canadian Living* magazine, and is the workshop in this book, as well.

Lois took me to the New Brunswick museum in Saint John. There I was totally enthralled to see the second oldest dated quilt in North America, made by Mary Morten in 1769, just one hour before it was to be removed to a new and inaccessible storage vault. I was impressed with the museum's quilt conservation practices: the white gloves, acid-free rolls, and temperature and humidity-controlled environment.

Then, stuffing ourselves into the van again for the relaxed trip to Prince Edward

INTRODUCTION: The Trip Story

Island, we visited the idyllic 120-acre farm of quilter **Iris Ethridge**, and couldn't drag ourselves away on the scheduled departure day. Iris's wall-hangings usually feature pure silk Prince Edward Island landscapes, or paper-pieced colour studies of traditional patterns presented in a jewel-like, contemporary way.

Our next destination was Nova Scotia, where our hosts were the gracious family of **Janet Pope**, who run a publishing shop downstairs in their residence. Janet's distinctive style of fibre art explores themes such as myths, legends, animals and music.

After the interesting Nova Scotia leg of our journey, we had a most entertaining six-hour ferry ride to Newfoundland to meet quilter **Sherry Bussey**. During the ride, our five-year-old Tess asked, out of the blue, "Do eagles bark?" It turned out she was concerned about meeting the Busseys' beagle. Both the dog and the family were anything but scary. We love Newfoundland, "the Rock," and felt at home because there are real hills, just like in our home province of British Columbia. Quilters will feel comfortable with Sherry's work because it has quite a traditional look to it. Her workshop helps machine-piecers to make accurate seams with minimal frustration.

This visit marked our trip's turnaround point. We asked Sherry to take a picture of my family, and I can clearly remember the ambivalent feelings, realizing we were beginning the return trip and would not be out this way for a long time. We got up in the middle of the night to catch the return ferry, and as we drove in that semi-darkness, we heard the good ol' CBC beginning its broadcast day with "O Canada." That poignant moment brought tears to my eyes. It re-emphasized the rightness of what we were doing. That turnaround marked the liberation of the true wishes of most of my family, too. If I thought they were having a great time already, it turned out to be only a drop in the bucket of ecstasy.

The trip transformed into a baseball trip! We made a detour to Cooperstown, New York, to see the Baseball Hall of Fame. The only quilting book I could find anywhere in Cooperstown was *Quilting*, by Canadian author Laurie Swim!

There was one more quilter to visit at this point, First Nations quilter **Alice Olsen Williams**, who lives in Ontario. We all enjoyed a short program of Native immersion with Alice and her family on beautiful Buckhorn Lake. Alice is devoted to honouring her Native traditions, and her quilts reflect this commitment. Even her workshop carries this message of pride, by using traditional beadwork designs to develop appliqué quilt patterns.

Without exception, each quiltmaker was an interesting person to visit. The photography/interview sessions went well (it would be an exaggeration to say they went flawlessly!). The weather co-operated with us every time we needed to photograph outside. But the purpose of the whole trip turned out to be much broader: brief immersions in diverse cultures, an education in geography, lessons in interpersonal coping skills, and, as it turned out, a chance for the whole family to live and breathe our other passion, baseball, for a while.

We saw a Montreal Expos home game, and then we heard that our very own Lynn Valley Little League baseball team from North Vancouver, British Columbia would be playing in the World Series in Williamsport, Pennsylvania. We *had* to make the detour to watch them play. The fact that we were only two and a half hours away from Intercourse, Pennsylvania, the heart of Amish quilt heaven, and I didn't even go there, just proves that the trip had become a baseball trip. On our homeward trip through Alberta, we toured the Spitz factory, where seasoned sunflower seeds (another baseball essential) are made.

By the time we crossed the Alberta/British Columbia border, however, we were getting anxious to return home. Someone on the CBC that day described our feeling perfectly by saying he was "luminous if not incandescent with gratitude." This is exactly how I felt when I got home and hugged my washer and dryer, then sank, exhausted but fulfilled into our big, wonderful, private bed.

Now that we're home again, we fondly recall those summer memories and realize how many intangible benefits we received. While transcribing the interview tapes and writing the book, I was lucky enough to relive each visit with the quiltmaker. After finishing the manuscript, I realized that my own work could also be included in the book. I added another chapter, with a workshop on blueprinting photos onto fabric, a technique I love to use in my own quiltmaking. Then, in early 1996, I was invited to teach in Yellowknife, Northwest Territories and Whitehorse, Yukon. In both places I discovered some exciting, innovative quilters who agreed to be part of the book, too. By this stroke of luck, I am able to introduce you to the work of **Pat White**, who lives in Haines Junction, Yukon Territory, and **Judy Farrow**, who lives in Yellowknife, as well as a taste of the work of some other northern quiltmakers.

Our once-in-a-lifetime journey across Canada strengthened my conviction that contemporary Canadian quilters offer a distinctive flavour in the pastiche of international fibre arts. As Canadian artists in all fields — from painting to writing to music — are making their mark globally, so are our quilters. Their work is commissioned and exhibited internationally, and they are being asked to teach workshops in many parts of the world.

So how can we characterize the Canadian style of contemporary quilting? The themes of persistence in the face of adversity, a dedication to family, the natural environment, strong social issues, and spiritual questing come to mind — this last theme strengthened by Native influences. There is also a strong commitment among contemporary Canadian quilt artists to master and explore unusual and innovative technical methods.

We should be proud of our unique artists and our country. Through the compilation of this book, I have been granted the gift of that remarkable insight. As you read *Quiltworks Across Canada: Eleven Contemporary Workshops*, I hope you, too, will sense the wonder of this beautiful, unspoiled country, will come to appreciate the quiltmakers and their quiltart, and will feel as though you are in the front row seat in their classrooms.

QUILTWORKS ACROSS CANADA

CHAPTER I

Gail Hunt

QUILTER & AUTHOR

With Workshop: Blueprinting Photos Onto Fabric

*"My subject matter is often family
or family history, because that is
what I know and care about."*

I think I have always been a quiltmaker, just waiting for a time to happen. As a young child I often involved myself with needle, thread and fabric. On the eve of my eighth birthday I tucked my embroidery under my pillow, then knelt on the bed to turn off the reading light. Half the embroidery needle inserted itself into my shin and the other half broke off, necessitating a trip to the hospital and three stitches. A few years later, in a poem written to me by a friend, I was characterized as a "fireside knitter" who would rather stitch than party. Is there a difference?

I chose Home Economics as my major at University. Perhaps I thought I would be able to design and sew for four years straight. "The Philosophy of Home Economics 450" and "Organizational Behaviour 221" were tolerated so that I could take "Textile Design 322," "Housing Design 420," and "Visual Arts 471."

Eventually I settled into becoming a high school teacher of home economics, science and photography. With very little idea of what I was doing, I even taught a quilting course during those years.

My appreciation of traditionally-made quilts was sharpened by the work of Ruby Adams, a Nova Scotian who made our family a total of four quilts in the traditional *Log Cabin* pattern. Her achingly tiny hand-quilting stitches on those quilts serve as a model for me still.

But it was not until 1988, when expecting my fourth child, that I was completely transformed into a quiltmaker. As it is with many other quilters, my conversion took place during an introductory sampler quilt course. Dolores Bell, the teacher, could not have known then that her gentle guidance would lead to my mega-compulsion and to increasingly crowded shelves of unfinished knitting, weaving and cross-stitch projects. She could not have known that I would never again sew on a button or make my children's clothes.

The following year, at a quilt exhibit at the Vancouver Museum, I came face-to-fabric with the other major influence on my quilting path. There I saw three quilts

Nancy Gobeil

made by British Columbia's Wendy Lewington Coulter which made my tears flow. The compelling images, unusual fabric and subtle messages drew me so far in that I could not erase them from my thoughts. My curiosity about the person who made them would not be assuaged until I met her. A few months later I did meet and even got to work with Wendy when she agreed to let me quilt a piece for an upcoming exhibit. Our sporadic communications continue to spur on my creativity.

Gail Hunt, Quilter & Author

Sometimes I feel that "real art," the good stuff, arises from an experience of pain. The pain might be a societal injustice, an emotionally wrenching family situation, or a life trauma. An artist must have something to say in order for people to listen. However, I believe that the artistic message can reflect contentment. In my case, for example, my upbringing in a safe, trusting environment, the luck of being born with the ability to achieve whatever I wanted, the good fortune to meet a mate with whom compatability grows each successive year, and the happenstance of having four healthy and competent children: all these lucky events conspire to make me content. I like to think it shows in my work.

Since my art does not speak in anger, and since I have the perspective to see that my troubles are insignificant in the broader context, I generally create highly personal quilts reflecting the contentment and safety which are emotionally satisfying to me. The subject matter is often family or family history because that is what I know and care about.

I work best to a deadline, and will squeeze the needed time out of my life if I'm faced with a quilt challenge, a quilt show deadline, a birthday or anniversary, a publication date, or a teaching engagement.

Into those busy family years since taking my first quilting course, I have sandwiched thousands of hours of quilt-related activities: taking classes and workshops, reading, experimentation, and making quilts. Since 1989, I have been an instructor of quilt-making for adults and children. Currently, I teach, lecture and judge throughout Canada and in the United States.

The compulsion to share my love of the craft has led to numerous volunteering opportunities as well. I was newsletter editor, then chairperson of our local Lions' Gate Quilters' Guild. A two-year stint as workshop convenor for the 440-member Fraser Valley Quilters' Guild coincided with a similar job convening workshops for the Canadian Quilters' Association/*Association canadienne de la courtepointe* biennial conference, called *Quilt Canada '96*. And during some of those years, I have been writing and editing for the *CQA/ACC Newsletter's "Teachers' Pages."*

All this volunteering and teaching does not leave much time for the actual sewing of quilts. My goal is to make at least one *real* quilt a year. I define a *real* quilt not by the standard definition: "three layers joined together with stitching," but rather by its importance in my life. If the quilt is calling out to me to be made, if it is for someone I love, or has significant meaning for me, and if I need to spend countless hours making it, then it is a *real* quilt!

In recent years, many of my *real* quilts have won awards in national and international juried shows. I like to enter them as a way of enhancing my own education, and I rely on the judges to provide some feedback. One valuable lesson I have learned from the process of entering shows is that every juror or jurying committee has different tastes. A quilter should not assume his or her work is inferior just because it has not been juried into a show or won an award. Two of my quilts, juried out of national shows, have subsequently won other important awards.

As I continue to gain insights into the broad world of quilting, my professional goals are to play a significant part in increasing the level of quilt education available to quilters, quilt teachers and judges. I want to design more quilts and write more articles and books. And I especially want to leave a significant body of quilted work for my children.

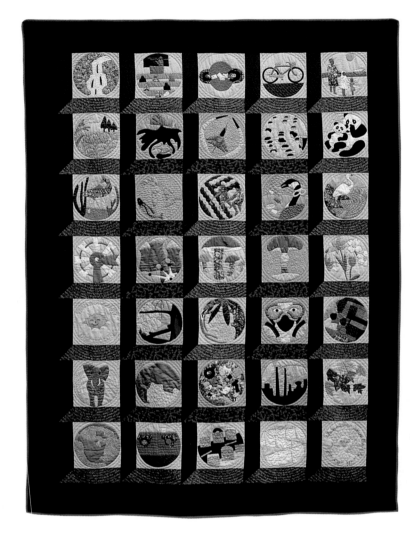

Whatever Man Sows, That He Will Also Reap (96"x72"), 1990

For many years, I was a peace activist. I was driven by fear for my children's future, and even questioned whether it was right for us to have children. Intimately tied to my philosophy of peace is my concern for the environment.

The idea for this quilt grabbed me and would not let go until I did something about it. The design starts from the centre and radiates to the perimeter, to parallel the way our attitudes need to start with the centre of our universe and expand to more global proportions.

In the centre, three green blocks depict the earth in its natural state: "Agrarian Africa," "Mushrooms," and "Quetzal in the Rain Forest." Surrounding the centre blocks are images of the earth, dead and dying and human activities that have facilitated this process. Some of the images juxtapose with nearby blocks; others stand independently. The red window frame suggests "danger, stop, fire, alarm, blood."

The outside blocks show images from a thriving earth: the Gorbachev/Bush summit meeting of November, 1989, alternate forms of energy and transportation, and protest and preservation.

In the black border, hourglasses are quilted in red to suggest we stop the destruction, and in green to suggest the greening of the sands of time. This piece is meant to be a hopeful statement, a promise to our children.

After 500 hours of work on this quilt, the last stitch (in red on one of the green hourglasses) was taken on our 15th wedding anniversary. I told my husband, Doug, that he could take the last stitch — it would symbolize his major contribution of tolerance and extra help on the domestic front — it would be a last stitch effort!

Whatever Man Sows, That He Will Also Reap (detail)

Gail Hunt, Quilter & Author

Family Album Quilt (56"x44"), 1991

During a Lions' Gate Quilters' Guild retreat, I followed the design format suggested in the book, One-of-a-Kind Quilts by Judy Hopkins. My theme blocks were laser-transferred photos of family, arranged in rough chronological order. When I was young, people suggested I looked like my paternal grandmother Florence, who was about seven years old in the uppermost photo. Although I did not know her well, I feel we are soulmates, and hope that I inherited some of her characteristics.

Family Album Quilt, back detail

Since being blessed with children, I've researched family history. The "family tree" is appliquéd onto the back; each leaf contains details about our family/ancestors.

Wishes (65"x78"), 1991

When my friend, the late Ruth McNiece, brought a little stitchery piece she had found to a guild meeting, I found the inspiration for my next piece. The stitchery piece depicted a young woman looking out from a window. Her hand pushed back the three-dimensional curtains, and ivy covered the wall outside her window.

I worked, one section at a time, on the house of my dreams, a bed and breakfast establishment I would love to have one day. From the windows, the members of our family look out. Behind each person are represented his/her current interests and future dreams. In my favourite season, fall, nasturtiums (without black aphids!) climb up the picket fence.

Wishes (detail)

I posed each person/dog the way I wanted them to appear in the piece, photographed them with slide film, then replicated the images in fabric and embroidery. Here, our son Brendan is depicted playing baseball, a major interest of his. In the background: a soccer ball, his viola, books, a baseball poster, a quilt, and a drafting table, which represented his interests and wishes at the time.

The wishes of the two youngest children, Tess and Liam, had to be guessed at, as they tended to copy their elder brothers, Rafferty and Brendan.

Gail Hunt, Quilter & Author

Waiting Panes (58"x50"), 1992

A former North American quilting contest, the "Labor of Love," spurred me on to do my first Christmas quilt. Here, Tess and Liam peer out the window in rapt anticipation. Santa and the reindeer are quilted with black thread in the night sky.

Waiting Panes (detail)

Judicial Gardens (each one 31"x25"), 1994

These pieces, made for the waiting room of my husband's law office, are loosely based on the colourwash explorations of English colourwash pioneer Deirdre Amsden.

A Quartet of Challenge Pieces

The creative stimulation of quiltmaking challenges, or contests based on a set of rules, fabrics or themes, always get me motivated to try something new. These four pieces were the results of challenges, each described below:

Some Summer (30" diameter), 1993

A challenge by the Lions' Gate Quilters' Guild was to use at least four of the five fabrics they provided, with an option of two more of my choice, and a theme of Indian Summer. My personal challenge was to machine-sew the fabrics so they looked like a woven straw hat. I discovered the weaving pattern in the tiles of a bathroom in Montreal.

Gail Hunt, Quilter & Author

Eagle Count: 3701 (24"x24"), 1994
Collection of Kathleen Bissett

For the past several years, the Canadian Quilters' Association/Association canadienne de la courtepointe (CQA/ACC) has issued a challenge to its members: Using at least four of the five fabrics provided and adding up to two of your own choice, make a 96" perimeter wall hanging, which will then be donated to the association and sold in a fund-raising auction. For the first time, I was not too late to get one of the challenge kits which contains the fabric and rules required. When I saw the blue/pink fabric provided, it reminded me of spawning salmon, so I thought about doing a salmon piece. When I heard that the highest ever count of bald eagles occurred on the Squamish River, because of the availability of their chum salmon feed, I knew what my quilt would be about. My personal challenge was to machine-piece all the eagles and salmon, rather than appliqué them, which is what I really prefer to do.

Happa Doo Doo (16"x26"), 1990
Collection of Dolores Bell

When B.C.'s Fraser Valley Quilters' Guild (FVQG) challenged its members to use only black and white fabric, with less than ten per cent of one other colour, piano keys and music seemed to be a happy, although predictable, choice. The musical staff is pieced, with the black lines being less than 1/16" wide. It was truly a challenge to beat those magically migrating black threads: they love to settle under the bright white fabric and make themselves known. This piece was named by our daughter Tess, two years old at the time, who couldn't say "Happy Birthday to you" yet.

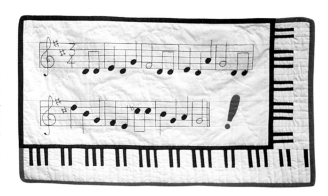

Fantasy Forest (33"x33" irregular), 1992
Collection of Anne Bodkin

Another FVQG challenge: This time we were to use a specific piece of fabric (in the centre of the hexagons) and at least five other fabrics. My personal challenge was to show the richness of the fan theme and to incorporate some textural fabric. The fan's skeleton is made from six lengths of wooden molding painted with gold model paint, then bolted together at the ends, and inserted into narrow channels sewn into the quilt.

A Piece on Canada (detail)

A Piece on Canada (52"x55"), 1993

After experimenting with photo-transfer *techniques for a couple of years, I became absorbed in the* cyanoprint/blueprint/sun-print *process, I revelled in what could be done with dyeing, painting, and parts of images, and I loved the way the resulting fabric handled (just like the original cotton). I am a fierce nationalist, so I made this* "Generation to Generation" *contest entry about Canada, using sunprinted images. The provinces and territories are interdependent yet distinct, just like the puzzle pieces. Since my family roots are based in Alberta, the triangular prairie points* frame the work.

Golden Marriage (56.5"x56.5"), 1994
Collection of Dick and Ruth Hunt

For my parents' 50th wedding anniversary, I used a variety of photo-transfer techniques to preserve memories from their life together. Quilted with hand-dyed gold quilting thread, the border has oak leaves and acorns to symbolize the strength and longevity of their marriage. Oak is Dad's favourite wood to work with, and fall is Mom's favourite season.

Within the border corner rings are quilted quotes about marriage, mistletoe (which symbolizes regeneration), and a note from each of Mom and Dad's four children with good wishes and memories about the marriage.

Golden Marriage (detail)

Blueprinting Photos onto Fabric

Level of Difficulty: All levels

O f all the methods of photo-transfer I've used and taught, the very old process of blueprinting (also called sunprinting or cyanoprinting) is the one which provides me with the most fun. With it I have been able to explore several options for my quilts. Its greatest appeal is that it feels like the original cotton when the photo-transfer is complete.

In this workshop I describe the basic technique. If you want to explore further, information is provided on some other options to try with blueprinting. For information on other types of phototransfer and suggestions for memory-quilt patterns, there are some excellent reference books listed at chapter's end.

M A T E R I A L S

■ **Rubber gloves**

■ **Fabric which has photosensitive chemicals applied to it**. By far the easiest way to acquire this is to order it from Blueprints-Printables (see Appendix #4: *Sources*). You may order their 56" wide sheeting a yard or more at a time, in white, turquoise or fuschia, or in precut squares, or they will treat fabric that you send to them, in your choice of colour/weight.

Another option, if you have access to a sunless room where you can stretch and treat the fabric, then let it dry before placing it in a lightproof bag, is to buy the necessary chemicals from a chemical supply house (see Appendix #4: *Sources*). This option is messy and unless you plan to do huge amounts of cyanoprinting, it is not even much cheaper. However, if you still wish to treat the

fabric yourself, see the directions in Appendix #7: *Chemically Sensitizing Fabric for Sunprinting*.

■ **A device to hold your negative firmly against the sensitized fabric** while it is being exposed to the sun. This could consist of a stiff plastic or

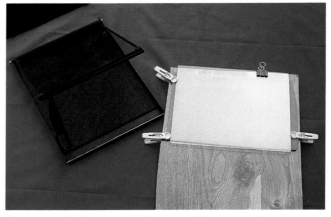

Photographer's contact printer and home-made version.

plywood base, some thin foam or layers of fabric, a piece of picture-frame glass, and some fold-back paper clips or clothespins. Or if you want to invest in the deluxe model, a photographer's contact printer, available in various sizes, makes the job a snap.

SUN! UV light is the only kind that can develop the print. If sun is not available just when you need it, a sunlamp is a distant second best. Sunlamps may be lurking in someone's attic or at a garage sale, but they are no longer considered safe for tanning, so are very difficult to find. You can still buy a UV lamp, but they are expensive and not as strong a UV source. The real, bright sun of midday is best, but you might discover interesting results by experimenting with different intensities of UV light.

A black and white negative of your photo(s), the same size as you want your sunprint to be. There are four options which work well:

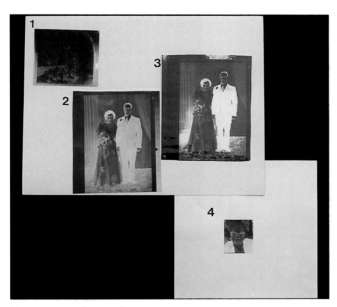

Four types of negatives.

1) You may already have **old negatives** large enough to see details (the example is 3"x3") .

2) You can take your original photo to a printing shop which does **half-tone negatives**. These are the same kind used by newspapers and magazines for printing photos and are basically a series of dots, denser in the

negative's dark areas, and sparser in the light areas. Ask for an **85 line screen**, which refers to 85 dots per inch. This will give you enough detail in the sunprint. This process usually takes a day or two for the half-tone negative to be ready.

3) A negative photocopy on transparent acetate. This is quicker and cheaper (about ¹/₃ the cost) than a half-tone negative, and the resulting sunprints are different, but equally acceptable. (See photo below. It also shows the results from layering a half-tone over a negative photocopy.) Ask for a dense emulsion (i.e. dark photocopy).

HALFTONE   PHOTOCOPY   BOTH

Compare results of different types of negatives.

If your original photo lacks contrast, you can ask to have the contrast increased. All Canon Color Laser Copiers are able to make these negative photocopies on acetate. The colour copiers can make either 8.5"x11" or 11"x17" size negatives.

HINT: Several photographs can be "ganged up" on an 8.5"x11" or 11"x17" sheet.

Gang up your photos to make the negative.

4) If you have access to a **photo scanner** connected to your computer you can produce a negative image, in the size you need, which can be printed out and then photocopied or printed directly on to a transparent sheet of acetate.

> **HINT: All negatives should be protected from scratches with a sheet of plain paper placed against the emulsion side. Negatives can be re-used as often as you wish.**

(**NOTE**: Your sunprint will only be as good as the negative you have. If there is very little contrast (i.e. lots of middle-tone greys but no blacks or whites) in the original photo, your negative, even with technical improvement, may lack contrast. You can sometimes lay a piece of clear acetate over the negative and "colour in" black with a permanent pen to make light areas whiter on the sunprint. If you are careful, you can even scratch some of the emulsion off to make the dark areas darker on the sunprint.)

T H E   S U N P R I N T

1 To determine the exposure time, make a test strip. Away from direct or reflected UV light, remove the sensitized fabric from the lightproof bag and cut a 2"x 6" strip from it before returning it to the bag. Your fabric will be some shade of green or brown, depending on the colour of the original fabric.

2 Place the test strip onto the contact printer base, and cover it with the negative (or as in the

2. Prepare to make a test strip.

sample, with an opaque object), emulsion-side down (in other words, the way you want the final image to appear so that it is not mirror-imaged). Place the glass on top of it all, and secure it so that the negative cannot move around during exposure.

3 Place a piece of paper or cereal box cardboard over ¾ of the test strip to block the sun, then take the whole unit outside to expose it. Orient the contact printer so it's at a 90 degree angle to the sun, and expose the fabric for 2 minutes. Then move the cardboard slightly so it covers half of the strip, and expose for 2 more minutes. Move the cardboard so it's only covering the last quarter of the test strip and expose for 2 more minutes. Finally, remove the cardboard entirely and expose the whole test strip for 4 more minutes. Take the contact printer inside.

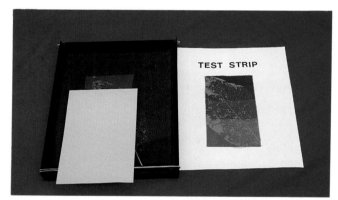

3. Place cardboard to block the sun.

4 Wearing rubber gloves, take the fabric test strip out of the contact printer, and rinse it under running water until no more yellow/green rinses off. Lay it flat to dry, or if you wish, it may be ironed dry on a special ironing pad or piece of cotton that you use only for that purpose. **From the dry test strip, you will be able to see what 4, 6, 8, and 10 minutes of exposure look like and choose an appropriate exposure time for your particular negative and design needs.** (**NOTE**: If you are using a sun lamp, place it about 18" away from the contact printer, start your exposure at 20 minutes, and change the increments to 5 minutes each. You will need to move the contact printer around under the sun lamp to avoid "hot spots" which expose unevenly.)

5 Now that you have determined the best exposure time, you are ready to **sunprint your whole photo.** Cut or rip a piece of sensitized fabric which is about ¹/₂" bigger all around than your negative. The fabric may be ironed flat, as long as you use a **dry iron** (no steam). **Make sure there are no loose threads or bits of fluff on the surface of the fabric.** Place the negative over the fabric and secure the contact printer as before. Expose the fabric to the sun for the required amount of time. You will notice the fabric changes from the green to a grey-blue to a blue-green during exposure. Rinse off the chemicals as before and observe the magic of sunprinting!

COLOUR CHANGE

5. Expose the fabric to the sun.

Your blueprints may eventually be washed if necessary, in a very low concentration of mild detergent, as long as it contains **no phospates**.

Those are the basics. Now for the frills, here are some supplemental techniques you may wish to try.

Changing the blueprint to a sepia-coloured print

If you are using old photos in a quilt, you may wish to give them an aged, yellowed look. This can be achieved by another bit of magic, and works best on fabrics that were tan-coloured or yellowed before being treated with sensitizing chemicals.

You will need:

1 tablespoon **phosphate** detergent dissolved in 2 cups lukewarm water in a plastic container

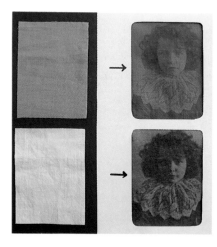

Depending on the result desired for your sepia-toned photo, your original fabric could be warm-toned or white.

Strong black tea made from 2 tea bags steeped in 2 cups boiling water for 5 minutes. Remove the tea bags, and pour the tea into another plastic container.

To do:

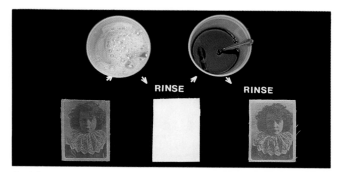

Swish the blueprint around in the phosphate, rinse, then swish in tea.

1 Swish the blueprint around in the phosphate detergent until the image disappears. (Yikes! Don't panic.)

2 Rinse the fabric thoroughly in running water. It's important to remove all traces of detergent.

3 Swish the fabric around in the tea until the image comes back! The longer you swish it around, the darker the tea stain becomes.

4 Rinse very thoroughly, to remove as much of the acid from the tea as possible. Acid causes future deterioration of the fabric.

Using other opaque objects to block the sun

Any opaque or translucent object placed on the sensitized fabric will block the sun. Beautiful shadowy leaves, seeds, or lace can impart a planned or accidental, yet pleasant effect. Where the object touches the fabric, the block to the sun's light will be complete, and the print will be white (or whatever colour the original fabric was), but if the object is not flat, the light will be reflected around the object to produce a partial or shadowy image. Try purchased 'confetti,' keys to your first car, pasta or plastic letters, handwritten notes on a transparency or a child's drawing photocopied onto a transparency, stick-on shapes, laser-cut stencils, onion bag netting, an oval frame made from cardboard, a typed message or wedding invitation photocopied onto a transparency, or . . . , or . . .

Any opaque object placed on the fabric will block the sun.

Adding colour to blueprints

Sometimes you don't want blue or sepia in your quilt, or you want a variety of colours. The transparent fabric dyes on the market, like Deka™ and Setacolor™ Transparent, can be successfully sponged or painted onto the blueprints or sepia prints, resulting in a variety of colours (e.g. blueprint + yellow = green). See *A Piece on Canada* in this chapter's quilt gallery.

When I wanted green cedar branches for a project, I dyed a blueprint green with Procion™ Fibre Reactive dye (see Chapter 4 for more information about dyeing). The result was a disaster; I could see no evi-

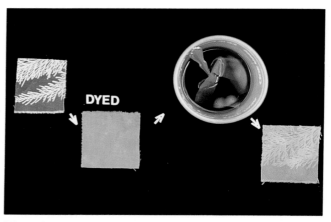

Blueprinted photos which have been dyed were restored with tea.

dence of the cedar branches. Then, since I had nothing to lose by further experimentation, I dipped it into tea, and sure enough, the image came back, just as it does with sepia tinting. A chemist would tell me that the soda ash used in the dyeing process removed the colour because it is the same composition as the phosphate detergent used in the sepia process.

There are other products on the market for sunprinting in different colours, such as Kwik Print™ (see Appendix #4: *Sources*) which produces tone-on-tone in many mixable hues.

Products which are suitable for "shadow prints" of opaque objects are Deka Silk™ and Setacolor™ Transparent, available in craft shops and graphic supply stores. To use these *heliographic* or sun-reactive dyes, the full-strength or diluted colour is applied with a sponge or brush to the fabric, which is then placed out in the sun on a calm day. Feathers, flowers, foliage, etc. are placed on top of the wet fabric while it dries. Those areas blocked by the opaque objects remain lighter in colour than the surrounding areas. Because the air must be able to circulate while the fabric dries, this method is not suitable for photographs, which require that the negatives be pressed firmly against the fabric.

Making labels for your quilts

Most quiltmakers now know the importance of documenting and labelling their quilts so that future generations will value them and understand their history. A sewn-on label with the relevant information about the quilt's history and its maker might include a photo of yourself. See Appendix #3: *Documentation, Care and Conservation of Quilts* for more suggestions about quilt labelling.

A FINAL NOTE : Once you have worked on the basics, consider using multiple images — or cutting up your sunprinted fabric to explore other pattern possibilities — or cutting up your negatives — or superimposing negatives together. You need not think of sunprinting only as a simple photo-transfer process. With it you could design your own fabric, or use it as inspiration for a quilt design. I wish you the joy I have experienced with sunprinting.

R E F E R E N C E S

Laury, Jean Ray. *Imagery on Fabric*. Lafayette, CA: C&T Publishing, 1992. ISBN 0-914881-56-6

Ritter, Vivian Howell. *Family Keepsake Quilts*. Wheatridge, CO: Leman Publications Inc., 1991. ISBN 0-943721-08-3

CHAPTER 2

Wendy Lewington Coulter

BRITISH COLUMBIA

With Workshop: Drawing for the Terrified and Machine Appliquéd Portrait

"I see the quilt as a metaphor for the creative resourcefulness necessary to survive as a woman in a patriarchal system. In quiltmaking, as in our lives, we are piecing together fragments and remnants in an attempt to form an integrated whole."

Her life's passion is exuded in her quilts. Her designs, formed with tiny perfect stitches, evolve into metaphors exploring human contradictions. Says Wendy Lewington Coulter: "I'm intimately connected with my quilts, and through them I examine issues of personal importance to me.

She says, "We must learn to trust our feelings and our instincts, and be willing to take risks for what we believe. My art is instrumental in this process. It's a place for me to have a conversation with myself, to notice what I am feeling, to process information, to organize, and to put some kind of order to chaos. I hope my quilts reflect some good thinking. They are my contribution to my world."

Only a heart of ice would not be warmed by the evocatively traditional designs used in many of Wendy's quilts. Only a heart of ice would be immune to the charm of fabric and thread that has been worked all over by expert hands. Only a heart of ice would not be moved by the compassion and love for all living things evident in her images. And only a heart of ice would not be further chilled by the messages of human suffering, of inequality, of environmental disaster, of technological power that are juxtaposed with the beauty of her quilts.

In a life fueled by the demands of family and by the confusion of circumstances, Wendy finds refuge and order in her quiltmaking. She and her partner Gary, a carpenter, are building a new home in rural Mission, British Columbia. For nearly a year they lived in two crowded holiday trailers with their family: school-aged daughters Anna and Claire, pre-schooler Nicola, and Gordon, a special needs adult.

Amid the pine and arbutus trees of coastal Lighthouse Park, in West Vancouver, Wendy feels at home.

18   *Wendy Lewington Coulter, British Columbia*

Magnificent first growth forests still occupy an estimated 60% of British Columbia's surface. With a high average annual coastal rainfall of 120 centimeters, it's an ideal environment for fast-growing vegetation.

Whenever she can, Wendy focuses on her creative work. For a mother, that opportunity usually arises in five-minute bites of time. But, says Wendy, "If I'm going around with idle hands, I could be quilting. I do hand-work while the children play." Now that she's back in an in-home studio, Wendy has resumed the regular quiltmaking routines that she established before the home-building project began. One day per week, she places Nicola into day-care while she focuses on some of the aspects of quiltmaking which require her full concentration.

"Until my third child was born, I quilted in every available scrap of time. I stayed up late, I got up early. When Nicola came along, I was just too tired. So that work day each week is very important to me. The kids have learned to respect my work."

Wendy is often invited to teach, lecture, create commissions, and exhibit. She has accepted these interruptions to her own quiltmaking with grace, because she identifies them as means to her professional goal: "being able to earn a living at what I love to do and feel good about my working life."

Wendy was born in British Columbia, a province she calls "one of the most stunningly beautiful places on earth." From the dramatically rugged western coastline, through the mountains, hills, lakes, forests and even desert in the interior,

Meares Island, looking northeast from Tofino. For the world, her country, and herself, Wendy hopes for "an awakening to the delicacy and splendor of nature, a true respect for the earth." Much of her art reflects this awareness.

Catherine Crouch

to the jagged Rocky Mountains on the eastern border, B.C. has much wilderness to explore. Perhaps because of this inspiring geography, combined with a mild climate, B.C. boasts many writers, visual and performing artists, and retired people. As a result, the culture is rich with variety, and the atmosphere is wholesome and relaxed.

While growing up, Wendy's interest in sewing was strongly influenced and encouraged by her mother who was a model of thrift, resourcefulness, and creativity for her daughters. Later, at Vancouver's Langara College, Wendy took a fabric arts course while working on her fine arts diploma. One of her classmates was well-known fibre artist Jeannie Kamins, who turned out to be an inspirational role model for Wendy.

In 1983, Wendy was inspired to make her first quilt for an art exhibition called "Active Vision: The Art of Living in the Nuclear Age." Wendy insists, "I did not intend to become a quiltmaker, but as I looked at historical examples of quilts during that project, I became very excited. My next idea for a piece was in the form of a quilt. Thirteen years later, I'm still making quilts!"

Based on her ever-expanding experiences in the art world, Wendy offers some advice for fabric artists: "Keep a journal/sketchbook and claim a space for your work. If you want to promote your work professionally, obtain good photos. Find and keep in touch with people who support and encourage what you do. Be proud of your work and make it a priority."

No Wife of Mine is Gonna Work (47"x35"), 1985

After having worked in the paid labour force full time for a number of years, Wendy says she was unprepared for the long and demanding hours of full-time housework and childcare. "Even less was I prepared for how this important work is discounted and undervalued by our society," she says. "The irony of the old cliché 'No wife of mine is gonna work' struck me with new force! I chose these words as a title for this piece to juxtapose against the images of working hands. While pointing to the cultural devaluation of women's labour, I also wished to portray the hands in a beautiful way which might serve to commemorate their invisible and relentless work."

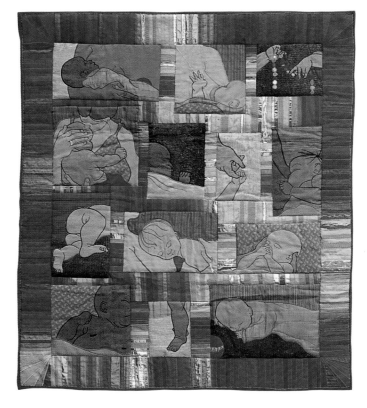

Baby Blanket (51"x45"), 1987

Wendy made this quilt while pregnant with her second daughter, Claire. "I wanted to create a piece which would interest a newborn baby. So instead of the usual pastels chosen for baby quilts, I chose intense, vibrant colours, and images of babies."

Wendy Lewington Coulter, British Columbia

Home Sweet Home (61"x72"), 1989 (below)

A variation of the traditional School House *quilt block pattern, the avenues between the rows of homey calico and plaid houses are dimly stamped in fabric ink with statistics on domestic violence:*

"One out of ten women in Canada is battered."
"Marital rape may afflict one in eight wives or more."
"40% of abuse begins during her first pregnancy."
"70% of wife battery occurs between 5 pm and 7 pm."
"90% of abusers have no criminal record."

(statistics are from "Wife Battering in Canada," published by the Canadian Advisory Council on the Status of Women.)

Home Sweet Home (detail)

This apparently safe, warm, and visually comforting quilt changes when the viewer becomes aware that it contains disturbing information. "By setting up these contradictions, I am attempting to create a tension which imitates the paradoxical reality of the problem of domestic violence," says Wendy.

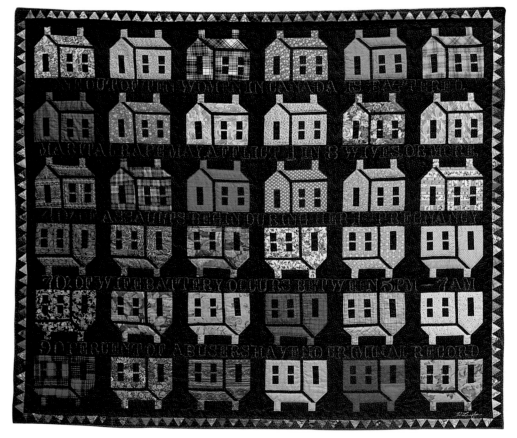

Wendy Lewington Coulter, British Columbia

Teacup Aunties (61"x48"), 1989

This quilt is a portrait of Wendy's great aunts, Rosa and Elsie. "In my family, we had a tradition that, yearly, from a girl's 13th birthday until her 21st birthday, she would receive a teacup and saucer from the collections of the older women in the family," says Wendy. "As neither aunt had daughters, I received many of their cups. In the quilt, I placed the aunts to make them appear to be floating in space, but also stepping onto the solid border. This symbolically represents the way my perspective changed on these women as I grew older. The broken and fragmented teacups flying in space symbolize the breaking of social conventions or rules which categorize and confine us according to age and gender."

A Piece of the Pie (70"x58"), 1990

Wendy's own design of a slice of pie in a repeated block format has colour-photocopied 'fillings' which represent aspects of our threatened environment. "These natural images are placed in a rigid, sliced-up way to show how humans have viewed the earth as a consumable commodity to be exploited at random, rather than as an interdependant whole to be cared for at all costs. I chose the pie image for its obvious relationship to the expression, 'Get your piece of the pie' and for its connection with pie graphs which divide up the whole.

A Piece of the Pie (detail)

Wendy Lewington Coulter, British Columbia

Art Object (48"x51"), 1991

"This quilt looks at how the male 'fine' art tradition, by objectifying, excluding, and defining women, has caused us to disregard our own artforms, to consider them as lower and of less consequence. At the same time it has disempowered us, and had us see our bodies not as active powerful agents of creativity, but as passive objects to be observed and judged always.

"By placing traditional 'fine' art images of women within the context of a quilt format, and by presenting the resulting object in a formal 'high art' manner, I am mixing up expectations about where we should expect to see what. The process of questioning is necessary to have art be a true reflection of human experience."

Wendy Lewington Coulter

Lovers and Fish (65"x45.5"), 1992

This quilt is about relationships between men and women and the contradictions and struggles within them. It is a celebration of the joy and pain which coexist between us, and a humorous look at the life and death approach we often take to romance. When I watch the salmon spawning every year, I am both in awe of their incredible tenacity and pitying of their apparent ignorance of impending fate. Somehow they remind me of my own mortality. The salmon represent the cycle of life and the mystery of creation."

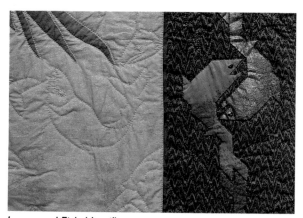

Lovers and Fish (detail)

Wendy Lewington Coulter, British Columbia

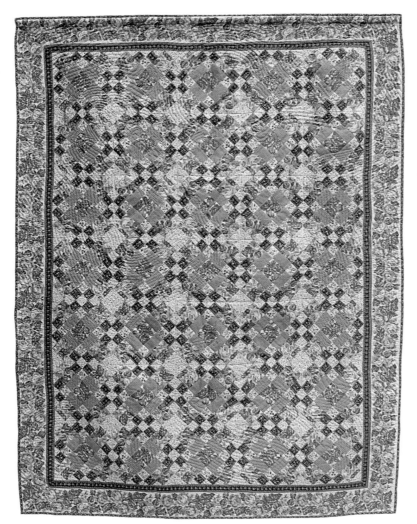

Heirloom Quilt (59"x44"), 1988

The comforting beauty of this classic quilt contrasts with the disturbing ugliness of its concealed message: patterns of behaviour such as domestic violence can be passed on from generation to generation, just like other family traditions and heirlooms. In the pink rectangles are typed quotes from a diary describing the personal and secret pain women and children experience when they are subjected to family violence. The pattern of the quilting stitches echos a police-style sidewalk chalk-drawing of a victim, which can be viewed best from the quilt's back.

"I wanted to juxtapose comfort with pain, love with alienation . . . elements which frequently coexist within families. The quilt as an intimate object, a bedcovering, is an important aspect of the message of this piece. It alludes to the issue of sexual oppression and violence within a structure where 'the privacy of one's own home' becomes a dangerous and inescapable threat."

Heirloom Quilt (detail)

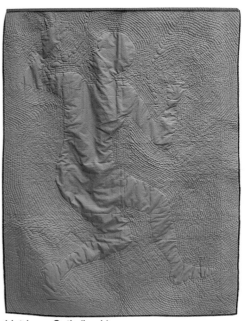

Heirloom Quilt (back)

Wendy Lewington Coulter, British Columbia

Watch It II (61"x52"), 1992

"During the last weeks of the Gulf War, I was in a hospital waiting room as my mother struggled with a life-threatening illness. I watched the news coverage which glorified technological advances in war-making, while minimizing the suffering of its victims. My intense emotions surrounding the potential loss of my mother, coupled with her very real physical and emotional pain, placed in bold relief the value of a single life. I reflected on how people would continue to suffer for years to come from this war.

"Watch It *is about the manipulation of minds by mass media. By presenting a collection of laser-copied images framed in televisions, I want to talk about our ability to compartmentalize information, and to see the world as a series of two-dimensional images. Choice of programs takes the place of significant political choice. Television becomes a substitute for real experience. The lasting quality of a quilt stands against the fleeting, transitory and disposable nature of television."*

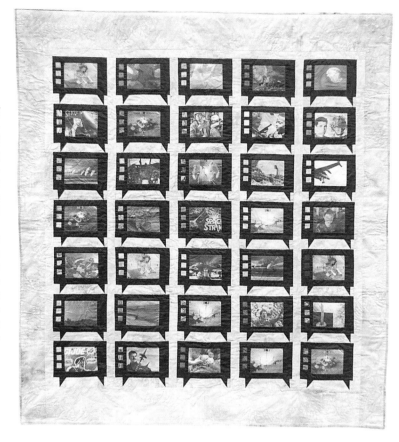

Wedding Ring (80"x71"), 1994

The traditional Double Wedding Ring quilt pattern is interpreted using printed cottons as well as fabric laser-printed with images from nature. Stamped on the quilt are words taken from traditional wedding vows: 'For better, for worse, for richer, for poorer, in sickness and in health, to love, to cherish, till death do us part.'

"I have made this piece in a spirit of love and hope which speaks of my desire that as human beings, we might make this kind of commitment in a much broader context than we traditionally have — to ourselves, to each other, and to the natural world, in the knowledge that we are inextricably bound to and dependent upon that world for our very survival."

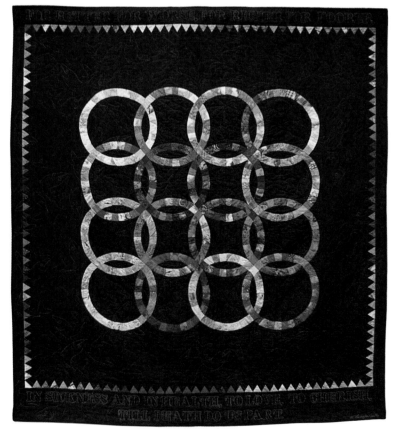

Drawing for the Terrified & Machine-Appliquéd Portrait

Level of difficulty: All levels (machine sewing)

In Part 1 of Wendy's workshop, you are guided through a drawing exercise designed to encourage non-drawers to practice "seeing." Based on the results of this exercise, Part 2 introduces the method of machine-appliqué that Wendy often uses in her quilts.

Part 1: Drawing for the Terrified

As children, we all made images freely: drawing, painting, creating fearlessly with whatever medium we were offered. At some point, as we learned to express ourselves "properly," "art" became more difficult, and many of us became fearful, intimidated, and downright reluctant to create art. Although most adults say they can't draw, and especially that they can't draw people, there are simple exercises anyone can practice to produce perfectly acceptable drawings, even of human figures.

In the photo below, Wendy guides non-drawer Maureen Clarke through this workshop's exercise as she draws using model Tess. The goal of this exercise is to place the emphasis on the act of observation, not on the results of your drawings. **You will create a**

design which will be seen separately and will not be compared to your source material. You do not need to be an artist to succeed at this exercise. If you can see, you can do it!

Although there are many kinds of drawing and design exercises, the blind contour exercise emphasizes the importance of **line**, which is especially suited to machine-appliqué work, since the stitching line is worked over the drawn line on the fabric surface. The blind contour method is so-named because the drawer is "blind" to the marks she is making. Her attention is focused on the model, rather than the drawing itself.

By practicing blind contour drawing, you will learn to have respect for line. As you translate your drawing into fabric, your stitching lines will no longer be a strictly utilitarian means of securing one fabric on top of another; they will become an essential and beautiful element of your design.

BLIND CONTOUR EXERCISE

1 Find a partner and take turns drawing each other. Or, if you are working alone, try a self-portrait using a mirror, set at a comfortable distance away from you.

2 Make sure you are comfortable, and that you have a sharp, soft (HB, B, 2B) pencil and a large piece of paper (newsprint is fine) to draw on.

3 Begin by carefully observing your subject for at least one minute. Trace your subject with your eyes, as if your eyes were a pencil drawing SLOWLY over each line as you observe it.

4 To begin drawing, choose a place to start on your subject. For example, you may choose to start with the line of a brow.

5 Place your pencil on your paper where you feel you would like to begin your first line. Take into account how much space you will need to accommodate your drawing. For example for a brow line on a face, you would probably choose to begin in the upper centre of the page.

6 Look at your subject, and, with your eyes, slowly follow the line of the subject you are drawing (i.e. brow). As you do this, move your pencil, **without looking down at your paper**, at the same rate and in the same direction as your eyes are moving. Do not lift your pencil until you complete this line.

7 When your first line is drawn, decide which line you will draw next, and place your pencil point at its beginning. Take your eyes off the paper, and draw with your eyes following the line on your subject, as in step 6. Remember, move eye and pencil simultaneously and slowly. Do not look down while you draw.

8 When one line appears to go "behind" or "underneath" another line, stop drawing and relocate your pencil to begin a new line. Do not go back over a line or stop a line in the middle. Rather than making "sketchy" lines, your goal is to make singular, complete lines.

Like this:　　　**Not this:**

9 You may give your lines character by varying the amount of pressure you apply while drawing. Some of your subject's lines may appear thicker and stronger at one point, then thin out. When tracing these lines, your pencil pressure will be heavier on the "thicker" lines, and will gradually ease on the "thinner" lines until ending very lightly.

10 Continue making lines in this way as you "trace" your subject entirely. One drawing may take 10 minutes to an hour or more.

10. Continue tracing your subject completely.

11 Consider repeating this exercise several times to build your skill and confidence. When you have one or more line drawings you feel satisfied with, choose one with a good potential for your machine appliqué. Think about these aspects:

- A simple drawing works best. Too many lines can be confusing and make your final piece seem busy.

- Look for enclosed areas, or make minor adjustments to your chosen drawing to create enclosed shapes which will become areas of fabric.

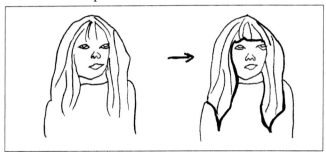

- How do you want your drawing situated in your final quilt? Do you want it cropped close, or surrounded by lots of space? Do you want your subject to the right or left of the composition?

> **HINT : You can experiment with various compositions using L-shaped black paper frames cut from tagboard. Moving the temporary frames helps your eyes block out unwanted sections, to "audition" prospective compositions.**

11. Decide on cropping.

12 When you have arrived at a satisfactory design and composition, you are ready for **Part 2: Machine-Appliquéd Portrait.**

Part 2: Machine-Appliquéd Portrait

M A T E R I A L S

- Your chosen **line drawing**

- **A piece of *stabilizer* material** such as Tear-away™ or Stitch 'n' Tear™, either iron-on or stitch-on, a little larger than your final appliqué. (See Appendix #4: *Sources*, for mail-order supplies.)

- **A piece of background fabric** on which you will appliqué your portrait. Wendy often chooses background fabric with interesting but subtle visual texture, such as hand-dyed silk. A pre-pieced background is also acceptable, if it suits your design goals.

- **A selection of fabrics**. A large variety of fabrics may be used, including metallics, plastics, velvet, corduroy, brocade.

> **HINT: Extremely stretchy fabric is best avoided.**

This technique adapts well to richly textured fabrics. Consider your fabric choices carefully. Colour can set a mood or feeling in a picture. Is there a variety of pattern and texture? Will you use solids? Consider larger-patterned or decorator prints. Fabric may be pieced, embroidered, painted, folded or otherwise manipulated before being appliquéd. Remember to turn a potential fabric over to see its "wrong" side; you might want to incorporate it as part of the "right" side!

- **A selection of threads, which contribute to the composition.** Will you use black thread exclusively for a cartoon-like effect? Will your threads contrast or harmonize with your fabric? Will the colour change throughout the design?

In the following examples, Wendy experiments with different fabric and thread choices for the same line drawing:

1) By using clear, solid colours outlined with black thread, a cartoon effect is created.

2) The unusual choices of print fabric add visual interest and texture, enhancing the representation of such images as hand, sky, etc. Notice that thread choice matches the fabric in *hue* (colour), but contrasts in *value* (darkness or lightness). This is important to emphasize *contour lines*.

3) Notice how contour lines are lost when thread colour and fabric colour are too similar. Orange silk works to imply sunset. Also see how well thermal undershirt fabric works with this technique. You can use almost any fabric to represent a motif through its colour and texture: metallic, brocade, corduroy, moderate stretch, silk.

4) Mood change is created here by using unusual prints. Notice variety in the scale (size) of the prints.

5) A harmonious colour scheme is created by choosing one multicoloured central fabric (in this case the shirt in the foreground), then harmonizing other fabric choices with it.

About your sewing machine: You need to feel confident that your machine can handle the satin stitch properly. Read the machine's manual to find out whether a special presser foot for embroidery is required to allow the extra bulk of the satin stitch to pass beneath the foot smoothly. According to the manual, is it advisable to adjust the machine's tension? Change your needle frequently, and be aware that machine appliqué produces copious amounts of lint under the throat plate. This affects the stitches produced, so you'll want to clean it away on a regular basis. An ideal satin stitch is quite dense, with no loops of bobbin thread showing on the surface. Practice making the satin stitch on a sample of fabric with a stabilizer ironed or basted on the back. Try the following satin stitch exercises: a varied width or undulating line, graduating smoothly from thin to thick, then abrupt variations, circles, squares, script, or open zig-zag with different thread colour overlays.

When you and your machine are confident satin stitchers, you are ready to begin your appliqué.

Practice making the satin stitch.

C O N S T R U C T I O N

I Transfer your design to the stabilizer *in reverse* (i.e. mirror image), since you will be stitching the lines from the back of the piece.

I. Transfer your design to the stablilizer.

2 Iron, pin or baste the stabilizer to your background fabric.

2. Iron the stabilizer to your background fabric.

3 Think of your design as layered. Some parts will appear to be behind others, and these will be stitched onto the background before the others. Decide on the order of sewing, and number the pieces in the right order if you wish. In this design, the face appears to be the bottom layer, so it will be put down first.

4 Pin the fabric you have chosen for the first layer (the face?) right side up, onto the front surface of the appliqué.

4a. Pin the first layer onto the front surface.

4b. Locate the design lines.

4c. Use pins to locate fabric boundaries.

5 From the back, lay down the first piece and machine-stitch its lines, using a straight stitch and a thread colour which matches the fabric piece.

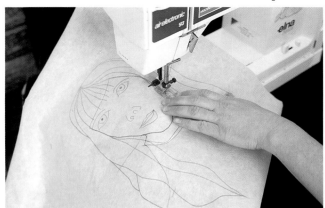

5. Machine stitch lines using a straight stitch.

6 From the front, use sharp scissors to cut away the excess fabric close to the stitching line.

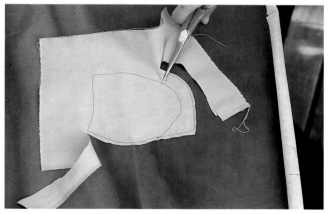

6. Cut away the excess fabric.

7 Machine-stitch the next piece (the dress in this example). Where there is no visible line to sew on (e.g. at the shoulder in the photo), estimate where it would be for the stitching.

7. Machine stitch the next piece.

8 From the front, trim away excess fabric as before, close to the stitching line.

8. Trim away excess fabric.

9 Repeat the last two steps until all the fabric areas have been laid down. Stitch over the other design line details (like the nose, eyebrows, hair). These lines will appear on the right side as guides for the satin stitch details.

9. Stitch over the design line details.

Consider using parts of large prints for some of the design features. In the sample, eyes and lips were taken from the marked areas of the larger print used for the dress, with the result that the colours harmonize well.

Use parts of large prints for design features.

10 Set your machine to a satin stitch setting, slightly wide to cover the raw edges (#3-5 on a scale of 0-5). From the right side of your work, with thread colour either harmonizing or contrasting, whichever you prefer, start by satin stitching one of the design lines which appears to be

10. Satin stitch one of the design lines.

covered by another design line (the shoulder in this case, which appears to be covered by the hair). The satin-stitching will be mostly on the top fabric, with just the outermost stitches on the background fabric.

11 Continue stitching along the design lines with satin-stitching, changing the thread colour and the stitch width according to the effect you want.

11. Continue stitching the design lines.

SOME HINTS: The waviness of hair suggests smoothly undulating widths, beginning and ending with narrow stitches. Facial feature lines might all be stitched using the same thread colour, with the exception of irises and lips. Stitching lines which are not covering raw edges can be varied, with facial details kept delicate, and finishing very thin, even using the "0" on the width scale.

12 When all the design lines have been covered with satin stitching, clip thread ends. Then, using the points of the scissors to carefully scrape out the corners of the tear-away stabilizer, remove the stabilizer from the back of the work. Press the appliquéd portrait flat.

12. Remove the stabilizer from the back.

13 Decide on the final cropping, and cut away any excess background fabric. Your portrait may be framed as is, or by adding pieced or solid borders, it could also be incorporated into a quilt. For suggestions on some finishing aspects of quiltmaking, see Appendix #1: *The Nutshell Guide to Finishing Your Quilt*.

This same portrait has been made up using all cotton fabrics, in a different colour scheme. Your interpretation of your own appliquéd portrait has endless possibilities.

One example of cropping

Another way to crop

R E F E R E N C E S

Edwards, Betty. *Drawing on the Right Side of the Brain*. New York: Jeremy P. Tarcher/Perigree, 1989. ISBN 0-87477-513-2

Penders, Mary Coyne. *Color and Cloth*. San Francisco: The Quilt Digest Press, 1989. ISBN 0-913327-20-4

CHAPTER 3

Laurrie Sobie

ALBERTA

With Workshop: 'Watercolour' Painting with Fibre

"Once you've allowed yourself the freedom of pushing over the first domino labelled 'traditional only,' it falls, revealing more and more exciting options."

Imagine a no-worry day with the warm sun bathing your face. That's the kind of feeling you get when you meet Laurrie Sobie and bask in her enthusiasm, hear her sunny voice, see her uplifting variety of quilts. The very characteristics that Laurrie possesses, her home province also possesses. With about 2000 hours of sunshine per year, Alberta leads the Canadian provinces for sunny disposition. It has the most diverse topography and climate: prairie in the east; the craggy Rocky Mountains in the west; the desert-like Badlands in the south; rivers, lakes and forests in the north. Hailstones the size of baseballs have broken all the greenhouses and skylights in Calgary, yet unpredictable warm chinook winds from the west can melt the harsh prairie winter within hours.

Such diversity is Laurrie's stock-in-trade. She has a firm traditional base of quilt-making behind her, but cannot make a quilt like anyone else's. She refuses to be bound by rules or pinned down to a single style. Instead, she "is always looking for options hiding around the corner. It kills me to make four identical placemats." Using hand, machine and adhesive *appliqué*, traditional *piecing*, extra-dimensional appliqué and piecing, net overlays, confetti colour bits, machine and hand-stitchery, dyeing, painting, *cyanoprinting* and whatever else she needs to produce her planned piece, Laurrie is proficient in a variety of traditional and contemporary techniques.

Laurrie is most renowned for teaching original design loosely based on a traditional block. She calls her approach "Decloning the Traditional Quilt." In 1986, she published

Laurrie's favourite Edmonton landmark is the Muttart Conservatory, a blend of ancient pyramid forms made of modern glass and steel materials.

Laurrie Sobie, Alberta

The Rocky Mountains, bordering Alberta and British Columbia, command attention.

a workbook with this name based on the philosophy that "once you've allowed yourself the freedom of pushing over the first domino labelled 'traditional only,' it falls in turn against the next, revealing more and more and still more exciting options." Her methods of helping students "look around that corner for options" include mirror tricks, scissor tricks and colour tricks—a veritable treasure chest of productive exercises.

Laurrie's students love her often bizarre sense of humour ("If you put me in a padded room, I could always quilt it"); her enthusiasm ("I don't teach anything I can't be enthusiastic about, because I'm being paid to give the very best I can give"); and her spontaneity ("When the flight attendant spilled coffee on the jacket I was finishing off with a knitted collar for a fashion show, I couldn't dry it in time for the show, so I just put on the jacket, carried the ball of wool, and wore the necklace of knitting needles onto the ramp. Sometimes you just have to be an actor and improvise!")

An Alberta field where sunflowers greet their namesake.

Laurrie Sobie, Alberta

In Alberta's Badlands (here Dinosaur Provincial Park), sandstone formations create a lunar landscape, where a great dinosaur graveyard has been unearthed.

With a full-time job in retailing, a grown daughter, Renée, and a dog, a cat, and a lovebird, all living at home, how does this energetic artist find the time to teach out of town four to six weekends a year, as well as maintain the long-standing biweekly University of Alberta faculty women's quilting class that has been her sounding board for the last 14 years? "I prioritize. I realized some time ago that I value *me*, and I have to do things for myself instead of everybody else. In doing so, I get peer recognition, which is so good for self-image at your lowest time. I look at the dust bunnies in the house and guilt sets in momentarily. Then somebody says, 'I loved your quilt' and I think, 'Oh well, the house can last another month or six'."

Does Laurrie have advice for quilters? "Look for the options. Read and look. Make a plan for a quilt. Do it at least three different ways before you cut it out in fabric." For herself, Laurrie says she is influenced more and more by her stitchery associates. She offers a class called "You stitch, I quilt, let's get together" to help eliminate tunnel vision and encourage students to become aware of more options with their quiltmaking, their stitchery and the combination of both. This tendency to look at all fibre as a potential medium may have had its birth in the two-year Fibre Arts program Laurrie completed at Grant McEwan College in Edmonton.

For inspiration, Laurrie is often spurred on by "an actual written challenge" (that's quilt lingo for a design contest); "It's good exercise for my brain, a challenge to my inner self." One memorable block Laurrie challenged herself to design was a stylized portrait of her friend Ethel Snow, which all Ethel's quilting friends interpreted in their own way to make a 50th birthday gift for the surprised subject.

We can expect more such gems from Laurrie's box of quilt treasures, but the only predictable treasure will be her delightful spontaneity.

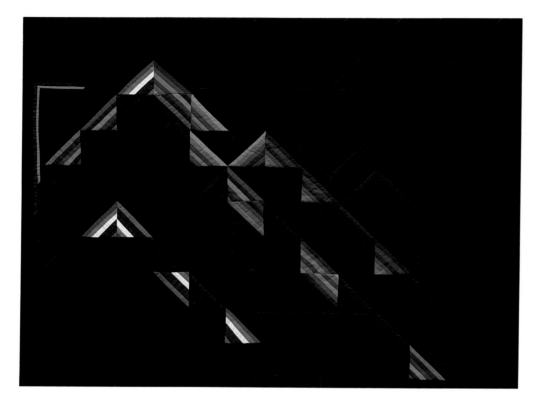

Amish Shadow Ranges (42"x55"), 1987. Collection of Dorise Broder

Begun in a workshop with Calgary quiltmaking teacher Anne Severson, this machine-pieced and machine-quilted work transforms the traditional Sunshine and Shadow *block so that it appears to form mountain peaks.*

Borealis Star (72"x72"), 1985

Laurrie's cousin used to have a toy: "You pressed and whirrr, flints would make sparks fly. By decloning a very traditional star design, this new star was born." The luminous sparks of colour are created with satin ribbons.

Borealis Star (detail)

Laurrie Sobie, Alberta

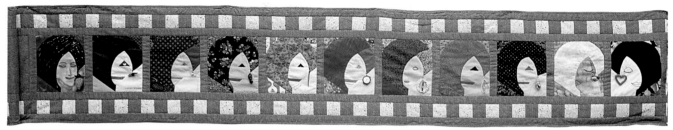

Ethel, by Friends (14.5"x190"), 1993 (detail)

The block was designed by Laurrie to commemorate Ethel Snow's 50th birthday, and the quilt was sewn by Ethel's friends.

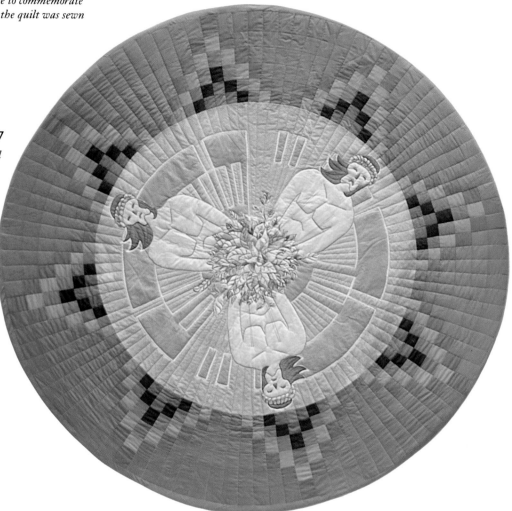

Sundance (68" diameter), 1987

By decloning the Sunshine and Shadow pattern I created a circle and a star instead of plain squares," says Laurrie. The central circle was printed using a cyanotype process, then hand-painted.

When I was researching plains Indians for this piece, I learned so much about how we have decimated all the tribes; we've killed their spirit. That's why I've made the heads look like skulls," explains Laurrie.

Sundance (detail)

Laurrie Sobie, Alberta

Clockworks (38"x42"), 1992
Collection of Barbara Fraser

A decloned version of the traditional six-wedged Kaleidoscope *block, Laurrie describes this quilt as a "colour value challenge," using many different techniques, including* trapunto, *with extra stuffing added in some areas, and three-dimensional insets which stand out from the quilt's surface.*

Sechelt 6:00 a.m. (47"x40"), 1993

Each year at a Sechelt, British Columbia quilting retreat, members are issued a challenge, which is always open to creative interpretation. The challenge which resulted in this piece decreed that we use triangles, and I creatively distorted my triangles where necessary. The seascape is the view I enjoyed each morning on my waterfront walks. In Sechelt 6:00 a.m., the marbled and hand-dyed patches are melded to the background, overlaid with netting, and machine and hand-quilted, with piping used for the binding and horizon line."

Laurrie Sobie, Alberta

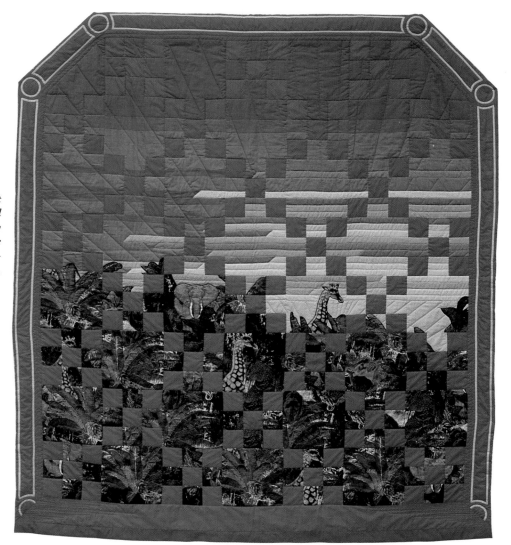

Pat's Pergola Dreams (80"x72"),
1989. Collection of Pat Letts

*"This was made as a wedding gift
for a friend whose father managed
an African gold mine. Armed with
the idea and 1 1/2 meters of a jungle
fabric, I decloned the traditional 9-
Patch block, and this trellised arbor,
or pergola grid layer appeared."*

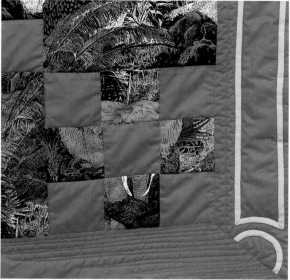

Pat's Pergola Dreams (detail)

Love Those Nasties (30"x42"), 1993

Another Sechelt retreat challenge, this work is about Laurrie's favourite flower — the strongly colourful, scented and sprawling nasturtium which "brightens up dark, shaded spaces."

I call the technique 'confetti fabric and machine embroidery'. (Note: see the technique in Laurrie's workshop, following.) The fabric is used like paint, applied with adhesive, covered with layers of netting, then stabilized and anchored by stitchery."

Laurrie Sobie, Alberta

Confetti Impressions: 'Watercolour' Painting with Fibre

Level of difficulty: Intermediate or confident machine-sewing beginner

Laurrie walks you through a workshop piece that samples some innovative techniques. No pattern is provided for this workshop, as precision is not important to the end result (aahh, that's a relief!). Experiment with your own landscape roughly based on a photo, or approximately copy Laurrie's example if you would rather not put on your creative cap today. For other examples of confetti technique, see *Love Those Nasties*.

M A T E R I A L S

Laurrie Sobie

- **Paper for full-size cartoon (drawing), pencil, pen, idea photo**

- **Muslin foundation fabric 2" larger all around than finished size desired.**

- **Rotary cutter and cutting mat, scissors**

- **Thermolam™ or needlepunched batting** the full size of your piece to add weight and firmness

- **A selection of suitable fabrics for the landscape shapes**. Laurrie loves the variegated, natural textured look of hand-dyed fabrics (see Appendix #4: *Sources* for suppliers of hand-dyed fabrics by mail; or you can experiment with dyeing your own landscape fabrics. See the workshop in Chapter 4 for recipe and tips.

Laurrie's **BEST TIP EVER** is to use spray starch on all your fabric after it has been preshrunk and dried. It restores the firm "hand" (that's fabric industry lingo for "feel") and makes all cottons, especially loosely-woven ones, more manageable for piecing, appliqué and machine or hand-embroidery.

- **Sheer nylon nettings, organzas** in different colours/ size of holes, sufficient for two or three layers.

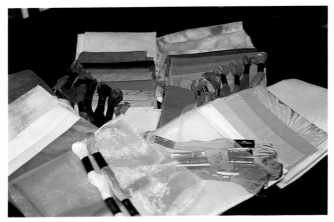

Shown here is a selection of fabrics and yarns grouped in seasonal hues, from left to right: winter, fall, summer, spring.

- **Assorted coloured threads, scraps of fabric, sequins, yarns**, in an assortment of colours you wish to 'paint' with. (**NOTE**: In the workshop piece Laurrie has chosen only whites and opalescent bits to suggest snow.)

- **WonderUnder™ or Heat n Bond™**(paper-backed iron-on adhesive)

- **Powdered adhesive** (such as Hot Stitch™)

- **Iron, ironing pad, teflon ironing sheet** to prevent adhesive sticking to iron and ironing board See Appendix #4: *Sources* for teflon ironing sheet.

- **Sewing machine capable of machine-embroidery.** Can the machine's feed dogs, used for gripping fabric from underneath, drop down below the throat plate or bed of the machine? Does it have an embroidery presser foot with a spring mechanism or can the pressure on the presser foot be released so that you can move the fabric freely under the presser foot?

- **Selection of threads for machine-embroidery.** Metallic, invisible, and rayon threads of various colours can all be useful. (Play with different thread colours and types on scraps.)

THE DESIGN

To achieve perspective and interest, Laurrie suggests you think in terms of layers, much like a pop-out greeting card which has a background, one or more mid-grounds, and a foreground. If you keep your design elements simple for a first project, you can more quickly achieve successful, encouraging results. Lightly sketch your design full-sized, in pencil, then when you're happy with the design, draw it in darker with a pen or felt pen.

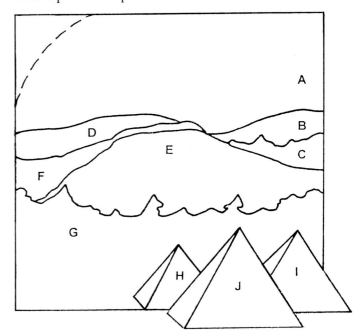

CONSTRUCTION

The Background

Pin the foundation muslin over the paper drawing or cartoon. Draw the background features onto the fabric with pencil.

1. Draw the features onto the fabric.

2 Lay the WonderUnder™ or Heat n Bond™ adhesive side up, over the cartoon, and draw, in pen, the background element which is furthest away (in this case, the sky).

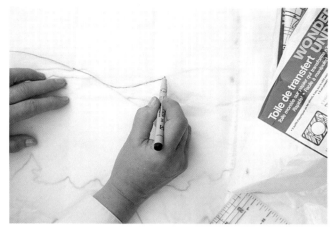

2. Draw the background element which is furthest away.

HINT: If you have a light table, or it's daylight and you can use a window to see the design lines through the paper, flip the cartoon to its reverse side and copy the pattern onto the paper side of the WonderUnder with pencil.

3 Cut out the paper-backed adhesive, adding approximately 1/2" extra allowance all around.

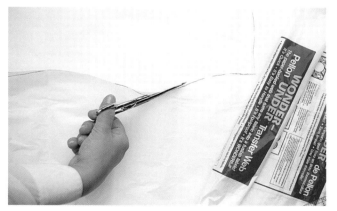

3. Cut out the adhesive, adding 1/2" extra.

4 Iron the adhesive to the *back* of the first fabric, according to directions which come with the adhesive, distributing the heat and pressure evenly over the piece.

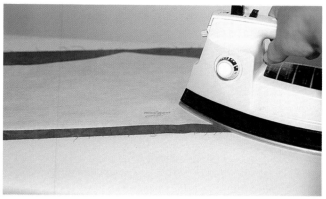

4. Iron the adhesive-backed fabric onto the background.

5 Peel off the paper backing.

5. Peel off the paper backing.

6 Iron the adhesive-backed fabric onto the background muslin, where the design lines indicate.

6. Iron the adhesive-backed fabric onto the background.

7 Add the next furthest element by repeating the adhesive procedure (in sample, the furthest hills).

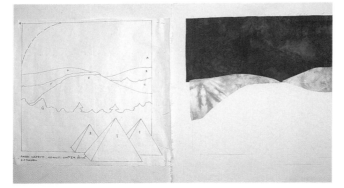

7. Add the next element.

(**NOTE**: from now on, the *tops* of the patterns have no extra allowance beyond the adhesive. In other words, the cutting line at the top will match the design line on the cartoon. Overlap this pattern by the 1/2" allowance before you iron it on.)

8 Add the third furthest element by the same procedure.

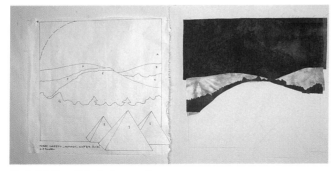

8. Add the third element.

9 Laurrie adds machine-embroidery to this line of trees to give more detail which suggests that it is

9. Add machine-embroidery.

closer. With the embroidery foot attached and the feed dogs lowered, you can control the stitching by the even, steady movement of the fabric. Check your machine's instruction manual for further hints on machine embroidery. Try some sample stitching on the same fabric weight and thickness to familiarize yourself with it before you work on your piece.

10 Continue adding the background layers until background is complete.

10. Continue adding the background layers.

The Mid-Ground

11 Laurrie cuts paper, swiss dot and yarn into tiny bits of confetti. With the addition of sequins, these bits will suggest swirling snow. Depending upon your composition, all manner of colours and materials could be used in this way.

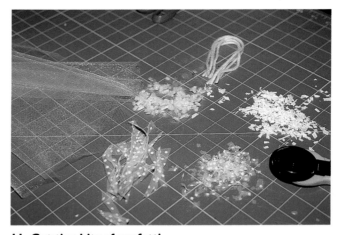

11. Cut tiny bits of confetti.

HINT: From now on, whenever you cut fabrics within the same colour family, gather up the tiniest scraps and seal them in a bag for the moment when you next feel the urge to be an impressionist fabric painter. The little bags look good on your shelf, and make you feel good because you didn't throw the scraps away.

12 With chalk, draw a rough guideline for the area you wish to 'paint' with confetti.

12. Draw a guideline for the confetti.

13 Cut netting pieces to cover those areas. Remove the pieces and set them aside.

13. Cut netting pieces.

14 Squeeze the powdered adhesive onto the marked areas.

14. Squeeze the powdered adhesive onto the marked area.

15 Sprinkle the confetti onto the adhesive.

15. Sprinkle the confetti onto the adhesive.

HINT: A toothbrush can help corral those elusive bits. However, it is suggested you do not use the same toothbrush for your teeth again.

A toothbrush can corral bits.

16 Replace the netting pieces over the confetti and powdered adhesive.

16. Replace the netting pieces.

17 Using a teflon ironing sheet, or the paper from the paper-backed adhesive, press the confetti layers together.

17. Press the confetti layers together.

18 Add a light dusting of powdered adhesive over the whole piece. Lay another netting

18. Lay another netting over the whole piece.

over the whole piece. Use a different texture and/or colour depending upon the effect you desire. Laurrie uses a sparkly organza to enhance the effect of glittering snow.

19 Press again over all with the iron and a teflon sheet.

20 Stitch over the surface with the machine, using regular, metallic or, as in Laurrie's sample, invisible thread. This stitching can be decorative (see *Love Those Nasties* detail) or functional, as in this sample. The netting does need to be secured with stitching, as the adhesive is only semi-permanent by itself.

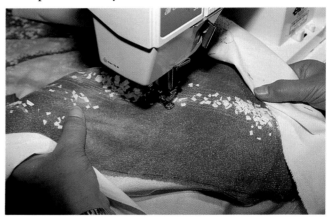

20. Machine-stitch over the surface.

21 Several jaggedly-cut layers of dark netting are machine-embroidered to the mid-ground behind the pyramids, and to the near mid-ground (left).

21. Machine-embroider netting to the mid-ground.

The Foreground

The Muttart Conservatory forms the foreground. Laurrie has chosen to represent the pyramids in metallic fabric, which is very often dimensionally unstable. To stabilize it, Laurrie does the following:

22 Using the template for each pyramid, without adding a turn-under allowance, cut 2 pieces of paper-backed adhesive, 1 piece of muslin, and 1 piece of Thermolam or other compact batting. Then, with the metallic fabric cut out **with** the $1/2$" turn-under allowance, layer the pieces according to this diagram:

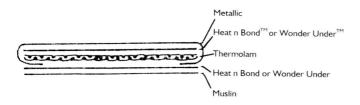

Iron one paper-backed adhesive to the Thermolam and one to the muslin. Remove the paper backings, then adhere the layers together.

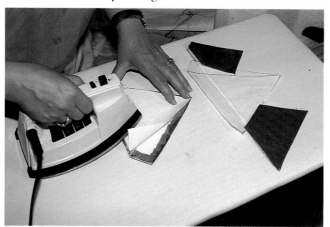

22. Adhere the layers together.

> **HINT: Metallic fabric will often melt or distort from the iron's heat. Always test the heat on a scrap and use a press-cloth.**

23 To add dimension to the pyramids, Laurrie machine quilts them.

23. Machine quilt the pyramids.

24 The two pyramids behind are hand-appliquéd to the background (see Chapter 5, page 91 for the hand-appliqué stitch). Before adding the third pyramid, Laurrie layers another swirl of net-sandwiched snow. This step adds to the illusion of perspective.

24. Hand-appliqué the pyramids.

To finish this piece, Laurrie has backed it with Thermolam™, trimmed the edges and curved the upper left edge, then sewn a facing or finishing piece around the perimeter, which is turned to the back and hand-stitched down. For general tips on finishing quilts, see Appendix #1: *The Nutshell Guide to Finishing Your Quilt.*

CHAPTER 4

Susan Andrews Grace

SASKATCHEWAN

With workshop: Introduction to Shibori Dyeing

"here I find the right words
to quilt a drunkard's path and embroider
convolvulus vines
on the white tablecloth and a sigh
that walks with me to and from the water"

—from "laps", by Susan Andrews Grace

aundry. Laundry is the thread that binds the elements of Susan Andrews Grace's story together. This mundane chore symbolizes a mother's nurturance, which is a common theme in Susan's early poetry. It symbolizes the maturation of her children, when they assert their independence by doing their own laundry. And it symbolizes the emergence of Susan's textile artistry, because her first studio was in the basement laundry room.

Not that Susan called it a studio at first. "I didn't really think of what I was doing as art. I just thought of it as working with cloth." After co-ordinating the construction of *The Peace Quilt* which now hangs at the Canadian Permanent Mission to the United Nations in New York, she "realized that the medium of textiles can have such effect. It seemed to me you could pack quite a wallop if you said something with textiles. All the traditional materials that are high up on the hierarchy of art materials, they can't say those things the way textiles can."

Susan says important things in her poetry, too. In fact, for her, "the visual stuff has to come after the writing." Coincidentally, it was a book by a quilter that convinced Susan to take her writing seriously. She tells the story of how, eighteen years ago, she and her husband, Gord, went to a computer conference in Toronto, where they stocked up on books to take home. "The last book I bought was in the subway station. It was *The Creative Woman's Getting It All Together At Home Handbook* by Jean Ray Laury, and I stayed up all night reading it on the hotel bathroom floor so I wouldn't keep Gord awake with the light on. I came home a changed woman. All I needed was that encouragement to take it seriously. That summer I went to a very good writing

Saskatoon, the city of bridges, sits in the centre of the Canadian prairies and has the same name as the wonderful wild berries famous here.

As the most fertile of the Canadian provinces, Saskatchewan's main export is wheat.

school, seven months pregnant with my third child, and started to write better poems." Her poems have since been published in two volumes, *Water is the First World*, and *Wearing my Father*, as well as in several anthologies, magazines, and on radio broadcasts.

Susan's formal training was as a nurse. "I went into nursing because I wanted to be an artist. I was going to support myself by nursing." Her only training in textile craft, art and writing has come by way of short courses and workshops, books, and trial and error. "I realize now that I have done a lot of things out of ignorance that I wouldn't have done otherwise, but they were good, and if I had had the proper training, I would have had to overcome the teaching." Once when Susan was attending a workshop, she had a long chat with Canadian quilter and art instructor, Anne Severson. "Anne talked to me about how she thought I'd trained myself well. By the time she'd finished it was as if she'd given me a diploma. It gave me licence to go ahead and do things. That's when I applied for and got an Explorations grant from Canada Council to do poems and quilts. I really jumped off the edge and became more interested in saying something with what I made."

The exhibition of quilted pieces that resulted from her grant-sponsored work was titled *Inside/Out*. It explored the interiors of quilts and the interiors of women's lives. In her artist's statement about this show, Susan postulates: "Perhaps quilts would like to bust out, blow up, be read, stand on their own, spill their guts, spin out, be at right angles to their smooth surfaces. The pieces explore such imagined desires on the part of quilts and also make statements about the lives of their makers and users, questioning all closed-in, contained reality." (See *Roll in the Hay*, *Umbilical Quilt*, and *Granny C*.) These installations were technically quilts, but Susan used such fillings as air, knives, hay, razor blades, barbed wire, articles of clothing. Through these incongruous interiors, Susan gives voice to women's domestic struggles. Family violence, economic pressures on the family, the invisibility of women's contributions to society ("Women do 80% of the world's work and receive less than 1% of the income"), relationships between men and women and mothers and children, women's health issues: all are fuel for Susan's textile and literary fires.

Although her writing and quilting relate to each other, Susan often felt a tension between them. "I hid one part of myself from the other. I'd go downstairs to put the laundry in and do a little bit of work on the side when I was supposed to be writing. I'd feel a little sneaky. I had myself divided into the writer upstairs and the closet quilter in the basement. I knew darned well one fed the other."

These days, Susan finds time to quilt late at night, "because I'd be up late anyway, worrying about my teenaged children, Katie, Thomas and Patrick. When they were little, I got up early in the morning. I've always put the children first, my work came a real close second, and Gord third. He's been happier since I stopped trying so hard to be a good wife." Many years ago, Susan and

Gord picked Saskatoon as the best city in Canada to raise a family. They appreciate it for its affordability, its amenities and its safety.

Increasingly, their children are becoming independent. One interesting accident occurred as a result of Thomas's independence in the laundry department. Susan had made a tufted wool batt quilt for him when he was little, and she always washed it carefully and laid it flat to dry. "At 15, Thomas decided he was going to do his own laundry, and he felt strongly that he could only get laundry clean with hot water. He washed his quilt in hot water, rinsed it in cool water, and threw it into the dryer. It shrunk perfectly to about 1/6th its size." The resulting textural piece has given Susan inspiration for her own shrink art. And the children's increasing competence is gradually making way for Susan to look after her own needs.

Susan gives an example of how her work nurtures her. "One night I had been working on a problem with the administration of our shared artists' studio space. When I came home late, the sink was full of dishes and I wanted to start dyeing in the sink. I thought, 'this house is stupid, it's such a mess.' Gord was out and he was supposed to be back. I thought, 'I could lead a single life.' I put on the gas mask to measure the dye powder, when Patrick came in asking for his allowance early and generally pestering me. I was trying to yell at him through the gas mask. And I thought, 'Why do I have to start work at what I love to do at 10:30 at night?' But, eventually I got to it, and it's such a restorative thing. By the time I was done, I was so happy with the way the wood grain dyeing had turned out that I thought, 'I've got such nice kids, they're such interesting people.' Gord came home, and I thought, 'What a nice man.' As I walked upstairs I thought, 'Isn't my living room nice'."

As a quilter, Susan's work may be said to go against the grain of traditionally-based and socially-acceptable forms. However, she has reconciled her need to create with this marginalization. Leopold Foulem, a ceramicist from Montreal told her, "When you're on the margins, you can have the most fun. You can do the most daring things because nobody ever pays attention anyway." Fun is what Susan likes having; her quilts

are often very humorous interpretations of serious subjects. "If you said what really happens in women's lives, for example, it would seem much too melodramatic. If you say it in a funny way, a tactile way, people pay more attention."

That's not to say that Susan doesn't respect the craft. "It bothers me when people do conceptual work without knowing proper technique. We need a healthy respect for what women have done in the past. I don't like sloppiness. It's important to understand your medium."

Susan has more advice for textile artists, gleaned from her reading and from other artists. From sculptor Joe Fafard regarding galleries and the buying public: "Don't go to them, let them come to you." From author Jean Ray Laury about creative experiences: "Don't pass up any opportunities." From fellow textile artist Jane Kenyon: "Go to every workshop that slightly interests you. You'll come back with something useful." From Canadian embroiderer Martha Cole: "Buy every tool and book you want." And from Manitoba artist Aganathea Dyck: "Work with materials and ideas you know." (Aganathea herself knew she was good at shrinking sweaters!)

Susan's current work continues to push out the barriers of quilt-art. She's dressing a series of thirteen 6-foot-high "tea cosies," some of them motorized, each in quilted/stitched clothing suitable to one archetype of a woman, such as 'healer,' 'whore' and 'priestess.'

We can look forward to much more humour and insight from this textile artist.

From Susan's poem, "it must be saturday morning":

> look I gave you a place to grow
> and milk from my body
> I wash your clothes   love you
> feel guilty   what more
> can you want?

UN Peace Quilt (7 ¹/₂' × 9'), 1986

A collaboration with Judy Fretz and several members of the international peace group, Ploughshares, resulted in this large work which now hangs at the Canadian Permanent Mission to the United Nations. "Helen Caldicott said, 'Do what you do for peace.' I had done a lot of things over the years that were not satisfying to me," says Susan. "With this project, I did what I did for peace, got immense satisfaction, and maybe it has done some good."

J. Fretz

Drunkard's Path (52"x40"), 1986

"I couldn't bear the thought of putting the quilt all together and have it look so regular, so unlike its name. So I made it into a real Drunkard's Path with a hodgepodge shape and I quilted it with messy journeys. The red 'dingle' [Susan's word] of cotton flannel is losing its stuffing."

Anne Simmie

Susan Andrews Grace, Saskatchewan

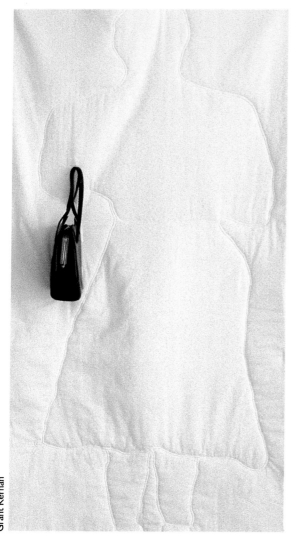

Grant Kernan

What Granny C. Left Behind (86.5"x72.5"), 1987

"My Grandma Cavanagh's leather purse is placed at right angles through this quilt, which is made of the finest cotton organdy. Grandma's shape is outlined in trapunto *quilting and her purse hangs on her arm, just as it did in real life."*

Granny C. (side detail)

Grant Kernan

Anne Simmie

Roll in the Hay (60"x17"x7"), 1987

"It was like the hay fell out of the sky for me. We were driving to a wedding as I was talking about how I was going to do this quilt, and there was a broken bale of hay on the highway. We drove 20 more miles before finally turning back to get the hay. When I stuffed the muslin channels with hay, I realized it could stand up by itself. With this quilt, part of a series, I'm examining the interiors of quilts and of women's lives."

Susan Andrews Grace, Saskatchewan

Domestic Bliss (small kitchen table size), 1991

"Two-parent families are supposed to be like the Cleavers, and that's a crock. The husband ends up having to work so hard to earn the money. [The pressure of the job is represented by the suspended axe.] [As well,] the woman at home is doing all that supportive work. The firm should really be paying for two people because there's no way he could do all that work if he didn't have all the support at home. This piece comments on the contradiction about how blissful domestic life is. It's a different kind of violence. I guess we were feeling the pinch around here when I made this quilt."

Grant Kernan

Grant Kernan

Umbilical Quilt (252" long, 2 ¹/₄" diameter, detail), 1987

"I just about turned my fingers inside out doing this. It's a double silk casing with coloured cords in it, placed on a blue quilt." says Susan. The 250" length of the cord symbolizes the ongoing connection between mother and child.

Thomas's Shrunken Quilt (36"x24"), 1993

A cotton quilt with wool batting, made by Susan, took on a sculptural texture when it was shrunk by her son, Thomas.

Grant Kernan

Brenda Pelkey

Grounded (24"x36"), 1989

The shibori-dyed cloth is quilted to a back that is larger, and the edges are not finished. It is anchored to the ground by a stone. One of a series called Wild Blue Flying Things.

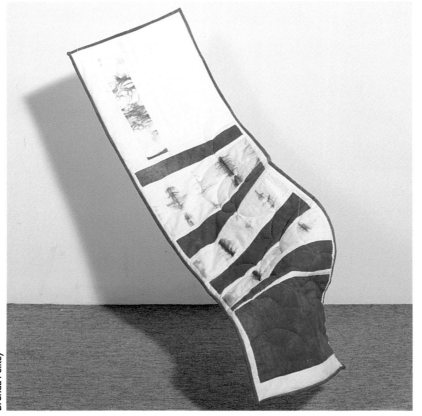

Brenda Pelkey

Snow on the Mountain (13.5"x 46.5"), 1989

Shibori-dyed pieces are hand-appliquéd to white diaper flannelette and then quilted. It is hung in space, as snow on the mountain sometimes appears to be.

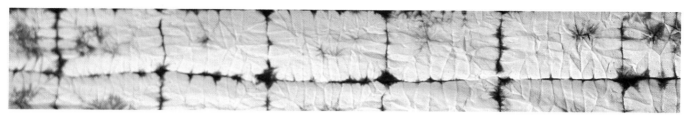

Introduction to Shibori Dyeing

Level of difficulty: Beginner

Although Susan does not normally teach, she has agreed to describe her shibori techniques for you in this workshop format. Shibori means a shaped resist. It is an ancient Japanese art, vaguely similar to tie-dye, but in a much more intricate and carefully preplanned stitching and wrapping interpretation.

In this workshop, Susan demonstrates two shibori patterns to make squares for a simple, two-colour quilt, using Procion™ MX dyes. **PLEASE, KEEP ALL CHEMICALS AWAY FROM CHILDREN AND PETS. IF YOU ARE PREGNANT, YOU ARE ADVISED NOT TO DYE FABRIC**, because breathing in airborne dye powder may affect the availability of oxygen to the fetus.

M A T E R I A L S

- **Fabric**. You may wish to prepare enough squares for a quilt top. If so, you will need 2.3 meters (2 ½ yards) of 115 cm. (45") wide fabric to cut 35 10.5" squares of preshrunk quilt-weight, non-permanent-press white 100% cotton. In the suggested quilt design, 18 of these will be dyed using a shibori resist, so you may wish to finish their edges by serging or edge-stitching (⅛" from edge).

- **High quality thread** for preparing the resist. Susan likes to use fine, unwaxed dental floss.

- **Disappearing marking pen** for fabric (optional)

- **Hand-sewing needle, thread snips**

- **Spray bottle filled with water**

For the dyeing, you will need access to a sink. If the fabric is not dye-ready, it may require 'scouring,' a step which requires a stove. Appendix #4: *Sources* lists mail-order suppliers for chemicals. The chemicals and utensils required are:

- **Soda ash** (also available at swimming pool chemical suppliers)

- **Salt** — almost any kind of table or pickling salt seems to work

- **Procion™ MX fibre-reactive dye, indigo blue**

- **Synthrapol™ detergent**

- **Plastic** to protect your work table

- **A kitchen timer**

- **Messy work clothes, rubber gloves, and a face mask.**

- **Stainless steel or enamel pot** to use on stove (if fabric needs scouring), measuring cups and spoons, small glass or plastic containers (the see-through ones that sherbet comes in are great), and a bucket to use as a dyepot. (**NOTE: ALL THESE UTENSILS SHOULD ONLY BE USED FOR DYEING IN THE FUTURE. KEEP THEM AWAY FROM YOUR FOOD PREPARATION AREA.**) You might write the measurements onto a clear plastic container with a permanent felt pen to use as your measuring cup.

Scouring the Fabric

You will need to scour the fabric if it is not "dye-ready."

To remove any finishes on the cotton so it will be more receptive to the dye, simmer it for 20 minutes in 2 tablespoons soda ash dissolved in 1-2 gallons water. Rinse thoroughly and dry.

The two patterns demonstrated are left, *ne-maki* (thread-resisted rings), and right, *mokume* (woodgrain).

For the Ne-maki:

(10 squares of cotton for sample design)

Finger-crease each square into square sixteenths.

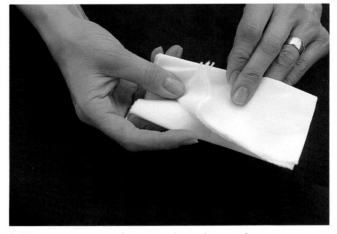

1. Finger-crease each square into sixteenths.

2 Finger-crease a square on-point (or draw on with disappearing marker) in the centre of each square, using the intersections of the grid to determine the square's corners.

2. Finger-crease a square on-point.

3 Thread a needle and tie a big knot at the end of the thread.

HINT: If you are using unwaxed dental floss, a wire needle-threader makes the job much easier.

Stitch around the central square with a running stitch. Susan prefers to use fine, unwaxed dental floss because of its strength. Here she uses a dark thread so it will show up better in the photograph.

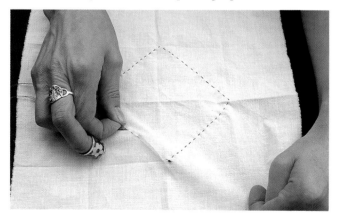

3. Stitch around the central square with a running stitch.

4 Pull up the thread from both ends as tightly as you can, and knot off firmly.

4. Pull up the thread tightly.

5 With a new length of thread, re-wrap where the running stitch is pulled tightly and knot. Continue wrapping tightly toward the centre so that the thread covers much of the white, but stop about 1" away from the centre. The closer the wrapping, the better the resist and the more interesting the pattern.

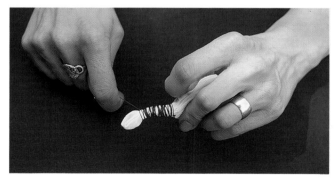

5. Re-wrap and knot.

For the Mokume:

(8 squares of cotton)

I With finger-creasing or disappearing marker, mark each square with parallel lines every ³/₄" to 1". For this pattern, slight unevenness improves the appearance of woodgrain, so don't worry if your lines aren't exactly parallel.

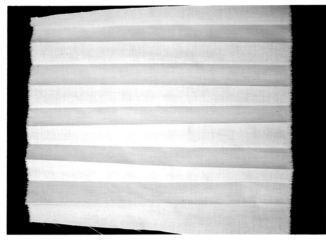

I. Mark each square with parallel lines.

2 Thread a needle with a length of dental floss that has a big knot at the end, and stitch along the marked lines in a running stitch.

3 Pull up the threads to gather, one at a time, **as tightly as you can**. Knot each thread.

3a. Pull up the threads to gather.

HINT: Spritz with water to make the bundle even tighter.

3b. Spritz with water.

D Y E I N G

The recipe used here is based on dyeing your 18 squares of fabric a dark indigo, which is the traditional shibori colour. This amount of fabric is about 1.4 meters (1 ¹/₂ yards). If you vary the yardage, all the amounts of chemicals and water must be varied accordingly to achieve similar results.

Most of the fun of dyeing your own fabric comes when you experiment. Although it's very difficult to repeat a pattern or colour exactly, you'll still want to keep a record of your recipe, the date, and a sample swatch of fabric, for future reference. Cotton fabrics, even 100% cotton, non-permanent-press, scoured fabrics, can vary considerably in their ability to be dyed.

I Wet the fabric in ordinary water. Squeeze dry.

WORKSHOP: Introduction to Shibori Dyeing

2 Measure 10 cups warm water into bucket.

2. Measure water into bucket.

3 Add 1/2 cup salt and stir till dissolved.

3. Add salt and stir.

4 Measure 1/2 cup lukewarm water into a jar. You **must put on your face mask, rubber gloves, and protective clothing**. Measure 1 1/2 tablespoons of the Procion™ MX dye powder and stir it into the water in the jar. There should be no breeze when you're doing this and no maskless people nearby.

4. Add dye powder.

5 Pour the liquid dye into the dye bucket. Rinse the dye jar with another 1/2 cup water and stir into bucket.

5. Pour the dye into the dye bucket.

6 Add your bound fabric squares, and stir and move them around in the dye bath almost continuously for 30 minutes.

6. Stir fabric squares in the dye bath.

7 Measure 2 tablespoons soda ash into 1 cup hot water. Stir until dissolved.

7. Measure soda ash into hot water.

8 Remove the fabric from the dyebath, then add soda ash solution to the dyebath. Stir.

8. Add soda ash solution to the dyebath.

9 Return fabric to the dyebath and agitate it for about 10 minutes. Leave fabric in dyebath for another 50 minutes, stirring it every 10 minutes. This is the stage where the dye "locks" onto the fibre, and it cannot be rushed. With fibre-reactive dyes like Procion™ MX, the depth of colour is determined by how much dye powder you use, not by how long you leave the fabric in the dyebath.

10 Remove the fabric from the dyebath and squeeze out extra moisture. Rinse it in lukewarm water till the water stays clear.

10. Rinse fabric till the water stays clear.

11 Add a capful or teaspoon of Synthrapol™ detergent to hotter water, and agitate the fabric around for a few minutes before rinsing in clear water for a final time. The Synthrapol™ helps prevent bleeding or migration of the dye.

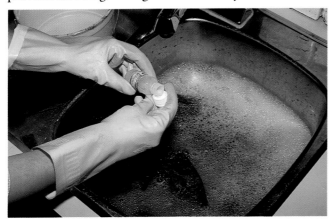

11. Add Synthrapol™ detergent.

12 If you thought all that was fun, you'll have a *really* good time removing the threads from the fabric and seeing magic unfold before your very eyes. Susan likes to see the little mound of threads grow higher and higher. She suggests a parallel with Carl Jung's advice to a sculptor: "Don't worry about the process, just concentrate on the chips on the floor."

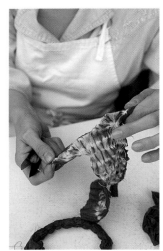

12. Remove the threads from the fabric.

13 Let the squares dry flat if possible. Traditionally, shibori is not ironed flat. The wrinkles add to the desirable texture.

QUILT TOP

Cut each square into four equal squares. Randomly arrange the *ne-maki* and *mokumi* squares with white (undyed) squares.

Sew the squares together with ¹/₄" seams. Take care to match your corners. You may choose to add borders to change the size of your quilt. For suggestions on finishing, refer to Appendix #1: *The Nutshell Guide to Finishing Your Quilt.*

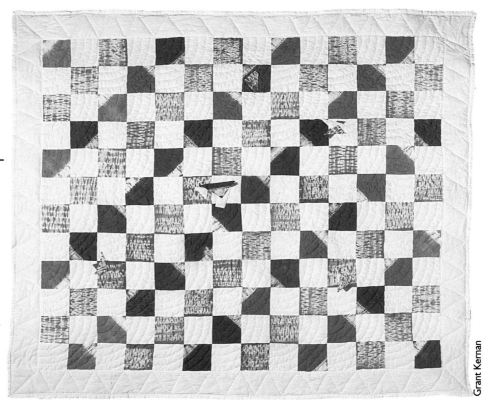

Grant Kernan

Workshop Quilt (54" x 63"), 1994

MORE PATTERNS

Susan offers some bonus ideas for patterns, described by photos:

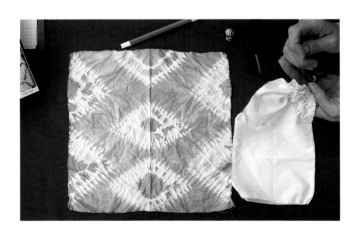

She demonstrates the use of a traditional shibori tool for making the little starburst dots so characteristic of traditional shibori.

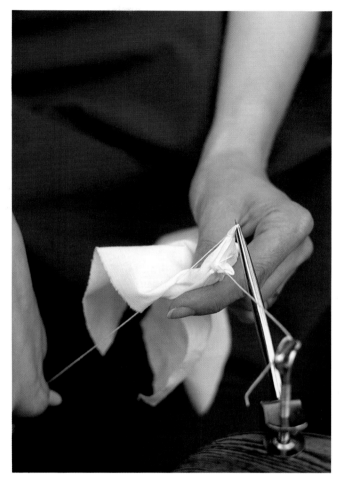

REFERENCES

Laury, Jean Ray. *The Creative Woman's Getting-it-all-together at Home Handbook.* New York: Van Nostrand Reinhold Co., 1977. ISBN 0-44224-704-4

Wada, Yoshiko, Rice, Mary Kellogg, and Borton, Jane. *Shibori, The Inventive Art of Japanese Shaped Resist Dyeing.* Japan: Kodansha International, 1983. ISBN 0-87011-559-6. Distributed in North America by Harper & Row.

CHAPTER 5

Carol Galloway

MANITOBA

With Workshop: Colour Value Wash and Hand-Appliqué

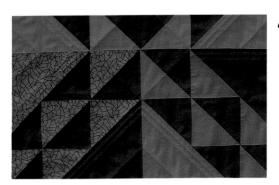

"No one should feel guilty about not finishing things started in a workshop, because knowledge is a goal in itself."

Contrary to a popular national myth, Manitoba is not one of the "western" provinces. This land of lakes occupies center-stage in Canada, in more ways than mere geography. Manitoba's capital city, Winnipeg, houses about half the province's population. It is famous for the world-class Royal Winnipeg Ballet, the Royal Canadian Mint which produces most of Canada's coinage, and for hosting "the windiest corner in Canada." It is also famous for the size of its mosquitoes.

This is not such a bad thing, particularly if you're an entomologist or a biological illustrator. In fact, it's the perfect environment in which to work. When quiltmaker Carol Galloway and her husband Terry bring giant moth larvae home to nurture to adulthood, then release into the neighbourhood, it's proof positive they are committed to the preservation of even the smallest living beings. And since they know when the mosquito larvae are due to hatch, they can plan their annual holiday accordingly!

First trained in fine arts, then pre-architecture, Carol eventually settled in to work as a biological illustrator and technician. Terry is an entomologist. Together with their two teenaged children, Andrew and Lindsay, they spent a year in New Zealand in 1991-1992 so that Terry could conduct entomological studies. Carol took the opportunity to concentrate on her long-standing interest in quiltmaking.

She says, "Away from many of the responsibilities which complicate my real life back home, I was almost totally free to immerse myself in quiltmaking. I joined two guilds and three home quilting groups, as well as an embroiderers' guild and a spinning and weaving group. I signed up for as many workshops as I could, and taught some while we were there, too. It was a dream come true, but many new friendships meant

---

Carol stands contentedly in bee territory, a field of flowering canola. The unearthly yellow of this crop is a frequent sight on the prairies. *Photo by T.D.Galloway.*

In the entomology lab, Carol draws fleas.

that leaving was painful. At least now I know how thin those international boundaries are, how easily they are crossed, and how similar to here life and people are on the other side of the world."

Carol credits some special quilting teachers for "leaving a lasting effect that goes beyond what they were teaching. From Canadian artist Laurie Swim came a more playful approach to design. Embroidery specialist Elizabeth Taylor prompted a more sculptural reaction to fabric. Quilting teacher Sue Spigel in New Zealand taught me to trust my instincts. And I was impressed by Canadian quilt artist and author Marilyn

The Fort Whyte Environmental Education Centre's marsh teems with animal life, most of it unseen below the water's surface or hidden within the rushes.

Carol Galloway, Manitoba

C.A.Galloway

Autumn gently settles on the tall grass prairie, near Gardenton, Manitoba.

Stothers's professionalism and focus. For me, her work legitimized quilts as an art form."

As a teacher herself, Carol is gaining fame for her awe-inspiring organizational skills. Furthermore, she encourages students to push themselves into new areas of quiltmaking, but also says "I think no one should feel guilty about not finishing a project started in a workshop, because knowledge is a goal in itself. I understand that some people are not their most creative under workshop conditions — I'm not myself." Carol is able to keep her class atmosphere relaxed and non-threatening.

Describing her design process, Carol says, "I find patterns of colour and texture particularly stimulating, but they are not enough in themselves. They get tucked away in the back of my brain until, for some inexplicable reason, they unite with an idea, a message I want to express or some method of reorganizing the colour or texture which is meaningful to me. When this union occurs, I'm very aware of it. The light bulb turns on. The idea is often not strong at first; it has to be coaxed along till I can grab hold of enough of it to start doodling a design or pulling out fabric. Then the process snowballs as the piece begins to dictate what comes next. It involves a lot of trial and error, maybe leaving it on the design wall for weeks while I work on another piece at a more settled stage of construction. As I work, my brain unconsciously stews on the design problems until decisions are made."

The subject matter of Carol's quilts often relates to those things she cares most about: "I feel very close to the Earth and am humbled by the power and beauty of its rhythms and cycles and patterns. I am afraid for the fragility of life. It is my love of all things natural and my concern for the future which I want to share through my quilts."

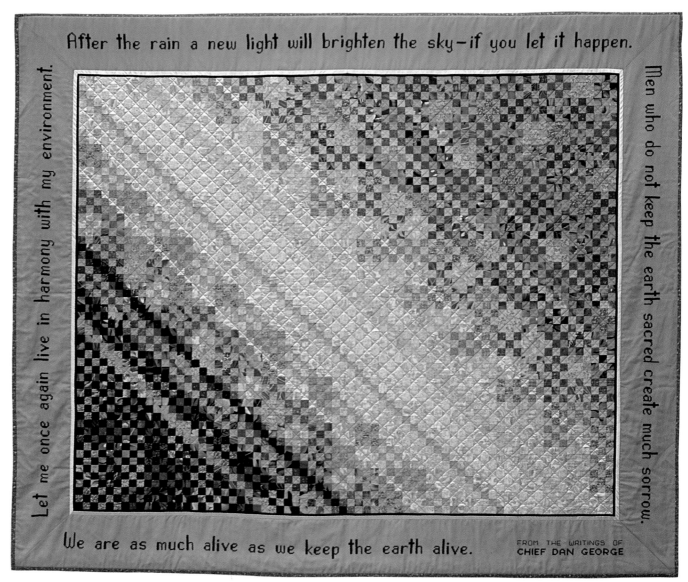

After the rain a new light will brighten the sky – if you let it happen.

Men who do not keep the earth sacred create much sorrow.

Let me once again live in harmony with my environment.

We are as much alive as we keep the earth alive.

FROM THE WRITINGS OF
CHIEF DAN GEORGE

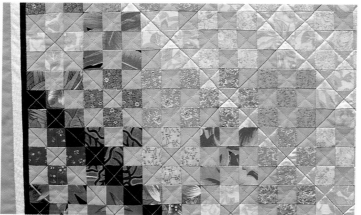

After the Rain (detail)

After the Rain (73.5"x85"), 1989

About her first original design, Carol says "At a time when I was facing a growing concern for the environment and the frustration of how to express it, I read and was moved by the writings of Chief Dan George. I wanted to bring his wisdom to a visual public, and to reflect my own love and concern for the natural world." The script on the borders is done with cross-stitch embroidery.

Carol Galloway, Manitoba

Cosmic Connections (41"x63"), 1990

This two-sided wall-hanging illustrates the opposing physical and spiritual forces in human nature.

Cosmic Connections *(back)*

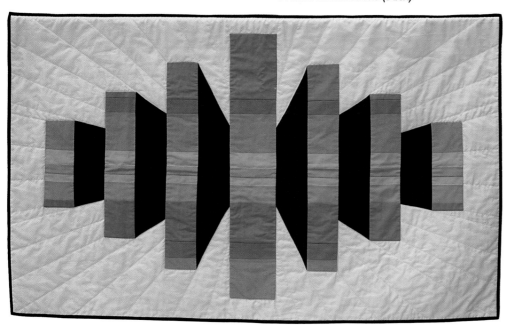

Reflections on Meech Lake (33"x54"), 1990

Carol made this hanging during the month when the Canadian prime minister Brian Mulroney met with provincial premiers at the Meech Lake retreat to negotiate a federal constitution which would be fair to all. "Most of us watching the progress of the talks on television felt as fractured as this flag, and worried that the power struggle among the parts was endangering the whole."

Carol Galloway, Manitoba

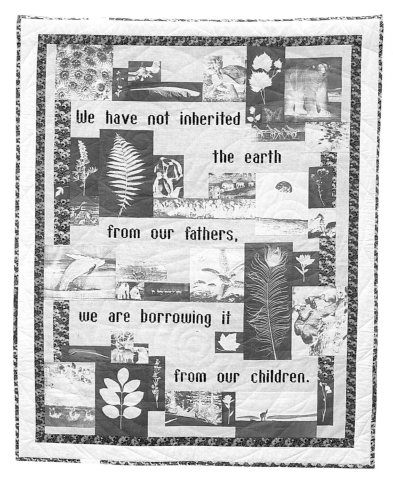

We have not inherited

the earth

from our fathers,

we are borrowing it

from our children.

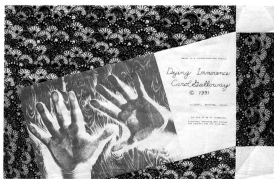

Dying Innocence (detail: back label)

Dying Innocence (69"x54"), 1991

Inspired by Native-American wisdom, the sunprinted panels combine with cross-stitching on burlap to "caution us to respect and treasure our home, our children's heritage," says Carol. "It is quilted in a ripple pattern because the actions of each of us have a ripple effect which either clashes with or augments the ripples created by those around us. The negative images suggest the memory of what was."

To underline the quilt's message, Carol incorporates her children's blueprinted handprints into the label.

Making Waves (59.5" x 59.5"), 1993

An original design based on the traditional block, Storm at Sea, the central block has been fractured as it moves outward. The fish print demanded to be included, which established the colour scheme. The aquatic theme continues with a 3-dimensional wave border. The quilt was machine pieced and quilted with metallic thread, in waves.

Carol Galloway

Carol Galloway, Manitoba

What's Black and White and Red All Over? (42"x34"), 1993

Entered into a show which required the use of a book or pattern published by That Patchwork Place, Carol chose the formula design technique described in One-of-a-Kind Quilts *by Judy Hopkins. Carol says, "I had been wanting to make a black and white wall quilt when I found the zebra print which provided the theme. To camouflage the zebra and enhance the puzzle idea, I included hand-dyed red fabrics."*

Carol Galloway

Carol Galloway

What's Black and White and Red All Over? (detail)

Carol Galloway, Manitoba

Carol Galloway

Aurora (60"x40.5"), 1994

"A true thrill on a dark prairie night is to stand outside as the aurora borealis dances across the sky in all directions, shimmmering pinks and greens and colours which defy naming. When I found the Spandex™ fabric streaked in all these fabulous colours, there was no question what it would be used for." The cotton fabrics were hand-dyed by Carol.

Carol Galloway

Aurora (detail)

Carol Galloway, Manitoba

Using Colour Value Wash and Hand-Appliqué

Level of difficulty: Advanced (machine and hand-sewing)

As further evidence of her interest in insects, Carol has designed a Viceroy butterfly in flight against the sun. All patterns are provided for you in this workshop so you will be able to complete *Flight of Fancy* without being a biological illustrator yourself. The background is composed of colour-washed strips of blue prints. "Colourwash" refers to the gradual change in value, or lightness or darkness of print fabrics. The blue background is machine-quilted in Carol's example, and the hand-quilted borders illustrate the life-cycle of the butterfly. Techniques used for the butterfly include hand-appliqué and *reverse-appliqué*.

Flight of Fancy (29.5"x29.5"), 1993

M A T E R I A L S

(**NOTE** : All fabrics should be washed and ironed. When ironing metallic fabric, follow manufacturer's special care instructions, as it can shrink, melt, or become dull from too much direct heat. Use of a press cloth may help.)

For the background, **a wide assortment** (between 12 and 89) **of blue cotton prints** is needed, ranging from very light, even a white or cream background with a blue print, through to a dark navy. If you use 12 different fabrics, each "round" of the octagonal background will use 8 pieces cut from one of your fabrics. If you have 89 different fabrics, each of the 8 pieces per "round" will be cut from a different piece of fabric. The strips used are 1 1/2" wide, and 3" to 12" long. A 3" square of your lightest fabric is required for the centre.

HINT: To increase fabric choices, try using the "wrong" sides of some fabrics.

1 meter (1 1/8 yards) black cotton for butterfly wings, border and binding.

.8 meter (7/8 yard) fabric for backing and hanging sleeve.

A piece of orange fabric for the butterfly, about 14" x 20". To enhance the effect of a light source behind the wings, Carol has hand-dyed her fabric so it deepens in intensity toward the wingtips.

A 10" square of silver metallic fabric for the spots on the wings

A 13"x 23" piece of lightweight cotton fabric to serve as a foundation for the butterfly

A 13"x 20" piece of cotton batting or *needle-punch batting* for padding the wings, a 32" square piece for the entire hanging, and a little loose polyester batting for the butterfly body.

A 26" square of tear-away *stabilizer* to use as a foundation for the octagon. If it needs to be pieced, try clear tape or loose hand-basting which can be removed later (see Appendix #4: *Sources*, for mail order sources). Lightweight paper can be used instead, or you might use a piece of light cotton fabric as the foundation, to be left in permanently.

A more textured piece of black fabric, like polyester crepe or cotton velveteen, about 3" x 8" for the butterfly body

Black beads (eyes), **black embroidery thread** (antennae)

Assorted blue, black and orange threads, metallic rainbow thread (Carol likes Sulky™ #142 7024) for border quilting

Drawing paper, lighter-weight paper for tracing the pattern to fabric, wax-free tracing paper or dressmaker's carbon

Clear quilting ruler, pencil, usual sewing supplies

CONSTRUCTION

Construction of the background

1 To prepare the octagon shape in the centre, mark the centre of the 26" square tear-away stabilizer foundation with two lines which cross at 90 degrees and are parallel with the edges of the stabilizer. With the aid of a clear ruler, draw a 2 ¹/₂" square in the centre (i.e. 1 ¹/₄" on each side of the two crossing lines). Draw two new crossing lines on the diagonal of the square to act as guides for drawing another 2 ¹/₂" square in the center, turned 45 degrees from the first. Draw the resulting octagon in darker.

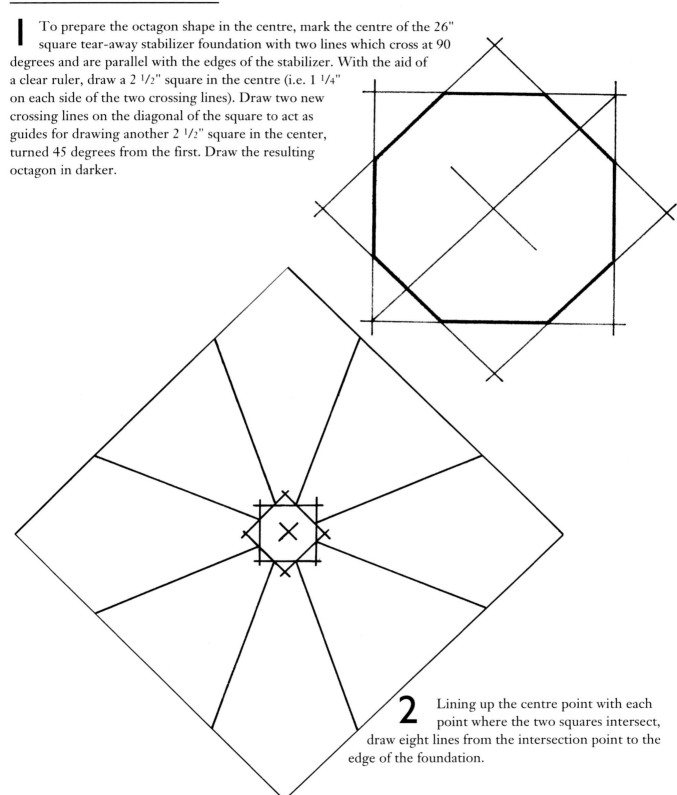

2 Lining up the centre point with each point where the two squares intersect, draw eight lines from the intersection point to the edge of the foundation.

3 With a sharp pencil, draw lines in 1" intervals to fill each wedge, echoing the central octagon.

4 Continue drawing these lines at 1" intervals until resulting octagon is 24 ¹/₂" across.

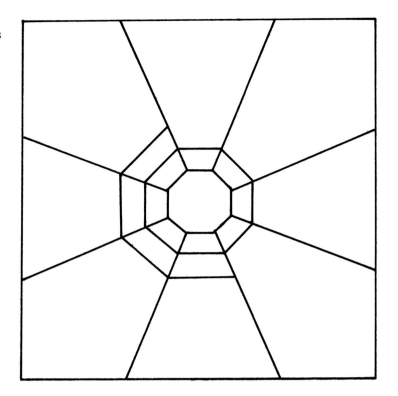

Selecting and cutting fabrics

Colour value is a term given to the relative lightness or darkness of a colour compared to those surrounding it. It is a measurement which ignores *hue*, *tint*, *shade*, *tone* and pattern or, perhaps more accurately, takes all of those things into account. The brain combines all of these elements to come up with a measurement of relative light and dark which is basic to all fabric selection, whether the project is a traditional block pattern, realistic representation or abstract design. The pattern of light and dark created will register with the viewer as surely as the pattern of colour.

5 Arrange the blue fabrics so that each is darker than the one before it.

HINTS: To see value rather than colour, it helps if you squint, take your glasses off, look through the wrong end of binoculars, turn off the room lights, use a peephole made for doors, look through transparent red acrylic (if there are no red-hued fabrics), or, as in this example, view through a camera out of focus. If one fabric stands out so there is not a smooth value transition, rearrange it so the transition will be smoother.

5. Arrange the fabrics by value.

View through a camera out of focus.

WORKSHOP: Using Colour Value Wash and Hand-Appliqué

6 Divide the fabrics into eleven piles of similar-value pieces. For her sample, Carol uses 89 different fabrics, so each pile has eight fabrics. If you are using only 12 fabrics (including the lightest value for the central octagon), each "round" of the octagon would consist of eight pieces cut from the same fabric.

7 From each of the 11 piles, cut 8 strips of fabric 1 1/2" wide and in the following lengths:

from the lightest-value pile:	3"
from the next darker pile:	4"
from the third (next darker):	5"
from the fourth:	6"
from the fifth:	6 1/2"
from the sixth:	7 1/2"
from the seventh:	8 1/2"
from the eighth:	9"
from the ninth:	10"
from the tenth:	11"
from the eleventh (darkest):	12"

8 Place your little piles of strips in order near your sewing machine. Trace the small central octagon to use as the pattern for the first piece to be sewn. Use your lightest-value fabric for this piece.

Sewing the background

9 Stitch the central octagon to the foundation, about 1/8" away from the edge.

9. Stitch the central octagon to the foundation.

10 Choose one of the 3" strips from the lightest pile, and press the 1/4" seam allowance to the wrong side along one long edge. Decide on the sewing order of the other 7 strips from the lightest pile, in such a way as to distribute the slight variations in value, colour and texture around the octagon.

10. Press the 1/4" seam allowance to the wrong side.

11 Place strip #1 in its "to-be-sewn" position, right side up along a flat side of the octagon. With its long raw edge along the parallel pencilled octagon, and its proposed seam line starting at one edge of the central fabric octagon, the strip will extend across into the next pencilled octagonal wedge.

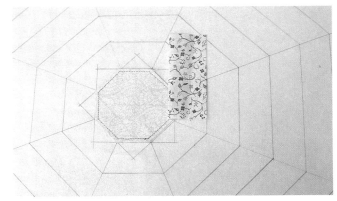

11. Place strip #1 in position.

12 Position strip #2, right side down, on top of the central octagon along the adjacent side (clockwise), so that its proposed seamline starts at one edge of the octagon and ends covering the first strip. While keeping the two strips in position, lift them up, open out the pressed-under seam allowance, and pin them together.

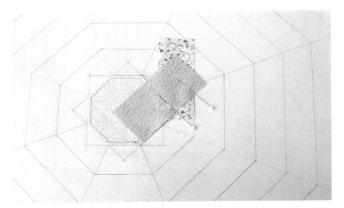

12. Position strip #2 and pin the two strips together.

13 Stitch the two strips together 1/4" from the raw edge of the second strip, as far as the pressed seamline of strip #1. Do not catch the seam allowance in your stitching.

13. Stitch the strips together.

14 Lightly mark the point on the fabric octagon where two 1/4" seamlines would intersect. Then, with a pin, match the end of the stitching (which joins the strips) to the point marked on the octagon.

14. With a pin, match the end of the stitching to the intersection point.

15 Lower the machine needle into the hole made by the last stitch on strip #2. Stitch one stitch forward, one stitch back, then stitch the rest of strip #2 to the octagon.

 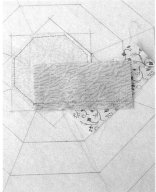

15. Stitch strip #2 to the octagon.

16 Trim away the triangle of excess fabric to prevent shadowing and bulk, then press strip #2 from the right side.

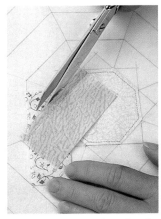 

16. Trim away triangle of excess fabric. Press strip #2.

17 Working clockwise, pin strip #3 right sides together to the next side of the octagon, covering the previous strip, and machine stitch the length of the strip. Trim and press.

17. Stitch strip #3, trim and press.

WORKSHOP: Using Colour Value Wash and Hand-Appliqué

18 Repeat the previous procedure with strips #4 to #8, pushing strip #1 out of the way before stitching strip #8 to the foundation.

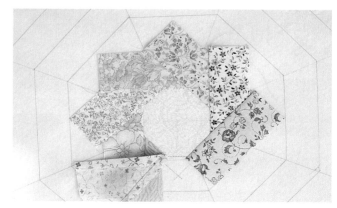

18. Repeat the previous procedure.

19 Fold strip #1 back into position, so that right sides are together, and pin into place over strip #8. Insert the machine needle into the last hole made by the partial seam joining strips #1 and #2, then do the forward-one-stitch-back-one-stitch trick to secure the stitches before stitching to the end of the seam of strip #1. (**NOTE** : This is awkward, on the first round especially, but it gets easier as the strips get longer on the subsequent rounds. An alternative method would be to hand-applique strip #1 to strip #8. Or, you may prefer to use the *Pineapple variation* of the Log Cabin block, in which four alternate strips are sewn on and pressed open, then the remaining four are sewn and pressed, covering the raw edges of the first four strips to complete the round. This Pineapple alternative would give a slightly different appearance to the pattern.)

19. Stitch the end of the seam of strip #1.

20 Trim away the triangles of excess fabric so you once again have an octagonal shape.

20. Trim away the triangles of excess fabric.

21 Organize the next darker pile of 4" strips for the second round so that you have a pleasing distribution of texture, value, and colour.

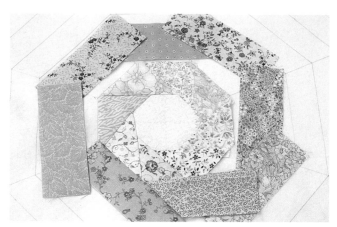

21. Organize the 4" strips for the second round.

22 Stitch this round in the same manner as your first.

22. Stitch the second round.

23 Stitch the rest of the rounds in the same manner until the resulting octagon is the desired size.

23. Stitch the rest of the rounds

Construction of the border

HINT : Subtle differences in colour can be noticeable when using black fabric, if you reverse the fabric back to front or change the fabric grain direction within a quilt. Cut the eight border pieces in the orientation that they'll be used, as described below.

24 Cut four strips of black, 3 3/4" x 10 1/2", two from the crosswise grain for the top and bottom, and two from the lengthwise grain for the sides. Label with "up" arrows, as they are cut. Stitch these to the four alternate sides of the octagon, then press open.

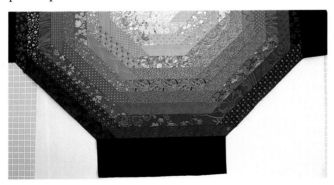

24. Cut four strips of black.

HINT: Very dark fabric often gets a "glazed" appearance from aggressive ironing. Press black fabric from the back only, or use a press cloth to prevent this permanent glazing.

25 Cut two 14" squares from the same side of the black fabric. Make a diagonal cut from top left to bottom right of one of these squares, and from top right to bottom left of the other square. Label the four resulting triangles with "up" arrows or appropriate numbers. Stitch these to the remaining four sides of the octagon. Trim away the excess from the black strips, then press. Square up the resulting piece by trimming, if necessary.

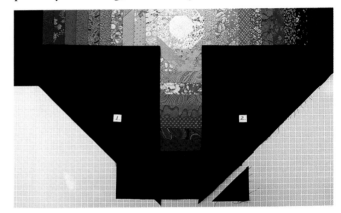

25. Stitch large triangles to the remaining four sides.

26 Taking care not to pull the octagon out of shape, remove the tear-away stabilizer from the back of the octagon.

Q U I L T I N G

Because of the three-dimensional quality of the butterfly, Carol recommends quilting the background before appliquéing the butterfly, as described below. In this way, the quilt will be less bulky and easier to manipulate for both machine and hand-quilting.

The Viceroy butterfly feeds on willow and poplar, so Carol has designed stylized willow leaves to wind around the border, and for each corner, a different stage of the butterfly's life cycle.

27 Onto lightweight paper, trace the full-sized patterns provided here, including the matching triangles and letters. Then, transfer the design to your quilt border, using pretested transfer paper or dressmaker's carbon.

WORKSHOP: Using Colour Value Wash and Hand-Appliqué

HINT : Before using the transfer paper, each colour should be tested for ease of removal on a scrap of the fabric you are planning to use. The wax-free type of transfer paper rubs off more easily, so may be traced with heavier pressure, using an inkless ballpoint pen for a fine line.

28 Prepare the quilt "sandwich." For tips on preparing the quilt sandwich, you may refer to Appendix #1: *The Nutshell Guide to Finishing Your Quilt.*

28. Prepare the *quilt "sandwich."*

HINT: Use fine, smooth, sharp "silk" safety pins from the drycleaner to temporarily hold the 3 layers together. A spoon is a useful tool to encourage the pin tips to the surface. Carol likes to use the grooves of a grapefruit spoon to guide the pin tip into the clasp.

29 Carol suggests machine-quilting the octagon to give strength to support the weighty butterfly. Using an *even-feed foot* on your sewing

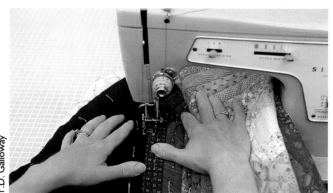

29. Machine-quilt the octagon.

machine, quilt the octagon, starting in the centre, and sewing "in the ditch" (along the seamline). Match the top thread to the shade of blue you are quilting on, and the bobbin thread to the backing fabric.

HINT : To avoid tying a lot of knots and having to conceal the thread ends, you might like to try gradually reducing the size of stitches to "0" in the last 1/4" of each quilting line. Then clip the threads to the stitching. This method takes practice before you use it on a quilt project.

30 Hand-quilt the border design, using metallic thread. Thread lengths of about 12" are most manageable.

30. Hand-quilt the border design.

HINT: As all metallic threads are not created equal, try out your threads on a sample to find one you enjoy using.

31 Bind the quilt, label it, and sew on the hanging sleeve at this point, if you wish, before appliquéing the butterfly. Refer to Appendix #1: *The Nutshell Guide to Finishing Your Quilt*, and Appendix #3: *Documentation, Care and Conservation of Quilts* for information about this step.

31. Bind and label the quilt.

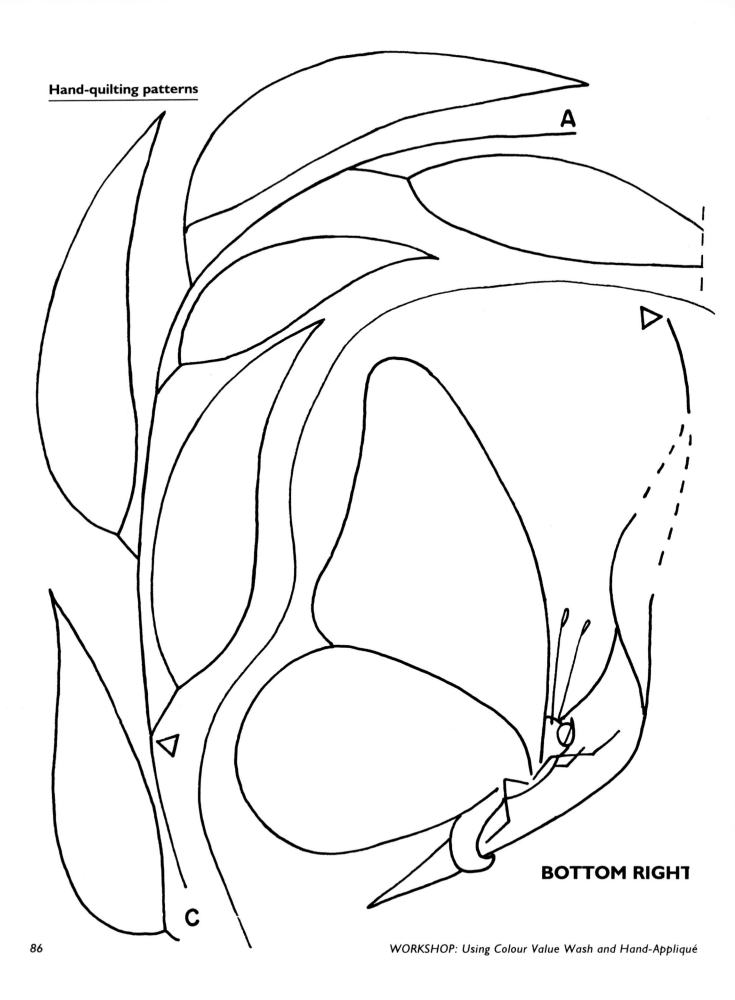

Hand-quilting patterns

A

▷

▷

C

BOTTOM RIGHT

WORKSHOP: Using Colour Value Wash and Hand-Appliqué

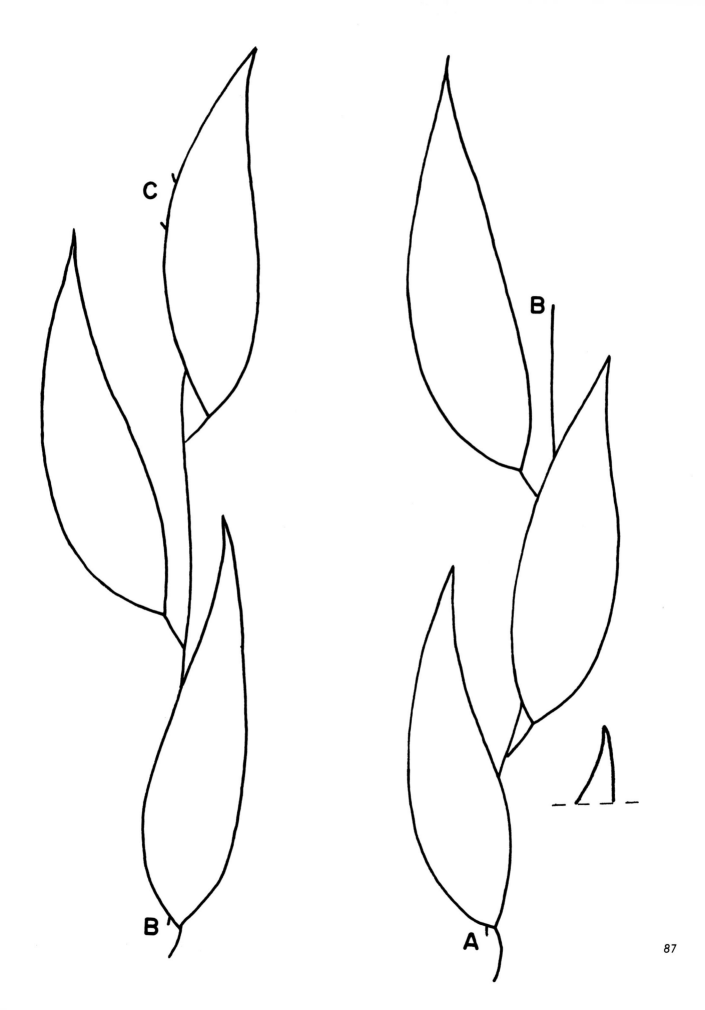

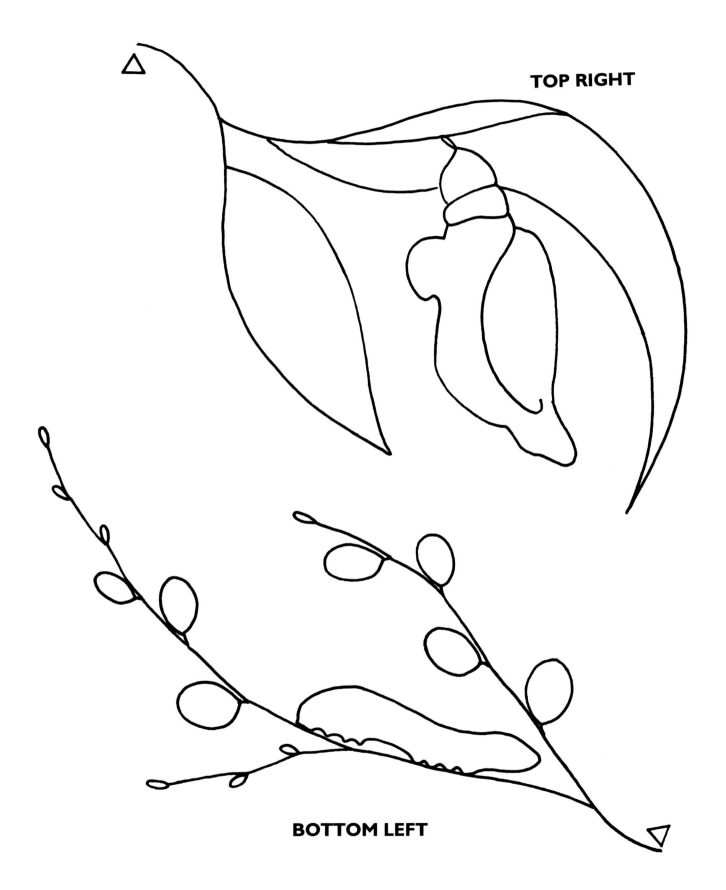

TOP RIGHT

BOTTOM LEFT

WORKSHOP: Using Colour Value Wash and Hand-Appliqué

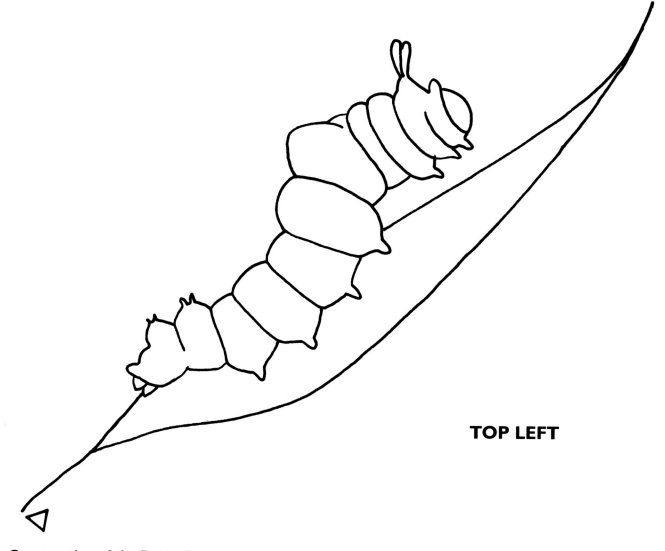

TOP LEFT

Construction of the Butterfly

Pattern preparation

32 Enlarge the butterfly pattern. For help with enlargement, see Appendix #5: *Enlarging Methods*. If you choose the grid method, use a 3" grid to draw your enlarged pattern from the ³/₄" grid pattern provided. (**NOTE** : The two halves of the butterfly have been drawn separately and are not identical.) Trace the pattern onto a second sheet of paper, which will be used to transfer the pattern onto the fabric and then cut up for pattern pieces.

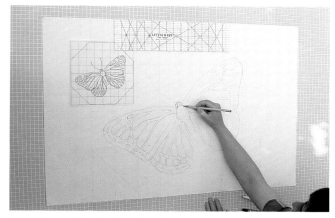

32. Enlarge the butterfly pattern.

33 Pin and transfer the pattern onto a piece of foundation fabric, using dressmaker's transfer paper.

34 Using a colour of transfer paper which can just barely be seen, trace the pattern of the wings onto your orange fabric. In the photo, the wing shapes are marked on the pattern in red, approximately 1/4" outside the area of orange.

Mark and cut the two halves of the butterfly separately.

33. Transfer the pattern onto foundation fabric.

WORKSHOP: Using Colour Value Wash and Hand-Appliqué

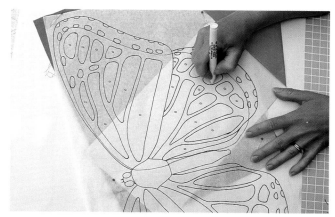

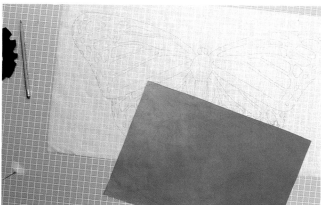

34. Transfer the pattern of the wings onto your orange fabric.

35 Mark and cut the metallic fabric for the butterfly's silver dots. As a guide, the areas marked in blue on the pattern in the photo extend approximately ¹/₄" beyond the area of silver dots.

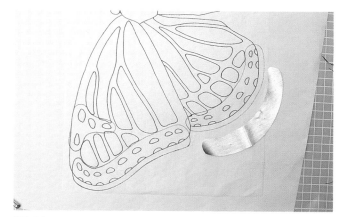

35. Mark and cut the metallic fabric.

36 On black cotton, individually mark and cut the four wing shapes, including the interior veins. Leave a turn-under allowance of ³/₁₆" where possible, and ¹/₄" around the outside of the wings.

Sewing the Butterfly

37 Position one piece of the orange fabric onto the marked foundation fabric, matching the markings, and pin. Position and pin the silver fabric, then the black (hindwing first; then the forewing). Hand-baste all these layers into position along the middle of the black wing veins to keep them from shifting, and remove pins.

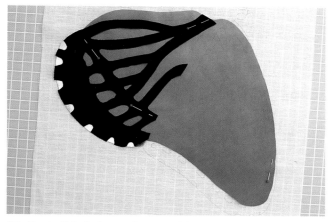

37. Baste fabric layers into position.

38 Beginning with a large central orange area, clip the concave curves and into the corners, ⁷/₈ths of the way through the turn-under allowance. Then starting with a long, straight section, and using

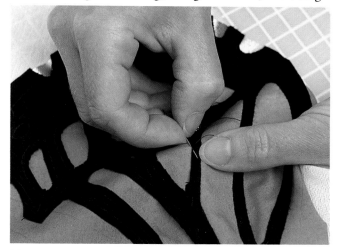

38. Appliqué the black fabric to the underfabric.

black thread, appliqué the black fabric to the underfabric. To do this, *needle-turn* and finger-press the edge along the markings, and blind-stitch to the matching markings below.

39 Appliqué the other three wings to the orange and silver with the foundation below, as in steps 37 and 38. Remove the basting stitches.

39. Appliqué the other three wings.

40 Using your drawing as a pattern (less 1/4" all around), cut two pieces of batting for placement under the left and right wing sections.

40. Cut two pieces of batting for the wing sections.

41 Tack the batting in place under the wings. From the back, trim as much as possible of the foundation fabric away from the butterfly shape, leaving a little bridge joining the two wings where the body will go.

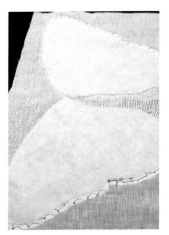 

41. Tack the batting in place under the wings.

42. Appliqué the butterfly to the background.

42 Position the butterfly on the quilted background as if it has been caught in mid-flight with the sun behind it, pin it in place, then appliqué it to the background. (**NOTE** : Take care to conceal knots under the butterfly, and catch only the top layer of the background to prevent unsightly stitches on the back of the quilt.)

43 Cut a body from the textured black fabric, using the tracing as a pattern, and adding 1/4" turn-under allowance. Stitch a line of fine running stitches across the body between the head and thorax, and also between the thorax and abdomen, and pull them gently to define the three body segments, before tying securely. Stuff a little batting under the body. (The photo shows the body from the wrong side.)

43. Make the butterfly body.

WORKSHOP: Using Colour Value Wash and Hand-Appliqué

44 Pin the body in place between the wings, then appliqué it to the background.

Carol Galloway

44. Appliqué the body to the background.

45 Stitch on the bead eyes, and embroider the antennae with a stem stitch, ending with one lazy daisy stitch for the little knob.

YOU'RE DONE!

R E F E R E N C E S

Amsden, Deirdre. *Colourwash Quilts.* Bothell, WA: That Patchwork Place, 1994. ISBN 1-56477-051-6

CHAPTER 6

Win Burry

ONTARIO

With essay: Whither Thou Goest: Sources of Inspiration

*"Our country is like a long laundry line.
It's impossible to get together."*

Our conversation begins in the peace and solitude of Win Burry's rural pine cottage in Ontario's Muskoka Lakes district. It is to this accessible cottage country that the inhabitants of the huge metropolitan Toronto area flock for weekends and holidays. Since Ontario has the largest population of all the provinces, getting to some less hurried environment is a priority for its citizens.

Here is where Win rests from the turmoil of her daily life. Here is where she reads philosophy and makes remarkable pictorial appliquéd quilts.

For four years, Win struggled with helping to manage the care of her terminally-ill mother. Before her mother's illness, her father was in poor health for many years. Win says, "We had 28 'last' Christmases after his heart attack." With her wry sense of humour, her love of books ("I'd die if I couldn't read!"), her quilting, and most importantly, her family, Win survives her trying times. Through these years she has emerged with a personal and spiritual philosophy as well as an optimism and love that fuels her creativity.

On average, Win makes one quilt a year. She signed up for her first quilting course in 1975 thinking, "If I learn to quilt I might be able to make banners." No banners are evident in Win's home, however. There are few quilts, either, because each quilt Win makes is given to her beloved family. Her husband Jamie, grown sons Guy, Donald and John, and daughter-in-law Liz, are usually the beneficiaries.

"It started with a graduation gift. When I bet Guy he wasn't going to get into the University of Toronto, he said, 'Would you make me a quilt if I do?' It was the first

Win Burry at her Lake Joseph cottage

Ottawa, Canada's capital city, is home to the Houses of Parliament.

Niagara Falls is Ontario's most popular tourist destination.

time I ever knew he was interested." Then her second son, Donald, requested a quilt based on the Native artists of the Woodland School, who were the first to use a pictographic or x-ray style of painting. It was Donald's encouragement that propelled Win so firmly into the study of Native spirituality. Finally, youngest son, John, who encouraged her to read a lot of books that he thought would inspire her, requested a quilt with "no tacky prints." This request marked a change to a more vibrant, graphic style in Win's work.

Fellow quilters in the York Heritage Guild admired her work and encouraged her. "It all goes back to your guild. They're the ones that get you launched," says Win. When eminent quilting instructor Virginia Avery visited a guild meeting and saw Win's Kenojuak's Owls, her enthusiastic response started a chain of events which exposed Win's work internationally.

Now Win enters her quilts into one major show every two years. In 1992 her evocative piece, *Distant Dreams* won a Judges' Choice award at Quilt Expo Europa III. She cites this award as one of the most emotional events in her quilting life. When Georgia Bonesteel, the host of the PBS series, *Lap Quilting* asked, "What does it feel like to win a ribbon in an international show?", Win was so stunned she said, "Well, um, pretty great, I guess."

"At inspiring quilting events such as Quilt Expo Europa you see the work that is being done in all the countries, like the Rumanian cot quilts the British quilters are making to send to Rumania, the quilts the Germans have done to raise money for world wildlife, and the AIDS project in the U.S.," says Win. "Quilting is a very large part of the women's movement. It isn't strident and it isn't pushy."

Win Burry, Ontario

With all the acclaim she receives for her work, Win could easily capitalize on her kudos. She gets letters asking for patterns and commissions. She says, "I don't want to market. These are made for my family. My quilts are me, they are my philosophy, they are from my heart. I couldn't turn around and say do it this way." Although she likes to speak to groups, she will not teach or commercialize her craft.

Win is willing to describe her quiltmaking process, however. "Usually, the design will begin with a vision that will come when I'm reading. I'll start sketching and eventually it will come. When I was in Denmark, I was drawing away on my next quilt and when I got to the conference, there was my piece. It was exactly what I had sketched. Somebody had made it, and it had not been shown before. This is why I believe there is a central supply up there and this person had tapped in before I had tapped in.

"As a child, I was considered not artistic. I did take one life drawing course as an adult. When the teacher came along and saw my work, he said, 'Chicken scratch, chicken scratch, too many lines, one line will do!' So I learned from that to draw with one line. And by the end of that course, he would look over my shoulder and say, 'Possible, quite possible.' So that was my art training.

"After sketching, I'll draw the design in small scale on to graph paper, then I'll just fold up my large paper into squares and draw roughly from the graph paper. I use a tracing from my large drawing as a pattern for cloth. Sometimes I'll cut out five, six, seven different fabrics that aren't right, and end up with a pile of rejections, but I have to cut it and put it in to see what it is really going to look like. As soon as a piece is made, I throw out my drawings, because I'm never going to make another one.

"I *machine piece* the background, and often the borders. The pieced work is anguish. I don't control my machine happily; it controls me. Then I hand-appliqué using the traditional *needle-turning* method, and cut away the extra fabric layers from behind. It was [Canadian quilting teacher] Ann Bird who suggested cutting away behind. She has been very supportive and has encouraged me along. To appliqué a moon or bullrushes, I'll baste around the edge, pull it tightly around a cardboard template and steam it to get the curves smooth. The cardboard is removed before I appliqué."

When Win is at the quilting stage, she says, "I have to count out the size 13 quilting needles, so I won't lose any. They're so small. There's one side of the needle that's easier to thread, and I use a dental magnifier that clips onto my glasses to see that side.

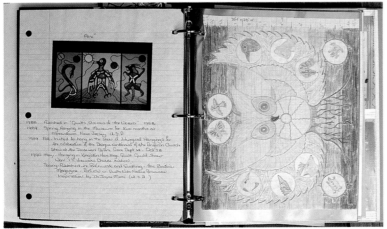 

Win documents her quilting life in well-organized notebooks. See Appendix #3: *Documentation, Care and Conservation of Quilts*, for more ideas to ensure your quilts can tell their own story in the future.

With a dental magnifier clipped to her glasses, Win demonstrates her quilting technique at the dining room table. She is working on *A Feather Upon the Breath of God*.

I'll take about three stitches at a time, and my first stitch is a titch longer than the next two, which makes 'dash dot dot' like a reverse SOS in morse code, so it's 'help, help, help' all the way across my quilts."

At home, Win says, "Fortunately I have a supportive husband who says, 'When are you going to get doing some quilting?' And my children like to see a mother who has an identity beyond them, who's not going to be on their necks all the time. I like to sit at that dining room table and have the young people come and chat."

Since her quiltmaking represents such a personal philosophy, why does Win exhibit her quilts and give lectures? "I meet people through it. It's a whole other world opening."

Win Burry

Communication (88"x68"), 1981
Collection of John Douglas Rogers Burry

Based on a print of the same name by Jackson Beardy, Communication *was a graduation gift to Win's youngest son John. John is a ham radio operator, a musician, a composer, and an avid reader, so communication is an appropriate theme. This quilt marks the beginning of Win's bold graphic quilting style.*

Kenojuak's Owls (72"x72"), 1984
Collection of Guy James Rogers Burry

When Win sent a photo of this quilt to Kenojuak Ashevak, in Cape Dorset, Baffin Island, Northwest Territories, the artist wrote her a letter in Inuit which Win had translated: 'I am so pleased that you won with my design. That's all I have to say, and good-bye even though I have never seen you before. I am happy.' Later, Win was able to meet Kenojuak at the Inuit Art Gallery in Toronto: "She hugged me and laughed. She was happy that I had done it."

Donald Standfield

Win Burry, Ontario

Donald Standfield

Amish Sweetgrass (43"x43"), 1985
Collection of C. James Burry

According to Win, Amish Sweetgrass *is based on the art style of Norval Morrisseau, the 'father' of the Woodland School, or pictographic style, of First Nations artists. Within the Thunderbird, protector, is the Shaman or holy man, and within the Shaman is the white circle which represents the 'light of Christ within', she says. "The four circles represent the four seasons, the four ages of man, and the four corners of the universe. They are bisected to show the duality of all things. The lines of communication show that everything is interdependent and goes on forever. The crown of thorns border represents the life and death of Christ."*

Pax (40"x72"), 1988. Collection of John Douglas Rogers Burry

This triptych depicts the triumph of good over evil. Says Win, "Peace comes within the souls of men when they realize their oneness with the universe and all its powers, and when they realize that the centre is really everywhere, it is within each of us."

Donald Standfield

Omega Point (32"x38"), 1988
Collection of C. James Burry

This quilt design is "based on [philosopher] Teilhard de Chardin's vision that the Omega Point is the point where all things come together in Christ," explains Win. "This work is our family tree using the symbolism of the Native medicine wheel. The owl is the only creature that can pass into the dream world and back and is considered to be a spiritual guide. Within his wings are the creatures from the medicine wheel that represent the individuals of our family. The creatures in the four circles outside the owl represent the four elements: frog (water), turtle (land), butterfly (air) and thunderbird (fire)."

Distant Dreams (49.5"x55.5"), 1991. Collection of Donald Alexander Rogers Burry

"A depiction of my own personal discovery of the oneness of all within the universe," says Win. "Mother Earth, [the figure is inspired by the art style of Maxine Noel], gazes into the crystal ball, sees herself reflected, and knows that peace comes when men realize their oneness with the universe and all its powers." The title, Distant Dreams, *is based on a poem written by Win at 15 years of age (Last stanza):*

How glad am I . . .
To have gazed into the soft stilly twilight
Of distant dreams where
I have seen, and known.

Donald Standfield

Whither Thou Goest (40.5"x51"), 1990
Collection of C. James Burry

The midnight moon's soft rays caress
Our Mother Earth and Father Sky,
And to the cadence of the pines
Wings softly beat their lullaby.
                        —Win Burry, 1990

"The Canadian geese mate for life and are therefore a
symbol of consummate friendship. The moon contains the
eye of the Shaman, at the centre of which is the white
circle symbolizing the light of Christ which is within
every atom of the universe."

Donald Standfield

A Feather Upon the Breath of God (50"x50"), 1993

"This mandala represents the oneness of all in the Light
of the Great Spirit. The Eagle represents the power of
the Great Spirit and his down feathers the breath of Life.
His protective wings embrace the Universe. The soul of
man reaches out and is released to soar with the Eagle,
forever free, A Feather Upon the Breath of God.

"The border quilting pattern between the stars is the
Buddhist symbol of the soul's pilgrimage through life.
The soul climbs through the four elements, to its purifi-
cation, from darkness into light. The title is inspired by
Abbess Hildegard of Bingen, Germany, a 12th century
mystic and prophet."

WHITHER THOU GOEST:
Sources Of Inspiration
ESSAY BY WIN BURRY

"Inspiration is the gentle listening to the wisdom of our inner being." —ANNE WILSON SCHAEF

"Inspiration comes very slowly and quietly."

—BRENDA UELAND

Our creative inspiration must be waited for slowly, slowly and then, as if the gods had spoken, we know the path. It is never an easy path but, as in the birth process, the outcome is worth all the effort. Each person finds her own sources of inspiration. Through any or all of our senses, music, the written word, paintings, architecture, the land, sea and air, the whole universe speaks to us. There is nothing that does not have the potential to inspire.

Why have I been influenced by Native art and philosophy to such a degree? Is it right to use the symbolism of another culture in my work?

Native art speaks so very profoundly to my soul. There are many other artists whose works inspire me (Monet or Tiffany, for example), but they do not express a spiritual philosophy. It is the spiritual aspect of Native art which has influenced me the most.

The Native peoples' belief in the oneness of man with his world, the feeling of wholeness, of not being divided from any part of our universe and all its powers, is what most influences me in my work. What we do to other creatures, plants, and all natural forms, we do to ourselves. This is a knowledge that makes me profoundly humble.

My spirituality is evolving constantly. I was raised in the Anglican Church, where the music and liturgy greatly influenced me. In my middle years, I began a study of the Quaker way of life which had been my paternal family roots. Again I was deeply touched. Then, when researching Native spirituality at the time I began making Native art style quilts, the beliefs seemed to blend with the Quaker approach. All of these influences, gradually absorbed through study and philosophical discussions, have enriched my own very personal beliefs.

The art which portrays Native philosophy tends to be strongly graphic and so is particularly amenable to the quilt medium. My adaptations of Kenojuak's and Morrisseau's art is done with public acknowledgement of my sources. Recently, the human forms in my work have been inspired by the work of Maxine Noel and my "moons" are styled on those in the paintings of Roy Vickers. All my work is made, with a great deal of love, for family members only. It is the love in the process which makes my work what it is. But Native American art has only recently taken on the European form of ornamentation to hang on walls. Their traditions were generally oral ones and their art decorated useful items: carved masks for religious ceremonies, beadwork and quillwork on garments and baskets, for example. Then, sometime around 1840, Zacharie Vincent, a Huron Native from the village of Lorette, near Quebec City, had his portrait painted by Antoine Plamondon. Vincent was so inspired by this experience that he made several copies for himself.[1] Later, Native culture seemed on the verge of extinction because the dominant European culture had banned Native ceremonies and discouraged Native language and socialization by educating Native children apart from their families. "Consequently, the long and sacred traditions that were the roots of ceremonial art ebbed to an unforgivable low as the artists . . . accepted Euro-Canadians' aesthetic tastes, their culture and their established order."[2]

In the early 1960s, there was a move by several individuals, including the late Jackson Pollock, to help preserve [native] culture in both writing and art. Pollock, a Toronto painter/dealer/critic, held an exhibition of the art of Norval Morrisseau, an Ojibwa artist.[3] Morrisseau's source of inspiration was the Indian rock paintings or pictographs from over 100 sites around the Great Lakes. Many of the pictographs are figured to be 400–500 years old, and are painted on rock faces using a mixture of pigment and possibly fish or bird egg. The drawings are frequently very high up on rocky cliffs and also under water, as water levels have changed over the centuries. There was also a linear type drawing on birchbark scrolls used by shamans or holy men to record sacred songs and ceremonies, which had a strong influence on Morrisseau's style.

By the very act of reproducing the pictographs, Norval Morrisseau, who is himself a shaman, was the first Native artist to break the centuries-old taboo against using the pictographs and scrolls for public display. Many others followed his example.

We are all influenced by others even though we may not even be aware of it. It is difficult to talk about subconscious inspiration without mentioning Carl Jung and his belief in the collective unconscious and archetypes. Jung believed that there are patterns common to all mankind, constant forms which appear in works throughout all societies and cultures. He called these fundamental forms archetypes. An example is the circle, the universal symbol of totality, bisected to show duality in the work of Morrisseau and in the Yin + Yang of the ancient Taoist Chinese culture.

The circle is so universal because it is an experience common to all mankind. We experience it in the day, the year, the circle of life. The sacred circle of the Hindu, the mandala, is used by many other cultures and belief systems: Zen's empty circle of enlightenment, Egypt's Ankh, and Venus's symbol in astrology, for example.[4] The examples of symbols which appear in many cultures are as numerous as the cultures in which they appear. Animals, objects in nature, colours, musical instruments, crosses, anything can be symbolized.

The pictographs of our Native peoples bear a very strong resemblance to those of the aboriginal people of Australia, those in the Atlas mountains of North Africa, the Palaeolithic cave paintings in Lasceau, France,5 and the Celtic Uffington White Horse in Oxfordshire, England.6

Our inspiration comes to us as individuals from a realm which is universal, from one "source." If people separated by continents and time have a similar vision, that is not surprising. Teilhard de Chardin's term noosphere describes "the layer of thought that hovers above nature and acts as a universal consciousness."7 When we create, we tap into this noosphere, the energy flows. The inspiration is as endless as the universe and as complete as the divine energy that is within it.

1. Elizabeth McLuhan and Tom Hill, *Norval Morrisseau and the Emergence of the Image Makers* (Metheun Publishers), page 11.
2. McLuhan and Hill, page 13.
3. Lister Sinclair and Jackson Pollock, *The Art of Norval Morrisseau* (Metheun Press).
4. J.C. Cooper, *An Illustrated Encyclopedia of Traditional Symbols* (Thames and Hudson, publisher), page 37.
5. Selwyn Dewdney and Kenneth Kidd, *Indian Rock Paintings of the Great Lakes* (University of Toronto Press), pages 19, 28, 61.
6. John Sharkey, *Celtic Mysteries – The Ancient Religion* (Thames and Hudson, publisher), figures 26 and 27.
7. Pierre Teilhard de Chardin, *The Phenomenon of Man* (Harper and Row, New York), 1965.

Adaire Schlatter

QUEBEC

With Workshop: Real Flowers from the Garden

"Imagination is like an elastic band; if you put it on a shelf, it rots, but use it and it stretches and stretches."

Crossing the border into Canada's largest province, a traveller is soon made aware of Québecois culture. Anglophone eyes notice road signs written in French, fast-food chains selling *poutine* (French fries sprinkled with white cheese curds and smothered in gravy), eye-catching fashions and historic architecture. The province's capital, Quebec City, was founded in 1608 and still retains a distinctive European flavour.

In the rural areas there is ample evidence that Quebecers know how to enjoy their leisure: most homes have verandahs equipped with bench swings and rockers which are occupied by keen observers of life.

For Adaire Schlatter and her husband, George, the several months they spend each year in the country at their rustic cottage on Lac Memphremagog, on the southern border of Quebec, allows them leisure in the ways they enjoy most. Adaire relaxes by tending her vibrant English country garden, and by quilting.

As a self-taught quilter, Adaire first produced "great quilts for the cottage: real toe-catchers" (referring to very large stitches) before deciding to take some courses. One of her early quilting teachers in Quebec was Sandi Pope, who asked Adaire to take over her classes when she moved out of the Montreal area in 1981.

Growing up in Winnipeg, Adaire had been exposed to professional craftspeople while her mother was president of the Canadian Handicrafts Association. "European crafters were in and out of the house all the time," she says. She grew up with artistic people around her; her mother was a tapestry weaver. Adaire herself went on to obtain

Adaire's favourite place to be is her hillside garden, from which many a quilt idea is born.

In Mansonville, Quebec, one of the few remaining round barns, circa 1910, still stands, unused.

a Bachelor of Interior Design degree in 1953 before moving to Quebec. There, she held various positions in the home decorating field as well as being an interior designer for Bell Canada.

All facets of quilting appeal to Adaire. Her own style could be described as "eclectic non-traditional," because she has a broad range of needlework skills, as well as an experimental nature. She is a sought-after conference teacher and quilt show judge in Canada, and has given generously of her time for guild executives and for convening exhibitions since 1981. Although her own quilting style has a distinctly contemporary appeal, she documents and studies historical quilts in the on-going Quebec Heritage Quilt registry. At last count, Adaire and her co-workers have documented and photographed over seven hundred quilts.

Her continuing study of quilts in Quebec has suggested a theory to Adaire. Many of the quilts she sees were brought there from out of the province. She believes the *habitants* came to the area with weaving expertise and that many of their bedcoverings were woven rather than quilted. Where quiltmakers would use strips and scraps of fabric to piece or appliqué a quilt, the weavers wove those strips of fabric into heavy fabric called *catalogne*. In those parts of Quebec where quiltmaking occurs, it is a relatively recent, fast-growing phenomenon. Adaire looks forward to watching regional quiltmaking trends develop and the quiltmaking tradition build in Quebec.

While teaching, in English or in French, Adaire has a relaxed, flexible approach. She'll suggest to students, "Don't be obsessed by the rules that you've learned. Let yourself open up and experiment. If you make an error, that's a learning experience. In many cases you can fudge it and in the process make it your own design." She paraphrases Somerset Maugham, "Imagination is like an elastic band; if you put it on a shelf it rots, but use it and it stretches and stretches."

Her own quilts reflect this flexibility. While all her work retains the essence of the traditional, Adaire can't make any pattern without changing it in some way, and more often she'll invent an original. She says, "Most of my pieces grow like topsy. I seldom know what the border is going to be like when I start the centre. I build from the background and fill in where it needs to be filled in. Maybe that's why I can't play chess. I can't think six jumps ahead."

Even though most of Adaire's quilts are done by handsewing, finding the time has not been so difficult for her. "I've always been independent and found time for me. I support myself mentally by quilting. It helps that I have the support from my husband, George. He's creative and always willing to help with opinions and physical setups wherever he can."

A typical three-storey walk-up, complete with ivy and lace curtains, on Montreal's St. Urbain Street

Close Pursuit (59"x69"), 1983
Collection of B. Schlatter

Adaire finds this quilt holds much personal feeling for her. "At the time it was my most successful pictorial quilt. My son was really involved in cycling, and he helped me by redrawing the legs so they depicted real cyclist's muscles. I think he was the first in my family to take my quilting seriously."

Close Pursuit (detail)

Adaire Schlatter, Quebec

Water, Forests, and Bridges (98.5"x76.5"),
1986

*Made for the Folk Art Pavilion at Expo '86 in
Vancouver as a touchable quilt, this piece incorporates various elements of Vancouver's environs.
Adaire was invited to demonstrate quilting skills
at Expo.*

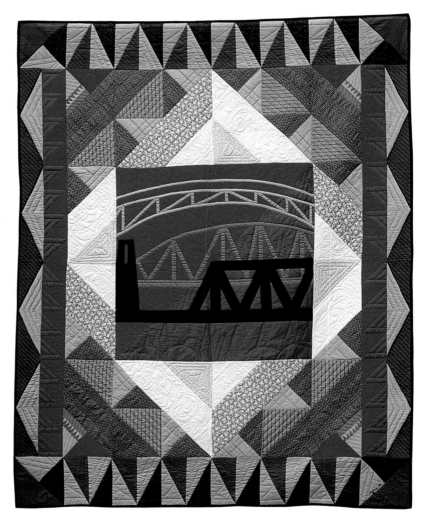

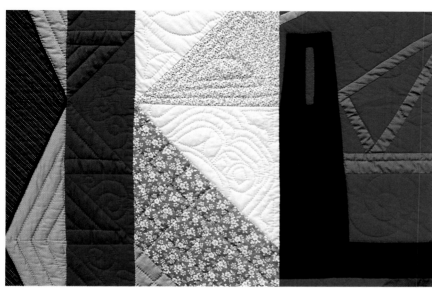

Water, Forests, and Bridges (detail)

Richard the Lionhearted (47"x55"), 1986

Living just north of Vermont, USA, Adaire often attends the Vermont Quilt Festival. On its 10th anniversary, she chose to honour its director, Richard Cleveland, and some of those quilting teachers who attended, by representing them in symbols that relate to their work or personalities. For instance: Blanche Young (Trip Around the World); Ann Bird (three birds); Yvonnne Porcella (clothing); Jean Ray Laury (house); Nancy Halpern (trees); and Jo Diggs (church).

Swans (42"x38"), 1989

Advertisements, with their powerful graphics, can often be adapted to a quilt design. Inspiration for this Celtic-style (continuous line) piece was an ad for a Swan Lake ballet.

Three Birds (25"x30"), 1990
Collection of Mr. and Mrs. K. Losch

Made in a workshop with Lucretia Romey, a New England artist, this design is based on sketches drawn by Adaire. The technique used was a flip-and-sew *method.*

Lizard (64"x47"), 1990
Collection of B. Schlatter

Adaire's daughter, a Canadian triathlete, was sponsored by "Lizard" sports clothing company. The lizard motif served as the inspiration for this design.

Icosahedron Unfolded (81"x49"), 1990

This design is based on the actual molecular structure of the common cold, found in the journal Trends in Biochemical Sciences.

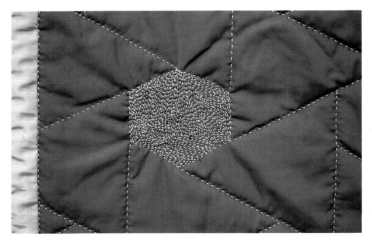

Icosahedron Unfolded (detail)

This quilting detail shows Adaire's humorous interpretation of a sneeze.

Adaire Schlatter, Quebec

Quilt Canada Workshop Sampler (41"x41"), 1990

A sampler *with a difference, this was made to showcase quilting techniques brought to Canada from other countries. In Adaire's workshop, "Transplanted Traditions," participants choose to sample one or two of these techniques. Quilting veterans should be able to find* Mola *from Panama, Pennsylvania* Amish *triangles,* Pa N Dau *from Indochina,* Mennonite *quilting.*

Flower Power (48"x50"), 1992

This piece, which won the Canada Quilts Magazine award of excellence at Quilt Canada '92, is the inspiration for Adaire's workshop.

Real Flowers from the Garden

Level of difficulty: Intermediate (with experience in hand-appliqué, see Chapter 5 for instruction)

Part of Adaire Schlatter's extensive "Touches and Textures" workshop is three-dimensional floral appliqué, a revived and reconsidered approach to realistic representation in quiltmaking. Adaire cites the stylized, formally symmetrical flowers of the Baltimore Album Quilts, circa 1860, as the "new" quilt embellishment of the 90s. "Be aware of their origins, then expand them using your own imagination," she says.

In this workshop, Adaire shows us part of the ever-changing, ever-growing process she uses to represent the flowers in her garden. Some of these ideas originated in the 1800s; many of them she has developed independently. No specific project is presented. Incorporate these techniques into your own design or change a floral arrangement to include three-dimensional flowers.

M A T E R I A L S

Real flowers from your garden, the neighbour's, the florist. The flowers which work well are large-petalled ones: the iris, tulip or daffodil in the spring, the fuchsia, bellflower, lily, or rose in summer, the cosmos sunflower in fall, poinsettia in winter, for example. Adaire has provided patterns for some of her favourite choices, to get you started.

Pencil and tagboard (lightweight cardboard) or cereal boxes, or plastic template material for making patterns

Some background fabric, solid or pieced, on which to work your floral magic

A selection of fabric scraps which speak "flower" to you. Here's where you may find a use for some very large painterly prints, like the blue-streaked morning glory in this example. Solids can also work well, as can small quilting calicos.

Include great fabrics that wouldn't normally be caught dead in a traditional quilt: seersucker, piqué, polyester organza, moiré, or satin. Learn to look at a section of a print. Hand-dyed fabrics with their irregular patterns and streaks make beautiful

flowers. See Appendix #4 for *Sources*, or Chapter 4 for dyeing techniques to make your own.

HINT: Lay a paper window, cut in the shape of your flower template over sections of fabric to audition for floral effect.

Various threads: regular threads for machine sewing and very fine embroidery, elastic thread, crewel yarn and embroidery floss, metallics, rayons, for embroidery

Some beads and findings such as floral wire stamens. A clear bead might represent a drop of dew to add to the realism.

A selection of permanent pens for drawing details on flowers

The usual sewing supplies (machine, pins, iron, etc.)

M A K I N G   F L O W E R S

The easiest way to figure out the shape of a flower is to use a real flower. Adaire's first example is the Carpathian harebell from her summer garden.

The Carpathain harebell

1 With the harebell it's possible to cut the flower so the blossom will lay flat. Trace around the edges of the flower to make a pattern on tagboard.

1. Make a pattern on tagboard.

2 Choosing appropriate fabric(s), lay them "right" sides together, then trace around the template. **Your traced line is the sewing line.** Cut out the fabric ⅛" to ¼" away from the sewing line.

HINT: The "lining", or inside, will also show in the 3-D flower, just as in the real flower, so choose a contrasting fabric, if appropriate. Remember to look on the "wrong" sides of fabrics for realistic floral effects.

3 Stitch the two layers together on the marked sewing line, using a small machine stitch (14-16 stitches per inch) and backstitching at each end. Leave a small opening for turning on a relatively straight edge. Clip the inside curves, almost to the sewn line. Sharp points may also be trimmed carefully, but not too closely.

4 Turn flower right side out. Press flat.

5 Handstitch the edges together with matching thread, closing the opening at the same time. Complete the bell with a little string "stem." Adaire has pulled the string to the inside of the bell, then frayed it to form the pistil, before tacking the blossoms to the stem.

6 Adaire makes her foxgloves in much the same way, but uses a narrow appliquéd stem, and adds drawn detail inside the blossom.

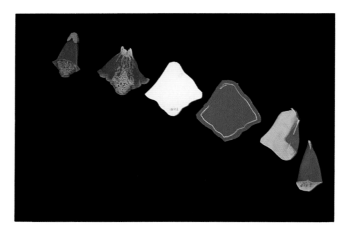

6. Make foxgloves.

7 Examine a fuchsia. The many petals of the inner blossom can be approximately copied with a length of satin, folded in half lengthwise, then tightly gathered on the raw edges. The four-pointed umbrella top for the fuchsia might be estimated, then gathered a little at the apex, before stitching the inner blossom and some wire stamens into the centre.

7. Make the elements of a fuchsia.

8 The Victoria flower is a delightful, low-relief blossom which nestles neatly into a quilted floral arrangement. Cut the petal piece using the pattern, press under 1/4" on one side, then gather the remaining side. Make 5 or 6 of these for one flower. Pin the gathered edges so they join in the centre, then appliqué the turned edges onto the background. The gathered edges may be covered by a circle of fabric with the edges turned under and a bit of stuffing inside.

8. Make a Victoria flower.

Stems are embroidered with the outline or stem stitch. More embroidery stitches are illustrated on page 123.

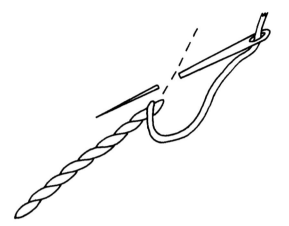

Stem stitch

9 Flowers with many small petals, like the daisy, cornflower, aster, and marigold can be realistic if you have suitable fabric. Use elastic thread in the bobbin and regular machine thread in the top of your machine, drop the feed dogs, and meander around the center of a layer or two of fabric. Trim to a round

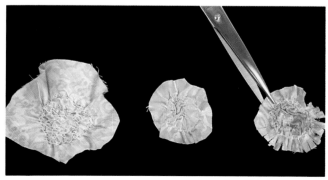

9. Sew with elastic thread. Clip and fray the edges.

shape, then clip the edges. Achieve a fluffier appearance by rubbing the clipped edges briskly to fray them.

10 Nasturtiums can look realistic if you sew separate petals. Vary the leaf sizes for a more realistic effect. The details are drawn and/or embroidered. Adaire has used the *couching* stitch to sew down 'rattail' cord for the stem.

Nasturtiums

10. Sew separate petals for nasturtiums.

11 Brightly-coloured zinnias look stunning when you use the old-fashioned ruching technique: Starting with a straight-grain strip of fabric 1 1/2" x 20", fold and lightly press the long edges in toward the centre, wrong sides together. With a needle and strong thread, running-stitch a zigzag pattern down its length. When you pull on this thread, the characteristic rounded petals of the zinnia will form as if by magic! You may pull the gathers tighter or loosen them, depending upon the effect desired. Lay the ruching onto the background in a spiral fashion, and tack down with matching or contrasting thread.

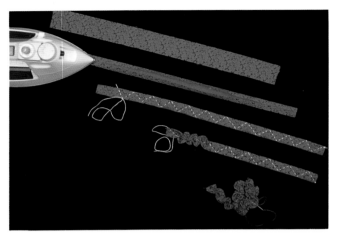

11.The ruching technique

Zinnias

12 The iris is a large-petalled flower which lends itself to 3-D treatment. Some parts are appliquéd flat to the background, then stuffed a bit before quilting. Other petals are faced, then pleated, and tacked into place. Leaves can be lifted off the surface, too, if they have been faced (or lined). Adaire uses a bit of bright yarn for the iris "beard."

Iris

13 Adaire shows the stuffed 3-D trumpet flower beside the flat version. Each new flower attempted provides a different construction challenge in order to make it realistic.

Trumpet flower

Patterns

(**NOTE**: Add seam allowances for all pattern pieces unless the seam allowances are noted on the patterns.)

Adaire takes the guesswork out of the above full-scale flowers by providing the patterns for you. She encourages you to let your imagination flow and try other flowers in your garden.

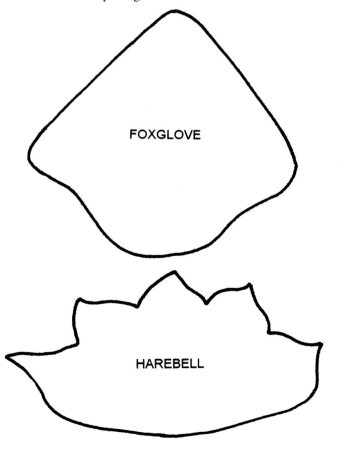

FOXGLOVE

HAREBELL

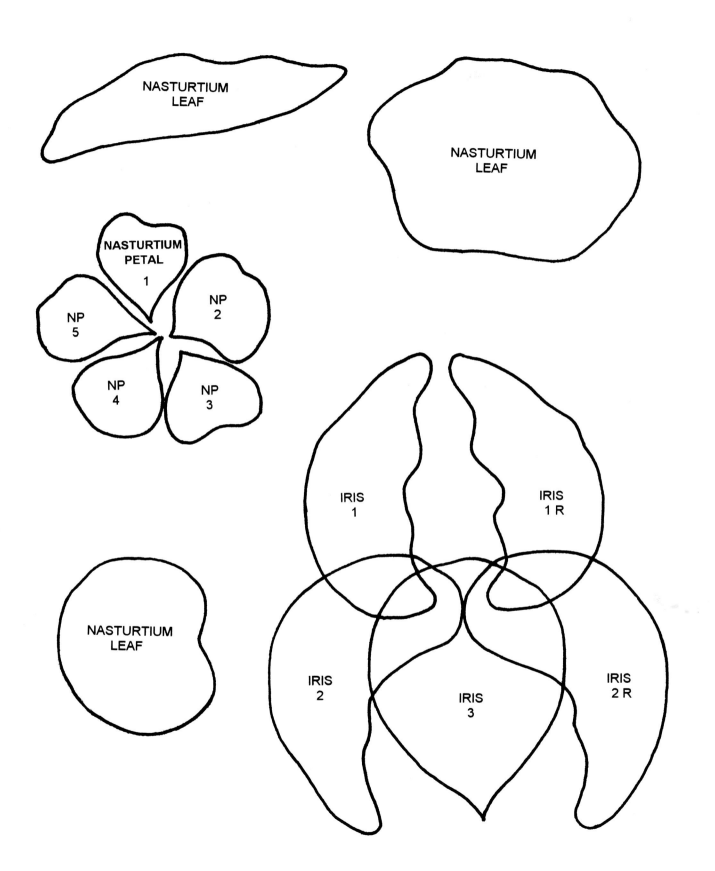

NASTURTIUM
LEAF

NASTURTIUM
LEAF

NASTURTIUM
PETAL

1

NP
2

NP
5

NP
4

NP
3

NASTURTIUM
LEAF

IRIS
1

IRIS
1 R

IRIS
2

IRIS
3

IRIS
2 R

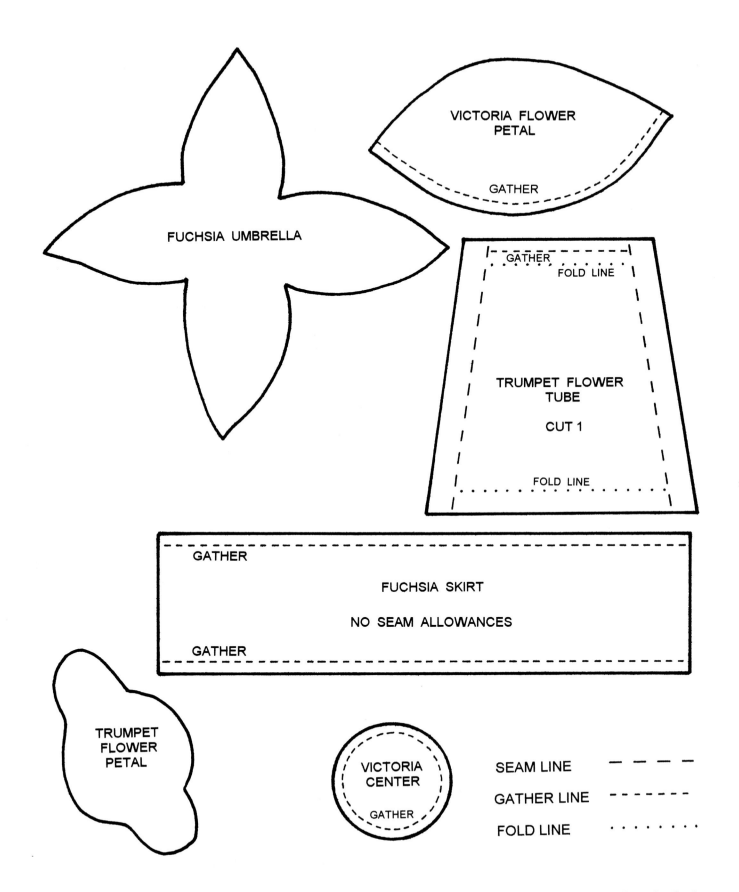

VICTORIA FLOWER
PETAL

GATHER

FUCHSIA UMBRELLA

GATHER
FOLD LINE

TRUMPET FLOWER
TUBE

CUT 1

FOLD LINE

GATHER

FUCHSIA SKIRT

NO SEAM ALLOWANCES

GATHER

TRUMPET
FLOWER
PETAL

VICTORIA
CENTER

GATHER

SEAM LINE   — — — —

GATHER LINE   - - - - -

FOLD LINE   · · · · · · ·

Embellishments

Beads or buttons for insects, dew drops, or anthers, combined with embroidery for insect legs, filaments, stems or tendrils can provide the finishing touches.

Some of the most commonly used embroidery stitches are shown below:

FRENCH KNOT

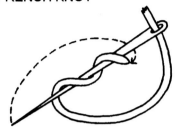

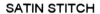

COUCHING

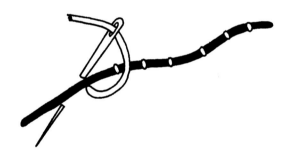

SATIN STITCH

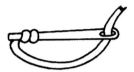

CHAIN STITCH

R E F E R E N C E S

Gaber, Susan. *Treasury of Flower Designs.* New York: Dover Publications, 1981. ISBN 0-486-24096-7

Montano, Judith. *Crazy Quilt Odyssey.* Martinez, CA: C&T Publishing, 1991. ISBN 0-914481-41-8

Moody, Mary. (Editor). *Flowers by Color.* New York: Mallard Press, 1990. ISBN 0-792-45267-4

Sienkiewicz, Elly. *Dimensional Appliqué: Baskets, Blooms and Baltimore Borders.* Martinez, CA: C&T Publishing, 1991. ISBN 0-914881-58-2

Also: seed catalogues and horticultural magazines have good colour photos of flowers.

CHAPTER 8

Lois Wilby-Hooper

NEW BRUNSWICK

With workshop: Canadian Seasons: A Scrap Quilt

"The pursuit of excellence is gratifying and healthy. The pursuit of perfection is frustrating, neurotic, and a terrible waste of time." —anonymous (on Lois's studio wall)

Fiercely proud of her New Brunswick heritage and sensitive to social and environmental issues, Lois Wilby-Hooper is a quiltmaker with strong opinions. Lois's quilts reflect her love and concern for her environment. Living as she does near the shores of the Bay of Fundy, which experiences the highest tides in the world, Lois's everyday existence is measured and influenced by the sea. She is haunted by the loss of the local fishing industry and the urban sprawl with its resulting loss of wildlife habitat. She says, "The bay is summer home to the last tiny remnant of northern Right whales. Through the environmental group, Friends of the Ocean, I recently 'adopted' a humpback whale named Patches. As a quilter, how could I resist with a name like that?"

Lois comes honestly by her needlework skills, but circuitously. She is a fifth-generation quilter on her Pennsylvania Dutch Loyalist mother's side, and her British father was a fine needleworker in his own right. As a small boy he was sickly, and when placed in a class of girls, he discovered he enjoyed doing all forms of needlework as much as they did. Lois, however, was too busy being a tomboy to learn at her parents' knees. It was not until she was an adult that her natural interest in historical textiles and costumes led to volunteer documentation work at the New Brunswick Museum, which in turn led her to the study of quilts. Lois learned she had a natural aptitude for quiltmaking, and her skills were self-developed over the next 18 years.

Lois relaxes at the newly-developed Irving Nature Park, on the shores of the Bay of Fundy.

At 1282 feet, this covered bridge at Hartland, New Brunswick, is the world's longest. The province boasts many of these "kissing bridges," graceful reminders of the past, where strolling lovers could find a bit of privacy.

Lois first made quilts to replace her grandmother's worn quilts which had kept her family warm. Then she moved on to develop more and more innovative designs, including abstract landscapes and traditionally-based scrap quilts. She began to realize that certain social themes she wanted to convey could be effectively communicated to viewers, along with the aesthetic and tactile charms of her quilts. With colour and design, Lois sympathetically addresses issues like domestic violence, loss of aboriginal lands and lifestyles, and depletion of the rainforest.

Finding time to quilt and teach is a real struggle for Lois. She and her husband David run a general contracting and roofing business from the ground floor of their Victorian-era home in Saint John. Orders, estimates, contracting subtrades, inspections, and the inevitable government red tape monopolize Lois's time for much of the year. Their children are grown and David, says Lois, "has never made the slightest objection to my leaving for workshops and conferences, even though they usually occur at an awkward time for business. He's entirely supportive of someone who can make a whole quilt, but who doesn't have time to sew on a button."

When Lois does sneak away to her studio, she puts on her favourite music for inspiration. She says, "I find that Bach's toccatas and fugues have just the right rhythm for machine-piecing. And all Stan Rogers's music speaks so strongly of the Maritimes and captures that elusive flavour of the life here. His song 'Make and Break Harbour' was the starting point for my series of harbour-themed quilts. I simmer things for a long time inside, then it gets out into fabric when the image coincides with the feeling."

The quilting tradition in New Brunswick started with the Loyalist settlers in 1783 and has continued unbroken since then. As a member of the large Kennebecasis Valley Quilt Guild, Lois observes high standards of craftsmanship, with traditional and especially blue-coloured quilts as predominant regional trends. "Saint John, being a major port, was always up to the minute in the latest European fabrics, so there is a rich textile heritage here, both for quilts and costume."

In her classes, Lois teaches by a maxim offered to her by fellow artist and close friend, Helen Brigham: 'If something is worth doing, it is worth doing badly.' "In other words," Lois says, "give yourself permission to experiment, try something different, and make mistakes." It took Lois a long time to gain that level of self-confidence. She didn't feel her work was valid until she received public acclaim when she showed her quilts. Lois also cites encouragement from Canadian quilter Ann Bird as a self-confidence builder. Ann told her, "It doesn't make any difference where you're from, or what your education is, you needn't feel intimidated. You have unique skills and talents, too."

A student in one of Lois's classes told a powerful wartime story, which she retells here: "During class break someone mentioned embroidery, and one of the students, a Danish-Canadian named Jenny, was encouraged to tell her 'tablecloth story.' In strongly-accented English, she quietly told us how she and her husband had owned a fishing boat in a small village on the Danish coast. During World War II, they made frequent trips to Norway, selling their fish and bringing back supplies for themselves and their neighbours. They also transported escaped Allied prisoners of war, British agents and members of the underground resistance in a secret compartment with a tiny opening on the deck. When they

Saint John is full of beautifully maintained heritage homes like this one.

were searched by the Germans at every port, Jenny would sit on a chair over the hatch, embroidering her tablecloth. And then, when her husband left the boat to arrange for transfer of the hidden passengers, Jenny would sit with her infant son on the deck under the watchful eye of the sentries. She would wait to signal the waiting passengers to slip over the sides the moment the soldiers turned their heads. After a stunned silence, Jenny was asked how such courage was possible. She replied simply, 'We were young and strong then'."

Sharing life's stories during classes or in her quilts is a compelling force in Lois's quilting career. For those who hear, there is much to learn.

Bali Hai Sunset (102"x87") (centre detail), 1986
Hand-quilting by Ruth Wilby

This piece evolved from a single piece of Indonesian batik given to Lois by a student. She cut sections, then re-pieced and combined them with printed and plain cotton to stretch the fabric enough to make a full-size quilt.

Blueberry Fields (31"x45"), 1993

"The colours in the barrens after the first frost have to be seen to be believed," says Lois. Much of New Brunswick is covered by fields too stony to grow anything less hardy than blueberry bushes. The wild berries have become a welcome source of income to those who are land-rich and money-poor.

Lois Wilby-Hooper, New Brunswick

Rain Forest (82"x56.5"), 1992
Hand-quilting by Ruth Wilby

To enhance the effect of the verdant, unspoiled jungle, Lois has added three-dimensional vines, insects, birds. "The rigid grid-work represents our efforts to restrain nature, which bursts forth regardless."

Snug Harbour (19.5"x42"), 1993

From Lois's harbour series, the pieced and hand-appliquéd scene was inspired by a calendar photo showing Seal Cove on Grand Manan island, the largest of the Fundy Isles. The fishing shacks nestle into the cove, beckoning the boats in.

Lois Wilby-Hooper

Saint John Harbour at night

Midnight Harbour (detail)

Midnight Harbour (25"x39"), 1992

The scene from Lois's kitchen window is a view of the harbour. At night, city lights reflect on the water, providing a mysterious quilt design.

Lost Meanings, Lost Dreams (52"x52"), 1993

"*Through a net of interlocked circles, an ancient symbol of eternity — the night sky — can be seen. The central star signifies the sun, source of all life,*" says Lois.

"*The top ring pattern is broken, showing the disruption of the Micmac and Maliseet cultures. Yet the pattern holds together despite the breaking of the bonds connecting the whole. The four rings suggest the four seasons as well as the recurring cycles of life.*

"*Through long adversity, the Micmac and Maliseet cultures survived in great part from the efforts of women practising their traditional arts. The sale of beadwork and quillwork supported families who had been deprived of their ancestral lands and lost their way of life. Though I mourn that which is lost, I rejoice in that which remains through their efforts. What the piece expresses for me is the underlying common themes of all races and a shared sisterhood. In spite of all that divides us, we are part of the whole.*"

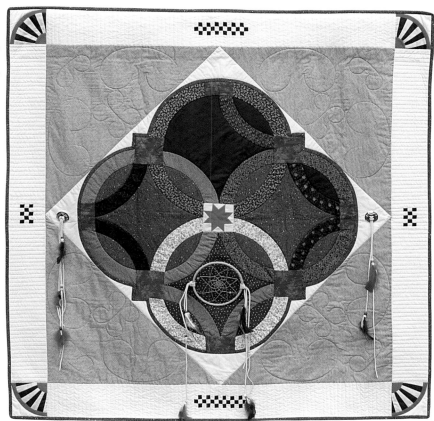

Star Charmer (69"x69"), 1993
Hand-quilting by Beth Barrett-Bowles

"*Though the phenomenon of the* charm *quilt revival is interesting, I never liked the haphazard arrangement of colours that often resulted. In this piece, inspired by American quiltmaker Judy Martin's* Star of the Orient *quilt, I developed a contemporary design which is more to my taste. Since I love heart designs, it was inevitable that they would creep into the arrangement of 555 different fabrics, as well as into the quilting design.*"

Lois Wilby-Hooper, New Brunswick

Canadian Seasons (86"x56"), 1987. Hand-quilting by Ruth Wilby

Featured in the January, 1990 issue of Canadian Living Magazine, *Lois's delightful scrap quilt takes a journey through the seasons, from winter at the bottom to a hint of the return of winter at the top. A pathway runs through the trees, inviting the viewer to wander over the Canadian landscape and enjoy the strong contrasts between the seasons.*

Lois Wilby-Hooper, New Brunswick

Canadian Seasons:
A Scrap Quilt

Level of difficulty: Confident beginner

Sort through your scrap collection and use up all those lovely cotton bits you couldn't bear to throw away. Each little tree consists of 3 or 4 triangles on an unbleached cotton muslin background. This twin-sized quilt could be expanded to a larger size by adding more trees and a border, or could be reduced to make a crib-sized quilt by using fewer trees. If you wish to further simplify the piecing, you have the option of making each tree from just one piece of fabric, rather than using 3 or 4 triangles. This workshop is featured by permission of *Canadian Living Magazine.*

M A T E R I A L S

Fabric amounts based on a twin-sized quilt. (All fabrics used need to be preshrunk.)

- **Template material**, such as lightweight cardboard, acrylic, or used x-ray film

- **Sharp pencil** for marking fabric and drawing templates

- **3.2 meters (3 1/3 yards) unbleached muslin** for background and binding

- **.5 meter (1/2 yard) total of assorted solid-coloured scraps** in greens, purples, browns, navy blue and black for the tree trunks. The darker ones are used in the winter range, and the lighter ones for the other seasons.

- **.9 meter (1 yard) total of assorted purples, mauves, light and dark blues, greys, and browns** for winter trees, in prints and solids

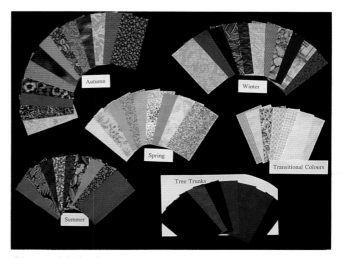

Choose fabrics by seasons.

- **.3 meter (1/3 yard) total of assorted lavenders, pale greens, off whites, pale pinks,** in prints and solids, for spring trees

- **1.2 meters (1 1/3 yards) total of assorted greens** in solids and floral prints for summer trees

- **.7 meter (³/₄ yard) total of assorted yellows, oranges, reds, and rusts** in prints and plains for autumn trees

- **.2 meter (¹/₄ yard) total of transitional light neutrals**

- **Sharp fabric scissors or rotary cutter with mat and rotary ruler**

- **Matching thread** (cream-coloured would be fine for piecing)

- **Sewing machine and the usual sewing supplies**

C O N S T R U C T I O N

Prepare templates

1 Trace pattern pieces onto paper, then glue the paper to lightweight cardboard. Or, trace onto transparent plastic template material. Cut templates out and label. Include the grainline on each template.

> **HINT: Used x-ray film makes an inexpensive template material, as it is semi-transparent and accepts a pencil line.**

Cut fabric

(**NOTE**: Line up the grainline arrows on the templates with the straight grain of the fabric.)

Cut strips from muslin.

2 From the unbleached muslin, cut 7 strips 6 ¹/₂" wide x 42" long. Trace around template A and cut to make 54 "A" pieces. Then, trace around template C and cut to make 26 "C" pieces.

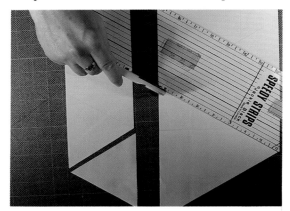

2. Cut "A" and "C" pieces.

> **HINT: If you are using a rotary cutter, layer the six strips together and mark only the top layer. Then six may be cut at a time.**

3 From the muslin, cut 7 strips 3 ⁵/₈" wide x 42" long. Trace around template B and cut to make 116 "B" pieces.

4 From the muslin, cut 15 strips the width of template E by 42" long. Mark and cut out 8 "E" pieces, thirty "F" pieces, 116 "G" pieces, and 26 "H" pieces.

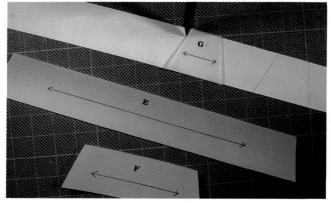

4. Cut "E," "F," "G," and "H" pieces.

5 Using template B, mark and cut "B" pieces from the season colours in these approximate quantities: 250 from "summer" fabrics, 170 from

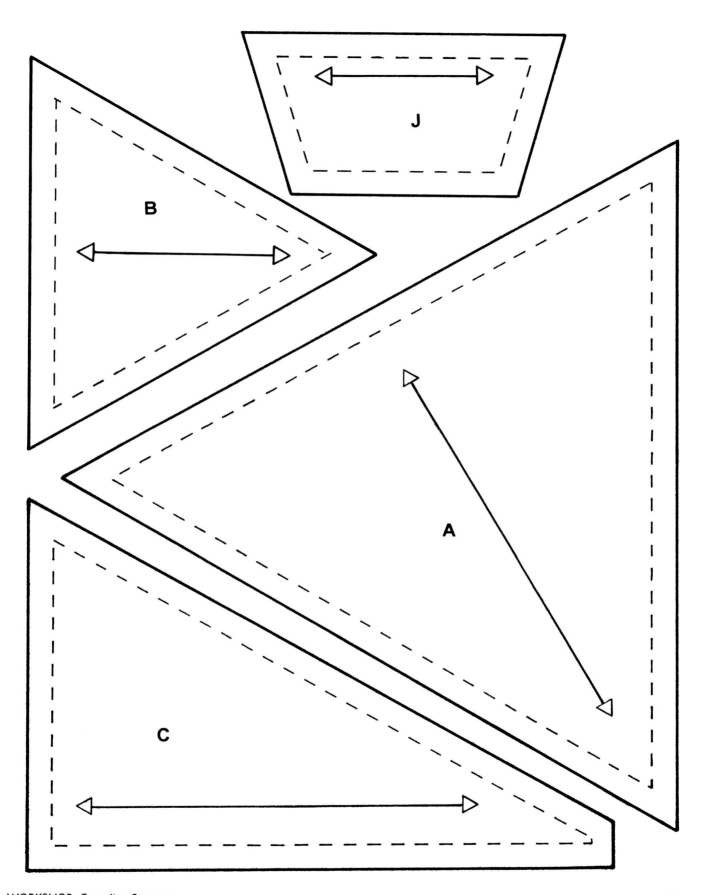

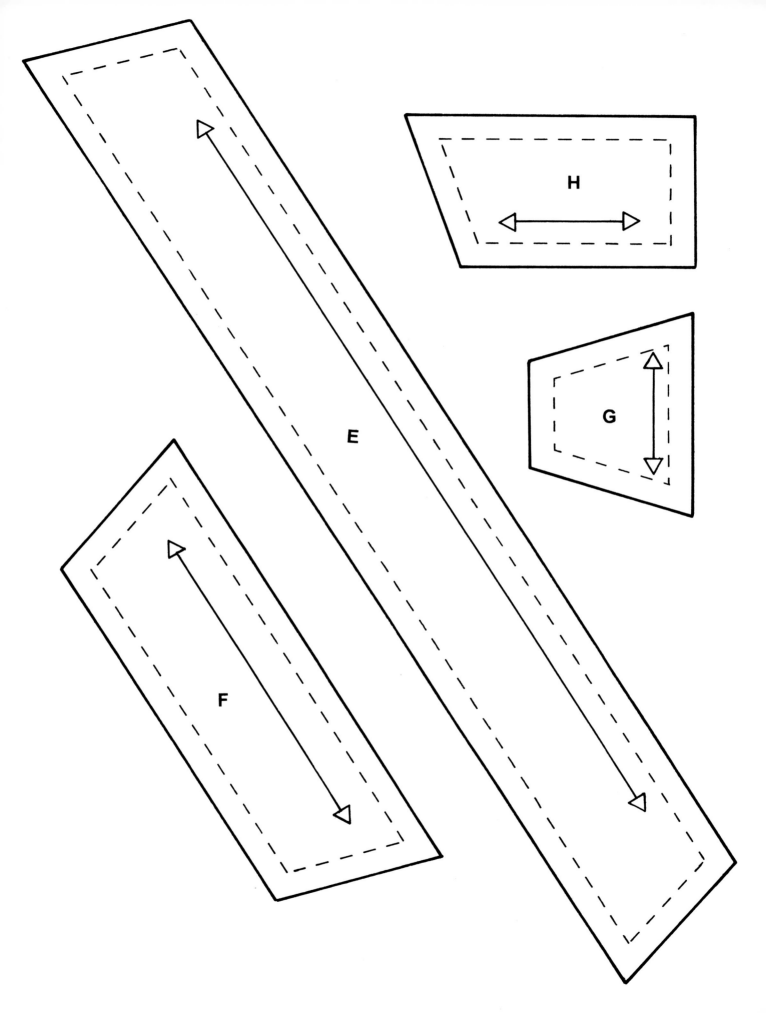

"winter" fabrics, 150 from "autumn" colours, 70 from "spring" fabrics, and 35 from "transitional" colours. (**NOTE**: Approximate quantities allow for choices when arranging your tree colours before sewing.)

6 Using template J, mark and cut approximately 170 "J" pieces from the tree trunk fabric.

6. Mark and cut 170 "J" pieces.

To piece

7 Referring to the piecing diagram on page 138 and the photo of *Canadian Seasons*, lay out one row of trees and background at a time.

> **HINT: If you have the space, hang a flannel sheet on a wall and pin the pieces you're considering onto the sheet. Then you will be able to stand back to "audition" your fabric choices, changing them around until you're satisfied with their arrangement.**

You will note that the three rows of "winter" trees are placed at the bottom of Lois's design, then there are 2 "spring" rows. Above those are 4 "summer" rows, and 3 "autumn" rows. Finally you'll see a transitional "autumn/winter" row at the top of the quilt.

You may also wish to use the transitional fabrics in other parts of the quilt. When changing from one season to the next, Lois has used some of one season's colours in the next season's row to make the transition fluid.

8 Check to ensure that your sewing machine has an accurate 1/4" seamline gauge. (To learn one method for checking your machine, see chapter 11, page180.) For tips on accurate machine piecing, refer to chapter 11's workshop. Lois's **BEST TIPS** concern machine care: Replace your needle frequently, oil the machine regularly, and refrain from sewing over pins, as this habit negatively affects the machine's timing.

9 Full trees are composed of 4 "B" pieces, and partially hidden ones are made with 3 of these "B" triangles. With right sides together, sew the little triangles for each tree unit together as planned, then press seams out from the centre triangle.

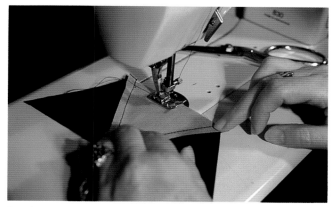

9a. Sew together triangles for each tree unit.

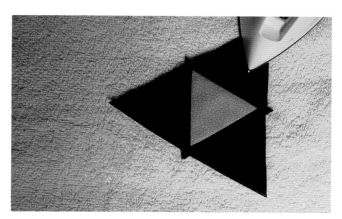

9b. Press seams out from centre of triangle.

10 Sew the small triangular muslin pieces to the tree units where needed in order to make a straight seam for joining to the next tree. Trim off the points. Press the seams toward the trees as you piece them.

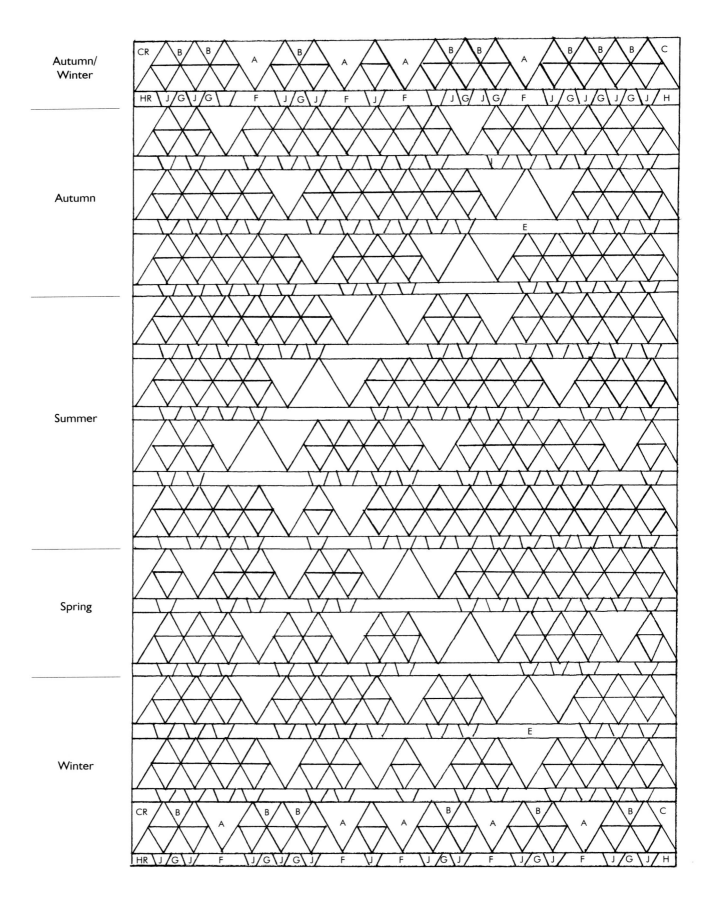

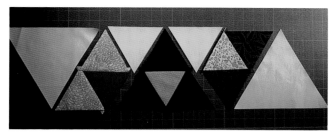

10a. Sew small triangles to tree units.

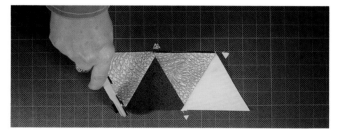

10b. Trim off points.

HINT: Pay close attention to grainlines: while constructing the quilt top, all pieces should have the grainlines going in the same direction. This consistency helps to make piecing easier and the resulting work will lay flatter.

11 Sew the tree units together into rows with straight diagonal seams, adding the muslin background pieces where they're needed. Trim off the points. Press the seam allowances toward the trees.

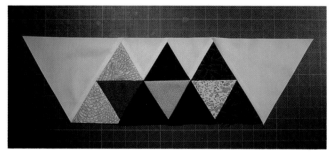

11. Sew the tree units together.

12 Piece the tree trunks (J pieces) into long strips with the E, F, G, and H muslin pieces, according to piecing chart, using the darkest tree trunk colours in the winter range. Press the seam allowances toward the trunks.

13 Join each row of trunks to the appropriate row of trees, centering each trunk to the base of each tree.

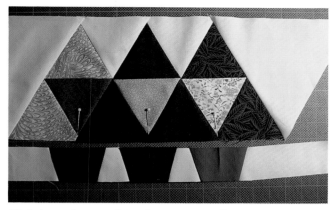

13. Join each row of trunks to a row of trees.

HINT: For a quick and accurate visual cue, fold each trunk in half and finger press the fold. Then, line up the folds with the centre points of the trees, marked here with pins, before pinning and stitching the rows together.

14 Sew the rows of trees together. From the back, press all these seam allowances upwards. **NOTE**: for general instructions on finishing, see Appendix #1: *The Nutshell Guide to Finishing Your Quilt.* When quilting, Lois suggests quilting closely around each tree *in the ditch.*

Be sure to label your quilt. For quilt conservation suggestions, see Appendix #3: *Documentation, Care and Conservation of Quilts.*

14. Label your quilt.

ENJOY CANADA'S SEASONS!

CHAPTER 9

Iris Ethridge
PRINCE EDWARD ISLAND

With workshop: A New Look at English Paper Piecing for Precision

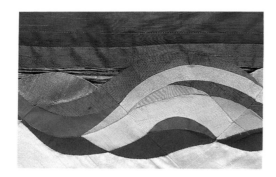

"Everybody has an urge to create and express, even if it remains undeveloped."

T here is a mysterious and compelling allure to Prince Edward Island, the smallest of Canada's provinces. Visitors 'from away' fall in love instantly with its relaxed lifestyle and the beauty of its rural coastal landscape. For Iris Ethridge and her husband Brian, a visit to the island in 1982 prompted a completely unplanned purchase of a farm near the birthplace of the island's most famous author, Lucy Maud Montgomery. "We spent more time buying a pair of socks than we did buying this place," says Iris.

When Iris and Brian took early retirement from their west coast teaching careers in 1987, they moved to their east coast farm with three cats, and adopted five more. They have renovated their old farmhouse into a convenient and comfortable retreat, where every available wall space seems to be covered with books. The horse barn is undergoing a transformation into a larger studio for Iris, and some of their 120 acres are farmed by a neighbour.

Making these changes in their lives has not slowed these adopted islanders down at all. Iris says, "I am interested in too many things, so I never have enough hours in the day. I make time somehow for what is most important to me." She reads voraciously, plays piano seriously, and works at her fibre art when she can. Since coming to live on PEI, Iris has been designing and selling sweaters in the very active tourist market, and some of her patchwork wall pieces are sold through an upscale craft gallery called The Dunes at nearby Brackley Beach.

Of the many excellent quiltmakers on the island, Iris is one of the special few whose work has a contemporary look. While based firmly in traditional technique (Iris works

Her hands uncustomarily idle, Iris relaxes on her farmhouse porch.

A section from one of Iris's theme notebooks shows the eclectic images she collects for design ideas.

No other province can boast so famous a house as Prince Edward Island's Green Gables, home of the legendary Anne, the energetic red-headed heroine of Lucy Maud Montgomery's novels.

almost exclusively with the old English method of *paper-piecing*), her work looks modern. A self-taught artist, Iris might see design ideas in books on folkart, abstract art, or gardening. She clips magazine pictures and makes sketches to file in her big three-ring themed binder. "Books have always been important to me and I find ideas in all sorts of unexpected places. For example, two recent sources of quilt designs have been a book on early medieval Europe, and another on prehistory, which is a book about fossils," she says. The island's pastoral scenery provides more inspiration for her designs (see *Dune with Marram Grass* and *20,000 Light Years East of Planet Earth*).

Iris's work looks modern, partly due to her choice of many solid-coloured silks as the material for her quilts. She shops in Vancouver's East Indian sari shops when visiting her grown daughter, Kath, and haunts the used clothing outlets in Charlottetown, PEI, looking for those jewel tones, that special lustre of a silk scarf, blouse, or tie peeking out from under a pile of clothes. She believes in using good materials ("I see a lot of really good workmanship executed on undeserving materials,") and recommends that we "try not to be enslaved by current fabrics [such as 100% cottons, designed specifically for quilts] which, although often fabulous, can have a homogenizing effect on quilters' work." Iris would like to work with wool more. "It seems to be a much neglected material in modern piecing," she says.

Iris believes that "everybody has an urge to create and express, even if it remains undeveloped." For herself, she says, "I have been aware of the pleasures of colour, pattern and texture for as long as I can remember, and quilting seems to offer the widest diversity of possibilities for exploring in these areas. Working with the paper-piecing process allows me to use skills that I've had since childhood in a new and contemporary way. I often seem to initiate the design process when I first wake up, develop the ideas during the day, and carry them out at night. I'll sit up half the night sewing, but it's not my creative design time."

One of the unique ideas Iris has come up with has not yet materialized: "I'd really like to introduce music into a quilt. Music is one of the really important elements in my life. I've thought about attaching bells, wind chimes, or hiding a tape recorder with a secret place on the quilt where it could be activated."

The sand dunes at Cavendish Beach on the north shore of the island remain peaceful and unspoiled.

Lobster Pots at North Rustico await the fisher's whim.

Iris brings imagination and sensitivity to her teaching as well. "Treating students in a respectful and friendly way, be they adult or younger, is a must. Being well-organized is an important strength." You'll see evidence of Iris's organizational skills in her workshop, *Paper-Piecing for Precision*.

Dune with Marram Grass (27"x43"), 1993, (center detail)

"Before coming to PEI, I had never seen such a place as the sand dunes at Cavendish Beach. The dunes lie behind a long white sand beach. On the windward side, the endangered piping plover builds its fragile nest, often having to repeat the task if a late winter storm washes the first one away. The marram grass anchors the sand. Its pale green spiky leaves suggested a traditional quilt block called, unaccountably, Widows. I like using a traditional block in a new context."

Dune with Marram Grass (27"x43"), 1993, (detail)

Kite (47"x35"), 1993
"I have always admired the beauty that emerges from the spareness and discipline of Amish quilt designs. In this little piece, the design and colour scheme are minimal, but I hope the effect is greater than the elements."

Iris Ethridge, Prince Edward Island

Particles (31"x43"), 1993
Collection of Sherrie Davidson

"I have a compulsion to make hexagons, which I try to ignore, not always successfully. Based on an Islamic design, which underwent much shifting and shuffling, this finished work did not bear much resemblance to the original concept. My husband, who for his leisure had been reading books on astronomy, took one look at the hanging and exclaimed, 'Particles!' I looked the word up, and found it was another name for 'quark.' So I looked up 'quark' and discovered that quarks have colours and 'flavours,' such as 'strange,' 'charm,' 'truth,' and 'beauty.' I decided I could not have found a nicer name, and perhaps it was not so far from the original intent, after all."

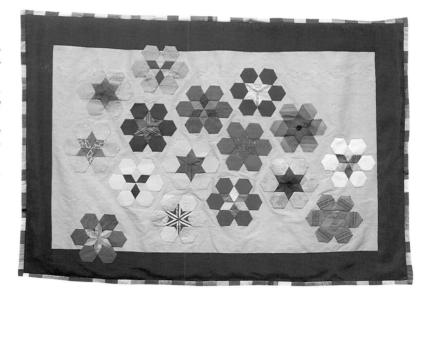

Particles (detail)

Drunk on Champagne (34"x34"), 1992
Collection of Sherrie Davidson

"I started this quilt while visiting Vancouver to see our daughter, Kath, who also does quilting. Like me, she collects silks, mostly exquisite pieces from the many East Indian cloth shops in that city. I raided her supply of fabrics and played with the traditional block, Drunkard's Path, to make this piece."

Drunk on Champagne (detail)

Iris Ethridge, Prince Edward Island

Triangles (Old Timer) (45"x36"), 1982-1993

"*I started this piece the year we bought the farm and were spending our first summer on the Island. I had brought some silk samples in Vancouver, and used them in my very first effort at paper-piecing. The quilt project kicked around for years, underwent various feline modifications when the cats decided to explore and play with it, and was finally completed in 1993. I have a sentimental liking for it, as it was my first.*"

Triangles (Old Timer) (detail)

20,000 Light Years East of Planet Earth (30"x25"), 1992
Collection of Jill Allman

"*When I finished this fun piece, it seemed to have a New Age flavour, which is not my field at all. Just for a lark, I gave it this silly name.*"

20,000 Light Years East of Planet Earth (detail)

A New Look at English Paper-Piecing for Precision

Level of difficulty: Beginner (hand-sewing)

The great advantage of paper-piecing is that it affords complete freedom to piece shapes that would be difficult by machine or with regular hand-piecing. It is such a simple technique that a child would experience success with it, using some basic shapes, yet complex designs by a more experienced quiltmaker can be made precisely using this 18th century technique. Any busy quilter will find the portability of this kind of handwork an asset.

THE DESIGN

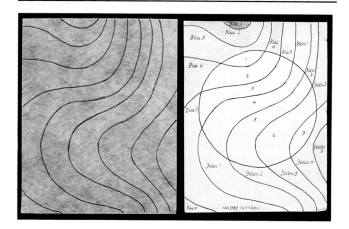

The source of the design idea for the small piece Iris demonstrates in this workshop "was the beautiful white sand of the Cavendish beach. The tide was going out, leaving the familiar patterns in the sand. I made a few sketches of the curves, very basic, just a starting point. The idea of tides suggested the moon,

so I drew a circle on one of my sketches. I liked the idea of the final design relating to the original source — sands, tides, the moon, and movement."

Iris offers some tips to help quilters work out their own designs. Small rough sketches of shapes or segments of forms you see in nature are a good starting point. Then, make several copies on a photocopier, enlarging some of them. Try some of these exercises with the copies:

Make a tracing on translucent paper, then by placing the tracing over one of your copies and moving it about, placing it at right angles, or upside down, you may see new ideas related to the basic idea.

Take one of your copies and cut it into 4 strips, or 4 square quarters. Rearrange them. Turn some upside down. In this way you see new juxtapositions of shapes.

Take several of your copies, placing them next to one another in different ways. Make them into a long strip. Make them into a big square. Make an irregular shape by slipping one partially under the other.

Take one of the copies and draw lines over it — horizontal, vertical, and diagonal — and see interesting new shapes emerge.

For your design, consider your abilities. If you are a beginning hand-sewer and are sampling this technique, sketch a simple design which might be used as a framed wall-piece, part of a larger quilt, or a cushion cover.

HINT : Try to avoid tiny sharp points in the design. They are the hardest to piece.

Enlarge your design to the desired size. Again, small is best for a beginner: you want to successfully complete your project. There are several ways you can enlarge. See Appendix #5: *Enlarging Methods* for illustrations of these methods:

the reliable old grid method

using a pantograph enlarging tool

applications of enlarging photocopiers

projection devices

Trace the enlarged design onto a sheet of white paper using a waterproof marking pen.

C O L O U R S

By this time your design, unless it is totally abstract, will probably suggest your colour range. Iris's design suggested shades of yellow and beige for the sand, blue for the sea, and creamy or silvery white for the moon.

HINT: Press the possible colours into ¹/2" folds, lay one next to the other, and view them through a little viewfinder. In this way, the colours are isolated, and seen just in relationship with one another.

Iris colours her full-size design, and sews together a sample palette of fabric swatches.

If the design itself does not suggest a colour scheme, you may find general help with choosing colours in Appendix #2: *An Easy System for Taking the Angst out of Fabric Selection.*

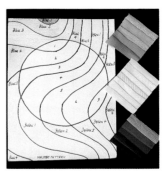
Iris's sample palette.

M A T E R I A L S

Freezer paper or iron-on stabilizer such as Totally Stable® , made by Sulky (available at fabric stores, or see Appendix #4: *Sources* for mail order). This is used in place of paper, although any light weight card paper or freezer paper will work in lieu of the iron-on stabilizer.

Basting thread of a contrasting colour

HINT: Red or black basting thread often leaves colour on fabric when removed. Choose a lighter colour.

Fabrics in your choice of colours. Iris prefers to use silk. She says, "I love the way it catches the light. It is a beautiful and exciting material."

HINT: The easiest fabric to piece is fine, firm 100% cotton.

A variety of threads to match your fabrics

Iron and ironing surface

Small, sharp scissors

Hand-sewing needles (sharps for basting, betweens size 10 for piecing is Iris's preference)

C O N S T R U C T I O N

1 Using a piece of iron-on stabilizer or freezer paper the size of your design, trace the design lines onto the **shiny** side of the stabilizer. If you are using light-coloured fabrics, do not use any heavy markings. Number the tracing lightly on the **matte** side of the stabilizer, relating the numbers to your colour key. (B1 for Blue 1, etc.)

2 Cut the stabilizer or freezer paper apart on the design lines as you need them. Iris starts with the blue pieces.

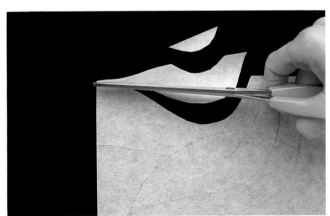

2. Cut the stabilizer on the design lines.

3 Iron your first piece of stabilizer, shiny side down, onto the back of your fabric. Use a medium hot iron. When placing the papers, it is best to place straight sides on the straight grain of fabric and curves on the bias, where possible. If there are to be several pieces cut from the same fabric, remember to leave $1/2$" between them for a turn-under allowance.

3. Iron stabilizer onto the back of your fabric.

4 Cut around each shape, leaving $1/4$" turn-under allowance all around. With the **tip** of your sharp scissors, clip curves (estimate $7/8$ ths of the way through the turn-under allowance.) Inside or concave curves especially need to be clipped.

4. Cut around each shape.

5 Turn the allowance over the edge of the paper, making sure you can feel the edge of the paper through the fabric. (**NOTE**: If you wish to sew a border to the design, leave all the outer edges unturned.) With a big messy knot on the end of your contrasting thread, start basting this allowance in place from the right side, so the knot will be easier to find when removing these stitches later.

5. Turn the allowance over the edge of the paper.

6 As each piece is prepared, place it in its correct position for the design on a flat surface near you. If you change your mind about a fabric choice, the iron-on template can be carefully peeled off and reused several times.

HINT : For a small design, or separate blocks, the tacky surface of a photo album page can hold the pieces steady for future piecing.

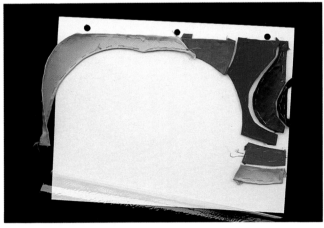

6. Place each piece in position.

7 Using your small needle, a tidy knot, and thread that matches the fabric as closely as possible, start to join two of the pieces together by hiding the knot inside the turn-under allowance.

7. Join the pieces together, hiding the knot.

8 Whipstitch the pieces, right sides together, matching up the straight side pieces (or use tailor's chalk to make matching lines across the two pieces while they still lie flat.) A **whipstitch** is a tightly spaced overcast stitch taken just on the edges of the pieces.

8. Whipstitch the pieces, right sides together.

9 When the whole design is assembled, remove the basting stitches.

9. Remove the basting stitches.

10 If you do not plan to quilt the piece and it is to be used as a decorative hanging, you may decide to leave the papers in to give the work body. In some 19th century quilts, we find that the papers have been left in, perhaps for added warmth. If you decide to remove the papers, they can be peeled off and used again, if intact.

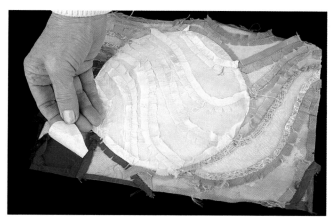

10. Remove papers if desired.

11 For finishing, Iris suggests you might appliqué the piece to a background fabric, or paper-piece a border, or stitch a border on by machine. Then, a piece of light batting can be sandwiched between the paper-pieced top and a backing fabric. The work can be quilted or simply tacked or tied, if it is for display purposes only. For suggestions on finishing your piece, you may wish to refer to Appendix #1: *The Nutshell Guide to Finishing Your Quilt.*

Here are some of the books Iris finds inspiring, from her vast collection of fine art books.

Janet Pope
NOVA SCOTIA

With workshop: Re-using Old Fabrics in Quilts

"An artist has a responsibility for interpreting images through her own psyche."

Born in New Brunswick, Janet moved at an early age to rural Nova Scotia, a province characterized as much by the charm and friendliness of its inhabitants as by its grand maritime heritage and dramatic coastline scenery. Janet's parents set up a publishing business and Janet, with older brother Robert and younger brother Doug, all worked in the family business before establishing art careers of their own.

Writing and art were encouraged by both parents, and the creativity of Janet's brothers was a strong stimulus. "Whenever we did something creative, our parents took it seriously. They were never indifferent. Before the demands of child-rearing and business became more pressing, my mother painted and my father did woodcarving. When art is in the air in a home, somehow it filters down," says Janet.

Janet painted before working with fabric. But her paintings did not express what she "had to say . . . they looked flat and amateurish, and although they have a certain charm, they lack richness of colour — they don't gleam, they don't have any luminosity."

Janet worked as a dressmaker for several years when she was making her first tentative experiments in large fabric hangings. But it was in 1986, when she saw an exhibition of wall hangings by Canadian quilter Laurie Swim at Dresden Galleries in Halifax, that her work was given a new impetus. Janet read Swim's book, *The Joy of Quilting*, and discovered the techniques outlined in the book were perfect for doing

---

One of Janet's favourite spots for thinking is near the Mt. Denson lighthouse, minutes from her home.

A saltwater marsh near
Blue Rocks, Nova Scotia

the elaborate curves and the figurative work that she was interested in. "So that was a real liberation," she says. "After I painted a picture I was always so frustrated. But when I finish one of my fabric pieces, there's a real satisfaction. My soul is at rest."

From the start, Janet's wallhangings garnered critical attention when they were exhibited in public. Her first series, *Animals and Music*, was shown at the Dresden Galleries in 1990. "The galleries where I've exhibited have been very open to fabric art, because it's an art form that's as expressive as painting, as sculpture, as any of the art forms. When I have a show, and see two, maybe three years of intense work all on the walls, it's very humbling and in another way it's empowering." The public snaps up Janet's quilts almost as soon as the last stitch is done. The exhibitions and a feature article on Janet's work in the magazine *Quilting International* have resulted in purchases and commissions for both public and private collections.

Much of what Janet has learned about professionalism was influenced by her brothers. Doug is the "idea man," a storehouse of ideas and suggestions for his siblings' art. Robert, who died in 1992 of a blood disorder related to cancer treatment, was very much the professional artist. Twelve hours before he died, he was selecting slides of his artwork for the Nova Scotia art bank. He was a model of discipline — always having slides labelled, resumé and press kit up to date, and work filed and organized. Janet's hanging, *Wounded Bird* is a memorial to Robert, and helped her to grieve his death.

How does the design process work for Janet? "It's a meditative train of thought, almost as if I lower a bucket into a deep well, deeper and deeper over the course of two or three days, and finally there's a splash. When I bring the bucket up, it starts to come out on the paper. My works are about a psychological, spiritual reality. I'm most creative in the summer and that's when I want to do a bold solar piece like *The Birth of Light* or *Roosters*. But when I've done a couple of solar pieces, I realize I have to change to a lunar one (*Moonamorphosis* and *Moonfish*), just to right the balance in my own nature."

Docks near Cheticamp,
Cape Breton Island

From her studio, which is across the hall from her fabric room, Janet views the flower beds and the meadow gently sloping down to the Avon River. She speculates that her work would be different if she lived in the city. "In the country, there's the rhythm of the seasons — the moon coming up and the tide going out. In the spring the whole earth is an eruption of new life. All the bird motifs in my work are very much a part of the surroundings here. We have radiant pheasants just walking across the lawn, summer and winter. You can't filter that out."

Janet recalls a specific day in 1988 when her style of fabric art changed abruptly, when she was able to achieve a new dimension and richness that she felt her painting lacked. "While I was waiting in the dentist's office, I picked up a magazine and read about South American Cuna Indian *mola* appliqué. This was a major thing for me because of the vibrant colours they use and the way black is used to intensify everything. The Cuna women used the embroidery on top as a decorative stitching, with many large fish and bird motifs which fill a whole piece." Other fibre techniques from which Janet draws inspiration are Victorian English *Crazy Patch*, the *Amish colour choices* and habits of recycling, geometric Navajo weaving, and intricate Japanese embroidery techniques.

"But," says Janet, "I don't think we should ever copy, unless it's an apprenticeship thing, where students copy the masters until they become skilled in the craft. An artist has a responsibility for interpreting images through her own psyche. We can use a technique [like mola appliqué] to do other things." Janet has developed her own distinctive style of art.

"Sometimes madness and the visionary are similar," she suggests. "Madness is a chaotic energy that isn't channelled. Art is a creative energy that is channelled into the craft and has an end result."

Janet Pope

Totem Sun (37"x21"), 1991
Collection of Acadia University, Wolfville, Nova Scotia

"I placed the figures one above another like a totem pole to create a path of vertical ascension from the human up to the cosmic, from fire up to light," says Janet.

"Because women in myths are often associated with fire and have traditionally been the ones who tended the fire for cooking and keeping their families warm, I placed a stylized fire goddess figure at the bottom. Next I put a red firebird to mediate between the earthly and the heavenly. And on top, I placed the gold sun, emblem of life and light."

Janet Pope

Wounded Bird (20"x22"), 1992
Collection of Peter and Janet Muttart

"I made this hanging a few weeks after my brother, Robert, died in 1992. He was only 35 years old; a remarkable artist who painted with force and compassion in the face of his long struggle with cancer. The wounded bird is a metaphor for his pain, his suffering, for his gifted life tragically cut short."

A Peacock's Cosmic Tail (39"x31"), 1991
Collection of Margaret Pope

"I want to convey the splendour of the universe, locked inside a mythical peacock's tail, which unfolds in all its swirling cosmological energy when the tail opens and spreads. I love the associations of beauty and rich shimmering colours that peacocks evoke."

Spider Weaves the World (28"x34"), 1991

From Janet's Creation series, this quilt is appliquéd with black twill tape and broadcloth. Janet says, "I wanted to celebrate the spider as a sister-creator so I made this hanging of a spider pulling the thread of life out of her body and weaving it into the web of life. It represents the fragile interconnectedness of all life forms."

Janet Pope, Nova Scotia

The Birth of Light (35"x40"), 1992
Collection of Nova Scotia Art Bank

"One of my most abstract hangings, this piece concentrates on a single image: light emerging from darkness. For the design to work for me, there had to be darkness in the light and light in the darkness. I pieced the background first, highlighting the largest swirls with a thin edging of gold fabric. In the same way I outlined the arms of the sun with black. Over it all, I machine-embroidered layers of gold thread to give a sense of pattern, motion, richness and density. The result is a mandala-like image, combining writhing energy with solid, monumental forms."

Moonfish (40"x45"), 1992
Collection of Dartmouth Regional Library

"The large fish in the center serves to link the moon and the sea. With its quarter-moon face, it is both a creature of ocean depths and a symbol of lunar power. Again, I used a lot of machine embroidery to add movement and flow. Over the outermost green border, I appliquéd navy seam binding in a pattern that suggests waves, fish, or possibly even a net."

Janet Pope, Nova Scotia

Bird Transformation: Crow Into Firebird (35"x41"),
1993. Collection of Bob and Cheryl Duff

"*This hanging is from my most recent series, Transformations. By dividing the space into panels, I could show how a crow transforms from an ordinary bird into a fully liberated, mystical and magical firebird,*" *says Janet.*

In the crow panel, the dark bird stands against a bright pink background. In the successive panels, the background becomes darker while the bird becomes progressively brighter and more dazzling.

Fleur de Lobster (detail)

Fleur de Lobster (20"x31"), 1993
Collection of Suzanne Lewis

"*Inspired by a set of 19th century French butter moulds I saw in a book once, this hanging shows a lobster transforming into a flower. The claws become the leaves, the tail becomes the root, and the antennae become the stamen. The panels have the formal aspect of botanical prints, yet the hanging never fails to make people smile.*"

Roosters (43"x36"), 1993
Collection of Zahi and Jenny
Deek

*"Although birds such as the phoenix
and the firebird appear again and
again in my work, I had never thought
of using roosters until Jenny Deek
commissioned a hanging with a rooster
motif. Her husband is Palestinian and
their surname, Deek, means rooster in
Arabic, so a fabric work with two
flaming roosters in it seemed both
evocative and appropriate. To bring
out the maximum luminosity of the
colours, I used a stained glass window
technique, outlining everything in
black. The abstracted pattern of flames
in the border echoes the fiery nature of
the birds."*

Roosters (detail)

Janet Pope, Nova Scotia

Moonamorphosis (34"x38"), 1993. Collection of Cynthia Fuller Davis

Moonamorphosis (detail)

Rags to Riches

Level of difficulty: Intermediate to Advanced (machine)

Janet Pope could earn her PhD in recycling. Nearly all her fabric art pieces were once ties, or other garments which showed little wear. Friends drop off great finds to Janet: her banker brings bags of ties he no longer needs, she looks for factory seconds which have interesting mistakes, and she goes often to *Matthew 25*, a little second-hand clothing outlet with a big heart.

At *Matthew 25*, all the ties that people donate are saved for Janet in garbage bags. Sometimes there will be a particularly special skirt or scarf in the bag. Dorothy LeGoffic, shown with Janet, and the rest of the volunteer staff take a keen interest in Janet's work. They love to see the riches she creates from a pile of discards.

Janet values ties for the way they reflect light and their deeply-saturated colours. They provide her with a vast range of colours and a manageable amount of fabric to work with.

Janet says, "When I'm commissioned to do a work for a particular person or family, I always ask if they have any fabric they want incorporated into the piece. It gives the hanging a personal history for them.

"By sharing with friends and supporting small local community organizations, one's work is rooted in the personal, caring female tradition that the needle-arts have been based on for millennia."

For this workshop, Janet shows you her basic techniques. She encourages you to use these techniques to produce a design of your own.

C O L O U R S

Janet washes all the ties/clothing she brings home, then sorts them by colour into baskets or onto shelves.

After sketching her design, Janet draws it freehand in full size.

Sorting through her ties, Janet looks for colours and textures which suit her design. "The jewel-tone shades look best against dark backgrounds. Black is an essential for highlighting and intensifying colour, and gives a rich stained-glass effect when placed next to ruby, emerald, sapphire, or gold. Balancing light and dark is all-important."

Once Janet has selected the colours desired for the background, she "can be freer in experimenting with the foreground colours."

Sort ties by colour and texture.

Select background colours.

MATERIALS

■ **Your full-size design**

> **HINT: If you draw 2 of these, one of them could be cut apart to be used for your pattern pieces.**

■ **A large assortment of ties, fabric scraps, garments** for recycling in the colour families you have chosen.

■ **A piece of foundation fabric** (light-coloured cotton) a few inches larger than the design

■ **Several pieces of facing fabric** (cotton or cotton/polyester) or yardage to back the appliqué pieces

■ **Light or medium-weight iron-on interfacing** to stabilize unmanageable fabrics

■ **Sharp scissors, iron and ironing surface, pins**

■ **Sewing machine** (Janet uses her faithful 1940s' Singer Featherweight with a no. 14 needle for everything, including machine embroidery)

■ **A variety of sewing machine threads**, in matching or selected contrasting colours.

■ **Some loose polyester stuffing**

PREPARING FABRICS

1 Cut the tie in half at the narrowest point.

1. Cut tie at the narrowest point.

2 Using the broader end of the tie, slide the scissors up the back seam, cutting the loose stitches in one quick motion. The interfacing falls out.

2. Cut stitches and remove interfacing.

3 Iron the tie flat. Some ties tend to retain their crease lines, so avoid these lines when cutting out pattern pieces.

4 To stabilize wobbly, slippery, or very lightweight fabrics, iron a light to medium interfacing to their backs, according to manufacturer's directions.

THE BACKGROUND

There is not much fabric in a tie so if a large area is to be covered, several ties must be pieced together. The advantage to this is that it creates pattern and movement, even if a monochromatic colour scheme is used.

Janet often uses the *crazy-patch* method of piecing backgrounds. This method is described in steps 8-12, below, and used in the outer border of *Moonamorphosis*, the workshop sample. However, for the large background in the centre of the quilt, Janet uses a form of **layering and machine-appliqué,** which provides the opportunity to use curvilinear shapes. This technique is described below in Steps 5 – 7.

5 Lay a length of your top fabric across the top of the foundation fabric. (**NOTE**: Janet does not use batting at this stage. The foundation piece will be covered by the quilt's backing, so it does not matter what it looks like.) This process is not an exact science. Rather, a creative decision is made with each piece of fabric chosen: Do I use this colour, or that one? Do I use a highly textured tie for interest, or do I want the transitions between each piece of fabric to be inconspicuous? Is a fluid curvilinear design consistent with the subject of my piece (for example waves or clouds) or would straight lines suit the feel of the piece (buildings or prairies)? Do I want a large piece of that fabric or a small accent piece?

In general, the background is not meant to hold the viewer's eye. Look at some of Janet's pieces to see how she has developed her backgrounds. In *Fleur de Lobster*, the background is solid black. For *Bird Transformation: Crow Into Firebird*, each background of the two smaller panels is made from a solid piece of fabric, while the larger one is pieced, crazy-patch style, in low contrast burgundies. In *Moonfish*, the centre is crazy-patched, then the round bubble shapes are **layered and machine-appliquéd**. And, with *Roosters*, crazy-patched background supports the floral motif, while the **faced-and-turned machine-appliqué**, described below in steps 13-22, complete the rest of the background.

If possible, before sewing anything down, try out the various fabrics to see how they look in relation to each other.

6 To prepare the next piece to be **layered and machine-appliquéd**, cut it in the shape desired, then press under an approximate 1/4" seam allowance.

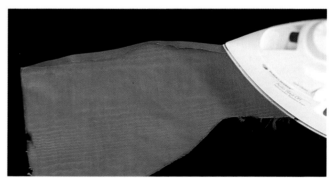

6. Cut shape and press 1/4" to the wrong side.

7 Pin the piece in place, then edge-stitch with matching thread close to the turned edge.

7. Edge-stitch the piece in place.

Repeat this process for subsequent pieces, fitting, cutting, and pressing, as needed, until the background is filled.

CRAZY-PATCHING

To add visual interest or to piece the background where curves are not desirable, the machine-sewn crazy-patch method can be used.

In *Moonamorphosis*, Janet uses this method to construct the border background and the moon, shown in the following steps:

8 Roughly sketch the pattern onto a piece of foundation fabric. Place one piece of fabric onto the foundation right side up, then the second piece right side down over the first. Stitch a straight seam through the 3 layers.

8. Stitch first pieces to the foundation.

9 Trim the excess fabric from behind the patch. Leave about 1/4" seam allowance.

9. Trim excess fabric from behind patch.

10 Press open.

10. Press open.

11 If desired, pre-piece a longer section before sewing it, right sides together, onto the foundation.

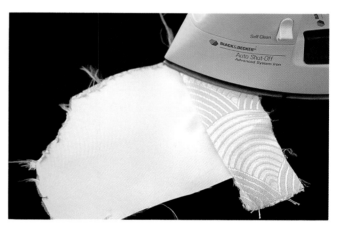

11a. Pre-piece a longer section.

11b. Sew section, right sides together, onto the foundation.

12 Continue sewing pieces on in this manner until your drawn shape is full (be sure to fill an extra 1" all around.)

12. Continue sewing pieces until shape is full.

THE FOREGROUND

The foreground generally provides the centre of interest. Janet's foregrounds contain large, boldly-coloured motifs which suggest lots of movement.

To achieve such fluid, dynamic curves, Janet uses a method of machine-appliqué described below:

13 Draw patterns from your original. They do not include seam allowances. Cut out the paper patterns.

13. Draw patterns and cut from your original.

HINT: Patterns can be numbered and labelled in sequence from the first to the last, if desired, according to the master design.

14 Pin your chosen fabric right sides together with a lightweight facing fabric. Draw the sewing line onto the facing fabric.

14. Draw the sewing line onto the facing fabric.

HINT: Whenever using light-coloured fabric, as in this case, make sure you use a light-coloured facing fabric, too, so that dark shadowing from the background does not show through.

15 Cut roughly around the 2 layers, leaving an approximate 1/4" seam allowance. Using matching thread in your machine, sew along the drawn line with medium to small stitches. For added strength, sew again within the seam allowance, a scant 1/8" outside the first line of stitches.

15. Sew along the seam line with small stitches.

16 Trim very close to the second line of stitching. As one edge of this piece is to be covered by the next piece, that whole edge can be left open to turn the piece right side out.

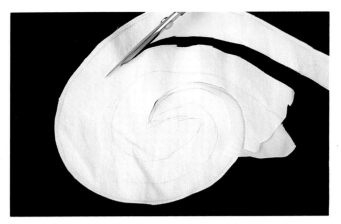

16. Trim close to the second line of stitching.

17 Turn and press the finished edge of this piece. Set it aside while you prepare the piece that will cover the raw edge.

17. Turn and press the finished edge.

18 Sew and trim the next piece the same way as the first. In this example, the design specifies an open edge at the bottom of this piece which allows the faced piece to be turned right side out.

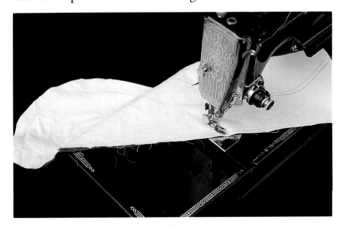

18. Sew and trim the next piece.

19 Press this piece flat.

19. Press piece flat.

20 Lay this piece over the first piece and pin together.

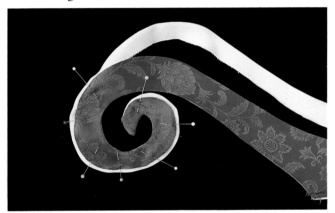

20. Lay piece over the first piece and pin together.

21 Using thread which matches the uppermost piece, stitch the unit together. (**NOTE**: another crescent-shaped blue piece forms part of this unit and has been stitched underneath already.)

21. Stitch the unit together.

22 The prepared unit is stitched onto its place on the quilt's background.

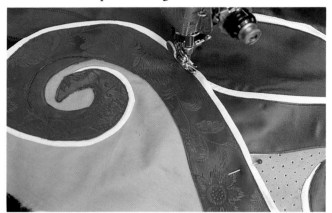

22. Stitch unit onto background.

FACED SHAPES

Many of Janet's appliqué pieces, such as the moons, birds, and fish in *Moonamorphosis*, do not have any open edges for turning the pieces right side out. To make these pieces, she uses the method shown below:

23 Cut one shape from the fabric (in this case the crazy-patched moon) and one from the facing fabric, as before.

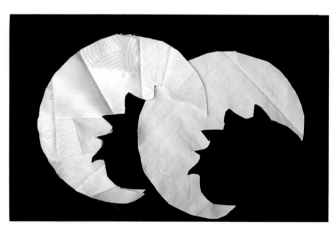

23. Cut shapes from fabric and lining.

24 Stitch with right sides together and trim as before, but this time do not leave an opening.

24. Stitch with right sides together and trim.

25 Lift the facing off the surface of the appliqué piece and make a slit through the facing fabric only.

26 Turn right side out. Press.

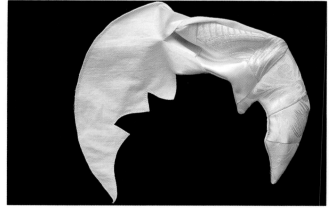

26. Turn right side out.

27 Janet adds dimension to some pieces by lightly stuffing them with polyester batting.

27. You may stuff the pieces with polyester batting.

28 Appliqué the piece onto the background as before, by edge-stitching with matching thread.

28. Edge-stitch piece with matching thread.

When all the machine-appliqué is completed, you may wish to add decorative details with machine embroidery, as Janet does.

Machine embroidery

Janet uses machine embroidery to fill empty spaces, to add detail, to modify a colour that is too bright, or to make a feature stand out.

You may use any decorative stitch and any kind of machine thread. This detail from *Crow Into Firebird* illustrates Janet's use of straight machine stitches only. She often stitches over and over when a stronger line is desired. Her trusty machine has no trouble getting through all the thicknesses of fabric she uses.

Janet says, "I think it's important never to lose sight of the fact that the most high-powered, technologically-advanced machine ever made is called the imagination."

Finishing details

After the top, including borders, is completed, Janet adds a heavy cotton or wool fabric as a batting to give the piece substance and stability. Underneath that she places a cotton backing and machine-quilts through all thicknesses. A last binding border is sewn on to finish the edges, wide enough at the top and bottom to create a sleeve for one-inch boards to be slipped through. Finally, picture-wire is stapled onto the top board and the work is ready to be hung.

R E F E R E N C E S

Chicago, Judy. *Embroidering Our Heritage: The Dinner Party Needlework.* Garden City, N.Y.: Anchor Books, 1980. ISBN 0-385-14568-3

Parker, Ann and Neal, Avon. *Molas: Folk Art of the Cuna Indians.* New York: Barren, 1977. ISBN 0-517-52911-4

Parker, Rozsika. *The Subversive Stitch: Embroidery and the Making of the Feminine.* London: The Women's Press, 1984. ISBN 0-7043-3883-1

Swim, Laurie. *The Joy of Quilting.* Markham, Ontario: Viking/Penguin Books, 1984. ISBN 0-670-800503

CHAPTER 11

Sherry Bussey
NEWFOUNDLAND AND LABRADOR

With workshop: Accurate Machine Piecing

"The most important thing in any class is for the student to get pleasure from what she is doing."

Y ou won't find a better example of an inventor inspired by necessity than Sherry Bussey of Pynn's Brook, Newfoundland. A Newfoundlander born and bred, Sherry has in many ways forged her own way as a quiltmaker as a result of the captivating isolation of living in a distant island province. Here is a coastal landscape unique among the provinces of Canada. Wind and surf erode the rocky shore in nature's own artwork. Frost and coastal windstorms produce the stunted, impermeable mats of balsam fir and spruce trees known as tuckamore. In some areas, fog thick enough to swim in hangs on every land form. In the spring months, huge slabs of ice broken off from northern ice masses roam down the coast. Islanders may awaken to a new wall of white outside their seaview windows. Here is wild beauty.

Since long before its accession to Canada in 1949, Newfoundland and its mainland component, Labrador, have suffered economic hardships. Influenced by frigid Arctic ocean currents, the harsh climate can seem unrelenting for most of the year. From this inhospitable environment spring warm and generous men and women who are strong of body and soul. Newfoundlanders have countered adversity with self-sufficiency.

This is the kind of independent spirit which leads citizens to pick any strip of unused, fertile public land to plant their gardens. It's the same need to live by their own means which leads Newfoundlanders to reject the many glorious provincial campgrounds in favour of "pitcamping," a phenomenon whereby gravel-pits near fish-laden lakes or streams blossom with campers and recreational vehicles. These apparently abandoned

Sherry stands by the restored fishing store at Broom Point, Newfoundland.

mobile communities come to life on sunny summer weekends, and save their inhabitants provincial camping fees.

Newfoundland's isolation has produced a separate culture with uniquely provincial dishes like "Fish and Brewis" and "Jigg's Dinner." The former is boiled cod with soaked and boiled hardtack bread drenched in scrunchions, made from fried salt pork, and molasses poured over all. The wonderful Marine Atlantic Ferry serves a Jigg's Dinner of salt beef and pease pudding made from dried peas, potato, cabbage, and turnip.

The same basic need to live by their own hard work leads most Newfoundlanders, like Sherry and her husband Bruce, to build their homes themselves, often with strong family support. Is there something in this pure, often bracing air which breeds such Canadians with a strong work ethic, a reserve of inner strength? Little wonder that any goal Sherry reaches for, she achieves by sheer effort.

Embarking on her quilting journey, Sherry was fortunate to have the early guidance of nearby quilting teacher Joan Penny-Flynn, who Sherry says, "gave me my most important technical experience. You certainly learned things the right way." Sherry's enthusiasm for the craft soon combined with her innate independence to produce quilts from her own designs. The quilting community in Newfoundland is still small, and Sherry's technical abilities and experi-

Tuckamore growth at the Arches, 400 million-year-old limestone formations near Cow Head, on the West Coast

The tip of the iceberg off St. Anthony

Calvin Hender

Sherry Bussey, Newfoundland and Labrador

ence as a school teacher were quickly recognized, so that she herself has become a popular quilting teacher in recent years.

As with many pioneers, the local scarcity of raw materials was little barrier to Sherry's indomitable quilting spirit. When good cotton fabric was unavailable, she brought quantities of it to Pynn's Brook herself. After buying a Bernina sewing machine, she became the local representative for Bernina. Now, in her home-based business, Patchworks, Sherry sells quilting supplies, teaches, and makes commissioned quilted pieces.

Working from home has allowed Sherry to fill a professional void she experienced after trading her eight-year teaching career for life at home with her newborn daughter, Sarah Lynn, in 1983. Now she pursues parenting, quilting, and part-time teaching with gusto. Bruce is a supportive partner who shares domestic tasks when he can. Sherry says, "Bruce has influenced much of my work." As a math instructor in college, "his mathematical background and interest in design has resulted in many collaborative efforts. One great advantage, too, is that he never complains about my compulsion to quilt."

Sherry seeks out experiences and challenges which help her develop her quilting skills. She says "Quilt Canada '92 [the biennial national conference of the Canadian Quilters' Association] opened my eyes to so many different possibilities. It was my first trip off the island since I started quilting, and in the space of a few days, I was exposed to more than in my previous seven years of quilting. Even though we have a growing number of quilters here, very few are doing contemporary work and rarely is there a workshop for experienced quilters. Recently, my quilting friends and I formed the 'Group of Six,' a support group which has been enriching. It encourages me to concentrate on my quilting."

For her classes, Sherry looks for ways to make them relaxing and allow individuals to be creative. "The most important thing in any class is for the student to get pleasure from what she is doing," she says.

What does the future hold for Sherry Bussey? "I'd like to find a style that is mine which would reflect this wonderful province that I call home."

Lighthouse at Lobster Cove Head in Gros Morne National Park

Amish Stars (97"x75.5"), 1992. Collection of Lynn Bussey

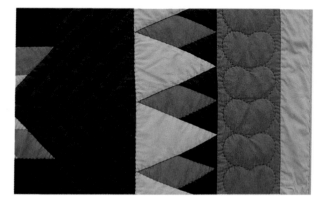

Amish Stars (detail)

Sherry Bussey, Newfoundland and Labrador

Scraps of Light (31"x24"), 1993

This is Sherry's first scrap quilt, machine-quilted in partial circles.

Going to the Chapel (26"x27.5"), 1993
Collection of Evelyn and Derek Locke

Inspired by Judy Hopkins' book One-of-a-Kind Quilts *and made as a wedding gift, this quilt is an example of an original design based on a strong traditional influence.*

Sherry Bussey, Newfoundland and Labrador

Troubled Waters (3'x15'), 1994. Collection of West Viking College

With a design based on the traditional quilt block, Storm at Sea, *the illusion of curved lines is reminiscent of waves rolling upon the Newfoundland beaches. The changes in colour represent the many hues apparent in the water, from the crystal white icebergs, through the blues and grays, to the subtle greens in the many untouched shallow coves.*

The codfish added to the surface contribute a mixed message. They were attached after the quilted water was complete, which indicates that they are not part of it, just as they are not presently part of the Newfoundland fishery. However, their presence on the quilt represents hope for future cod stocks and a re-emergence of the fishing industry, which is necessary for our livelihood.

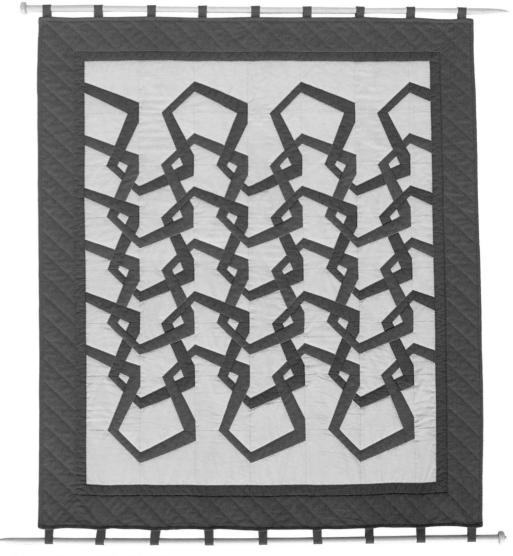

Primary Stitches (48"x40"), 1993

Sherry Bussey, Newfoundland and Labrador

Let's Knit a Quilt with Accurate Machine Piecing

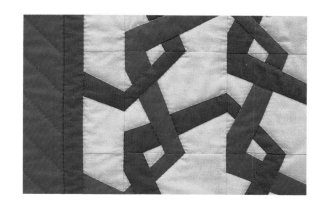

Level of difficulty: Intermediate

H ere's an original Sherry Bussey design inspired by artist M.C. Escher. Using one set of templates (full-sized patterns provided), make multiples of four different blocks by a method of "slash and insert." Depending on how you put the blocks together, you can make either a "knitted" quilt or a "woven" quilt (the "woven" option requires an additional two templates, labelled C1 and C2). The woven piecing is described in Part 2 of the workshop.

WORKSHOP PART 1: A Knitted Piece

M A T E R I A L S

Template material, indelible pen, ruler

Rotary cutter and mat, 6" square rotary ruler (optional), 6"(+) long rotary ruler

Sharp fabric-marking pencil (for example, Berol Verithin™ silver)

Pins, sewing machine, iron and ironing surface

Fabric in three colours: In this sample,
- The background yellow requires 1.2 meters (1 $1/4$ yards)

- The red and blue contrast colours for "stitches" requires .3 meter each ($1/3$ yard).

- The inner blue frame: .2 meter ($1/4$ yard)

- Outer red border, .4 meter ($1/2$ yard)

- Binding (double layer), .3 meter ($1/3$ yard)

- Backing fabric: 1.2 meters (1 $1/4$ yards)

Your fabrics need to be prewashed and ironed.

HINT: Test for colour-fastness by placing a small wet piece of each fabric onto a white paper towel and leaving to dry. If paper towel stays white, it's safe to use the fabric in your quilt.

C O N S T R U C T I O N

Cutting

Copy the template patterns onto your template material. Label A1, A2, A3, B1, B2, B3. Transfer the grainline markings and cut out templates.

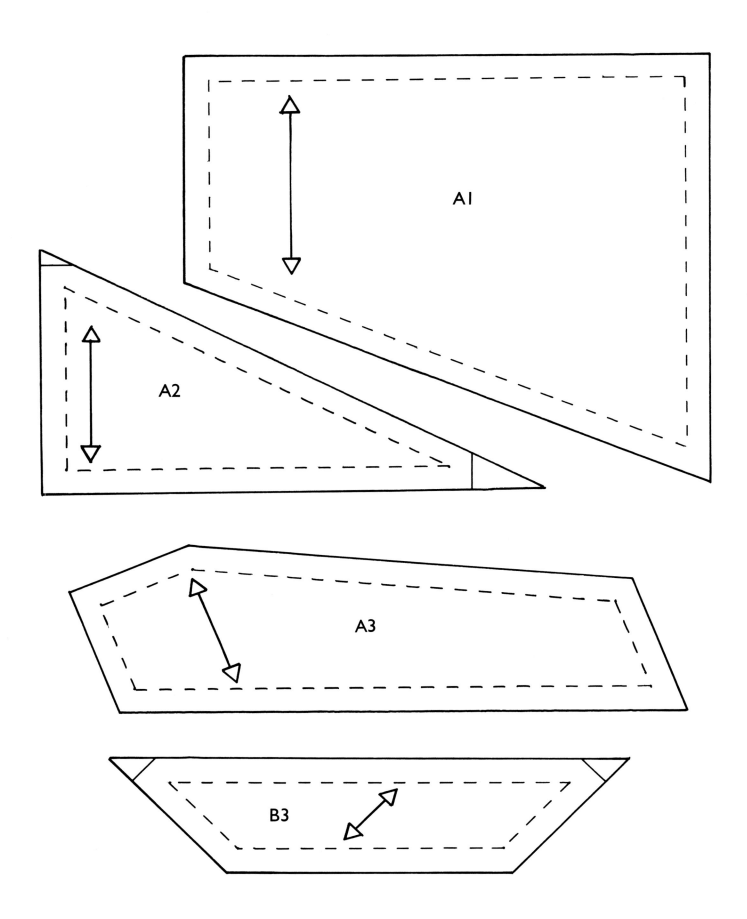

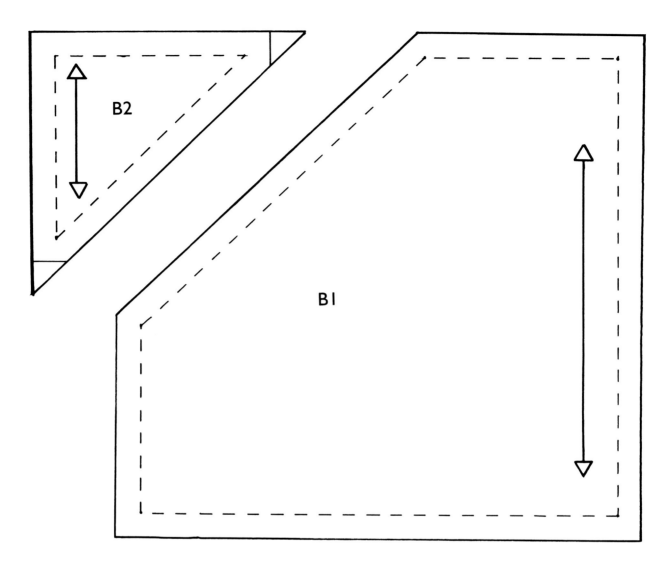

2 All blocks start with 5 ¹/₂" squares of the background fabric (yellow in Sherry's sample). To make the illustrated quilt, cut 56 squares.

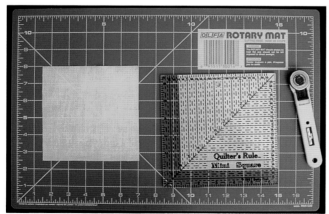

2. Cut 56 squares.

3 From **each** contrast colour cut 18 B3s, 21 A3s, and 18 reversed A3s (A3rs). If you're using solid fabrics, you will not need to reverse the template to cut the A3r pieces.

For instruction purposes, we'll call the lighter contrast colour ONE (red in sample) and the darker one colour TWO (blue in sample).

Sewing

To piece a block, think of the contrast pieces as being stacked on top of each other. The piece at the bottom of the stack is the first one sewn. The new block is then cut and the next piece is sewn in. Then the next cut is made and finally the top piece is sewn in to complete the block.

Four different blocks are arranged according to the diagram on page 184 to make the "knitted" piece. **The piecing of block #1 is illustrated in these photographs**. The steps for piecing the other blocks are then listed under the diagrams of the blocks.

4 Using templates A1 and A2, mark and cut along cutting lines. Remove and discard the resulting sliver.

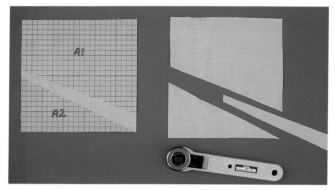

4. Cut along cutting lines.

5 Mark the seam corners of all pieces ($^1/_4$" in from the sides) with a sharp pencil.

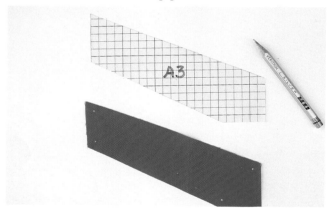

5. Mark the seam corners.

HINT: Poke a hole in the templates with a large safety pin or needle at the seam corners so marking is quick and accurate.

6 Placing A1 and an A3 of contrast fabric colour ONE right sides together, match the marked seam corners by inserting pinpoint through them.

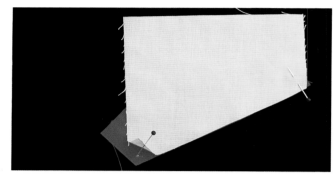

6. Match the marked seam corners.

HINT: To avoid having the pieces shift as you pivot the pin, leave the pin sticking through the markings at a right angle as you insert another pin directly beside it.

7 Stitch a $^1/_4$" seam.

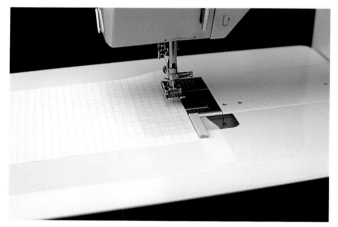

Use graph paper to find an accurate $^1/_4$" seam.

HINT: To train your machine to guide you to a perfect $^1/_4$" seam, feed it a piece of $^1/_4$" graph paper. Insert the needle along the gridline which is $^1/_4$" away from the cut edge of the paper. Then a piece of molefoam or narrow masking tape can be stuck to the throat plate exactly along the cut edge of graph paper.

7. Stitch a ¼" seam, joining A1 to A3.

HINT: Feed the end of the seam under the presser foot with the pin tip to ensure the seam remains a consistent ¼" to the very end.

HINT: Whenever you leave off sewing a seam, sew into a little fabric scrap and leave it under the presser foot to start the next seam. This prevents the thread from pulling out of the needle when you start up, and it prevents wasting thread at the end of every seam.

8 Stitch piece A2 to the other edge of A3.

8. Stitch A2 to A3.

9 Press the seams toward the contrast piece.

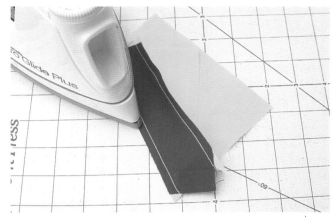

9a. Press seam as shown.

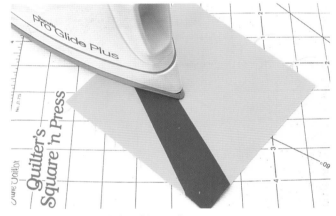

9b. Flip block to right side and press.

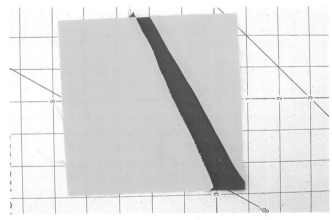

9c. Press seam allowances toward contrast colour.

HINT: Sherry's method of attaining smooth, straight seams is to press the seam as it's sewn from the wrong side, then, while it's still warm, flip the piece to the right side to press.

10 Using the block diagram as a guide, slash and remove the next sliver of fabric. In Block #1, templates A1 and A2 are used again for this step.

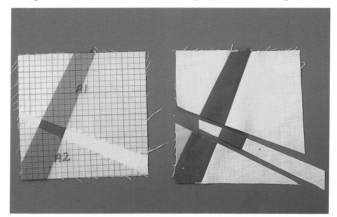

10. Slash and remove the next sliver of fabric.

11 Insert a contrast colour TWO piece, cut from template A3.

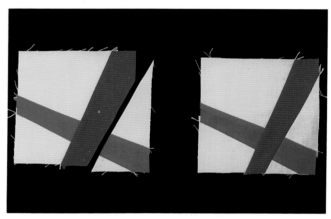

11a. Insert a contrast colour TWO piece.

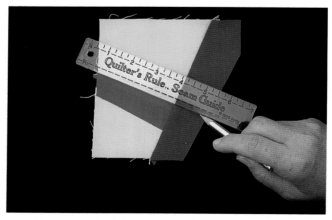

11b. Use quilter's ruler to mark the intersection points.

HINT: To ensure the first contrast piece still lines up, use a quilter's ruler to mark the intersection points where the piece will match up when you sew the second seam.

12 Using the block diagram as a guide, slash and remove the next sliver. For Block #1, this time use templates B1 and B2.

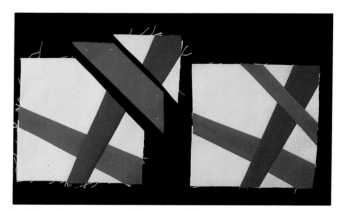

12. Slash and remove the last sliver.

13 Insert contrast colour ONE piece cut from template B3. You have completed block #1. For the sample in the diagram, you'll need 5 more of these.

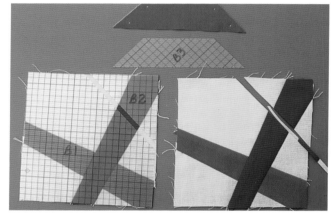

13. Insert contrast colour ONE piece.

In the photograph on the next page, Block #1 is placed beside its twin in the 4-block grouping. You will need 6 of each of the blocks for the sample piece. For the abbreviated construction steps of all 4 blocks see below the diagrams of those blocks.

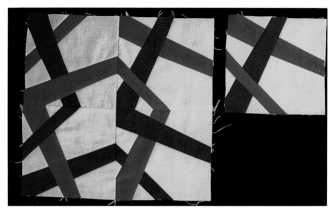

BLOCK #1

1 Using A1 and A2, slash and insert A3 of contrast colour ONE.

2 Using A1 and A2, slash and insert A3 of contrast colour TWO.

3 Using B1 and B2, slash and insert B3 of contrast colour ONE.

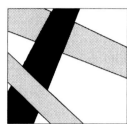

BLOCK #2

1 Using B1 and B2, slash and insert B3 of contrast colour ONE.

2 Using A1 and A2, both reversed, slash and insert an A3r of contrast colour TWO.

3 Using A1 and A2 (both reversed), slash and insert an A3r of contrast colour ONE.

BLOCK #3

1 Using B1 and B2, slash and insert B3 of contrast colour TWO.

2 Using A1 and A2, slash and insert an A3 of colour ONE.

3 Using A1 and A2, slash and insert an A3 of colour TWO.

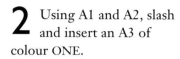

BLOCK #4

1 Using A1 and A2, both reversed, slash and insert an A3r of contrast colour TWO.

2 Using A1 and A2, both reversed, slash and insert an A3r of contrast colour ONE.

3 Using B1 and B2, slash and insert B3 of contrast colour TWO.

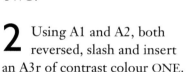

When you've completed 6 of each of the 4 blocks, label them "Block #1, Block #2," etc. and set them aside, while you piece the outside blocks.

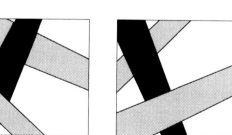

OUTSIDE BLOCKS

Sherry has completed the appearance of knit stitches by making incomplete versions of Blocks #1, #2, #3 and #4 for the blocks around the 24 central blocks. In the **PIECING DIAGRAM** below, the steps required to piece each of the outside blocks is described.

> **HINT: As you piece each block, pin it in place according to the piecing diagram onto a bulletin or cork board, or slap it onto a large piece of flannelette taped to a door, wall, or window close to your work area. This allows you to see the piece as it knits together, and you'll be able to visually check for correct piecing.**

PIECING DIAGRAM

When all the blocks are constructed, sew them together into rows.

	#2 step 3	#1 step 3	#2 step 3	#1 step 3	#2 step 3	#1 step 3
	#4 step 1,2	#3 step 1,2	#4 step 1,2	#3 step 1,2	#4 step 1,2	#3 step 1,2
#1 step 1	#2	#1	#2	#1	#2	#1
#3 step 3	#4	#3	#4	#3	#4	#3
#1 step 1	#2	#1	#2	#1	#2	#1
#3 step 3	#4	#3	#4	#3	#4	#3
#1 step 1	#2 step 1,2	#1 step 1,2	#2 step 1,2	#1 step 1,2	#2 step 1,2	#1 step 1,2
#3 step 3	#4 step 3	#3 step 3	#4 step 3	#3 step 3	#4 step 3	#3 step 3

If you use the marking and pinning tips as before, each block should meet at the points. Sew the rows together to complete the top.

Because of design considerations, Sherry has cut off 2 ½" from the left-hand side of the quilt top. You may wish to do this, too, before adding borders.

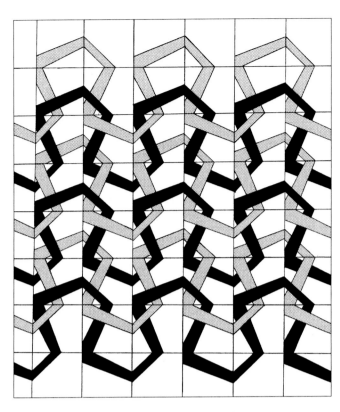

ADDING BORDERS

A 1-inch wide frame from contrast colour TWO and a 3-inch wide border from contrast colour ONE completes the sweater (I mean quilt top). The cutting measurements and order of sewing for the border pieces are:

> **HINT: Be sure to measure your own quilt top before cutting, to ensure that it is the same size as the sample.**

1 Cut and sew 2 - 40.5" x 1.5" strips to sides.

2 Cut and sew 2 - 35" x 1.5" strips to top and bottom.

3 Cut and sew 2 - 42.5" x 3.5" border strips to sides.

4 Cut and sew 2 - 41" x 3.5" border strips to top and bottom.

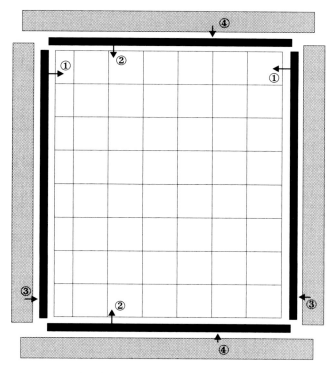

For tips on finishing quilts, see Appendix #1: *The Nutshell Guide to Finishing Your Quilt*. Sherry has continued the knitting theme for Primary Stitches by hanging it by fabric "stitches" on two wooden "knitting needles."

WORKSHOP PART 2:
Try a Woven Piece

Autumn Weaves (26"x21"), 1993

Autumn Weaves (detail)

BLOCK #5   **BLOCK #6**

#5	#6	#5
#5	#6	#5
#5	#6	#5
#5	#6	#5

By adding two more templates (C1 and C2) to your repertoire, you can transform your knit stitches into warp and weft.

Fabric requirements for the small 12-block version:

– Background fabric: .3 meter (¹/₃ yard)

– Contrast colour 1 and 2: .2 meter (¹/₄ yard) each

– Inner narrow border: .1 meter (¹/₈ yard)

– Outer border: .2 meter (¹/₄ yard)

– Backing fabric: .5 meter (⁵/₈ yard) or a 23"x28" piece

C U T T I N G

1 Cut 12-5 ¹/₂" squares of the background fabric.

2 From each contrast colour cut 4 of A3, 8 of A3r, and 12 of C2.

3 From contrast colour TWO, cut 4 of B3.

4 From contrast colour ONE, cut 8 of B3.

C O N S T R U C T I O N

Just two block layouts make the woven piece:

BLOCK #5: (8 required)

1 Using B1 and B2, slash and insert B3 (contrast colour TWO).

2 Using A1 and A2 (both reversed),slash and insert an A3r of contrast colour ONE.

3 Using A1 and A2 (both reversed),and slash and insert an A3r of contrast colour TWO.

4 Using C1, cut away the two corners, then sew in the two C2s, one of each contrast colour, as per diagram.

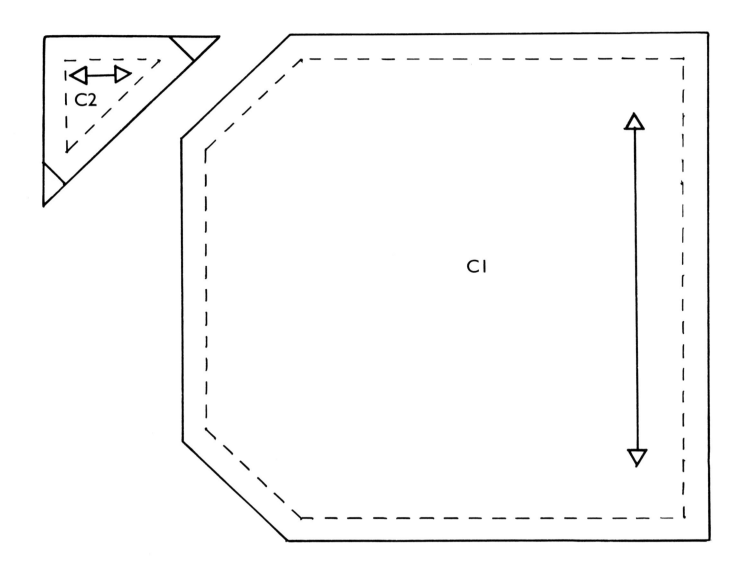

BLOCK #6: (4 required)

1 Using A1 and A2, slash and insert A3 (contrast colour ONE).

2 Using A1 and A2, slash and insert A3 (contrast colour TWO).

3 Using B1 and B2, slash and insert B3 (contrast colour ONE).

4 Using C1, cut away the two corners, then sew in the two C2s, one of each contrast colour.

R E F E R E N C E

Schattschneider, Doris. *Visions of Symmetry - Notebooks, Periodic Drawings, and Related Work of M. C. Escher.* New York: W.H. Freeman and Company, 1990. ISBN 0-7167-2126-0

CHAPTER 12

Quilters From Canada's North

Canada's vast north, generally defined as north of 60° latitude, stretches from the Atlantic Ocean to the Arctic Ocean and almost to the Pacific Ocean in its southwest. Above the treeline which runs diagonally across the Northwest Territories, from northwest to southeast, much of the land is barren treeless tundra or marshy plain that is nearly always frozen. While an unaccustomed eye might see ice and snow for nine to twelve months of the year, a northerner might describe subtle differences in the quality of the ice from one day to the next, or the delicate flora which shows itself in spring's abundance.

Because of the territories' proximity to the North Pole, the sun shines up to 24 hours a day in the summer. The "Land of the Midnight Sun" transforms into the "Land of Night at Noon" in the winter months. Second only to mining, tourism is an ever-growing industry in Canada's north. Visitors flock to the territories for adventure and to see pristine wilderness. They troop to observe the *aurora borealis*, or Northern Lights, a magical shimmering curtain of colour in the sky created by solar winds flowing through the earth's magnetic fields.

The inhabitants of the north are resilient. In remote areas, physical survival is hard-won, and every nuance of the land is perceived, absorbed and used in the battle for daily existence. Nearly half of the population is aboriginal. The first known people to inhabit the land were the Dene or Athapaskans, who came from Asia as long as

The view from inside an igloo

Judith Farrow

25,000 years ago. The Inuit peoples are thought to have arrived 4,000 to 8,000 years ago. The other large group of aboriginal people is the Métis, a mixed native and white people. The non-native people, largely Caucasian, are descended from explorers, gold rushers or missionaries, or they are more recent arrivals. There are nine official languages recognized by Northwest Territories.

Craft-making in the north is well-developed, because the indigenous peoples have handmade useful items of beauty for centuries. Bone, sinew, fur and stone are traditional materials. In more recent years, other materials have been added to the craftperson's repertoire. A quilter's eye would notice and appreciate the wool melton cloth coats, hand-appliquéd with wolf, caribou, whale, polar bear and hunting motifs.

Quiltmaking, while not a traditional craft in the Arctic, enjoys growing popularity. In Yukon Territory in the west and Northwest Territories in the central and eastern part of Canada's north, several quilters are doing innovative work. Some of them share their art with us here.

Lloyd Freese

Spring comes brilliantly in the foreground of the St. Elias Range, Kluane National Park, Yukon.

Judy Farrow
NORTHWEST TERRITORIES

"The north crystallized things for me. You research, then jump in and do it. My quilting began the same way."

I t would be a whole lot quicker to describe Judy Farrow by what she is not, because only one word springs to mind: passive. Describing who she is takes more time. Judy was born to a Canadian father and an English mother. Growing up in the industrial city of Birmingham, England, she spent a lot of her spare time escaping the city into the mountains of North Wales where her passion for rock-climbing developed. Through climbing and instructing others to climb, Judy met Malcolm, married him and came to Canada. Poring over maps of the Arctic, she had always had a fascination for her father's homeland. Judy says, "There was always this link between the British Isles and the Arctic explorers. A good many of them were British and the whalers and their names are still present on the maps today."

Judy and Malcolm spent three years in Montreal obtaining their Canadian teaching qualifications. When they were both offered high school teaching jobs in Frobisher Bay (now called Iqaluit) on Baffin Island in the eastern arctic, they went with the expectation that they would be there for a few years to try it out. Twenty-five years later, they are still living in the Northwest Territories, although they moved to Yellowknife in 1986 with their daughter Justine, who was born in 1982.

In Yellowknife, Judy works for the Métis Nation, Northwest Territories Environmental Division as Project Coordinator for the Northern Contaminants Education Program. She researches and designs educational materials, on environmental contaminants and how they get into the food chain, for use in schools and adult education centres across the north. She says, "It is interesting and challenging work."

But Judy says, "This is not the north. Where we live now, on the shores of Great Slave Lake, is sub-Arctic northern boreal forest. My north will always be the eastern Arctic, Baffin, because it is tundra, above the treeline. The north can be flat, it can be mountainous, it can be rolling Precambrian hills, or raised alluvial beaches.

"First impressions of the north are of a vast barren land where nothing can survive. But time and careful observation soon show that relatively only a small number of

By Yellowknife's famous Wildcat Cafe, Judy Farrow copes with -30° Celcius temperatures, typical of winters here.

In spite of long sunny days, ice and snow remain significant features of an Arctic summer. Iceberg remnants washed up on the beach often have stunning sculptural qualities.

Judith Farrow

species survive here, but survive they do extremely well. The colours are wonderful, too. In the north, the extreme angle of the sun's rays does something to the quality of the light. It gives these extraordinary qualities to the landforms. One of my favourite artists, even before I came to Canada, was Group of Seven painter Lawren Harris. I was in love with his paintings, the snow landscapes, with their purples, blues, viridian, but I thought he had taken the colours and imposed them on the landscape. These colours could not possibly exist except in his imagination. But when I moved north, it was a great revelation to me. I remember particularly one day walking on the beach in Frobisher Bay in September. The tide was coming in and because the sea was just beginning to freeze, it made the shoreline particularly treacherous. Salt water when it freezes is much more slippery than fresh water. I was walking along being very careful how I placed my feet, and I began to notice that the ice was not white, not even just blue, but purple and green. Here were Lawren Harris's colours, colours I had not believed. That was a wonderful thing to me."

One of the greatest influences on Judy's interest in art was her mother. "When I was 14, my mother decided that she was going to art school. In those days, the concept of a mother going to school was novel. Mom shared a lot of her art assignments with me, and although I could not take art myself because I was in the science stream at school, the art side of me never left."

Another significant influence on Judy's art was the botany course Philosophy of Natural Systems. Judy says, "This class allowed me to bring together my ideas on art and science. I will always be grateful to my professor, Rolf Sattler at McGill University, for putting these links into context for me.

"When I moved north there were these visual experiences that I needed to record somehow. I decided I wanted to be a photographer. In the early 70s in the small community of Frobisher Bay you couldn't just sign up for a course. You had to do it yourself. For 15 years I had ordered my staple groceries once a year to be brought in on the 'sea lift ship' that keeps the eastern Arctic supplied. There was a lot of planning

Judith Farrow

Arctic conditions sometimes dictate the method of transportation. Judy and Malcolm often travelled with their dog team. This scene was photographed at midnight on south Baffin sea ice in spring. Sea ice does not break up and clear until mid-July.

and lead time required for any project. One day I sat down, listed what I needed in the way of camera and darkroom equipment, and I ordered it from Hong Kong. I got two whole mail bags, all to myself, when the photography equipment arrived. The north crystallized things for me — you research, then you jump in and do it. My quilting began the same way.

"I have always felt the need to create visual objects with my hands. I fancied myself as a batik artist after taking a class at the Yellowknife Guild of Crafts. I messed up on a batik that was important to me, and rescued it by adding batting and stitching in an area that wasn't very interesting." Next she made the quilt *Half an Owl* and says about the process, "I enjoyed the design concept, fabric choice, the challenge of construction, the rhythm of quilting and the finished product." In 1990, soon after making her first quilt, Judy applied for and received a Northwest Territories Arts Council grant to make three quilted wall hangings that used batik and patchwork as design elements. She did some research to learn more about quilting, then jumped in and made them.

Judy says, "I have a grasshopper mind. Ideas just seem to pop into my head. My design concepts come from the northern landscape that has been my home for the last 25 years. I think we are more free up here. We do our own thing."

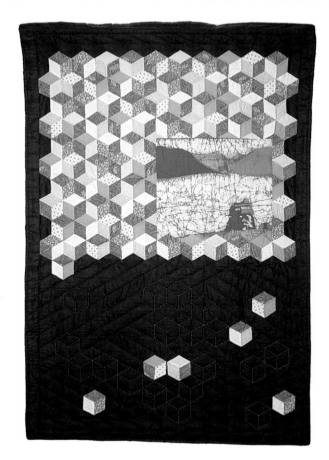

Spring Sea Ice (60" x 40"), 1991

In the Arctic spring, there is a time when the snow has melted from the land, yet the ice remains on the sea. It's a time when the travelling is good and the days are long. This quilt is a celebration of this time. The batik in this piece could be a fjord anywhere on Baffin Island, overlooked by an inukshuk, or stone cairn. The sea ice is represented by a Tumbling Blocks *design. The blocks are destined to fall off and melt into a quilted ocean.*

Half an Owl (50" x 50"), 1990

"This wall hanging was my first quilt. I enjoyed making it so much, I decided to make more."

Wild Cat Cafe Log Cabin (60" x 57"), 1992. Collection of Louise Roy

The Wildcat Cafe, a fine log cabin, was built and owned by Willie Wylie and Smokey Snout in 1937. It was later taken over by Mah Gow and became Yellowknife's first Chinese restaurant. It closed in the early fifties. After extensive reconstruction and renovation the Wildcat was reopened in 1979 by the Old Stope Association.

An original batik of the Wildcat Cafe is incorporated into a traditional Log Cabin patchwork pattern. The contrasting browns and whites used in the patchwork evokes the idea of a log cabin amidst winter snow. The Log Cabin patches are arranged in a 'Barn Raising' set.

Four Seasons of Great Slave
(65" x 106"), 1991

"After living for 15 years above the treeline, trees take on a new significance. It's a love-hate relationship. You like them, like old friends you haven't seen for a while, but they do get in the way of what you want to look at.

"Symbolic patchwork trees undergo seasonal colour changes. It's no accident that there are twice as many winter trees as any other season. The four seasons are represented by whimsical batik landscapes and birds. Snow geese for spring, loons on the lake mean summer for me, and for some reason I always notice the eagles in fall. Of course ptarmigan for winter, but what about the ubiquitous raven, a bird for all seasons? I haven't forgotten the raven, can you find it?"

Judith Farrow

Four Seasons of Great Slave, detail

Bear on Thin Ice (29" x 33"), 1992

Polar bears are the world's largest carnivores reaching weights close to a ton. In spite of their tremendous size and weight they are very adept at moving on thin sea ice. They lie on the ice assuming a prone position, thus spreading their great weight, and half crawl, half shuffle over the ice. Lying like this they can look like a floppy, cuddly child's toy bear.

Sea ice is safe to walk on as long as it is white. As it gets thinner it changes colour, getting progressively darker until almost black, at which point it becomes unsafe.

This wall hanging depicts a great bear on thin ice. Incorporated into the border is a traditional patchwork pattern known as Bear's Paw.

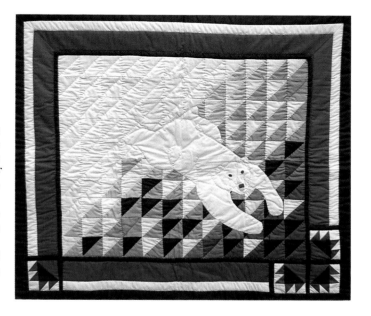

Pat White

YUKON

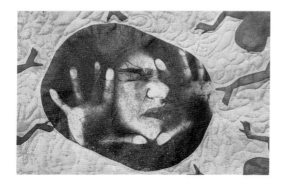

"I quilt to dispel the myths of quilting."

Many people go to the Yukon to seek adventure. In Pat White's case, adventure seeks her. When she blows into town, the very air is charged and ruffled.

Pat moved to Haines Junction, Yukon in 1992 from Alberta, with her husband Darryll and their young adult children Krista, Jason and Jennifer. Also at home are an ever-changing assortment of visitors as well as Mr. Beazley the cockapoo and Samantha the cat, who figure largely in this adventure story. When the children were younger, Pat would periodically kidnap them from school for a day's adventure: How many grizzly bears can we find in one day? How many streams can we ford in the four-wheel drive before we get stuck? Where can we hike today to see something we've never seen before? Pat is well-qualified to show anyone the sights, as her summer job has been guiding in the magnificent Kluane National Park.

Pat has been quilting for 23 years and says, "I only believed in bed quilts until about four years ago. Now I make only wall quilts." She has exhibited locally, nationally and internationally, and has achieved some degree of recognition for her work. For the past eight years, Pat has been teaching classes for quilters and other artists in Alaska, Yukon, and Alberta. She says, "I love everything about this fibre medium, from the tactile quality of the fabrics to the texture created in a quilting line. I enjoy the interplay of colour and design in creating stories and the duality of working in a medium traditionally relegated to the realm of 'a woman's hobby.' My quilts are strongly grounded in traditional techniques and design, yet push the limits in colour, combinations of techniques, and subject matter. Now I quilt to dispel the myths of quilting."

Several years ago, in an effort to achieve effects not possible with commercially-available fabrics, Pat began to paint and dye her own fabrics. The colours in the resulting fabrics are so vibrant and unusual that she has begun to meet the demand to sell her dyed fabrics and to teach dyeing to other fibre artists. One day, while Pat was

Pat White and Logan the Llama take a winter walk by Paint Mountain. Llamas are used as pack animals on guided hikes in the mountains. Logan was named after Canada's highest mountain, found in the Yukon. (Photo by Lina Tremblay)

An interior mountain in Kluane National Park. Much of central and south Yukon is mountainous.

Lloyd Freese

repackaging dyes in a tidy, organized assembly line, the family's new cat jumped onto the counter. She playfully batted a sealed container of blue Procion® MX powdered dye off the counter. It was caught in mid-air by Mr. Beazley, who ran into the living room, bit into it and flipped it into the air, causing the powder to shower onto the grey carpet and the dog. After one hour of rinsing the dog in the bathtub, Pat left to get more shampoo. Mr. Beazley jumped out of the tub and ran into the living room, shaking the blue dye onto every surface on his way. Days of cleaning later, Pat is ready to take the story of the Great Northern Carpet Caper on the road with her personal testimonial on the joys of Synthrapol® detergent and how it has brought a deeper meaning to her life.

Like a growing number of geographically-isolated quilters, Pat has gone out of her way to explore surface design opportunities. She belongs to several organizations like the Surface Design Association, and has taken an advanced workshop at the Quilt Surface Design Symposium in the United States. She applied for and received an Advanced Artist Award from the Yukon government to attend a week-long workshop with internationally-known quilt artist Michael James.

In an effort to become connected to other people in her areas of interest, Pat embraces new communications technology for its simplified access to the rest of the world. Pat White, cyberquilter, recently suspected a deadly virus had been downloaded with a file via her modem. No amount of effort on her part could restore her computer to its former health. She mourned its death, and considered Darryll's suggestion that cryogenics would allow for its maximum preservation ("his exact advice was to throw it into the nearest snowbank"). One final attempt at resurrection found the problem: There was just too much stuff on it. A technician repaired it and Pat is once again on-line.

Pat puts so much energy into everything she does that friends, relatives, neighbours and colleagues consider her behaviour to be hyperactive and even occasionally bizarre. For one quilt project, she needed to paint keys. She laid her keys out on the lawn and

Quilters from Canada's North

bent over them with a paintbrush. The neighbours thought she was painting her lawn! When she worked on the collaborative quilt with Yukon artist Janet Moore, they would start the day with 18 pairs of scissors, and work so feverishly that every pair was covered up by fabric and lost. Then there was the day she was to drive a visitor to the studio. She cleaned the debris from the truck and threw it and her only set of car, house and studio keys into the dumpster, to be found much later by the ever-patient Darryll. And when it comes to social causes, Pat is an active volunteer and appointed arts board member who will advocate for human needs, especially for the needs of artists. She comments wryly, "I'm easy to wind up, but I try hard not to allow myself to get dragged in. I don't want to be mad all the time."

As founding chairperson of the Kluane Quilters' Guild, fellow quilters accept Pat for what she is: an innovative artist who embraces and shares traditional and contemporary techniques and an energizer whose enthusiasm and love of adventure is contagious.

Louise Breneman

Frosty morning, Haines Junction. On a mid-day in mid-winter, temperatures plunge to -50° to -55° Celcius, creating otherworldly effects with frost and snow.

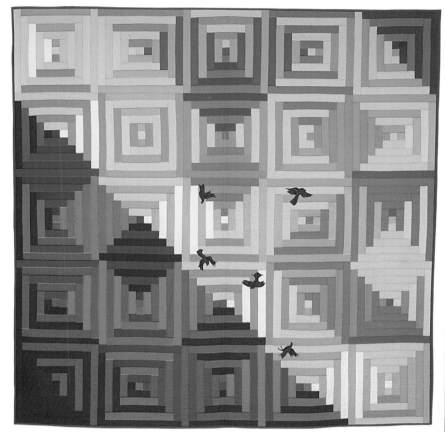

Crashing Ravens (77"x77"), 1994

"Crashing Ravens is a survival story. The ravens on the surface of this quilt move from darkness into the light, struggling to allow themselves the freedom of movement necessary to take flight. The ravens are women. Ravens are for me a symbol of freedom, playfulness and survival. Women have survived through harsh conditions and continue to do so."

Crashing Ravens, detail

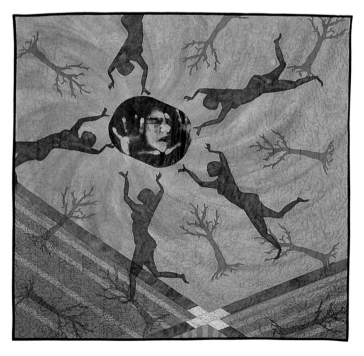

Isis (45"x45"), 1995

"Isis is part of an ongoing series in which I am exploring human individuality in the context of broader society. In particular, I am looking at our compulsion to unthinkingly follow the mainstream regardless of how our souls speak to us. This quilt is about the commercialization of spirituality and how we, as women, fear our own inherent wisdom and power. I am exploring ways to take responsibility for making the necessary connections which enable me to become a powerful, active participant in my own life, rather than passing this responsibility to some external source."

Light of Life (49"x43"), 1995

"*Light of Life began when a friend asked me to create a quilt which included an image of her beloved sled dogs. Although I did not know her well at the time, I admired my friend's courage, wisdom, and strength, and as I reflected on this, the quilt took on a life of its own. She had told me about how she had danced under the Northern Lights, which coincided with my vision of dancing women and ravens being interchangeable symbols of strength, joy and freedom.*"

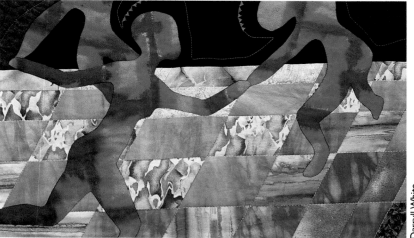

Light of Life, detail.

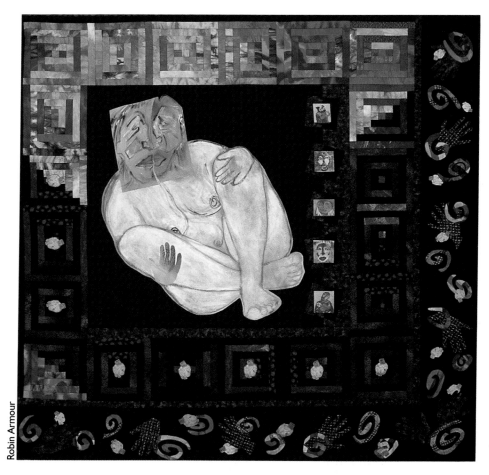

No Comfort (80"x80"), 1996
Collaborative work by Janet
Moore and Pat White

"This quilt is a result of a collaboration between Yukon artist Janet Moore and me. Janet paints big bold nudes and smaller figures that I recognized as images I wanted to work with. To this end, I asked Janet to work with me.

"When we started to work on the quilt, we did not know where this decision would take us. As we worked with the material we told stories to each other. We would meet at the studio and work for 24 hours straight and then, exhausted, go our separate ways, work alone for awhile and meet again to once more coax the images out and arrange them in solid form in our material world.

"This work began as a grief quilt. As we shared our experiences, the quilt was transformed into one that dealt with the loss of innocence and the way in which this has affected our self-images and body images as women. The story told also touches on the resonance of childhood memory and how sometimes these images surface into adult reality. We finally came full circle and realized that indeed we had made a grief quilt.

"I believe that Janet's portraits and our sharing of stories has allowed me the opportunity to strengthen and clarify my own repeated choice of images."

No Comfort, detail

No Comfort, detail

A Selection of Northern Quilted Works

Many of the innovative quilters who live in the north reflect their surroundings in the subject matter of their quilts. A select few of these works are presented here.

She Walks in All Weather (41"x50"), 1996.
By Carol Pettigrew, Whitehorse, Yukon

Carol Pettigrew developed a teacher training program for second language acquisition to assist First Nations elders pass their languages on to the next generations. In order to better understand what the learners are going through, Carol took lessons in Northern Tutchone, Big Salmon dialect, for one hour per day for ten years. At the end of her learning, her instructor said she was doing very well. Now she could speak as well as a four-year-old. The communication between Carol and her instructors over many years has helped her to learn that, "The land is the context for meaning in the language." Until she made a study of native plants, she didn't realize how intimately they were connected with the cycles and the seasons. Carol prints fabrics with the shadows of native plants and says, "I like to think something of their essence is captured in the fabric. I hope the fabrics are treated well."

Carol gains strength for her quiltmaking and for writing poetry at her remote and wild retreat, 3½ hours' drive from Whitehorse. Here, within range of the world's largest non-polar ice fields, she says, "Solitude in the company of the landscape is all I need to heal. Then it creates for me a source of inspiration and creative energy." About this quilt Carol says, "Something of the power and spirit of Kim Mosher's bear pattern appealed to me. The quilted lines are ancient native symbols for weather and the location of the baby Bear's Paw block indicates the bear is female."

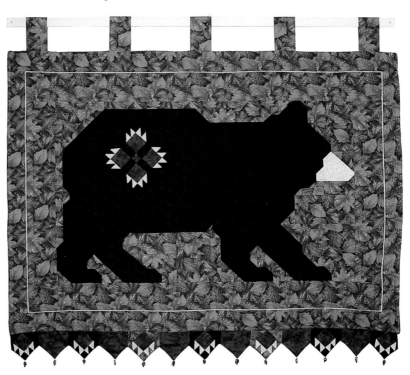

Fractured Rock and Atlin Mountain (28.5"x 34"), 1995
By Shirley Connolly, Atlin, British Columbia

Shirley Connolly lives in the small town of Atlin, 50 kilometres south of the Yukon border, and accessible by road only through the Yukon border. From the picture windows of her log home she has a panoramic view of Atlin Lake. She sees the rugged mountains that edge its western shore and rocky outcroppings nearby that are rooted against winds that sometimes howl fiercely from a great glacier at the southern reaches of "AHTLAH," the great water of the Tlingit Indians. This powerful landscape inspired the creation of Fractured Rock and Atlin Mountain. It evolved from a Fractured Landscape class she took with American quilting instructor Katie Pasquini-Masopust at Santa Fe, New Mexico.

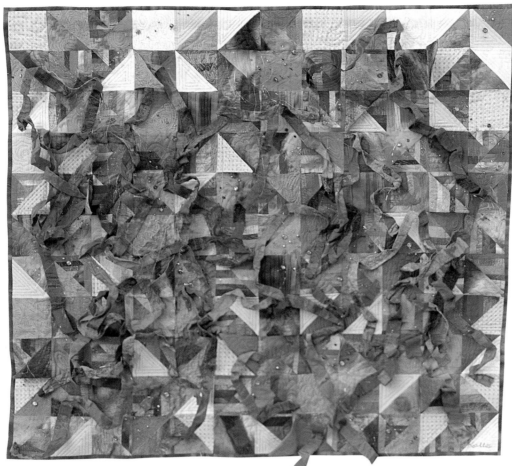

Plea for Compassion
(41.5"x 38.5"), 1996
By Linda Kallos
Yellowknife, Northwest
Territories

"I will always remember and be touched by my dear late son Steven's kind and generous heart. Steven fought a courageous battle with schizophrenia — a disease which takes the mind but not the soul.

"The texture added to this piece at random represents the bizarre and strange behaviour that people suffering from mental illness often exhibit to the world. The jewels and colour beneath represent the precious and beautiful hearts and souls which are so often forgotten. These people need acceptance, understanding and love.

"The six squares suspended from — and very much attached to — the quilt are representative of the family members (Mom, Dad, Sarah, Josh, Celeste and Sebastian) who will always love and cherish Steven's memory."

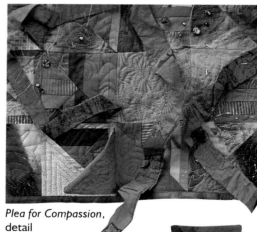

Plea for Compassion,
detail

Inukshuk #1 (28" x 36"), 1996
By Shawna Lampi-Legaree
Yellowknife, Northwest Territories

"The imagery of an Inukshuk fascinated me when I moved to Iqaluit on Baffin Island. The Inuit use these rock cairns to mark important places and to show the way home. The overcast sky with gently falling snow and the wind swirls show a typical prelude to a raging blizzard. Even when the storm is over, the Inukshuk is ready to help weary travellers on their way."

Northern Perspectives II (20.5" x 26"), 1996
By Tina Cresswell
Yellowknife, Northwest Territories

"In the dark days of winter we look forward to the few hours of sunlight we have. Out my office window I can watch both sunrise and sunset in the southeast and southwest. The sky is black. A vibrant orange/pink glow starts on the horizon. Depending on vapour in the air, this strip of colour may break into bars, but by and large the bars have straight lines. The rest of the sky is still black. Suddenly, a bright orange/pink sun appears, popping up from nowhere. It rises fully in only a minute or two, accompanied by vibrant stripes of colour which finally light up the black sky. In the afternoon I watch the same process in reverse.

"I have tried to find this colour, but didn't get the feel of it until I saw the Nancy Crow fabric that I used in the border. After I took Gail Hunt's Pictorial Construction workshop, I knew what method I would use to give this piece the shimmering light it needed.

"I will do more wallhangings in the Northern Perspectives series. There is so much opportunity for imagery up here."

CHAPTER 13

Alice Olsen Williams

FIRST NATIONS

With workshop: Celebrating Women's Work — Adapting Traditional Beadwork

"We see things differently than dominant culture people do. We have a special relationship to the land and to the creation."

Alice Olsen Williams, daughter of an Anishinaabe mother and a Norwegian father, was born at Trout Lake, homeland of her mother's people, in northwestern Ontario. Alice says, "Anishinaabeg can refer to all First Nations people of North and South America. 'Ojibwa' is a Cree word used by white people to name us [our specific nation]. It means boogieman or monster. It is not our word for ourselves."

Until she was sent to all-white schools, Alice spoke Anishinaabe. In recent years she has reimmersed herself in her Anishinaabe culture to relearn her first language so she can talk about the beliefs and values to other people. She says, "I really believe women are the heartbeat of the nations. They pass on the nuances of all the culture to their children and grandchildren. That's why in the centre of my quilts I have animals or topics that are intimately involved with the lives of the Anishinaabeg. And then, deliberately, on the outside I try to have the conventional quilting blocks that were developed by those women who came from Europe and made quilting a tradition in North America." This European influence represents her father's contribution to her heritage.

Alice learned to sew at an early age. "My mother had us make doll clothes and we had to take tiny, tiny stitches, so when I took quilting I didn't have to learn that. My first local quilting teacher was Orlean Morrison who was very encouraging so that you

---

In the Williams's yard sits the sweat lodge frame, made from bent maple saplings. It is covered with canvas and infused with steam from healing water on hot rocks during the sweat lodge ceremony, which forms part of the Anishinaabe healing process.

A view of Alice's studio.

felt what you had done was good." Later, at a week-long course at the Haliburton School of Fine Arts, another Canadian teacher and quilt artist, Margaret Stephenson-Coole, was to introduce more skills than Alice could grasp all at once. But she kept her notes so when she encounters something that she remembered Margaret taught, she can go back and look it up.

Alice developed a unique style. "For four years I quilted traditional blocks. When I was quilting I said to myself, 'I love this work so much. How can I make it my own so when people see my work they know it was done by an Anishinaabe woman?' I wasn't so much concerned that they know it was done by Alice Olsen Williams. And it took me a long time to evolve how to do that. I'm not satisfied with how I draw, so it was important for me to ask an Anishinaabe person to help me with that because we see things differently than dominant culture people do. We have a special relationship to the land and to the creation. We depict the spirit of the animal or tree in x-ray vision or pictographic style. Norman Knott [a Curve Lake artist] gave me some loon and geese forms. He shared his talents with me so I could move on to do what I wanted to do, because that's the kind of people we are. We share those gifts that are given to us by the Creator."

Alice and her family share liberally with the many friends and relatives who visit their modern, open-design home on Buckhorn Lake, near Peterborough, Ontario. Alice and her husband Doug provide the home base for the comings and goings of their four grown children: son Keesic and daughters Donna, Sagateh, and Sarah. Their adored grandchildren, far-away Devin and Alysha and nearby Amelia, complete the family unit.

In this enriched setting you may, on occasion, find Alice's students gathered for classes. Her airy studio provides inspiration from both inside and outside the windows. Alice believes "there's a flame in each one of us and a person like me is there to put some kindling on that flame." When people ask her to teach, she says, "I owe that to people because I have that skill that's been given to me." Many parents can relate to the story about Alice's eldest daughter who was never interested in sewing before she moved away from home. "She tells me she signed up for a quilting course, when she could have got it for free here!"

People also come to buy Alice's quilts. "I don't make them to sell," she says, "but if someone wants to buy them, they're there. If people buy a quilt from me I feel it's because they know it's Anishinaabe and it touches them that way."

One of her customers was her friend, the late Canadian novelist Margaret Laurence, who Alice met in 1974. Alice had read Margaret's book, *The Diviners*, "and the life of that little girl, Morag, reminded me of my own life. I really felt that Margaret Laurence and I were kindred spirits. And I called her and cried and cried and she waited for me to stop. She seemed to under-

Alice's evening view of Buckhorn Lake, as seen from the house

stand that I had to do this. I thought she was Anishinaabe." That phone call led to years of friendship between Alice's family and Margaret. Margaret had commissioned a loon quilt, but was diagnosed with her terminal illness before Alice completed it, so Alice lent Margaret one of her own quilts. It comforted both of them, and acted as a communication bridge during the difficult time when the author was dying.

About her professional evolution as a quiltmaking teacher, Alice says, "I have that special situation where I could use quilting as a way of teaching our language, have it as a credit course and at the same time use it as a medium for political analysis and social awareness, where women get together and talk about what we can do about the inequities of this society."

Increasingly, Alice uses her quilt art to mourn Mother Earth's demise, to protest societal inequities between men and women, to rail against racism, to celebrate Anishinaabe beliefs and traditions, and to express the beauty of women's work. She now incorporates her interpretation of the traditional medicine wheel or *Pimaatisiwin Circle* into each of her quilts. Each section of the wheel represents some of Mother Earth's elements and the teachings associated with them. *Pimaatisiwin* is the aim or hope of living a good life on this earth. "This symbol helps me to recognize and be thankful for the gifts of life, which have been given to me."

The *Pimaatisiwin Circle*, here basted and ready to applique onto a quilt top, is symbolic of many of the foundations of Anishinaabe teachings, according to Alice Olsen Williams. The green (sometimes brown) circle surrounding the centre circle "represents our Mother, the Earth, life and continued life."

The red stands for the East for the Anishinaabeg, for spring and new life, for the life-giver food, the animals and the plants that have shared their lives so that we may have a good life on this Earth. So the East teaches us about sharing.

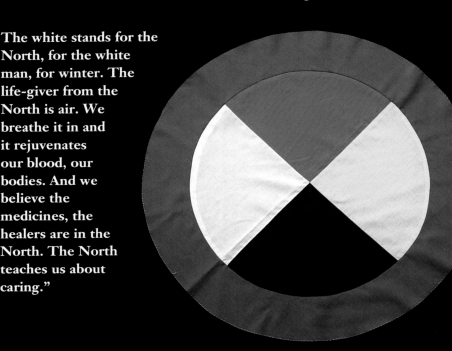

The white stands for the North, for the white man, for winter. The life-giver from the North is air. We breathe it in and it rejuvenates our blood, our bodies. And we believe the medicines, the healers are in the North. The North teaches us about caring."

The yellow stands for the South, for the yellow [Asian] race, for summer. We believe that the sun is the life-giver from the South. The sun teaches us about patience, because it takes all day to go around the earth [according to the teachings], and gives us warmth. The special gift of the South is the trees, which grow up tall and straight. We are supposed to live our lives like that. We live with honesty and the South talks to us of relationships, which take time and patience.

The black stands for the West, for the black race, for fall. The life-giver from the West is water. We are told to look after the water. It is a sacred healer, the life-blood of the Great Mother. When we drink water, we drink in the healing qualities of the water. The West teaches us to walk on the earth with kindness.

Starblanket and Fires (77" x 77"), 1992
Hand-quilting by Lydia Kelder

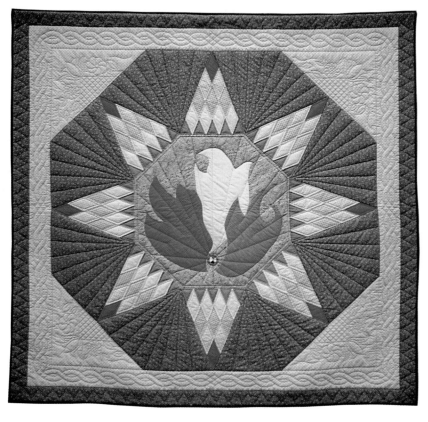

Alice says, "The Starblanket is a source of healing and represents the teaching of how the Peace Drum came to the Anishinaabeg. She retells the story:

At one time, our men had fallen into aggressive, war-like behaviour. Their songs, dances, drums, and dreams were inspired by greed and war, contrary to the teachings of the Creator. This way of life caused anguish, fear, and disrespect among the populace.

One day, a certain young Anishinaabe-Kwe was alone in the bush, meditating, when a Sky Being came to her. This Spirit Being told the young woman that the men in her society had to change their dreams, drumsticks, dances and medicines into visions and instruments of peace. Because the young woman would be the one to bring the message of peace to her people, the Sky Being gave her the instructions and all the meanings attached to making the original Peace Drum. She took these teachings to the Anishinaabe men and so helped her society to live in peace and harmony and balance with the Creation.

The three flames in the centre of the star represent the body, mind and spirit, the past, present and future, and the morning, noon, and night.

Flowers at the Petroglyphs (40.5" x 39"), 1990

"Not far from our home at Curve Lake First Nation is a spot sacred to our people," says Alice. "Several generations ago, Anishinaabeg came to that area and left sacred drawings in the soft rock. The bright yellow fabric with the black markings reminds me of the life-giver, the sun, shining down on the petroglyphs."

Alice Olsen Williams, First Nations

Family Outing (53" x 68"), 1987

"The water represents humility: water gives life to all living things and yet always seeks the lowest spot to show how humble she is. Sometimes when I work with the windows open, the loon's lively calls pull me outside."

Family Outing (detail)

"For Norman Knott, the artist who designed these loons, when there's that red in the loon it represents the life-blood. The black represents bone structure, the framework."

We Are All Crying: A Quilt for 1992 (46" x 84"), 1992

"*The North is placed at the top of this Medicine Wheel because it is the white man who has spread himself all over the world, bringing grief, destruction, exploitation, hate and carelessness. People cry and mourn over the destruction, represented by the factories gobbling the Earth's gifts.*"

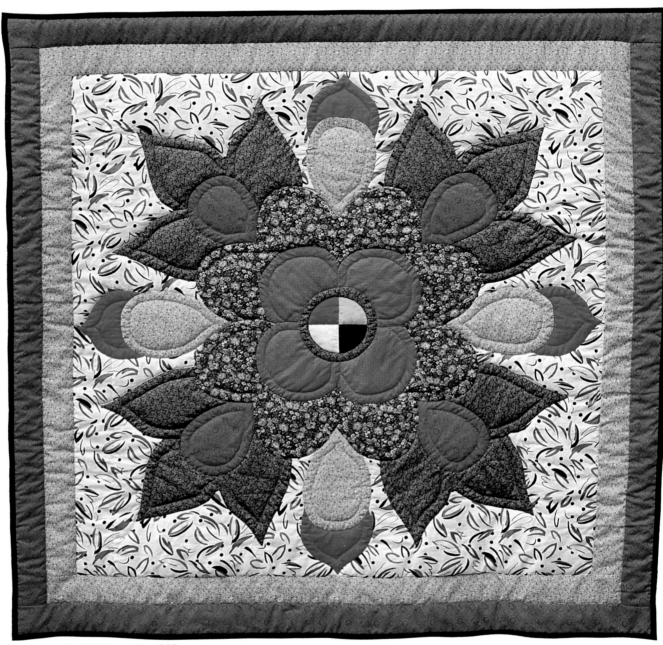

Bouquet to Gail I (56" x 56"), 1993

Celebrating Women's Work—Adapting Traditional Beadwork Designs to Quilts

Level of difficulty: Beginner

Using a paperfolding technique with bold simple shapes derived from Anishinaabe beadwork, Alice honours the work of her foremothers. Traditional beadwork pieces feature bold solid floral motifs. It is this matrilineal creativity that Alice celebrates in her workshop.

M A T E R I A L S

8.5" x 11" white paper

Soft-lead pencil

Large format paper, such as newsprint or tracing paper, for full size of appliqué and paper patterns

HINT: In the true spirit of making do, tape smaller pieces together.

Dark black pen

Template material. Cereal boxes are great.

A selection of brightly-coloured, pre-washed 100% cotton fabrics, background fabric the size desired. (For tips on fabric selection, see Appendix #2: *An Easy System for Taking the Angst out of Fabric Selection*.)

Hand-sewing appliqué needles

Threads that match your fabrics

T H E   P A T T E R N S

Start by folding your paper in half, then quarters, then eighths.

1. Fold your paper in eighths.

2 Draw a small circle in the centre. Alice works freehand but you may choose to use a compass if your circles look more like eggs. This is where Alice's personal symbol, the Pimaatisiwin Circle, might go.

2. Draw a small circle in the centre.

3 Referring to the photo or an actual sample of beadwork for suggestions of floral shapes, draw with a soft-lead pencil a shape within two of the folds of paper (i.e. ¹/₈ th of the area). For *Bouquet to Gail I*, Alice uses a half heart for this first round of shapes.

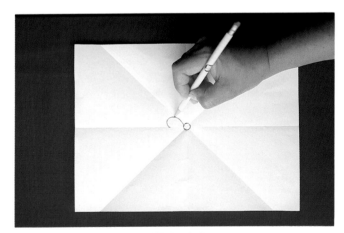

3. Draw a shape within 1/8th of the area.

4 Fold the paper and rub with your fingernail over the line you've just drawn. A faint mirror-image replica of the line will appear beside it.

4a. Fold the paper and rub with your fingernail.

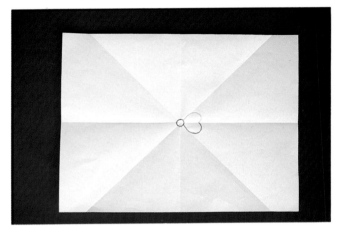

4b. A faint replica of the line will appear.

5 Draw this line in with the pencil.

5. Draw this line in with the pencil.

6 Refold on another line, rub, and draw the line darker. Fill in the first round of shapes this way.

6a. Refold on another line.

6b. Draw the line darker.

6c. Fill in the first round of shapes.

7 Starting with a new shape, repeat the process for another layer of floral shapes.

7. Repeat the process for another layer of floral shapes.

8 Continue to add layers of floral shapes. When you have completed the design to your satisfaction, you're ready to enlarge it to the size desired for your quilt.

8. Continue to add layers of floral shapes.

9 Fold the large paper into eighths as you did with the small paper. Then, working by eye as Alice does, draw your shapes into the larger format.

9a. Draw your shapes into the larger format.

This time, instead of rubbing the pattern onto each eighth, you may wish to fold the paper, then draw the mirror image when holding the paper up to a window so you can see the dark lines through the light paper.

9b. Complete the 'cartoon' or large drawing.

HINT: A dining room table with the leaves removed, a sheet of glass laid over top, and a desk light shone up from underneath makes a great "light table" at night.

10 Copy each different shape and cut out to make your paper patterns.

10. Cut each different shape to make your paper patterns.

HINT: If you have a complex design, you may wish to label each pattern piece and corresponding shape on the master pattern, A,B,C, etc.

11 For a longer-lasting template, outline or glue the paper pattern onto a piece of lightweight cardboard, like a cereal box, and cut out a template.

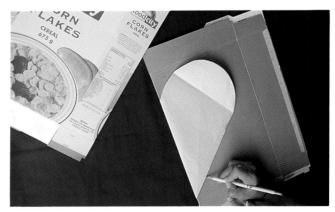

11a. Glue the paper pattern onto cardboard.

11b. Cut out a template.

A P P L I Q U É   P I E C E S

1 For some of the pieces, such as the heart-shaped motif, Alice has chosen to fold her fabric into quarters and cut four layers together on the fold.

1a. Mark four layers for cutting.

First, the turn-under line is marked around the template, then the fabric is cut approximately ¼" away from the marked line.

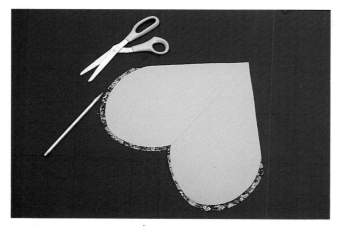

1b. Cut approximately ¼" outside marked line.

1c. Unfold.

2 Each of the appliqué pieces is turned under on the marked line, then finger-pressed and basted. Alice joins the appliqué pieces together into a unit, before applquéing them to the background.

2a. Turn under the seam allowance and baste.

Shown here is the wrong side and the right side of equal appliqué units that Alice has basted together for another quilt. She is preparing them for appliqué onto another quilt top with a circular design, similar to the one pictured. (**NOTE**: Alice does exceptionally fine even basting, which should not be mistaken for quilting stitches in this example!)

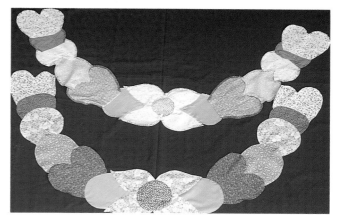

2b. Baste units together. (Shown from wrong side and right sides)

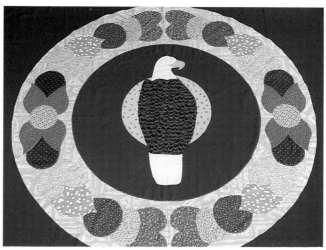

2c. These pieces are ready to be appliquéd to another quilt.

To learn how to do the appliqué stitch, please refer to Chapter 5, page 91. For tips on finishing quilts, see Appendix #1: *The Nutshell Guide to Finishing Your Quilt.*

APPENDICES

The Nutshell Guide to Finishing Your Quilt

You Have A Beautiful Quilt Top, Now What?

1 If you're making a rectangular quilt, **check to ensure that the top is "square"** by measuring diagonally corner to corner on **both** diagonals. If measurements are not the same, you may be able to resew some seams to adjust for accuracy.

2 **Clean up your act.** Make sure the seams are all **pressed** the way you want them. Trim any long thread ends (particularly if the quilt has any light-coloured fabrics, because thread ends shadow through them). Pick up all the loose threads with a clothes brush or masking tape wrapped around your hand.

3 **Cut backing and batting** at least 2" larger all around than the quilt top. For the backing, use quilt-weight cotton yardage, seamed if necessary, rather than sheeting; it's easier to hand-quilt.

4 **Layer the quilt "sandwich."** To a large, clean, flat surface (a gym floor if you have it!), **tape the backing, right side down. Lay the batting over the backing,** smoothing out lumps (but do not stretch the batting). **Centre the quilt top, right side up, over the batting,** and smooth it gently with your hands, from the centre out.

5 To prepare the 3 layers for quilting, **pin them together** with "silk" safety pins (from the drycleaners or a quilt shop) or **baste them together** on a 4"– 6" grid, from the centre out.

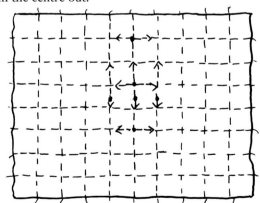

6 Remove the tape from the backing, then roll the edges of the backing and batting up over the quilt top. Secure with more basting or pins. This step prevents the edges from being frayed or shredded while quilting.

7 If you choose to **tie** your 3 quilt layers together, embroidery floss or crochet cotton works well. To tie, **use a square knot** (every 4" on a grid works well for polyester batting) and leave a tail about 3/4" long. Most people have their "tails" showing on the quilt top.

If you choose to **hand-quilt** your layers together, practice your quilting stitch on a sample first. Whole books are written on the quilting stitch, but since this is a nutshell, suffice it to say that the quilting stitch is a running stitch, sometimes follows a design predrawn on the quilt top, is ideally the same size as each stitch preceeding and following it, and has no knots or large stitches showing on the top or back. (Beginning and ending knots are "popped" into the batting.) Most quilters use a portable quilting hoop or frame to hold the layers taut while they hand-quilt.

If you choose to machine-quilt, practice on a sample first. (Again, whole books are written about machine quilting.)

In general, any quilting method you choose should be done from the quilt's centre out, to prevent unsightly puckers or unsquare corners.

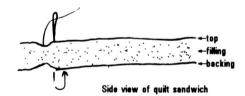

Side view of quilt sandwich

8 **Handbaste the edges of the quilt together.** Trim batting and backing to 1/2" larger than the top.

9 **Bind the edges** with double binding cut from the straight grain of the fabric. (If you have a curved edge, cut from the bias of the fabric.) Cut the binding fabric 2 1/2" wide by the length of the perimeter of the quilt. Where it is necessary to piece the lengths of binding fabric, seams should be on the bias, or 45° angle. Press a centre fold along the whole length of the binding, wrong sides together. Stitch the raw edges of the binding to the quilt edges, onto the quilt's top, ending with a backstitch 1/4" from end. At the corners, allow an extra 1/4" fold at binding to provide excess for smooth mitering. Fold the binding to the quilt's back, match the fold to the sewn line, and hand stitch binding in place.

10 **Sign and label your work.**

A P P E N D I X   2

An Easy System for
Taking the Angst out of Quilt Fabric Selection

North Vancouver's well-loved quilting teacher, Dolores Bell, offers these general guidelines to students in her sampler classes, when they are not sure where to begin:

1 Choose your favourite colour. The pleasure of sewing with a colour you love will encourage you to finish the quilt.

2 To begin, select an "idea" fabric, or multicoloured print, that contains your favourite colour plus two or three other colours.

3 Next, choose four or five fabrics that blend with your "idea" fabric. When doing this, consider:

— The **value** (lightness and darkness) of the colour. Dark and cool colours (violets, blues, greens) appear to recede in a quilt design, while light and warm colours (yellows, oranges, reds) come forward. The greater the value contrasts in a design, the stronger the impact of the design.

— The scale of your prints. Your quilt will appear more interesting if you use blender fabrics. Blenders use a variety of print scales rather than solid colour fabrics. A balance of small, medium and large prints, as well as stripes, polka dots, plaids, pictorial prints and border prints suggests movement.

Often the beginning quilter avoids very large floral prints, but once these fabrics are cut up into pattern shapes, the bits and pieces of the large print provide a wonderful "flowing" across the surface as the viewer looks for the portions of the large scale prints.

4 Stack your favourite "run" (group of harmonious fabrics), then step back and squint at it to make sure you have a satisfactory value change.

5 100% cotton is "quilter friendly." Prewash your fabric to check for colourfastness and to preshrink.

6 The most important factor in choosing fabric and colour for quilts is that it please **you**, the quiltmaker. If you are happy with your fabric run, you are on your way to making a beautiful quilt.

APPENDIX 3

Documentation, Care and Conservation of Quilts

DOCUMENTATION

When you make a quilt, you know where, why and when you made it. Perhaps no one else knows. In order to save information for posterity, every quilt needs to be labelled with, at the very least, your name and the date that you made it.

Your heirs will appreciate and respect the quilt more if they know some of its history. They will think of you every time they look at or cuddle under the quilt. If quilt historians of the future have a chance to see your handiwork, they will be thrilled to be able to identify the maker and the date.

Consider documenting even more of the story of your quilt. If you count the hours it takes to make a quilt, if your life is somehow influenced by quilting, or if the quilt itself speaks about your life experience, if the quilt has won awards, been in exhibitions, or served a special purpose in your life or the life of some other person(s): **write it down**, in a journal, in a documentation binder, or on the quilt itself. While a quilt may appear to be commonplace to someone who doesn't know its story, it can speak volumes if its history is known.

There are countless ways to label the quilt itself. Some historians suggest sewing a label onto the quilt's back **before** quilting it, so that if it were lost or stolen it would be difficult to erase evidence of its ownership. Labels can be made by writing with permanent markers (like Pigma® pens) onto fabric, by embroidery, by phototransfer, by typing directly onto fabric (heatsetting with an iron recommended), by incorporating information **on the front of the quilt**, as part of the design.

Information which you could include on the label: **who made it, where it was made, when it was made, who was it made for, why it was made, when the maker was born, who is to inherit it, care instructions, and who contributed to the design, selection of materials or construction of the quilt.**

Be sure to take photos of the quilt, whether you plan to give it away or keep it. If you should lose the quilt in a flood, fire or robbery, such a photo (and other documentation) may help establish its value, or provide you with pictorial reference should you choose to recreate it.

CONSERVATION

Perhaps you have made a quick baby quilt which is meant to be used and laundered frequently. Such a quilt will be loved and eventually discarded. There may be other quilts which are meant to be loved **and cared for**, because you have spent the time to make an heirloom quilt or you have been the recipient of an heirloom quilt. Most quilt lovers have seen or heard of an example of disregard for quilts: the packing "blanket" dragged from place to place in a pickup truck, the dog's birthing blanket, the art quilt used at the beach to deflect the sparks from the fire. By public education and careful documentation, we can contribute to the increased longevity of these treasures.

Textile conservators in museums and quilt historians are becoming more conservative in their advice to staff, collectors, and owners of quilts, about cleaning textiles. Some of their advice follows:

CLEANING

Cleanliness is not as important as the safety of the textile.

Do not wash (or wet clean) an old quilt without research about whether it should be done at all. Be aware that the colours may bleed, stitches may break, batting may bunch or become matted, and fibres may be weakened, and you may not be able to get it clean anyway.

If you must wet-clean an heirloom quilt, follow these guidelines:

1) Place an old sheet in the bottom of a bathtub, then fill the tub with lukewarm water to which a small amount of no-phosphate quilt detergent (e.g. Orvus, Dawn) has been added.

2) Lower the loosely-bunched quilt into the water.

3) Using the sheet to lift and support the quilt, gently swish the quilt around.

4) Let the water drain out of the tub, then lightly squeeze excess moisture from the quilt and sheet.

5) Using the sheet, lift out the quilt, then refill the tub with clear water.

6) Replace the sheet and quilt and gently swish again to rinse.

7) Repeat the rinsing procedure until the rinse water is clear.

8) Gently squeeze the excess moisture from the sheet and quilt.

9) Spread the sheet and quilt together over grass which is not exposed to direct sunlight. Let it dry flat, turning the quilt once if desired.

2 **Do not dry clean** a quilt. Not enough is known about the effect of the chemicals which remain in the textile after cleaning. Over time, these chemicals may cause deterioration of the fibre.

3 If the quilt smells musty, **lay it on a clean sheet out of direct sunlight to air it.**

4 To remove surface dirt, place a square of nylon screen over the quilt while you **vacuum** through it with the upholstery attachment. Move the screen around with the vacuum as you clean the front and back of the quilt.

5 Neither the yellowing of white fabrics nor the fading of colours can be reversed by any means. Damage from mould is permanent also.

STORAGE

If a quilt is not on display or in use, the best storage system would be to lay it flat on a disused bed, in a dark, humidity and heat-controlled room. This is not practical for the average quilt owner. Since moisture, heat, insect and rodent pests, light, and dirt are a healthy quilt's worst enemies, we can store quilts in ways that will reduce exposure to these factors.

1 **Store the quilt flat,** if possible, to reduce pulling on the stitches. Cover with an old sheet. Second best would be to **store it rolled onto an acid-free storage tube and wrapped with washed cotton or acid-free tissue** (see Appendix #4: *Sources* for conservation supplies). Third best would be to **fold in thirds with well-washed cotton or acid-free tissue** in the folds, then wrapped in more tissue or acid-free boxes and stored on a shelf with ventilation (refold occasionally to prevent permanent folds). All quilt storage areas should be cleaned and checked for pests or moisture accumulation on a regular basis.

2 **Do not store in direct contact with wood.** All woods release oils and acids which cause deterioration of fibres. Wood sealed with plastic paints is acceptable.

3 **Do not store in attics, basements or garages** unless they are humidity and temperature regulated.

USE OR DISPLAY

1 **On beds,** keep quilts away from direct or reflected sunlight, and from a steady source of humidity or excessive heat. To reduce stress on the stitches, do not tuck the quilts under the mattress or habitually sit on one section of the quilt.

2 **For wall display,** sew a cotton tube along the top of the quilt's back, then insert a rod or sealed wooden slat to distribute the quilt's weight evenly. Avoid hanging quilts on outside walls in your home. Change wall quilts every 6 months to give the stitches a rest time.

REFERENCES

Armstrong, Nancy Cameron. "British Columbia Heritage Quilt Project: Quilt Care and Conservation."

Canadian Conservation Institute. CCI Notes: 13/1, "Textiles and the Environment." Ottawa: Canadian Conservation Institute, 1992.

Canadian Conservation Institute. CCI Notes: 13/2, "Flat Storage for Textiles." Ottawa: Canadian Conservation Institute, 1993.

Canadian Conservation Institute. CCI Notes: 13/11, "Fibre Information." Ottawa: Canadian Conservation Institute, 1988.

Canadian Conservation Institute. CCI Notes: 13/13, "Commercial Dry Cleaning of Museum Textiles." Ottawa: Canadian Conservation Institute, 1990.

Sources

Books: Basic Quiltmaking Information

There are many excellent books on the market about basic quiltmaking. One of these is *Your Quilting Primer* by Barbara Koroluk, **ISBN 0-9693666-0-4,** available at many quilt shops, or by writing to: Lormac Publications, 2425 Tolmie Street, Vancouver, BC V6R 4C4. Phone: 604-224-3693.

Mail-order: General Quiltmaking Supplies

Many retailers who sell supplies for quiltmaking would be happy to sell by mail-order. To find out the quilt shops' locations and phone numbers, look in the Yellow Pages of the cities near you. Or, subscribe to *Canada Quilts Magazine*, PO Box 39, Station A, Hamilton ON L8N 3A2, to identify quilt shops which suit your needs. The shops listed below specialize in mail order, and produce catalogues or fabric swatches. Most of them are retail shops, too, so please pay them a visit if you are in the area (call first to confirm).

Fabrics:

Crocus Creek Quilt Shop
Box 4745, Whitehorse, YT. Y1A 4N6
Phone: 403-668-7699, Fax: 403-668-7693
(swatch club)

From My Studio
PO Box 36011, Castledowns
Edmonton, AB. T5X 5V9
(hand-dyed fabric)

Rocky Mountain Quilt Company
Box 2, Site 11, RR#5
Calgary, AB. T2P 2G6
Fax: 403-279-6041
("fat eighths" by colour families)

General Quiltmaking Supplies/ Notions, Including Fabrics:

A Great Notion Sewing Supply Ltd.
100 - 5630 Landmark Way
Surrey, BC. V3S 7H1
Local Phone: 604-533-2891
Local Fax: 604-533-7563
Orders: 1-800-309-2829, Fax: 1-800-204-4117

The Fabric Sandwich
Box 1749, Grand Forks, B.C.
V0H 1H0
Phone: 250-442-2998
(fat quarter fabric club)

The Hobby Horse
RR#5, Georgetown
ON. L7G 4S8
Phone: 905-877-9292, Fax: 905-877-4522
Orders: 1-800-565-5366

Quilters' Fancy Limited
2877 Bloor Street West
Toronto, ON. M8X 1B3
Phone: 416-232-1199 Orders: 1-800-363-3948
(including quilt design software)

Satin Moon Quilt Shop
517 Pandora Ave.
Victoria, BC. V8W 1N5
Phone: 250-383-4023 or 1-800-345-3811 (orders)
Fax: 250-920-7670

The Quilting Bee
1026 St. Mary's Road
Winnipeg, MB. R2M 3S6
Phone: 204-254-7870, Fax: 204-254-7895

Sew Fancy
RR#1, Beeton
ON. L0G 1A0
Phone: 1-800-739-3629

Wineberry Fabrics
Unit 105, 6351-152nd Street
Surrey, BC. V3S 3K8
Phone: 604-597-7934, Fax: 604-597-1388
Orders: 1-800-803-8991

Needleworks North
Box 5964, Whitehorse
YT. Y1A 5L7
Phone/fax: 403-633-4924
(Collectable thimbles and tools by mail-order)

CHAPTER 1

Canadian Quilters' Association/*Association canadienne de la courtepointe***
PO Box 22010, Herongate Postal Outlet
Ottawa, ON. K1V 0C2

Pretreated blueprinting fabric:

Blueprints — Printables
1504 #7 Industrial Way
Belmont, CA 94002, USA
Phone: 1-800-356-0445
Fax: 415-594-0936

Kwik Print chemicals:

Light Impressions
439 Monroe Ave.
Rochester, NY
14607-3717, USA

CHAPTER 3

Pat White
Haines Junction, YK. Y0B 1L0
Phone 403-634-2030, Fax: 403-634-2304
e-mail: white@mariposa.whfip.yknet.yk.ca
(Hand-dyed fabrics, various textures)

Valerie Hearder
Box 279
Mahone Bay, NS
B0J 2E0
(Fibreglass Teflon pressing sheet)

CHAPTER 4

Dyes and Chemicals (mail order):

Pat White, above, sells a kit which includes all materials needed for the chapter workshop, Shibori dyeing. She also sells dyes and chemicals separately.

EHB Designs
132 Rosedale Valley Road
Toronto, ON. M4W 1P7
Phone: 416-964-0634

Maiwa Handprints
#6-1566 Johnston St. Granville Island
Vancouver, BC. V6H 3S2
Phone: 604-669-3939

Opulence Silks & Dyes Ltd.
1428 Roxbury Road
North Vancouver, BC. V7G 1X7
Phone: 604-929-4440 or 1-800-288-9597

APPENDICES

Archival storage materials:

Look in the Yellow Pages under artists' materials and supplies. The following suppliers have mail-order catalogues:

R. Bury Media & Supplies Ltd.
B5-4255 Arbutus St.
Vancouver, BC. V6J 4R1
Phone: 604-731-3439, Fax: 604-736-7492
(all types of acid-free archival storage materials)

Opus Framing Ltd.
1360 Johnston Street
Vancouver, BC. V6H 3S1
Phone: 604-736-7028
BC: 1-800-663-6953
Outside BC: 1-800-663-6953. Fax: 604-731-3519

Study, contemporary/historical quilts, documentation, quarterly newsletter:

Canadian Quilt Study Group
c/o Nancy Cameron Armstrong
1109-160A Street, White Rock, BC
V4A 7G9
Phone: 604-538-7551
E-mail: armstr@ibm.net

Pantograph enlarging tool:

Try graphic suppliers in the Yellow Pages, or for mail-order:

Lee Valley Tools Ltd.
PO Box 6295, STN. J
Ottawa, ON. K2H 8K7
Phone: 1-800-267-8767

Chemicals to treat fabric for blueprinting:

Photographers' Formulary
PO Box 950, Condon
Montana. 59826, USA
Phone: 1-800-922-5255

Enlarging Methods

1 **Enlargement by Grid**: This age-old method is time-consuming, but takes minimal equipment: paper, ruler, and pencil. You can draw some permanent grids, 1/4" and 1/2", on see-through acetate, or use template plastic which has 1/4" grid marked on it to lay over your original. Draw your larger grid onto the drafting paper. Then, square by square, draw the enlarged version from the original.

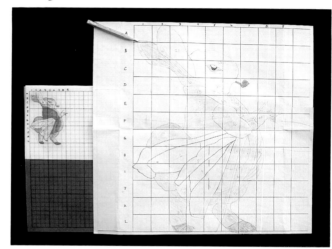

1. Enlargement by Grid

HINT: Use the 1" grid on your rotary cutting mat as a guide for drawing a 1", 2" or larger grid onto your drafting paper.

2 **Pantograph**: This set of four bars is screwed together at strategic locations. It has a stylus to follow the figure you are enlarging, and a pencil lead to draw onto your copy. It clamps to the table, and can be adjusted to the amount of enlargement you need. It does not handle huge enlargements, because it is restricted by its extension length, but can be a useful tool for block-sized enlargements. It is recommended that you do not copy directly from a treasured photograph, as the stylus may scratch it. Instead, try a photocopy or acetate overlay. This handy tool can be purchased at drafting supply stores. Or see Appendix #4: *Sources* for mail-order.

3 **Photocopier**: Ah, this indispensable bit of technology! It can enlarge your sketch or photo with so little pain. There are even machines that can enlarge on one sheet of paper up to 36" wide. Look in the Yellow Pages in your nearest city to find out who has one of these large format machines. Then, by taping your enlarged photocopy onto a window (during the day) and placing the tracing paper over it, you can copy your design, simplifying it if necessary.

4 **Slide Projector**: If you have access to a slide projector, drawing directly from a slide projected onto your paper is the simplest, quickest method of enlarging to any size.

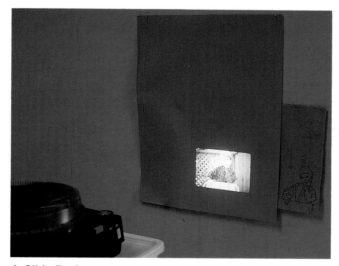

4. Slide Projector

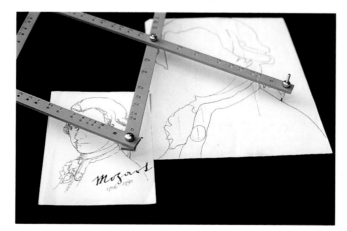

2. Pantograph

5 **Opaque Projector**: These hardy dinosaurs from the public schools are awkward and unwieldy to use, but they do a great job of enlarging a photo, drawing, etc. The room needs to be quite dark to use this device. There are hobby-sized projectors advertised in the backs of magazines. They use a 60 watt light bulb, and handle small (3"x3") photos. A new generation of smaller, more efficient projectors is beginning to show up in some institutions.

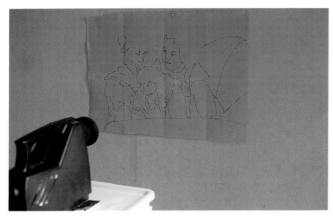

5. Opaque Projector

6 **Overhead Projector**: By copying the outlines of your photo onto a piece of transparent acetate, the resulting image can be projected onto your drafting paper with an overhead projector.

A P P E N D I X 6

A Survey of Canadian Quiltmakers

As part of my research for this book, I have conducted an informal, not-at-all scientific survey of 213 quiltmakers from many parts of Canada. At guild meetings, conferences and quilt shows, voluntary participants answered written questions about themselves.

Are all quilters older tea-drinking cat-owners? Of course not. But there were some surprising results from this small sampling of opinions about important and trivial questions. Tune in:

Pets

28% of respondents were cat owners (although more than one questioned whether the cat or the human was the 'owner'.) 26% of respondents were dog owners, 11% had both dog and cat, and 40% had neither.

Age

Of those who bravely stated their age, 19% were 40 or under, 31% were aged 41-50, 29% were 51-60, 19% were 61-70, and 1% were over 70. The youngest respondent was 22, the oldest 79.

Marital Status

79% of respondents were married, compared with 9% single, 9% widowed, and 2% divorced.

Children

46% of respondents had children who were living at home. Most of these (87%) had one or two children at home, while 11% had three or four, and one respondent had 6 children living at home. 10% of the children were preschool-aged, 34% were elementary-aged, 39% were high-school-aged, and a whopping 41% were adult children.

Tea or Coffee?

A crucial question determined that 44% of respondents preferred to drink tea, while 48% preferred coffee.

How Long Quilting?

When asked "How long have you been quilting?" 2% responded less than a year, 9% 1-2 years, 26% 3-6 years, 18% 7-10 years, and 45% over 10 years (the average length of time in this last group was 19.4 years, with the most experienced quilter responding that she has been quilting for 72 years!)

How did you learn?

Most quilters learned about quilting from classes (58%). The next most common source of education was books and magazines (37%), then friends (12%), guild (12%), family (8%), self (5%) and TV (3%).

Traditional or Contemporary?

41% of respondents consider themselves to be "traditional," 9% "contemporary," 36% both traditional and contemporary, and 15% found it "hard to say."

Membership

86% belong to a guild, 49% to the Canadian Quilters' Association (these first two results would be influenced by the fact that the survey was conducted during guild meetings and CQA events). 26% belong to a U.S. quilting organization, and 8% listed no organized group affiliation.

Design

When asked about quilt design, 44% prefer to use traditional or published patterns, 37% prefer to do their own design, 45% like to use an adaptation of another's design, and 7% like all of the above.

Preferred Methods

44% prefer piecing over appliqué, while 10% like appliqué better, and 46% like both techniques equally.
20% prefer machine sewing, 48% prefer hand-sewing, and 32% like both equally.

Workshops

The average number of workshops or classes taken by respondents "in the last year" was 3.5.

Competitions

48% of respondents have entered a quilting competition ("challenges" are the most commonly mentioned form), while 52% have not.

Some comments indicate strong opinions about competition, such as the following: "I don't believe that competition produces more creativity—all studies to date have shown that supportive, shared environments which encourage growth and support artistic development do not benefit from pitting people or skills against each other. Competitions exist to feed the industry, not feed creativity."

The following are more positive about competition: "I have entered because I like to get the critiques" and "It was a very positive experience for me."

Cultural Correctness in Quiltmaking

The responses to the open question "What is your opinion about the use of cultural images/motifs by a quiltmaker not of that culture?" fell into these categories:

Agree with the use of images from any culture	35%
Agree with the use of images, with reservations	1-28%
Disagree with the use of images from any other culture	6%
No opinion	24%
Neutral opinion	7%

Some of the many thoughtful responses are sampled below:

In the category: Agree with the use of images from any culture:

"A way to have more insight on a different culture."

"Isn't quilting about sharing?"

"I am a Canadian of Japanese ancestry, and I feel that non-Japanese should feel free to use Japanese motifs."

"It is one way of bringing people of different cultures closer, making one another aware and respect the cultural differences"

(Not sharing) "would stifle both the artist borrowing and the culture itself because it must grow and adapt to remain relevant, otherwise it dies."

"People should not be pigeonholed in their own culture."

"The use of other cultures' motifs shows respect and admiration for the other culture — a compliment!"

In the category: Agree with the use of images, with reservations:

"As long as you aren't claiming to be Amish or Native Indian, or African, etc., you can use those techniques to explore ideas."

"Respect and understanding of the images/motifs is essential."

"I would have no objection to an image from my culture, e.g. Celtic cross, being used as long as it's not in a desecrating manner."

"I do object to copying the art of another culture for the sake of profit. I do not have any problem with copying as a way to learn to use materials and techniques and understand symbols— as a way of exploring and understanding another culture."

"Any taboos or limitations observed by that culture should be respected, and the source of the borrowed elements should be acknowledged."

"You must understand and feel it within your soul — otherwise the piece is dead and may confuse future historians."

In the category: Disagree with the use of images from any other culture:

"Seems somewhat opportunistic."

"I like traditional pattern to stay traditional vs. others diluting it so it loses its original flavour."

"They can express the emotion and traditions of their own people best."

"Exploiting cultural art for profit is objectionable and I believe can only be dealt with through education of the buying public."

A P P E N D I X   7

Chemically Sensitizing Fabric for Sunprinting

WARNING: These chemicals can be fatal if swallowed, and caustic if in contact with your skin. They must be kept away from children and animals. Do not use them in any food preparation area, nor use the same utensils for any other purpose, particularly food preparation. The solutions should be mixed inside a safebox or chemical hood, to prevent inhalation of the powders, then stored for up to six months in a locked, light-proof cabinet.

You will need the following: (See Appendix 4: *Sources* for chemical suppliers)

- A sunless room with space to stretch or hang the fabric while it is treated and dried. Whatever room you use should have adequate ventilation, a floor which could be dripped on and possibly stained.

- A sheet of plastic covered with newspapers to protect the floor

- A clothesline to hang fabric for treating or two lines to stretch the fabric while treating. Clothespins.

- A wide (3-4") sponge craft brush to paint the chemicals

- Rubber gloves

- Metric weigh-scales with two pieces of paper to place chemicals on for weighing

- 50 grams Ferric Ammonium Citrate (green powder)

- 25 grams Potassium Ferricyanide (orange crystals)

- 12 fluid ounces distilled water

- 1 capped jar to keep the mixed chemicals in, large enough to accommodate sponge brush and 12 fluid ounces.

- 1 stirring utensil (glass, plastic, or stainless steel)

- A homemade safebox to contain spills and protect you from breathing in powders. This may have an open bottom to allow it to be placed over the jar and measuring utensils.

A homemade safebox

- Washed and ironed cotton or silk fabric in your choice of colour. (White, muslin, pale skin tone, or tan are suitable choices for portraits. However, any colour of fabric will work, depending on your quilt project. Fabrics may be dyed before applying chemicals.) Do not wash fabric in detergents with phosphates, unless you rinse it very thoroughly afterwards.

- A lightproof bag to store sensitized fabric

Mixing the chemicals:

1 Place chemicals, pre-measured hot water (12 oz. in jar), weigh scales with papers, and stirring utensils onto protected counter or table. Place safebox over all.

2 With rubber gloves on, insert your hands into holes cut into the sides of the safebox. Open the chemical containers. Weigh out 25 grams of Potassium Ferricyanide, then stir into the water till it's dissolved. Then weigh out 50 grams of Ferric Ammonium Citrate and sprinkle onto the surface of the water as you stir to dissolve. Cap the chemicals. Place the lid on the solution. Remove your hands from the safebox, and rinse the gloves well under the tap. Lift the safebox away from the chemicals.

Applying the sensitizing chemicals to fabric:

3 Stretch the fabric onto a protected surface or between two taut lines. Paint the solution onto the fabric with the sponge brush, first horizontally, then vertically, to ensure complete coverage. Cap the lid of any leftover chemical (better to use it all up).

4 Wash all surfaces and utensils with sudsy water immediately, as stains are impossible to remove after they have been exposed to light.

5 Leave treated fabric to dry overnight. A hairdryer may be used to hasten the drying process.

6 When dry, fold and place the fabric into a black plastic or foil (lightproof) bag. Tape it closed and label it, especially with colour of the original fabric and the date.

APPENDIX 8

A Directory of Canadian Quilting Professionals

For further information, including detailed resumés, course descriptions, samples, photos, or rates from any of these professionals, you may contact them directly. All photographs are by the artists, unless otherwise stated.

Karen Atkin
Box 17, Minett, ON. P0B 1G0
Phone/fax: 705-646-7396

Karen does commissions and offers workshops in machine-pieced landscapes with pieced borders, curved and straight-line perspective piecing, and machine-applied bias stained glass.

**Passage Island
(100'x84") 1991**

Sherry Bussey (see Chapter 11)
Box 9 Site 5 RR#1
Deer Lake, NF. A0K 2E0
Phone: 709-686-2392

Avis Caddell
11275 Hickory Drive
Sidney, BC. V8L 5J9
Phone: 250-655-0275

Available for commission work, trunk shows and teaching, Avis specializes in *2-day Colourwash, Colour Design.*

Victorian Fancy

Wendy Lewington Coulter
(see Chapter 2)
10079 Dewdney Trunk Road, RR#2
Mission, BC. V2V 5X4

Wendy designs, creates and exhibits art quilts. She teaches and lectures on a variety of subjects, judges in a variety of media, and has extensive experience creating original commission work.

Helen Courtice
362 MacDonald Street,
Penticton, BC. V2A 4C9

Helen's love of quilting has led her in many directions. She's had commissions, but prefers to work without restrictions and decide later whether to sell a piece. Most recent works are wall-hangings inspired by photos.

Summer Sunset at Crescent Beach (36"x50")

Judith Dingle
140 Evelyn Avenue
Toronto, ON. M6P 2Z7
Phone: 416-766-9411

Trained teacher, full-time textile artist, 3 lectures, 14 workshops. Specializes in *Crazy, Log Cabin Variations, Art Quilts, Wearables, 3-D*, etc. Judith's work has been widely documented and exhibited worldwide.

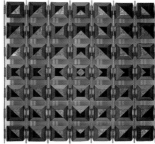

**Around the World (48"x48")
3-D quilt, silk, cotton, wood, screening**

Susan Duffield
1631 Barrett Drive
Sidney, BC. V8L 5A9
Phone: 250-655-3855

Susan teaches fine hand and machine appliqué incorporating hand-dyed and painted cottons and silks, exotic fabrics, stuffed work and 3-D flowers.

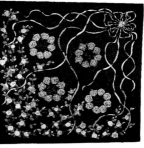

Ribbons 'n Roses 1995

Gary McKinstry

Iris Ethridge, (see Chapter 9)
New London, Kensington, PE. C0B 1M0
Phone: 902-886-2744

Decorative hangings in silk and other natural fibres. Mixed media: appliqué, fabric collage, hand and machine embroidery.

Judy Farrow (see Chapter 12)
Midnight Sun Designs
Box 1273, Yellowknife, NT. X1A 2N9
Phone: 403-873-5462, Fax: 873-4401
E-mail: farrow@internorth.com

Traditional and contemporary quilts with original batik design features. Workshops: *Introduction to Batik, Bear On Thin Ice: Interpreting the North in Quilt Design.*

Carol Galloway, (see Chapter 5)
79 Macalester Bay
Winnipeg, MB R3T 2X6.
Phone: 204-269-9566, Fax: 275-5308
E-mail: cgallow@MTS.Net

Creative development encouraged in relaxed workshops for guild, retreats, shops. Beginner through advanced, mainly non-traditional hand and machine work, colour. Commissions accepted.

Pam Godderis
4804 Claret Street N.W.
Calgary, AB. T2L 1C1
Phone: 403-284-3591
Fax: 284-4109

Internationally-known teacher and lecturer specializing in creative workshops on: *Designing Original Quilts* and *Clothing Embellishment, Colour* (introductory and advanced classes), *Machine Embroidery and Appliqué.*

Frost Panes - Night (48.5"x49.5") Silver leaf and machine piecing

Susan Andrews Grace (see Chapter 4)
419 10th St. East
Saskatoon, SK. S7N 0E1

Offers workshop: *Writing About Your Art*

Valerie Hearder
Box 24, Mahone Bay
NS B0J 2E0
Phone: 902-624-8181
Fax: 624-9401

A well-known teacher on the international quilt scene, Valerie wrote *Beyond the Horizon: Small Landscape Appliqué* featuring her original techniques and designs.

Betty Howe
Penticton, BC
Phone: 250-493-7920

As an artist/quilter, Betty makes and sells original pictorial quilts and framed combination paint and quilt pieces. She offers workshops: *Designing an Original Pictorial Quilt* and *Colour Basics* and *Perspective in Quilts.*

Reflections of a Quilter

Gail Hunt (see Chapter 1)
Pacific Quiltworks Ltd.
4740 Mountain Highway
North Vancouver, BC. V7K 2Z9
Fax: 604-990-9161, Email: ump@unix.infoserve.net

Judges, offers workshops, writes and lectures on a variety of quilt-related topics, especially pictorial/landscape quilts, phototransfer techniques, professional development, Canadian quilters.

Rosemary Makhan
3264 Whispering Pine Road
Burlington, ON. L7M 2R3
Phone: 905-335-3762

CQA teacher of the year in 1993, Rosemary teaches workshops on appliqué and piecing, as well as *Raised Flower Techniques, Crazy Quilting, Pictorial Watercolour,* and *Trapunto.*

Rose Sampler Supreme

Judy Martin,
Box 29, Bay Estates, RR#1
Sheguiandah, ON. P0P 1W0
Phone: 705-368-3819

A maker of exhibition quilts, Judy is available for lectures and workshops. "My work is filled with meditative handwork. The finished piece thus exists not only as a visual image but also seems to capture for me a certain period of time."

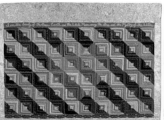

***Gaea Enthroned* Triptych, Cottons, silks and metallics, Hand-painting, machine-piecing, hand appliqué, embroidery. Collection of Ontario Government.**

A. Joyce McKinnon
135 Kensington Drive
Thunder Bay, ON. P7C 2A4
Phone: 807-577-9866

Joyce offers wall quilts for sale and teaches the following workshops: *Strip-pieced Landscapes, Postage Pets and Others, Tuck Quilts,* and *Quilted Vests.*

True Courage (51.5"x65")

Pat Menary
Schoolhouse Cottage
RR#1, Innerkip
ON. N0J 1M0
Phone: 519-469-9087

Pat teaches miniature quilts which use traditional handpiecing or machine-pieced foundation methods. Her trunk show, *Miniature Madness* consists of a growing collection of over sixty miniature quilts.

Judy Morningstar
Box 820
Deloraine, MB. R0M 0M0
Phone/fax: 204-658-3564

Judy's non-traditional art quilts are in private and corporate collections around the world. Her workshops encourage creativity without compromising good workmanship. Commissions are accepted.

Fire! **Collection of Cancade Fire**

Sylvia Naylor
25 Howe Island Ferry Road
Kingston, ON. K7L 4V1
Phone: 613-547-4213
Fax: 547-0734

Sylvia creates pictures and quilted hangings incorporating free machine and hand-embroidery and many fabric painting techniques. She is an experienced fibreartist and teacher.

Garden of a Golden Afternoon **(36"x28") 1994**

Marianne Parsons
RR#1 S16/C5
Oliver, BC
V0H 1T0
Phone: 250-498-2370

Zinnias **(46"x53"), detail, 1995**

1995 CQA Teacher of the Year, Marianne makes contemporary quilted pieces, writes about quilt topics, teaches classes in designing, drafting, figures, innovative use of fabrics.

Jocelyne Patenaude
4470 Mayfair Avenue
Montréal, Québec
H4B 2E3
Phone: 514-481-3731

Jocelyne, BFA Concordia University, is an artist/quiltmaker, writer, lecturer and

Taboo **(55' x 51"), detail, 1995**

teacher whose quilts have won many awards in Canada, the USA and Europe. Her interests include aesthetic, symbolic and metaphorical aspects of quiltmaking.

Carol Pettigrew
Box 4146
Whitehorse, YT. Y1A 3S6
Fax: 403-668-4197

Using sun-sensitive dyes, Carol makes one-of-a-kind fabric pieces which use native Yukon plants as their subject matter. Most of the pieces come with mythical, spiritual and medicinal stories about the plants.

Kay Phillips
2756 Brimley Road
Agincourt, ON M1V 1K2

1992 CQA Teacher of the Year, Kay as a passion for innovative contemporary machine-piecing techniques. Her infectious enthusiasm and fine-tuned motivational skills make her lectures and classes both educational and inspirational.

Janet Pope (see Chapter 10)
Box 425, Hantsport
NS. B0P 1P0
Phone: 902-684-9129, Fax: 684-3685

Artist Janet Pope creates rich and textured wallhangings from vibrant fabrics that explore spiritual and mythical themes. Commissions both public and private are welcome.

Gail Hunt

Sunprinted Fabric Pieces

Suttle Reds **(42"x36") cotton, machine-pieced, machine-quilted**

Donna Pringle
RR#3 S3/C2
Oliver
BC
V0H 1T0
Phone: 250-498-3656

Poppies was a commission developed from photographs. Donna does wallhangings and quilts in traditional or contemporary original designs, and machine or hand-quilts them.

Janet Rice-Bredin
Morning Glory Designs
274 N. Algoma Street
Thunder Bay, ON. P7A 5A6
Phone/Fax: 807-346-8087

Janet is an award-winning contemporary quiltmaker, teacher, judge and juror. She uses music, science, landscapes and gardens for her inspiration.

Giverny I **(41.5"x45"), 1995**

Susan D. Russell
1703 Hampshire Road
Victoria, BC. V8R 5T7
Phone: 250-595-6365

"The recognition of the art quilt as a viable art form in Canada excites me. While I love to work with colour, hue and texture, saying as much as possible with a minimum of detail is my main objective."

'Tis a Gift to be Simple
(56.5"x56.5") 1993

Adaire Schlatter (see Chapter 7)
418 Alexandra St.
St. Lambert, PQ. J4R 1Z5
Phone: 514-671-3271

Adaire enjoys sharing her expertise and knowledge of the art of quiltmaking through workshops, lectures and demonstrations with any group, large or small.

Donna Schneider
679 Clifton Road S.
Kelowna, BC V1V 1A7

A quilting instructor since 1992, Donna teaches Mary Ellen Hopkins's *"It's Okay..." Seminars I, II and III* and *Advanced Machine Quilting*. She team-teaches these classes with Laurie Turik.

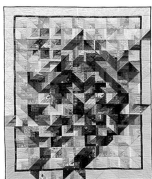

Jayne Willoughby Scott
894 Currandale Court
Victoria, BC. V8X 4Y2
E-mail: scottsway@pinc.com

A quilting and design instructor, Jayne has exhibited nationally and internationally since 1989. Many of her award-winning quilts make social statements. She explores textural and embellishment techniques.

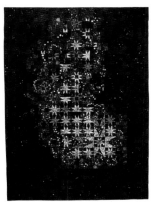

Gail Hunt

How I Wonder What You Are
(80"x58")

Carol Seeley
c/o Boston Pizza
1309 North Island Highway
Campbell River, BC
V9W 2C9
Phone: 250-923-8875

Carol, quiltmaker and teacher, provides custom, show-quality heirloom machine quilting services, original quilting patterns. Write for quilting sample and further information.

Laurrie Sobie (see Chapter 3)
4220 - 110 Street
Edmonton, AB. T6J 2T5

Laurrie's eclectic experience across many mediums contributes to a willingness to explore and innovate. This is the gift she strives to pass on in her workshops.

Marilyn Stewart Stothers
630 Cloutier Drive
Winnipeg, MB
R3V 1T9
Phone/fax: 204-269-7794

Originator, author and publisher of the book, *Curved Strip-Piecing — A New Technique*; workshops and lectures of surface designing and non-traditional quiltmaking; commissions; judging; jurying.

Winnipeg Art Gallery

Shadows in the Garden
(55.5"x44.5") 1995.

Laurie Swim
2586 Kepler Road, RR#1
Elginburg, ON. K0H 1M0
Phone: 613-545-0661
Fax: 545-1360

Visual Artist: site-specific commissions for interiors; Author: *The Joy of Quilting* (1984), *Quilting* (1991) and *The Joy of Quilting on CD-ROM* (1996); Lectures and Workshops.

Dancing Dress (18"x24"), **Silk, cotton, hand-appliquéd, machine quilted**

Laurie Turik
679 Clifton Rd. S
Kelowna, BC. V1V 1A7

A quilting instructor since 1992, Laurie teaches Mary Ellen Hopkins's *"It's Okay..."* Seminars I, II and III and *Advanced Machine Quilting*. She team-teaches these classes with Donna Schneider.

Marilyn Turner
59 Kearney Lake Road, Halifax NS. B3M 2S9
Phone: 902-443-8418
E-mail: af727@ccn.cs.dal.ca

A Dew Like That of Hermon (triptych: 100"x60", 100"x90", 100"x60"), Collection of Atlantic School of Theology

Quiltmaker and teacher with a particular interest in all facets of hand-dyeing, block-printing, shibori, dye painting and cyanotype. Original designs, sometimes computer aided.

Judy Villett
9942- 86 Avenue
Edmonton, AB. T6E 2L7
Phone: 403-439-6031 (studio)
439-3510 (home)

Judy is a well-known Western Canadian teacher, judge and designer. Current workshops: *Colour Wheel Basics*, which includes fabric kit and original colour wheel pattern, and *Beginner-Advanced Colourwash.*

Garden Window, 1995

Jean Weller
2482 Panorama Crescent
Prince George
BC. V2K 4B9

Jean accepts commissions for panel coats, 12th century Tibetan sleeveless coats of simple shapes which permit the use of many designs and techniques to create one-of-a-kind wearable art.

Western Panel Coat (back)

Angelika Werth
801 Park Street
Nelson, BC. V1L 1H2
Phone 250-352-2752

Angelika started her brassiere series in 1992. Inspiration for these nine quilts was an interview on CBC with Sheila Copps, on women and breast cancer.

Waiting for Adam (68"x51")
1994, Brassieres, silk

Pat White (see Chapter 12)
Box 2062
Haines Junction
YT. Y0B 1L0
Phone: 403-634-2030
Fax: 634-2304
Email: pwhite@mariposa.whfip.yknet.yk.ca

Lois Wilby-Hooper (see Chapter 8)
90 Prince St.
Saint John
NB. E2M 1P1

Lois teaches machine-pieced miniatures, various landscape techniques, colourwash. She does original designs, will teach for retreats, and accepts commissions.

Alice Olsen Williams (see Chapter 13)
Pimaatisiwin Quilts
Curve Lake First Nation
Curve Lake
ON. K0L 1R0

Alice teaches, offers lecture and trunk show *"The Spirit of My Quilts"*, sells quilts and wall-hangings, accepts commissions.

Michelle Wilman
Mamamania Vintage Buttons
618 - 18th Avenue N.W.
Calgary, AB. T2M 0T8
Phone: 403-284-3266
Fax: 289-6524
E-mail:nr@cadvision.com

Contact Michelle for a dynamic speaker, inspiring teacher, and button catalogue.

Self Portrait

Amish quilts quilts made by the Old Order Amish, an Anabaptist Christian sect which, in the United States is centered in Lancaster County, Pennsylvania and surrounding states. *Amish quilts* generally refer to the quilts made by the Amish in the late 1800s and early 1900s, characterized by the use of only solid colour fabrics, bold, graphic, non-representational designs, precise piecing, and exquisite hand-quilting.

appliqué *(v. or n.)* to apply a cut-out shape of fabric onto background fabric with hand or machine stitching, or the shapes so applied

Bear's Paw block

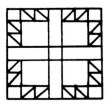

blueprint an image made by printing on sensitized paper or fabric, using exposure to ultraviolet light (from the sun) to develop the negative image. Blueprinting was invented by English astronomer John F.W. Herschel in 1840, and was used universally to print architectural drawings in characteristic blue colour.

charm quilt a pieced quilt made from charm squares, or donated pieces of fabric. A true charm quilt does not include any piece of fabric more than once.

contour line in drawing, a line that represents an edge of a shape

crazy-patch the piecing and appliqué, by hand or machine, of odd-shaped and irregularly-sized pieces of fabric. Victorian *Crazy-patch* is characterized by elaborate embellishment with embroidery and the addition of lace, charms, beads, appliqués, and buttons. It was made popular by Queen Victoria in the late 1800s.

cyanoprint another name for blueprint. In colour photography, dyeing and painting, cyan (a blue-green) refers to one of the three primary, mixable colours. The other two are magenta (a purplish pink) and yellow.

decloning in quilting, a term coined by Laurrie Sobie describing the alteration of a traditional quilt block so that it evolves into a unique pattern or design

Drunkard's Path block

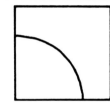

even-feed foot a presser foot for a sewing machine which has grip, either from teeth-shaped projections or from a rubbery substance, to pull the top fabric through the machine at the same rate as the bottom fabric. Sewing machines have feed-dogs, or metal teeth, to pull it through from underneath.

flip-and-sew a method of sewing two pieces of fabric right sides together through a foundation or backing fabric, sometimes with quilt batting between the pieces and the backing. After the seam is sewn, the top fabric is flipped right side up, and the next piece to be joined is placed right sides together over it. The next seam is sewn, then the top pieced flipped right side up, etc.

heliographic reacting to the sun's light. Heliographic fabric dyes become more intense as they dry in direct sunlight, so that any opaque or translucent object placed on the fabric blocks the sun's light, and produces a lighter colour in the blocked area, creating what is commonly called a "shadow print."

hue colour, as in red, green, blue, etc.

in the ditch the location of a line of quilting stitches directly beside a seam joining two patches of fabric, in the depression caused by the seam

Kaleidoscope block

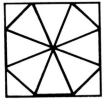

Log Cabin block

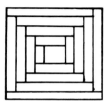

machine-piecing sewing pieces of fabric together with the sewing machine

Mennonite quilts quilts made by members of the Mennonite sect, an Anabaptist sect similar to the Amish. Old Order Mennonites, who shun modern technology, are concentrated in Waterloo County, Ontario, and their quilts are usually made with traditional designs using polyester fabrics or polyester/cotton blends.

Mola intricate reverse appliqués made by the Cuna Indians of Panama for use on clothing, characterized by bold solid colours and black, and assymetrical designs based on nature

needle-punched batting a filling for quilts, garments and accessories, which is held together by its own fibres which have been pushed through the batting's thickness by needles. Needle-punched batting tends to retain its even thickness through repeated use and washings, rather than bunching up.

needle-turning a traditional method of doing appliqué, where the raw edge of the piece being appliquéd is turned under with the needle just before the stitch is taken with the needle

9-Patch block

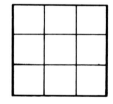

Pa N Dau intricate reverse appliqués made by nomadic Mong Chinese needleworkers originally from Indochina, for use in clothing. The appliqués are characterized by the use of bright solid colours and black, as well as symmetrical, geometric designs embellished with geometric embroidery.

photo-transfer refers to a number of processes which transfer photographs onto fabric to be used in quilts

piecing sewing fabric pieces together by hand or machine, to make a quilt top

Pineapple variation block

prairie points an edge treatment for quilts which looks like a series of overlapped triangles. Prairie points are made of squares of fabric folded twice. One corner of the resulting triangle is placed between the two matching corners of the next triangle, and sewn into the seam which joins the quilt top to the quilt back.

quilt sandwich the layers of a quilt, usually a backing fabric, a filler and a quilt top

quilting commonly used to describe the whole process of making a quilt. The quilting refers to the stitches, either by hand or by machine, which join the layers of the quilt sandwich together permanently.

reverse-appliqué the process of cutting away the top fabric to expose the background fabric, then sewing the edge of the top fabric onto the background fabric

sampler a quilt made of a selection of different traditional blocks or techniques, often made to learn basic quiltmaking techniques

Schoolhouse block

shade a pure hue with black added

stabilizer any fabric, paper, synthetic or starch used to hold fabric firm while it is being stitched. Stabilizers prevent unsightly puckers from developing, and help maintain the shape and size of the piece being stitched. Some stabilizers remain in the quilt, some are removed by water, heat, or tearing away after stitching.

Storm at Sea block

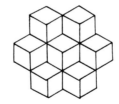

Sunshine and Shadow block

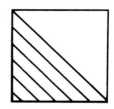

Sunshine and Shadow design refers to the placement of small like-coloured patches of fabric in concentric diamonds over the surface of a square quilt top

sunprint blueprint

template a pattern used to cut pieces of fabric for a quilt, with or without seam allowances or turn-under allowances. Templates may be made of paper, hard or soft plastic, metal, used x-ray film, cardboard, etc.

tint a pure hue with white added

tone a pure hue with grey added

trapunto an area of a quilt with extra batting or stuffing in it for emphasized relief, usually between lines of quilting stitches, but sometimes between an appliqué and the background fabric

Tumbling Blocks

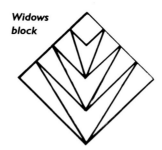

value darkness or lightness, sometimes referred to as colour value, but which is independent of colour and is more accurately referred to as colourless value

Widows block

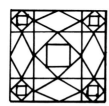

I N D E X

THE GREAT
COMPOSERS AND
THEIR WORKS

THE GREAT COMPOSERS AND THEIR WORKS

THEIR WORKS

VOLUME II

NICOLAS SLONIMSKY

Edited by Electra Yourke

SCHIRMER BOOKS
AN IMPRINT OF THE GALE GROUP

For permission to reprint some of the material in this collection, the author gratefully acknowledges the Los Angeles Philharmonic Association and *The Christian Science Monitor.*

Schirmer Books
An Imprint of the Gale Group
1633 Broadway
New York, NY 10019

Library of Congress Catalog Card Number: 99-42808

Set ISBN: 0-02-864955-9
Volume 1: 0-02-865474-9
Volume 2: 0-02-865475-7

Printed in the United States of America

Printing Number

2 3 4 5 6 7 8 9 10

Library of Congress Cataloging-in-Publication Data

Slonimsky, Nicolas, 1894–1995
     The great composers and their works / Nicolas Slonimsky ; edited
by Electra Yourke.
         p.   cm.
     ISBN 0-02-864955-9 (set). — ISBN 0-02-865474-9 (v. 1). — ISBN
0-02-865475-7 (v. 2)
     1. Music—History and criticism. 2. Music appreciation.
I. Yourke, Electra.   II. Title.
ML160.S48   2000
780′.9—dc21   99-42808
                                                                     CIP
This paper meets the requirements of ANSI/NISO Z.39.48–1992 (Permanence of Paper).

TO DAVID R
—*è ben trovato*

CONTENTS

VOLUME I

V O L U M E   I I

XVIII SERGEI PROKOFIEV: His Signature—SRG PRKFV
(1891–1953) 563

ORCHESTRAL MUSIC

OTHER WORKS

PETER ILYICH TCHAIKOVSKY
(1840–93)
Poet of Cheerful Melancholy

THE WORLD OF Peter Ilyich Tchaikovsky was confined and compressed within himself, and the music that he wrote was an explosive complaint that somehow gave him the sense of full life and even exaltation. He composed an enormous amount of music in a great variety of forms, and yet every work seemed to come to him as a trial.

An indefatigable correspondent, he poured out his feelings in his letters with extraordinary frankness. He also gave an insight into his philosophy of work. "The worst is to yield to the reluctance to work," he wrote. "I have set myself a rule to force myself to accomplish something every morning until I achieve a favorable frame of mind for work."

And again:

A true artist cannot sit idly on the pretext that he is not inclined to work. If one waits for an inclination, it is easy to lapse into laziness and atrophy. One must be patient and have faith that inspiration will surely come. This phenomenon happened to me this very morning. Had I succumbed to my lack of desire for work, I would not have accomplished anything. But faith and patience never abandoned me, and I became possessed with this incomprehensible fire of inspiration, which comes no one knows whence, and thanks to which I know in advance that everything I write today will have the faculty of penetrating the heart and leaving a lasting impression. I have learned how to conquer myself.

He adds an interesting observation on Russian composers at large: "I am happy to say that I do not follow in the footsteps of my Russian colleagues who, lacking self-confidence and tenacity, prefer to take a rest and to put off their work at the slightest provocation."

Scherzo (It.). A joke, jest; an instrumental piece of a light, piquant, humorous character. Also, a vivacious movement in the symphony, with strongly marked rhythm and sharp and unexpected contrasts in both rhythm and harmony; usually the third movement.

Pianissimo (It.). Very soft.

The struggle with himself was the principal motive of Tchaikovsky's music. He was obsessed with the idea of inexorable fate. One of his earliest symphonic works is entitled *Fatum* (fate). The theme of fate permeates his Fourth Symphony, his Fifth, and his Sixth, the *Pathétique*. To Tchaikovsky, happy times were always in the past, misery in the present, with Fatum in the future. But if despair is the rule of the world and of art, then what is the source of the gay dances and sparkling **scherzos** in Tchaikovsky's symphonies? Even in the *Pathétique*, which ends on a tone of depression, in the lowest reaches of the instrumental range, in **pianissississimo** (pppp), there is a scherzo full of infectious exhilaration and rhythmic fire.

If we were to compile a table of musical statistics, then Tchaikovsky's music would show a mournful mood, as exemplified by a decisive preponderance of minor **modes** and drooping **cadences**, with the main melodic line constantly falling in symmetric sequences. The overture to Tchaikovsky's opera *Eugene Onegin* contains perhaps the longest falling sequence of this nature in any musical composition, and of course the key is **minor**. But somehow Tchaikovsky's melancholy muse has brought artistic satisfaction, and hence happiness, to millions of people everywhere.

Tchaikovsky had many devoted friends, and he loved company, but he was afraid of strangers, and was particularly wary of admirers who thrust themselves at him with compliments that he detested. Once in Hamburg, when he was enjoying a happy anonymity, a Russian tourist sought him out, dispensing fulsome expressions of admiration. Tchaikovsky decided to leave town earlier than he expected, just because of this unwelcome encounter.

Among Tchaikovsky's intimates were his brothers, his sister and her family, some of his colleagues, his former pupils, and that extraordinary woman who played such a role in Tchaikovsky's life, Nadezhda von Meck. Tchaikovsky's correspondence with her began as a result of a commission that she asked him to accept, at a plainly exorbitant fee. In subsequent years she sent Tchaikovsky a regular and very generous subsidy, which enabled him to work and travel without financial worries. The relationship was strange. It was mutually agreed that they should never see each other face to face, but it appears from Madame von Meck's letters that she was not at all averse to a personal meeting. When they both happened to live in Florence at the same time, she even suggested that Tchaikovsky should visit her villa while she was absent. But Tchaikovsky's morbid fear of social involvements made him refuse all these advances, as gently as he could. "One should not see one's guardian angel in the flesh," he

Mode. The distinction between a major key (mode) and minor key (mode).

Cadence. Rhythm; also, the close or ending of a phrase, section, or movement.

Minor. A key, as in A minor.

explained, and their correspondence continued by messenger across the city.

There are composers who address their creations to the world with deliberate intent, in quest of universal acceptance. They eliminate subjective elements as a price of coveted success. But as often as not they do not succeed, because communicative power cannot be adjusted. Tchaikovsky wrote music out of his full heart, even when he wrote pieces commissioned for a special purpose, such as his ballets. And his very personal art became cosmopolitan in its appeal. His first ballet, *Swan Lake*, demanded a combination of dance music in the Italian style prevalent in Russia at the time, with some elegiac qualities. The story, taken from a German folktale, was tragic, which gave Tchaikovsky an opportunity to write music in his favorite symphonic style. The theme of the swan, with its poignant minor cadence, is one of Tchaikovsky's simplest and yet most profound inspirations. But *Swan Lake* also abounds in wonderful waltzes and other dance episodes; the ballet of little swans, in the lightest instrumentation, is one of the most popular numbers in the score. Tchaikovsky wrote another ballet from the world of fairy tales, *The Sleeping Beauty*. And one of his most cheerful works, the children's ballet *The Nutcracker*, was written at the same time as his most tragic score, the *Pathétique*.

Symphony No. 4 in F Minor, Op. 36 (1877–78)

Tchaikovsky began the composition of his Fourth Symphony in Moscow in May 1877, and finished it in Italy during the season 1877–78. The composition of the symphony was interrupted by a tragic event in Tchaikovsky's life, his unnatural marriage. Some commentators explain the disparity of treatment between the dramatic opening and ostentatiously gay **finale** as paralleling Tchaikovsky's moods of dark gloom, when he determined to marry, and his relief when he was liberated from

Finale (It.). The last movement in a sonata or symphony.

A mon meilleur ami

Fourth Symphony in F Minor, Op. 36

I

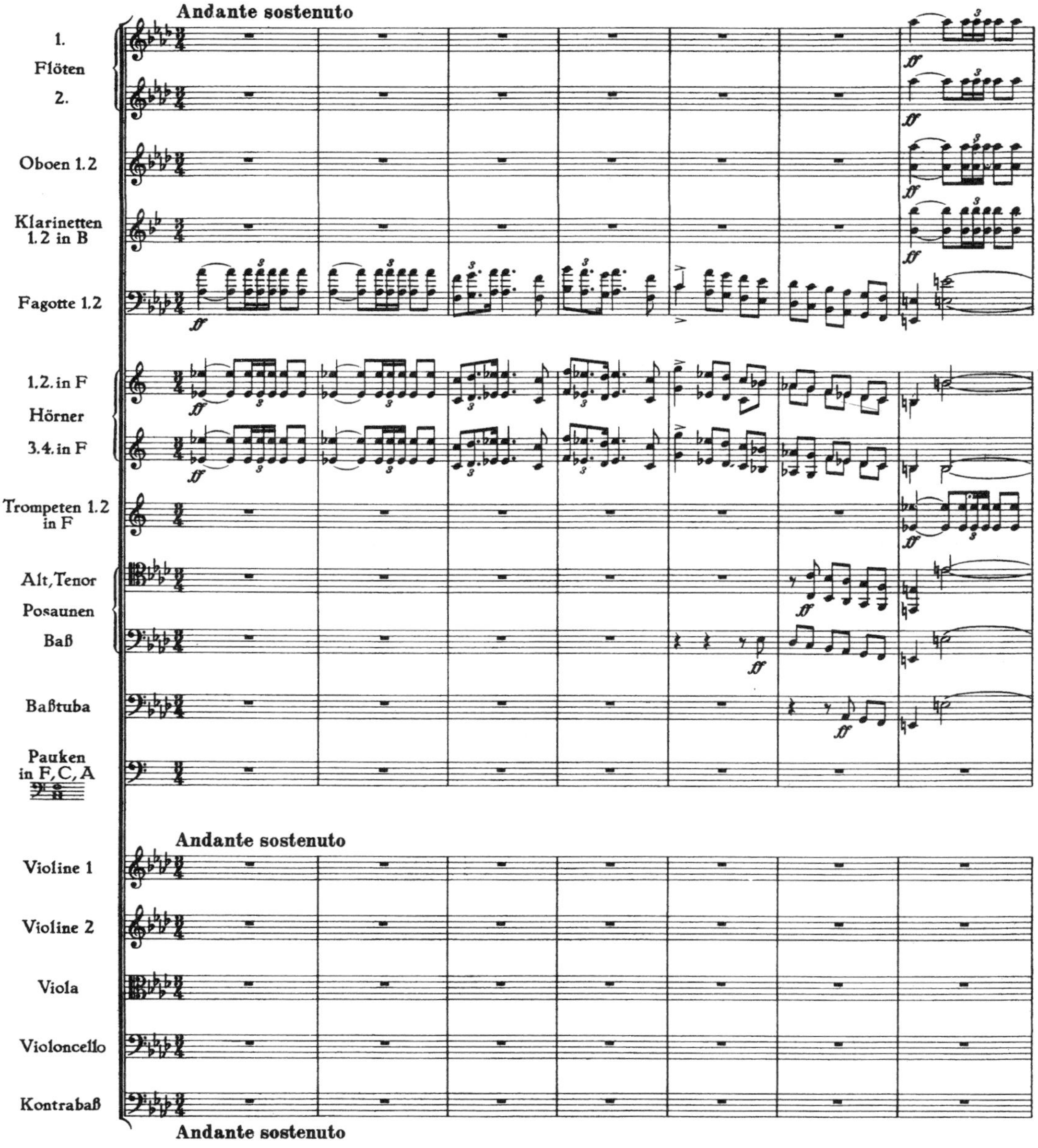

his marital bonds. However, it must be remembered that sketches of the symphony were made before the wedding ceremony, and that the rest of the work was devoted to details and orchestration without changes in the original conception.

The symphony is dedicated to Madame von Meck, although her name does not appear on the title page. The dedication merely reads, "To my beloved friend." In his letter to Madame von Meck of February 17, 1878, Tchaikovsky explained the introductory **motive** as the nucleus of the entire symphony, a Fatum, something less than inexorable fate, and more than an accident of misfortune. The only salvation from Fatum is the life of dreams, which is characterized by a livelier rhythmic motive of the first movement.

Motive. A short phrase or figure used in development or imitation.

The second movement of the symphony is merely another phase of nostalgia and melancholy. It is full of reminiscences of the young days and the realization that life has passed. The third movement, a Scherzo, in which an extraordinary effect is achieved by strings playing **pizzicato**, is a reflection of capricious moods. "All of a sudden a group of tipsy moujiks appears in the picture, and there is a street song." (This description corresponds to the **trio** of the Scherzo.) "Then, somewhere far off, passes a military parade." (This refers to **tempo primo**, after the Trio, before the second appearance of the principal motive of the Scherzo.)

Pizzicato (It.). Pinched; plucked with the finger; a direction to play notes by plucking the strings.
Trio (It.). A piece for three voices or in three parts.
Tempo primo (It.). At the original pace.

The finale of the symphony opens with a joyful theme, which is alternated with a theme of the Russian folk song "A Birch Tree Stood in the Meadow." The song is very old, and was first published in 1790 in the collection compiled by the Czech musician J. G. Pratsch. Tchaikovsky did not change either the melodic outline or the essential harmonization of the Pratsch version. He gave the description of the finale in these words: "If you find no reason for joy in yourself, look at others. Go to the people. See how they can make merry." But the theme of the Fatum intrudes again. The conclusion is a compromise: "Be gay with other people's joy. Life is tolerable after all." However, Tchaikovsky's program should not be accepted too literally. He wrote to Madame von Meck on the spur of the moment, but a month later, in a letter to Taneyev, he corrected himself: "My symphony is of course programmatic. But this program is such that it is utterly impossible to formulate it. It would arouse ridicule, and appear comical."

It is interesting to note the progress of Tchaikovsky's work on the symphony, which he reported in his letters to his brothers. He wrote to Anatol from Venice on December 15, 1877, "I slept very well, and from early morning set to work on the symphony." A few days later he wrote, "I am very much satisfied with the symphony. It is beyond doubt the best work I have written, but the progress is not without difficulty, particularly in the first movement." On December 23 he wrote to Anatol, "I have finished today the most difficult part of my symphony, the first movement," and on the following day,

> My nerves have amazingly calmed down. I sleep very well, but every night, before going to bed, I drink beer or a couple of glasses of cognac. My appetite is as usual, that is, excellent. All this is thanks to the symphony, and also to the monotonous life in Venice and the absence of all distraction, which has enabled me to work so determinedly and assiduously. When I wrote my opera, I did not experience the sensation the symphony gives me. In the opera I write at random, reckoning that it may come off well, and then again it may not. But the symphony I write in full consciousness that this is a work quite out of the ordinary, and the most perfect in form of all my compositions.

On December 26 he informed Anatol: "I worked from morning to lunch, and from lunch to dinner time without respite, and only took a walk in between. I have almost finished the third movement of the symphony." On the next day he re-

Tchaikovsky Timeline

1840	Born in Votkinsk, Russia
1859	Graduates from law school in St. Petersburg
1861	Enters Anton Rubinstein's newly established music institute (later, St. Petersburg Conservatory)
1866–78	Serves as professor of harmony at Moscow Conservatory
1868	Completes first mature composition, *Fatum*, a symphonic poem; considers marriage to opera singer Desirée Artot
1868–74	Writes music criticism for various Moscow newspapers
1869	Begins work on overture-fantasy *Romeo and Juliet* (completed in 1880)
1875	Piano Concerto No. 1 receives world premiere in Boston, under Hans von Bülow
1876	Visits first Bayreuth Festival; completes ballet *Swan Lake*
1877	Contracts short-lived marriage with a conservatory student, Antonina Milyukova; attempts suicide
1877–78	Visits Italy, Switzerland, Paris, Vienna; composes Fourth Symphony, dedicated to his patron, Nadezhda von Meck
1878	Composes opera *Eugene Onegin*
1888	Composes Symphony No. 5
1889	Composes ballet *The Sleeping Beauty*; von Meck withdraws her patronage

(continued)

**Tchaikovsky
Timeline (cont.)**

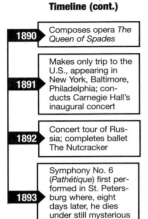

1890 Composes opera *The Queen of Spades*

1891 Makes only trip to the U.S., appearing in New York, Baltimore, Philadelphia; conducts Carnegie Hall's inaugural concert

1892 Concert tour of Russia; completes ballet The Nutcracker

1893 Symphony No. 6 (*Pathétique*) first performed in St. Petersburg where, eight days later, he dies under still mysterious circumstances

Fortissimo (It.). Extremely loud.

ported again: "Finished the Scherzo. Feel very tired." Finally, writing to Anatol from San Remo on January 7, 1878, he stated: "Yesterday and today I worked without getting up, and finished my beloved symphony. My health is perfect. I feel fine."

The first performance of the symphony took place in Moscow on February 22, 1878. Nikolai Rubinstein, the brother of Anton, conducted. Tchaikovsky was in Florence at the time, but Madame von Meck was present at the performance, and wrote Tchaikovsky enthusiastically about it. On November 25, 1878, the Czech conductor and composer Eduard Nápravník conducted the symphony in St. Petersburg. Modest Tchaikovsky described this performance in a letter to his brother:

> If it is at all possible that a symphonic work should produce a furor, then your symphony did it. After the first movement the applause was moderate, about to the extent of applause after the first movement of a Beethoven or Schumann symphony. After the second movement there was much more acclaim. Nápravník was compelled to acknowledge it by bowing. After the Scherzo there were outcries in **fortissimo**, stamping of feet, and demands for an encore. Nápravník bowed several times, but the noise would not subside, until he finally lifted his conducting scepter; then there was a silence, which yielded to your pizzicatos. After that there was more shouting, recalls, bows, etc. The concluding chords of the Finale were accompanied by handclapping, shouting, and stamping of the feet. Here I flew out of the hall like a bomb, and in fifteen minutes I was here in my study, with a pen in my hands.

When the Fourth Symphony was produced in Berlin in 1897, already after Tchaikovsky's death, the Berlin critics were uncommonly caustic. The *Kleines Journal* wrote: "Tchaikovsky's symphony is a tittle-tattle in motley orchestration, the contents of which look astonishing enough in the classical form. . . . I found the whole very boring. The external orchestral splendor could not conceal the inner bareness of the work. The tomfooleries of the Russian composer irritated me. . . . The chaotic brass and the abuse of the kettledrums drove me away." The *Berliner Tageblatt* was equally condemnatory:

> Even if we ignore the traditions of our masters, there should be a limit if the word "symphony" is to have any meaning at all. . . . Tchaikovsky substitutes for a musical idea phrases, sometimes of the most formidable kind. Still worse are his melodies when they appear at all clearly. There were themes which might be pleasant enough in the **operetta** theater, but which under the circumstances affected me repulsively, so much more so because their **contrapuntal** treatment sought to lend them the false glamour of nobleness. Most disagreeable was also the obstinate adherence to repeated rhythmic figures, which seem to persecute the composer like fixed ideas. The same semi-Asiatic taste is shown in the instrumentation, which changed from distressing dullness to cheap gaudiness.

Operetta (It.), **opéette** (Fr.). A "little opera"; the poem is in anything but a serious vein; music is light and lively, often interrupted by dialogue.

Contrapuntal. Pertaining to composition with two or more simultaneous melodies.

In America the Fourth Symphony was produced by Walter Damrosch, the pioneer conductor who introduced many great works to the American public. The first performance took place in New York City on the Friday "public rehearsal," January 31, 1890. The *New York Evening Post* wrote interestingly on the occasion:

> The Fourth Tchaikovsky Symphony proved to be one of the most thoroughly Russian, i.e., semi-barbaric, compositions ever heard in this city. The keynote of the whole work is struck by the Rienzian blare of brass, which opens it, and which recurs at intervals. There is an extraordinary variety in the orchestral colors, some of which are decid-

edly too loud for a symphony. If Tchaikovsky had called his symphony "A Sleigh Ride Through Siberia," no one would have found this title inappropriate.

The reviewer of the *Musical Courier* commented:

> Tchaikovsky's symphony was in parts a disappointment. One vainly sought for coherency or homogeneousness; indeed the work might better be labeled a **suite**, for all the organic variety appreciable in the four movements. . . . In the last movement the composer's Calmuck blood got the better of him, and slaughter, dire and bloody, swept across the storm-driven score. Then, as if to do penance for his musical sins, he winds up the work with a weak and vapid choral, in which musical platitudes abound.

Suite (Fr.). A set or series of pieces in various (idealized) dance forms. The earlier suites have four chief divisions: the Allemande, Courante, Saraband, and Gigue. Also referred to as Classical Suite, or Baroque Suite; the modern orchestral suite is more like a divertimento.

At the first Boston performance, on November 27, 1896, the *Boston Globe* remarked: "At times the musical tumult is deafening and sound inharmonious. The kettledrums are liberally woven into the score, and there are musical combinations of an eccentric nature in abundance."

As late as 1904, Tchaikovsky's Fourth Symphony was still debatable. Louis C. Elson, reviewing a performance by the Boston Symphony Orchestra in the *Boston Evening Transcript* of March 28, 1904, called the symphony "labored and grandiloquent."

As is often the case with great composers and great works, they start out in the estimation of the official musical judges as barbaric and eccentric, and only later are universally accepted. When the point of saturation is reached, there is a feeling of surfeit, and the music is relegated to summer concerts for the large public. Then, after a pause of a decade or two, there is a rediscovery. In Russia Tchaikovsky was in decline after the Revolution, as a representative of gloomy defeatist moods, only to come back with a vengeance as the protagonist of the Internationale of universal human emotion. In the Anglo-Saxon countries, Tchaikovsky is a perennial companion whose glory has never been dimmed with the public. But it is only recently that serious composers of England and America have discovered that Tchaikovsky was not only a neurotic sentimentalist, but also a classic of Romantic emotionalism.

Manfred *Symphony, Op. 58 (1885)*

The *Manfred* Symphony was first performed in Moscow on March 23, 1886. Tchaikovsky wrote to his benefactress and epistolary friend Madame von Meck: "I believe that Manfred is my best composition." But Tchaikovsky expressed the same opinion about several of his other works, notably about the *Pathétique* Symphony. As it happened, *Manfred* never matched his other symphonic scores in musical significance or in public acclaim.

The subject of *Manfred* was inspired by the famous mystical poem by Lord Byron, who exercised tremendous influence on Russian poets and musicians. Tchaikovsky provided the following résumé of Byron's poem:

> Manfred wanders in the Alps. Beset by the fateful problems of human existence, tormented by the burning feeling of hopelessness and by memories of his hideous past, he suffers cruel distress. He seeks solace in the mysteries of magic and communication with the powerful force of Hell. But nothing can give him [the] oblivion he seeks in vain. The memory of dead Astarte, whom he passionately loved, gnaws at his heart. There are no limits, there is no end to Manfred's infinite despair.

Manfred is described as a symphony in four tableaux, but it is not ordinarily included in the catalogue of Tchaikovsky's symphonies. Like most of Tchaikovsky's programmatic works, *Manfred* is set in a minor key. The first movement consists of several episodes, clearly demarcated by protracted pauses. The

Lento (It.). Slow; calls for a tempo between andante and largo.

first episode, **lento** lugubre, portrays Manfred with a strong leading motive in fortissimo; the second, moderato con moto, provides a moment of tranquillity; the third, andante, evokes memories of Astarte, bringing new tortures to Manfred's soul. The initial theme is invoked again. The movement concludes with spasmodic chords of ultimate despondency.

The second movement, Vivace con spirito, is a scherzo. While wandering in the mountains Manfred summons the fairy of the Alps, who appears in the rainbow of a waterfall; the music sparkles in Tchaikovsky's colorful instrumentation. The third movement, Andante con moto, set in the pastoral time signature of 6/8, pictures the bucolic scene of rural life. The shepherd's pipe is heard in the woodwinds. Gradually a dancing spirit enters the music, and a climax is reached through continuous rhythmic escalation. A somber note is struck when Manfred makes his appearance. But the sound of the church bell brings about a mood of peace. The movement ends in diminutive pianississississimo.

The fourth and last movement, Allegro con fuoco, illustrates the orgiastic ritual of the subterranean world. Manfred enters during a bacchanal; this moment is signaled by the appearance of his leading motive. The infernal spirits try to expel

Fugato (It.). A passage or movement consisting of fugal imitations not worked out as a regular fugue.

Cadenza (It.). An elaborate passage played or improvised by the solo instrument at the end of the first or last movements of a concerto.

Chorale. A hymn tune of the German Protestant Church, or one similar in style.

him. An energetic **fugato** reflects the agitation provoked by Manfred's intrusion. Undeterred, he implores the rulers of hell to summon Astarte. She appears and promises to end Manfred's torments. A protracted harp **cadenza** suggests a celestial intervention. A solemn **chorale**, based on Manfred's motive, is heard, symbolizing the attempt of reconciling Manfred to the Church. There is a contrapuntal insertion of the medieval Doomsday chant, Dies irae. Manfred receives absolution and dies in peace.

Symphony No. 5 in E Minor, Op. 64 (1888)

In one of his notebooks, Tchaikovsky jotted down his ideas for the Fifth Symphony: "Introduction: Complete submission to

Fate or, what is the same, to the inexorable judgment of Providence. **Allegro**: Doubts, laments, reproaches to X.X.X." Who was "X.X.X." to whom Tchaikovsky addressed his complaints? No biographer would venture a guess. "Should I perhaps throw myself into the arms of Faith?" Tchaikovsky asks. "A ray of light?" he notes in the sketches for the second movement of the Fifth Symphony, and he answers his query on the same page, in the bass part: "No, there is no hope."

Allegro (It.). Lively, brisk, rapid.

All Tchaikovsky's symphonies, except the little-known Third Symphony, are set in minor keys, a characteristic trait for the melancholy composer. The Fifth Symphony is in E minor, in four movements. The first, **Andante**, in 4/4 time, states the "fate motive" in the low register. The introduction is followed, after a pause, by allegro con anima, the theme of complaints and reproaches, in 6/8 time. Chordal explosions—implosions would be a more fitting word—interrupt the progress of thematic development. The harmonic sequences are **plagal**, conveying the sense of obliquity and indecision. A "ray of light" shines through in a candid major tonality, but it is immediately polarized by rhythmic interference in its melodic phase, resulting in a disquieting syncopation, even though the tempo is marked molto più tranquillo.

Andante (It.). Going, moving; moderately slow tempo.

Plagal mode. A church mode in which the final keynote is a fourth above the lowest tone of the mode.

The second movement, Andante **cantabile** con alcuna licenza, in D major, in 12/8 time, sings out lyrically. It is contrasted by a bright theme in F-sharp major, which the eminent British musicologist Sir Donald Francis Tovey calls "the chief topic of the most impassioned climaxes in this movement." It comes therefore as a shock to find, on Tchaikovsky's own authority, that he used in this melody the street cry of a Moscow vendor of salami and sausages. Old Russians may still recall the familiar singsong: "Kol-ba-a-saaaa . . . Soo-see-ski . . ." Tchaikovsky marks the tune **dolce** espressivo. The idyll is disrupted by the new intrusion of Fatum. The salami-sausage theme is engulfed in the stream of ominous brass, and with it are swept away all tentative smiles and all gladness of heart.

Cantabile (It.). "Singable"; in a singing or vocal style.

Dolce (It.). Sweet, soft, suave; a sweet-toned organ stop.

The third movement, Allegro moderato, in A major, is a waltz, an unusual symphonic ingredient. But Tchaikovsky felt that a waltz was no less entitled to social recognition in a symphony than the minuet, which is a dance of the same measure. Tchaikovsky's waltz, of course, is not of the salon variety, but a melodic invention which is soon wrapped up in ingenious melodic and rhythmic variations.

The finale opens solemnly in an andante maestoso. The key is E major, a proper cyclic counterpart to the initial E minor of the first movement. It is followed by an Allegro **vivace**, containing four distinct themes, built in **sonata form**. The oppressive pessimism of the concept of Fatum is here seemingly dispelled by the marchlike tones of the music. But the melodic and rhythmic configuration of the march is the ubiquitous Fatum motive. A titanic struggle is waged in the concluding pages of the symphony. Whether humanity wins against the blind force of destiny remains a question for philosophical analysts to settle.

Vivace (It.). Lively, animated, brisk.

Sonata form. Usually used for first movements of classical symphonies, sonatas, and chamber works, with exposition, development, and recapitulation.

Symphony No. 6 in B Minor, Op. 74 (Pathétique) *(1893)*

Tchaikovsky, the "melancholy genius" of Russian music, was haunted in his life and in his work by the inexorable specter of fate. It is of psychological significance that five of Tchaikovsky's six symphonies are set in minor keys, traditionally associated with the feeling of sadness. For students of musical morphology, it may be of interest that the nuclei of the opening themes of the last three symphonies are all confined within the somber interval of the minor third. In his original outline of the work that was to become the *Pathétique*, Tchaikovsky planned to limn in tones the entire course of human life. "The first movement," he wrote, "is all in upswing, self-assurance, action; the second portrays love; the third is disappointment; the finale is Death, ultimate dissolution." Other jottings in Tchaikovsky's notebook relating to the

Sixth Symphony in B Minor

("Pathétique"), Op. 74

I

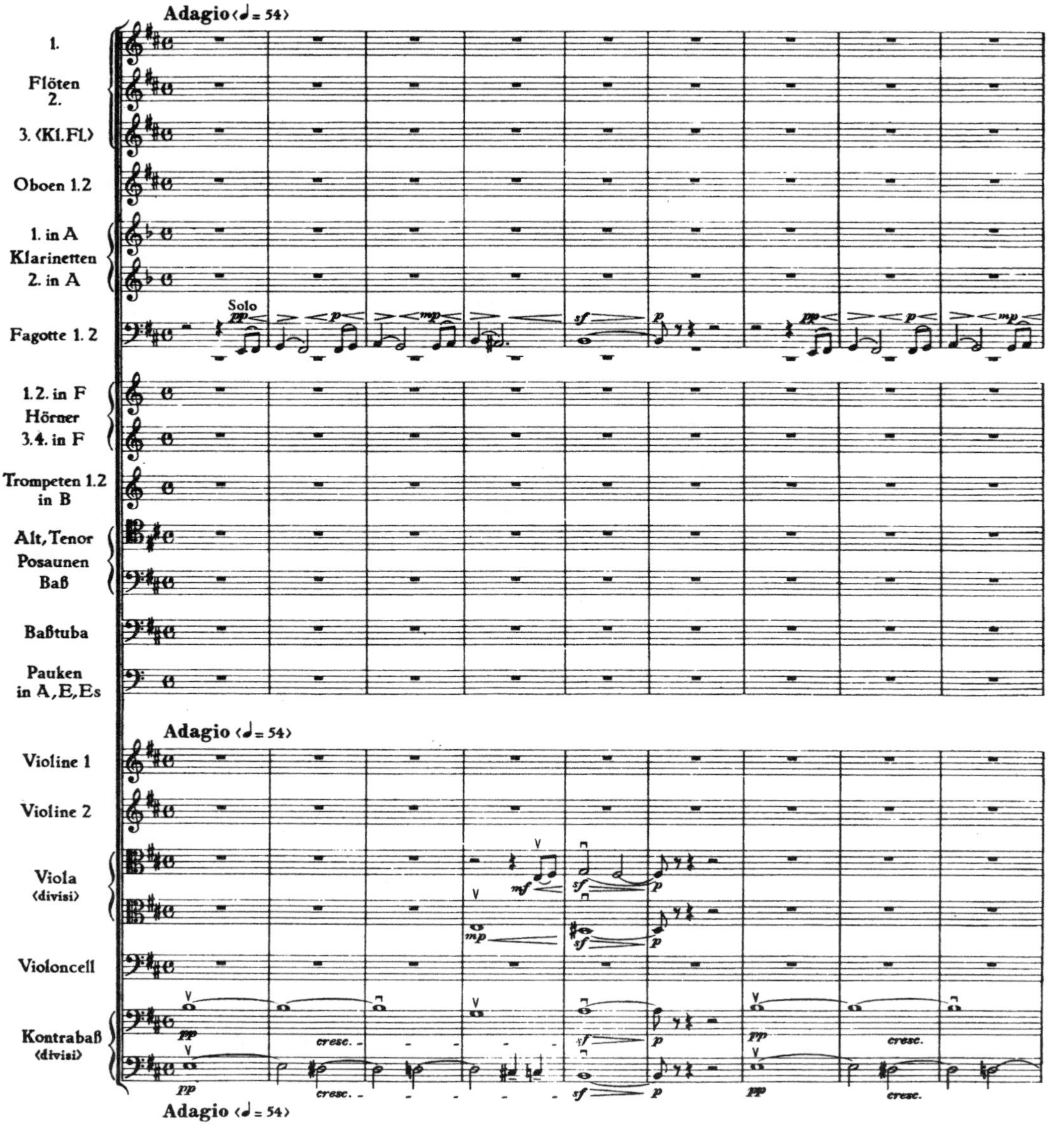

planned symphony are typical: "This motive asks the questions Why, What for, For what reason?"

He confided to his favorite nephew Bob Davidov, to whom the *Pathétique* was eventually dedicated:

> The program of my symphony shall remain an enigma to all. It is very subjective, and while composing it in my mind during my trip to Odessa I often wept bitterly. On my return home I set to work with such determination that in barely four days I had the first movement completely done. Half of the third movement was also finished. There will be much that is novel in the form. For instance, the finale will be not a loud Allegro, but a long Adagio.

Bob Davidov did not respond to his uncle's impassioned communications, and Tchaikovsky voiced his displeasure: "I intended to dedicate my new symphony to you, but now I must reconsider, to punish you for not writing for such a long time. But still I believe it is my best work, and I love it more than any of my musical children." Tchaikovsky did not carry out his threat; the score bears Davidov's name in the dedication.

The veil over the "enigma" of the *Pathétique* is lifted in a passage in the first movement, when suddenly, like a memento mori, the trombones intone the mournful chant from the Russian Mass for the Dead, "Let him rest in peace with the Saints." Was it a premonition of his own death? But Tchaikovsky was only fifty-three in 1893 when the Pathétique was completed, although he looked much older. (He was very much disturbed when an American reporter described his age as about sixty during his concert tour in the United States in 1891.) Professionally, socially, and musically, he was very active; in the summer of the fateful year 1893 he traveled to England to receive a doctor's degree in music at Cambridge University; a photograph taken of him in cape and gown shows a cheerful countenance.

Tchaikovsky asked his friend, the conductor Vasili Sa-
fonov, to play over the symphony with his orchestral class at
the Moscow Conservatory in order to check on details and on
the accuracy of copy. Apparently, the report was satisfactory,
and Tchaikovsky went to St. Petersburg to conduct the first
performance of the work. The premiere took place on October 28, 1893. The title, *Pathétique*, was suggested to him after
the performance by his brother and biographer Modest, and
Tchaikovsky accepted it at once.

What happened immediately after the performance was
the essence of tragedy. A cholera epidemic was raging in St.
Petersburg at the time. Tchaikovsky's mother had died of the
disease. Apparently, Tchaikovsky incautiously drank a glass of
unboiled water; the dread symptoms of the infection set in.
Within a few days, Tchaikovsky was dead. Rumors spread almost at once that Tchaikovsky deliberately exposed himself to
contamination. The "enigma" of the *Pathétique* became clear
to morbidly romantic Russians; the "memento mori" of the
trombones, the victory of death in the finale, all this must
have presaged Tchaikovsky's determination to kill himself.
Once before, he had defied Fatum when he walked into the
chilly Moskva River with the intention of catching a deathly
cold.

The opening **adagio** of the *Pathétique* sets a funereal
mood. After a moment of eloquent silence, the principal
theme becomes the nucleus of a moving musical particle in Allegro non troppo. The music plumbs the depths and scales
the heights of Romantic lamentation. It is in the process of development that the chant from the Russian Mass for the Dead
is heard. Then a contrasting lyric theme appears, letting a ray
of sunlight enter the dark landscape. Despite the profound
emotional turmoil of the music, Tchaikovsky observes the conventions of sonata form; the two contrasting themes are properly developed; there is an abundance of secondary motives.
The **recapitulation** is opulent in its sonorities.

Adagio (It.). Slow, leisurely; a slow movement.

Recapitulation. A return of the initial section of a move-ment in sonata form.

The second movement, Allegro con grazia, is in 5/4 time, unprecedented in symphonic annals, which moved the ineffable Vienna critic Eduard Hanslick to say that "it upsets both the listener and the player," and to suggest that Tchaikovsky could, were be not so perverse, have arranged it "without the slightest inconvenience" in 6/8 time by merely adding a beat to each bar and changing quarter notes to eighth notes. To Russians, on the other hand, there is nothing unnatural in 5/4 time, for it often occurs in Russian folk songs. If the second movement is a scherzoid waltz in quintuple time, the third, Allegro molto vivace, is a scherzo-march in **tarantella** time. The march is built on a progression of perfect fourths, a procedure not fully developed until the twentieth century. Here Tchaikovsky appears as a precursor of modern devices.

Tarantella (It.). A southern Italian dance in 6/8 time, the rate of speed gradually increasing; also, an instrumental piece in a very rapid tempo and bold and brilliant style.

The finale, Adagio lamentoso, opens with a remarkable trompe l'oreille, in which the pathos-laden melody is divided in cross-counterpoint between the violins, with the lower strings similarly arranged. The entire movement is a continuous cry of despair, a musical portrait of Tchaikovsky sobbing on the train while thinking of the music to come. The melodies are in a state of perpetual fall along the notes of the principal scale of B minor, a key which in Romantic music is associated with sorrow and death. An ominous sound of the tam-tam enhances the mood of depression. In the coda the descending violins stop as if asphyxiated, one note short of the **dominant**, and the low wind instruments have to supply the missing F sharp below the violin range.

Dominant. The fifth tone in the major or minor scales; a chord based on that tone.

Piano Concerto No. 1 in B-flat Minor, Op. 23 (1875)

Concerto (It.). An extended multi-movement composition for a solo instrument, usually with orchestra accompaniment and using (modified) sonata form.

Tchaikovsky's First Piano **Concerto** had its world premiere not in Russia, not in any European country, but in Boston, Massachusetts! An extraordinary displacement, which occurred as a result of an equally extraordinary rebuke Tchaikovsky received from the director of the Moscow Conservatory, Nikolai Rubinstein, brother of the director of the St. Petersburg Conservatory, Anton Rubinstein.

Tchaikovsky describes the circumstances in a highly emotional letter to his financial benefactress, Nadezhda von Meck. "In December 1874 I composed a piano concerto," he wrote.

> Since I am not a pianist, I intended to consult a professional virtuoso for advice about technical details, pianistic writing, awkward passages, etc. An inner voice warned me against approaching Nikolai Rubinstein, as a judge of the purely mechanical aspect of my concerto, for I suspected that he would take an opportunity to show off his egotistical side. But he is the best pianist in Moscow, and I knew that he would have been deeply offended had I gone to someone else for advice. So I asked him to go over the concerto with me and give me advice regarding the piano part. It was on Christmas Eve of 1874. We both were invited to a Christmas party, and Rubinstein suggested to use the time before the evening to play over the concerto in a classroom of the Moscow Conservatory. I came with my manuscript, sat at the piano and played the first movement. There was no response whatsoever on Rubinstein's part, not a single word. You cannot imagine the sense of intolerable foolishness when a person serves to a friend a dish of his own concoction, and the other eats it without saying a word!
>
> Rubinstein's eloquent silence was significant. He seemed to be saying: "My good friend, how can I discuss details when the very essence of your music is repugnant to me?" I armed myself with patience and played the work to the end. Again silence. I rose and asked: "Well, what do you think?" Then Rubinstein let loose a torrent of words, at first in a soft tone of voice, but gradually assuming the thundering tones of Jove. My concerto, he said, was absolutely worthless, impossible to play; tech-

nical passages were trite, clumsy, and so awkward that they could not be fixed. Musically, too, my concerto was poor, banal, and furthermore borrowed from this or that work by someone else. There were perhaps two or three pages that could be salvaged, he went on, but the rest must be either discarded entirely or completely revised. A stranger happening to step in by chance would think that I am some sort of maniac, an incompetent and uneducated scribbler who annoys a famous musician with his trashy productions.

I felt stunned and insulted. I left the room in silence and went upstairs, unable to utter a word from excitement and anger. Rubinstein followed me and, noticing my distress, called me to another room. Then he reiterated his opinion that my concerto was impossible to play, and indicated numerous places which required radical alterations. He added that if I revised my concerto according to his requirements by a certain date, he would give me the honor of performing it at one of his concerts. To this I replied: "I will not change a single note and will have the work published as it stands now." And this is exactly what I did.

The original dedication of the concerto was to Rubinstein, but after the rebuke Tchaikovsky received from him, he rededicated it to the German pianist and conductor Hans von Bülow, who had previously shown interest in having Tchaikovsky's music performed. Von Bülow acknowledged the receipt of Tchaikovsky's manuscript and wrote him warmly about the high quality of the music. But apparently he hesitated to present it before the classically minded audiences in Germany. He was making an American tour, and took this opportunity to try out the new work on Americans, who might not be as sensitive as the Germans. And so it came to pass that on October 25, 1875, von Bülow played the world premiere of

Tchaikovsky's famous concerto with a pickup orchestra in Boston.

But the Bostonians, nurtured on German music, did not take too kindly to Tchaikovsky's "Asiatic" melodies and wild rhythms. The cultured *Boston Evening Transcript*, read by all proper Bostonians, opined: "This elaborate work is, in general, as difficult for popular apprehension as the name of the composer. There are long stretches of what seems, on the first hearing at least, formless void, sprinkled only with tinklings of the piano." The *Boston Journal* voiced similar sentiments: "Tchaikovsky is unmistakably a disciple of the new school, and his work is strongly tinged with the wildness and quaintness of the music of the North. Taken as a whole, his Piano Concerto appeared interesting chiefly as a novelty. It would not soon supplant the massive productions of Beethoven, or even the fiery compositions of Liszt, Raff and Rubinstein."

Dwight's Journal of Music, published in Boston by John Sullivan Dwight, the eminently respectable arbiter elegantiarum of the Boston scene (and Boston was, of course, the "hub of the universe"), added a note of puzzlement: "This extremely difficult, strange, wild, ultra-modern Russian concerto is the composition of Peter Tchaikovsky, a young professor at the Conservatory of Moscow. . . . We had the wild Cossack fire and impetus without stint, extremely brilliant and exciting, but could we ever learn to love such music?" Bostonians, and Americans at large, ended up liking this music very much indeed. Its broad introductory theme was transmogrified by Tin Pan Alley into the popular song "Tonight We Love!" Bemoaning the fact that Tchaikovsky never profited by this posthumous fame, a Hollywood tunesmith put out a song entitled "Everybody's Making Money but Tchaikovsky!"

The key of Tchaikovsky's First Piano Concerto is listed as B-flat minor, but that tonality is outlined only at the very beginning of the concerto and is treated as the **submediant** of D-flat major, inaugurated by the piano solo with wide-ranging

Submediant. The third scale tone below the tonic; the sixth degree.

plangent tonic triads. Then the famous principal theme is sounded in the orchestra, while the piano continues to play its sonorous rhythmic chords. Then the soloist picks up the main tune, adorning it with melodic encrustations. There follows a brilliant cadenza. The initial section of the first movement, allegro non troppo e molto maestoso, concludes on a pause, and an Allegro con spirito is ushered in, in the nominal key of the concerto, B-flat minor. A tender-sweet flute introduces an expressive theme, which is further developed in one of the numerous piano cadenzas in the movement. The concluding part is in the homonymous key of B-flat major.

The second movement, Andantino semplice, in D-flat major, is a typically Tchaikovskian barcarole, swaying gently on the surface of the water. It is **antiphonally** constructed, with the flute and the oboe playing **dolcissimo**, accompanied by piano solo in **syncopated** rhythm. Even in this short movement Tchaikovsky finds room for several piano cadenzas.

The third and last movement of the concerto, Allegro con fuoco, in the principal key of B-flat minor, begins like a fiery scherzo. Gradually, it accumulates a tremendous amount of kinetic energy. There are several climactic points. Finally, a majestic coda is reached in the key of B-flat major, with pyrotechnical displays of bravura octaves in the piano solo. Von Bülow reported to Tchaikovsky that on his American tour he had to repeat the finale. Tchaikovsky was greatly pleased. "The Americans must have a healthy appetite," he wrote. "Imagine, von Bülow had to play the entire finale of my concerto as an encore! Nothing like that could ever happen in Russia!"

Francesca da Rimini, *Symphonic Fantasia, Op. 32 (1876)*

On October 26, 1876, Tchaikovsky wrote to his brother and biographer, Modest:

Antiphonal. Responsive, alternating.
Dolcissimo (It.). Very sweetly, softly.
Syncopation. Shifting of accents from strong beat to weak beat or between beats.

I have just finished my new work, a fantasy on Francesca da Rimini. I wrote it with love, and the love came off rather well. As to the storm, one could write something that would come closer to Doré's drawing. [The French artist Gustave Doré made drawings to Dante's *Divine Comedy,* in which Francesca is a figure.] However, correct estimate of the piece cannot be made until it is orchestrated and performed. . . . Did I tell you that I began taking cold baths every morning? You have no idea how beneficial it is to my health. I never felt as well as now (knock wood). This circumstance (that is, the cold water) has and will continue to have influence on my writings. If there is anything fresh and new in Francesca, it is due to a large extent to cold water.

In Tchaikovsky's original manuscript, now preserved at the Tchaikovsky Museum in Klin, there is the following program note, paraphrasing the episode from Dante's "Inferno":

Dante, accompanied by Virgil's shadow, descends into the second realm of hell's abyss. The air is here filled with lamentations, shouts, and cries of despair. The storm rages in gravelike darkness. An infernal whirlwind rushes through, carrying in its rounds the souls of those whose reason was darkened by a love passion in their lives. Among innumerable human souls, Dante's attention is attracted by two beautiful images, locked in embrace, Francesca and Paolo.

Deeply affected by the heart-rending spectacle of the two young souls, Dante addresses them, and wants to know what crime led to this horrible punishment. Francesca, in tears, recounts her sad tale. She loved Paolo, but was against her will given in marriage to the hateful brother of her lover, the one-eyed hunchback, jealous tyrant of Rimini. The yoke of a forced marriage could not eradicate Francesca's tender passion for Paolo. Once they read together the romance of Lancelot. "We were alone," Francesca said, "and we were reading in peace. Often we paled, and our anxious eyes met. A single moment was our ruin. When the happy Lancelot finally gained his first kiss of love, Paolo, from whom nothing will part me now, touched my trembling lips with his, and the book that opened to us the mystery of love fell from our hands." At that moment, Francesca's husband made a sudden appearance, and killed her and Paolo with his dagger. Having told her story, Francesca, still in Paolo's arms, is carried away by the savagely raging storm. Shaken by inexpressible pity, Dante faints, and falls down as one dead.

The program given in the printed edition of the score contains the Italian text from Dante's "Inferno," beginning with the lines: "Nessun maggior dolore che ricordarsi del tempo felice nella miseria" ("There is no greater sorrow than to remember the happy times in misery"). Tchaikovsky often quoted these lines in his letters to his brothers, particularly during the tragic interlude of his unsuccessful marriage.

The structural plan of *Francesca da Rimini* is simple. There are three divisions played without pause. The first and the third portray the fury of the storm, in **chromatic** harmonies and powerful dynamics. The middle section represents Francesca's sad story. It opens with an unaccompanied solo of the clarinet. The theme is later taken by the flutes with the oboes, the violins, and the cellos, and, finally, by the combined string instruments against the background of the rest of the orchestra. There is another motive, similarly developed, and there are rhapsodic episodes with harp passages. The fanfare is sounded, there is a crashing chord, and the storm breaks out with renewed fury.

Francesca da Rimini was performed for the first time in

Chromatic. Relating to tones foreign to a given key (scale) or chord; opposed to diatonic.

Moscow on March 10, 1877, with Nikolai Rubinstein conducting. The success was great. Even more successful was the performance in St. Petersburg on March 23, 1878. In the volume of Tchaikovsky's family letters published in 1940, we find the report of the St. Petersburg performance written by Tchaikovsky's brother Anatol: "Francesca had enormous success, there was no end to the applause. . . . After the concert we had tea at the Davidovs [Carl Davidov (1838–89), the famous cellist and director of the St. Petersburg Conservatory]. Carl has asked me to write you that in his opinion Francesca is the greatest work of our time."

The composer and pianist Sergei Taneyev, to whom the score of *Francesca da Rimini* is dedicated, reported more opinions: Eduard Nápravník, who conducted the performance, liked the work very much, but found it a bit too long. The composer César Cui liked the introduction. Rimsky-Korsakov did not like the themes, but liked the work as a whole. Tchaikovsky's friend the critic Hermann Laroche was restrained in his estimate; he thought the music was too much like Liszt's, and that symphonic poems were not Tchaikovsky's genre.

Variations on a Rococo Theme for Violoncello and Orchestra, Op. 33 (1877)

The characterization "rococo" gives a clear indication of Tchaikovsky's intentions in this set of attractive variations for violoncello and orchestra. "Rococo" comes from the word *rocaille*, suggesting shell-like rock ornaments, elegant, charming, decorative, in soft blue or rose colors, like a girl's figure painted by Greuze or a pastoral landscape by Fragonard. The Variations had its first performance in Moscow on November 30, 1877.

After a brief introduction, the theme Moderato semplice, is sounded by the cello solo. Its rhythm suggests a **gavotte**, a dance favored during the innocent age when the Rococo flour-

Gavotte (Fr.). A Gavot; an old French dance in strongly marked duple time (*alla breve*), beginning on the up-beat.

ished in prerevolutionary France. There are seven variations in all; they are all distinguished by simplicity and virtuosity. The first two variations are in the same tempo as the original theme. But the third variation, Andante sostenuto, assumes an air of Russian melancholy. The fourth variation, Andante grazioso, resumes its Rococo character. The fifth variation, Allegro moderato, affords the solo cello a display of easy virtuosity, with opulent cadenzas adding brilliance to Rococo elegance. The sixth variation, Andante, is by contrast a Russian meditation. The final, seventh, variation, Allegro vivace, serves as a coda, rushing forward with joyous precipitation.

Violin Concerto in D Major, Op. 35 (1878)

Tchaikovsky wrote his Violin Concerto during March and April 1878, at Clarens, a peaceful little town on Lake Geneva. The composition of the concerto followed immediately after the Fourth Symphony, and the opera *Eugene Onegin*. It was a very dramatic period of Tchaikovsky's life. He had just thrown off the burden of an unnatural marriage, and was obsessed with the fear that the true cause of its failure would become generally known.

Financially, Tchaikovsky felt secure through the rich annuity that the beneficent Madame von Meck was giving him, first under the pretext of commissioned works, and later as an outright gift. Madame von Meck's admiration for Tchaikovsky's genius was warmed by the sympathy she felt for his unsuccessful marriage, and in her letters she pictured Tchaikovsky's wife as a person unworthy of bearing his name, a person who failed to understand his greatness. In accepting this version of the story, Tchaikovsky nevertheless could not help feeling that he was something worse than a hypocrite. Only with his brothers he could be frank, for they knew. Thus, Tchaikovsky's life was split; the facade gave no hint of the interior.

By nature, Tchaikovsky was morbidly introspective. He found pleasure in condemning himself. In the Tchaikovsky

Museum at Klin there is an old volume in Latin, in which Tchaikovsky wrote on the title pages "Stolen from the Palace of the Doges in Venice by Peter Ilyich Tchaikovsky, State Counselor and Conservatory Professor." This flaunting, in the privacy of his own self, of a minor criminal offense is very characteristic of Tchaikovsky's mentality. In his work, however, Tchaikovsky was amazingly efficient. No matter what his state of mind, he could write fast, without deviating from the original idea. Diffident and self-condemning though he was in life, in his art he was always sure of himself. The evidence of his manuscripts shows an orderly procedure, with no loose ends, no incomplete designs.

The Violin Concerto was dedicated to the famous violinist Leopold Auer. It is ironic that Auer should have shown so little interest in the work, and let it gather dust, until Adolf Brodsky picked it up, and played it in Vienna on December 4, 1881. For Leopold Auer was the teacher of a flock of Russian violinists, who made Tchaikovsky's concerto their favorite pièce de résistance. Brodsky's performance in Vienna was not an unqualified success. The Viennese critic Eduard Hanslick, famous for his invective, wrote harshly of it. Tchaikovsky said he could never forget this review, and no wonder; for Hanslick wrote that the violin was not played, but beaten black and blue. He also remarked that there is music that one can hear stink, and that the last movement of the concerto, so odorously Russian, belongs in that category.

The concerto opens with a theme of the first violins, in D major, 4/4. After a short introductory period, the kettledrum, basses, cellos, and the bassoon play a **tremolo** on the dominant, a time-honored device to create suspense, in anticipation of the principal subject. Here the violins of the orchestra give away the rhythmic pattern of the coming violin solo. The solo begins with a few preliminary flourishes, and then announces the theme. There is a rapid development, with the soloist playing in virtuoso style. The orchestra

Tremolo (It.). A quivering, fluttering, in singing; an unsteady tone.

sounds vigorously rhythmed chords. After a brilliant display of technique, the solo violin announces the second theme, of a lyrical character.

The movement grows, there are three, four, and six notes to a beat. The solo violin is now at the height of its virtuosity. The orchestra supports it by rhythmical chords, first on the beat, then syncopated. The flutes and violins sing out the lyrical theme, while the soloist carries on in virtuoso manner. There is more "business," to use stage parlance, and the entire orchestra strikes the first theme in the dominant, to the accompaniment of the fanfares of the wind instruments. The solo violin has a long period of rest, and then comes in with brilliant variations on the first theme, in a new key, C major. Once more the orchestra takes over the theme, this time in F. The soloist and the orchestra exchange vigorous chords. The orchestra now keeps the dominant A in the bass, a clear indication of the impending return of the original key.

Stop. On the violin, etc., the pressure of a finger on a string, to vary the latter's pitch; a *double stop* is when two or more strings are so pressed and sounded simultaneously.

Trill. The even and rapid alternation of two tones which are a major or minor second apart.

The violin plays a brilliant cadenza, employing all its technical resources—double, triple, and quadruple **stops**, **trills**, and runs. The cadenza ends on a trill, and the flute announces the first theme of the movement. This is the recapitulation, but Tchaikovsky would not use this formality of a sonata form without coloring and embellishing it, to make the recapitulation a new edition of the exposition. But the outline is clearly recognizable. Once more, we hear the rhythmically spaced orchestral chords. And then comes the second theme, now in the tonic key.

The solo violin plays the lyrical second theme on the G string. A chromatic run brings the theme an octave higher, and higher still, to the limits of the effective range of the violin. We recognize the syncopated chords in the orchestra. Then the orchestral violins play the lyrical theme, chromaticized, and otherwise modified, while the soloist plays rapid passages. The tempo is stepped up, paralleling the corresponding section of the exposition, and the final portion of the movement is reached. It is marked allegro giusto. The square-by-square rhythm of the solo violin, four sixteenth notes to a quarter, is punctuated by the chords of the orchestra. The rhythm narrows to six notes to a beat. The concluding più mosso has some material similar to *Eugene Onegin*, the opera that Tchaikovsky wrote shortly before the concerto.

The lyrical second movement is more Italian than Slavic, and the Italian designation, **Canzonetta**, is not an accident. It opens with an introduction for wind instruments. Then the solo violin plays the unassuming theme, in G minor, 3/4 time. The flute repeats the theme with added trills. Then the solo violin resumes, playing a contrasting melody, to the accompaniment of the strings, and later of the woodwinds. After some transitional passages, the solo violin returns to the original theme of the Canzonetta, with parenthetical interpolations from the clarinet and the flute. The violin leaves off with a trill, and the woodwinds repeat the introduction. There is some interplay of instrumental colors in slow tempo, and the movement ends in pianissimo.

Canzonetta (lt.), **canzonet.** A solo song or part-song; a brief instrumental piece.

The finale enters at once, in the original key of D, in 2/4 time. The orchestra starts in vigorous dancing rhythm, and the solo violin plays a cadenza, preliminary to the main subject. The solo violin holds the foreground, with the woodwind instruments quick repartees, now and then. A running scale leads to a new, "Russian" theme, played by the solo violin against the thumping fifths of the **violoncellos**. It must have been this theme that moved Hanslick to remark that he detected the strong smell of Russian boots. However that may be, here is a dance for dance's sake. The theme is played over and over in the violins, the horn, and the bassoons. Then there is an interlude in a slow tempo, with the oboe and clarinet playing a lyrical theme, bearing only rhythmical affinity to the thumping Russian motive. The solo violin and the violoncellos echo this new lyrical figure. Then the solo violin whips up the tempo, and brings back the first theme of the finale.

Violoncello (lt.). A four-stringed bow instrument familiarly called the cello.

Rondo (It.). An instrumental piece in which the leading theme is repeated, alternating with the others.

The form is clearly a **rondo**, with two principal themes, and episodes, patterned after the themes. The orchestra presents the first theme in various keys, and modified to the intervals, while the solo violin interjects brilliant arpeggio passages. The "Russian" theme returns in G major. The flutes take it over, while the solo violin plays variations. But all resources of the violin technique are not yet exhausted, and the theme is played in octaves, and in harmonics. Once more, the oboe and the clarinet have their interlude, participated in by the solo violin. In the final section, both themes appear in various guises. The concerto ends in a rousing fortissimo.

Overture "1812," Op. 49 (1880)

Battle pieces are the most ancient, the most obvious, and the most profitable art forms. They always glorify, and they are always composed by nationals of the winning party. One of the best-known battle pieces, *The Battle of Prague*, continued inexplicably in popularity for a century after the composer, one Francis Kotzwara, a Czech-born violinist at the King's Theatre in London, had hanged himself in a London brothel, on September 2, 1791. Another popular battle piece was *Battle Gemmappe*, a sonata by François Devienne, who ended his days in an insane asylum near Paris. In America, Francesco Masi, "author of several fugitive compositions," wrote *The Battles of Lake Champlain and Plattsburg,* a Grand Sonata for the Piano Forte, respectfully dedicated to the "American Heroes Who Achieved the Glorious Victories." Finally there is the *Battle of Marengo*, a military piece by Bernard Viguerie, whose claim to pioneer achievement is the special effect for the sound of the cannons "to be expressed by stretching the two hands flat on the three lower **octaves**, the hand to be kept on the keys until the vibrations are nearly extinct." In all these pieces, galloping horses are portrayed by the device known in music history as the Alberti bass. Another feature is an "attack with swords" or, in later pieces, with bayonets.

Octave. A series of eight consecutive diatonic tones; the interval between the first and the eighth.

There is an obligatory section in a minor key entitled Cry of the Wounded. The end is usually a grand fanfare. The most famous orchestral battle piece is Beethoven's Wellington's Victory; in it the cannon is represented by two bass drums.

Tchaikovsky wrote the Overture "1812" in 1880 for the dedication of the Temple of Christ the Savior on Red Square in Moscow (be it noted parenthetically that Red Square was the ancient name of the Kremlin Square, in old Russian the word for "red" also meaning "beautiful"). The composition was written at the instigation of Nikolai Rubinstein. Tchaikovsky had no enthusiasm for writing the commissioned work. "There is nothing more distasteful to me than to compose music for special occasions," he wrote to Madame von Meck from Kamenka on September 28, 1880. "What can one write for an inauguration of an exposition except banalities and noisy commonplaces? But I have no heart to refuse Rubinstein's request and so, willy-nilly, I will have to embark on a disagreeable task." On October 10, he reports to Madame von Meck: "My muse is so benevolent to me of late that I have completed two pieces with great speed, namely, an **overture** and a **serenade** for string orchestra. I am orchestrating both pieces. The overture will be very loud and noisy, but I was writing it without a warm feeling of affection, and there will probably be no artistic value in it." The proposed performance on Red Square did not materialize. Yet with this public performance in mind, Tchaikovsky had included in the score a real cannon, such as is used in the theater for sound effects, and a battery of church bells.

The Overture "1812" depicts the epic event of the victory over the "invasion of twelve nations," as the Napoleonic armies were described in Russian popular phraseology. The faith in victory is symbolized by the opening prayer, "Save, O Lord, your people, and bless their treasure." Further, there appears the Russian song "At Father's Gates" and the Russian national hymn. On the French side is the "Marseillaise." The

Overture. A musical introduction to an opera, oratorio, etc.

Serenade. An instrumental composition imitating in style an "evening song," sung by a lover before his lady's window.

"Marseillaise" grows in volume until it reaches a climax, the occupation of Moscow in September 2, 1812. But the Russian song is heard undiminished. It is now a people's campaign. The invader is ejected. The "Marseillaise" now appears in minor, while the prayer and the national hymn return in triumph.

Tchaikovsky was accused of anachronism for the inclusion of the "Marseillaise" and the Russian National Hymn. The "Marseillaise" was not the popular hymn of Napoleon's imperialist armies, and the Russian National Hymn was not composed until 1833. Tchaikovsky might have replied with the words of Tolstoy in the epilogue to *War and Peace*.

> The discrepancy of my description of historic events with the account of historians is not an accident. It is inevitable. The historian and the artist depicting a historical era have two entirely different objectives. The historian is concerned only with the result of an event, while the artist is interested in the event by itself.

Coda: Tchaikovsky Rediscovered in His Dwelling Place—Notes of a Visit to the Tchaikovsky Museum in Klin

Klin is a small town near Moscow. Many changes have swept through Russia in the last century, but Klin has changed little. There were a few buildings of modern architecture when I visited the town in 1935, but it was an old-fashioned droshky that brought me from the railroad station. The rain fell on the horse with the same even rhythm that Russian rain has always possessed—nothing violent, nothing capricious, but a steady, determined precipitation.

There was a feeling of gratitude in my heart when I observed how little modern times had affected the quiet and, in itself, unimportant town. But it was important to me, as indeed it is to all musicians, since Klin was for many years the home of the great Russian composer Peter Ilyich Tchaikovsky. There he lived and worked. In Klin he composed his Sixth Symphony, the *Pathétique*. The cottage he occupied was lovingly preserved by the Russian people.

Entering that cottage, we are introduced into the private world of Tchaikovsky. On the wall over his bed there was a picture that had hung there for some sixty years. It was a landscape, painted by an artist who was not great but whose sincerity of sentiment made up for lack of mastery—a Russian woman who was deeply moved when she heard the nostalgic second movement of Tchaikovsky's Violin Concerto. Tchaikovsky was devoted to the picture, for he appreciated the sentiment that had inspired it.

There were objects connected with Tchaikovsky's daily activities, the incidental minutiae which help to reconstruct the temporal aspect of a great musician's life. There was his silk dressing gown, hanging from a peg near the bed; a pitcher and basin—there was no running water in Tchaikovsky's Klin; a kerosene lamp and some utensils of everyday use. Of more direct interest were the numerous photographs of Tchaikovsky's friends, inscribed to him. They left little space on the walls they decorated. The bookshelves were filled with books and the printed editions of Tchaikovsky's music. And, finally, in the center of the large drawing-room, stood an instrument of Tchaikovsky's muse, a grand piano.

I asked the custodian of Tchaikovsky's house—or perhaps I should call him curator, for the cottage was officially named "house-museum"—whether I might play on the piano. The curator himself seemed to be a personage of Tchaikovsky's world. His features strangely resembled those of the great musician to whose memory he dedicated himself. Perhaps instinctively, he trimmed his beard after the Tchaikovsky manner, because he thought it was the most dignified mode. Well, he cordially permitted me to run my fingers over the keyboard that had once

Nocturne (Fr.). A piece of a dreamily romantic or sentimental character, without fixed form.

felt the imprint of Tchaikovsky's hands. I played the C-sharp Minor **Nocturne**, which I had learned as a boy in Russia, and which to this day personifies Tchaikovsky for me more even than his symphonies. There is a perfection in this nocturne that is rarely matched, a cyclical form with two sections in minor, separated by a page in major. When the melody returns in the last part, it is sung by the left hand, while the right runs a measured scale upward and then downward in a swift cascade. As I played, the curator's Tchaikovskylike face smiled—in approval, so I hoped. Playing Tchaikovsky, in Tchaikovsky's house, on Tchaikovsky's piano, was a responsibility, even though there was no audience or music critic present.

But later on that day, there was an audience. It was a group of eager young boys and girls who were being conducted by the curator through the Tchaikovsky House-Museum, and introduced to the world of great music composed long before these young people were born. The curator played some of Tchaikovsky's music on a gramophone. It was an old machine that he used, with an old-fashioned loudspeaker of corrugated metal, and with that unearthly squeak that former generations of phonograph enthusiasts must have ignored. And so did the present audience, listening in reverence, without disparagement. Somehow that old gramophone, and even that squeak, seemed to strengthen the illusion of being near Tchaikovsky's world, an illusion that would have been destroyed by the incongruous perfection of a modern machine.

Toward the end of the day, the curator unlocked the metal containers in which Tchaikovsky's manuscripts were preserved, and I was allowed a glimpse into the inner sanctum of Tchaikovsky's musical thinking. Here was his opera *Pique Dame*. I knew every note of it. How strange: Could it be that this **aria**—which had always seemed to me something hewn unalterably from rock—could it be that Tchaikovsky had at first hesitated over the melodic line? There were other era-

Aria (It.). An air, song, tune, melody.

sures and alterations that fascinated me. So that was the way such music was written!

I left Tchaikovsky's house with a feeling of having traveled into the past, of having been a member of Tchaikovsky's circle of friends. The house was a symbol of Russian culture, its strength, its poetry, its continuity. No storm, it seemed to me, would ever strike that unimpressive cottage, so far removed from the highways of modern life. But a storm did engulf Tchaikovsky's world. It was a man-made storm, led by men in uniforms riding on motorcycles. They reached Klin, in their sweep toward Moscow, as part of an ambitious plan to subjugate and repress the national development of Tchaikovsky's homeland. In apprehension and anticipation of this invasion, the museum's curator had removed to a safe distance the manuscripts in metal containers, had tried also to send off Tchaikovsky's library. But there was no time for that. The invaders arrived, emptied the half-packed cases, and threw the books in the snow. They were not interested in either destroying or stealing Tchaikovsky's books and music. To them the house-museum was but a shelter for their bodies, a shelter for their motorcycles. They would have burned the house in their retreat from Klin, but they were driven off too rapidly to destroy.

Some weeks later, the invasion's tide receded and work was resumed in the museum. The rooms were cleaned; the broken-down motorcycle left behind by the invaders was removed from Tchaikovsky's drawing room. Again, during visitors' hours, came eager boys and girls to listen to Tchaikovsky's music. The pictures were once more restored to their accustomed places on the walls. Tchaikovsky's world, after a tempest, was once more returned to its calm and timeless existence.

Presenting the Great
NIKOLAI RIMSKY-KORSAKOV
(1844–1908)

"THIS IS A COMPOSITION BY RIMSKY, arranged by Korsakov," announced a disc jockey on the air. His naïve blunder was rather an understatement, for there is enough variety and color in Rimsky-Korsakov's music for several composers. No other composer can equal Nikolai Rimsky-Korsakov in the sheer brilliance of his orchestra, and the moderns, beginning with Debussy, followed his lead in treating instrumental colors. Yet to him music was music and nothing else, and he disliked extraneous explanations of his melodic phrases. When he conducted a concert of his works in Paris, early in the century, an enthusiastic lady asked him after the concert, "Please tell me,

Maître, what was your clarinet saying?" Rimsky-Korsakov replied, with the greatest show of politeness, "It said, 'I am not an oboe.'"

In his autobiography, which is a model of modest yet informative writing, Rimsky-Korsakov tells us that he became conscious of music before he was two years old; at four, he could beat the toy drum strictly in measure while his father played the piano. In the spirit of a game, the elder Rimsky-Korsakov would suddenly change the tempo, but the boy would immediately catch on, and follow the new rhythm. He also had the sense of **absolute pitch** from his earliest childhood, so that he could name any note played for him on the piano without looking. Despite his unusual absorption with music, he was a lively boy who liked to climb on the roof and on trees. Indoors, he entertained himself by harnessing chairs for horses. He imitated a watchmaker by putting on eyeglasses, made of cardboard, and taking apart an old watch. He read books of adventure, and loved to spend time with geographic maps and astronomic charts.

At eighteen, Rimsky-Korsakov entered the naval academy and sailed abroad on the clipper *Almaz* ("amber"). He traveled to Gravesend, England, and later to America, visiting New York, Washington, and other coastal cities. He gratefully notes in his autobiography that "the Americans took us to Niagara Falls at their own expense as an act of hospitality accorded to Russians by their transatlantic friends." That was the time of the Civil War, and Rimsky-Korsakov followed the events with the greatest interest, all his sympathy being in favor of the Northern states and President Lincoln. The only musical instrument the mariner-musician took with him on board ship was a mouth harmonica. He found an American sailor, one Thompson, who could play on the violin, and together they amused themselves by playing American songs. The *Almaz* continued to Rio de Janeiro and then proceeded southward, intending to return to Russia via Cape

Absolute pitch. Ability to name instantly and without fail any note struck on the piano keyboard or played on an instrument. This is a rare, innate faculty, which appears in a musical child at a very early age, distinct from "relative pitch," common among all musicians, in which an interval is named in relation to a previously played note. Also known as "perfect pitch."

Horn and the Pacific. But mechanical trouble developed and the clipper was summoned back by the Mediterranean route.

Upon his return in 1865, Rimsky-Korsakov began to compose music seriously and with great concentration. He became friendly with a group of young composers whose names are now familiar to every music lover—Mily Balakirev (1837–1910), César Cui (1835–1913), Alexander Borodin (1833–87), and Modest Mussorgsky (1839–81). Balakirev was the acknowledged leader of the group. Cui, of French descent, was an expert in military fortification, and music was to him a pleasant hobby; Borodin was a young professor of chemistry—he had a laboratory in the neighboring building, and would often interrupt composition and run over to see that his chemical utensils were in working order. Mussorgsky was employed in the Department of Forestry, and had little time to compose. The technique of composition was not coming easily to Rimsky-Korsakov, Borodin, and Mussorgsky; only Balakirev and Cui possessed the mastery of the art, and they were deferred to by the rest for their superior knowledge.

One fine day the group decided to present their symphonic works at a public concert. After that event, the Russian writer and lover of the arts, Vladimir Stasov, referred to the five composers as "the mighty little company [handful]." Rimsky-Korsakov thought this nomination was "tactless," but the variant form, "the Mighty Five," has been accepted by music historians. Among the composers who were grouped almost accidentally as the Mighty Five, Rimsky-Korsakov was the most professional, and indeed professorial. Curiously enough, Balakirev and Cui, who were regarded as superiors by their comrades-in-arms, have made little impact on subsequent musical developments; the mentor of the group, Balakirev, stopped composing midway in his long life. The stature of Mussorgsky, who was too erratic for a professional musician and always

Rimsky-Korsakov Timeline

1844 Born in Tikhvin, near Novgorod

1856 Enrolls in Naval School in St. Petersburg; befriends composers Mily Balakirev, César Cui, Alexander Borodin

1862 Upon graduation, sails on clipper ship *Almaz* for three-year voyage

1865 Returns to Russia, settles in St. Petersburg; First Symphony premiered, conducted by Balakirev

1871 Begins lifelong association with St. Petersburg Conservatory, teaching composition and orchestration

1873-84 Serves as head of the military orchestra of Russian Navy

1874 Makes conducting debut at charity concert for victims of Volga famine, with first performance of Third Symphony

1882 *The Snow Maiden* produced in St. Petersburg

1883-94 Serves as assistant director of Court Chapel, leading chorus and orchestra

1886–1900 Conducts annual concerts of Russian symphonic music

1888 Premieres the *Easter Overture*

1889 Conducts two concerts of Russian music at World Exposition in Paris

1890 Completes (with Glazunov) Borodin's unfinished opera *Prince Igor*

(continued)

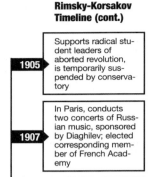
Fugue. Contrapuntal imitation wherein a theme proposed by one part is taken up equally and successively by all participating parts.

aware of his technical inadequacy, rose to extraordinary heights. Rimsky-Korsakov became one of the greatest masters of Russian music and a superb technician in the art of composition.

And so Rimsky-Korsakov became a master of music. Still in his twenties, he was appointed a professor at the St. Petersburg Conservatory, and later became its director. He was extremely conscientious in going over his students' exercises, which he read note by note, and offered detailed advice for improvement. Many of his students became important composers in their own right, and the traditions of Rimsky-Korsakov's teaching endured in Russia. Never a professorial pedant, he possessed a keen sense of humor. One of the most delightful compositions of Russian light music is a collection of variations written by Rimsky-Korsakov, Borodin, Cui, and others on the theme of the old-fashioned Chopsticks. In his contribution to this humorous collection, Rimsky-Korsakov managed to combine Chopsticks with a **fugue** on the name of Bach, which in German notation spells out the notes B-flat, A, C, and B-natural.

Tall, bespectacled, bearded, quiet in manner, friendly but not too convivial in company, a model husband, an affectionate father, Rimsky-Korsakov was the veritable personification of an old-fashioned Russian intellectual. Rimsky-Korsakov led a sedentary life in St. Petersburg. He was a modest man. He declined the proffered doctorate of Cambridge University, because he did not regard himself as a scholar. But he was unyielding in matters of principle. His personal integrity was absolute. When the czarist regime ordered the expulsion of a number of students at the St. Petersburg Conservatory who had been accused of holding an unauthorized political meeting, Rimsky-Korsakov registered a vehement protest, and as a result was himself relieved of his position as director and professor. But he refused to abandon his pupils and continued to give them private lessons at home.

Rimsky-Korsakov was adamantly against unauthorized cuts in his operas. When Diaghilev proposed drastic cuts in his Paris production of *Sadko*, because French audiences would not sit through a long opera, Rimsky-Korsakov wrote him in anger: "If to the dressed-up but feeble-minded Paris opera-goers who drop in at the theater for a while and who are guided in their opinions by their venal press and their hired claque, my *Sadko* in its present state is too heavy, then I would rather not have it done at all."

Rimsky-Korsakov's musical conscience made him his own severest critic. Being human, he had his moments of creative fatigue, when he seemed unable to work productively, but he regarded such dereliction of duty as unwarranted self-indulgence. He was at his happiest in the final stages of **orchestration**. "What can be more satisfying than final scoring!" he wrote to a friend. "When I begin to orchestrate, everything becomes crystal clear and precise in harmony, rhythm, melodic line, even in secondary parts. The soul is calm for the thread of the composition has been woven in, and in a way the work already exists. And what a pleasure to correct unsatisfactory passages and polish up rough spots! As for the hopelessly bad sections, one simply gets used to them, and they cease causing irritation." This is, indeed, "an ode to professionalism and technique," as Rimsky-Korsakov's son Andrey described it.

Orchestration. The art of writing music for performance by an orchestra; the science of combining, in an effective manner, the instruments constituting the orchestra.

The great innovation of Rimsky-Korsakov and his friends of the Mighty Five was the use of Russian national subjects in their operas and **symphonic poems**. Before them, Russian music followed the models of the Italian and German masters—even the great Glinka could not get away from Italianate inflections. But Rimsky-Korsakov did not slavishly borrow from Russian folk songs. Rather, he wrote new melodies that sounded like genuine folk songs. This fooled one of his critics, who asserted that the best melody in Rimsky-Korsakov's opera *The Snow Maiden* was the shepherd's song, which, so he said, was really a Russian folk tune. Rimsky-Korsakov wrote a letter

Symphonic poem. An extended orchestral composition which follows in its development the thread of a story or the ideas of a poem, repeating and interweaving its themes appropriately; it has no fixed form, nor has it set divisions like those of a symphony.

to the editor of the paper, asking the critic to tell what Russian song that was. Of course, there was no reply to that.

Rimsky-Korsakov's music is extremely graphic. The growth of a magic forest is musically depicted in *The Snow Maiden* by a sequence of notes, one to a beat, then two, three, and four to a beat. In his symphonic **suite**, *Scheherazade*, the story-telling of the Sultan's wife is represented by a recurring **motif** of the solo violin which seems to articulate words in singing notes. In his *Capriccio espagnol* he catches the rhythm of Spain more effectively than any native Spanish composer ever did. The rhythmic waves of the ocean and the frolics of the fish in *Sadko* unroll a musical seascape that one can almost perceive visually. Sometimes Rimsky-Korsakov imitated animal sounds as close to nature as the tempered musical scale could afford. His rooster's elaborate cock-a-doodle-doo could arouse a barnyard to sudden activity before daybreak. And there is also a family canary whose song he copied for another instrumental solo.

Rimsky-Korsakov's musical personality conceals a paradox. How could this typical Russian music teacher, who led such an uneventful life, have produced such resplendent pageants of sensuous color as *Scheherazade* and *Le Coq d'or*? The answer is that orientalism is part of the Russian musical heritage. Rimsky-Korsakov's Orient was the Near East, comprising countries with which Russia had a common frontier and a flourishing trade. This music was to Russia what Cuban dance rhythms are to the United States, an exotic stimulant. By a curious process of reversion, Rimsky-Korsakov's quasi-Oriental music spread in Asian countries by means of recordings and over the radio, and actually began to influence the lands that provided the original inspiration. The music of Rimsky-Korsakov is now, literally and figuratively, in the public domain. It is used and abused in pseudo-Oriental shows and in popular songs, its carefully balanced harmonies filled with extraneous notes, its flowing melodies deformed and cut to

Suite (Fr.). A set or series of pieces in various (idealized) dance forms. The earlier suites have four chief divisions: the Allemande, Courante, Saraband, and Gigue. Also referred to as Classical Suite, or Baroque Suite; the modern orchestral suite is more like a divertimento.

Motif. A short phrase or figure used in development or imitation.

meet the exigencies of the medium, its masterly instrumenta-tion blatantly inspissated. What a cry of anguish would Rimsky-Korsakov have emitted at such ignominious treatment at the hands of musical barbarians!

It is an accepted maxim that a deeply felt national art in-evitably becomes universal art. Rimsky-Korsakov's music, so profoundly Russian, has spread to the four corners of the world. And now, his melodies speak as clearly to Americans as they do to Russians; to the English as to Italians; to Australians as to the Hindus. It is difficult for a foreigner to learn the Russ-ian language; it is easy to learn and to enjoy Russian music as presented, in marvelous colors, by Nikolai Andreievich Rimsky-Korsakov.

Quintet for Piano, Flute, Clarinet, French Horn, and Bassoon in B-flat Major (1876)

Before Rimsky-Korsakov became a classic, he was regarded in some circles as almost a revolutionary. Eduard Hanslick, the famous Vienna critic, once described him as belonging to "the extreme left wing of the Russian school." The asymmet-rical rhythms in Rimsky-Korsakov's operas caused great trou-ble to performers. Singers used to study the rhythms of eleven quarter-notes in some of his operatic choruses by reciting "Rimsky-Korsakov sovsen sumasoshol" (Russian for "Rimsky-Korsakov is completely mad"), which contains eleven syllables.

Chamber music. Vocal or instrumental music suitable for performance in a room or small hall.

Quintet(te). A concerted in-strumental composition for five performers; a composi-tion, movement, or number, vocal or instrumental, in five parts; also, the performers as a group.

In order of popularity, the works of Rimsky-Korsakov range from his symphonic suite *Scheherazade* through ex-cerpts from his operas to his songs. His **chamber music** is virtually unknown. One such forgotten work is his **Quintet** for Piano, Flute, Clarinet, French Horn, and Bassoon. It was written in 1876, for a contest of the Russian Musical Society. Rimsky-Korsakov describes, in *Chronicle of My Musical Life*, the nature of this work:

I composed the quintet in three movements. The first was in the classical style of Beethoven; the second, **Andante**, contained a fairly good fugue for the wind instruments, with a free contrapuntal accompaniment in the piano part. The third movement, **Allegretto** vivace, in **rondo** form, contained an interesting passage: the approach to the first subject after the middle section. The flute, the French horn and the clarinet by turns play virtuoso cadenzas, according to the character of each instrument, and each is interrupted by the bassoon entering by octave leaps. After the piano cadenza, the first subject finally enters in similar leaps.

Andante (It.). Going, moving; moderately slow tempo.

Allegretto (It.). Quite lively; moderately fast.

Rondo (It.). An instrumental piece in which the leading theme is repeated, alternating with the others.

Writing many years later, he admitted that the quintet did not express his real individuality. It was neatly copied and sent to the jury of the Russian Musical Society, along with another work, a sextet (Rimsky-Korsakov submitted two manuscripts to have a better chance to win). But the prize went to Eduard Nápravník, a Czech conductor and composer who settled in Russia. Rimsky-Korsakov's sextet got an honorable mention; the quintet received no reward at all. Rimsky-Korsakov explained that Nápravník's work, a trio, received an admirable performance by Leschetizky, though playing at sight from manuscript, whereas Rimsky-Korsakov's quintet was mangled by a poor pianist. "The fiasco at the contest was undeserved," Rimsky-Korsakov wrote, "for it pleased the audience greatly when it was subsequently performed at a concert of the St. Petersburg Chamber Music Society."

The May Night *(1878–79)*

The May Night is Rimsky-Korsakov's second opera. He wrote it in 1878–79, at a time when he was fascinated by stories of the fantastic and the supernatural. For his libretto he selected a tale by his favorite writer, Nikolai Gogol. The story deals with the youthful love of the Ukrainian boy Levko for the beautiful Hannah; Levko's father, the village elder, is himself infatuated with the girl and refuses to allow his son to marry her. There are several comic characters: the wine distiller, the scribe, the village drunkard. The fantastic element is represented by a drowned Polish maiden who comes out at night from the water and helps Levko in his romance by producing a magically contrived letter from the chief commissioner ordering Levko's father to have the marriage of Levko and Hannah celebrated without delay under heavy penalty for disobedience.

Rimsky-Korsakov used many passages of Gogol's prose without alterations in the recitatives and even in the arias. The result was that the opera acquired a colloquial flavor. There was no attempt at operatic realism in the manner of Mussorgsky, but rather an adaptation of the common speech to a melodic line written according to purely musical considerations.

The first performance of *The May Night* took place at the Mariinsky Theater in St. Petersburg on January 21, 1880, under the direction of the invariably strict and meticulous Czech conductor Eduard Nápravník. Rimsky-Korsakov, who once described Nápravník as "an inimitable wrong-note detective," was not particularly happy about the way the conductor interpreted his operas, and he resented the cuts made by Nápravník at subsequent productions of *The May Night*. The opera was not too successful at the Mariinsky Theater. It was revived by a Moscow opera company in 1892 and for a time attracted good audiences, but it was eventually replaced in the repertory by Leoncavallo's *I Pagliacci*, "a swindling score created by a modern musical careerist," as Rimsky-Korsakov ruefully described it.

Capriccio espagnol, *Op. 34 (1887)*

The most effective Spanish pieces for orchestra have been written by Frenchmen and Russians. Rimsky-Korsakov's Spanish suite of five pieces, played without pause and entitled, for want of a better description, *Capriccio espagnol*, is a particularly brilliant example of Russian Spanish orchestration. In a letter to V. Yastrebtzev, Rimsky-Korsakov's Boswell and "phonographic and photographic" biographer, as he was known in Rimsky-Korsakov's family, Rimsky-Korsakov writes: "How strange! It seems that I like to orchestrate better than to compose." In his *Chronicle of My Musical Life*, Rimsky-Korsakov points out the difference between a "well-orchestrated piece" and a "brilliant composition for orchestra." He puts his *Capriccio espagnol* in the latter category, a piece conceived for orchestra and inseparable from orchestral timbres. Instrumental **cadenzas**, the role of percussion, figurations and **embellishments**, all these, he maintains, are not mere elaborations and exercises in **tone color**, but integral parts of the whole.

The composition of *Capriccio espagnol* was completed on August 4, 1887. A year later, *Scheherazade* was written. These orchestral works mark the conclusion of a period in Rimsky-Korsakov's evolutionary style, which he defines by two characteristics, the attainment of a virtuoso style in orchestration, without Wagner's influence toward the enlargement of sonorous means, and the lessening of purely **contrapuntal** writing. In place of elaborate **polyphony**, Rimsky-Korsakov makes increasing use of melodic ornamentation, and its logical outgrowth, the art of variation. The first performance of *Capriccio espagnol* was given in St. Petersburg at one of the series of Russian Symphony Concerts, on November 12, 1887, conducted by Rimsky-Korsakov himself. (The date of October 31, 1887, given in the dictionaries and orchestral program notes, is the old-style date of the Russian calendar, which in the nineteenth century was twelve days behind the West's.)

Capriccio espagnol obtained a great success at its initial performance, and quickly became a repertoire piece. Its hispanicism is, of course, external, but the stylization of Spanish

Cadenza (It.). An elaborate passage played or improvised by the solo instrument at the end of the first or last movements of a concerto.

Embellishment. Also called a grace; a vocal or instrumental ornament not essential to the melody or harmony of a composition.

Tone-color. Quality of tone; timbre.

Contrapuntal. Pertaining to composition with two or more simultaneous melodies.

Polyphonic. Consisting of two or more independently treated melodies; contrapuntal; capable of producing two or more tones at the same time, as the piano, harp, violin, xylophone.

Serenade. An instrumental composition imitating in style an "evening song," sung by a lover before his lady's window.

Semitone. A half tone; the smallest interval in the Western scale.

Minor. Latin word for "smaller," used in music in three different senses: 1. A *smaller* interval of a kind, as in minor second, minor third, minor sixth, minor seventh; 2. A key, as in *A* minor, or a scale, as in *A* minor scale; 3. A minor triad, consisting of a root, a minor third, and a perfect fifth above the root.

Dominant. The fifth tone in the major or minor scales; a chord based on that tone.

Tonic. The keynote of a scale; the triad on the keynote (tonic chord).

Fandango (Sp.). A lively dance in triple time, for two dancers of opposite sex, who accompany it with castanets or tambourine.

melodies and rhythms is remarkably effective. The name of the opening dance, Alborada (from the Latin and Spanish word *albor*, "whiteness, dawn") is often defined as "morning serenade." But since a **serenade** is itself an evening song, Alborada is a "morning evening song," which is as complicated a description as Erik Satie's *Crépuscule matinal (de midi)* ("morning twilight at noon"). Rimsky-Korsakov's Alborada is an explosive orchestral dance in A major, duple time, with several instrumental solos for contrast. It leads to a movement entitled Variations, in F major, in slow 3/8 time. The horns announce the theme, and the first variation, given by the strings, is followed by an instrumental colloquy between the English horn and the French horn. Then the orchestra enters in full. A flute solo marks the transition to the next movement, which latter is a return of the Alborada, a **semitone** higher. The orchestration is, of course, different—a fact that justifies the repetition.

The next movement is a series of instrumental cadenzas under the general title Scene and Gypsy Song. The Gypsy-ness of the song is indicated by a sort of illegitimate Mixolydian or Hypoaeolian mode, derived from a **minor** scale, with the **dominant** serving as a **tonic**. This mode has done excellent service in nineteenth-century music as an "ersatz" for non-tempered Oriental or Near-Eastern scales. There is a parenthetic flourish in the opening fanfare for horns and trumpets, and there is a flight of ornament in the ensuing violin cadenza. The flute and the clarinet play flourishes and ornaments in their turn, and finally the harp spreads a luxuriant foliage of scale passages with the triangle's metallic assistance. The Gypsy Song proper enters in the violins.

The movement gains in definiteness of rhythm, leading to the last number of the suite, an Asturian **fandango**, in A major, triple time, the theme announced by the trombones. The derivation of the name *fandango* has been traced by amateur etymologists to the playing on the lute (*fidicinare*), but it seems that the dance and the name were brought to Spain from the West Indies. The rhythm is similar to that of the **bolero**, but it has been said that while the bolero intoxicates, the fandango inflames. Rimsky-Korsakov felt the necessity of a well-rounded form very strongly, and could not resist the urge to return to the scene of the first act, to the initial theme and key. Accordingly, the Alborada returns suddenly, and the piece ends in the spirit of its beginning.

Bolero (Sp.). A Spanish national dance in 3/4 time and lively tempo (*allegretto*), the dancer accompanying his steps with castanets.

The treatment of Spanish melodies in Rimsky-Korsakov's *Capriccio espagnol* has become a model for some Spanish composers. Yet Rimsky-Korsakov himself borrowed his materials for this work from a collection of songs by the Spanish composer José Inzenga, retaining not only the melodies and the rhythms of the originals, but the harmonization as well, much as Bizet used the "Chanson Havanaise" by Yradier for his "Habanera" in *Carmen*.

Symphonic Suite: **Scheherazade ("After 'A Thousand and One Nights'"), *Op. 35* (1888)**

A composer's physical appearance seldom provides a clue to his musical style. Rimsky-Korsakov's case confirms this adage. He wore a professorial beard, led a dignified life, was a good family man, and proved himself a fine administrator during his tenure as director of the St. Petersburg Conservatory. This is a drab life story, out of character with the luscious sound of his exotic music, filled to the brim as it is with quasi-Oriental melodies fashioned in serpentine spirals and colubrine convolutions.

In the total absence of filmable amours and licentious behavior in Rimsky-Korsakov's disconcertingly placid life, the caliphs of Baghdad-on-the-Hollywood-Hills, eager to make use of his technicolorful music, performed a pogonotomy on his chin and, dipping a greasy hand into a barrel of schmaltz, came up with a spectacular movie version of the Russian master's life. In it, a clean-shaven Rimsky-Korsakov lounges in an

SCHEHERAZADE.
Suite symphonique.

I.

N.Rimsky-Korsakow, Op.35.

Algerian bistro and, enraptured by a sultry, dark-eyed ecdysiast, jots down on the back of a menu the score of a belly dance, which is performed the next night by a large Algerian orchestra. But what is this music? It is *Scheherazade*, electrically amplified, stuffed with saxophones and topped with bongos! This is the Rimsky-Korsakov Hollywood likes to chew gum by. Rimsky-Korsakov's family tried to protest against this outrage, but in vain. There is no copyright protection for Russian music, and it is wide open to such depredations.

Scheherazade is by far the most popular symphonic score by Rimsky-Korsakov. Its four movements represent tales told by Scheherazade to her uxoricidal Sultan Schahriar, who, with the nonchalance of a Henry VIII, puts his wives to death after their first night together. The sultana stays the hand of doom by a serial recital of 1001 Arabian tales, keeping the sultan in suspense at the most dramatic point of her story, so that his curiosity is aroused and he cannot afford to have her done away with.

The connecting link of all four movements is a violin solo representing Scheherazade's introduction to each tale. The action opens with a series of mighty unisons in the orchestra, portraying the stern sultan. It is followed by a series of modally disposed triadic progressions in the woodwinds. Scheherazade's violin solo introduces the first tale, that of "The Sea and Sinbad's Ship." The seas roll gently in **barcarole** time, 6/4, in the aquamarine key of E major. Tropical fish pass in colorful array in the woodwinds, as Sinbad's ship sails smoothly upon Rimsky-Korsakov's waters.

The second movement tells the story of "The Kalandar Prince." It is set in the maritime tonality of B minor, the key of yet another sea piece, Mendelssohn's overture *The Hebrides (Fingal's Cave)*. Scheherazade's violin solo is heard again. The main movement is a **Scherzo**, with the saturnine bassoon assigned the role of the narrator of the adventures of the exotic prince.

Barcarole (Ger.). A vocal or instrumental piece imitating the song of the Venetian gondoliers.

Scherzo (It.). A joke, jest; an instrumental piece of a light, piquant, humorous character. Also, a vivacious movement in the symphony, with strongly marked rhythm and sharp and unexpected contrasts in both rhythm and harmony; usually the third movement.

The third movement is a romance recounting the simple story of a sentimental love of a young prince for a young princess, projected by the violins in the bland key of G major, in gentle 6/8 time. In the background are heard the tintinnabulations of a tinkling triangle and a jingling tambourine.

The finale is a festive drama. Scheherazade and her violin open the curtains on the great festival of the fabled city of Baghdad, **Allegro** molto e frenetico, in the principal key of E minor, in barcarole time of 6/8. But a tempest is brewing on the troubled ocean. A Leviathanlike trombone roars defiance of reckless sailors, and is echoed by an anxious trumpet. Sinbad's ship founders on the rocks with a fearful bitonal crash. As the storm subsides, the soft chords of the opening are heard again, and Scheherazade concludes her last Arabian tale on the highest harmonics of the violin.

It is hard to believe that *Scheherazade* was damned in the American press as an abomination of musical desolation. "The Russians have captured Boston!" cried the American music historian Louis Elson in 1905. "The Scheherazade engagement began with a bombardment of full orchestra, under cover of which the woodwinds advanced on the right. A furious volley of kettledrums followed, bringing up the trombone reserves and the remaining brasses. At this, the entire audience, including some very big guns, surrendered."

Le Coq d'or (The Golden Cockerel): *Introduction to the Wedding Procession (1906–7)*

Rimsky-Korsakov's opera *Le Coq d'or* was the last and musically most remarkable of his operas. The score introduces modernistic procedures far beyond the habitual language of Rimsky-Korsakov's music: **whole-tone scales**, polyharmonies, combining augmented **triads** and **diminished-seventh chords**, and **arabesques** teetering on the edge of **atonality**.

Rimsky-Korsakov did not live to see the production of *Le*

Allegro (It.). Lively, brisk, rapid.

Whole-tone scale. Scale consisting only of whole tones, lacking dominant and either major or minor triads; popularized by Debussy.

Triad. A "three-tone" chord composed of a given tone (the root), with its third and fifth in ascending order in the scale.

Diminished-seventh chord. A chord consisting of three conjunct minor thirds, outlining a diminished seventh between the top and bottom notes.

Arabesque. A type of fanciful pianoforte piece; ornamental passages accompanying or varying a theme.

Atonality. The absence of tonality; music in which the traditional tonal structures are abandoned and there is no key signature.

Coq d'or on account of a squabble with the Imperial censorship office regarding some verses in the libretto, taken verbatim from a fairy tale of Pushkin's. Russia had just suffered a humiliating defeat in its war with Japan; a powerful revolutionary movement against the regime of the lassitudinous Czar Nicholas II was in full swing. The picture of a mythical czar, constantly dropping off to sleep (Nicholas II was somewhat narcoleptic), dallying with an Oriental princess (the affair of Nicholas II with the ballerina Kszesinska was freely reported in underground pamphlets), indulging in absurd diplomacy that led to disaster, was too close to Pushkin's tale and Rimsky-Korsakov's opera for comfort. The concluding verse, "The fable is false, but there is a lesson in it for certain people," was an invitation to draw embarrassing parallels, and the czar's censors wanted it deleted. Rimsky-Korsakov refused to submit to alterations, but they were finally made in the posthumous production of *Le Coq d'or* in Moscow on October 7, 1909. The original version was not restored until after the Revolution of 1917.

The coq d'or of the title refers to a weather vane in the shape of a rooster, presented to the czar by an astrologer (whose part is given to a **countertenor** singing **falsetto**, imitating the voice of a human gelding) to ward off aggression. The coq d'or is magically sensitive to movements of armies across the border. When all is well the cockerel crows the all-clear signal to the czar: "Reign lying on your bed!" But when hostilities threaten, it sounds a vociferous cock-a-doodle-doo, waking up the lackadaisical czar and alarming his somnolent kingdom. Elated, the czar promises the astrologer any reward he wishes, but is dismayed when the canny magician demands the czar's slinky bride in payment for his radar rooster. "What use is a girl to him?" asks the puzzled monarch. But the astrologer insists, and the czar, losing his patience, strikes him dead with his scepter. Thereupon the rooster takes off from his perch, alights on the czar's head and pecks him to death in the medulla oblongata.

Countertenor. A male singer with an alto range.
Falsetto. The highest of the vocal registers.

GUSTAV MAHLER
(1860–1911)
Musical Prometheus

THE LIFE AND MUSIC OF Gustav Mahler can be fully understood only in the setting of his time and place, prewar Vienna, Januslike in its dual aspect of the gay capital of the waltz, and the seat of heavy intellectualism and searching philosophy. This was the city of Franz Lehár, and also of Freud; of the pleasure-loving royalty and of the tragic Mahler. It must be understood that at that time the Wagnerian wave was still rolling strong; composers did not merely write music: they created philosophies, founded religions. Although Mahler invariably denied that his **symphonies** had a program or a story behind them, each work was a chapter in his struggle with himself or, as he believed, a struggle with some mystical evil force.

Symphony. An orchestral composition in from three to five distinct movements or divisions, each with its own theme(s) and development.

Nietzsche once said that music of genius throws sparks of images. Mahler's music belongs to his category. Bruno Walter, the famous conductor, who was a protégé of Mahler, gives this evaluation of Mahler as a musician: "He was a great man whose visions, aspirations, and emotions reached to the utmost boundaries of human understanding. His musical inspiration came from his deep humanity and love of nature. But as a composer, he produced works that can be understood from a purely musical standpoint." As a composer, Mahler aroused controversy. Hostile critics assailed the alleged diffuseness of form and unconscionable length of his symphonies. Then the tide turned inexplicably and he came to be regarded as one of the greatest symphonists of his time.

Mahler's symphonicism is philosophical, proceeding from a guiding idea and developing as freely as human thought itself. He was not fearful of repetition when the musical ideas required emphasis, or of free association as a source of inspiration. His music was not all introspection and profundity; the emotional turbulence of his symphonic writing alternated with moments of hedonistic insouciance, signaled by the sudden intrusion of Viennese waltz tunes. In his philosophical moods, he probed eternal verities; in his topical digressions, he was an interested observer of the real world around him. For all his mystical strivings, Mahler retained in his music a vivid sense of local habitation, his beloved Viennese countryside. In each of his symphonies there is a welcome breath of fresh air from the fields, suggesting the simple melodic turns of rustic songs. In this, Mahler was a true heir of Beethoven, who also knew how to relax the philosophical profundity of his music with a gay rhythm or a folklike tune.

In selecting texts for his song cycles, Mahler, in common with his fellow Romanticists, was irresistibly drawn to poets obsessed by morbid hopelessness, grim anticipation, forlorn fatefulness. Yet these poets, and Mahler, who set their words to music, let a gleam of ultimate hope shine through the darkest of moods. Typical in this respect is Mahler's song "At Midnight." As the poet lies awake, no star smiles at him from the black firmament; he feels he is entrusted with the battle of all humanity, but his powers are too weak, and he surrenders the task into the hands of a greater power that keeps eternally the vigil of midnight. And the music, torn with long suspended **dissonances**, reflects this mood with trumpet sounds, concluding in a triumphant major key.

Dissonance. A combination of two or more tones requiring resolution.

Mahler was the last Romantic composer in the last refuge of romanticism, Vienna. The First World War killed the spirit of old Europe, the nonchalant gaiety, the poetic sentimentality, and the Romantic conviction that subjective art has objective significance. His life and his music were two facets of the same spirit. Not as unsuccessful as his spiritual brother, Anton Bruckner, he made his life much more tragic than it was. Mahler was a great conductor and as such could gather financial rewards that would have been denied him had he been only the composer of complex and rarely performed symphonic works. But the afflatus of tragedy made Mahler's physical life precarious.

Universality of gifts is a Romantic ideal. Mahler approached this ideal, for he was a great interpreter of music at the conducting podium as well as a composer of extraordinary power. During his lifetime, he was known principally as director of the Vienna Opera, where he enjoyed great respect and wielded great power. Human frailty received little sympathy from Mahler. Once, when an opera soprano missed a rehearsal on account of trouble with her vocal cords, Mahler remarked: "What vocal cords? I never knew she had any." In Rome, he lectured the orchestra men on discipline and, with the aid of an Italian dictionary, accused them of *indolenza* and even *stupidità*, whereupon the orchestra went on strike. It took considerable diplomacy to patch up the quarrel and avoid the cancellation of the concert. As the musical director of the New York Philharmonic, Mahler had his difficulties with management and the all-powerful women's committee that held the purse strings and therefore ruled over the affairs of the orchestra. "In Vienna even the Emperor did not dictate to him," his wife Alma declared. "But in New York he had ten women ordering him about like a puppet." But Mahler never yielded to these pressures, and imperturbably maintained his Olympian air.

Chorus. A company of singers; a composition sung by several singers; also, the refrain of a song.

In the Romantic era, striving for greatness was quantitative. Berlioz and Liszt started the fashion by augmenting the orchestral and **choral** sources in their descriptive symphonic works. Wagner expanded the operatic form to tremendous proportions. Mahler's art owed much to Liszt and Wagner; to his symphonies he attached grandiose subtitles such as *Titan*, *Resurrection*, *The Giant*, and *Tragic*. His huge symphonies were often attacked as elucubrations of a self-deluded mind hermetically sealed from musical reality.

But in his own self Mahler was in a state of constant turbulence. In the margin of his unfinished Tenth Symphony he wrote: "Madness takes possession of me. . . . It destroys me, and I forget that I exist." Mahler's madness was not certifiable—it was the madness of a creative personality that tried to seize more fire from the heavens than Prometheus himself.

SYMPHONIES

Symphony No. 1 in D Major (Titan) *(1883–88)*

Mahler assigned programmatic titles to most of his symphonies, but later took them off and declared his works to be in the category of absolute music, independent of imagery or psychological content. He was twenty-eight years old when he completed his First Symphony, which he called *Titan*, with reference to the novel of that name by the Romantic writer Jean Paul Richter.

In its final form, following the classical model, Mahler's First Symphony is in four movements. (The original version of the work had five movements.) The **tempo** marks, in German: "Slowly, dragging"; "Powerfully turbulent"; "Solemnly and measured, without dragging"; and "Tempestuously stirring." Within these four movements, Mahler assembles a variety of sentiments and expressions, from the subjective and philosophical to folklike grotesquerie.

He gave the title "Spring Without End" to the first movement. Bucolic moments animate the score. There is even a cuckoo call. The second movement, a **scherzo**, includes rhythms of Moravian dances and a waltz, a reminiscence of his youth, for Mahler was born in Moravia, then a part of the Austro-Hungarian Empire. The third movement was originally entitled "March in the Manner of Callot," inspired by an engraving of the seventeenth-century French artist Jacques Callot, in which the body of a dead hunter is taken to the grave, accompanied by dancing animals celebrating their freedom from his hunt. The last movement represents the apotheosis of the human soul emerging from darkness.

Tempo (It.). Rate of speed, movement; time, measure.

Scherzo (It.). A joke, jest; an instrumental piece of a light, piquant, humorous character. Also, a vivacious movement in the symphony, with strongly marked rhythm and sharp and unexpected contrasts in both rhythm and harmony; usually the third movement.

Symphony No. 4 in G Major (Humoresque) *(1899–1901)*

For a long time after Mahler's death, his symphonies virtually disappeared from the concert repertory and were cultivated only by partisan admirers among conductors, principally Willem Mengelberg and Bruno Walter. Then the tide turned spectacularly. Mahler's music, so unashamedly Romantic in its essence and in its musical language, somehow found a resonance in the new generation. His symphonies were resurrected and he was proclaimed one of the greatest symphonists of all time.

Mahler gave grandiose programmatic subtitles to many of his symphonies; an exception was his Fourth Symphony, which he originally planned to name *Humoresque*. It was to be in six movements, each with a definite program: "The World as an Eternal Present"; "The Earthly Life"; "Caritas"; "Morning Bells"; "The World Without Trouble"; "The Heavenly Life." Some elements of this first scheme remained in the final product, which comprised four movements.

Mahler conducted the first performance of the Fourth Symphony in Munich, on November 25, 1901. The first movement is marked *Bedächtig, nicht eilen* ("Deliberately, unhurried"). It opens with an extraordinary exaltation of four flutes accompanied by sleighbells, conjuring up a pastoral scene so often represented in Mahler's symphonies. The main theme of the movement is in vigorous G major; the second theme, even more assertive, is in the **dominant**, thus suggesting the key relationship of orthodox **sonata form**. But within this traditional framework, Mahler indulges in a constant change of mood and manner, indicated by such romantic expression marks as "Fresh," "Broadly sung," "Flowingly." In the **fortissimo** ending, Mahler instructs the oboes and clarinets to hold bells up, a device common in horns and trumpets employed to achieve greater sonority, but rarely, if ever, applied to woodwind instruments.

The second movement, *In gemächlicher Bewegung, ohne Hast* ("In an easy motion, without haste"), is a leisurely scherzo, in 3/8, in the key of C minor. Here Mahler introduces an unusual innovation, a scordatura (i.e., discordatura, mistuning) in the first violin solo, with all four strings tuned a whole tone up in order to achieve greater brilliance. The violin thus becomes a transposing instrument. Scordatura is common in Baroque music (Vivaldi uses it in his violin concertos), but in symphonic works it is exceptional. Novelty always tempted Mahler. The mood of the scherzo is that of a wistful Viennese **Ländler** dance. A mournful horn signal is echoed by an angst-laden figure in the oboe. The lachrymal flatted **submediant** is in evidence when the movement modulates into a major key. Formally, there are five sections, three

Dominant. The fifth tone in the major or minor scales; a chord based on that tone.

Sonata form. Usually the procedure used for first movements of classical symphonies, sonatas, and chamber works; may be used for other movements as well.

Fortissimo (It.). Extremely loud.

Ländler (Ger.). A slow waltz of South Germany and the Tyrol (whence the French name "Tyrolienne"), in 3/4 or 3/8 time.

Submediant. The third scale tone below the tonic; the sixth degree.

scherzolike expositions, and two triolike interludes separating them.

The third movement, *Ruhevoll* ("Peacefully"), in the key of G major, in 4/4 time, is the one that Mahler described as "spherical," in the sense of a continuous surface of sounds, without a beginning or an end, an idea that is advanced by ultramodern composers of the last third of the twentieth century. Mahler's vision was prophetic. The movement is in the form of free variation, in five distinct divisions, each based on a theme bearing a morphological likeness to the other four. Regarding this movement, Mahler said to Natalie Bauer-Lechner that it represents the first set of true variations he had ever written, variations that really vary, as real variations ought to do. He described his own idea of the movement: "The music is pervaded by a divinely merry and profoundly mournful melody so that you can only laugh and weep listening to it."

The fourth movement, *Sehr behaglich* ("Very leisurely"), in 4/4 time, is set in the principal key of the Symphony, G major. This is the movement that has a **soprano** solo, another unusual element. The words are from the collection of German folk songs *Des Knaben Wunderhorn*, arranged and rephrased by Mahler. A stern warning is inserted in the score: "It is of the greatest importance that the singer should be accompanied with utmost discretion." Among instrumental novelties there are **glissandos** in the cello part. The text justifies Mahler's visual impression of "perpetual cerulean blue" in the music, which was intended to portray "the heavenly life":

> Wir geniessen die himmlischen Freuden, d'rum tun wir das Irdische meiden. Kein weltlich' Getümmel hört man nicht im Himmel! Lebt Alles in sanftester Ruh! Wir führen ein englisches Leben! Sind dennoch ganz lustig, ganz lustig daneben!

> We enjoy the heavenly pleasures, thus we avoid the earthly things. No worldly strife is heard in Heaven! All

Soprano (It.). The highest class of the human voice; the female soprano is also known as *treble*.

Glissando (It.). A slide; a rapid scale. On bowed instruments, a flowing, unaccented execution of a passage. On the piano, a rapid scale effect obtained by sliding the thumb, or thumb and one finger, over the keys.

lives in most gentle restfulness! We live an angelic life! Yet we are quite cheerful, quite cheerful as well!

Symphony No. 6 in A Minor (Tragic) *(1903–5)*

The Sixth Symphony is frequently referred to as Mahler's *Tragic* Symphony. He conducted its first performance in Essen on May 27, 1906. Romantic commentators found in it the expression of an unequal struggle of a human soul against a hostile destiny.

The work is in four movements. The first movement, **Allegro** energico, in 4/4 time, is in the key of A minor. The principal theme is built on a vigorous descending melodic leap of an **octave**, which may be interpreted as the "motive of destiny." The development introduces seraphic melodies that form a contrasting group of thematic materials. Throughout, there is an alternation of minor and major **triads**, symbolizing the duality of pessimism and optimism.

The second movement is a scherzo. The rhythm undergoes a series of singular variations, suggesting a mischievous poltergeist at play. An ironic mood pervades this movement, with a sad smile behind the dancing notes. The third movement, **Andante** moderato, is a bucolic vignette, with an optimistic outlook depicted in the resonant major keys of E and E-flat. Hunting horns and tinkling cowbells paint a pastoral landscape in the background.

The finale is counterposed to the first three movements, equaling their combined length. There is an abundance of new thematic materials, interspersed among recollections of the motive of destiny originally sounded in the first movement. The strokes of a heavy hammer illustrate the finality of the unequal struggle. The thematic alternation of major and minor **tonic** triads emphasizes the conflict. The symphony ends in resigned submission.

Mahler was given an ovation at the first performance and

Allegro (It.). Lively, brisk, rapid.

Octave. A series of eight consecutive diatonic tones; the interval between the first and the eighth.

Triad. A "three-tone" chord composed of a given tone (the root), with its third and fifth in ascending order in the scale.

Andante (It.). Going, moving; moderately slow tempo.

Tonic. The keynote of a scale; the triad on the keynote (tonic chord).

was recalled eight times to the podium. The critics were not as enthusiastic. An American correspondent contributed a disdainful report in the *Musical Courier* of New York. "Mahler's Sixth Symphony," he wrote, "contains not one original thought. One hears a few notes of Tchaikovsky's B-flat-minor concerto, of *Carmen*, of the *Faust* Overture by Wagner. Mahler patches together these stray scraps from ancient and modern music with a conventional thread or two of his own, making a heterogeneous crazy quilt of music." This stood in open contradiction to an intelligent review in a Vienna newspaper written by Julius Korngold, who found in the symphony "a colossal structure built up in a thoroughly thematic style, and at the same time in a strict unity of sentiment, which Mahler designated as a tragic one." But even Korngold had misgivings. He thought that the music had a "nerve-wracking intensity that operates like an alarm."

Symphony No. 8 in E-flat Major (Symphony of a Thousand) *(1906–7)*

Mahler's Eighth Symphony, the last that he conducted himself, was advertised before its world premiere in 1910 in Munich as "The Symphony of a Thousand," for indeed the number of performers was in the vicinity of a thousand—an orchestra of 150, two mixed choruses aggregating to 500 voices, a children's choir of 350, and 8 soloists. The German papers grumbled against the high-pitched promotion, which they found in "echt amerikanischer" bad taste. But Mahler was above such mundane preoccupations, intent only on the adequate preparation of the immensely difficult and long work, rehearsing each instrumental and choral group separately for weeks before putting the whole ensemble together. The "Symphony of a Thousand" was not even a real symphony. It consisted of two parts, the first sung in Latin to the text of a medieval hymn, and the second in German to selected passages from the last act of Goethe's *Faust*, with its enigmatic conclusion: "All that

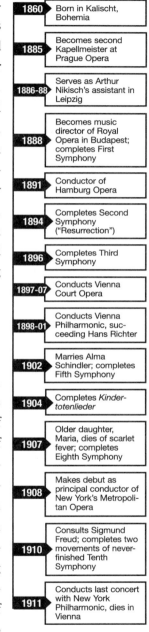

Mahler Timeline

1860	Born in Kalischt, Bohemia
1885	Becomes second Kapellmeister at Prague Opera
1886–88	Serves as Arthur Nikisch's assistant in Leipzig
1888	Becomes music director of Royal Opera in Budapest; completes First Symphony
1891	Conductor of Hamburg Opera
1894	Completes Second Symphony ("Resurrection")
1896	Completes Third Symphony
1897–07	Conducts Vienna Court Opera
1898–01	Conducts Vienna Philharmonic, succeeding Hans Richter
1902	Marries Alma Schindler; completes Fifth Symphony
1904	Completes *Kindertotenlieder*
1907	Older daughter, Maria, dies of scarlet fever; completes Eighth Symphony
1908	Makes debut as principal conductor of New York's Metropolitan Opera
1910	Consults Sigmund Freud; completes two movements of never-finished Tenth Symphony
1911	Conducts last concert with New York Philharmonic, dies in Vienna

passes is but a parable. All that is unattainable is the true event. The eternally feminine draws us near."

Its first performance was a triumph for Mahler; the large Exposition Concert Hall in Munich was filled with admirers, detractors, and the curious. Richard Strauss sat in the front of a box and read the piano score through a lorgnette. The musicians in the audience were impressed. The newspaper dispatches were purple with metaphors: "Flames seemed to dart from Mahler as he conducted. A thousand wills obeyed his will." But some professional music critics were openly derisive in their reviews. "Eight trumpeters and four trombone players stood up in a row at the top of the platform and blew for all they were worth into the faces of the audience," wrote an American observer. "There was also a gentleman who played on a large concert grand piano. He was very industrious. I know it because I saw him. Unfortunately, in the general clamor, none of his notes even got as far as my ear."

VOCAL MUSIC

Songs of a Wayfarer (Lieder eines fahrenden Gesellen) *(1883–85)*

The cycle of four songs, *Songs of a Wayfarer* was Mahler's first significant work, written when he was in his early twenties, to his own texts. They are songs of frustrated love, a frequent theme of German poetry. The music is remarkable, for it contains virtually all of Mahler's melodic, rhythmic, and harmonic elements later developed in his symphonies—the characteristic transitions from momentary exhilaration to depressive sadness, the use of folklike dance rhythms, the ambivalence of major and minor modes, revealed particularly in his predilection for the lowered **subdominant** in major keys.

Subdominant. The tone below the dominant in a diatonic scale; the fourth degree.

The first song, "Wenn mein Schatz Hochzeit macht" ("When my Beloved Marries") portrays the distress of a lover

Songs of a Wayfarer
Lieder eines fahrenden Gesellen

1 Wenn mein Schatz Hochzeit macht

whose beloved is married to another. Mahler described the various effects and actions on that sad day: "I go into my little room, darkened room, and I weep over my treasured one," but still he calls her "little blue flower" and "sweet little bird." But "all songs are now gone!"

The second song, "Ging heut' morgen übers Feld" {"This Morning I Walked over the Field"), is an ode to nature, a union with life in the fields. There are musical links in it with the finale of Mahler's Fourth Symphony and the "youth" movement in *The Song of the Earth*.

The third song, "Ich hab' ein glühend Messer" ("I Have a Glowing Knife"), pictures the poet with a glowing dagger of pain in his heart, that "cuts so deeply into every joy and every desire." When he looks at the sky he sees the two blue eyes of his beloved there; when he ventures into a yellow field he sees her again; and when he awakens from his dream, he hears her silvery laughter.

The fourth song, "Die zwei blauen Augen" ("The Two Blue Eyes"), is another variation on the theme of love: "The blue eyes of my dear treasure sent me out into the faraway world, into the silent night." He falls asleep under a tree, which bestrews him with blossoms. This brings him back to life, and everything is good again. But the final third in the music is the minor third.

Songs of the Death of Children (Kindertotenlieder) *(1901–4)*

To Gustav Mahler, music was a language so profoundly human and at the same time so impenetrably arcane that he could fully accept Schopenhauer's aphorism that a person who can understand the message of music will achieve the knowledge of ultimate mysteries of the universe. Mahler's whole life seemed to exemplify this theomachy through music. He wrestled with the gods. The music he wrote was to him a phenomenon that might affect the destiny not only of himself, but

Kindertotenlieder
Songs of the Deaths of Children

1 Nun will die Sonn' so hell aufgeh'n!

also of others. He blamed himself for the death of his infant child, which occurred shortly after he wrote his *Songs of the Death of Children* to extremely morbid texts dealing with the death of small children. On the margins of the manuscript of his unfinished Tenth Symphony he scrawled: "Devil! Come and take me away with you, for I am accursed!" Even his sense of humor had a morbid turn. Asked whether he was satisfied with a performance of one of his works, he replied, "Do not speak of it! The very thought makes me turn in my grave!"

For the texts of his song cycle he selected five poems by Friedrich Rückert. Rückert, a nineteenth-century German poet, some of whose verses were set to music by Schubert and Schumann, wrote the poems after the death of his own two children from scarlet fever. Mahler set them to music in 1902, and arranged them for orchestra three years later. When Mahler's own daughter, Maria Anna, died, also of scarlet fever, at the age of four in 1907, he said that it was perhaps a defiance of fate to have written the songs. Indeed, the German originals touch the ultimate in irremediable grief. Here are the mottoes of the five songs:

1. Now the sun will rise so brightly as though no disaster struck in the night. Misfortune happened to me alone. The sun shines on all.
2. Now I know why your eyes reflected these dark flames. I did not suspect then that the beam was already directed there, where all light is born.
3. When your mother enters the door, I turn my head, not toward her, but toward the place near the threshold where I used to see your dear little face when you joyfully came in, O, my little daughter.
4. Often I think they have merely gone out. Soon they will be back in the house. The day is bright! O do not be anxious! They merely took a longer walk.
5. In such a storm, I would never let the children out of the house! Yet they have been taken away, and I did not dare to say a word.

Chromatic. Relating to tones foreign to a given key (scale) or chord; opposed to diatonic.

Mahler's musical settings of Rückert's poems reveal a rare affinity of feeling between poet and musician. The **chromatic** and **diatonic** steps in the melody are used with literal correspondence to pervading anguish or imagined hope, and the instrumental accompaniment often picks up the singing line in the middle of a phrase, as if to express the speechlessness of words. The last song ends with an otherworldly lullaby: "They rest there, in storm, as in a mother's house." Mahler makes this notation in the published edition of the songs: "These five songs are intended as one inseparable unit, and in performance their continuity should not be broken by applause at the close of any of the songs, or by any other interference."

Diatonic. Employing the tones of the standard major or minor scale.

The Song of the Earth (Das Lied von der Erde) *(1907–9)*

Bruno Walter, Mahler's friend and interpreter, tells a strange story that could have come from Edgar Allan Poe:

> While at work in his cottage in Toblach, [Mahler] was suddenly frightened by an indefinable noise. All at once something terribly dark came rushing in by the window, and when he jumped up in horror, he saw that he was in the presence of an eagle which filled the little room with its violence. The fearsome meeting was quickly over, and the eagle disappeared as stormily as it had come. When Mahler sat down, exhausted by his fright, a crow came fluttering from under the sofa and flew out.

Bruno Walter thinks that this episode happened at the time Mahler was composing *The Song of the Earth*, and that Mahler referred to the work as a symphony in songs: "It was to have been his Ninth. Subsequently, however, he changed his mind. He thought of Beethoven and Bruckner, whose Ninth had marked the ultimate of their creation and life, and did not care to challenge fate. He turned to the Abschied [Farewell— the last movement] and said: What do you think of it? Will not people do away with themselves when they hear it?"

But Mahler did write a Ninth Symphony, and even started on a Tenth. As to *The Song of the Earth*, it is not numbered among Mahler's symphonies at all. It must therefore be considered, as Mahler said to Bruno Walter, a symphony of songs, separate from his purely symphonic works.

The selection of texts to these songs is also characteristic for the spirit of prewar Europe. It was a set of Chinese poems, translated into German. Chinese poetry and Japanese art were extremely popular among European intellectuals who believed there was in the Orient an immediacy of feeling, a spirit of communion with the eternal that no Westerner could approach. The selection of poetry cannot, therefore, be accidental, and must be regarded as part of the design. All songs of *The Song of the Earth* are united by a single motto, a descending progression of three tones, A—G—E. These three tones may be regarded as a part of the Chinese **pentatonic scale**, but there is no evidence that Mahler made this connection. The motive was not used explicitly; rather it was Mahler's private magic formula, which he employed in various forms, in **augmentation** (that is, played twice as slowly) or **diminution** (twice as fast). It also appears in the **retrograde** motion, and in ascending intervals, through inversion. All three notes appear together in the concluding chord of the entire work, signifying unity. The symbolic quality of *The Song of the Earth* is thus plainly indicated; yet the movements are greatly diversified, from deep pantheistic contemplation to simple earthly joys.

There are six songs. The first is a "Drinking Song of the Misery of the Earth." The horns give the opening theme, which is built on the three notes of the leading motive. The violins present the leading motive in still another transformation. Tonality is clearly maintained throughout the first movement, but the **modulations** are frequent and sudden. The pessimistic refrain of the song "Dark is life, and so is death," is heard in a lugubrious phrase in G minor.

Pentatonic scale. A five-tone scale, usually that which avoids semitonic steps by skipping the fourth and seventh degrees in major and the second and sixth in minor.

Augmentation. Doubling (or increasing) the time value of the notes of a theme or motive, often in imitative counterpoint.

Diminution. The repetition or imitation of a theme in notes of smaller time value.

Retrograde. Performing a melody backwards; a crab movement. Also, one of three standard techniques in twelve-note composition (retrograde, inversion, transposition) wherein all notes of a set are played in reverse (i.e., backward).

Modulation. Passage from one key into another.

The second movement, or the second song, is entitled "The Lonely One in Autumn." It opens in D minor, and the characteristic indication in lieu of the tempo mark is "Somewhat dragging. Tired out." Against the background of muted violins, the oboe intones sadly the three notes of the leading motive. The **contralto** sings the song of loneliness and soul fatigue. The minor keys are remarkably prevalent.

Contralto (It.). The deeper of the two main divisions of women's or boys' voices, the soprano being the higher; also called alto.

The third song, "Of Youth," is one of the most optimistic utterances in symphonic literature, the scherzo of this symphony of songs. The orchestration abounds in woodwind color, and the impression of childish delight is heightened by the high register of the entire piece. Also, the Chinese pentatonic scale is used in this movement explicitly, imparting to the piece a definite local color.

The fourth movement is entitled "Of Beauty." The text of the song describes young maidens at play, and once more the pentatonic scale is explicitly employed. There are rhythmic figures that suggest a light dance. This and the third movement constitute the two spots of sunshine in Mahler's pessimistic symphony in songs.

The fifth movement is called "Drunkard in Spring." But the drinking is not gay, it is an escape from life's trouble. The theme is gay but wry, with melodic intervals distorted to express bitterness in artificial gaiety.

The sixth movement is "The Farewell." This is the movement that Mahler thought would inspire suicidal thoughts. The song describes the death of the day, when the sun sets, and the world falls asleep. The oboe, to which Mahler is wont to give his saddest tunes, plays solo against a subdued orchestra. The rhythm grows less distinct, and the feeling of farewell is achieved by a gradual fading away of all music. *The Song of the Earth* closes on a C-major chord with an added sixth. This added sixth is, of course, the high note of the leading motive, A—G—E.

The Song of the Earth was performed posthumously in

Munich, on November 20, 1911, six months and two days after Mahler's death; Bruno Walter conducted. The reception of the work and the estimate of its place among Mahler's works varied considerably. Ernest Newman, reviewing Walter's recording in the *Sunday Times of London* of November 27, 1939, places this music very high:

> *Das Lied von der Erde* is not only Mahler's greatest work, but one of the supreme creations of German music. In its special sphere—that of the mutual interpenetration of the two worlds of musical beauty and philosophic contemplation—it is without a rival since *Parsifal*. Not even *Parsifal*, indeed, moves us more profoundly than the long final section of *Das Lied von der Erde*, the concluding pages of which are without a doubt the saddest of all music.

On the other side of the balance is Philip Hale, who summed up Mahler's status in a review in the *Boston Herald* of October 17, 1931: "A strange figure in the symphonic field; a man of great moments but, as Rossini said of Wagner, of dreadful half-hours." "He was looked upon as a great artist, and possibly he was one," commented the *New York Tribune* after Mahler's death, "but he failed to convince the people of New York of the fact, and therefore his American career was not a success. We cannot see how any of his music can long survive him." The *New York Sun* said cryptically: "If he had gone to afternoon teas, he would have been more popular, and would be alive today."

CLAUDE DEBUSSY
(1862–1918)
Poet of Musical Impressions

THE FRENCH POET Stéphane Mallarmé (1842–98) wrote: "To name an object is to suppress three quarters of the enjoyment of a poem; this enjoyment consists of the happiness of divining the meaning little by little. To suggest—that is the dream." The music of Claude Debussy responds to these sentiments. Its melodies are ethereal; its suggestions are dreamlike. Music historians call him an Impressionist by analogy with the art of painting in small brush strokes. In his musical impressions, Debussy is attracted by the lesser manifestations of nature; the waves rather than the ocean; the gentle wind rather than the tempest; half-awakened human sensations rather than grand passions; the moon rather than the sun.

The titles of Debussy's works reflect this charm of the minuscule and elusive: "Footsteps in the Snow," "Mists," "The Shadows of the Trees," "Sounds and Perfumes," and "The Goldfish." In his most celebrated piece, "Clair de lune," Debussy paints the silvery moonbeams in delicate tones. The initial musical phrase seems motionless; its serenity is not disturbed when **arpeggios** begin to roll underneath like a mirrored image of the immobile moon in the sky. In that exquisite creation *Prélude à l'après-midi d'un faune* (*Prelude to "The Afternoon of a Faun"*), inspired by Mallarmé's poem, it is the pastoral flute that sets the mood of poetic dalliance; from that phrase, Debussy develops a charming miniature "in nostalgia and in light, with finesse, with yearning, with richness," as Mallarmé described the music in a letter to Debussy after hearing it for the first time.

Arpeggio (It.). Playing the tones of a chord in rapid, even succession.

In Debussy's symphonic sketch *La Mer*, the dialogue of the wind and the sea is at times turbulent, but the dynamic surgings are of brief duration, pulsating rhythmically without drowning the listener in a heaving tide of water music. The opening movement, "From Dawn to Noon on the Sea," draws a tonal picture of infinite delicacy, and yet the impression is precise. In his opera *Pelléas et Mélisande*, he depicted Maeterlinck's tragedy of love by indirection, in subdued colors, but the magic of this tonal understatement makes the music all the more impressive, and the emotions more penetrating than in conventional operatic writing.

This subtlety of impressions required the formation of a new musical language. Debussy developed his own melody, in poetical musical phrases, in free rhythm, in shimmering tonalities. He moved his harmonies in parallel motion, which was a radical departure from conventional practice. He emancipated discords and abolished the resolutions of dissonant chords prescribed by academic rules.

In search of fluid tonality, Debussy turned to a scale of **whole tones**, proceeding in uniform steps outside of either

Whole tone. A major second.

major or **minor** keys. From the Orient, he adopted the **pentatonic scale**, such as can be played on the black keys of the piano. One of his piano pieces is written in the **whole-tone scale**, with the middle section in the pentatonic scale on black keys. When he wished to evoke the archaic past, Debussy used the ancient modes, such as can be represented by scales played on white keys starting on other notes than C. In his harmony he applied the consecutive fifths, which were common in the simple music of the remote past, forbidden in classical harmony.

Debussy's orchestration was similarly unconventional; he favored unusual combinations of instruments. He gave most of his telling melodies to the gentle flute; his violins often hovered in high **treble**. He divided instrumental groups into several sections, so that each player had an individual part to perform. He was not building in large sonorities; rumbling basses and sounding brass had little attraction for him. He muted his horns to change their tone color; he relished the **pizzicato** strings and the plucked harp. In his orchestral tone paintings, each note had an individual importance; there was no filling out for external effect.

Such innovations, and such recessions to the old, came as a shock to Debussy's contemporaries. He was called an anarchist of music. He was accused of renouncing melody and of converting harmony into perpetual discord. Alarmed by the growing influence of Debussy's music on a new generation of composers, a group of French music theorists published a symposium of opinions under the pointed title *Le Cas Debussy* (*The Debussy Case*), in which Debussy was denounced as a false prophet. Numerous academic musicians expressed the conviction that Debussy's music was nothing but a symptom of decadence, and that it would never exercise lasting influence. Now that Debussy has become a classic of modern music, this little book makes strange reading.

Debussy excels in tonal miniatures and in half-spoken

Minor. Latin word for "smaller"; in minor keys, the third of the scale forms an interval of a minor third from the root.

Pentatonic scale. A five-tone scale, usually that which avoids semitonic steps by skipping the fourth and seventh degrees in major and the second and sixth in minor.

Whole-tone scale. A scale consisting only of whole tones, and therefore lacking the dominant and either major or minor triads; popularized by Debussy and his followers.

Treble. Soprano. *Treble clef:* the *G* clef.

Pizzicato (It.). Pinched; plucked with the finger; a direction to play notes by plucking the strings.

emotions. But he was also capable of great gaiety and of picturesque evocation of festive moods. There is nothing in contemporary orchestral writing that can rival the excitement and the beauty of Debussy's symphonic picture, "Iberia" (from *Images*). This music has more Spanish verve than many scores by the Spanish composers themselves. Debussy makes the violins sound like guitars; the players are instructed to take their instruments from under the chin, put them in their arms, and imitate the guitar by strumming the strings.

Exotic faraway lands fascinated Debussy. When he visited the Paris Exposition in 1889, it was not the Eiffel Tower (which was then inaugurated) that attracted him, but the Burmese dancers with their chimelike **gamelans**. He had never traveled to the Orient, but his imagination was stirred by its life and manners. For the cover of the published score of *La Mer,* he selected a Japanese print representing a breaking wave.

Debussy possessed a keen sense of humor. In his piano **suite**, *Children's Corner* (the original title is in English), he parodies the piano exercises of good old Clementi in a movement entitled "Doctor Gradus ad Parnassum." And in the last movement, "Golliwog's Cakewalk," written in the style of early American ragtime, he pokes fun at Wagner by introducing a motive from *Tristan and Isolde*, followed by musical laughter in the treble.

Debussy's art and his new technique are inseparable. His musical impressions could not be set within the framework of nineteenth-century ideas. He revolutionized music without in any way destroying the values of the old. No composer in the new century was unaffected by the profound change that Debussy brought about on the musical scene.

Prélude à l'après-midi d'un faune *(1892-94)*

In the annals of modern music, Debussy occupies an exalted niche as the founder of the French Impressionist movement. Debussy himself deprecated the term; he insisted that he was

Gamelan. A typical Indonesian orchestra, variously comprised of tuned gongs, chimes, drums, flutes, chordophones, xylophones, and small cymbals.

Suite (Fr.). A set or series of pieces in various (idealized) dance forms. The earlier suites have four chief divisions: the Allemande, Courante, Saraband, and Gigue. Also referred to as Classical Suite, or Baroque Suite; the modern orchestral suite is more like a divertimento.

a composer in the classical tradition of French music. In his later years he liked to add to his name the simple words "musicien français."

The word "impressionism" originated as a derisive neologism describing the manner of painting in Monet's picture *Sunrise, an Impression*, exhibited in 1863 in the Salon des Refusés, after it was rejected by the Paris Salon of acceptable art. Monet's innovation in his "impression" consisted in the subjective treatment of a landscape, in which the image is intentionally thrown out of focus and the lines are blurred so as to bring out the psychological aspects of the scene as perceived by the painter's eye and mind. Impressionism thus challenged the cardinal principles of classical and Romantic art—realism of representation and naturalism in detail.

Rather than be offended by the sarcastic designation, Monet and his group accepted it as an effective slogan, and openly declared themselves Impressionists. This was not the first time that contemptuous sobriquets had been adopted as honorific by their targets. *Sans-culottes*, literally "without knee-breeches," was a demeaning appellation used by French aristocrats for the poor of Paris, but it was picked up as a fighting cry by the disenfranchised populace. The Ashcan School, as a group of realistic American painters of the first decade of the twentieth century was collectively described by the critics, became the title of an honorable chapter in the history of American art. For that matter, "baroque," originally meaning "bizarre," "ungainly," or "tasteless," has been glorified in its application to the sublime art of Bach and Handel.

Is the analogy between French Impressionist art and the music of Debussy at all valid? Analytically, yes. In Debussy's works, as in the paintings of Monet, Manet, Degas, and Cézanne, subjective impressions of objective sounds and lights are recorded with free strokes of the brush; melodic and rhythmic lines are drawn in evanescent curves; the colors themselves are attenuated, often coalescing into a neutrality of complementary hues.

Paul Verlaine describes the essence of impressionism with penetrating intuition in his *Art poétique,* counterposing to the classical precept "est modus in rebus" (Horace's *Ars Poetica*) a refined concept of "la chanson grise où l'indécis au précis se joint" ("the gray song where the indistinct merges with the precise"). And, in a single expressive line, he sums up the aesthetic code of Symbolist poetry and Impressionist art alike: "Pas la couleur, rien que la nuance!" (No color, nothing but shades!) The formula fits Debussy's music to perfection: in it, the indecisiveness of the design is joined by the precision of execution. The gross colors are abandoned, and the fine nuance is installed as a chief artistic aim. Just as the eye is trained to differentiate between light and shadow in Impressionist art, so the ear is disciplined to register and absorb the measured quanta of sonic impulses in Impressionist music. Yet Debussy's melodic curves are nowhere discontinuous, and the melorhythmic particles are integrated in a musical wave in uninterrupted emanation.

Debussy was a master of subdued sonorities, emulating Verlaine's "chanson grise" in the gray but luminous radiation of his instrumental writing. Even his most disagreeable critic, Camille Bellaigue (who was Debussy's classmate at the Paris Conservatory), had to admit grudgingly that Debussy's music "fait peu de bruit" ("makes little noise"), but, he added malevolently, the small noise it makes is "un vilain petit bruit" ("mean little noise").

Triad. A "three-tone" chord composed of a given tone (the root), with its third and fifth in ascending order in the scale.

The technique of musical impressionism comprises many novel procedures: parallel progressions of **triads**, dominant-seventh chords and dominant-ninth chords; whole-tone scales, causing a temporary suspension of the sense of tonality; free application of unresolved dissonances; individualized instrumentation with unusual combinations of instruments; and, finally, abolition of academic conventions such as the development and **recapitulation**, in favor of a more supple associative process of composition.

Recapitulation. A return of the initial section of a movement in sonata form.

In no other work of Debussy is the spirit of impressionism revealed more poetically than in his *Prélude à l'après-midi d'un faune,* a symphonic eclogue inspired by the poem of Stéphane Mallarmé. Mallarmé, a Symbolist poet par excellence, paints a faun not as a familiar wood sprite of Greek mythology, but as a psychologically disturbed spirit of modern times, beset by anxieties and uncertain of his emotions. The faun reflects on the events of the afternoon of the previous day, reminiscing about his dalliance with sensuous nymphs. He tries desperately to perpetuate these elusive images before they vanish with the substance of his dreams. But were the ravishing creatures present in the reality of that afternoon, or were they the feverish figments of his superexcited imagination? Unable to resolve his doubts, the faun fashions a syrinx from reeds growing by the lake, and he plays upon it a hymn to love.

The *Prélude à l'après-midi d'un faune* was first performed at a concert of the Société Nationale de Musique in Paris on December 23, 1894. A curious notice appeared in a theatrical annual for that year: "The poem of Mallarmé, which inspired Debussy, is so sadistic that the management decided not to print it in the program book, because young girls attend these concerts."

Mallarmé was profoundly impressed by Debussy's music. "It extends the emotion of my poem," he said, "and it recreates the scene much more vividly than color could have done in painting." He inscribed his book of poems to Debussy with the following quatrain:

> Sylvain d'haleine première
> Si ta flûte a réussi
> Ouïs toute la lumière
> Qu'y soufflera Debussy!

It is interesting that in this inscription Mallarmé equates light with sound: "Sylvan of primal breath, |/| even if your flute has been successful,|/|listen to all the light|/|that Debussy will breathe into it."

The instrumentation of the *Prélude à l'après-midi d'un faune* is remarkable. There are no trumpets, no trombones, and no drums. The only instrument to mark the rhythmic caesura is a pair of antique cymbals. The flute is the faun, accompanied by other flutes, oboes, an English horn, clarinets, bassoons, four horns, two harps, and strings. The opening flute solo evokes the sound of a panpipe in undulating convolutions. Despite its fluctuating **chromatics**, the tonality, E major, is clearly outlined at cadential points. A contrasting theme arises in the violins; it is a spacious **diatonic** melody, limning the elusive and distant nymphs. Again the melancholy faun intones his dolent air, evoking Mallarmé's lines: "Ne murmure point d'eau que ne verse ma flûte au bosquet arrosé d'accords" ("No water murmurs except that which pours from my flute and sprinkles the plants with its harmony").

The ending is remarkable. Two horns join a solo violin in three-part harmony, forming a series of four mutually exclusive triads comprising all twelve notes of the chromatic scale. This is an intriguing anticipation of the dodecaphonic future of the new century.

Chromatic. Relating to tones foreign to a given key (scale) or chord; opposed to diatonic.

Diatonic. Employing the tones of the standard major or minor scale.

Pelléas et Mélisande *(1893, 1898, 1901–2)*

This work was Debussy's masterpiece, a lyric drama in five acts and twelve tableaux, which portrays with translucent penetration the peripeteia of Maurice Maeterlinck's poignantly symbolic play.

Debussy began the work in August 1893, completing the original score two years later. However, he then revised the score, completing a second version in 1898. He reorchestrated the second version in December 1901, and then finally composed some further symphonic interludes shortly before the first performance of the work on April 28, 1902.

Debussy's musical setting is of startling originality and

concentrated power of latent expressiveness. The voices sing the poetic lines according to the inflections of natural speech, following every nuance of sentiment in a continuously diversified declamation. The melodic curves tend toward their harmonic asymptotes in tangential proximity and form chords of quasi-bitonal consistency, the modal intervalic progressions with their concomitant cadential plagalities imparting a nostalgically archaic sound to the music. The frequent parallel motion of triadic units, seventh chords and ninth chords provide instant modulatory shifts, extensive vertical edifices in fourths and fifths reposing on deeply anchored **pedal points**, giving stability in fluidity, while the attenuated orchestra becomes a multicellular organism in which the instrumental solos are projected with pellucid distinction echoing the text in allusive symbolism (when light is mentioned, the strings are luminously tremulous; for water, harps respond). The psychologically adumbrative motives reflect the appearances of dramatic characters in graphically imprecise identifications.

Pedal point. A tone sustained in one part to harmonies executed in the other parts.

Two weeks before the dress rehearsal of the production, the Paris daily *Le Figaro* published an open letter from Maeterlinck sharply denouncing both Michel Carré's libretto and Debussy's setting and expressing a wish that the production should result in a "prompt and resounding failure." His wrath was aroused because Debussy preferred Mary Garden in the title role to Georgette Leblanc, Maeterlinck's common-law wife.

After the public dress rehearsal on April 28, many critics reacted favorably to the production. Still, there were some who were less-than-impressed, including Arthur Pougin writing in *Le Ménestrel*:

> The public is tired of hearing music which is not music; it is weary of this heavy, continuous declamation, without air and light; it is sated with this unsupportable abuse of chromatics, thanks to which all sense of tonality disap-

pears along with the melodic sense. . . . Rhythm, melody, tonality—these are three things that are unknown to M. Debussy. His music is vague, without color or nunace; without motion, without life. . . . What a collection of dissonances, sevenths and ninths, ascending even by disjunct intervals! . . . Very pretty! No. I will never have anything to do with these musical anarchists!

Nocturnes *(1892–99)*

Debussy composed his orchestral suite *Nocturnes* between 1892 and 1899. In a program note, he or someone speaking on his behalf pointed out that the title had nothing to do with the conventional form of nocturne as glorified by Chopin, but seeks to reflect the gradually diminished light of day before its nocturnal darkening. The first movement, *Nuages*, suggests such a twilight mood with clouds moving slowly in gentle two-part counterpoint, the kind of intervallic construction that suggested to some overeducated commentators a similar procedure in some of Mussorgsky's music; there is a justification for this parallel, for Debussy spent several months in Russia in his youth as a house pianist in the employ of Madame von Meck, the benefactor of Tchaikovsky, and was exposed to Russian music. Madame von Meck made him play a lot of her beloved Tchaikovsky, but later he picked up some Mussorgsky scores which produced a more lasting impression on him.

If *Nuages* is properly affiliated with twilight moods, the second part of the suite, *Fêtes*, is anything but nocturnal. Debussy's program note describes it as a festival of rhythm, dancing in the air, with bursts of sudden light. A procession passes through the festival and becomes a part of it; a luminous dust pervades the scene.

The third movement, *Sirènes*, is even more remote from nocturnal inspiration. It is scored for a women's chorus and orchestra. The chorus is wordless; the sirens did not have to lure Ulysses with articulate verbal exhortations. They sing in a curious undulation of major seconds, a manner calculated to produce a mesmerizing effect, which fits perfectly into the notion of what sirens must have sounded to the imagination of a French musician of the fin de siècle.

So distinct is the final movement of *Nocturnes* in its manner and instrumentation that it was not put on the program together with the two other movements at the first performance of the suite by the Lamoureux Orchestra, conducted by Camille Chevillard in Paris on December 9, 1900. The complete work, including *Sirènes*, was first produced by the same orchestra in Paris on October 27, 1901.

String Quartet, Op. 10 (1893)

During the desperate days of the German offensive in the First World War, Debussy proclaimed his national faith by signing, after his name, "Musicien français." Indeed, Debussy was a French musician to the core. To understand Debussy and his music, it is necessary to reconstruct the peculiar ambiance of literary and artistic France at the end of the century, the Paris of Baudelaire, Verlaine, and Mallarmé. The dictum of Mallarmé, whose poetry inspired Debussy's *Prélude à l'après-midi d'un faune*, might well be applied to the music of Debussy: "To name an object is to suppress three-quarters of the enjoyment of the poem, the pleasure of guessing step by step; to suggest is our aim."

But suggestion must also be imbued with logic, like the method of induction in mathematics: departing from a proved relationship between two initial members of a series, to establish this relationship for the entire series. Robert Jardillier, an ardent Debussyist, quotes this line of Verlaine, "cette fantaisie et cette raison," in discussing Debussy's Quartet:

> Reason? It is symbolized by the adoption of a cyclical theme, which pervades the entire Quartet, a close relative of the cantus firmus which unified the medieval Mass.

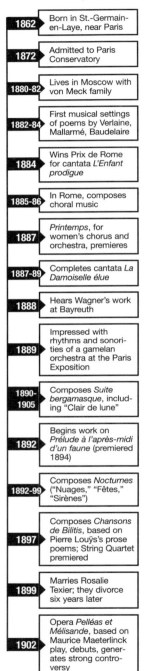

Fantasy? This theme undergoes so many modifications that it is hardly recognizable. It engenders, in the second movement, a sort of furtive Andalousian dance. It gives birth, an instant later, to an infinitely melancholy Andante. All this is bathed in vibrant harmony. This harmony was deemed revolutionary, but that was not its essence. Whether he invoked the pre-Raphaelite virgin, the night of Baudelaire, the park of Verlaine, or the fawn of Mallarmé, whether he gave free rein to his imagination in a string quartet, Debussy showed himself capable of offering, better than anyone else, a key to the life of dreams.

Indeed, the transfigurations of the theme of the quartet are audacious in the extreme. Here the danger of monotony is no less great than the opposite danger, of variegation to the point of the loss of identity. Debussy combats both dangers by deploying an extraordinary range of harmonic and rhythmic variety, still keeping the intervallic integrity of the theme. This theme is stated explicitly at the very opening and recurs, with almost no changes of outline, in all four instruments in the first movement of the quartet, against the varied counterpoint of the rest of the voices, or in the splendid isolation of a solo figure against a shimmering foil of accompanying harmonies. Because the theme of the quartet is based on the interval of the tritone, the feeling of tonality is fluid. But tonality is never abandoned; indeed, a key signature is given in every movement, and the quartet itself is marked as being in the key of G minor. The whole-tone scale, which became so important in Debussy's later works, and which, by its very nature, is tonally neutral, for no dominant and no common triad can be built in it, appears in the quartet but incidentally.

The String Quartet is the only work of its kind Debussy ever wrote. The medium of chamber music, and particularly that of an ensemble of homogeneous instruments, held little attraction for Debussy, whose imagination craved the palette of an orchestra, or an Impressionist poem for a vocal setting. The quartet was performed for the first time by the Ysaÿe Quartet, to which it was dedicated, on December 29, 1893, at a concert of the Société Nationale in Paris. The reception was a mixed one, but there were no cries of outrage such as greeted, several years later, the production of *Pelléas*.

Paul Dukas, Debussy's fellow Impressionist, gave a fine appreciation of Debussy's Quartet:

> All is clear and neatly outlined, despite the great freedom of form. The melodic essence of the work is concentrated, but possesses a rich flavor. It impregnates the harmonic tissue with penetrating and original poesy. The harmony itself, despite its great audacity, never shocks. Debussy delights in the succession of full harmonies, in dissonances without crudity, more harmonious indeed, in their complexity, than the concords themselves. Debussy's melody treads as though on a sumptuous, cunningly ornamented carpet, full of exotic colors, but devoid of gaudiness and discord.

At the first performance of the quartet in Boston, Edward Burlingame Hill, an early champion of French music in America and himself an eminent composer in an idiom that may be called American Impressionism, wrote in the *Boston Evening Transcript* of March 11, 1902:

> It is not difficult to appreciate the enthusiasm of the few for Debussy. This Quartet, while decidedly, even audaciously, ultra-modern, is coherent and logical: it shows originality of form without departing too rhapsodically from convention. It is wonderfully subtle poetic music, and seems almost totally new in quartet idiom. Without degenerating into so-called orchestra style, there are many new and startlingly beautiful color effects.

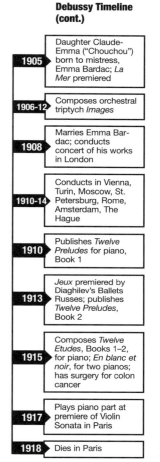

Debussy Timeline (cont.)

1905 — Daughter Claude-Emma ("Chouchou") born to mistress, Emma Bardac; *La Mer* premiered

1906-12 — Composes orchestral triptych *Images*

1908 — Marries Emma Bardac; conducts concert of his works in London

1910-14 — Conducts in Vienna, Turin, Moscow, St. Petersburg, Rome, Amsterdam, The Hague

1910 — Publishes *Twelve Preludes* for piano, Book 1

1913 — *Jeux* premiered by Diaghilev's Ballets Russes; publishes *Twelve Preludes*, Book 2

1915 — Composes *Twelve Etudes*, Books 1–2, for piano; *En blanc et noir*, for two pianos; has surgery for colon cancer

1917 — Plays piano part at premiere of Violin Sonata in Paris

1918 — Dies in Paris

Symphonic Suite: La Mer *(1903–5)*

When Debussy asked the composer Erik Satie (1866–1925) which part of *La Mer* he liked best, Satie replied: "The first movement, 'From dawn until noon,' particularly about a quarter of eleven." Assuming that the dawn broke in Paris at six o'clock, the spot in the music at a quarter of eleven in the first movement of *La Mer* would come at one of the loveliest passages of the work, when the divided cellos play the motive of the sea. Satie had made a good choice.

In a letter written at the time of the composition of *La Mer,* Debussy said that he had always loved the sea and was destined to be a sailor. Yet he never made a prolonged sea voyage, and his cross-Channel trips to England were infrequent. *La Mer,* a symphonic suite of three movements, is a series of fleeting images of the sea in Debussy's mind.

He revealed some hesitancy about the titles of the three movements. His first idea was to name them as follows: "Mer belle aux îles sanguinaires" "Jeux de vagues," and "Le vent fait danser la mer." The title of the second movement remained, but the first movement was renamed "De l'aube a midi sur la mer" and the third, "Dialogue du vent et de la mer." Debussy completed the score on March 5, 1905, and the first performance took place on October 15, 1905, at the Lamoureux Concerts in Paris, under the direction of Camille Chevillard.

Debussy disliked the word "impressionism," with which his music was tagged, even though the term was accepted as honorable by French painters, to whom it was first applied. His musical language is Impressionist only in the sense that it does not derive from the formal elements of classical music. It is revolutionary in content. Disregarding sacrosanct conservatory rules, Debussy employs parallel progressions of unresolved dissonances, consecutive fifths, and that intriguing exotic scale of whole tones. He dispenses with the classical development of principal subjects, and the subjects themselves are reduced to essentials. A fleeting wave of sound, rushing forward with passionate vehemence, replaces the carefully fashioned type of Baroque melodies; a languorous recession of the melodic line signals the conclusion of the musical phrase. And since dissonances are emancipated, the demarcation between formal sections becomes indistinct, and the flow of music acquires a sense of perpetual transition. Because of the unstable equilibrium of structure, subtle details and dynamic gradations assume great importance in Debussy's music. This is the world in which, as the poet said, "le précis et l'imprécis se rencontrent."

In the first movement, "From Dawn until Noon on the Sea," the panorama of Debussy's ocean unrolls with gentle waves breaking at the shore. The hours from dawn to noon are compressed into a few minutes of music in the score with uncanny hydrological accuracy; the ocean grows lyrical as the day advances, and the melody of the divided cellos sings the enchantment of the sun approaching the meridian. The orchestra regains its undivided strength, without ever attaining the grossness of **fortissimo**.

The second movement, "Play of the Waves," is the Impressionist equivalent of a **scherzo**. The orchestra is split into sparkling sections; luminous motives break into prismatic fragments. The continuity of the coruscating interplay remains unbroken to the end.

The last movement, "Dialogue of the Wind and the Sea," starts with a powerful gust of wind in the bass register. The sea is portrayed by a tense chromatic motion underneath the tonal surface, which remains unruffled. But as the kinetic energy of the wind increases, the music becomes turbulent. There is an interesting transformation of the melody of the sea into a progression of whole tones. The waves of sound increase in amplitude, in constant affirmation of tonal grandeur. The work ends triumphantly in a sonorous apotheosis of major tonality.

Why did this magnificent work arouse so much indigna-

Fortissimo (It.). Extremely loud.

Scherzo (It.). A joke, jest; an instrumental piece of a light, piquant, humorous character. Also, a vivacious movement in the symphony, with strongly marked rhythm and sharp and unexpected contrasts in both rhythm and harmony; usually the third movement.

tion on the part of otherwise enlightened critics on both sides of the Atlantic? In Paris, in a collection of violent dissenting opinions published under the title *Le Cas Debussy,* Debussy was called a "déformateur musical." When *La Mer* reached the United States, the revulsion toward the music was universal among professional music critics. Louis Elson, a respectable American pedagogue and music critic, wrote with a degree of misplaced wit:

> It may be possible that in the transit to America the title of this work has been changed. It is possible that Debussy did not intend to call it *La Mer,* but *Le Mal de mer,* which would at once make the music as clear as day. It is a series of symphonic pictures of seasickness. The first movement is *Headache.* The second is *Doubt,* picturing moments of dread suspense, whether or no! The third movement, with its explosions and rumbling has now a self-evident purpose. The hero is endeavoring to throw up his boot-heels.

The *New York Post* wrote: "Debussy's music is the dreariest kind of rubbish. Does anybody for a moment doubt that Debussy would not write such chaotic, meaningless, cacophonous, ungrammatical stuff, as in *The Sea,* if he could invent a melody?" The *New York World* shrugged its Atlas shoulders: "New York heard a new composition called *The Sea,* and New York is probably still wondering why. The work is by the most modern of modern Frenchmen, Debussy. Compared with this, the most abstruse compositions of Richard Strauss are as primer stories to hear and to comprehend."

Two Dances for Harp and String Orchestra: Danse sacrée, Danse profane *(1904)*

During the first decade of the twentieth century, Debussy was the most controversial figure in Paris. He attracted fanatic supporters and he found equally fanatic opponents. The viewpoint of admirers was clear: they welcomed the creation of a new art, and the innovation of music by sonorous suggestion rather than formal composition. The opponents were equally strong in their convictions. They accused Debussy of spreading a musical anemia through the destruction of formal ties that hold a musical composition together. Camille Saint-Saëns (1835–1921) could not reconcile himself to Debussy's music even after Debussy was dead. He wrote in 1920 that Debussy's works resemble music no more than the palette used by an artist in his work resembles a painting. Even the composer and pianist Ferruccio Busoni (1866–1924), who was anything but a musical Tory, said that Debussy's music is like the picture of a beautiful sunset; it fades when one looks at it too closely. The judgment of posterity upon Debussy's music is neither enthusiastic acceptance nor a definite rejection. Debussy has assumed his role as a historic figure. Contemporary musicians rarely imitate his style, but without Debussy behind them, even neoclassical composers of today would not be able to write music effectively.

The great Debussy is represented by *Pelléas et Mélisande*, *La Mer*, some of the *Préludes*, and most of his songs. The Two Dances for Harp and String Orchestra, composed in 1904, are lesser known. These dances were written especially for the chromatic harp, which was new at the time. The first dance is called *Danse sacrée*; the second is *Danse profane*. This antimony of moods is expressed in Debussy's music not by an exaggerated piety of sentiment for the sacred dance, or the savagery of movement in the second, but impressionistically, by suggestion. The harmonic and melodic idiom is interesting because it represents a complete catalogue of characteristic devices employed in French Impressionist music. The *Danse sacrée* employs neomodal progressions in block chords, with a sprinkling of whole-tone scales in the middle section. The *Danse profane* is couched in the Lydian mode, obviously with reference to the ethos of ancient Greek music in which the Lydian mode was regarded as effeminate and lascivious. It is followed by passages in the pentatonic scale. The harmonic idiom includes dominant-ninth chords and progressions of diminished-seventh chords; there are successions of parallel triads. The sonority of both pieces is reduced by the limitations of the harp.

The critical reception of the dances after their first performance at the Cologne concerts in Paris on November 6, 1904, was mixed. The critic of *Le Ménestrel* found "des jolis effets, des recherches amusantes" but complained about the overdose of whole-tone scales. But another critic commented on "an ultrarefined art, idealistic and sensual, absolutely new and of unique gracefulness." From the camp of irreconcilable anti-Debussyists came a growl:

> In M. Debussy's music, dissonance has become the rule and consonance the exception. Consequently those who admire the former style applauded his Deux Danses for chromatic harp and orchestra; whilst the devotees of the latter type of music made grimaces. . . . His musical plan has no architectural quality; it is vague, hazy, disturbing, almost morbid. Its counterpart in Impressionist painting is to be found in . . . canvases where the subjects are so submerged in a misty atmosphere as to be barely visible, and where suffering seems to be the dominant note.

Jeux *(1912)*

Debussy was a thorough Parisian who took great interest in all things passing on the Paris scene, from Symbolist poetry to Art Nouveau, from exotic Oriental music, which he heard at the Paris Exposition, to popular American dances at the vaudeville. He himself was an *homme nouveau,* eager to take part in the artistic events of the new century.

JEUX

One of the most spectacular cultural manifestations in the Paris of Debussy was Serge Diaghilev's Ballets Russes. It gave the French a look into the artistic soul of "la Russie mystérieuse," at the time when the two nations were politically united in an *entente cordiale.* When Diaghilev approached Debussy with a request to write a ballet score for his enterprise, Debussy readily agreed. The product was *Jeux,* described by Debussy as a "poème dansé."

The "jeux" of the title were tennis games. The scene opens on an empty garden at dusk, with dim electric streetlights providing illumination. Suddenly a tennis ball flies across the stage. A young man in a tennis jacket runs after it. Two girls appear and begin to dance. The young man asks one of the girls to dance with him, and the other watches them with some envy. He then dances with the second girl; this time it is the first girl who is jealous. Finally, all three engage in a round. But another tennis ball flies onto the stage. Like frightened children, all three scurry off in different directions.

The novelty in *Jeux* was its scenario, taken from contemporary life rather than from mythology or fairy tales, which were the main sources of the classical French ballet. The ballet was produced by Diaghilev's troupe at the Théâtre des Champs-Elysées in Paris on May 15, 1913. The choreography was by Diaghilev's star dancer, Vaclav Nijinsky (1890–1950), who also mimed the part of the tennis player. Tamara Karsavina and Ludmila Schollar were the two girls. Pierre Monteux conducted the orchestra. The production was successful, but it was completely overshadowed by the sensational première of Stravinsky's *Le Sacre du printemps,* which took place two weeks later at the same theater.

The score of *Jeux* is a typical Debussyan creation. Its kinetic energy, like that of a tennis ball, is instantly spent in a resilient impact, and just as quickly renewed in another burst of musical saltation. Its dynamic scheme is an expertly recorded oscillograph, marked by a series of brief inflations and deflations of well-calibrated sonorous matter, with moments of equipoise between swiftly changing scenes of action.

The ballet opens with an atmospheric **prelude** (*très lent*), in 4/4 time, on a landscape of static emptiness. Woodwinds intone soft whole-tone harmonies (*doux et rêveur*), imparting an air of dreamy sweetness. The horns give out *sons d'écho*, hovering over immobile muted strings. The tranquillity of the scene is suddenly invaded by palpitating Spanish rhythms in rapid 3/8 time, sending off flights of chromatic *étincelles* and scintillations of major seconds in the muted violins. It is the initiation into a dance, with lambent **glissandos** in the harps and avian trills in the flutes. Evanescent solos appear in the woodwind section, with recurrent implosions generating asymmetric sparks of rhythmic energy. In an episode (*ironique et léger*), a babbling bassoon indulges in a garrulous solo, leading to a climax (*joyeux*).

The music becomes emotionally charged (*toujours plus passionné*), harps splashing, trumpets chanting, and trombones rumbling underneath, with the metal clang of the triangle, tambourine, and cymbals conjuring up the sound of a distant festival. Agitation mounts, reaching a climax (*violent*). But a détente supervenes, with divided violins sliding downward. There is a brief pause, followed by a choreographic envoi with a murmuration of strings (*très doux*) and a susurration of piccolos (*le plus doux possible*), with horns and trumpets (*lointain*, "distant") and the timpani (*très lointain*). A shimmering motion is suddenly suspended, and the orchestra, supplemented by the xylophone and **celesta**, converges on a unison A in a luminous sonic spark.

Six épigraphes antiques *(1914)*

Antiquity attracted the modern composers at the turn of the twentieth century as strongly as the mystery of exotic life in the Orient. Remoteness in space or time supplied the psychological impetus in the search for new means of expression and

Prelude. A musical introduction to a composition or drama.

Glissando (It.). A slide; a rapid scale. On bowed instruments, a flowing, unaccented execution of a passage. On the piano, a rapid scale effect obtained by sliding the thumb, or thumb and one finger, over the keys.

Celesta. Percussion instrument consisting of tuned steel bars connected to a keyboard.

new techniques of composition. This state of mind was particularly pronounced in France, and most especially in Paris. In this fascination with spatial and temporal distance, the French musicians of the Impressionist group were encouraged by symbolism in poetry and similar trends in painting.

The invocation of exotic antiquity was never literal among French poets and musicians. Rather, in a true Impressionist manner, they conjured up a vision of music in dreamlike memories of something never seen. The pentatonic scale served both for the pipes of Pan and the doll-like dances of the Orient. The whole-tone scale was an artificial creation, but it was for this very reason suitable for poetic visions. Formations of consecutive triads or major ninth-chords, favored by Debussy and his contemporaries, were suggestive of the luxuriance of primitive dalliance. Thus modern devices helped to recreate a picture of graceful antiquity. French Symbolist poetry, which inspired Debussy, was saturated with the essence of eroticism; the imagined freedom of love in remote times and remote lands exercised its own powerful attraction.

The poet Pierre Louÿs asked Debussy in 1899 to write a score of background music for his Grecian poems *Chansons de Bilitis*. The poems were to be recited and mimed. Debussy obliged and wrote a suitably fugacious score for two harps, two flutes, and celesta. The first reading of the poems took place in Paris on June 7, 1901. Much later, Debussy set the same cycle of poems to music for voice and piano, without making use of musical materials of the incidental music of 1901.

In 1914, Debussy extracted six of the ten pieces of incidental music for *Chansons de Bilitis* and arranged them for piano four hands. They were published under the title *Six épigraphes antiques*. Debussy himself wrote the descriptive subtitles for these pieces. He performed them for the first time, with the composer Jean Roger-Ducasse, in this four-hands version in Paris on March 15, 1917. In a letter to his publisher Durand, Debussy said that he had intended to arrange the suite for orchestra. He was too ill to carry out his intention. The symphonic version was eventually produced by the Swiss conductor Ernest Ansermet, who had an intimate understanding of Debussy's orchestral style. Ansermet's score bears this dedication: "To the memory of Claude Debussy I dedicate this work in which I have tried to fulfill a wish that had been his."

The first "epigraph" is entitled "Pour invoquer Pan, dieu du vent d'été." Here Debussy makes Pan play the panpipe in the pentatonic scale; the music is evanescent in its attenuated sonorities. The second piece, "Pour un tombeau sans nom," is unquiet, as behooves an evocation of a nameless tombstone. Hyperchromatic **melismas** color the music, and there are frequent passages in whole-tone scales. The ending is caducous, transitory, and volatile in its dissonant substance. The whole-tone scale is again in evidence in the third piece, "Pour que la nuit soit propice." The prayer for a propitious night is accentuated by distant drumbeats and chromatic arabesques.

Melisma. A melodic ornament with more than one note to a syllable.

Quite different in mood is the fourth piece, "Pour la danseuse aux crotales." The dancer with castanets of the title is Cybèle, the nature goddess of the Greeks, attended by armed female Corybantes raging through the forest in orgiastic abandon. Debussy sees Cybèle through the mist of legend and the music is almost tranquil in its Grecian modalities. But there are furious, though brief, explosions of passion; chromatic tones intrude, forming jarring dissonances. The ending is on a thirdless seventh-chord.

The fifth epigraph, "Pour l'Egyptienne," is Orientalistically flavored. The melody is sinuous in its wistful **arabesques**. The rhythm is nervously dotted; the harmonies are austere in their open fifths. The ending is a static aureole. The last piece is titled "Pour remercier la pluie au matin." The gratitude for rain in the morning is expressed by alliteration. Rapid streamlets descend in chromatic passages; then the raindrops are more

Arabesque. A type of fanciful pianoforte piece; ornamental passages accompanying or varying a theme.

Pentatonic scale. A five-tone scale, usually that which avoids semitonic steps by skipping the fourth and seventh degrees in major and the second and sixth in minor.

widely spaced, presently assuming **pentatonic** configurations. The ending is a reminiscence of the pipes of Pan of the opening. Thus Debussy unifies the six disparate epigraphs by the invocation to the patron of shepherds and hunters, the lover of nymphs, the player upon the syrinx, the god of nature's music.

RICHARD STRAUSS
(1864–1949)
Richard the Second

IN HIS EARLY CAREER, Richard Strauss was often described by journalists and critics, half facetiously, half admiringly, as Richard the Second, the first Richard being, of course, Wagner. As in most such sobriquets, this nomination has a particle of allegorical and historical truth. Wagner had created a new stage genre of music drama, in which characters and ideas were identified by individual themes, the **leitmotivs** ("leading" motives) of the Wagnerian lexicon. Strauss transplanted Wagner's musical identification tags to the domain of symphonic music, primarily as **tone poems**. Each was a complex of leading motives, intertwining, overlapping, expanded, contracted, fragmentized, melodically and rhythmically altered, moving in a fantastic **counter-**

Leitmotiv (Ger.). Leading motive; any striking musical motive (theme, phrase) characterizing one of the actors in a drama or an idea, emotion, or situation.

Tone poem. Also called "symphonic poem"; an extended orchestral composition which follows the thread of a story or the ideas of a poem.

Counterpoint. Polyphonic composition; the combination of two or more simultaneous melodies.

Polyphonic. Consisting of two or more independently treated melodies; contrapuntal; capable of producing two or more tones at the same time, as the piano, harp, violin, xylophone.

Program music. A class of instrumental compositions intended to represent distinct moods or phases of emotion, or to depict actual scenes of events; sometimes called "descriptive music," as opposed to "absolute music."

point of instrumental entries. A fanatical coterie of musicians and litterateurs assembled around Strauss and saluted him as a prophet of new German music. Special manuals were issued for first performances of his tone poems, profusely illustrated with musical examples, to guide the listener, like musical Baedekers, through the labyrinth of Straussian thematic **polyphony**. Strauss, with a robust Bavarian sense of humor, treated these efforts lightly. He was undoubtedly aware of his great role as a musical innovator, but he never regarded himself as a messiah, and had little need for self-appointed exegetes. He once calmed the distress of an erudite listener who found himself without a printed guide at a concert by saying that listening could be done by ears alone.

In these works Strauss established himself as a master of **program music** and the most important representative of the nascent era of musical modernism; as such, he was praised extravagantly by earnest believers in musical progress and damned savagely by entrenched traditionalists in the press.

In 1894, Strauss conducted the premiere of his first opera, *Guntram*, for which he also composed the text. The leading soprano role was performed by Pauline de Ahna; she was married to Strauss a few months later, and remained with him all his life. While engaged in active work as a composer, Strauss did not neglect his conducting career. In 1894, he succeeded Hans von Bülow as conductor of the Berlin Philharmonic, leading it for a season, and in 1896 became chief conductor of the Munich Court Opera.

Strauss's works of the period included the sparkling *Till Eulenspiegel's Merry Pranks* (*Till Eulenspiegels lustige Streiche*); *Thus Spake Zarathustra* (*Also sprach Zarathustra*), a philosophical symphonic poem after Nietzsche; *Don Quixote*, variations with a cello solo after Cervantes. He conducted the first performance of his extraordinary autobiographical symphonic poem *A Hero's Life* (*Ein Heldenleben*, 1899), in which the hero of the title was Strauss himself, while his critics were represented in the score by a cacophonous charivari. For this exhibition of musical self-aggrandizement, he was severely chastised in the press.

For his first visit to the United States, he presented the premiere performance of his *Symphonia Domestica* at Carnegie Hall (1904). The score represents a day in the Strauss household, including an **interlude** describing, quite literally, the feeding of the newly born baby. The reviews in the press reflected aversion to such musical self-exposure. His opera *Salome*, to the German translation of Oscar Wilde's play, had its American premiere at the Metropolitan Opera in 1907. The ghastly subject, involving intended incest, seven-fold nudity, decapitation followed by a labial necrophilia, administered such a shock to the public and the press that the Metropolitan Opera took it off the repertoire after only two performances. Scarcely less forceful was Strauss's next opera, *Elektra*, to a libretto by the Austrian poet and dramatist Hugo von Hofmannsthal, in which the horrors of matricide were depicted with extraordinary force in unabashedly dissonant harmonies.

Strauss then decided to prove to his admirers that he was quite able to write melodious operas to charm the musical ear. This he accomplished in his next production, also to a text of Hofmannsthal, *The Cavalier of the Rose* (*Der Rosenkavalier*), a delightful **opéra bouffe** in an endearing popular manner. Turning once more to Greek mythology, Strauss wrote, with Hofmannsthal again as librettist, a short opera, *Ariadne on Naxos* (*Ariadne auf Naxos*), which he conducted for the first time in 1912 and later expanded into a full-length work (1916).

His next work was the formidable and quite realistic score *An Alpine Symphony* (*Eine Alpensinfonie*, 1915), depicting an ascent of the Alps, and employing a wind machine and a thunder machine in the orchestra to illustrate an alpine storm. With Hofmannsthal, he wrote *The Woman Without a Shadow* (*Die Frau ohne Schatten*, 1919), using a complex plot heavily endowed with symbolism. Subsequent works included *Inter-*

Interlude. An intermezzo; an instrumental strain or passage connecting the lines or stanzas of a hymn, etc.

Opéra bouffe (Fr.), **opera buffa** (It.). Light comic opera.

mezzo (1924), *The Egyptian Helen* (*Die ägyptische Helena,* 1928), and *Arabella* (1933), his last collaboration with von Hofmannsthal.

When Hitler came to power in 1933, the Nazis were eager to persuade Strauss to join the official policies of the Third Reich. Hitler even sent him a signed picture of himself with a flattering inscription, "To the great composer Richard Strauss, with sincere admiration." Strauss kept clear of formal association with the Führer and his cohorts, however. He agreed to serve as president of the newly organized Reichsmusikkammer in 1933, but resigned from it in 1935, ostensibly for reasons of poor health. He entered into open conflict with the Nazis by asking Stefan Zweig, an Austrian Jew, to provide the libretto for his opera *The Silent Woman* (*Die schweigsame Frau*, after Jonson). It was produced in 1935, but taken off the boards after a few performances. His political difficulties grew even more disturbing when the Nazis found out that his daughter-in-law was Jewish.

During the last weeks of the war, Strauss devoted himself to the composition of *Metamorphosen*, a work for string orchestra mourning the disintegration of Germany. It contained a symbolic quotation from the Funeral March of Beethoven's *Eroica* Symphony; in 1945 he moved to Switzerland. Although official suspicion continued to linger after the war regarding his relationship with the Nazi regime, he was officially exonerated. A last flame of creative inspiration brought forth the deeply moving Four Last Songs (1948), for **soprano** and orchestra, inspired by poems of Herman Hesse and Joseph von Eichendorff. With this farewell, Strauss returned to his home in Germany, where he died at the age of eighty-five.

Undeniably one of the finest master composers of modern times, Strauss never espoused extreme **chromatic** techniques, remaining a Romanticist at heart. His genius is unquestioned as regards such early symphonic poems as *Don*

Soprano (It.). The highest class of the human voice; the female soprano, or treble, has a normal compass from c^1 to a^2.

Chromatic. Relating to tones foreign to a given key (scale) or chord; opposed to diatonic.

Juan and *Thus Spake Zarathustra*; many of his operas have
attained a permanent place in the repertoire, while his Four
Last Songs stand as a noble achievement of his Romantic inspiration.

Symphonic Poem: Don Juan, *Op. 20 (1888–89)*

In the dictionary of musical invectives, Strauss occupies many
pages. Every symphonic poem he wrote was a signal for the
critics of the two hemispheres to make use of their choicest
vocabulary of abuse. Strauss stood up well under this bombardment, but suffered most damaging blows from his admir-
ing commentators who published catalogues of themes and
fragments of themes used by Strauss, together with the meaning of each of these motives. It is fashionable among contemporary composers to deny literary implications in their music,
but Strauss could hardly do that, for the very titles of his tone
poems—*Don Juan*, *Death and Transfiguration*, *Till Eulenspiegel*, *Thus Spake Zarathustra*, *Don Quixote*, and *A Hero's
Life*—are literary.

Don Juan is the first of Strauss's tone poems, if we disregard the earlier orchestral work, *Macbeth*, which has not been
retained in the active repertoire. Strauss wrote *Don Juan*
when he was twenty-four years old, and conducted its first
performance at Weimar on November 11, 1889. The program
carried a quotation from the poem "Don Juan" written by the
morbid Austrian poet, Nicolaus Lenau. The portion of Lenau's
poem published in Strauss's score pictures a romantic Don
Juan, insatiable in his conquests. He expresses the desire to
die from a kiss on the lips of the last of his women. He elevates
the plurality of his affections to a dogma and poeticizes the
manifold charms of beautiful womanhood. He cries, "Out and
away to new and new conquests." But he is reconciled to
death, a lightning from above that finally strikes a deadly blow
to his love power.

Don Juan.

Tondichtung von Rich. Strauss, Op. 20.

This poem, representing the hero as a tragic figure frustrated by his easy triumphs, is the only program that Strauss ever acknowledged, which did not prevent Wilhelm Mauke from expanding the action of Strauss's symphonic poem into a detailed catalogue of places and people, following the text of Lenau in its entirety. According to Mauke, Don Juan makes three conquests in Strauss's symphonic poem, which lasts altogether eighteen minutes in performance. The first conquest is easy, and takes only seventy bars in **allegro** molto con brio. The opening theme is termed a "storm of delight." The second theme represents the philosophical concept of the multiplicity of womanly essence. Then comes the upsurging Don Juan theme, followed by the theme of the first victim, whom Mauke identifies as Zerlina or, as he affectionately calls her, Zerlinchen. But this conquest leaves a feeling of disgust and lassitude expressed in dreary chromatics. The second conquest starts on the ninth chord in **pianissimo**. The intended victim is a blonde countess, who lives in a villa one hour's ride from Seville, but there is no Spanish atmosphere in the music. There is a theme of "nameless delight" in the uppermost regions of the violin range. The affair with the countess takes eighty-nine bars, ending in an E-minor crash. The third and tragic love is Anna. She is a G-major creature, but the chromatics of disgust are **contrapuntally** projected against her theme at the very outset. A new Don Juan theme is introduced—a call to new conquests—but it is caricatured by diminution in the tinkling glockenspiel. He goes to a masked ball (cachinnating chromatics in the woodwinds). Then comes death by the sword of Don Pedro. Don Juan's blood flows slowly down the **tremolos** of the violins. He expires in E minor.

Don Juan reached America on October 31, 1891, when Arthur Nikisch conducted it at the concert of the Boston Symphony Orchestra. Philip Hale wrote with his usual caustic wit in the *Boston Post*:

Allegro (It.). Lively, brisk, rapid.

Pianissimo (It.). Very soft.

Contrapuntal. Pertaining to composition with two or more simultaneous melodies.

Tremolo (It.). A quivering, fluttering, in singing; an unsteady tone.

He uses music as the vehicle of expressing everything but music; for he has little invention, and his musical thoughts are of little worth. This symphonic poem is supposed to portray in music the recollections and regrets of a jaded voluptuary. Now, granting that music is capable of doing this, what do we find in this composition? There are recollections, not of Don Juan, but of Liszt and of Wagner. There are also regrets, but the regrets come from the hearers. There is plenty of fuss and fuming; but is there any genuine passion or any real terror from the beginning to the end? Besides, Don Juan was more direct in his methods. His wooing was as sudden and as violent as his descent to the lower regions. According to Strauss, he was verbose, fond of turning corners, something of a metaphysician, and a good deal of a bore. When he made love he beat upon a triangle, and when he was dyspeptic he confided his woes to instruments that moaned in sympathy.

Eleven years later, *Don Juan* was played again by the Boston Symphony Orchestra. This time, Hale, who had a prodigious memory for other people's writings but not for his own, wrote enthusiastically in the *Boston Journal* of November 2, 1902: "A daring, brilliant composition: one that paints the hero as might a master's brush on canvas. How expressive the themes! How daring the treatment of them! What fascinating irresistible insolence, glowing passion, and then the taste of Dead-Sea fruit!"

Symphonic Poem: Till Eulenspiegel's Merry Pranks, *Op. 28 (1894–95)*

An early biographer of Richard Strauss, writing in the *Musikalisches Wochenblatt* of April 1897, when Strauss was in his thirties and just beginning to amaze the world, relates an interesting episode of Strauss's apprentice years. His father,

Franz, was an excellent player on the French horn, and knew other orchestral instruments well. He taught Strauss never to force an instrument to play beyond its natural capacities. Once, looking over an orchestral score written by his son, he suddenly turned toward him and gave him a slap on the face. "Lausbub," he exclaimed, "so you are writing a high B flat for the flute! Mozart and Beethoven never used it; neither should you." Strauss had great respect for his father as educator and musician, and he remembered his lessons well. When he needed wider range of **tone color**, he had a new instrument made. Thus, in *An Alpine Symphony*, Strauss wanted a low instrument of the tone color of the oboe. The English horn would not do, for it was associated with pastoral scenes, as in the famous solo in the *William Tell* Overture. Strauss then asked Heckel, the instrument maker in Berlin, to construct a special instrument, which he called the **heckelphone**.

Strauss imagined all horn players to be as good as his father. He wrote a **concerto** for horn and orchestra, under his father's inspiration. In *Till Eulenspiegel*, he entrusted to the horn one of the most difficult solo passages ever written for the instrument. It is said that Strauss got the idea of this solo from listening to the first horn player of the Weimar Orchestra practice before each rehearsal. When at the first rehearsal of *Till Eulenspiegel* the horn player complained about the difficulty of the passage, Strauss replied, "Nonsense! I heard you practice it every morning."

Strauss completed the composition of *Till Eulenspiegel's Merry Pranks* (*Till Eulenspiegels lustige Streiche*) on May 6, 1895, and the first performance took place in Cologne on November 5 of the same year. The composition is defined by Strauss himself as an escape, but in the low regions of the double bassoon and the double basses, Till's fate is already sealed. The fateful rhythm, dash and dot, is pounded by the entire orchestra. The kettledrums strike, and the bass drum. Till's motive is in all the flutes, and all the clarinets, helped out by a

Tone-color. Quality of tone; timbre.

Heckelphone. A double-reed instrument somewhat misleadingly called the baritone oboe; gives out a rich, somewhat hollow sound.

Concerto (It.). An extended multi-movement composition for a solo instrument, usually with orchestra accompaniment and using (modified) sonata form.

trumpet and the violins, but each time it is answered by the sepulchral chords of the brasses.

As a last resort, Till decides to joke his way out. There is a merry dance tune, but it is of short duration, and soon gives way to a plaintive cry of the oboe. A lyrical reminiscence follows: Till's whole life passes in his mind. The horn plays its difficult passage, and there is an interlude of pastoral serenity. But grim reality interrupts these dreams. Till is on the march to his destiny. His theme is sounded in the entire orchestra; the march becomes a gallop, a gallop to the gallows. The tumult ceases. There are lugubrious lifeless fifths in the low wind instruments. They are marked *drohend*, "menacing," and they are then filled with equally lugubrious **minor thirds.** The execution drum beats a roll. There is a stifled outcry of the small clarinet, but only funereal fifths answer it. The small clarinet shrieks out in the last agony, and all is over. There are drops of muted strings. The epilogue commemorates the gentleness of Till, and a tribute is paid to his soul by the reiteration in full orchestra of his motive.

Minor third. An interval of three half tones.

Symphonic Poem: Thus Spake Zarathustra, *Op. 30 (1895–96)*

Also sprach Zarathustra is the first example of an orchestral composition purporting to expound a system of religious philosophy. The full title reads: *Also sprach Zarathustra, Tondichtung, frei nach Friedrich Nietzsche (Thus Spake Zarathustra, tone poem, based loosely on Friedrich Nietzsche).* Nietzsche's book, *Also sprach Zarathustra,* bore the subtitle, *A Book for All and None.* It was published in 1892, post-mentally, so to speak, for by that time Nietzsche was completely insane.

Strauss was fascinated with Nietzsche's book, and set to work on his tone poem a few years after its publication. He conducted the first performance of *Also sprach Zarathustra* in Frankfurt on November 27, 1896. He had this to say to an inquiring writer regarding the score: "I did not propose to write philosophical music or to portray Nietzsche's great book in tones. I merely intended to convey by musical means an idea of the development of the human race through its various stages, religious and scientific, culminating in Nietzsche's vision of the superman."

It must be noted that in Nietzsche's book, Zarathustra is not the legendary Persian religious teacher, but merely a convenient spokesman for Nietzsche's own philosophy. The image of Zarathustra came to him, or so it was said, during a walk in the woods near the Silvaplana Lake in the Engadine, when he came in sight of a towering crag. It impressed him as a symbol of the overwhelming grandeur of man's spirit, the footprint of the superman, which was to transcend man in the course of Nietzschean mystical evolution.

A lengthy passage from Nietzsche's book is quoted in the score:

At the age of thirty, Zarathustra left his home at the lake and went into the mountains. His solitude raised his spirit and sustained him for ten years without weariness. But one morning he awoke at dawn and addressed the sun in these words: "Great Star! You would never be happy except for the satisfaction of knowing that people benefit from your light. For ten years you rose to shine in my cave dwelling. You would have wearied of your light and of your journey were it not for me, for my falcon, and for my serpent. We waited for the sunrise each morning and blessed you for your bounty. And now I am weary of my own wisdom, like the bee that has gathered too much honey. I would gladly give away the fruits of my knowledge to other men of wisdom so that they could indulge once more in their follies, and to the poor so that they could profit from their riches. To accomplish this duty I must descend into the depths of the earth, as the sun does when setting behind the ocean, to shed its light upon the nether regions. Oh resplendent star! I must follow you, and go down to men beyond the sunset. Bless me therefore, oh impassive orb, for you can look without envy even on the greatest happiness. Bless the overflowing cup, so that the water shining with golden light may carry everywhere the reflection of your splendor. But the cup is empty again, and Zarathustra must once more become a man." Thus it was that Zarathustra's journey into the depths began.

The music describes Zarathustra's journey. A brief outline is inserted in the score:

First movement: Sunrise. Man feels the power of God (Andante religioso). But man retains his yearning. Second movement: Man plunges into passion, but finds no peace. Third movement: Man turns toward science, and tries in vain to solve life's riddle in a fugue. Pleasant dance melodies are heard, and man becomes his individual self again. His soul soars aloft, letting the world sink beneath him.

German mystical philosophy is often impenetrable. Nietzsche atones for the nebulousness of his own ideas by his linguistic inventiveness (he introduced the word "Übermensch"—"superman"—into international vocabulary), his imaginative metaphors, the power of his aphoristic style, and the stimulating effect of his surprising oxymoronic appositions.

The orchestration of *Also sprach Zarathustra* is on a grand scale, containing, in addition to the ample contingent of strings and wind instruments, a bell, two harps, and an organ. The dominating tonality is C major, mystically associated with purity of thought, because of the all-white, accident-free visual appearance of C major on the musical staff.

The opening of the tone poem is marked by a mysterious rumble in the nethermost regions of the orchestra anchored on C, with the bass drum supplying an ominous roll of thunder. The trumpet announces the cardinal theme of the work, the motive of nature's riddle, consisting of the ascending notes C—G—C. The organ enters with the ponderous resonance of declarative power. The kettledrums pound out the **tonic** and the **dominant**. The music portends a weighty development.

These introductory measures mark the beginning of Zarathustra's journey as retailed in Nietzsche's vade mecum. The first stage of the journey is reached in "Von den Hinter-weltlern," treating of those who live behind the world of human reality in constant search for ontological permanence. Since this quest is tortuous, the music acquires the patina of **modal** uncertainty, moving through minor harmonies which color also the motive of nature's riddle, which recurs here. And since rational speculation fails under such chaotic conditions, religion steps in, with a quotation of a Gregorian melody, "Credo in unum deum."

The qualification in the title of the work, *"freely after Friedrich Nietzsche,"* gives Strauss the freedom to select passages from Nietzsche's book suitable for musical representation. The Wagneromantic flow of triadic melodies, saturated with mellifluous harmonies in a sea of chromatic abundance, characteristic of all tone poems of Strauss, makes *Zarathustra* sound more like the all-too-human Straussian personages Don Juan, Don Quixote, or Strauss himself in *Ein Heldenleben*, rather than the Nietzschean superman.

After the eerie mysticism of the music, there is a return to terrestrial emotions in the sections entitled "Von der grossen Sehnsucht" ("Of Great Yearning") and "Von den Freuden und Leidenschaften" ("Of Joys and Passions"). No sooner does the human element expand into self-enjoyment than the plaintive voice of the oboe makes itself heard in "Grablied" ("Song of the Grave"), a lugubrious reminder of ultimate dissolution, when even memories vanish. To illustrate this passing of the cherished scenes of youth and love, themes of previous movements are recalled in pale brilliance.

Tonic. The keynote of a scale; the triad on the keynote (tonic chord).
Dominant. The fifth tone in the major or minor scales; a chord based on that tone.

Mode. The distinction between a major key (mode) and minor key (mode).

If life ends in dissolution and memories are obliterated in the grave, there is solidity in the secular blandishments of scientific thought, portrayed in the next section, "Von der Wissenschaft" ("Of Science"). Quite appropriately, science is expounded by means of a scholastic **fugue**. The subject of the fugue is remarkable. It opens with the motive of nature's riddle, C—G—C, rising in the solemnity of the bass. Beginning with the third note, the theme traverses all twelve different notes of the chromatic scale in a formation of four mutually exclusive **triads**, two major and two minor. This anticipation of the Schoenbergian method of composition is of historical interest, but it is rudimentary and incomplete, since the essential Schoenbergian ramifications of **inversion**, **retrograde** motion, and inverted retrograde are lacking.

The following optimistic episode, "Der Genesence" ("The Convalescent"), leads to a hedonistic "Tanzlied" ("Dance Song"). The song of the dance is a Dionysian waltz, illustrating Nietzsche's humanistic vision: "Now at last the lover's songs are awakened. And my soul, too, is a lover's song."

The concluding section of *Also sprach Zarathustra* is a darksome epitaph, "Nachtwanderlied" ("Song of the Night Wanderer"). The midnight bell counts off its foreboding twelve strokes. The night is quiet, and the wanderer marches slowly toward the daybreak in the "world behind the world." He reaches the empyrean heights in the chord of B major in the upper woodwinds, but far beneath it, in the Stygian depths of the basses, there is sounded the motive of nature's riddle, C—G—C. This superimposition, barely broken off by rests, of two unrelated tonalities is the earliest example of the use of bitonal harmony. Its symbolism, in Nietzschean terms, has moved many a Straussian eschatologist to magnificent verbosity. Strauss himself, prudently, stood aloof from these propaedeutical exercises, preferring to leave the final judgment to the listeners—and the critics.

This judgment proved severe. At its first appearance, *Also*

Fugue. Contrapuntal imitation wherein a theme proposed by one part is taken up equally and successively by all participating parts.

Triad. A "three-tone" chord composed of a given tone (the root), with its third and fifth in ascending order in the scale.

Inversion. The transposition of one of the notes of an interval by an octave; chord position with lowest note other than root.

Retrograde. Performing a melody backwards; a crab movement. Also, one of three standard techniques in twelve-note composition (retrograde, inversion, transposition) wherein all notes of a set are played in reverse (i.e., backward).

sprach Zarathustra shocked the innocents, offended the purists, and fired the faithful with enthusiasm. Alas and lackaday! In the last third of the twentieth century the work no longer produces any of these strong emotions, and—the ultimate indignity—is even pronounced a bore. Harold C. Schoenberg, reviewing a performance of the work in the *New York Times*, in March 1968, called it, unfeelingly, an "overscored monstrosity," adding, "It used to be an effective vehicle for orchestra. But this vehicle has long since run out of gas."

For unregenerate Straussians, it is easier to bear the contumely and the spittle of spite showered on *Also sprach Zarathustra* when it was a novelty, for such reactions could be attributed to the Victorian obtuseness of the critics. After its first English performance, the *Times of London* described the work as "a hopeless failure, whatever its value as a philosophical treatise," in which "the possibilities of cacophony seem to be exhausted." The *Boston Herald* painted a Boschlike landscape in the guise of a critical review:

> If the interpretation given by Strauss is in any way reliable, Zarathustra was possessed of pulmonic powers of a rhinoceros, and shouted his "Thus Spake" through a megaphone of brobdingnagian proportions. The work is unhealthy; it suffers severely from basstubaculosis and its utterances are too often basstubathetic. The score is at its worst in the Dance Song, a species of symbolic waltz, ushered in with unheard-of caterwauling with a gruesomeness of execrably ugly dissonance—a realistic tone-picture of a sufferer from the worst pangs of sea-sickness.

The *Boston Gazette* was similarly picturesque:

> In *Also Sprach Zarathustra* the genius of Strauss is merciless; it possesses huge lungs and stands close to one's ear. When a man is awakened by an entire city tumbling about his ears, the blowing up of a single building by ni-

troglycerine passes unnoticed. The composer plays the part of the howling dervish; he whirls madly about until he becomes hysterical, and then he bellows.

Finally, this nosegay from the *New York Evening Post*:

Nietzsche, though he lives in a lunatic asylum, is one of Germany's favorite philosophers, and his crazy, rambling works have even been translated into English. Strauss, like Nietzsche, is impotent to create anything new, but as you cannot abuse people in music, he abuses the divine art itself. His mind seems to be an absolute desert as regards tangible musical thoughts. What he does invent is new cacophonies.

Fantastic Variations: Don Quixote, *Op. 35 (1896–97)*

Strauss brought the Wagnerian system of leitmotivs to such a degree of complexity that it became a veritable catalogue of musical identification marks, and he elevated the genre of tone poem to the highest point of artistry. The greatest among these tone poems–*Don Juan*, *Death and Transfiguration*, *Till Eulenspiegel*, *Thus Spake Zarathustra*, *Don Quixote*, *A Hero's Life*—were all written by Strauss between the ages of twenty-four and thirty-four, a remarkable achievement. All received their inspiration from literary sources.

Perhaps the boldest in conception and in execution is *Don Quixote*. Its subtitle, *Fantastic Variations on a Theme of Knightly Character*, has an ironic ring, but no greater tribute has ever been given in an art form to the immortal Knight of the Sorrowful Countenance. Don Quixote himself is incarnated in the solo **violoncello**, a curious selection, but superlatively fitting at the hands of a master like Strauss. The character of Sancho Panza, Don Quixote's clumsy but faithful henchman, is confided to a solo viola. Don Quixote may therefore be described as a double concerto for cello and viola with

Violoncello (It.). A four-stringed bow instrument familiarly called the cello.

Don Quixote.

Fantastische Variationen
über ein Thema ritterlichen Characters.

Introduction.

Richard Strauss, Op. 35.

orchestra. Strauss completed the score of Don Quixote on December 29, 1897. The work was performed for the first time in Cologne, from manuscript, with Friedrich Grützmacher as solo violoncellist and Franz Wüllner conducting, on March 8, 1898. Strauss himself conducted it ten days later in Frankfurt, when Hugo Becker was the violoncellist.

The intricacy of contrapuntal involvements in the score among a multitude of thematic elements is staggering. An exegesis of twenty-seven pages was compiled by Arthur Hahn to guide the listener. So literal were the literary allusions in this brochure that the compiler even perceived in the dissonant harmonics of the introduction "an admirable characterization of Don Quixote's notorious tendency to draw wrong conclusions." The main divisions of the score are formed by a lengthy Introduction, a Theme with variations, and the Finale. The variations faithfully represent the most important incidents in the famous Cervantes romance.

In the Introduction, marked "chivalrously and gallantly," a typically Straussian soaring motive introduces the hero. There are dreams in the woodwinds, but there are also evil forces arrayed against Don Quixote by chromatically scheming magicians. The instruments are muted, even the bass tuba, creating a phantasmagoria of blending sonorities. Madness and chivalry collide in discordant harmonies. But Don Quixote is now determined to devote himself to the rescue of the helpless and the innocent.

Glissando (It.). A slide; a rapid scale. On bowed instruments, a flowing, unaccented execution of a passage. On the piano, a rapid scale effect obtained by sliding the thumb, or thumb and one finger, over the keys.

The theme portrays Don Quixote idealistically. The solo violoncello intones the identifying motive of the hero in a minor key. It is followed by the mundane appearance of Sancho Panza, set grossly in outspoken major. A set of variations follows. The first introduces Don Quixote's ideal lady, the ineffably beautiful Dulcinea. She is in danger from rotating windmills, and Don Quixote rushes to her defense. He is knocked down by the sails, represented by the harp **glissando** and the drums. The second variation portrays another battle. But the enemy army turns out to be a flock of sheep. There are ingenious effects of muted brass representing a chorus of bleating sheep. The harmonic cloud of dust is panchromatic.

The third variation is a philosophical discussion between the master and the henchman. The cello is idealistic in its calm proclamation of the aims of chivalry; the viola expresses doubts, and soon becomes so insistent in its demands for peaceful life that the cello is forced to summon the entire orchestra to silence the impertinent henchman. In the fourth variation Don Quixote confronts a procession of penitents. Although they sing sacred chants, he believes they are robbers, and lunges at them. He is thrown off his horse. Exhausted, he falls asleep. A dream of sweet Dulcinea descends on Don Quixote in the fifth variation. The tremolos of the woodwinds and muted strings accompany his vision.

Don Quixote finally meets his Dulcinea in the sixth variation. But she is not the ideal woman of his dreams: Sancho Panza cruelly deceived him by passing a common country girl for his beloved. Don Quixote is sure that her transformation was effected by the black arts of his enemies, and he is ready to fight them. The seventh variation carries Don Quixote and Sancho Panza through the air on a wooden horse, in their imagination, of course. Here Strauss introduces the wind machine into the orchestra, which reinforces the blowing chromatics in the flutes, and the whistling glissandos in the harp. In the eighth variation they take a ride in a boat, to the strains of a **barcarole**.

Don Quixote finally confronts, in the ninth variation, the Two Magicians, his greatest enemies. In reality they are itinerant monks, harmlessly conversing in a duet of bassoons. He attacks them and puts them to rout. The tenth variation sets the end to Don Quixote's adventures. In his last battle, he is defeated by the Knight of the White Moon and returns home to die. The Finale is without strife. The tremolos in the muted strings mark the last feverish excitement; one more idealistic

Barcarole (Ger.). A vocal or instrumental piece imitating the song of the Venetian gondoliers.

sigh in the cello and Don Quixote de la Mancha is dead. His epitaph is brief; the final chords of the cadence speak of eternal peace.

Symphonic Poem: A Hero's Life, *Op. 40 (1897–98)*

Ein Heldenleben (*A Hero's Life*) was the last of the great series of symphonic poems of Richard Strauss, all of which were composed still in the nineteenth century, each one a masterpiece in its own right: *Don Juan*, *Death and Transfiguration*, *Till Eulenspiegel*, *Thus Spake Zarathustra*, and *A Hero's Life*. The first of these Strauss wrote as a mere youth of twenty-three; the last, when he was thirty-four. The very title, *Ein Heldenleben*, with its obvious autobiographical connotations, shocked the contemporary public. Its post-Wagnerian idiom, with free use of unresolved dissonances, revolted respectable music critics. The appearance of *A Hero's Life* was greeted with an outpouring of righteous indignation.

> Richard Strauss indulges in a self-glorification of the most bare-faced kind. The hero's antagonists are described by him with the utmost scorn as a lot of pigmies and snarling and yelping bowwowing nincompoops. The composer's progressing impotence, however, is most plainly perceivable in the section devoted to his wife. She is represented by a solo violin, which is not a bad insinuation, as much as to say that she plays first fiddle in his life. But the climax of everything that is ugly, cacophonous, blatant and erratic, the most perverse music I ever heard in all my life is reached in the section "The Hero's Battlefield." The man who wrote this outrageously hideous noise is either a lunatic, or rapidly approaching idiocy.

Thus spake the *Musical Courier* of New York in 1899.

Concerning the harmony employed in *Ein Heldenleben*,

a Boston music critic opined that "the attempt to play in two different keys at the same time is as disastrous as the attempt of two railroad trains to pass each other on the same track." Even the urbane Philip Hale expressed shock at the self-appreciation expressed by Strauss in *Ein Heldenleben*. "This tone poem," he wrote, "might be justly entitled 'A Poseur's Life,' and a blustering poseur at that."

And finally, here is a bouquet of florid invective from the pen of Richard Aldrich of the *New York Times* in 1905: "In no other work has Strauss so deliberately affronted the ear with long-continued din and discord or . . . so consciously used ugliness in music to represent conceptions of ugliness, as in *Ein Heldenleben*."

Richard Strauss began the composition of *Ein Heldenleben* in Munich on August 2, 1898, and completed it on December 27, 1898, in Charlottenburg. Strauss conducted the first performance of the work from manuscript in Frankfurt on March 3, 1899. The subtitle is *Tondichtung (Tone Poem)*, an appellation popularized by Strauss. By definition, a tone poem is a narrative in poetic language. Examined impartially at this point of time, *Ein Heldenleben* appears almost traditional in its structure. It begins and ends in the key of E flat major. Its harmonic, melodic, rhythmic, and orchestral elements are entirely within the rational confines of late-nineteenth-century music. The orchestra is huge, but no more so than the orchestra of Wagner or Bruckner.

Ein Heldenleben has a definite story to tell, and it is told with imagination and wit. It may be argued, in fact, that, far from being an outrageous exhibition of self-inflation, *Ein Heldenleben* may be a subtle parody on a composer in the role of a self-made personage from the *Eroica*.

An admirable custom existed in nineteenth-century Germany: whenever a new musical composition of importance was performed, a detailed guide profusely illustrated with musical examples was published for distribution among the

Strauss Timeline (cont.)

1935 *Die Schwiegsame Frau*, with libretto by Jewish writer Stefan Zweig, performed in Dresden, then withdrawn; resigns as president of Hitler's Reichsmusikkammer

1936 Composes Olympische Hymne for Berlin Olympic Games

1948 Exonerated by Allies of all Nazi-related associations

1949 Returns to Germany, dies in Garmisch-Partenkirchen

listeners. For *Ein Heldenleben*, an impressively voluminous guide was compiled by Friedrich Rösch; it contained seventy thematic illustrations, in addition to a descriptive poem by a volunteer admirer. Yet Strauss told Romain Rolland: "No program of any kind is needed. It is sufficient to know that in this tone poem the hero is fighting off his adversaries."

Ein Heldenleben consists of six distinct sections. The first represents the hero. His theme breathes the eloquence of nobility. According to the exegesis by Rösch, the theme itself comprises four motives illustrating the various attractive sides of the hero. The theme soars ever higher until its heroic character is well established. Then there is a pause on an unresolved dominant seventh chord. It serves as a prelude to a section dealing with the hero's antagonists. They are jabbering enviously, not to say cacophonously, on the piccolo, the flute, the oboes, the English horn, and the tubas. They try to demean the hero by the device of thematic diminution, that is, by halving the note values of the hero's theme. He is dismayed by this impertinence, but soon regains his composure and repels the chromatic assaults of his enemies. He is now free to return to the serenity of his private life. He turns the full power of his affection to his feminine companion, represented by a solo violin. She does not seem to appreciate the hero's attention. The expression marks over the violin part vary from "somewhat sentimental" to "coquettish," "nagging," and "angry." But soon the solo violin becomes tender and loving. Clamorous voices are still heard in the background, but the love duet has now reached the point of appassionato, and the defeated antagonists can no longer disturb the hero's contentment.

Augmentation. Doubling (or increasing) the time value of the notes of a theme or motive, often in imitative counterpoint.

Still, like Don Quixote in the preceding tone poem of Strauss, the hero must challenge his new enemies. There are flourishes of trumpets backstage announcing the battle. The hero's theme soars aloft, in **augmentation**, to avenge the former attempt of his enemies at the diminution of his glory;

they now wilt in chromatic impotence. The battle rages on with drums accentuating its ferocity. But the hero's theme is now triumphantly sounded in the potent brass. His victory is total.

The time has now come for the hero's mission of peace. He recalls his earlier musical conquests. Self-quotations appear successively from his previous tone poems, from *Macbeth*, *Don Juan*, *Thus Spake Zarathustra*, *Death and Transfiguration*, *Don Quixote*, *Till Eulenspiegel*, and his early opera *Guntram*. Industrious calculators accounted for twenty-three of such self-quotations in all. Did Richard Strauss, at the young age of thirty-four, deliberately try to glorify himself by such means? Or was he indulging in a ponderous jeu d'esprit? He was a complex personality, capable of taking a skeptical view of himself as well as of the world. The indignation of the critics against his outrageous presumption in picturing himself as a hero posted in the center of the musical universe may have been the demonstration of their own lack of humor.

Symphonia Domestica, *Op. 53 (1902–3)*

Richard Strauss had a genius for a creating a musical sensation. He was also the product of an era in which egotism was elevated to the plane of mystical solipsism. The individual was placed above society. God was abolished, and the superman assumed the vacated deistic functions. With a fine mixture of self-aggrandizement and irony, Strauss painted a self-portrait as a hero in his tone poem *A Hero's Life*, and watched with amusement the outraged reaction to his effrontery. After all, he had anticipated it when he depicted his detractors by the cackling cacophony of uneuphonious brass in that work.

In the *Symphonia Domestica* (*Domestic Symphony*) Strauss raised the curtain of his family life, and dedicated the score "to my beloved wife and our young one." He conducted the world premiere of *Symphonia Domestica* at a concert of his works in New York on March 21, 1904. An analytical study, provided by devout Straussians, lists sixty-seven distinct motives identifying various aspects of the characters that pass the scene during twenty-four hours in the life of the Strauss family. Since it was a matter of common gossip in knowledgeable circles that Frau Pauline de Ahna Strauss ruled the household with a whim of iron, there were amused whispers concerning the idyllic musical phrases that Strauss assigned to his imperious spouse. A Boston music critic put the rumors into print when he wrote: "If *Symphonia Domestica* were a true biographical sketch, we fancy that the wife would be portrayed on trombones and tubas while the husband would be pictured on the second violins."

The work is an immense revolving musicorama, subdivided into four sections, which correspond to four symphonic movements. After a sonatomorphic opening, there is a development, a **reprise**, a Scherzo, an **Adagio**, and a finale. The paterfamilias is sympathetically introduced by a genial motive in the cellos. But there are more sides to his nature. Strauss magnanimously admits in specific markings in the score that he may be absent-minded, unsocially introspective and at times even temperamental. Frau Strauss is depicted with uxorious deference by a gentle phrase in the violins, grazioso. But there are other sides to her nature, too, which are not grazioso, for she may be capricious, moody, and self-willed, as Strauss dutifully points out in his interlinear comments. The most affectionate musical characterization is reserved for the baby, whose sweet lallation is sounded by the oboe d'amore. Aunts and uncles come to visit the Strauss family and to admire the baby's looks and intelligence. "Ganz der Papa!"—Just like Daddy!—exclaim the aunts through the medium of muted trumpets. "Ganz die Mama!"—Just like Mommy!—opine the uncles on muted trombones, horns, and woodwinds. (The words of these breathless interjections are noted in the score.) The loving

Reprise (Fr.). A repeat; reentrance of a part or theme after a rest or pause.
Adagio (It.). Slow, leisurely; a slow movement.

relatives depart, and the parents take advantage of the lull to have a moment of play with the child in a vivacious scherzo. But it is late in the day, a lullaby is sung, and the baby is put to bed, wrapped up in warm clothes and covered with blankets and shawls, according to the barbarous precepts of Victorian pediatricians.

It is now seven o'clock, signalized by seven silvery bell strokes on the glockenspiel. The child is asleep and the parents are alone. An expressive adagio introduces a "Liebesszene" ("Love Scene"), with the motives of the married couple intertwining in a blissful marital **counterpoint**. An emotional upsurge illustrates the growth of mutual passion, culminating in a soaring **fortissimo**. The flutes out of breath, the whispering harps and the moan of stifled violins sul ponticello draw a veil on the scene of love. The night passes quickly, and in minutes of symphonic time, the clock strikes seven again. The baby wakes up and emits a demanding cry in the woodwinds and muted trumpets. Father, annoyed by this vocal intrusion, makes a grumbling remark, eliciting a counterremark from Mother. A "lively quarrel" ensues in the form of a double fugue, with the baby furnishing a treble in dissonant counterpoint. But lo! Here is the milkman. A bottle of warm milk pacifies the child, the fugal contretemps subsides, and all is well. Strauss makes amends to Frau Strauss with a cello offering. Then they go to the window to greet the morning son.

"I see no reason why I should not write a symphony about myself. I find the subject as interesting as Napoleon, or Alexander the Great," Strauss said to Romain Rolland in reply to a baffled inquiry. Some critics were unconvinced by his argument. Henry T. Finck, of the *New York Evening Post*, an inveterate old fogey who viewed modern trends in music with constant alarm, voiced the suspicion that *Symphonia Domestica* was nothing more than "a clever method of courting publicity." He denied even the illustrative validity of the music, claiming that the child's motive suggested "a megalosaurian

Counterpoint. Polyphonic composition; the combination of two or more simultaneous melodies.
Fortissimo (It.). Extremely loud.

monster rather than a Bavarian baby." "The whole thing," he concluded, "might be called as appropriately *A Trip to Constantinople*, or *A Day at Vladivostok*."

Salome *(1903–5)*

Strauss wrote his one-act opera Salome to the text of a play by Oscar Wilde of that name. The subject was extremely daring for the period, dealing with the apocryphal story of the beautiful dancer Salome who tries to lure John the Baptist into intimacy. The saint curses her in repulsing her unspeakable advances. Herod, who is infatuated with Salome, asks her to dance for him. She consents on condition that he would grant her a wish. She then performs her Dance of the Seven Veils. Having thrown off the last veil, she demands from Herod the gratification of her desire, namely the head of John the Baptist. Horrified, Herod nevertheless carries out his promise. John is beheaded, and his head is brought to Salome on a platter.

Then follows one of the most shocking scenes ever enacted in the theater. Salome speaks to the inanimate head, taunts the saint and kisses his lips. Herod is appalled by this exhibition and orders his soldiers to slay her. The curtain falls.

For this play, Strauss wrote an amazing score, abounding in unresolved dissonances and orchestrated in the most extraordinary manner. The vocal parts, too, were written without regard for traditional operatic singing. The singers were required to master a totally new technique of melodramatic narrative with an angular melodic line and palpitating asymmetrical rhythms.

No wonder, then, that after the first performance of *Salome* by the Dresden Court Opera on December 9, 1905, there was an outcry against the opera. In 1907 the Metropolitan Opera produced *Salome* in New York, arousing such a hullabaloo that the management was forced to take the opera off the boards. The *New York Times* published a letter to the editor by a doctor of medicine which contained the following passage: "I am a man of middle life who has devoted twenty years to the practice of the profession that necessitates a daily intimacy with degenerates. I say that *Salome* is a detailed and explicit exposition of the most horrible, disgusting, revolting and unmentionable features of degeneracy that I have ever heard, or imagined." New York music critics assailed *Salome* for its unresolved dissonances.

"Strauss has a mania for writing ugly music," said the *New York Sun*.

> What more natural than that he should cast about for a subject which imperatively demands hideous din to correspond with and justify his concatenated discords? And what more natural than that the noisome Salome should seem an ideal companion for his noisy music? The presentation of such a story is ethically a crime; Richard Strauss's music is aesthetically criminal or at least extremely coarse and ill-mannered. There is one consolation. Thanks to the prevailing dissonance nobody knows whether the singers sing the right notes, that is, the notes assigned to them, or not.

And he concludes the review with this proclamation: "If this be art, then let the music of the future find her mission in the sewer, pesthouse and brothel."

Der Rosenkavalier *(1909–10)*

Hugo von Hofmannsthal was Strauss's most imaginative collaborator and he wrote the libretto of *Der Rosenkavalier*, which was produced in 1911. The intricacy of the plot, with its manifold entanglements, amatory cross-currents, disguises, and contrived mistaken identities, is in the most extravagant manner of eighteenth-century farce. The action takes place in Vienna in Mozart's time. The personages embroiled in the comedy are the Feldmarschallin (the wife of the field marshal), a young count whom she takes as a sporadic lover, an aging Baron, and a nubile lady whom the ineffable baron proposes to marry.

According to the quaint custom of the time, the prospective bridegroom must send to his betrothed a young messenger carrying a rose: this is the Rose Cavalier of the title. The Feldmarschallin selects her young lover for this role. What neither she nor the baron could foresee was the instant explosion of youthful love between the Rosenkavalier and the young lady. The situation becomes further confused when the Feldmarschallin orders the young Cavalier of the Rose to put on a servant girl's dress to conceal his presence in her bedroom. Dressed as a girl, the Rosenkavalier attracts the attention of the foraging aging Baron and, to save the situation, agrees to a tryst with him. As if this were not enough to bemuse the spectator beyond all rational tolerance, the part of the Rosenkavalier is entrusted to a mezzosoprano, so that when he (in actual appearance and physiological gender, she) changes his/her dress, the actress singing the role of the Rosenkavalier reverts, in this process of double transvestitude, to her original god-given gender.

The finale of the opera unravels the numerous strands of the plot when the police arrive as a proverbial deus ex machina. The Feldmarschallin shames the Baron into a behavior befitting his age and status, and she herself gives up the Cavalier of the Rose, who is awarded the welcome prize in the person of the Baron's intended bride. The music redeems the nonsense of the plots of Strauss's comic operas. The Viennese waltzes that enliven the score of *Der Rosenkavalier*, albeit anachronistically for a play that takes place in the eighteenth century, are gorgeous. After the morbid and somber scores of *Salome* and *Elektra*, Strauss proved to his critics that he could produce an opera full of brilliance, wit, and novel musical invention.

The first performance of *Der Rosenkavalier* took place in Dresden on January 26, 1911. A thematic guide was issued for the production, tabulating 118 leading motives employed in the score. The opera won an immediate acclaim; a symphonic suite extracted from the score became a favorite on concert programs.

ARNOLD SCHOENBERG
(1874–1951)
A Musical Prophet

ON HIS SEVENTY-FIFTH BIRTHDAY, Arnold Schoenberg sent a circular letter to his friends and admirers, opening with the anguished words, "To be recognized only after death!" The letter is a bitter summary of the life of a star-crossed genius. Schoenberg recalls in it the question he was asked when he was in the Austrian Army in World War I: "Are you the famous composer Arnold Schoenberg?" and his reply: "Somebody had to be, and nobody wanted to, so I took it on, myself." In the same letter, he quotes a prediction he made in 1912: that the second half of the century would make amends by excessive praise for the lack of understanding that his work received in the first half of the century. The biblical flavor of these declarations is in harmony with Schoenberg's messianic complex. For he truly regarded himself as both a martyr crucified by his professional enemies and music critics and the savior of music as formulated in his new dodecaphonic testament. The miracle of Schoenberg's phenomenon was that his lofty prophecy was completely vindicated.

All his life, Schoenberg was acutely conscious of his destiny as a musical reformer. But being a realist, he knew that the struggle for a new language of composition would be cruel, and that he would suffer greatly for his daring. Performances of his works were occasions of wild disturbances. The critics called him a musical anarchist, fabricator of cacophonic antimusic, a de-composer. Like other reformers of genius, Schoenberg had devoted disciples and ardent friends. Two of his pupils, Alban Berg and Anton Webern, achieved great fame on their own merits. But even composers from an entirely different world of music showed curiosity regarding Schoenberg's revolutionary theories. The great Puccini once made a special trip to Florence to hear Schoenberg's song cycle *Pierrot lunaire*, in which the lines are recited in a singsong fashion, half spoken, half sung, to the accompaniment of a strange-sounding little group of instruments. Schoenberg was profoundly moved by this sign of interest on Puccini's part.

Schoenberg was a philosopher in his attitude toward life, but he was also a fighter. In his early days in Vienna, to ensure fair play for modern music, he organized a Society of Private Musical Performances, from which the critics were excluded, and applause was not allowed. At the concerts of Schoenberg's society, all kinds of modern music was presented, not only works by ultramodernists, but also by less radical composers. But Schoenberg soon left Vienna for Berlin.

As the twentieth century advanced, seeking subtler means of musical expression, Schoenberg abandoned the convention of tonality. He wrote melodies that were strangely angular; they leaped and skipped, dangled in deliberate hesitation, hovered with calculated uncertainty over a dissonant chord, broke in a zigzag, or fell precipitously after a sudden ascent. His harmonies arranged themselves into unusual tonal groups, with a distinct preference for dissonance. The **key signature** disappeared, for there was no longer any key in Schoenberg's music, which was atonal; even transitional occurrences of triads, particularly the assertively strong major **triads**, became infrequent. Rhythm was free, but the division into measures separated by bar lines to designate **meter** was preserved even in his most advanced works.

It is interesting to observe that, before the twentieth century, every piece of music ended on a chord containing no more than three different notes, and forming a perfect concord, either a major or a minor triad. No such restriction existed for Schoenberg and his modern contemporaries. Any chord, no matter how dissonant, could mark the end of a composition. Emancipation of **dissonance** was Schoenberg's slogan, immeasurably widening the range of expression in his music.

Parallels with modern art, and even with modern mathematics, suggested themselves. If Schoenberg's melodies are no longer rectilinear in a classical way, neither, in geodesics, is a straight line the shortest distance between two points. If space is curved, forming an unthinkable hyphenated entity with time, then Schoenberg's dissonant harmonies and free rhythm correspond more closely to the musical reality of modern life.

In Expressionistic paintings, realism gives way to subjective image building, in which optically distorted shapes of familiar objects or human figures seem to reach deeper than conventional art. Schoenberg was also a painter of singular power; his self-portrait, with the keen eyes fixed at infinity, is a remarkable example of psychological expressionism, depicting a face both anguished and aggressive, ironic and firm. Schoenberg also painted a savage caricature in oil, portraying

Key signature. The sharps or flats at the head of the staff.

Triad. A "three-tone" chord composed of a given tone (the root), with its third and fifth in ascending order in the scale.

Meter, metre. In music, the symmetrical grouping of musical rhythms. In verse, the division into symmetrical lines.

Dissonance. A combination of two or more tones requiring resolution.

a surrealistic monster with bloated features, bulbous nose, and purple blotches on the cheeks. It bore the title, *The Critic*. His paintings, cognate with Blake and Goya, but perhaps more directly influenced by Impressionists of the prewar era, are subjective visions.

With the gradual dissolution of formal principles of old music, Schoenberg faced the necessity of creating a new musical organization, for his mind demanded order. He described this new organization as "composition with twelve tones related only to one another." Each musical work must be based on a theme containing all twelve different notes. This theme, or **tone row**, appears in four guises—in its original form, in an **inversion** (in which the direction of the melodic line is reversed), in **retrograde** motion (played backward), and in retrograde inversion (the inverted melody played backward). Since each of these four forms can be transposed to any note of the **chromatic scale**, the grand total of possible derivatives is forty-eight.

The twelve-tone row determines not only the melody, but also **counterpoint** and harmony. Twelve is a very divisible number, so that the twelve notes of the basic theme or any of its derivatives can be conveniently arranged in two, three, four, or six parts. In florid counterpoint, the notes may skip diagonally from one voice to another. In vertical structures, full chords are formed from the basic thematic materials. Thus the tone row unifies all three aspects of composition—melody, counterpoint, and harmony.

There are 479,001,600 possible permutations of twelve different chromatic notes, and a twelve-tone composer—or, to use the more highfalutin term, a dodecaphonic composer—has a rich selection of tone rows at his disposal. Some of these tone rows are beautiful, dodecaphonically speaking; some are not. Aesthetic standards of beauty in this new musical language may be different from the classical ideals, but they are nonetheless valid.

Tone row. The fundamental subject in a twelve-tone composition.

Inversion. The transposition of one of the notes of an interval by an octave; chord position with lowest note other than root.

Retrograde. Performing a melody backwards; a crab movement. Also, one of three standard techniques in twelve-note composition (retrograde, inversion, transposition) wherein all notes of a set are played in reverse (i.e., backward).

Chromatic. Relating to tones foreign to a given key (scale) or chord; opposed to diatonic.

Counterpoint. Polyphonic composition; the combination of two or more simultaneous melodies.

Schoenberg was extremely sensitive in safeguarding the rights to his method of composition. He reacted vehemently to the claims of Josef Matthias Hauer, an Austrian musician who went so far as to have a rubber stamp made with the words, "the sole inventor and despite all pretensions by untalented imitators the true initiator of twelve-tone music," which he appended to his signature in correspondence. Schoenberg objected violently to Thomas Mann's attribution, in his novel *Doktor Faustus*, of Schoenberg's method to the mythical syphilitic German composer Adrian Leverkühn. In a lengthy letter to the *Saturday Review of Literature* he excoriated Mann for this impropriety. "Leverkühn is depicted from beginning to end as a lunatic," Schoenberg fulminated. "I am seventy-four and I am not yet insane, and I have never acquired the disease from which this insanity stems." Schoenberg also raised the specter of an encyclopedia published in the year 2060 crediting the discovery of the twelve-tone method to Leverkühn or to Thomas Mann himself. Mann tried to assuage Schoenberg's wrath by adding a note of acknowledgment of Schoenberg's dodecaphonic priority in a new edition of *Doktor Faustus*, but he made an egregious faux pas in referring to Schoenberg as "a contemporary composer." This only added fire to Schoenberg's fury. "I wanted to be noble to a man who was awarded a Nobel Prize," Schoenberg wrote, glorying in the pun, and added acidly: "In two or three decades one will know which of the two was the other's contemporary."

Schoenberg was attacked as a cerebral composer who reduced music to a soulless game of numbers, and yet he always insisted on the paramount importance of talent, even in twelve-tone composition. When this writer submitted to Schoenberg a musical treatise purporting to exhaust all workable melodic patterns, dodecaphonic and otherwise, Schoenberg answered in a friendly postcard, but added significantly: "You have in all probability organized every possible succes-

Schoenberg Timeline

1874	Born in Vienna
1894	Studies counterpoint with Alexander von Zemlinsky
1898	Converts to Protestantism for professional reasons
1899	Composes *Verklärte Nacht* for string sextet
1901-3	Lives in Berlin, launches artistic cabaret, Überbrettl, teaches at Stern Conservatory
1907	Vereinigung Schaffender Tonkünstler, which he organized with Zemlinsky in Vienna, premieres Chamber Symphony No. 1
1908	Composes Second String Quartet, last work (with one late exception) with key signature
1909	Composes first atonal work, first of three Piano Pieces, Op. 11
1910	Appointed to faculty of Vienna Academy
1911	Completes influential theoretical text *Harmonieliehre*
1912	Premiere of Five Pieces for Orchestra in London; conducts premiere of *Pierrot lunaire* in Berlin, after 40 rehearsals
1913	First complete performance of *Gurre-Lieder* by Vienna Philharmonic
1918	Organizes Society for Private Musical Performances
1924	Articulates 12-tone compositional method, exemplified in Piano Suite, Op. 25

(continued)

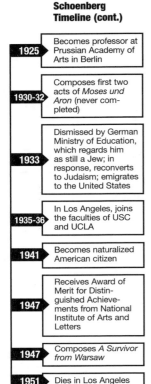

Oratorio (It.). An extended multi-movement composition for vocal solos and chorus accompanied by orchestra or organ.

sion of tones. This is an admirable feat of mental gymnastics, but as a composer I must believe in inspiration rather than in mechanics."

Schoenberg was a philosopher-musician. He argued from the particular to the general. Even in his purely didactic works, such as his *Harmonielehre (Theory of Harmony)*, he formulated the rules as inductive steps into universal concepts. He was not, however, an intellectual hermit. He did not remove himself from the world around him. He was a participant in life and had an interest in people. He was an excellent tennis player. He also had some quaint ideas for practical inventions. A list of his projects included a musical typewriter, a proposal for equitable transfer fares on Berlin streetcars, and a recipe for pumpernickel bread.

Much has been said and written about Schoenberg's presentiment of a personal and general catastrophe, as evidenced by his paintings, his writings, and his music. Subsequent events must have strengthened this morbid faith, for no sooner had Schoenberg, in 1925, settled down in Berlin as a professor at the Prussian Academy of Arts than the Hitlerian cataclysm burst over his non-Aryan and modernistic head. Under the stress of a double stigma, he had to leave Germany for France. The shock of a new discrimination led him, probably in the spirit of an emphatic demonstration, to return to the religion of his youth, which he had relinquished thirty-five years earlier. Momentarily in Paris, he responded to a call from America, the last country offering refuge to European undesirables regardless of creed.

There is something biblical in Schoenberg's spectacular martyrdom. In his early life, shuttling between Vienna and Berlin, revered by disciples, derided by scurrilous critics, he was the very picture of a prophet of the faith. Not content with music, he pursued literature and poetry, in the most esoteric form of expression. His poetry, such as the book to *Die Jakobsleiter (Jacob's Ladder)*, an **oratorio** begun during the war days (but left unfinished), is abstruse and, to the uninitiated, irritatingly tangential. His choice of words for his **monodramas**, operas, songs, and song cycles is of the same tantalizing sort, when you seem to grasp the meaning at one moment, only to see it fade into distressing nonsense at another. Often, coarse matter succeeds evanescent symbolism—thus, an early song of Schoenberg's, as yet not out of Wagnerian indentures, ends with the words, "I think of my dog." In one song, Schoenberg "feels the air of other planets," yet in his monodramas he is earthly. A metaphysical woman with child, a strangely unjealous "lover to be," these visions of his operas are as difficult to grasp as a stranger's dream. They were certainly excellent material for easy burlesque, as newspaper critics of both hemispheres discovered to their advantage.

Monodrama. A dramatic or musical presentation with a single performer.

It is fantastic that a mind as relentlessly logical as Schoenberg's was also prone to common superstition. He regarded it as an ill omen that he was born on the thirteenth of the month of September, 1874, and the consciousness of this numerical accident developed into acute triskaidekaphobia. To be sure, he rationalized it as a numerological set of probable concomitances, but the seriousness with which he proceeded to eliminate number thirteen from his references, even to the point of skipping the thirteenth measure from the numbering of bars, is extraordinary. When he noticed that the number of letters in the title of his opera *Moses and Aaron* added up to thirteen, he deleted the second *a* in Aaron, despite the fact that the spelling with two *a*'s was standard in German from the time of Luther. When he reached the age of seventy-six, a friend jocularly pointed out to him that the sum of the digits of seventy-six was thirteen. Schoenberg became quite disturbed at this, and remarked that he might not live through the year. His premonition was only too true. On July 13, 1951, during his last illness, he suffered a collapse, but his mind was clear. He observed to his wife that all would be well if only he would survive the fateful thirteenth, but he died—thirteen minutes before midnight.

Verklärte Nacht (Transfigured Night), *Op. 4 (1899)*

"I personally hate to be called a revolutionist. . . . I possessed from my very first start a thoroughly developed sense of form. There was no falling into order because there was never disorder. There is no falling at all, but on the contrary, there is an ascending to higher and better order." So wrote Arnold Schoenberg to the author from Hollywood, California, on June 3, 1937, in reply to an inquiry regarding his style of composition. A study of Schoenberg's works confirms his self-estimate. His evolution was logical in the Hegelian sense. Proceeding from Wagnerian and Brahmsian roots, Schoenberg's musical language developed into the method of composition with twelve tones related "only to one another" (Schoenberg's own definition of his epoch-making dodecaphonic system).

String quartet. A composition for first and second violin, viola, and cello.

Schoenberg began his career as a composer with a work of utmost serenity, a **String Quartet** in D major, which was performed in his native Vienna in 1897. The formidable Eduard Hanslick wrote a remarkably benevolent review of the piece in which he said half facetiously, "It seems that a new Mozart is growing up in Vienna." It was fortunate for Hanslick that he did not live to hear the new Mozart's later music.

Schoenberg was twenty-five years old when he wrote his first important score, *Transfigured Night* (*Verklärte Nacht*) for string sextet. It was first performed in Vienna on March 18, 1902. In 1917 Schoenberg arranged it for string orchestra; he made another revision of the score in 1943. Ironically, this early work remained Schoenberg's most frequently performed composition. His atonal and dodecaphonic works written during the subsequent fifty years exercised a tremendous influence on composers of all lands, but audiences at large did not give them emotional acceptance.

Transfigured Night is a rare example of a **chamber music** work with definite literary connotations. It is inspired by a poem of Richard Dehmel, on a subject that was rather bold for its time. A man and a woman walk through a darkening forest. The key is that of D minor, often associated in Romantic music with woods and fields. The opening measures, in their measured tread, vividly suggest people walking. There is an interruption of the mood, a *Luftpause* (pause for breathing), which Schoenberg indicates by a V sign in the score.

So close is the music to the letter of the poem that many melodic passages follow precisely the syllables of the verse. The woman confesses to her lover: "Ich trag' ein Kind und nicht von dir" ("I carry a child, but not from you"), and the melodic rhythm follows the words as in a *Lied*. Her lover urges her not to give way to the consciousness of guilt. The passage is marked "soft, tender, warm." The music soars, the tension rises in chromatic entanglements. After an episode in melancholy F minor, there is a modulation into sunny E major, with a strong **pedal point** supporting the new tonality. The mood varies between *etwas ruhiger* and *etwas unruhiger*, from "somewhat quiet" to "somewhat unquiet." Wagneromantic **gruppetti** are catapulted to higher notes. The music grows more agitated, with **modulations** into remote keys. With tremendous emphasis, the string instruments reach **fortissimo** in long, protracted metrical divisions. From these emotional heights, there is a tonal descent to the major tonic in D, dissolving in **pianississimo**. There is a return to the primordial phrase. The strings are muted in **tremolo** passages, moving in the direction of the darkly bright key of F-sharp major. Here the violins sing a motive in rhythmic concordance with the prosody of the corresponding words in the poem, "Das Kind das Du empfangen hast sei deiner Seele keine Last" ("The child that you have conceived should on your soul not be a burden").

Chamber music. Vocal or instrumental music suitable for performance in a room or small hall.

Pedal point. A tone sustained in one part to harmonies executed in the other parts.
Gruppetto or **gruppo** (It.). Formerly, a trill; now, a turn. Also, any "group" of grace notes.
Modulation. Passage from one key into another.
Fortissimo (It.). Extremely loud.
Pianissimo (It.). Very soft.
Tremolo (It.). A quivering, fluttering, in singing; an unsteady tone.

Tonic. The keynote of a scale; the triad on the keynote (tonic chord).

The measured beats of the pedal point on the **tonic** D reflect the renewed steps of the lovers. As the moon follows them on their walk, the radiance of their love makes the unborn child one that belongs to both. The "transfigured night" of the title vibrates with the white splendor of D major. The

Arpeggio (It.). Playing the tones of a chord in rapid, even succession.

tonal harmony is enhanced by rolling **arpeggios** supported by deep-seated pedal points, and the paroxysm of luminous emotion recedes into inaudible euphony.

When Richard Dehmel heard *Transfigured Night*, he was moved to write to Schoenberg: "I expected to recall the motives of my poem in your wonderful sextet, but I soon forgot about my words, so bewitched was I by your music. Oh the most beautiful sound! Oh, the reverberation of the maker of words! . . ."

Gurre-Lieder *(1900–1903; 1910–11)*

Schoenberg's early life in Vienna was hard. At various times he served as a bank clerk and conductor of workers' choruses. He eked out his meager income by orchestrating the operettas of his more fortunate fellow composers. In 1902 he moved to Berlin, where he enjoyed better living conditions. The evolution of his style took him to the borders of tonality, until the sacrosanct foundations of tonal harmony began to crumble and the sturdy tonic-dominant ganglion became atrophied. It was in Berlin that he had his first taste of critical

Symphonic poem. An extended orchestral composition which follows in its development the thread of a story or the ideas of a poem, repeating and interweaving its themes appropriately; it has no fixed form, nor has it set divisions like those of a symphony.

abuse. His innocuous early **symphonic poem** *Pelléas and Mélisande* (inspired by the same drama by Maurice Maeterlinck as Debussy's great opera) was described in a respectable music journal as a long protracted wrong note. His Chamber Symphony No. 1 provoked the same journal to remark that it should be renamed the "Chamber-of-Horrors Symphony."

As Schoenberg's style grew in complexity, the critical chorus became increasingly shrill in its invective. In 1928, a Berlin writer demanded that Schoenberg be relieved of his teaching position as a protective measure against the musical corruption of the young. Terms like "cacophony," "musical anarchy," "lunacy," "charlatanism," and similes like "cat music" and "a bomb in a poultry yard," became habitual critical expressions whenever Schoenberg's works were performed. Riots erupted at Schoenberg's concerts. On one occasion a critic so completely lost his self-control that he began swinging his cane violently, and broke a window. Charged with disturbing the peace, he claimed intolerable musical provocation in his defense, and was released.

During the years of his struggle for subsistence in Vienna, Schoenberg undertook the composition of his most grandiose score thus far, *Gurre-Lieder* (*Songs of Gurre*), scored for an immense ensemble comprising five soloists, three men's choruses, mixed chorus, and a huge orchestra consisting of twenty-five woodwind instruments, twenty-five brass instruments, four harps, **celesta**, and a rich assortment of percussion instruments including a set of iron chains, as well as a large contingent of strings. In order to accommodate all these parts Schoenberg had to order special manuscript paper with forty-eight staves. He completed virtually the entire score in an amazingly short time between March 1900 and April 1901. But owing to the pressure of the daily routine of working for a living, Schoenberg put off the completion of the orchestration, and it was not until 1911 that the entire score was finally ready for publication and performance. The first performance of *Gurre-Lieder* took place in Vienna on February 23, 1913, under the direction of the greatly esteemed opera composer Franz Schreker, and it was received enthusiastically. But the occasion had the character of an almost retrospective event, stylistically speaking, for in the meantime Schoenberg had written such innovative scores as *Pierrot lunaire* and had moved toward the emancipation of dissonance with his atonal piano pieces.

Gurre-Lieder is an oratorio in three parts. The text is by the Danish poet Jens Peter Jacobsen, who wrote the Gurre

Celesta. Percussion instrument consisting of tuned steel bars connected to a keyboard.

poems in 1868 at the age of twenty-one. Schoenberg used the German translation by Robert F. Arnold. The story, derived from Scandinavian sagas, is preoccupied with the tragic, symbolic, and supernatural occurrences in the castle of Gurre, on the Esrom Sea in North Zealand, the seat of the Danish King Waldemar, who reigned in the fourteenth century. He fell in love with Tove, a commoner. When the queen discovered his infatuation, she had the girl murdered. The entire action of the poem represents the dream of the dead by the dead. Waldemar rides at night toward Gurre, where Tove waits for him. The dove of the forest announces Tove's death. The King is also dead, but his heart beats wildly in his lifeless body. The dove describes the scene at Tove's sepulchre, with the Queen standing by in repentance for her deed and the King staring at Tove's mute lips. In the second part of *Gurre-Lieder* Waldemar hurls bitter imprecations at God for robbing him of his dearest creature. The third and last part represents the wild hunt in the forest. Waldemar summons the bones of his slaughtered armies, but his men urge him to let them return to the peaceful dreams of their graves. The speaker reads the epilogue, calling on nature to restore life after the spectacle of death.

The shadow of Wagner hangs mightily over Schoenberg's score. As in Wagner's operas, the principal motives possess a deceptive folklike simplicity in their unambiguous triadic structure, but the harmonies are effluent and full of multiple suspensions. At climactic points, these tonal edifices acquire a measure of dissonance that Schoenberg described as "an excursion into the harmony of the future." Also Wagnerian are the resonant cadential 6/4 chords marking the moments of eschatological revelation. But in the method of application of these Wagneromorphic elements, Schoenberg forms an original style presaging the ultimate dodecaphonic developments. Specifically Schoenbergian is the utilization of the old **polyphonic** devices of thematic **augmentation**, diminu-

Polyphonic. Consisting of two or more independently treated melodies; contrapuntal; capable of producing two or more tones at the same time, as the piano, harp, violin, xylophone.

Augmentation. Doubling (or increasing) the time value of the notes of a theme or motive, often in imitative counterpoint.

tion, and motivic fragmentation in the plexus of dissonant counterpoint.

The orchestration is hyper-Wagnerian. The score includes Wagner tubas and such rare instrumental subspecies as the bass trumpet and the double-bass trombone. A historical innovation occurs in the third part of *Gurre-Lieder*, where the trombone **glissando** is introduced for the first time. When, in America, Schoenberg heard a jazz trombonist execute a glissando, he remarked to a friend, "I invented this sound in *Gurre-Lieder*."

The harmonic motto of the entire work consists of a major triad with an added sixth. This chord, in E-flat major, is outlined in the opening measures of the orchestral introduction. The thematic significance of the harmony is strikingly confirmed by the fact that the same chord, in C major, concludes the entire work. It is interesting to note that the C major triad with an added sixth is also the final chord in Mahler's *The Song of the Earth*. Debussy used the same cadential ending much earlier, as did the untutored ragtime piano players. The expansion of triadic harmony was in the air, and it is idle to attempt to establish the priority of its usage or to trace mutual influences.

After the orchestral prelude comes the first song of Waldemar. It is shaped in a simple, melodic style, but there is a premonition of the later Schoenbergian developments in the bold intervallic leaps of the solo part. In Tove's song, there is an intercalation of the **whole-tone scale**, a progression much in favor early in the century, which was also a harbinger of **atonality**. The next poem depicts Waldemar's dramatic ride to the castle of Gurre, culminating in the cry, "Waldemar has seen Tove!" Here Schoenberg lets the entire orchestra swell with luscious harmonies and heave with emotionally charged melodies, until a ringing climax is reached in a Wagneromorphic apotheosis of love. The dialogue between Waldemar and Tove continues, now dramatic in its concentrated chromati-

Glissando (It.). A slide; a rapid scale. On bowed instruments, a flowing, unaccented execution of a passage. On the piano, a rapid scale effect obtained by sliding the thumb, or thumb and one finger, over the keys.

Whole-tone scale. Scale consisting only of whole tones, lacking dominant and either major or minor triads; popularized by Debussy.
Atonality. The absence of tonality; music in which the traditional tonal structures are abandoned and there is no key signature.

cism, now lyrical and tender in its diatonic simplicity. Waldemar's impassioned exclamation, "Du wunderliche Tove!" is perhaps the most eloquent Wagnerophilic passage in the entire score.

A symphonic interlude follows the love-death dialogue between Waldemar and Tove. It is a true **tone poem**, bearing strong affinity with the music of Richard Strauss, without following specific Straussian procedures. Schoenberg's excursion into the harmony of the future takes place here in a coloristic episode, with muted violins bowing near the bridge in a massive convergence of secundally related inversions of major triads. The effect epitomizes Schoenberg's concept of *Klangfarbe*: "tone color." The symphonic **interlude** serves as a transition to the fateful poem of the forest dove reciting the course of the tragic events.

The second part of *Gurre-Lieder* comprises Waldemar's song, notable for its systematic exploitation of the minor- seventh chords on the **supertonic**, **mediant**, and **submediant** degrees of the major scale. These usages are also Wagnerian in origin, traceable particularly to *Lohengrin*. Similar harmonies permeate the third part of the work, opening with a section entitled "Wild Hunt." It is in this division, in the orchestral accompaniment to the "Song of the Peasant," that the famous trombone glissando appears in the score.

One of the most striking numbers in the finale is the "Melodrama" (a German term applied to inflected vocal recitation accompanied by instruments), in which the Speaker delivers his exhortation on the rebirth of nature. In a letter to Alban Berg, who prepared an extensive analytic guide for the first performance of *Gurre-Lieder*, Schoenberg emphasizes the difference between this inflected *Sprechstimme* (speech-voice), which outlines the rhythm and stress, and the full-fledged Sprechmelodie ("speech melody," or intonation), in which intervallic proportions are indicated with precision, as exemplified by *Pierrot lunaire*.

Tone poem. Also called "symphonic poem"; an extended orchestral composition which follows the thread of a story or the ideas of a poem.

Interlude. An intermezzo; an instrumental strain or passage connecting the lines or stanzas of a hymn, etc.

Supertonic. The second degree of a diatonic scale.
Mediant. The third degree of the scale.
Submediant. The third scale tone below the tonic; the sixth degree.

Gurre-Lieder concludes with a solemn **chorale** for full chorus, "See the Sun," set in the radiant key of C major, a tonality that has so often been used by composers as a symbol of purity of soul and redemption from sin. It must be left to students of musical semasiology to account for the psychological association that exists between the spiritual concept of goodness and saintliness and the notational accident of the absence of sharps and flats in the key signature, which results in the visual "whiteness" of the music. This association must have been very strong even to Schoenberg, if he was moved to end *Gurre-Lieder* in that key. It is all the more striking that when he arrived at the formulation of his logically hermetic method of composition with twelve tones related only to one another, he imposed the first and strongest taboo on the C major triad.

Chorale. A hymn tune of the German Protestant Church, or one similar in style.

Chamber Symphony No. 1, Op. 9 (1906)

No other composer shook the world of music as violently as Arnold Schoenberg. Performances of his works invariably provoked an outburst of anguished indignation on the part of the music critics. Sample quotations are "Schoenberg's opus is not merely filled with wrong notes, but is itself a fifty-minute-long protracted wrong note"; "Schoenberg's music is the reproduction of the sounds of nature in their crudest form"; "The endless discords, the constant succession of unnatural sounds, baffle description"; "Schoenberg's music is the last word in cacophony and musical anarchy, the most earsplitting combination of tones that ever desecrated the walls of a music hall"; "The Schoenberg piece combines the best sound effects of a hen yard at feeding time, a brisk morning in Chinatown, and practice hour at a busy conservatory"; "New exquisitely horrible sounds . . . the very ecstasy of the hideous. . . . The aura of Arnold Schoenberg is the aura of original depravity, of subtle ugliness, of basest egoism, of hatred and contempt, of cruelty and of the mystic grandiose."

Schoenberg never flinched from the barrage of malice and invective, which went on for nearly fifty years. In his letter of acceptance of the 1947 Award of Merit for Distinguished Achievement, bestowed upon him by the National Institute of Arts and Letters, he went so far as to credit his critics with encouraging him to continue his struggle. He writes:

> I never understood what I had done to make them as malicious, as furious, as cursing, as aggressive—I am certain that I had never taken away from them something they owned: I had never interfered with their rights. . . . Maybe I myself failed to understand their viewpoints. But I have one excuse: I had fallen into an ocean, into an ocean of overheated water, and it burned not only my skin, it burned also internally. And I could not swim. At least I could not swim with the tide. All I could do was to swim against the tide—whether it saved me or not. . . . When you call this an achievement, I do not understand of what it might consist. That I never gave up? I could not—I would have liked to. . . . Maybe something has been achieved, but it was not I who deserves the credit for that. The credit must be given to my opponents. They were the ones who really helped me.

Schoenberg's role is historic, for he established a new rational system of composition. It is the technique of twelve tones, in which a complete musical work is derived from a unique tone row of twelve different chromatic notes. He arrived at the formulation of the twelve-tone technique by a series of logical steps. His early music was the product of post-Wagnerian chromaticism; it led to the abandonment of all preconceived tonality. The last step was the organization of the atonal fabric into a rational system of monothematic composition based on a twelve-tone row.

Schoenberg's Chamber Symphony No. 1 belongs to the

period of transition from fluid tonality to atonality, with chordal harmonies built on fourths rather than on classical thirds. The basic tonality is retained; the form is clearly traceable to the classical **sonata** and the orchestration adheres to the established practices of early modernism. Even the dissonances are sparingly used, and ultimately resolved. The conclusion of the work is in the same key as the beginning, E major.

But even this mild music aroused a storm of criticism after its first performance in Vienna on March 31, 1913. The Berlin music weekly, *Signale*, reported as follows: "Fifteen brave musicians gave us an opportunity to hear Schoenberg's Chamber Symphony. It would be more suitable to call it the 'Schreckenkammersymphonie.'" The *Musical Courier* in its Berlin dispatch echoed these sentiments:

> Schoenberg has once more baffled the critics and public, this time with his Chamber Symphony for fifteen solo instruments. In order to give the listeners an opportunity to become accustomed to and to find the meaning in the unintelligible mixture of sounds, the whole work was gone through twice, but its interest did not seem to be increased even by this stringent measure. The audience sat perfectly silent as if stunned.

One Berlin critic compared the harmonic structure of the work to a field of weeds and turnips mixed together, and the general opinion was that the composition was a most unaccountable jumbling together of abnormalities.

It is interesting to note that when the Chamber Symphony was performed for the first time in New York on November 14, 1915, at a concert of the Friends of Music conducted by Stokowski, the newspaper comment was surprisingly restrained. One headline even proclaimed: "Schoenberg's Music Is Received Kindly."

Sonata (It.). An instrumental composition usually for a solo instrument or chamber ensemble, in three or four movements, connected by key, contrasted in theme, tempo, meter, and mood.

Pierrot lunaire, *Op. 21 (1912)*

In the history of the arts there are works of curious destiny. They are creations of small dimensions, often esoteric, and romantically vague. Their purpose is circumscribed. Yet, by some imponderable quality, they inspire more than a small circle of initiates, and become a center of attention and discussion. Often they exercise a subtle but lasting influence. In literature such a work was Baudelaire's collection of poems, *Les Fleurs du* Mal, which, in Victor Hugo's words, created a "frisson nouveau," a new thrill. In painting, there was Manet's picture *Le Dejeuner sur l'herbe*, which became a storm center in the Paris "Salon of the Rejected."

In music, such a work is Schoenberg's *Pierrot lunaire*. It is a set of "thrice seven" melodramas, short poems by Albert Giraud, translated into German by Erich Hartleben. The scoring is extremely tenuous, employing the piano, flute (interchangeable with piccolo), clarinet (interchangeable with bass clarinet), violin (interchangeable with viola), and cello. The poems are not sung, but spoken along a given melodic line. The music is not necessarily a reflection or illustration of the text. At times it deliberately deflects from the meaning of the words in the poems. Thus in "Serenade," Pierrot is pictured as playing on the viola, but the setting is for cello, and when the word "**pizzicato**" occurs in the text, the cello continues to play **arco** (i.e., with the bow).

The idiom of *Pierrot lunaire* is expressionistic. The subjective world of the moonstruck Pierrot is here made into a private reality, which a breath of oxygen would instantly destroy. Expressionism in poetry is reflected by integral chromaticism in music, with chromatic tones now crowding narrowly, then dispersing widely through several **octaves**, creating the feeling of tenseness or spaciousness, according to the design of each piece. This is the language of atonality: there is no determinable key, and the acoustically sharp intervals, major sevenths and minor ninths, prevail over milder dis-

Pizzicato (It.). Pinched; plucked with the finger; a direction to play notes by plucking the strings.
Arco (It.). Bow. *Arco in giù*, down-bow; *arco in su*, up-bow.

Octave. A series of eight consecutive diatonic tones; the interval between the first and the eighth.

DER ERSTEN INTERPRETIN
FRAU ALBERTINE ZEHME
IN HERZLICHER FREUNDSCHAFT

DREIMAL SIEBEN GEDICHTE

AUS ALBERT GIRAUDS

PIERROT LUNAIRE

(DEUTSCH VON OTTO ERICH HARTLEBEN)

Für eine Sprechstimme
Klavier, Flöte (auch Piccolo), Klarinette (auch Baß-
Klarinette), Geige (auch Bratsche) und Violoncell

(MELODRAMEN)

von

ARNOLD SCHÖNBERG

Op. 21

PARTITUR

U. E. 5334

Aufführungsrecht vorbehalten — Droits d'exécution réservés

UNIVERSAL-EDITION A.-G.

WIEN Copyright 1914 by Universal-Edition LEIPZIG

Aufführungsrecht vorbehalten.
Droits d'exécution réservés.

I. Teil.

1. Mondestrunken.

Arnold Schönberg, Op. 21.

Universal-Edition Nr. 5334. 5336.

Stich und Druck von Breitkopf & Härtel in Leipzig.

sonances. But this chromatic idiom does not yet constitute the logical system in which the twelve tones of the chromatic scale are arranged in a fundamental series. This twelve-tone technique was not elaborated by Schoenberg until twelve years later.

The twenty-one pieces of *Pierrot lunaire* were written between March 30 and September 9, 1912. It took forty rehearsals to bring the work to performance, which took place in Berlin on October 16, 1912. *Pierrot lunaire*, like every epoch-making work, met with derision on the part of the music critics. The American correspondent for the *Musical Courier* described the music as "the most ear-splitting combination of tones that ever desecrated the walls of a Berlin music hall," and the critic of the *Börsencourier* in Berlin exclaimed in mock horror: "If this is the music of the future, I pray my Creator not to let me live to hear it again."

1. "Mondestrunken" ("Moonstruck") speaks poetically of the wine that the moon pours nightly on the waves of the sea, the wine that we drink with our eyes (piano, flute, viola, and cello).
2. "Colombine." The poem extols the "pale blossoms of the moonlight, the white wonder roses" (piano, flute, clarinet, and viola).
3. "Der Dandy" ("Dandy"). The poem treats the figure of Pierrot, the "silent dandy of Bergamo," standing by the fountain in moonlight (piano, piccolo, clarinet).
4. "Eine blasse Wäscherin" ("A Pale Washerwoman"). The poem describes the whiteness of the washerwoman's arms, and of the linen she washes at night (flute, clarinet, and violin, marked "without any expression," and in pianissimo throughout).
5. "Valse de Chopin." An atonal melodic pattern with a Chopinesque élan. The poem dwells on the melancholy charm of a waltz that is like a pale drop of blood coloring the lips of an ailing man (piano, flute, and clarinet/bass clarinet).
6. "Madonna." A poet's appeal to the mother of all sorrows (flute, bass clarinet, and cello, with piano accompaniment in the last measures).
7. "Der kranke Mond" ("The Sick Moon"). Speaking voice

Passacaglia (It.). An old Italian dance in stately movement on a ground base of four measures.

with flute, in a nostalgic, but not tragic, poem of the desperately sick moon.

8. "Nacht" ("Night"). Subtitled "**passacaglia**," which implies the constancy of the thematic pattern, the song is an invocation to the black night. The voice is assigned, by exception, three singing tones in the deep register (piano, bass clarinet, and cello).

9. "Gebet an Pierrot" ("Prayer to Pierrot"). The prayer to restore the gaiety of life to one who has forgotten how to laugh (clarinet and piano).

10. "Raub" ("Theft"). Tale of Pierrot's nightly thieving after the ducal rubies, the bloody drops of bygone fame (flute, clarinet, violin, and cello).

11. "Rote Messe" ("The Red Mass"). Pierrot's blasphemous Mass at eventide (piccolo, bass clarinet, viola, cello, and piano).

12. "Galgenlied" ("The Song of the Gallows"). The condemned man's vision of his last mistress, the withered hussy with a long neck, about to strangle him (piccolo, viola, cello, and piano).

13. "Enthauptung" ("Decapitation"). Pierrot looking in deathly anguish at the unsheathed Turkish sword of the crescent moon, imagining himself being decapitated by it (bass clarinet, viola, cello, and piano).

14. "Die Kreuze" ("The Crosses"). The poet's verses are the crosses on which he is bled (speaking voice with piano, later joined by flute, clarinet, violin, and cello).

15. "Heimweh" ("Homesickness"). In nostalgic mood, Pierrot utters plaintive cries, like the sighs from an old Italian pantomime (clarinet, violin, and piano).

16. "Gemeinheit" ("Outrage"). Pierrot bores a hole in Cassander's skull, while his cries rend the air, stuffs his "authentic Turkish tobacco" into the hole, sticks a reed at the base of the skull, and puffs contentedly (piccolo, clarinet, violin, cello, and piano).

17. "Parodie" ("Parody"). A matron in love with Pierrot is cruelly exposed to light by the playful moon, aping her shining hairpins with its beams (piccolo, clarinet, viola, and piano).

18. "Der Mondfleck" ("Moonspot"). Pierrot takes an evening walk in search of adventure, and the moon puts a white spot on his jacket, which will not come off even though Pierrot tries to scrub it off till early morning (piccolo, clarinet, violin, cello, and piano).

19. "Serenade." Pierrot saws away on his viola with a grotesquely long bow. When Cassander, enraged by this noise at night, bids him stop, he grabs him by the collar and fiddles on his bald pate (cello and piano).

20. "Heimfahrt" ("Journey Home"). Subtitled "Barcarolla," the poem describes Pierrot's homeward journey southward to Bergamo, with the moonbeam for a rudder and a water lily for a boat (flute, clarinet, violin, cello, and piano).
21. "O alter Duft ("O Olden Fragrance). The poem recites the charm of old tales, which enchant the senses, and dispel gloomy moods (flute, clarinet, violin, cello, and piano).

Arnold Schoenberg describes the recording of the work as follows:

The ensemble which recorded *Pierrot lunaire* has been chosen with great care because of the high quality of preceding ensembles that played this piece. Eduard Steuermann, whose performance seems to be unsurpassable, was the first to play the piano part in 1912. He participated in almost all subsequent performances in Italy and France. He also belonged to the ensemble of the Verein für musikalische Privataufführungen (Society for Private Performances in Vienna), which, under the direction of Erwin Stein and my direction, played about one hundred performances in the last twenty years. Erika Wagner-Stiedry has performed the vocal part since that time (with a few exceptions, of which I want to mention particularly the great Marie Gutheil-Schoder), and this proves the great satisfaction her performance has always given me.

It may be interesting to mention that Hans Kindler, now conductor in Washington, D.C., was the first cellist who mastered the enormous difficulties of the cello part in an unforgettable manner. Other cellists who subsequently achieved world fame: Emmanuel Feuermann (with Klemperer conducting), Gregor Piatigorsky (with Arthur Schnabel at the piano, and Fritz Stiedry conducting), Benar Heifetz, the former cellist of the Kolisch Quartet, have played the cello part. I must not forget also the clarinet of Victor Polatschek, now of the Boston Symphony Orchestra.

But a special word must be said about Rudolf Kolisch. I have to discount the fact that he is my brother-in-law; what counts is that he was my pupil; what counts still more is that he has played the violin and viola part in *Pierrot lunaire* since 1921, together with Erika Stiedry and Eduard Steuermann; and what counts most is that he participated in every one of the two hundred rehearsals from the very beginning to the very end, although after the first five rehearsals he had no need for them for himself. He knows this music better than I myself know it, and I was indeed happy that he was the one who prepared the new ensemble for this recording.

I, personally, may admit that my humble contribution to this recording is, perhaps, the spirit in which I composed the work, which is, of course, within the competence of the author. Among conductors who directed performances of *Pierrotlunaire* are two composers, Darius Milhaud, Louis Gruenberg, the well-known German conductor Hermann Scherchen, and two American orchestra leaders, Frederick Stock of Chicago and the great pioneer, Leopold Stokowski.

Mr. Posella (flute), Mr. Kalman Bloch (clarinet) and Mr. Stefan Auber (cellist) have helped to keep the performance on a level satisfying to the most refined and critical connoisseur.

Orchestration of Two Chorale Preludes by Bach (1922)

Schoenberg regarded his own music as a logical stage in the historical development of composition. Accordingly, he believed that classics must be viewed from a modern point of view. In a letter to Fritz Stiedry dated July 31, 1930, he explained: "Our present musical concepts necessitate clarity of the motivic procedures in both the horizontal and the vertical dimensions. We need this transparency in order to examine the musical structure. Taking into consideration these circumstances, the transcriptions I made of Bach's works was not only my right but my duty."

Schoenberg selected two of the best-known Bach chorale preludes—"Schmücke dich, O liebe Seele" ("Deck thyself, my soul, with gladness") and "Komm, Gott, Schöpfer, heiliger Geist," ("Come, God, Creator, Holy Ghost)—both based on Eucharistic Lutheran hymns dating back to the early years of the Reformation. The spiritual power of the former moved Schumann to write to Mendelssohn when he heard him play it in the St. Thomas Church in Leipzig (where Bach was organist a century before): "The melody seems interlaced with garlands of gold, and breathed forth such happiness that were life deprived of all faith, this simple chorale would restore it to us."

In his orchestration of this chorale prelude Schoenberg was extremely faithful to Bach's original. There are no gratuitous alterations or additions in Schoenberg's score. He retained the key of E-flat major used by Bach. The chorale melody is given to cello solo, an instrument Schoenberg knew because he played it, as an amateur. The cello presents the five strains of the chorale in a finely balanced dialogue with the orchestra. The score contains a rich assortment of instruments Bach never used, among them **glockenspiel**, triangle, and celesta, but they serve as decorative embellishments to emphasize the rhythmic pattern and do not conflict with the harmonic structure of the work.

Glockenspiel (Ger.). A set of bells or steel bars, tuned diatonically and struck with a small hammer. Also, an organ stop having bells instead of pipes.

The second chorale prelude, "Komm, Gott, Schöpfer, heiliger Geist," is orchestrated by Schoenberg with greater boldness than the first in the application of instrumental colors. The melody is given to the oboe and the high clarinet in E flat. The pentachordal cadence descending from the **dominant** to the tonic of C major is played by four horns in fortissimo. The theme subsequently is given to the trombones,

Dominant. The fifth tone in the major or minor scales; a chord based on that tone.

tuba, and bassoons in unison, while the rest of the orchestra provides the ornamentation. The chorale prelude ends in full sonorities.

A Survivor from Warsaw, *Op. 46 (1947)*

Like Mahler, whom he admired so greatly, Schoenberg was born in the Jewish faith, but was converted to Protestantism. The anti-Semitic horrors unleashed by Hitler moved Schoenberg to return to the religion of his forebears. In a ceremony held in a Paris synagogue on July 24, 1933, Schoenberg once more became a Jew. *A Survivor from Warsaw* is an anguished expression of Schoenberg's newly found Jewish consciousness. The work was commissioned by the Koussevitzky Foundation. He completed the composition in twelve days, between August 11 and August 23, 1947. However, its first performance was given not by Koussevitzky with the Boston Symphony Orchestra, but by the Albuquerque Civic Symphony Orchestra under the direction of Kurt Frederick, on November 4, 1948.

Schoenberg was singularly proud of his proficiency in English and frequently engaged in argument with American-born friends about the proper usage of words and idioms. The title *A Survivor from Warsaw* was his own. His publishers felt that the preposition "from" was an unidiomatic rendering of the German "von," and suggested changing it to "of." Schoenberg did put "of" in the manuscript, but inserted a derisive exclamation point in parentheses after it to indicate his disagreement. Eventually he prevailed, and the score was published with the Germanic "from" in the title.

Schoenberg wrote his own English text for the work, and its curious syntax intensifies the sense of unreality, terror, and hopelessness of the situation. The narrative is based on reports Schoenberg received from actual survivors of the hideous hell in the Warsaw sewers where the Jews were hiding. It tells a moving story of the persecuted people who, at the point of death, summon their last courage and together intone the Hebrew prayer Shema Yisroel.

The scoring is for narrator, men's chorus, and orchestra. The narrator's part is written in *Sprechgesang*, inflected speech which Schoenberg introduced in *Gurre-Lieder* and developed in *Pierrot lunaire*. Its notation is unusual. The relative pitch of the syllables of the text is indicated by varying positions above and below a single central line, but sharps and flats are placed in front of these indeterminate notes, giving the visual impression of a musical staff. The final Hebrew prayer, however, is in regular five-line notation.

The work is written according to Schoenberg's method of composition with twelve tones. No more fitting medium can be imagined for this agonizing subject, with "squeezed octaves" resulting in the thematic supremacy of the atonal major sevenths, and with the classical tonic-dominant relationship of a perfect fifth replaced by the **tritone**, the "diabolus in musica" of the medieval theorists. The chromatic dispersal inherent in the dodecaphonic technique may well have assumed in Schoenberg's mind the symbolic significance of the diaspora of Israel. The illustrative power of the music is further enhanced by the use of a large section of percussion instruments in the score. It is significant, however, that Schoenberg shuns the obvious dramatics of the military drum. When the Nazi Feldwebel (sergeant) shouts, "In a minute I will know how many I am going to deliver to the gas chamber!" the accompaniment is ominously subdued, limited only to strings.

Schoenberg's text of *A Survivor from Warsaw*, with German sentences interpolated in the original, is as follows:

> I cannot remember everything. I must have been unconscious most of the time; I remember only the grandiose moment when they all started to sing, as if prearranged, the old prayer they had neglected for so many years—the forgotten creed!

Tritone. The interval of three whole tones.

But I have no recollection how I got underground to live in the sewers of Warsaw so long a time.

The day began as usual. Reveille when it still was dark—get out whether you slept or whether worries kept you awake the whole night: you had been separated from your children, from your wife, from your parents, you don't know what happened to them; how could you sleep?

They shouted again: "Get out! The sergeant will be furious!" They came out; some very slow, the old ones, the sick men, some with nervous agility. They fear the sergeant. They hurry as much as they can. In vain! Much too much noise, much too much commotion and not fast enough!

The Feldwebel shouts: "Achtung! Still gestanden! Na wird's mal, oder soll ich mit dem Gewehrkolben nachhelfen? Na jut; wenn lhr's durchaus haben wollt!" ["Attention! Stand still! How about it, or should I help you along with a rifle butt? All right, if you want."]

The sergeant and his subordinates hit everyone: Young or old, strong or sick, guilty or innocent—It was painful to hear the groaning and moaning.

I heard it though I had been hit very hard, so hard that I could not help falling down. We all on the ground who could not stand up were then beaten over the head.

I must have been unconscious. The next thing I knew was a soldier saying, "They are all dead!" Whereupon the sergeant ordered to do away with us.

There I lay aside half conscious. It had become very still—fear and pain. Then I heard the sergeant shouting: "Abzählen!" ["Count off!"]

They started slowly, and irregularly: One, two, three, four. "Achtung." The sergeant shouted again: "Rascher! Nochmals von vorn anfangen! In einer Minute will ich wissen wieviele ich zur Gaskammer abliefere! Abzählen!"

["Faster! Once more, start from the beginning. In a minute I will know how many I am going to deliver to the gas chamber! Count off!"]

They began again, first slowly: One, two, three, four, became faster and faster, so fast that it finally sounded like a stampede of wild horses, and all of a sudden, in the middle of it, they began singing the Shema Yisroel.

MAURICE RAVEL
(1875–1937)
Poet of Simplicity

MAURICE RAVEL'S FATHER was a Swiss engineer, and his mother was of Basque origin. The family moved to Paris from the Lower Pyrenees when he was an infant. He began to study piano at the age of seven and attended the Paris Conservatory until 1895, when he left at the age of twenty. That same year, he completed work on his song "Un Grand Sommeil noir," the ***Menuet*** *antique* for piano, and the ***Habanera*** for two pianos (later included in the *Rapsodie espagnole* for orchestra). These pieces already revealed great originality in the treatment of old modes and of Spanish motives, but Ravel continued to study, returning in 1897 to the Conservatory to study with Gabriel Fauré (composition) and André Gédalge (counterpoint and orchestra-

Minuet (Fr.), minuet. An early French dance form, distinguished by the symmetry of its musical structure.

Habanera (Sp.). A Cuban dance, in duple meter, characterized by dotted or syncopated rhythms.

Dissonance. A combination of two or more tones requiring resolution.

Diatonic. Employing the tones of the standard major or minor scale.

Pandiatonicism. A modern term for a system of diatonic harmony making use of all seven degrees of the scale in dissonant combinations.

Whole-tone scale. Scale consisting only of whole tones, lacking dominant and either major or minor triads; popularized by Debussy.

Augmentation. Doubling (or increasing) the time value of the notes of a theme or motive, often in imitative counterpoint.

Triad. A "three-tone" chord composed of a given tone (the root), with its third and fifth in ascending order in the scale.

tion). Ravel's well-known *Pavane pour une infante défunte* for piano was written during that time (1899).

By 1905, Ravel had written a number of his most famous compositions and was regarded by most French critics as a talented disciple of Debussy. No doubt, Ravel's method of poetic association of musical ideas paralleled that of Debussy; his employment of unresolved **dissonances** and the enhancement of the **diatonic** style into **pandiatonicism** were techniques common to Debussy and his followers. But there were important differences: whereas Debussy adopted the scale of **whole tones** as an integral part of his musical vocabulary, Ravel resorted to it only occasionally. Similarly, **augmented triads** appear much less frequently in Ravel's music than in Debussy's. In his writing for piano, Ravel actually anticipated some of Debussy's usages.

Where Debussy's progress was uneventful through the years of his academic study, Ravel had to fight against the conservatism of academic circles. Four times he applied for and was denied the Grand Prix de Rome, a coveted prize not only because of the attendant honors, but because it gave the opportunity to a young composer to write in financial comfort in a villa in Rome. His rejection stirred a scandal, particularly when the six candidates were announced, and they all turned out to be pupils of one professor at the Paris conservatory who was influential in Academy circles.

The "Ravel case" soon became a cause célèbre: far from being pushed back by the decision, Ravel gained tremendously in popularity. Even his former critics rallied to his cause. Ravel was a very modest man, but under certain circumstances he showed great pride. He revealed this pride during a discussion in the musical columns of the Paris newspapers of his dependence on Debussy. Ravel wrote to the influential critic of *Le Temps*, pointing out that his *Jeux d'eau* established a new pianistic technique of his own, quite independent from Debussy, and gave chronological data to support his statement.

In Paris, elsewhere in France, and soon in England and other European countries, Ravel's name became well known. For many years, he was regarded as an ultramodernist. But inspired evocation of the past was another aspect of Ravel's creative genius: in this style are his *Pavane pour une infante défunte*, *Le Tombeau de Couperin*, and *La Valse*. Luxuriance of exotic colors marks his ballet *Daphnis et Chloé*, his opera *L'Heure espagnole*, the song cycles *Shéhérazade* and *Chansons madécasses*, and his virtuoso pieces for piano, *Miroirs* and *Gaspard de la nuit*. Other works are deliberately austere, even ascetic, in their pointed classicism: the piano **concertos**, the **Sonatine** for piano, and some of his songs with piano accompaniment. For Diaghilev's Ballets Russes he wrote one of his masterpieces, *Daphnis et Chloé*; another ballet, *Boléro*, commissioned by Ida Rubinstein and performed at her dance recital at the Paris Opéra on November 22, 1928, became Ravel's most spectacular success as an orchestral piece.

Ravel never married, and lived a life of semiretirement, devoting most of his time to composition. He accepted virtually no pupils, although he gave friendly advice to Vaughan Williams and to others, but he was never on the faculty of any school. Not a brilliant performer, he appeared as a pianist only to play his own works, often accompanying singers in programs of his songs. Although he accepted engagements as a conductor, his technique was barely sufficient to secure a perfunctory performance of his music. When World War I broke out in 1914, he was rejected for military service because of his frail physique, but he was anxious to serve; his application for air service was denied, but he was received in the ambulance corps at the front. His health gave way and, in the autumn of 1916, he was compelled to enter a hospital for recuperation. In 1922 he visited Amsterdam and Venice, conducting his music, and in 1923 he appeared in London. In 1926 he went to Sweden, England, and Scotland, and he made an American

Concerto (It.). An extended multi-movement composition for a solo instrument, usually with orchestra accompaniment and using (modified) sonata form.

Sonatina (It.), **sonatine** (Ger.). A short sonata in two or three (rarely four) movements, the first in the characteristic first-movement form, abbreviated.

tour as a conductor and pianist in 1928, returning to Paris to complete the commission for a dance piece, ***Boléro***.

Following his American tour, an honorary degree of doctor of music was conferred upon Ravel by Oxford University. (In the Latin text of the diploma he was described as "Musarum interpretes modorum Daedalus Mauritius Ravelius.") This year of *Boléro* marked the peak of Ravel's worldly success. It was also the year during which he felt the ominous signs of an incipient cerebro-vascular disturbance. His mind was alert, but he was beset by what he called "une tristesse affreuse." He suffered from amnesia. Once, he could not remember his own name. His doctors spoke alarmingly of "apraxia" and "dysphasia." He began to lose the ability to write notes or words. He knew the individual letters that made up each word he wanted to write, but he could not remember the order in which they occurred. His speech became disarticulate. A friend described his state as a procession with muted fifes and muffled drums, on a mental journey into the night.

In a desperate effort to save Ravel, brain surgery was performed. No tumor was found; Ravel's condition was due to arteriosclerotic degeneration of a main cerebral blood vessel. The operation was futile; Ravel sank into a coma and died a few days later. At his funeral, the writer Colette said, "He was deprived of memory, lost the power of speech and ability to write. He died stifled, while there still surged within him so many harmonies, so many memories of bird songs and guitars, of dancing and melodious nights."

An ironic postscript to Ravel's life was the posthumous fate of his royalties, which grew to considerable sums of money owing particularly to the success of his fascinating tour de force, *Boléro*, based on a single theme and never, except in the last measure of the coda, diverging from the basic key of C major. Ravel left his estate to his brother, who in turn bequeathed it to his housekeeper; she married a peasant from central France who survived her and received millions of francs of revenue from music he could not understand. There was a litigation on the part of Ravel's distant cousins, but the French law of inheritance of property by a lawful spouse prevailed.

ORCHESTRAL MUSIC

Alborada del gracioso *(1908);* Rapsodie espagnole *(1919)*

It has been said that the best Spanish music has been composed by Frenchmen. The Spanish pieces of Bizet, Chabrier, and Debussy seem to sustain this paradoxical notion; the music of Isaac Albéniz, Eduardo Granados, and Manuel de Falla may be more authentically Spanish, but French works in the Spanish vein seem to possess an impetuous élan that has an immediate appeal to the listener. Ravel felt very close to Spain; he was born on its border at Ciboure, in the Basses-Pyrénées, on March 7, 1875. His mother was of Basque descent; as a child Ravel could actually speak the unspeakable Basque language. His father was a mechanical engineer from Switzerland who played a role in the manufacture of early motor cars. Marveling at Ravel's precise technique in instrumental writing, someone remarked that he wrote music with the lapidary care of a Swiss watchmaker. Ravel never attained perfection, or even competence, as a performer; he played piano poorly, and had to use the notes and a page turner even when accompanying a singer in his own songs. He was even more inept as a conductor, and his sense of pitch was defective. But with myriad pianists and conductors to perform Ravel's music, the lack of his own capacities at the keyboard or on the podium was not of any consequence.

Among Ravel's works in the Spanish vein, *Alborada del gracioso* is one of the most succulent. *Alborada* is an early-

Ravel Timeline

1875	Born in Ciboure, Lower Pyrénées
1889	Enters Paris Conservatory
1895-97	Leaves Conservatory to compose vocal and piano works; returns to study with Fauré
1899	Composes *Pavane pour une infante défunte* for piano; conducts premiere of Shéhérazade overture in Paris
1900-05	Competes for but fails to receive prestigious Grand Prix de Rome, causing scandal
1912	*Daphnis et Chloé* performed by Diaghilev's Ballets Russes
1914	Rejected for military service in World War I; serves in ambulance corps
1916	Leaves ambulance corps owing to frail health
1922-23	Conducts his music in Amsterdam, Venice, London
1925	Opera *L'Enfant et les sortilèges* premiered in Monte Carlo
1926	Visits Sweden, England, Scotland as conductor/pianist
1928	Tours U.S.; best-known work, *Boléro*, commissioned by Ida Rubinstein for her dance recital, premiered in Paris
1929	Begins to suffer effects of debilitating brain disease
1937	Undergoes unsuccessful brain surgery, dies nine days later in Paris

morning song, as contrasted with *serenade*, which is an evening song. *Gracioso* is the Spanish word for a graceful jester. *Alborada del gracioso* is therefore a jester's salute at dawn. The piece is gracefully symmetric, with evocative, melodious sections contrasted with exciting dance rhythms. It was originally a part of Ravel's piano suite *Miroirs*; Ravel orchestrated it at a later time in his inimitable colorful manner. The orchestral version of the *Alborada del gracioso* was performed for the first time in Boston on February 16, 1921.

Rapsodie espagnole is another work of Ravel's rooted in Spanish melodies and rhythms. It is an orchestral suite in four movements: "Prélude à la nuit," "Malagueña," "Habanera," "Feria." The "Prélude" opens with a wistful descending **tetra-chord** on muted strings, establishing the mood of the entire piece. It is echoed by wind instruments, all in muted colors, concluding with an improvisation on the English horn.

There follows a brilliant *malagueña*, a dance from southern Spain suggesting the rhythms of a **fandango**. It progresses gradually from subdued sonorities to explosions of rhythmic energy. The next movement is a *habanera*, set in a characteristic Cuban rhythm evoking the time when Spain dominated the Caribbean islands. The last movement, "Feria," is a spectacular Spanish fiesta set in a dual meter, 6/8 and 3/4 time, with conflicting stresses made more beguiling by coloristic instrumental devices, including such effects as **glissandos** on natural harmonics in the viola and the cello. The work was performed for the first time in Paris on March 15, 1908, at a concert conducted by Edouard Colonne.

Ravel is often paired with Debussy as an initiator of a new harmonic and instrumental style of composition, but he is rarely described as an Impressionist composer. His music does not employ the luxuriant sonorities typical of Debussy's orchestral palette; on the contrary, Ravel is very careful in assigning his effects with a minimum of purely pictorial displays. Unlike Debussy, who favored parallel harmonic progressions

Tetrachord. The interval of a perfect fourth; the four scale-tones contained in a perfect fourth.

Fandango (Sp.). A lively dance in triple time, for two dancers of opposite sex, who accompany it with castanets or tambourine.

Glissando (It.). A slide; a rapid scale. On bowed instruments, a flowing, unaccented execution of a passage. On the piano, a rapid scale effect obtained by sliding the thumb, or thumb and one finger, over the keys.

and cultivated the whole-tone scale, Ravel retained the classical tonalities, combining melodies and chords in pandiatonic
superstructures.

Valses nobles et sentimentales *(1912)*

In May 1911, the Société Musicale Indépendante in Paris decided to test the critical capacity of the audience and professional music critics by giving a "concert without the names of
the composer." Several works of the modern school were accordingly presented anonymously, among them, and for the
first time, Ravel's *Valses nobles et sentimentales*. Emile Vuiller-
moz, one of the initiators of the concert, described the event
in the memorial publication *Maurice Ravel par quelques-uns
de ses familiers*, issued in Paris in 1939:

> Ravel was in a loge in the midst of a group of society dilet-
> tantes who habitually swooned when they heard even
> two bars of Ravel's music. Heroically faithful to his oath as
> a conspirator, the composer of *Valses nobles et sentimen-
> tales* had not forewarned them that his unpublished work
> was included in the program. When they heard this com-
> position played with an imperturbably serious mien by
> Louis Aubert, the composer's sycophantic companions
> began to jeer, hoping to give Ravel pleasure by assailing
> ferociously these "ridiculous pages." Stoically, but no
> doubt somewhat bitterly, Ravel accepted these remarks in
> silence, but I am not sure whether he ever forgave me for
> unwittingly placing him in so awkward a situation that
> night.
>
> Machiavellian to the end, we distributed among the
> listeners little slips of paper, with the request to name the
> composers of the pieces played. The results of this refer-
> endum were terrifying. The professional critics cautiously
> abstained from voting, and the next day they failed to
> publish a single word about this evening that must have

been so disconcerting to them. As to the rest, they naively ascribed works, in which the personality of our extreme modernists was clearly reflected, to Mozart, Schumann, Chopin, Gounod, Wagner, or Mendelssohn. No one perceived the hand of Ravel in this succession of waltzes, which bear so clearly Ravel's distinctive imprint.

An American writer heard Ravel play the *Valses* in Paris a year later and recorded his impressions of the man and the artist in the pages of the *Musical Courier*: "He is a very boyish-looking little man, and you wonder to look at him, at his tremendous force and passion as a composer. . . . There seems to be a strangely fascinating discordant note added to nearly every harmony. You wonder constantly how he does it, and why it is so delightful." The "fascinating discordant note" is the added sixth, which Ravel particularly favors in the *Valses*. And Ravel liked to use a parallel row of six-five chords over a pedal tone, a procedure that, to an untutored ear, gives an impression of a recurring discordant note. The rhythms of several of the *Valses nobles et sentimentales* anticipate *La Valse*, written seven years later. Some of the harmonies and dynamic effects of the earlier work have also found application in *La Valse*, but the similarity is that of allusion rather than of identity.

Ravel orchestrated the work for the Russian dancer Trouhanova, who gave a dance recital in Paris on April 22, 1912, with Ravel's *Valses*, under the new title of *Adélaïde, ou Le Langage des fleurs*. The scenario, written by Ravel himself, was an imaginative tale from the early nineteenth century, and dealt with the young courtesan Adélaïde, the old Duke, and the young lover, Lorédan. The lovers exchange flowers, each of which has a meaning. The score bears an epigraph from Ravel's favorite poet, Henri de Régnier: "le plaisir délicieux et toujours nouveau d'une occupation inutile" ("the delicious and always new pleasure of a useless occupation"). There is a fine point of irony in this quotation, which supplements the irony of the title.

Daphnis and Chloé: *Suite No. 2 (1913)*

The sobriquet "Swiss watchmaker of music" refers to Ravel's exquisite equilibration of instrumental sonorities and close attention to the minuscule nuances of dynamics. Another relevant detail in this definition is to Ravel's Swiss family origin, for his father was a Swiss engineer who invented a steam automobile.

His name is commonly bracketed with that of Debussy as initiators of the Impressionist idiom in composition. The term may be applied to Debussy's music by analogy with French Impressionist paintings, but Ravel's art tends toward **neoclassicism**. His harmony is more precise than the fluid modulatory language of Debussy, and he rarely makes use of the elusive whole-tone scale, with its tonal instability. Rather, he stylizes archaic modes, never abandoning the implicit tonality.

In *La Valse*, Ravel invokes the scene of waltzing couples in Vienna; in *Boléro*, he distills and integrates the rhythms of Spain. His scores are choreographic par excellence. His ballet *Daphnis and Chloé* was produced by Diaghilev's Ballets Russes in Paris on June 8, 1912. Ravel extracted two symphonic suites from this ballet, of which the second is by far the more popular. The scenario is derived from a bucolic love story. Daphnis, the shepherd, is asleep in front of the grotto of the nymphs. Other shepherds appear seeking Daphnis and Chloé, who also tends a flock of sheep. They need the sanction of Pan for the consummation of their love. In pantomime, they reproduce the magic story of Pan's love for the nymph Syrinx and, by doing so, they become lovers themselves.

The second symphonic suite of *Daphnis and Chloé* comprises three scenes; Dawn, Pantomime, and General Dance. Dawn is portrayed by a delicate murmuration of flutes and clarinets supported by two harps glissando. The annotation in

Neoclassicism. A revival, in twentieth-century compositions, of eighteenth-century (or earlier) musical precepts, exemplified by many of the post-WWI works of both Stravinsky and Schoenberg.

DAPHNIS ET CHLOÉ

Une prairie à la lisière d'un bois sacré. Au fond, des collines. A droite, une grotte, à l'entrée de laquelle, taillées à même le roc, sont figurées trois Nymphes, d'une sculpture archaïque. Un peu vers le fond, à gauche, un grand rocher affecte vaguement la forme du dieu Pân. Au second plan, des brebis paissent. Une après-midi claire de printemps. Au lever du rideau, la scène est vide.

Introduction et Danse religieuse

(+) *La clarinette basse doit avoir un mi ♭. Sinon prendre le ton de La.*
The bass clarinet should have an E♭. Otherwise use the instrument in A.

the score reads: "Not a sound but the murmur of brooks of dew that flows from the rocks." The birds are heard, illustrated by three solo violins and the **trills** of the piccolo. In the meantime, the melody of the dawn after its inception in the divided double basses spreads into the upper strings and the lower woodwind instruments. The **roulades** of the piccolo represent the shepherd's pipe, soon answered by the high clarinet representing another shepherd. The tide of assembled sonorities rises as Daphnis and Chloé fall into each others' arms.

The rivulets of fluid sonorities in the woodwinds and the harps, and the silvery cataracts of the **celesta** subside, and the Pantomime begins, with Daphnis representing the god Pan and Chloé playing the part of the lost nymph Syrinx. The nymph escapes from Pan, who tries to reach her. As she vanishes, Pan plucks some tall flowers and fashions a panpipe from the stems. His melancholy song is intoned by the flute, accompanied with the utmost gentleness by muted strings. The nymph yields to the fascination of Pan's languorous plaint and appears before him. A General Dance follows to celebrate the imagined reunion of Pan and Syrinx. The lovers swear their undying fidelity with two sheep as witnesses. The bacchantes enter the scene and start a dance, shaking tambourines, striking cymbals, and drumming insistent rhythms. The sonorous wizardry of the General Dance is achieved by the constant ebb and flow of dynamic strength, vanishing to the threshold of audibility and then mounting to plangent **fortissimo**.

Trill. The even and rapid alternation of two tones which are a major or minor second apart.

Roulade (Fr.). A grace consisting of a move from one principal melody tone to another; a vocal or instrumental flourish.

Celesta. Percussion instrument consisting of tuned steel bars connected to a keyboard.

Fortissimo (It.). Extremely loud.

Le Tombeau de Couperin *(1920)*

There are two equally important directions in modern French music: innovation and restylization. Ravel, equipped with an exquisite sense of values and a precise science of musical equilibration, was as expert in reviving the French past as he was in building its musical future.

Le Tombeau de Couperin is Ravel's tribute to France's

greatest Impressionist—for, indeed, Couperin was a precursor of impressionism. Long before Virgil Thomson began painting symphonic portraits at musical sittings with live subjects, Couperin wrote a series of pieces for **clavecin** in which he subtly pictured the girlish characters of the Timid One, the Indiscreet One, and even the Irritating One. In the midst of the aesthetic fight for the acceptance of French impressionism, Jean Cocteau recalled Couperin in defense of Erik Satie; the public is shocked by the titles of Satie's pieces, he declared, but accepts "the most cockeyed" titles of Couperin: *Le tic-toc choc, Les culbutes Ixcxbxnxs, Les Coucous bénévoles,* and *Les Trésorières surannées.*

Clavecin (Fr.). A harpsichord.

Ravel's tribute to Couperin is more of a handshake of two kindred spirits across 207 years of time than an offering on Couperin's glorified tomb. The music of Ravel is a twentieth-century counterpart of Couperin's. The manner and the attitudes are the same; the idiom is tonal, touched up with a pandiatonic brush, and seasoned with droplets of **chromatic** harmony. Ravel wrote this suite as a set of six piano pieces in 1914–17; he later orchestrated four of them, and they were performed for the first time by the Pasdeloup Orchestra in Paris on February 28, 1920.

Chromatic. Relating to tones foreign to a given key (scale) or chord; opposed to diatonic.

Le Tombeau de Couperin, as an orchestral suite, contains four movements: Prélude, **Forlane,** Menuet, and **Rigaudon.** The Prélude begins in a murmuring hurly-burly of the woodwinds, punctuated by plucked strings. A chromatic descending line helps to sustain the even motion, in which the strings soon join. A feeling of stability comes from the **pedal points** in the transition; the hollow fifths in parallel progressions suggest an archaic detachment. The dynamics are subdued, and then a sudden **crescendo** wells up to a climactic chord of the thirteenth. After a few scattered figurations and a protracted trill, the Prélude comes to an end.

Forlane (Fr.). A lively Italian dance in 6/8 or 6/4 time.
Rigaudon (Fr.), **rigadoon.** A lively French dance, generally in 4/4 time, that consists of three or four reprises.
Pedal point. A tone sustained in one part to harmonies executed in the other parts.
Crescendo (It.). Swelling, increasing in loudness.

The Forlane is a stylization of an old dance of Italian origin that is close to a **gigue** in rhythm. It is a gay dance, and Ravel

Gigue (Fr.), **giga** (It.). A jig.

keeps its original gaiety in soft instrumental colors as a nostalgic reminiscence of another era. The Menuet has a characteristic recessive bass, leading to a cadential construction every
fourth bar. The **tonic**-dominant pedal point is the ground for
the middle section, following the classical formula. The
rigaudon is a seventeenth-century dance of southern France;
it was often adopted in the classical suite. Ravel modernizes it
in a spirited manner. The harmonic texture is pandiatonic, so
that not a single accidental mars the initial eight bars of the
score. The middle section approaches the rhythm of a polka.
The Rigaudon ends with a decisive flourish in clear C major.

Tonic. The keynote of a scale; the triad on the keynote (tonic chord).

La Valse *(1920)*

The original title of *La Valse* was simply *Wien*, German for Vienna. It is a pity that this title was not allowed to stand. "Wien"
evokes in the mind a definite picture of the carefree, amorous
atmosphere of the imperial city that the indefinite title *La
Valse* fails to convey. When the title was changed, it was necessary to add an explanatory note, in which the locale of the
scene was marked with deliberate latitude: an imperial court
circa 1855. The score is subtitled choreographic poem, which
shows that Ravel had in mind a ballet interpretation of the
music. He marks the places in the score in which the waltzing
crowd appears through the rifts in the clouds, and the fortissimo passage where the light of the chandeliers suddenly illu-
minates the scene.

La Valse was performed for the first time at the Concerts
in Paris on December 12, 1920. Ravel was often late in completing his scores for a previously arranged performance, and
this explains the mistakes in Ravel's chronology, which are unfortunately found in the monographs by Ravel's Boswell,
Roland-Manuel, who also gives a premature date for *La Valse*,
January 8, 1920.

The misdating of the first performance was the more unnecessary since Roland-Manuel was in close touch with the

Opening to Ravel's *La Valse*

progress of Ravel's work on *La Valse*. On January 17, 1920, Ravel was unexpectedly nominated chevalier of the Legion of Honor. He refused to accept the nomination. "Quelle histoire ridicule," he wrote to Roland-Manuel, "Who could have played this trick on me? And *Wien* must be completed by the end of the month. Have you noticed that the Legionnaires are similar to morphine addicts, eager to force others to share their passion, perhaps to justify it in their own eyes?" "The end of the month" referred to in Ravel's letter was January 1920, and so *La Valse* could not conceivably have been performed on January 8.

The elimination of "Wien" from the title of *La Valse* has misled the critics. In one of those vague reviews with more literary allusions than relevant analysis, the critic of *Le Ménestrel* gives this description: "To the grace and languor of a Carpeaux is here opposed the anguish of Prud'homme: 'We are dancing on a volcano.' This bacchanal has in its joy something foreboding, like drunkenness betraying a debility, perhaps by the dissonances and shocks of orchestral colors. . . ."

Henry Prunières is much more scholarly and much more literary. Writing in La Revue musicale, he gives a specific program of *La Valse*.

A classical Viennese Waltz, or rather a phantom of a waltz in a dream. Crushed with fatigue after the ball, one falls asleep, and the rhythms just heard haunt him. Indistinct at first, they gradually take shape. Shreds of phrases emerge, the melody is organized, and the waltz appears, quite simple, a bit caricatured, a waltz of Johann Strauss and Offenbach. It sweeps the couples, it hurries along, pressed, out of breath, hesitating for a moment, but never stopping. . . . The dancers whirl, the heads are dizzy, the walls, the floors vibrate. The gyrating hallucination reaches a paroxysm. Suddenly, awakening comes, or perhaps a plunge into unconsciousness, and all disappears. Never has Ravel's art been more perfect. This is a tour de force, this waltz that lasts twelve minutes without an episode, without a stop. Inexhaustible verve animates this whole piece, written with a dizzy virtuosity, and visibly to the great enjoyment of the author himself.

Alfredo Casella, who was closely associated with Ravel, describes *La Valse* as "a masque of human life, with its pomp and glory, its luxury of sight and sound, its hours of golden youth, one generation treading upon the receding footsteps of another."

Eight years after the composition of *La Valse*, Ravel wrote his famous *Boléro*, which he himself described as an "orchestral crescendo lasting seventeen minutes." *La Valse* is also a continuous movement, but it seethes in constant dynamic oscillation, never approaching the constancy of the key and rhythmic pulse that characterize *Boléro*. Ravel varied his technique, but whatever technique he used, his art of precision and immediate effectiveness never failed him.

Orchestration of Pictures at an Exhibition, by Modest Mussorgsky (1922)

Modest Mussorgsky wrote his suite for piano, *Pictures at an Exhibition* in 1874 as a tribute to the memory of his friend, the Russian painter Victor Hartmann. Each number of the suite illustrates one of Hartmann's drawings or water colors. The very name of Hartmann has vanished into oblivion, and is preserved for posterity only through the glory of Mussorgsky's music.

Pictures at an Exhibition was brilliantly arranged for orchestra by Ravel in 1922, on a commission from Serge Koussevitzky, for a fee of 10,000 francs. Koussevitzky performed it for the first time in Paris on October 19, 1922.

Mussorgsky's suite is a leisurely musical promenade through a gallery of Hartmann's pictures. Brief interludes between each pair of pictures represent a walk from one to the next. A thematic musical promenade opens the gallery. The first painting is *Gnomus*, a dwarf-shaped nutcracker. In Ravel's orchestration, the music is punctuated by the sounds of rattles and whiplashes, as nut fragments fly apart under the impact of the gnomus. After a promenade, the viewer is conducted to Hartmann's Italian drawing *Il Vecchio Castello*. The image of an old Italian castle is depicted in the music by a melody in a minor mode. In Ravel's orchestration, the theme is played by the alto saxophone.

After another promenade, the scene shifts to the Garden of the Tuileries in Paris, with children playing happily in the sunlight. The next picture presents a striking contrast. A clumsy Polish oxcart, *Bydlo*, hobbles on the cobblestones of a village road. It rumbles by with uncouth noise, and then disappears in a cloud of musical dust. Ravel assigns the theme of the rough-wheeled vehicle to the bass tuba, a most fitting instrument for such an object.

Another promenade introduces the "Ballet of Unhatched Chickens in Their Eggshells." There is a lot of scratching inside and a lot of cracking sounds as the eggshells break up and let the chicks emerge into the world of light. Ravel's orchestration makes the most of the amusing "ballet," with expert use of the celesta, harp, and high woodwinds.

We next are confronted with a painting of sociological significance, a grotesque sketch entitled *Samuel Goldenberg and Schmuyle*. These personages are Polish Jews, one rich, the other poor. The rich Jew is appropriately pompous, sermonizing his unfortunate companion in an orientalized mode with its rich proliferation of augmented seconds in a minor mode. In Ravel's orchestration, the rich Jew orates in imposing unisons in the lower register, while the poor Jew pipes dejectedly on a muted trumpet.

From Poland we cross to a market scene in Limoges, France, with French housewives bickering and haggling, chattering and jabbering in perpetual commotion. There follows a solemn tableau, *Catacombae*. In sepulchral tones, Mussorgsky invokes Hartmann's spirit to guide him through the ancient Roman catacombs. In an ensuing chorale, "Cum mortuis in lingua mortua," Mussorgsky communes "with the dead in a dead language." Bidding farewell to the land of the dead, Mussorgsky plunges into a revelry of Russian folklore in *A Hut on a Hen's Legs*, where dwells the hideous Russian witch Baba Yaga. The music is full of demoniacal **tritones** and sharply dissonant major sevenths. Baba Yaga rides the broomstick through the stormy skies on an avalanche of scales.

Tritone. The interval of three whole tones.

Then, without a break, the music leads to the grand finale, *The Great Gate of Kiev*. This is an apotheosis of Holy Russia, with church bells pealing and religious chants intoned with devotional fervor. The motive of the opening promenade returns, dressed up in opulent harmonies. Ravel's orchestration is resplendent in depicting the golden glory of Mussorgsky's Russia.

Pictorially, *The Great Gate of Kiev* was a sketch drawn by Hartmann for an arch to be erected in Kiev to commemorate the escape of Czar Alexander II from an assassination attempt engineered by Russian nihilists. But the second attempt, in 1881, succeeded, and the great gate of Kiev was never built. Mussorgsky died in the same year, at the age of forty-two, a victim of acute alcoholism.

Boléro *(1928)*

In 1928, Ravel made a grand tour of the United States as conductor in programs of his own works. He wrote to a friend from Los Angeles in February:

> The sun shines in full splendor; it is a wonderful city decked in flowers, and I hate to think that it will be cold again when I come back to Paris. But the triumphs are fatiguing. In Los Angeles, I actually avoided seeing people; besides, I was dying of hunger. I made a trip to Hollywood, the city of the cinema, and met various stars,

among them Douglas Fairbanks, who fortunately speaks French.

During his entire American tour, Ravel's mind was preoccupied with a commission he had accepted from the danseuse Ida Rubinstein, who wanted him to write a Spanish-colored symphonic movement for her modern dance recital. Ravel decided on a bold idea: to build the entire work on a single theme in the single tonality of C major, without any change in the rhythm of the underlying accompaniment. The theme assumed a bilateral form, the first section progressing along the C-major scale, the second beginning on B-flat and descending slowly toward the dominant G in a flatted **Phrygian** cadence. Despite these tonal alterations, the fundamental harmony remains firmly anchored on C, with the remarkable exception of eight bars before the **coda**, when a sudden **modulation** into E major is effected.

Ravel called the piece *Boléro*, even though some of his Spanish friends grumbled that it was more like a fandango or a *seguidilla* in character and rhythm. Ravel himself described the *Boléro* as "a rather slow dance, uniform in its melody, harmony and rhythm," the latter being tapped out continuously on the drum. The only element of variety is supplied by the orchestral crescendo. Asked for his own opinion about the value of *Boléro*, Ravel replied, ruefully: "Malheureusement, il est vide de musique." Devoid of music or not, *Boléro* became Ravel's most celebrated work, spreading his name and fame across the five continents.

The first performance of *Boléro* took place at the Opéra in Paris, on November 22, 1928, produced by Ida Rubinstein, who was also the dance soloist. The scene was set in a realistic Barcelona café, with a voluptuous dancer surrounded by a group of men, shouting encouragement and voicing their delight.

Formally, *Boléro* is a veritable tour de force. It consists of eighteen **variations**, each employing either the first or the sec-

Phrygian mode. A church mode corresponding to the scale from *E* to *E* on the white keys of the piano.
Coda (It.). A "tail"; hence, a passage ending a movement.
Modulation. Passage from one key into another.

Variations. Transformations of a theme by means of harmonic, rhythmic, and melodic changes and embellishments.

Oboe d'amore (It.). Literally, "oboe of love"; an oboe that sounds a minor third below the written notation; used in many old scores, and also in some modern revivals.

ond part of the bilateral subject, and each in a different orchestration. The first eight variations are given largely to eight solo instruments: flute, clarinet, bassoon, small clarinet, **oboe d'amore**, muted trumpet, tenor saxophone, and soprano saxophone. In the subsequent variations, the "orchestral crescendo" is created by the doubling of instruments and the accretion in sonority of the accompanying rhythmic figures. The ninth variation is remarkable from the acoustic standpoint. In it, a French horn solo, supported by the celesta, is accompanied in the high treble by two piccolos, forming the sixth and the tenth overtone of the melody. Ravel specifically indicates that the high notes are to be played **pianissimo**, as actual **overtones**, which are weaker the higher they are. Visually, the passage looks like a progression of consecutive parallel triads in open harmony, but acoustically, in proper performance, the overtones should not be heard as harmonic ingredients, but are calculated to produce a magical alteration in the **tone color** of the solo instrument, converting it into a sort of hyperhorn.

Pianissimo (It.). Very soft.
Overtone. Harmonic tone.

Tone-color. Quality of tone; timbre.

The tenth variation combines the oboe, the oboe d'amore, the English horn, and the clarinet in its melodic projection. The eleventh is a trombone solo; the remaining variations increase the contingent of the participating instruments. In the last variation, the piccolos, trumpets, saxophone, and violins intone the second section of the subject in mighty vociferation. It is this last variation, before the coda, that contains the extraordinary modulation into E major. C major returns for an abrupt ending on a Phrygian cadence.

WORKS FOR SOLO INSTRUMENT AND ORCHESTRA

Tzigane *(1924)*

The musical greatness of Ravel is twofold. He conjures up images of sensuous subtlety, or else he stylizes the artifacts of yesterday, recreating the musical past as though seen through a memory-dimming refractor. To some aestheticians, stylization is an inferior art. Others argue that it is a prerequisite of artistic self-renewal, that without constant adaptation of the past to the present there is no continuity in art.

In appreciation of his mastery, Ravel has been called the "Swiss watchmaker of music." But he was also attacked as an artificer out of touch with the real world. The *Manchester Guardian* wrote about Ravel in April 1924:

> Never was an artist more fastidious, more afraid of all that is crass and gross, and never a composer so precious, so remote from nature, so anxious to avoid all plain-speaking human sympathy. If ever a man was born at the wrong time, that man is Ravel. He belongs spiritually to the artificial eighteenth century. To him, trimmed hedges and glittering waterworks are nature, while fragile Sèvres shepherdesses come as near humanity as he wishes to get.

Ravel was conversant with porcelain shepherdesses, but also with waltzing bon-vivants and warm-blooded Gypsies, as shown in *La Valse* and the famous *Boléro*. His *Tzigane* (the title means a Gypsy, with specific reference to Gypsy musicians), a *rapsodie de concert* written for the Hungarian violinist Yelly d'Aranyi, is the stylization of a type of music reputed for its reckless spirit and orgiastic abandon. No fragile Sèvres shepherdess is the Gypsy songstress of Ravel's *Tzigane*!

When Ravel played the piano part of *Tzigane* for the first time, with d'Aranyi, at a London concert of his works 1924, the critics were frankly perplexed. "One is puzzled to understand what Ravel is at," wrote the *London Times*. "Either the work is a parody of all the Liszt-Hubay-Brahms-Joachim school of Hungarian violin music, or it is an attempt to get away from the limited sphere of his previous compositions, to infuse into his work a little of that warm blood it needs." The *Manchester Guardian* was unqualifiedly enthusiastic: "*Tzigane* is an astounding bravura piece, full of the most wonderfully telling effect. Ravel has once again proved his unique gift of exploiting instrumental resources and finding new and entrancing sound-values. But there is more in this work, which toys delightfully with some Hungarian conventions and remolds them into something new and fascinating."

In 1925, Ravel orchestrated the piece and it was performed in Amsterdam by Samuel Dushkin with the Concertgebouw Orchestra conducted by Willem Mengelberg. After its Boston performance, H. T. Parker, the critic of the *Boston Evening Transcript*, wrote: "It is difficult to believe that Ravel would mock, much less parody, with Gallic adroitness, the rhapsodies of technique and tone, the extravagance of feeling, common enough in these Gypsy violinists. Rather, he would outdo them at their own game, with a variety of invention, a subtlety of exaction, beyond their less cerebral powers." Every critic commented upon the extraordinary difficulty of the solo part. "If it is a joke," observed Philip Hale, "not many violinists can play it on the audience."

Tzigane opens with a long **cadenza** for violin alone. It is intervallically constructed upon the so-called Gypsy scale. From the outset, there is an abundant display of modern virtuoso technique, with difficult progressions, harmonics, and double, triple, and quadruple **stops**. After the violin has come to an end of its exertions, there is a cadenza for the harp, projected against the "Parisian" bitonality of C and F-sharp major. These two cadenzas serve as preliminaries to the principal section, **Moderato**. The violin has a dancing Gypsy tune. Then the clarinet comes in with another Gypsy melody, accompanied by the violin solo in ethereal harmonics. Later, the violin picks up the clarinet's tune and, after some intensive reiteration of its Gypsy intervals, arrives at a cascading cadenza. There is a brief pause, and once more the Gypsy dance is resumed,

Cadenza (It.). An elaborate passage played or improvised by the solo instrument at the end of the first or last movements of a concerto.

Stop. On the violin, etc., the pressure of a finger on a string, to vary the latter's pitch; a *double stop* is when two or more strings are so pressed and sounded simultaneously.

Moderato (It.). At a moderate tempo or rate of speed.

this time with the oboe playing the original violin tune. The orchestra has a dancing interlude; the violin plays difficult harmonics, and then, as though for relief, glides in fifths over the open strings, fortissimo. Now the harp plays sonorous glissandos, while the violin is trilling its Gypsy refrain. Then comes the section marked **grandioso**, in which the violin plays an imposing singing air. Finally, the soloist starts on its last dash, with 488 sixteenth notes in changing velocities, coming abruptly to a stop, and ending the vertiginous dance.

Grandioso (It.). With grandeur; majestically, pompously, loftily.

Concerto for the Left Hand (1931)

Amputation of an arm is a most distressing event, but by a quirk of fate, it contributed to the creation of several excellent piano concertos for the left hand alone. The amputee in the case was Paul Wittgenstein, the Austrian pianist who lost his right arm on the Russian front in the First World War. He was taken prisoner and spent some unpleasant time in Omsk, Siberia, before being repatriated in 1916. Nothing daunted, he developed an extraordinary virtuosity for the left hand alone. Being a member of a rich family, and having been reared in a philosophical milieu (his brother was the famous logician Ludwig Wittgenstein), he decided to convert a misfortune into an artistic fortune. Accordingly, he commissioned several contemporary composers, among them Richard Strauss, Ravel, and Prokofiev, to write one-arm piano concertos.

Such works are not unknown in the piano repertory. Scriabin wrote a couple of charming pieces for left hand alone when his right hand was disabled as a result of excessive practice. And there was a Hungarian composer named Géza Zichy who lost his right arm in an hunting accident and proceeded to write left-hand piano pieces; he played his three-hand arrangement of Liszt's Rákóczy March with Liszt himself providing his own functional two hands.

It so happened that Ravel was already at work on a two-arm piano concerto when he accepted Wittgenstein's commis-

Lento (It.). Slow; calls for a tempo between andante and largo.

Allegro (It.). Lively, brisk, rapid.

sion. The left-hand concerto is a single movement, symmetrically segmented into three sections: **lento**, **allegro**, lento. Ravel was at the time very much impressed by (then novel) jazz music, which he heard during his American trip in 1928; the allegro in the left-hand concerto is alive with jazz and blues rhythms. Ravel points out that the work is actually monothematic, and that a keen ear can easily perceive the intervallic and rhythmic turns common to both the fast middle section and the outer slow sections. The concerto was performed by Wittgenstein in Vienna on November 27, 1931; later, Ravel coached a two-armed French pianist, Jacques Février, to play the work, and he performed it in Paris on January 17, 1933.

Concerto for Piano and Orchestra in G Major (1932)

Ravel was working on two piano concertos in 1930, and they could be no more distinct in style if two different men had written them. One was really half a concerto, commissioned by the Austrian pianist Paul Wittgenstein, who had lost his right arm on the Russian front during World War I. The one-armed concerto was, despite its limitation, filled with opulent impressionistic harmonies. The second concerto, for both hands, was Ravelesian in a surprising sense. It breathed the air full of invigorating ozone, as though refreshed by the peals of a rhythmic thunderstorm. The electric sparks exploding throughout the pages of the concerto are those of American jazz, which Ravel absorbed during his American tour in 1928. Listening to this music, one might be tempted to say that the great Ravel became infatuated with the sound of Gershwin's *Rhapsody in Blue*. But jazz was not entirely a novelty to French musicians at the time; a Negro jazz band played an engagement at the Casino de Paris as early as 1918.

The Concerto in G Major was first performed by Marguerite Long in Paris on January 14, 1933, with Ravel himself conducting the orchestra. It is in three movements. The first,

Allegretto, leaps into action at once in a state of hyperthyroid euphoria, with the piano playing bitonal arpeggios, the right hand on white keys, and the left on black keys. The mood changes suddenly; the piano projects a meditative solo, leading to an episode reminiscent of Ravel's early *Pavane pour une infante défunte*, with its archaic modalities and a sense of timeless serenity. **Syncopation** erupts again; there is an expansive ascent of chordal harmonies along the **pentatonic scale**, Gershwinian in its unabashed songfulness. Then the musical landscape is shifted once more in a virtuoso display of pianistic technique, with trills and thrills painted with a lush brush on an Impressionistic palette of tones.

The second movement, **Adagio** assai, is, by contrast, highly restrained. Ravel told Marguerite Long that it took him many days to find the proper mold for this movement. The piano plays unaccompanied for thirty-three bars; the gemmation of the austere melody and its florification are remarkable. The orchestra picks up the tonal thread, while the piano indulges in scale runs. The **antiphony** between the soloists and the orchestra is maintained in perfect balance to the end.

The third and last movement, **Presto**, is a glorified fanfaronade, interrupted by shrill outcries in the high register of the woodwinds. The bustle continues without letup; the percussion section, which includes wood blocks and slapstick, is busy. Jazzy bits of color are splashed in glissando trombones. There is a tremendous buildup of tempo and sonority in the coda, and the concerto ends with declarative concision.

Syncopation. Shifting of accents from strong beat to weak beat or between beats.
Pentatonic scale. A five-tone scale, usually that which avoids semitonic steps by skipping the fourth and seventh degrees in major and the second and sixth in minor.
Adagio (It.). Slow, leisurely; a slow movement.

Antiphonal. Responsive, alternating.

Presto (It.). Fast, rapid; faster than "allegro."

CHAMBER MUSIC

String Quartet in F Major (1903)

When the Kneisel Quartet gave the first American performance of Ravel's String Quartet in F Major in New York on December 11, 1906, the music aroused wonderment among New

York music critics. History repeats itself with monotonous regularity. Going over a stack of clippings from the time of Berlioz down to the time of Arnold Schoenberg, one finds the same sort of incomprehension, dubious brand of humor, and polysyllabic invective. These critical outbursts have a semblance of humanity in them when they are directed against revolutionary works like Stravinsky's *Le Sacre du printemps*. But the innocent music of Ravel's String Quartet lacks revolutionary elements, and it is baffling that the New York music critics of 1906 should have been perturbed by it. Yet the adverse judgment was unanimous. Wrote the *New York Tribune*:

> M. Ravel is content with one theme which has the emotional potency of one of those tunes which the curious may hear in a Chinese theatre, shrieked out by an ear-splitting clarinet. This theme serves him for four movements during which there is about as much emotional nuance as warms a problem in algebra. In the second movement, which stands for the old-fashioned **scherzo**, the four viols essay the noble language of the banjo effectively. This, we suppose, is the cerebral music, and the psychical music that we read about in the dithyrambs sung by the young men of France.

Scherzo (It.). A joke, jest; an instrumental piece of a light, piquant, humorous character. Also, a vivacious movement in the symphony, with strongly marked rhythm and sharp and unexpected contrasts in both rhythm and harmony; usually the third movement.

The reviewer added, with sesquipedalian humor, that Ravel's music was "a drastic dose of wormwood and assafoetida," which caused a "horripilation of nerves," and he complimented the audience on its tolerance: "The audiences of the Kneisel Quartet are a gentle and well-bred folk. Even when music revolts them they do not utter catcalls or throw missiles at the performers. Instead, they give a respectful hand to the musicians, evidently crediting them with good intentions."

The New York critics were not alone in being nonplussed by Ravel's simple music. The *London Times* wrote on December 7, 1907, after the first performance of Ravel's String Quartet in England: "There is no recognizable principle of construction, and the only wonder is how the thing is kept going so long without a principle." In the same review, Ravel's piano pieces are dismissed in the following words: "The *Jeux d'eau* is another piece of the descriptive order of no kind of musical interest, but *Pavane* [*pour une infante défunte*] has some faint suggestions of the antique." In according some merit to *Pavane*, the London reviewer must have anticipated the time when the piece was to be converted into a popular song.

Ravel's String Quartet was performed for the first time in Paris, on March 5, 1904, at a concert of the Société Nationale, under the auspices of the famous Schola Cantorum. The Société Nationale was not devoted exclusively to the cause of modern music. In fact, its organizers fought shy of extreme examples of modernity so that eventually the more modern members bolted, and formed a new organization definitely modernistic in its aspirations, under the name Société Musicale Indépendante.

Charles Koechlin writes in a letter to the author of *Music Since 1900*:

> The Société Nationale had been very useful to French art, but since about 1900 it found itself under the influence of Vincent D'Indy. While pieces of mediocre students of the Schola Cantorum were performed at the Society's concerts, works of real value were often rejected. Even Ravel was accepted with suspicion, and at the first performance the whole clan of the Schola was hostile to the point of impoliteness.

Still, the quartet was performed, and D'Indy praised the music in a public statement.

Ravel's String Quartet is in the orthodox four movements. The first movement is Allegro moderato, marked *très doux*. It is in **alla breve** time. The melodic idiom is strictly **diatonic**,

Alla breve (It.). In modern music, two beats per measure with the half note carrying the beat; also called "cut time."

Diatonic. Employing the tones of the standard major or minor scale.

but the modulatory plan is very free, with parallel progressions typical of the French school. The second movement is in double time, 6/8 and 3/4, which results in cross-accents. This is a characteristic rhythm of Iberian and Ibero-American national dances. The third movement is slow, in changing meters. The fourth and last movement is quick and agitated. It opens in the rhythm of 5/8, and subsequently alternates with 5/4 and 3/4. The concluding harmonic progression is an ascending series of major chords on a root progression of minor thirds. This progression became a cliché of modernism, and was used to good effect in Hollywood movie music.

Sonatine (1905)

Written in 1905, Ravel's Sonatine for piano is of simpler texture than his *Jeux d'eau*, written several years earlier. The first movement, in a modal style imparting pastoral serenity, is designed in miniature. Both hands operate in the high register (G clefs in both staves is a typical Ravel imprint); dynamics are subdued; the movement is very short, but it includes the formal elements of a **sonata**, with the three sections—**exposition**, **development**, and **recapitulation**—clearly recognizable. The second movement, a modified Minuet, maintains the poetic air of miniature writing: it is a stylization of the old dance, rather than its literal reproduction. The third and last movement is an animated **Rondo**, and is the longest movement of the **Sonatine**. The left hand is again placed in the treble, which, as in the first movement and partly in the second, creates and sustains the air of poetic miniature.

Introduction and Allegro (1906)

The Introduction and Allegro is, in essence and form, a concertino, or little concerto, for harp, accompanied by flute, clarinet, and **string quartet**. Ravel wrote it in 1906, when he was thirty-one years old. Jules Renard, the French writer, noted in

Sonata (It.). An instrumental composition usually for a solo instrument or chamber ensemble, in three or four movements, connected by key, contrasted in theme, tempo, meter, and mood.

Exposition. The opening of a sonata movement, in which the principal themes are presented for the first time.

Development. The working out or evolution (elaboration) of a theme by presenting it in varied melodic, harmonic, or rhythmic treatment.

Recapitulation. A return of the initial section of a movement in sonata form.

Rondo (It.). An instrumental piece in which the leading theme is repeated, alternating with the others.

Sonatina (It.), **Sonatine** (Ger.). A short sonata in two or three (rarely four) movements, the first in the characteristic first-movement form, abbreviated.

String quartet. A composition for first and second violin, viola, and cello.

his diary on November 19, 1906, in reference to Ravel: "a musician of the advance-guard, for whom Debussy is already an old beard." This is, of course, a literal translation: the French *vieille barbe* means a back number, a has-been, and the fact that Debussy wore a beard and Ravel was always close-shaven has no bearing on the case. Jules Renard's remark is interesting in that many critics accused Ravel of imitating Debussy, who, consequently, could not be just an old beard for him. Ravel, a man of great modesty, was moved to protest the allegations in a letter to the music critic of *Le Temps*, pointing out that he had used a style of writing usually associated with Debussy before Debussy did so, and gave dates in support of his claim. At the same time, he reiterated his profound respect for the elder master.

In the light of history, Ravel is bracketed with Debussy as representative of French impressionism. The term impressionism itself originated in 1874, when Claude Monet exhibited his picture *Impressions*, and the critic Louis Leroy, in the French publication *Charivari*, called Monet and his followers "impressionists" in derision. The name stuck, and was later applied to Debussy and the modern school of French music. The Impressionist school developed a musical style, characterized by subtly changing moods, languorous melodies, and highly individualized instrumentation.

The Introduction opens with a duet between the flute and clarinet. The strings enter in expressive pianissimo, and the harp is heard in brilliant **arpeggio**. The word "arpeggio" itself comes from *arpa*, which is Italian for "harp." The cello introduces a broad melody against the shimmering pianissimo of the violins, flute, and clarinet. The movement grows in tempo and sonority, only to subside again, marking the transition to the principal part, Allegro.

Allegro opens with a harp solo. The flute picks up the melody, to the accompaniment of plucked strings (pizzicato) in the violins. The melody is passed from one instrument to

Arpeggio (It.). Playing the tones of a chord in rapid, even succession.

another; there is a gradual increase in sonority until a climax is reached.

The flute and clarinet play, accompanied by strings pizzicato. The principal theme makes a brief appearance, and is reduced to a seesaw figure of two notes. There is an interplay of instrumental colors. The movement grows more animated. The harp resumes, accompanied by plucked strings and fluid arpeggios in the flute and clarinet. The vestigial two-note figure is heard again, then the clarinet plays the melody in full against the strings pizzicato. The bell-like harmonics of the harp are heard; the movement grows in force, reaching a sonorous climax. The violins, having climbed to the high register, descend chromatically.

Webster's Dictionary defines the word "cadenza" as "parenthetic flourish, or flight of ornament." This definition has a fine literary sound, but it fails to mention that a cadenza should contain material drawn from the principal themes of the composition. This harp cadenza does. There are reminiscences from the opening duet of the woodwinds, and the cello tune from the Introduction. The bell-like sounds are the harmonics. After a full quota of "parenthetic flourishes," the harp plays the Allegro theme, accompanied by the trills of the entire ensemble. The melody is passed to various instruments, the movement recedes, then flares up again, and there are short interludes for the harp solo. The final reiteration of the principal melody in variation form in the harp, accompanied by pizzicato strings, leads to a brilliant conclusion.

BÉLA BARTÓK
(1881–1945)
Modern Janus

THE CAREER OF Béla Bartók is a striking illustration of modern society's willful neglect of a great composer. We are all familiar with the tales of poverty of men of genius in bygone times, but it is peculiar that lessons of history could not be learned in the twentieth century.

Béla Bartók was a renowned figure in modern music when he made his way to the United States from his native Hungary. World War II was already raging; friends provided Bartók and his wife with enough funds to reach neutral Portugal. Mrs. Elizabeth Sprague Coolidge, the munificent American patroness of music, paid his transatlantic boat fare and an honorarium for an appearance at the Coolidge Festival in Washington. But other concert engagements were rare and difficult to obtain, and critical reviews in the American press were curiously hostile. Thanks to the efforts of members of the music department at Columbia University, Bartók obtained an appointment to classify a collection of Serbo-Croatian folk songs, at an annual salary of $2,500. But soon the special funds ran out and Bartók lost his job. He declined an offer to teach a summer course in composition at a midwestern college, on account of the rudimentary state of his English. He proposed to teach piano instead, but no one was interested in engaging a famous modern composer in such a capacity. "Never in my life," he complained in a pathetic letter to a friend in 1942, "since I have been on my own, earning my living from the age of nineteen, have I been in such a horrible financial situation. Where can I find pupils or a teaching job?"

A Hungarian compatriot in New York, who ran a small phonograph company, arranged for Bartók to record some of his piano music. To help Bartók out, he deliberately inflated the royalty statement and sent Bartók a substantial check. The following year, Bartók made recordings for the Columbia Phonograph Company, and was outraged when he received a modest check corresponding to the actual number of records sold. He promptly decided to sue, arguing that if a small outfit, owned by a Hungarian refugee, could do so advantageously with his records, it was obvious that the wealthy Columbia Phonograph Company was out to cheat him of his rightful income. It was with some difficulty that the conspirators who had engineered the unrealistic royalties in the first place dissuaded Bartók from filing the suit.

The story of Bartók's financial predicament finally reached the press. The *New York Times* published an article, "The Strange Case of Béla Bartók," which raised the question as to why a master of such stature could not be assured a subsistence minimum in the richest country in the world.

In the meantime, Bartók's health deteriorated. He suffered from a variety of ailments—asthma, arthritis, stomach ulcers, periodic fever, acne. To these was added dread leukemia. The little great man weighed only eighty-seven pounds before he died in a New York hospital on September 25, 1945. The funeral expenses were paid by the American Society of Composers and Publishers, but for several years there was not enough money to erect a tombstone on his grave.

Despite his disheartening experiences, Bartók was well aware of his position in music history. He even anticipated posthumous honors that might come his way. In his will he inserted a stern injunction not to have a Budapest street named after him as long as there were places bearing the names of Hitler and Mussolini. The injunction proved to be unnecessary. The Nazi and Fascist street signs were swept away by the course of events, and a street was named after Béla Bartók. The Hungarian post office honored Bartók's memory by issuing a series of airmail stamps with his portraits.

The great Hungarian composer began playing the piano in public at the age of eleven. At the Royal Academy of Music in Budapest, he studied piano with Istvan Thoman and composition with Hans Koessler, graduating in 1903. His earliest compositions revealed the combined influence of Liszt, Brahms, and Richard Strauss, but he soon became interested in exploring the resources of national folk music, which included not only Hungarian melorhythms but also elements of other ethnic strains in his native Transylvania, including Romanian and Slovak. He formed a cultural friendship with Zoltán Kodály, and together they traveled through the land collecting folk songs; then his interest in folk-song research led him to tour North Africa in 1913.

Bartók toured the United States as a pianist from December 1927 to February 1928 and gave concerts in the So-

Bartók Timeline

1881	Born in Nagyszentmiklós, Hungary (now Romania)
1892	First public performance as a pianist
1894	Family moves to Pressburg (now Bratislava)
1899-1903	Attends Royal Academy of Music in Budapest
1904-06	Travels collecting folk songs with Zoltán Kodály; publishes first collection
1910	First String Quartet premieres in Budapest
1913	Tours North Africa
1919	Serves as member of musical directorate of the short-lived Hungarian Democratic Republic; becomes deputy director of Academy of Music
1926-39	Famous piano pieces for students, *Mikrokosmos*, in six volumes, appear
1927-28	Tours U.S. and Russia as concert pianist
1934	Resigns position at Budapest Academy of Music to concentrate on ethnomusicological research
1940-2	Emigrates to U.S.; receives honorary degree from Columbia University; continues folk-song research
1944	Concerto for Orchestra, commissioned by Koussevitzky the previous year, premiered
1945	Dies in New York; Third Piano Concerto and Viola Concerto completed posthumously by his student, Tibor Serly

viet Union in 1929. He resigned his position at the Budapest Royal Academy of Music in 1934, but continued his research work in ethnomusicology as a member of the Hungarian Academy of Sciences, where he was engaged in the preparation of the monumental *Corpus Musicae Popularis Hungaricae.*

In his own compositions he soon began to feel the fascination of tonal colors and impressionistic harmonies as cultivated by Debussy and other modern French composers. The basic texture of his music remained true to **tonality**, which he expanded to **chromatic** polymodal structures and unremittingly dissonant chordal combinations; in his piano works he exploited the extreme registers of the keyboard, often in the form of tone clusters to simulate pitchless drumbeats. He made use of strong asymmetrical rhythmic figures suggesting the modalities of Slavic folk music, a usage that imparted a somewhat acrid coloring to his music. The melodic line of his works sometimes veered toward **atonality** in its chromatic involutions; in some instances he employed melodic figures comprising the twelve different notes of the chromatic scale; however, he never adopted the integral techniques of the twelve-tone method.

Bartók was not a prolific composer. He never wrote a symphony, and his other works are of moderate dimensions. But he was a fervent experimenter in novel sonorities. He gave particular prominence in his scores to instruments of percussion and indeed the piano itself became a percussion instrument in his technique. His renunciation of the pianistic luxuriance of Chopin, Liszt, and Debussy in favor of an austere, almost ascetic mode of expression required compensation in the subtlety of nuances. Dynamic contrasts assume in Bartók's piano writing a special significance. The frequent utilization of the extreme registers, high and low, imparts a drumlike timbre to the sound; chords grow by accretion of **dissonance** rather than by expansion of harmonies. The

Tonality. A cumulative concept that embraces all pertinent elements of tonal structure; a basic loyalty to tonal center.

Chromatic. Relating to tones foreign to a given key (scale) or chord; opposed to diatonic.

Atonality. The absence of tonality; music in which the traditional tonal structures are abandoned and there is no key signature.

Dissonance. A combination of two or more tones.

asymmetrical rhythms in rapid successions of even time units build up nervous tension. But despite the percussive character of Bartók's piano writing, in slow movements, there is a genuine lyrical quality achieved by unadorned melodic modalities, with folklike inflections.

Far from being a cerebral purveyor of abstract musical designs, Bartók was an ardent student of folkways, seeking the roots of **meters**, rhythms, and **modalities** in the spontaneous songs and dances of the people. Indeed, he regarded his analytical studies of popular melodies as his most important contribution to music. Even during the last years of his life, already weakened by illness, he applied himself assiduously to the arrangement of Serbo-Croatian folk melodies of Yugoslavia from recordings placed in his possession.

He was similarly interested in the natural musical expression of children; he firmly believed that children are capable of absorbing modalities and asymmetrical rhythmic structures with greater ease than adults trained in the rigid disciplines of established music schools. They can learn new accents, intervals, and harmonies as easily as they learn a new language. His collection of 153 piano pieces—entitled, significantly, *Mikrokosmos*—was intended as a method to initiate beginners into the world of unfamiliar tonal and rhythmic combinations, a parallel means of instruction to the Kodály method of schooling. In this remarkable collection, a modern child—and a modern teacher—will find a comprehensive exposition of the entire wealth of modern musical resources, an anthology of little masterpieces demonstrating the use of **pentatonic**, **diatonic**, and chromatic scales arranged in asymmetric rhythms and dissonant **counterpoint**.

Literally, *Mikrokosmos* means "the little world," but it may also, in Bartók's sense, mean the world of the little ones. The first four books of *Mikrokosmos* contain mostly pieces and exercises for beginners. But even in the simplest pieces, Béla

Meter, metre. In music, the symmetrical grouping of musical rhythms. In verse, the division into symmetrical lines.

Mode. Any scalar pattern of intervals, either traditional to a culture or invented.

Pentatonic scale. A five-tone scale, usually that which avoids semitonic steps by skipping the fourth and seventh degrees in major and the second and sixth in minor.

Diatonic. Employing the tones of the standard major or minor scale.

Counterpoint. Polyphonic composition; the combination of two or more simultaneous melodies.

Bartók follows a method of his own. There is no insistence on C major as the fundamental tonality, which is characteristic of most piano courses, so that the student develops a C major complex and measures all other modes and scale patterns against this chosen key. Instead, the modal feeling is established from the very first steps. There is no raising of the seventh in the **minor** mode, and the semicadences fall freely on different degrees of the modal scale. The rhythm, too, is freed from the symmetric rigidity of the common collections of piano exercises, and is composed of note values in changing patterns.

Melodic statements in Bartók's music are short, often abrupt, and they are developed not by baroque exfoliation but by spatial juxtaposition and temporal compression and extension. They are derived from the basic patterns of popular songs and dances of the Hungarian, Bulgarian, Romanian, and Turkish ethnic groups which make up the musical melting pot of Bartók's native Transylvania. They are modal and usually confined within the first four or five notes of the scale. Bartók's polyphony is rough-hewn; **canonic** and fugal progressions in his music are motivic rather than germinal. These cellular thematic proteins are constantly activated by the powerful enzymes of Bartók's rhythms, which are also of Balkan origin. They are asymmetrical, compounded of unequal groups of equal note values.

The insistent pounding on a single tone with unperiodic stresses is an inherent idiomatic trait of Balkan folk music, and Bartók uses the cumulative energy of such reiterated beats as an aesthetic sledgehammer to enthrall and subjugate even the most antagonistic listener. His harmonic usages are wide-ranging, including simple triadic constructions and congested globules of dissonant sounds employed functionally as single units. Acoustically harsh minor seconds and major sevenths often replace the classical thirds and **octaves** in Bartók's counterpoint, while the ambiguous **tritone** becomes the cor-

Minor. Latin word for "smaller," used in music in three different senses: 1. A *smaller* interval of a kind, as in minor second, minor third, minor sixth, minor seventh; 2. A key, as in *A* minor, or A scale, as in *A* minor scale; 3. A minor triad, consisting of a root, a minor third, and a perfect fifth above the root.

Canon. Musical imitation in which two or more parts take up, in succession, the given subject note for note; the strictest form of musical imitation.

Octave. A series of eight consecutive diatonic tones; the interval between the first and the eighth.

Tritone. The interval of three whole tones.

nerstone of both his melody and his harmony, superseding the tonic-dominant fifth.

Duke Bluebeard's Castle *(1911; revised 1912, 1918)*

Bartók was thirty years old when he wrote his only opera, *Duke Bluebeard's Castle*. It was first performed in Budapest seven years later, on May 24, 1918. The legend of Bluebeard was immortalized by Charles Perrault in his celebrated *Mother Goose Tales (Les Contes de la mère l'Oye)*, published in 1697. Besides Bluebeard, the collection contains such famous nursery stories as "Cinderella," "The Sleeping Beauty," and "Little Red Riding Hood." Perrault's version of the Bluebeard story takes the familiar form of a rescue tale. When Bluebeard's latest wife, driven by curiosity, disobeys his stern order, and opens a secret door, she finds behind it the heads of Bluebeard's slain wives. Her own life is saved by the opportune arrival of her brothers. The Bluebeard tale has been elaborated by numerous writers, and made the subject of several operas. The most notable modern interpretation is found in Maurice Maeterlinck's play, in which Bluebeard appears as a victim of his own fears whose wives, except the last, eventually come to his aid in a mystical reincarnation.

Bartók's librettist, Béla Balázs, treats the tale of the sextuple murderer as a neomedieval mystery play wherein Bluebeard's last wife, who is called Judith, induces him to open all the doors voluntarily. The action is focused on the castle itself rather than its inhabitants. Judith follows Bluebeard of her own volition, impelled by the desire to let the light of day shine into the segregated chambers. Blood pervades the scene, and is illustrated in the score by a motive based on the narrow intervals of the minor second. The first chamber contains instruments of torture; the second is an armory; the third yields a treasure trove of jewels; the fourth is a flower

5

HERZOG BLAUBARTS BURG
A kékszakállú herceg vára

Béla Bartók, Op. 11.

Prolog des Barden

Sinnender Sage
Verborgene Klage,
Verwesender Worte unsterblicher Sinn
Ist heute das Spiel, dessen Künder ich bin,
Ihr Herren und Damen.

Alte Geschichten
Ergötzen und richten.
Wen?_ Euch und mich, heut' Auge in Auge,
Wer von uns fehlte, wer von uns tauge,
Ihr Herren und Damen.

Was Sehnsucht streute,
Dess bleiben wir Beute.
Nicht unser Meinen, nicht unser Toben
Entscheidet die Lose_ ob unten, ob oben,_
Ihr Herren und Damen.

Drum: was wir heut spielen,
Gilt uns und noch vielen.
Wo ist die Bühne? Wer sieht Euch zu?
Was treibt Euch hasten, was gibt Euch Ruh,
Ihr Herren und Damen?

(Der Vorhang hebt sich)

Regös prologusa

*Haj regö rejtem
Hová, hová rejtsem
Hol volt, hol nem: kint-e vagy bent?
Régi rege, haj mit jelent,
Urak, asszonyságok?*

*Im, szólal az ének.
Ti néztek, én nézlek.
Szemünk pillás függönye fent:
Hol a színpad: kint-e vagy bent,
Urak, asszonyságok?*

*Keserves és boldog
Nevezetes dolgok,
Az világ kint haddal tele,
De nem abba halunk bele,
Urak, asszonyságok.*

*Nézzük egymást, nézzük,
Regénket regéljük.
Ki tudhatja honnan hozzuk?
Hallgatjuk és csodálkozzuk,
Urak, asszonyságok.*

(A függöny szétválik a háta mögött)

Der Barde: Geigen beginnen, lasset das Sinnen.
A regös: Zene szól, a láng ég, Kezdődjön a játék.

Andante ♩ = 92

Piano

Hört nun · und seht; und geht es zu Ende, und hat es
gefallen, so reget die Hände, Ihr Herren und Damen.
Szemem pillás függönye fent.   Tapsoljatok
majd   ha   lement,   Urak,   asszonyságok._

Ein Schloß,_ muß ich's nennen? Ihr solltet es kennen!
Noch seht Ihr es kaum, doch bald sollt Ihr's hören....
Régi vár, régi már Az mese, ki róla jár, Tik is hallgassátok.

Mächtige, runde, gotische Halle. Links führt eine steile Treppe zu einer kleinen eisernen Türe. Rechts der Stiege befinden sich in der Mauer sieben große Türen: vier noch gegenüber der Rampe, zwei bereits ganz rechts. Sonst weder Fenster, noch Dekoration. Die Halle gleicht einer finstern, düstern, leeren Felsenhöhle. Beim Heben des Vorhanges ist die Szene finster, der Barde verschwindet in ihr.
Hatalmas kerek gotikus csarnok. Balra meredek lépcső vezet fel egy kis vasajtóhoz. A lépcsőtől jobbra hét nagy ajtó van a falban; négy még szemben, kettő már egész jobboldalt. Különben sem ablak, se disz. A csarnok üres sötét, rideg, sziklabarlanghoz hasonlatos. Mikor a függöny szétválik, teljes sötétség van a színpadon, melyben a regős eltünik.

Meno mosso ♩ = 72

Universal-Edition Nr. 7026

garden; the fifth reveals a magnificent landscape; the sixth is a lake of tears. The last door hides three of Bluebeard's wives, who are still alive. But Judith must follow them into darkness. Bluebeard remains alone. The conclusion admits of diverse interpretations; perhaps the wives are only memories in Bluebeard's mind awakened by Judith, who becomes a memory herself in the end.

Bartók's opera breaks away completely from both the Baroque Italian genre and the Wagneromorphic music drama, but it retains the principle of leading motives, or **leitmotiv**. The blood motive in jarring minor seconds is omnipresent. Other motives are responsive to the situations depicted on the stage. A fanfare is sounded when the armory door is opened; the glitter of the jewels is reflected in the shimmering **tremolos** in the strings, as are also the flowers in the garden. The murder motive is represented by the giant strides of vacuous fifths moving in chromatic ascension, with resulting differential **semitones** that recall once more the blood motive. At a climax, the fifths overlap to form chords of major sevenths arrayed in parallel motion.

It is interesting to note that although Bartók wrote the opera in 1911, when Debussian impressionism was the dominant influence among modern composers, he was reluctant to adopt any of the favorite devices of the French modern school: **whole-tone scales**, the luscious dominant-ninth chords, the voluptuous unresolved suspensions over **diminished-seventh chords**. The orchestration, too, is devoid of coloristic scoring characteristic of the Impressionist palette. The music of Bartók's opera is austere, almost ascetic in its economic choice of musical resources. The only extrinsic effect is the use of a pentatonic motto at the opening and at the close of the opera. The pentatonic scale is of course an ancient Magyar modality, and is also a ubiquitous tonal matrix of ancient civilizations. In this reference, Bartók may have inten-

Leitmotiv (Ger.). Leading motive; any striking musical motive (theme, phrase) characterizing one of the actors in a drama or an idea, emotion, or situation.

Tremolo (It.). A quivering, fluttering, in singing; an unsteady tone.

Semitone. A half tone; the smallest interval in the Western scale.

Whole-tone scale. Scale consisting only of whole tones, lacking dominant and either major or minor triads; popularized by Debussy.

Diminished-seventh chord. A chord consisting of three conjunct minor thirds, outlining a diminished seventh between the top and bottom notes.

tionally emphasized the national and the universal meaning of his work.

The Miraculous Mandarin: *Suite (1918–19)*

Béla Bartók possessed an instinctive feeling for the diversity and the richness of folk music, but as a composer shaped by twentieth-century ideas, he sought new methods of musical self-expression. After an inevitable period of academic romanticism, he felt the fascination of French impressionism. The idea of painting nature in subjective terms, the new techniques that emancipated dissonance and allowed free interchange of tonalities, modalities, and rhythms, took possession of him. He wrote symphonic music marked by the delicacy of Impressionistic half colors.

But the brutal impact of the First World War dispersed the mists of the Impressionistic palette. In its stead came the psychologically tortured Germanic art, which became known as expressionism, and which split the scale into its common denominators in an atonal penumbra. On the opposite side of the aesthetic ledger, musicians experienced the assault of fauvism, a sophisticated savagery that affected primitivistic postures. The euphony of impressionism, the tense chromaticism of expressionism cohabitated, but never blended, with powerful earthy dissonant harmonies and grotesque asymmetrical rhythms of neoprimitivism; musical folklore provided physical material for this primitivistic explosion.

The music of Bartók combined these twentieth-century techniques, and the spontaneity of his folkloric inspiration imparted a sensation of natural vitality and concrete strength. Wit and warmth were the attributes of his style, while intervallic angularity became part of his modernistic lyricism. Above all, his music radiated deep conviction and individualistic self-assurance. The score of Bartók's pantomime *The Miraculous Mandarin* belongs to his Expressionistic period. Its subject is both surrealistic and symbolic: the supremacy of sensual passion and its triumph over death itself. When lust is assuaged, the body dies. He wrote the score of The Miraculous Mandarin between October 1918 and May 1919, during the worst phases of the Hungarian Civil War.

The story of *The Miraculous Mandarin* deals with a prostitute and a company of pimps, who lure susceptible men, then rob them. The first customer, an impecunious gentleman, is bounced out. He is followed by a young student who is also short of money. But he is handsome and the girl dances with him free of charge. Then the Mandarin appears, obviously prosperous and obviously passionate. He dances with the girl, but she is horrified by his hideous embraces. Her confederates leap upon him, rob him of his money, and attempt to murder him. They try to suffocate him under a pillow, they stab him repeatedly, but he still refuses to succumb. They hang him from a chandelier, but it collapses. The girl, affected by the Mandarin's will to survive, decides to submit to him. At last his desire is gratified; his wounds begin to bleed, and he dies.

The first performance of *The Miraculous Mandarin* was given in Cologne on November 27, 1926, but the police prevented a second performance. An attempt was made to produce the pantomime in Budapest for Bartók's fiftieth birthday in 1931, but after the final rehearsal, the production was banned. Even after the **libretto** was revised to eliminate the more lurid situations, no theater would risk announcing a performance.

Libretto (It.). A "booklet"; the words of an opera, oratorio, etc.

Bartók extracted an orchestral suite from the music of the pantomime, and it was played by the Philharmonic Society in Budapest on October 15, 1928, under the direction of the eminent conservative composer Ernst von Dohnányi. Then the war came and Bartók fled to America. The permissive postwar era removed all moralistic objections to the story of *The Miraculous Mandarin*, and the pantomime had numerous posthumous performances in Europe, and some in America.

The musical idiom of the score of *The Miraculous Mandarin* is starkly dissonant, but at the same time extremely economical. There is no gratuitous agglomeration of discords. The melodies are free of academic key relationship but they retain the sense of modality, often joining groups of notes from different modes. As a result there is a sense of tonal obliquity, ideally suited for a grotesque subject. Expected octaves are squeezed to major sevenths or expanded to augmented octaves, and perfect fifths are reduced to tritones, the cornerstones of the modern idiom, harmonically in bitonal conjunctions and atonally in melodic writing. The Mandarin himself is introduced by a scale of the augmented octave.

Most interestingly, Bartók assigns a pentatonic subject to the Mandarin when he meets the prostitute, as an ethnic allusion to his Chinese ancestry. But this pentatonic melody is harmonized by two rows of noncoinciding tritones, forming excruciatingly dissonant combinations. There are also lyric passages, but the lyricism is acidulated. The orchestration is luxuriant in its effective use of instrumental timbres, and its commentaries on the stage action are most eloquent; some passages suggest lust in a strikingly naturalistic manner. The score of *The Miraculous Mandarin* is a classical example of the modern musical usage.

Concerto for Piano and Orchestra No. 1 (1926)

Dissonance. A combination of two or more tones requiring resolution.

Consonance. A combination of two or more tones, harmonious and pleasing, requiring no further progression to make it satisfactory.

Béla Bartók's genius was twofold. As an ardent collector of folk songs among the diversified ethnic groups in his native Transylvania, he acquired a profound understanding of popular melodies and rhythms that form the foundation of all musical developments. As a composer whose imagination was stimulated by a modern environment, he evolved a musical language in which **dissonances** are treated on equal terms with **consonances**. To listeners brought up on the obsolescent notion that music must be euphonious, Bartók was incomprehensible. "If the reader were so rash as to purchase any of Béla Bartók's compositions," wrote Frederick Corder, a British musician, in an article entitled "On the Cult of Wrong Notes" and published in *The Musical Quarterly* of 1915, "he would find that they each and all consist of unmeaning bunches of notes, apparently representing the composer promenading the keyboard in his boots."

In historical perspective, it is clear that Bartók had revolutionized the art of piano playing. A professional pianist himself, he knew the resources of the instrument. But instead of emulating the refined nuances of the French masters of Impressionistic techniques or contributing to the emasculation of the piano by epicene neo-Baroque practices, Bartók restored the primary function of the keyboard as a medium of percussive sonorities. His piano music, in which the rhythmic impulse determines its course, is concise, terse, and curt.

Bartók wrote three piano concertos, of which the first is technically the most complex. Bartók gave its first performance as soloist in Frankfurt on July 1, 1927, with Wilhelm Furtwängler conducting the orchestra. The concerto is in three movements: Allegro moderato, Andante, and Allegro molto. Bartók described the tonality of the work as E minor, but it is E minor only in the Bartókian sense, for the crucial **mediant** is missing in the tonic chords, with the noncommittal **supertonic** placed in its stead. Although the harmonic fluctuation and the prevalence of dissonances make the key signature gratuitous, Bartók occasionally makes use of it in the score, perhaps to indicate that he does not exclude tonality on principle.

The first movement, Allegro moderato, introduces its principal theme by the process of gradual assembly of prefabricated segments. Diatonic and chromatic passages form contrasting episodes in the development section, with triadic progressions in parallel motion sustaining the sense of basic tonality. Meters and rhythms are in a constant flux of asym-

Mediant. The third degree of the scale.
Supertonic. The second degree of a diatonic scale.

Eighth note. Equal to one-half of the duration of a quarter note.

metrical patterns, with the **eighth note** serving as the least common denominator. The recapitulation echoes the relationship of the tonic and the dominant of the exposition, but metrical alterations give it a novel aspect. The movement comes to a natural close when all viable melodic, harmonic, and rhythmic elements of the original thematic material are exploited to their full potential.

The second movement of the concerto, Andante, is a study in percussion sonorities, in which the piano is antiphonically counterposed to an ensemble of drums and other instruments. Bartók gives detailed instructions in the score for the proper method of obtaining the required sound effects: the manner of striking a suspended cymbal on the rim from below, centrifugal and centripetal glissandos on the drumheads, etc. The piano itself becomes an instrument of percussion, with an emphasis on clarity and dynamic variety. As for harmonies, Bartók builds them by gradual encrustation and deposition of additional tonal elements. In this movement, dominated as it is by hard and clearly demarcated rhythmic units, the harsh major sevenths and the impinging minor seconds become the vertebrae of the harmonic skeleton.

Toccata (It.). A composition for organ or harpsichord (piano), free and bold in style.
Ostinato (It.). Obstinate; in music, the incessant repetition of a theme with a varying contrapuntal accompaniment.

The finale, Allegro molto, is an impetuous **toccata**, in which the initial motoric impulse generates a relentless rhythmic **ostinato**. Motivic fragments appear and disappear, congregate and segregate, integrate into large sonic columns and disintegrate in a rhythmic collapse. Each additional note in a chord, each alteration in the rhythmic pattern, each dynamic differentiation, each intercalation of rests, is of thematic import. In Bartók's music even silences are singularly eloquent.

Concerto for Piano and Orchestra No. 2 (1930–31)

Bartók wrote three piano concertos; the third was his last completed work. The Second Piano Concerto represents a syncretism of many elements: the ethnic musical folkways of southeastern Europe, classical polyphonic devices, dissonant counterpoint, **polytonality** and **polyrhythmy**. The concerto is in three movements: Allegro, Adagio—Presto, and Allegro molto. There are no key signatures.

The first movement, Allegro in 3/4 time, opens with a trumpet solo playing a folklike tune. This tune later appears in the forms of inversion and **retrograde inversion**. In the inverted form the direction of intervals is reversed without changing the rhythmic formula. The visual design of retrograde inversion (which is identical with inverted retrogression) can be obtained by turning the original theme upside down, or by looking at the inverted form in the mirror without turning the page upside down, the reflection supplying the retrograde image. The rhythmic pulse is firm, the dominating metrical unit being a quarter note. Canonic imitation is rampant. The piano is exercised in bland scale passages, but harmonically the idiom is increasingly dissonant. In the recapitulation the subject is inverted. There follows a long **cadenza** for piano solo, in which the subject appears in the horns in retrograde inversion, imitated by trumpets and trombones, and leading to a sonorous **coda**.

The second movement begins in Adagio, with a perpendicular structure of naked Gregorian fifths. The upper levels then diverge from the lower, leaving a gap in the middle. The scheme is further developed in **chorale**-like tones. This serves as an introduction to **Presto**, with the solo piano occupying the forefront, playing scales bitonally in minor sixths—a favorite device of Bartók—and in seconds. There are strettos and fugatos; parallel progressions reach greater consistence through harmonic inspissation, eventually expanding into tone clusters, with the right hand striking fistfuls of black keys, and the left of white keys. (Tone clusters were invented by the American composer Henry Cowell; Bartók, respecting Cowell's priority, wrote him for permission to use this device in the Second Concerto.) The movement ends cyclically with an epilogue of fifths.

Polytonality. Simultaneous use of two or more different tonalities found in modern music.

Polyrhythm. The simultaneous occurrence of several different rhythms.

Retrograde inversion. A standard technique in twelve-note composition wherein all notes of a set are played in a reverse succession which also mirrors the original set.

Cadenza (It.). An elaborate passage played or improvised by the solo instrument at the end of the first or last movements of a concerto.

Coda (It.). A "tail"; hence, a passage ending a movement.

Chorale. A hymn tune of the German Protestant Church, or one similar in style.

Presto (It.). Fast, rapid; faster than "allegro."

The third and last movement, Allegro molto, is set into motion by a big boom on the bass drum. The piano solo resumes its customary scale playing. Bartók makes a virtue of repetitive use of unadorned percussive figures; the kettledrums beat a primitivistic tattoo of two notes, C and E flat, and the piano responds in the kettledrum register with a syncopated figure on E flat and G flat. It takes a long time before the piano rises to higher reaches of the keyboard; on its way it plays a brusque duet with the bass drum. The soloist atones for this dalliance by plunging into parallel scales in major thirteenths. A churchly interlude breaks up the motion for a brief moment, but with celerity and alacrity the piano and the orchestra make their final run toward the ending in **fortissimo**, in the clearest G-major key.

Music for String Instruments, Percussion, and Celesta (1936)

Written for the Chamber Orchestra of Basel, Switzerland, and first performed there on January 21, 1937 under the direction of its founder Paul Sacher, Music for Strings, Percussion, and Celesta is in four movements: Andante tranquillo, Allegro, Adagio, and Allegro molto. The Andante tranquillo opens with a minuscule **fugue** in muted strings; its subject is serpentine in its chromatic involution. A brief but still very slow **stretto** follows. The subject is combined with its own **inversion**, accompanied by a shimmering display of celesta colors. The second movement, Allegro, is, by contrast, full of driving energy. The momentum never slackens. The melodic structure is polymodal, but centripetally directed towards C, which is the final note of the movement.

The Adagio begins with a xylophone solo in a rhythmically varied reiteration on a single high note. The strings command the melodic ground, with numerous trills, **glissandos** and flutelike effects, while the piano, the harp, and the celesta provide a floating accompaniment. The movement ends as it

---

Fortissimo (It.). Extremely loud.

Fugue (fewg). Contrapuntal imitation wherein a theme proposed by one part is taken up equally and successively by all participating parts.

Stretto (It.). A division of a fugue in which subject and answer follow in such close succession as to overlap.

Inversion. The transposition of one of the notes of an interval by an octave; chord position with lowest note other than root.

Glissando (It.). A slide; a rapid scale. On bowed instruments, a flowing, unaccented execution of a passage. On the piano, a rapid scale effect obtained by sliding the thumb, or thumb and one finger, over the keys.

began, with the xylophone solo on the same high F. The last movement, Allegro molto, is an exposition of alternating sonorities and intervallic groupings. It concludes energetically on an A-major chord.

Concerto for Violin No. 2 (1937–38)

The greatness of Bartók lies in the innovative quality of his instrumental works. He was fascinated by the asymmetric rhythms of the Magyar, Romanian, and Slavic folk songs of Transylvania, where he was born, and his works reflect many of these materials. Bartók was a brilliant pianist, but he also had profound knowledge of other instruments. He wrote his First Violin Concerto at the age of twenty-six, but did not take steps toward its publication or performance. A movement from this early concerto was incorporated into another work.

In 1937, the Hungarian violinist Zoltán Székely commissioned Bartók to write a violin concerto for him. Bartók set to work with enthusiasm, and completed the concerto on December 31, 1938. Székely played its first performance on April 23, 1939, with the Concertgebouw Orchestra of Amsterdam, Willem Mengelberg conducting. Although no identifying number was attached to the concerto in the published score, it was subsequently listed as No. 2, to take cognizance of Bartók's earlier violin concerto.

The score bears no key signature, but the opening and the ending are centripetally directed toward B major. It is in three movements: Allegro non troppo, Andante tranquillo, and Allegro molto. The form is classical, but the language is modern. In the violin part, Bartók applies the principle of polymodality, largely developed by himself. By shifting the basic modality, he is able to effect instant modulation; by interpolating chromatic tones he creates coloristic images. His harmonies are translucid despite their dissonant texture. Surprisingly, he incorporates, early in the first movement, a twelve-tone motive. It is not worked out according to the

Schoenbergian dodecaphonic method, but it is not an accidental insertion, for it reappears in the third movement, with some of the notes of the series in simple permutation. Most important of all, in his Second Violin Concerto, Bartók succeeds in creating a new type of modern virtuoso piece, brilliant in technique and highly effective in performance.

Contrasts *for Violin, Clarinet, and Piano* *(1938)*

Béla Bartók's music has a percussive quality, for percussion is the essence of rhythm; but instead of applying actual percussion instruments, Bartók used special effects: the high treble, or the lowest bass register of the piano keyboard; **pizzicato** of the violin, asymmetric **syncopation**. Against this background, his melodies appear unhindered by accompaniment, thus securing the optimum of expressive power.

Contrasts, his **suite** of three pieces for violin, clarinet, and piano, was written especially for Joseph Szigeti and Benny Goodman. The manuscript bears the date: Budapest, September 24, 1938. These are studies in contrast. The first movement is the Hungarian counterpart of American blues. The violin and piano provide the steady accompanying figure for the flourishes of the clarinet, and then the violin takes up the theme, while the clarinet plays **arpeggios** in quickly changing tonalities. After a slower interlude, the movement is resumed in syncopated rhythm against the booming glissandos of the piano. There is a passage in which the theme is played canonically against its own inversion—a favorite device of Bartók's. A brilliant and difficult clarinet cadenza leads to a conclusion.

The second movement is a short and slow chorale in the two solo instruments, punctuated by darksome trills in the bass. The third piece is a fast dance, opening with the fifths of a mistuned violin, with the E string lowered a semitone and the G string raised to G sharp. However, there is another vio-

Pizzicato (It.). Pinched; plucked with the finger; a direction to play notes by plucking the strings.

Syncopation. Shifting of accents from strong beat to weak beat or between beats.

Suite (Fr.). A set or series of pieces in various (idealized) dance forms. The earlier suites have four chief divisions: the Allemande, Courante, Saraband, and Gigue. Also referred to as Classical Suite, or Baroque Suite; the modern orchestral suite is more like a divertimento.

Arpeggio (It.). Playing the tones of a chord in rapid, even succession.

lin in reserve, which the player is instructed to pick up when normal tuning is required, much as the clarinet player changes from an instrument in A to one in B-flat.

The clarinet, and then the piano, introduce a dancing rhythm in even notes, punctuated by cross-accents. The interval of the diminished fifth, the tritone, produced by the special tuning of the violin, dominates the melodic texture of the movement. There is the characteristic **canon** between a fragment of the theme and its inversion. The movement then comes to a short stop, and resumes in an uneven meter of thirteen eighths in a bar. There are convergent and divergent progressions in the Lydian mode, which is the only mode that has the tonic interval of the tritone. Once more there is a pause, and the rhythmical interplay between the violin and the clarinet, and the right hand with the left hand of the piano, presents a double canon with the thematic fragments in direct and inverted forms. The violin (the one normally tuned) has a long cadenza. The movement ends brilliantly with an abrupt chord.

Canon. Musical imitation in which two or more parts take up, in succession, the given subject note for note; the strictest form of musical imitation.

Concerto for Two Pianos and Orchestra (1940)

The Concerto for Two Pianos and Orchestra is a transcription of Bartók's Sonata for Two Pianos and Percussion, composed in the summer of 1937 in Budapest, and first performed by Bartók and his second wife, Ditta, in Basel on January 16, 1938. In December of 1940 he transcribed it for two pianos and orchestra; this version of the work was first performed by the Royal Philharmonic Orchestra in London on October 14, 1942. Sir Adrian Boult conducted; the soloists were Louis Kentner and Llona Kabos. The *Musical Times* of London commented briefly: "This may be the music of tomorrow; it is difficult to see how it can ever be the music of any considerable public." The first American performance followed on January 21, 1943, by the New York Philharmonic conducted by Fritz

Reiner; the piano parts were performed by Bartók and his wife.

The Concerto for Two Pianos represents the culmination of Bartók's techniques in writing for the piano treated as a percussion instrument, with a percussion ensemble regarded as an integral part of the orchestra. The concerto is in three movements: Assai lento, Lento ma non troppo, and Allegro non troppo. There is no key signature, but in the spiraling modalities formed by asymmetrical intervallic structures, shifting tonal foci are clearly present. In the opening movement, the principal motive is a convoluted figure filling in the chromatic tones within the compass of a tritone. The music acquires momentum by intervallic accretion, inversion, and canonic imitation. The agitation grows until the tempo reaches the Allegro molto. Amid polytonal collisions, clear major triads are flashed. A grandiose declaration, un poco maestoso, is made. A rolling motion leads to a fugue charged with static electricity. Kinetic energy accumulates; the pianists cross the keyboards in opposite directions. Sonorous harmonic blocks are hewn out of thematic materials. A powerful coda brings the movement to a conclusion.

The second movement, Lento ma non troppo, is an elegy. The initial melody oscillates slowly along shifting modal modes. Then a nervous quintuplet appears, pulsating rapidly, increasing in strength and speed, and soon reaching the uppermost register of the keyboard in fortissimo. A series of dissonant chords is set in motion in the piano parts, while the thematic quintuplets maintain their rhythmic pulse in the orchestra. The nostalgic melody returns; the quintuplet motto echoes it. The ending is very slow and very soft.

The third movement, Allegro non troppo, is a brilliant rondo. It embodies most of Bartók's favorite pianistic devices: rapid polymodal passages traversing the entire keyboard, triadic parallelisms, multiple dissonant trills, crisp arpeggiated chords. The coda is remarkable: limpid major triads diverge in the twin pianos, ending in an unadulterated C major.

Concerto for Orchestra (1943)

Béla Bartók found a haven in America from devastated Europe at the outbreak of World War II and spent his American years, until his death in New York in 1945, in difficult financial circumstances. He was a master pianist, but not the possessor of the fashionable abilities of a romantic virtuoso. He was a teacher of great stature, but did not fit into the easygoing curriculum of American music schools. His compositions, difficult to perform, were not commercially lucrative. His reputation among musicians and music scholars was high—but not his income. When he fell ill, his personal circumstances became even more distressing, and his predicament was openly discussed in the press. Serge Koussevitzky commissioned him to write a symphonic work and offered a modest down payment, but Béla Bartók was reluctant to accept the money, afraid that because of his illness he would be unable to complete the work. Koussevitzky was persuasive and solicitous, and Béla Bartók accepted the commission, completed the score in October 1943, and named it the **Concerto** for Orchestra. Koussevitzky conducted the first performance of the Concerto for Orchestra with the Boston Symphony on December 1, 1944. In his program annotations, Bartók explained that the title referred to the virtuoso treatment of the instrument, so that there is always a temporary soloist playing a miniature concerto with orchestral accompaniment. The Concerto for Orchestra was destined to become his most popular work.

The Concerto for Orchestra is in five movements: Introduzione, Giuoco delle coppie, Elegia, Intermezzo interrotto, and Finale. The first movement opens with sylvan murmurs in the strings and flutes; a gently swaying motion leads to a **scherzo** in **rondo** form the ending is abrupt and tonally clear. The second movement, "a game of pairs," begins and ends

Concerto (It.). An extended multi-movement composition for a solo instrument, usually with orchestra accompaniment and using (modified) sonata form.

Scherzo (It.). A joke, jest; an instrumental piece of a light, piquant, humorous character. Also, a vivacious movement in the symphony, with strongly marked rhythm and sharp and unexpected contrasts in both rhythm and harmony; usually the third movement.

Rondo (It.). An instrumental piece in which the leading theme is repeated, alternating with the others.

with a side-drum solo. The title gives the clue to the structure of the music, which is a series of duos of wind instruments paired at different intervals, the bassoons in sixths, the oboes in thirds, the clarinets in sevenths, the flutes in fifths, the muted trumpets in major seconds. The time signature is 2/4, another pair. The third movement, an elegy, is marked by an effusion of melismatic **arabesques** and canonic imitations.

The fourth movement, an "interrupted **intermezzo**," is a burlesque with the thematic interval of the tritone imparting wry humor to the music. The "interruption" occurs with the sudden intrusion of a rather insipid tune, which turns out to be the military German theme from Shostakovich's "Leningrad" Symphony. This tune ruled the radio waves at the time Bartók was composing his Concerto for Orchestra, and annoyed him. He disguised it somewhat, and made it sound even closer to the original source, the song "Dann geh' ich zu Maxim" from Lehár's operetta *The Merry Widow*. The quotation is introduced by a mocking glissando in the trombones and followed by a chromatic cascade of the woodwinds.

The Finale opens like a glorified military march with a deliberate atonal twist. The main part of the movement is a rapid rondo, which includes a vigorous fugue going through ingenious telescopic contractions and expansions of the subject. The concluding section of the Finale mobilizes all the resources of the orchestra. It is also the most varied movement rhythmically, but it is maintained within the metrical framework of 2/4. Bartók also provided an alternative and more emphatic ending in which the descending figure of the original version is replaced by an ascending run of three and a half octaves, along the **Lydian mode**, reinforced by a vesuviating glissando in the horns and trombones.

Arabesque. A type of fanciful pianoforte piece; ornamental passages accompanying or varying a theme.

Intermezzo (It.). A light musical entertainment alternating with the acts of the early Italian tragedies; incidental music; a short movement connecting the main divisions of a symphony.

Lydian mode. The church mode that corresponds to the scale from *F* to *F* on the white keys of the piano.

IGOR STRAVINSKY
(1882–1971)
Perennial Revolutionary

IGOR STRAVINSKY! This name has a metallic ring to it that has long outgrown purely musical associations. It has become a symbol of the urbanistic, geometric, lapidary modern age. Poets rather than musicians find the most expressive words to define the music of Igor Stravinsky; despite its complexity it speaks a direct language to the uninitiated. Musicians whose formative period belongs in the nineteenth century cannot accept Stravinsky wholeheartedly, for Stravinsky's every note negates the heritage of the immediate past.

Stravinsky starts his musical career with an academic symphony, and he enters the peak of maturity (which is reached at fifty-four, if we are to believe Aristotle) in the academy of classical knowledge. *Apollon Musagète*, *Oedipus Rex*, *Perséphone*—in these subjects Stravinsky finds the greatest freedom of abstraction, the static beauty that is germane to absolute music. Between these two academic solstices, there has passed a season of greatest storms, luxuriant growths, and spectacular upheavals. *The Firebird*, a sumptuous panorama of Russian fairy tales on a direct line from Rimsky-Korsakov's tradition, marks the ascent of Stravinsky's star in Paris, where it was performed at the Diaghilev ballet on June 25, 1910.

Nine years later Stravinsky revised this score and chastened it. It is interesting to compare the two orchestrations, the first abundant with harps, celestas, woodwinds; the second stripped to the essentials, the celesta replaced by a percussive pianoforte, the woodwinds reduced, the development and transitional passages cut. It is a bowdlerized edition of a great work, and yet, under Stravinsky's knife, the overorchestration of the first version is convincingly shown. In *The Firebird*, behind the Russianizing orientalism of the idiom, there is the true Stravinskian color: the **tritone** plays a greater role in melodic constructions than with any of Stravinsky's precursors, but as yet is not extended onto the harmonic plane, and so stops short of **bitonality**.

Tritone. The interval of three whole tones.

Bitonality. Harmony in two different tonalities, as *C* major and *F* sharp major played simultaneously.

May, 1911. In Rome Stravinsky finishes *Petrushka*. The bitonality comes to fruition, the C major is combined with F-sharp major. The syncopating rhythm, which had appeared in *The Firebird* in the "Infernal Dance of Kashchei," is here carried to its ultimate potentiality—the destruction of the main beat, leaning, so to speak, on a vacuum. Some tunes used in *Petrushka* are from Russian folk music; there is also a French **chansonette** and a Viennese waltz.

Chansonette (Fr.). A short song of a light nature.

March 8, 1913. Stravinsky marks the date at the end of the score of *The Rite of Spring* (*Le Sacre du printemps*). The simple bitonality of *Petrushka* is submerged under more inclusive harmonies. Two clarinets play at the interval of the major seventh instead of the octave. The distinction between the major and the **minor** key is obliterated. A new "frictional" tonality contains both the major and minor **triads**. The rhythm and meter merge in the "Danse sacrale," and the main beat is relegated into a fiction by being deprived of any substance. The drums themselves are syncopating. The peak of effective complexity has been reached.

Thursday, May 29, 1913. The first performance of *The Rite of Spring*. It is accompanied by a scandal, about which too many legends have been formed. It is said, for instance, that Saint-Saëns, perplexed by the sound of the opening solo of the bassoon, in its highest register, mockingly inquired: "What instrument was that?" and, told it was a bassoon, rose and went home.

The war. Stravinsky is in Switzerland. He finishes *The Nightingale* (*Le Rossignol*), an opera on a pseudo-Chinese tale by Hans Christian Andersen. But already a change is apparent—the time of large orchestral works has passed. The war requires wartime music, reduced, stripped to an economical minimum. Stravinsky meets Charles-Ferdinand Ramuz, the Swiss novelist, who suggests a half-mystical story about a soldier, the devil and the fiddle. Stravinsky dreams a dream: a Gypsy woman gives breast to a child, and at the same time plays the violin with the entire length of the bow. Stravinsky uses the melody of the dream—and the manner of playing with the entire bow—for his *Soldier's Story* (*L'Histoire du soldat*), scored for only seven instruments.

The armistice approaches. From America the first sounds of jazz are heard. Stravinsky composes the chamber work *Ragtime*. The main beat is reinstalled. It is almost a recantation of his prewar syncopation. Ramuz, in his informal way, notes down his impressions of Stravinsky at that period: his professorial punctiliousness, his pointed neatness, his calligraphic writing, his table with multicolored inks and freshly sharpened pencils on it. Ramuz credits Stravinsky with an invention: that of a roulette that traces the five-line staff on paper . . . a convenient gadget.

Minor. Latin word for "smaller," used in music in three different senses: 1. A *smaller* interval of a kind, as in minor second, minor third, minor sixth, minor seventh; 2. A key, as in *A* minor, or a scale, as in *A* minor scale; 3. A minor triad; consisting of a root, a minor third, and a perfect fifth above the root.

Triad. A "three-tone" chord composed of a given tone (the root), with its third and fifth in ascending order in the scale.

June 13, 1923. Ernest Ansermet, the Swiss mathematician-conductor, directs the first performance of *The Wedding* (*Les Noces*). Four pianos, thirteen percussion instruments, voices, choruses. Every singing note, spoken word, and percussive sound are here scientifically placed in position, so as to contribute to the maximum efficiency of the whole. Impressionism here suffers its last defeat. The rhythms and meters are crossed, the bar lines overridden. Here, as in *The Soldier's Story*, a written meter means nothing but an arithmetical fiction. In fact, there is no common meter for the entire ensemble. The conductor should here conduct one rhythm with one hand, and another rhythm with the other hand; or, better still, robot conductors should be installed, beating the smallest unit, and marking the true downbeat for each group.

Small operas, *Renard* and *Mavra*, continue the tradition of *The Soldier's Story* and *The Wedding*. Harmonically speaking, the idiom is tonal. The superposition of the **tonic** upon the **dominant** and the free use of all degrees of the **diatonic** scale only emphasize the feeling of tonality. This feeling of tonality grows more and more definite.

Finally, Stravinsky's mind turns to the fountainhead of tonality; his Octet for Wind Instruments recreates the idiom before Bach. With the Piano **Concerto** (1924) Stravinsky launches the movement in modern music that has been so erroneously designated as a movement "back to Bach." No, Stravinsky goes back much further than Bach. His works, in which a religious note is beginning to sound not only in the titles but in the dedications themselves, indicate his growing fascination with theological music of the Middle Ages. Already in *The Wedding* there is a feeling of the medieval Organum, as in the successive fourths of the prayer. The reversion to the Latin language in *Oedipus Rex* is also significant. Medieval Latin exercised a great influence on the musical line. In fact, hymnal **melos** was often a mere function of the vocables of the text, so that there were even special **neumes** adaptable

Tonic. The keynote of a scale; the triad on the keynote (tonic chord).

Dominant. The fifth tone in the major or minor scales; a chord based on that tone.

Diatonic. Employing the tones of the standard major or minor scale.

Concerto (It.). An extended multi-movement composition for a solo instrument, usually with orchestra accompaniment and using (modified) sonata form.

Melos (Gk.). The name bestowed by Wagner on the style of recitative employed in his later music dramas.

Neumes. Signs used in the early Middle Ages to represent tones.

to certain classes of sounds. Stravinsky's request to Jean Cocteau to have a Latin text written to *Oedipus Rex* clearly indicated his predilection for certain forms of a very definite historical and ideological moment. *Oedipus Rex* is thus a modern Passion play, to a pagan subject, in the holy language of Christian Rome.

The *Symphony of Psalms* bears an inscription, "ad majorem Dei gloriam," which is also indicative of a tendency. Stravinsky works to restore music to its former position as an accessory to a loftier purpose—*theologiae ancilla*. In form, this music may be classical, or even Romantic. In each case it will recreate the theological spirit as reflected in this or that century. That it is a renaissance of a renaissance does not mean that it has to be inferior. Great music has been written in the spirit of a revival of a preceding period. Those that bemoan Stravinsky's present trend underrate his power of rising above commonly insurmountable barriers.

The Nightingale (Le Rossignol) *(1908–14)*

The Chinese emperor is dying and his life is supported by the singing of the nightingale. But when the Japanese ambassador thoughtlessly presents the emperor with a mechanical nightingale, the real bird flies away, and the emperor's health declines dangerously. As a discordant funeral march is played, the real nightingale is brought in, and the emperor regains his strength. The moral seems to be that things natural cure all ills. The opera, produced in Paris in 1914, is extremely dissonant, with harmonies built on the tritone and the major seventh. The element of ***atonality*** is employed with grotesque effectiveness.

Atonality. The absence of tonality; music in which the traditional tonal structures are abandoned and there is no key signature.

The Firebird: *Suite (1910; revised 1919, 1945)*

For his 1910 season of the Ballets Russes, a remarkable enterprise that played Russian music with a cast of Russian dancers

ВСТУПЛЕНИЕ   *Introduction*

Introduction to Stravinsky's *Firebird*

all over the world except Russia itself, its great impresario Serge Diaghilev needed a ballet score with a Russian folk flavor. In St. Petersburg, he approached Anatol Liadov, composer of delectable symphonic miniatures that figuratively smelled of the Russian soil, but Liadov was notoriously indolent, and nothing came of the project. The name of young Igor Stravinsky was then brought out as a possible substitute. Stravinsky was a student of Rimsky-Korsakov's during the last years of the master's life, and had absorbed the inimitable coloring of Rimsky-Korsakov's orchestra that suited the Russian folk tales so well. For Stravinsky's ballet Diaghilev suggested the subject of the Russian folk hero Ivan Tsarevich, the monster Kashchei and the magical Firebird. The final title, in French, was *L'Oiseau de feu*, described as a "conte dansé."

Stravinsky describes the circumstances attending the composition of *The Firebird* in his autobiography:

> Towards the end of the summer of the year 1909, I received a telegram which upset all my previous plans. Diaghilev, who had just arrived in St. Petersburg, asked me to write the music to *The Firebird* for the season of The Ballets Russes at the Paris Opéra in the Spring of 1910. The offer was flattering. I was chosen among musicians of my generation to collaborate in an important enterprise. . . . I worked on the score with frenzy, and when I finished it, I felt the necessity of rest in the country before going to Paris.

Stravinsky completed the score in St. Petersburg on May 18, 1910, a month before his twenty-eighth birthday, and dedicated it to Rimsky-Korsakov's son Andrey (1878–1940). It was his last work written in Russia. *Petrushka* and *The Rite of Spring* were composed abroad.

The Firebird was produced by Diaghilev and the Ballets Russes in Paris on June 25, 1910. The French composer

Gabriel Pierné conducted the orchestra. Stravinsky writes in his *Chroniques de ma vie*: "The spectacle was warmly applauded by the Paris public. Of course, I do not attribute this success entirely to my music: it was equally due to the sumptuous scenery of the painter Golovin, the brilliant interpretation of Diaghilev's dancers, and the talent of the ballet master." The ballet captivated the Parisians by the exotic exuberance of its rhythm and the splendor of its instrumentation. Among the innovations in the score was a **glissando** on the harmonics in the strings covering the range of the first twelve overtones of the natural series.

In 1919 Stravinsky revised the score, eliminating much of its panache, reducing the opulent orchestral apparatus to a practical minimum, scuttling the supernumerary instruments, excising ornamental passages, eliding **cadenzas**, deleting paraphernalia, in sum, plucking the flaming plumage of the Firebird and divesting Kashchei of some of his brassy terrors. But the loss in flamboyance is compensated in this revised version by greater compactness and functional solidity.

That was the time when Stravinsky, watching the economic disruption of the European world from his refuge in Switzerland, thought that the era of huge orchestral conceptions was past, that it was imperative to limit the medium to a practical level. In that new orchestration he, so to speak, returned the luminous feather to *The Firebird*. With the deleted passages for the harps, the celesta, and the bells went also the light that "shone like an untold number of candles." And that is why the early version of the score is still by far the more popular among conductors and orchestras.

The story of *The Firebird* follows the classical Russian folk tale in essential details. Ivan Tsarevich captures the Firebird as she picks the golden apples in the enchanted garden of the fearsome Kashchei the Immortal. She begs him to release her in exchange for one of her magic feathers. Thirteen royal princesses, captives of Kashchei, appear and dance around.

Glissando (It.). A slide; a rapid scale. On bowed instruments, a flowing, unaccented execution of a passage. On the piano, a rapid scale effect obtained by sliding the thumb, or thumb and one finger, over the keys.

Cadenza (It.). An elaborate passage played or improvised by the solo instrument at the end of the first or last movements of a concerto.

Ivan falls in love with one of them and follows her into Kashchei's castle, but is seized by the guards. He waves the magic feather and the Firebird appears at his summons. She reveals to him the secret of Kashchei's immortality, which is hidden in an egg kept in a casket. Ivan smashes the egg; Kashchei perishes, his captives are set free, and Ivan marries his beloved princess.

Stravinsky handles his musical materials in this score with a mastery that still astounds. The Introduction, depicting Kashchei's garden, imparts an air of mystery; its principal melody is embanked within the interval of the tritone, so beloved by Russian musical story tellers because of the demonic associations inherited from the medieval symbolism of the tritone as diabolus in musica. The Dance of the Firebird is a tableau vivant in gorgeous chromatic harmonies. By contrast, the Round of the Princesses enchants by the diatonic purity of its music. The Infernal Dance of Kashchei and his subjects is charged with syncopated energy. The Berceuse is a poetic vignette. The Finale unleashes the entire wealth of orchestral resources bearing forth an oriflamme of triumphant sonorities.

Igor Glebov, the Russian critic, said of the score of *The Firebird*: "Stravinsky has indeed caught the luminous golden feather in this fairy tale. The entire score of *The Firebird* sparkles with the rainbow colors of precious stones and orchestral timbres." This luminous quality places *The Firebird* on the borderline of impressionism, with its tonal *chatouillement* ("tickling") and coloristic pointillism.

Petrushka *(1911)*

Stravinsky tells in his autobiography that one of the most important dates in his life was the Siloti concert in St. Petersburg, at which Diaghilev, the great Russian impresario, was present, and heard an early Stravinsky piece for orchestra. It was on

Stravinsky Timeline

1882 Born in Oranienbaum, near St. Petersburg

1905 Begins lessons in orchestration with Rimsky-Korsakov

1908 Composes orchestral fantasy *Fireworks* for wedding of Rimsky-Korsakov's daughter

1910 First collaboration with Serge Diaghilev's Ballets Russes, *The Firebird,* staged in Paris

1911 Settles in Paris (with frequent trips to Switzerland); second ballet for Diaghilev, *Petrushka,* is premiered

1913 The revolutionary *Le Sacre du printemps* (*The Rite of Spring*), with choreography by Vaclav Nijinsky, is produced in Paris, causes riots

1914 Lyric fairy tale *Le Rossignol,* after Hans Christian Andersen, produced by Diaghilev

1918 Composes narrated dance work *L'Histoire du soldat,* inaugurating series of smaller-scale works

1920 Neoclassical ballet *Pulcinella* premiered at Paris Opéra

1925 Piano soloist in U.S. premiere of Piano Concerto, with Boston Symphony Orchestra under Serge Koussevitzky

1927 First performance of opera-oratorio *Oedipus Rex* in Paris

1928 *Apollon Musagète* (*Apollo*), pantomime for string orchestra, first heard at Library of Congress

(continued)

February 6, 1909 and as a result of this hearing, Diaghilev decided to commission Stravinsky to do some orchestrations of Chopin for his Paris season. For the following season, Diaghilev asked Stravinsky to write an original ballet, based on the Russian fairy tale "The Firebird." Stravinsky wrote for this ballet a music gorgeously Russian. When it was produced by Diaghilev in Paris on June 25, 1910, Stravinsky was only twenty-eight years old, and it was a beginning of a long association with Diaghilev, which determined Stravinsky's career up to the very time of Diaghilev's death in 1929. Stravinsky left Russia to write Russian music in France, Switzerland, and Italy, and eventually became a French citizen.

Petrushka was Stravinsky's second ballet written for Diaghilev. It did not assume the shape of a ballet at once. For a time, Stravinsky toyed with the idea of composing a short piece for piano and orchestra, in the manner of Weber's Konzertstück (Concert Piece for piano). It was to be a compressed piano concerto, and the piano part was largely ready, when Stravinsky decided to put a new meaning into the piece. Stravinsky describes the genesis of the score in his autobiography:

> In composing *Petrouchka* I wanted to experiment with a work for orchestra, in which the piano would play the predominant part, a sort of Konzertstück. I conceived a clear vision of a puppet turned loose with a cascade of demoniacal **arpeggios** to which the orchestra responds by menacing fanfares. There follows a terrible brawl resulting in a pitiful defeat of the poor puppet. After completing my **burlesque** piece, I took long walks by the shores of the lake of Geneva, thinking of a title that would express in a single word the character of my music. And then, all of a sudden, I was seized with joy: Petrouchka! The eternal unlucky hero of puppet shows. I had found my title!

Arpeggio (It.). Playing the tones of a chord in rapid, even succession.

Burlesque. A dramatic extravaganza, or farcical travesty of some serious subject, with more or less music.

"Petrushka" is a diminutive for Peter, used by Russian peasants, but specifically it is the name of a puppet popular at Russian fairs after Lent. Thus, Petrushka is the counterpart of a character in the English Punch and Judy show. He is usually the pathetic lover who gets beaten up by the villain, and is thwarted in all his enterprises. He is quarrelsome without cunning, and aggressive without caution. However, it was not Stravinsky's intention to write a musical biography of Petrushka, in the manner of Strauss's *Till Eulenspiegel*. Stravinsky's score is a panorama of the Russian pre-Lent festival *Maslenitza* (literally, "butter time"). There are many sideshows in Stravinsky's ballet: the organ grinder, the magician with his flute, a dancing bear. Among the crowds there are two categories of typical visitors: children's nurses and coachmen. Petrushka's tragedy is a part of the show. He quarrels with the Moor over the love of a ballerina, and gets his skull cracked.

Stravinsky completed the composition of *Petrushka* in Rome, on May 26, 1911. The ballet was produced by Diaghilev in Paris on June 13, 1911, and its success was instantaneous, but quite lacking in the riotous quality that accompanied the production of *The Rite of Spring*. The three scores, *The Firebird*, *Petrushka*, and *The Rite of Spring* constitute the "Russian" period in Stravinsky's evolution. In all three, the subjects are intensely Russian, and in *Petrushka* Stravinsky actually uses the themes of popular Russian songs in the score, the only work in which he does so openly. There are Russian melodies in *The Wedding*, which he wrote during the years of the world war and after the armistice, but these melodies are original. *The Soldier's Story*, composed in 1918, employs Russian rhythms but makes no direct use of actual melodies. The Russian period of Stravinsky comprises the years from 1910 to 1924, after which he changed his style to a special type of classical writing.

The expressly Russian style of *Petrushka* did not deter composers of many nations—French, Spanish, Americans—

Stravinsky Timeline (cont.)

1930 Composes Symphony of Psalms for fiftieth anniversary of Boston Symphony Orchestra

1934 Becomes French citizen; composes ballet *Perséphone*, with narrator, commissioned by Ida Rubinstein

1937 *Jeu de cartes: Ballet in Three Deals* first performed at Metropolitan Opera in New York

1939-40 Delivers Charles Eliot Norton lectures on poetry at Harvard University

1940 Following death of first wife, Catherine Nosenko, marries longtime mistress, dancer Vera de Bosset

1942 Ringling Brothers commissions *Circus Polka*, for a young elephant

1944 Prevented from performing his arrangement of "The Star-Spangled Banner" because Massachusetts law forbids "mutilation" of national anthem

1946 Composes *Ebony Concerto* for Woody Herman; attends first performance of *Symphony in Three Movements* in New York

1951 Completes *The Rake's Progress*, conducts premiere in Venice

1945 Becomes U.S. citizen

1957 *Agon*, ballet for twelve dancers employing 12-tone method, first staged in Los Angeles

1962 *The Flood*, for narrator, mime, singers, dancers, broadcast by CBS-TV

1971 Dies in New York

from imitating its harmonic and even rhythmic idiom. The impact of *The Rite of Spring* on creative musicians was even greater, affecting young talents as well as composers of established reputation. When Stravinsky abandoned the Russian style and adopted a classicism bordering on academicism, musical opinion followed him in that change. However, it may be that Stravinsky himself followed the changes necessitated by the economic and political reorganization after the First World War, and in one case, that of *The Soldier's Story*, he declared his intention to reduce the apparatus of modern orchestra to an efficient minimum so as to make frequent performances possible without great expenditure of money.

The subtitle of *Petrushka* reads: *Burlesque Scenes in Four Tableaux*, which establishes the character of the score as stage music. Yet, the orchestral **suite** from *Petrushka* has proved extremely effective without the visual theater, although early critics of the score, in Europe and America, wrote that ballet action was essential to illustrate the music. Similarly, *The Rite of Spring* and *The Firebird* stand by themselves as effective orchestral suites. Historically, Stravinsky was right in acknowledging Diaghilev as the animator of his creative work, but the ballet was to Stravinsky merely a medium of expression, and his music, divorced from action, remains undiminished in its artistic power.

Alexandre Benois, the coauthor with Stravinsky of the libretto of *Petrushka*, called it "a street ballet," because its action reflects the street life of old Russia. The first and last scenes take place at the Admiralty Square in St. Petersburg during the reign of Czar Nicholas I in the 1830s. The season is the Shrovetide, or Mardi Gras, when Russians of all classes gorged themselves on food in anticipation of a long Lent. (Regular contests in gluttony used to be held at that time for the greatest consumption of bliny, buttered pancakes; one story had it that a merchant held a record of 120 bliny in one day, but he died the next morning.) The second scene is in

Suite (Fr.). A set or series of pieces in various (idealized) dance forms. The earlier suites have four chief divisions: the Allemande, Courante, Saraband, and Gigue. Also referred to as Classical Suite, or Baroque Suite; the modern orchestral suite is more like a divertimento.

Petrushka's room, and the third is in the apartment of the Blackamoor, Petrushka's successful rival in love. He enters the Blackamoor's room in the middle of a love scene with the ballerina, and is ignominiously thrown out. In the final scene, the puppets engage in an open fight. Petrushka is struck down by the Blackamoor with his scimitar and falls piteously to the ground. The spectators are horrified, but the puppeteer reassures them that Petrushka is merely a creature of wood and sawdust. He carries Petrushka's broken remains off the stage as darkness descends on the scene. Then comes an unexpected climax. Petrushka's ghost suddenly appears on the top of the theatrical booth and thumbs his nose at the public. There is a mystical exchange of roles; Petrushka becomes the master of the show, and the puppeteer his servant.

Stravinsky wrote his very Russian score in Switzerland, completing the manuscript in May 1911, when he was only twenty-eight years old. The first performance took place at Diaghilev's Ballets Russes in Paris, on June 13, 1911. Pierre Monteux was the conductor. The choreography was by Mikhail Fokine. The part of Petrushka was interpreted by the most celebrated of all Russian dancers, Vaclav Nijinsky (1889–1950). Shortly after the Paris production of *Petrushka*, Alexandre Benois wrote an impassioned account in a daily St. Petersburg newspaper of the history of the ballet, and of his own part in it:

> In my unbounded admiration for the unquestionable genius of Stravinsky's music, I was quite willing to minimize my own part in the creation of *Petrouchka*. The subject of the ballet was entirely Stravinsky's idea, and I only helped him to organize it in a concrete dramatic form. But the **libretto**, the cast of characters, the plot and the dénouement of the action, as well as a number of other details, were almost wholly mine. My share in the production, however, seems trivial in comparison with Stravinsky's music. When at a rehearsal Stravinsky asked me who

Libretto (It.). A "booklet"; the words of an opera, oratorio, etc.

should be listed as the author of *Petrouchka*, I replied without a moment's hesitation, "You, of course." Stravinsky objected to this verdict and insisted that I should be named as the actual author of the libretto. Our combat de générosité was resolved by putting both our names on the program as co-authors, but I succeeded in having Stravinsky's name placed first, despite my alphabetical precedence. Still, my name appears twice in the score, because Stravinsky decided to dedicate *Petrouchka* to me, which touched me infinitely. . . . From my earliest childhood I carried the vivid memories of the riotous turmoil and merrymaking of the "plain people" of St. Petersburg at the Shrovetide, the peepshows and the excitement of the street fair, where my friends used to come "to learn what Russia really is like." These unforgettable scenes of a vanishing world remain dear and near to me in many ways. Some will say that these memories are colored by the remoteness of my childhood, and that in reality it was just dirt, brawling, and lust. Naturally, these street fairs were not idyllic events conforming with the bittersweet ideals of virtue so dear to our temperance societies. But no matter how much drunkenness, how much crudity there was in these scenes, the street life had its own rights, and set its own rules of conduct and its own code of decency.

The perception of *Petrushka* by the Parisians was a far cry from the scandal that greeted the production of Stravinsky's *The Rite of Spring* two years later. "*Petrushka* is a marvel," reported the critic of the Paris journal *Comœdia*.

It is simply astonishing. Apart from an abundance of musical themes, original and classical, and a profusion of fantastic rhythms, Stravinsky's orchestration is extraordinary. Instrumental timbres flow in a stream in a most uncommon way, creating among the audience a sense of inexpressible exhilaration. Not a single measure is wasted. And what boldness in handling of the instruments! What eloquence! What life! What youthfulness!

Among musicians who were enthralled by Stravinsky's youthful exuberance was Debussy, but he sounded a note of caution to posterity. In a letter to a friend he wrote:

> I saw Stravinsky the other day. He is a spoiled child who sometimes sticks his fingers into the nose of music. He is also a young savage who sports extravagant cravats, kisses women's hands while stepping on their toes. In his old age he will be insufferable, that is to say that he will not tolerate any other kind of music than his own. But at the moment, he is incredible!

Petrushka was not only an amazing spectacle and an extraordinary ballet. It also set a landmark of modern music from the purely technical standpoint. The score contains the first consistent use of bitonality, the "*Petrushka* chord," as it came to be known, which combines the polarized keys of C major and F-sharp major, the two tonalities standing at the opposite ends of the vertical axis in the cycle of scales. This bitonal combination had a pianistic origin, for *Petrushka* was originally conceived by Stravinsky as a **Konzertstück** for piano and orchestra. Stravinsky experimented at the keyboard, playing on the white keys with his right hand and on the black keys with his left, resulting in a series of bitonal arpeggios.

Konzertstück (Ger.). A concert piece, or a short concerto in one movement and free form.

The melancholy theme of "Petrushka's Cry" also contains elements of C major and F-sharp major. Besides these original inventions, Stravinsky freely borrowed melodic and rhythmic materials from Russian folk songs, mostly from collections published by Tchaikovsky, Rimsky-Korsakov, and others, fashioning them with ingenious alterations to suit his purposes. There are also in the score of *Petrushka* a couple of dance tunes borrowed from Joseph Lanner. One such borrowing ended up in an embarrassment. Stravinsky picked up a popular song which he heard played on a barrel organ. It turned out to be a music-hall chansonette fully protected by copyright. As a result, Stravinsky was obliged to pay a royalty to the publishers of the song each time *Petrushka* was performed.

The Rite of Spring (Le Sacre du printemps) *(1911–13)*

Stravinsky completed the manuscript of the piano version of *The Rite of Spring* in Clarens, Switzerland, and wrote in the score, in blue and red pencil: "Today, Sunday, on the 17th November, 1912, suffering from an unbearable toothache, I finished the music of *The Rite of Spring*." This was the most fruitful toothache in music history. No composition written since 1900 produced a comparable impact on the evolution of modern musical thought than *The Rite of Spring*. Even though it is a typically Russian product (its subtitle is *Scenes from Pagan Russia*), composers of all lands have, in one way or another, been deeply moved and inspired by its music.

The first performance of the work took place at the Théâtre des Champs-Elysées in Paris on May 29, 1913, produced in its original conception as a ballet commissioned to Stravinsky by Serge Diaghilev, the impresario of the famous Ballets Russes. The original Russian title is, in literal translation, *The Sacred Spring*. The French title, under which it was produced, is *Le Sacre du Printemps*, and the English most commonly used, *The Rite of Spring*.

The Paris production gave rise to a riot without precedent in the annals of music. Just what happened exactly has been reported in numerous contradictory accounts, most of them unverifiable. Jean Cocteau, not a very reliable witness, reported that the old Comtesse de Pourtalès stood up in her loge and, brandishing her fan, exclaimed, "This is the first time in my sixty years that I was taken for a fool." In his postcard

ЧАСТЬ ПЕРВАЯ
ПОЦЕЛУЙ ЗЕМЛИ
Вступление

FIRST PART
A KISS OF THE EARTH
Introduction

Introduction to Stravinsky's *Rite of Spring*

sent to Maximilian Steinberg, Rimsky-Korsakov's son-in-law, from Neuilly, a suburb of Paris, and dated 3 July 1913, Stravinsky presents a more sanguine report of the occasion:

> I was very much satisfied with the way *The Rite of Spring* sounded in the orchestra; I was happy, really happy to

hear this long awaited symphonic setting. Nijinsky's choreography was unsurpassable. But there was plenty of trouble at the performance, at times reaching the point of actual fist fights. We will have to wait a long time for the public to be accustomed to our language, but I am absolutely convinced that what we have accomplished was right, and this gives me strength for further work.

On the picture side of the postcard Stravinsky, who was then recovering from an attack of typhoid fever, wrote: "This is my room where I spent many desperate hours in dreadful agony."

The reaction to *The Rite of Spring* in the press was that of a catatonic shock. "Never was the cult of the wrong note practiced with so much industry, zeal and fury," wrote Pierre Lalo (nephew of the composer Édouard Lalo), in *Le Temps* of June 3, 1913. American music critics joined the chorus of condemnation after *The Rite of Spring* was performed in the United States. W. J. Henderson, in the *New York Sun*, called Stravinsky "a cave man of music." A writer in the *Boston Herald* of January 27, 1924, burst into verse:

> Who wrote this fiendish *Rite of Spring*,
> What right had he to write the thing,
> Against our helpless ears to fling
> Its crash, clash, cling, clang, bing, bang, bing?
> And then to call it *Rite of Spring*,
> The season when on joyous wing
> The birds melodious carols sing
> And harmony's in everything!
> He who could write *the Rite of Spring*,
> If I be right, by right should swing!

Saint-Saëns, the grand *seigneur* of French music, who attended the performance, was reportedly stunned by the opening bassoon solo. "What instrument is this?" he whispered to a friend. "Why, the bassoon, of course," the other answered, "If this is a bassoon, then I am a baboon," Saint-Saëns remarked, and haughtily left the theater. This introductory bassoon solo is indeed a marvel. Set in the highest register of the instrument it makes the player feel like a puffer fish about to explode from inner pressure when pulled out of the water. But the melody itself is simple; it was in fact taken by Stravinsky from an old collection of Lithuanian folk songs.

The ballet is in two parts: "The Kiss of the Earth" (usually translated "Adoration of the Earth," which changes the subject into the object) and "The Great Sacrifice." In the introduction, the music is made predominantly by wind instruments entering **canonically** in varied and sometimes dissimilar thematic configurations. The opening scene proper, "Spring Fortune-telling" (thus the Russian title, variously rendered as "Spring Auguries" or "Harbingers of Spring"), marked by stomping **dissonant** chords in the string with cross-accents punctuated by blurting and burning French horns, while gentler figures are given out by the English horn and the bassoons. Soon the high winds join the proceedings, the flutes and clarinets tonguing a series of fluttering chromatics.

The fortune-telling leads to "Dances of Smartly Dressed Girls" (usually, and misleadingly, translated "Dance of Adolescents"), redolent of Russian folk-song refrains. Another change of scene, and we are witnessing a brutal "Abduction Game," with its truncated meters, pullulating rhythms and asymmetric chordal ejaculations. It is followed by a serene **interlude** as a preface to "Spring Rounds." The tunes are stunted and slow in starting off, but when the point of saturation is reached, an eruption of myriad coruscating tonal particles ensues. The serene **entr'acte** returns as a transition to yet another game, "Contest Between Two Camps," in which two groups contend in a millennial Russian bowling match in which gnarled logs, stood on end in a row, are toppled over by whittled bats. The themes are made up of three or four notes of the diatonic

Canon. Musical imitation in which two or more parts take up, in succession, the given subject note for note; the strictest form of musical imitation.

Dissonance. A combination of two or more tones requiring resolution.

Interlude. An intermezzo; an instrumental strain or passage connecting the lines or stanzas of a hymn, etc.

Entr'acte (Fr.). A light instrumental composition or short ballet for performance between acts.

scale, evoking the melodic patterns of the oldest known Russian songs.

Another shift of scene, and there begins a "Procession of the Oldest and Wisest Chief." His hoary wisdom is introduced by hollow-sounding brasses against a constant unaltering drumbeat. The procession stops abruptly. After an intermediate soft discord in the strings, the earth itself is stirred to a dancing measure. The Russian title is untranslatable; it can be paraphrased as "The Stepping Out of the Dancing Earth." The terrestrial solo is solid: the main beat is relentlessly driven into the ground. But above the quaking bass there is a proliferation of secondary seismic activities throwing up enormous boulders of blunt sonorities. With the dance of the earth the first part of the ballet comes to an end.

The second part, "The Great Sacrifice," opens with a reedy murmuration in the wind instruments; the strings, too, affect a similar sound, expressly marked **flautando**. This introduction leads to the scene entitled, in Russian, "Maidens' Secret Rites and Walking in Rounds" (usually translated as "Mysterious Circles of the Adolescents," although this translation leaves out the crucial reference to the feminine gender unavailable in English adjectives). A girl is elected to be honored by the multitudes, and a festive dance follows, "Glorification of the Chosen Maiden" (in Russian the suffix indicates the gender). The conventional prettiness and harmonious shapeliness that such a subject might suggest are of course totally absent from this scene of pagan ritual; the meters are apocopated, the strong beats are asymmetrically distributed, and the themes are outcries of elemental vital forces.

The scene ends as abruptly as it began. The next tableau is "Appeal to the Forefathers" (a more accurate translation than the usual "Evocation of the Ancestors"). The music conjures up the visions of Russian pagan idols, the stolid stony statues that once lined the banks of the Dnieper River at Kiev before they were hurled down about A.D. 1000, when Russia

Flautando (It.). A direction in violin music to play near the fingerboard so as to produce a somewhat "fluty" tone.

became nominally a Christian nation. The next scene depicts the "Ritual Action of the Human Ancient Ancestors." The musical action is limited to the low instrumental register of the orchestra; the melodic resources are reduced to a few notes; but before the terminal petrifaction sets in there is an explosion of latent energy in the high reaches of the wind instruments.

The Rite of Spring concludes with an overwhelming "Danse sacrale" ("Sacred Dance"). The choreography indicates the sacrifice of the chosen maiden, but the Russian title reads simply "The Great Sacred Dance," with the subtitle "The Chosen One." The "Danse sacrale" interrupts its ruthless drive to allow a rhythmically relaxed and metrically steady section. Then its savage progress is resumed and, after a fertilizing scratch on the Cuban gourd, the *guiro*, *The Rite of Spring* comes to a shattering close on a multiple discord anchored in the lower depths of the brasses and strings and nailed down by a blow on the bass drum. The finale is the most complex section of the entire score.

For 1913, when *The Rite of Spring* was first presented to the public, this cataract of unrelieved discords within a network of fantastically entangled rhythms was an overwhelming experience, beyond the powers of most musicians to grasp. For many years, only Pierre Monteux, who led the first performance of the ballet and its first performance as a purely symphonic score, was able to cope with the formidable difficulties of this finale. Much later, Stravinsky himself rewrote the finale, smoothing down the thorny rhythms and rearranging the instrumentation. But in the meantime a whole generation of young conductors arose to whom the difficulties under which Koussevitzky and his contemporaries labored and faltered were elementary. Most conductors perform *The Rite of Spring* from memory.

Is it any wonder that *The Rite of Spring* outraged the world of 1913 still basking in pristine innocence before the wars? The crashing assault of the orchestral dissonances coupled with the exotic Russian choreography, in which the great Nijinsky was the star, administered a shock that was too much to bear. For several decades *The Rite of Spring* was unacceptable in Stravinsky's native land, not because he was an émigré (so was Rachmaninoff, whose popularity never waned in Russia despite his outspoken hostility to the Revolution), but because of the nature of its musical language. In 1959, Leonard Bernstein conducted *The Rite of Spring* in Moscow, nearly forty years after its previous Russian performance, and another performance was given in Russia during Stravinsky's visit there in 1962. It was only in 1965 that the Soviet State Publishing House finally issued the full orchestral score of *The Rite of Spring*.

The Wedding *(*Les Noces*) (1921–23)*

Cantata (It.). A small-scaled multi-movement vocal work with instrumental accompaniment.

Stravinsky described this work, called *Svadelka* (*Little Wedding*) in Russian, as "choreographic scenes with singing and music." Since it is performed on the stage, it occupies an intermediate position between **cantata** and opera. First produced for Diaghilev's Ballets Russes in Paris in 1923, it is scored for chorus, soloists, four pianos, and seventeen percussion instruments. The music is rooted in Russian folk song, but the harmonic and **contrapuntal** realization is propulsive and acrid, while always keeping within the diatonic framework of tonality. The libretto consists of four scenes tracing the rituals of a peasant betrothal and wedding.

Contrapuntal. Pertaining to composition with two or more simultaneous melodies.

Octet for Wind Instruments (1923)

Throughout his extraordinary career Stravinsky anticipated the spirit of the musical times, and by so doing became the leader of generations of composers. He then legislated the new aesthetic development and by force of his conviction made it inevitable. No sooner had the music world accepted the shattering innovations of *The Rite of Spring* than Stravinsky reversed his course and turned back to Bach, or even further into the past. This past was also the future, the plus and minus signs of the temporal function intersecting in the present.

The portents of the new departure from the luxuriant style of Stravinsky's early ballets appeared at the time of the First World War. The war, Stravinsky believed, made the huge modern orchestra obsolete for economic reasons; besides, the lavish productions of the velvet era of the young century became aesthetically unacceptable. It seemed to be purposeless to dispense musical sonorities with an extravagant disregard for their utility, when the same artistic message could be conveyed more cogently with less expenditure of instrumental means. Finally, and most important, there was a challenge. Large panoramas of sound are notoriously easier to design than compact drawings in the Gothic or Baroque manner. For a master of the musical craft, the task was to create *multum in parvo*, not *parvum in multo*.

Highly significant of this period was Stravinsky's revision of his sparkling ballet score *The Firebird*. He plucked the score of its flaming feathers, dimmed the rainbow colors of the orchestra, eliminating decorative passages and other luscious delights. The new score may possess superior consistency and organization, but unregenerate music lovers kept faith with the incandescent virgin version, leaving the revision to the watchers of trends.

Stravinsky's new aesthetic code found its perfect realization in his Octet for Wind Instruments. Stravinsky reveals that the composition of the work was inspired by a dream in which he found himself surrounded by a group of instrumentalists playing some attractive music. The only thing he could remember upon awakening was that there were eight instruments in the ensemble. The very next morning he began the composition of the Dream Octet for flute, clarinet, two bassoons, two trumpets and two trombones. He completed the score in Paris on May 20, 1923, and conducted its first performance at the Koussevitzky concerts at the Opéra in Paris on October 18, 1923. Jean Cocteau described Stravinsky's appearance on the podium as that of an "astronomer preoccupied with the solution of a magnificent instrumental calculation made with the aid of silver numbers."

Octet. A composition for eight voices or instruments.

The **Octet** is a study of musical self-sufficiency. Every note counts; each Baroque trill performs a necessary function. The form is exquisitely balanced; the melodies arch their intervallic components with calculated precision. Yet within this circumscribed art there is room for a variety of expressive means. As in Baroque music, the mood changes readily from lyricism to drama, from elegiac contemplation to propulsive virility. The instrumentation, from bassoon to flute, from bass trombone to trumpet, provides a complete range of useful registers in wood and brass. Artful coupling of homonymous or heteronymous instruments contributes contrapuntal richness to the texture.

Sinfonia (It.). A symphony; an opera overture.

Tema con variazioni (It.). Composition in which the principal theme is clearly and explicitly stated at the beginning and is then followed by a number of variations.

Mediant. The third degree of the scale.

Chromatic. Relating to tones foreign to a given key (scale) or chord; opposed to diatonic.

The work is in three movements: **Sinfonia**, **Tema con variazioni**, and Finale. In the Sinfonia, the least common denominator of the metrical division is a sixteenth note. The meters vary; a frequent grouping is the alternation of bars of 2/8 and 3/16. The idiom is strongly tonal, and modulations are effected by carefully prepared shifts of inner voices. Equivocal **mediants** (third scale-steps), typical of Stravinsky's harmonic writing, provide the link between homonymous major and minor triads. Canonic imitations become increasingly frequent. Acrid **chromatics** create somber interludes, but the texture is never opaque.

The second movement, Tema con variazioni, is remarkable in its syllogistic development. There are five distinct variations, of which the first returns twice. The theme itself is formed of permutations of four notes within a major third, leaving out the middle note to avoid a suggestion of chromatic filling. The theme is subjected to melodic and rhythmic translocations, giving rise to dancing measures—a conventionalized polka, a fast waltz, as well as a lyrical romance.

The Finale is centered on C major, with the principal measure of 2/4. The pulse is often asymmetrical; a dancing chorale combines austerity with Baroque hedonism. Tonal elaborations result in the formation of a **pandiatonic** web. The work comes to a close on a tonic 6/4, which traditionally serves as the antepenultimate chord in an authentic cadence. Stravinsky leaves it unresolved; in his neo-Baroque domain, it is more consummate, more expressive, more challenging in its finality.

Stravinsky deemed it advisable to give to his public, stunned and embarrassed by his recession, the reasons for the revaluation of his former values. "My Octet is a musical object," he wrote in 1924.

Pandiatonicism. A modern term for a system of diatonic harmony making use of all seven degrees of the scale in dissonant combinations.

This object has a form and that form is influenced by the musical matter with which it is composed. The differences of matter determine the differences of form. One does not do the same with marble that one does with stone. My Octet is made for an ensemble of wind instruments. Wind instruments seem to me to be more apt to render a certain rigidity of the form I had in mind than other instruments—the string instruments, for example, which are less cold and more vague.

Oedipus Rex *(1927; revised 1948)*

Igor Stravinsky has been many things to many people. He was the magnificent conjurer of symphonic fairy tales; the shatterer of the earth in his prodigious ballet scores; a disciplined scholar who initiated his private renaissance of classical forms; the enlightened technician of twentieth-century methods, and a musical philosopher who succeeds in uniting, with Aristotelian logic, the disparate elements that enter the art of composition.

At Stravinsky's hands, the oldest forms become new, and the newest forms become traditional. His "Russian" stage works—*Petrushka*, *The Rite of Spring*, *The Wedding*—were first produced outside Russia. Their impact affected the evolutionary course of modern music in national cultures of many lands. Neoclassical trends observable for several decades of European and American music were in part the consequence of Stravinsky's revival of ancient forms. It was not inconsistent with these developments that Stravinsky should have eventually adopted the strong discipline of the method of composition with twelve tones related only to one another. Yet through all these avatars, the essential Stravinsky persevered. There are rhythms, there are melodies, there are harmonies, there are orchestral and vocal devices in Stravinsky that are common to all his works. His stylistic departures, digressions, and detours seem to be the converging roads to the essential Stravinsky.

Perhaps the most formalized, and thus the purest, work of Stravinsky is *Oedipus Rex*, an opera-oratorio in two acts, after Sophocles. *Oedipus Rex* is written to the text by Jean Cocteau—the Jean Cocteau of 1927, Catholic and mythologist. He had run the gamut of human infatuations, embracing a faith which, to the overcynical, may have appeared as his latest perversity. Cocteau was anxious to narrate to the world a story well known; of things dead, he would speak in a dead language. Latin is the Esperanto of the true Catholic—but Cocteau's proselytism is of recent date and his schooldays remote. Therefore a Monsieur J. Danielou is entrusted with the task of translation. Mindful of the audiences that may be shy of classical learning, Cocteau retranslates Danielou's ecclesiastical Latin into telegraphic French. The Latin diction is carefully supervised; the performers are advised against minor mousetraps and admonished to harden the consonants, replace the dental *c* by the guttural *k*, sound a broad *u*.

The production, as originally intended, was to combine

aspects of both opera and oratorio. Singers were to be placed in fixed positions, except the incidental characters of Soothsayer, Shepherd and the Messenger. Stylized costumes and scenery were to be employed, but entrances and exits were symbolically signalized by drawing, or withdrawing, curtains behind which the principal characters were placed. The cast included Oedipus (tenor), Jocasta, his mother (mezzo-soprano), Creon, her brother (bass-baritone), Tiresias, the Soothsayer (bass), the Shepherd (tenor), and the Messenger (bass-baritone). A speaker was also included to give a running account and interpretation of the events. The first performance of *Oedipus Rex* took place in Paris on May 30, 1927, as oratorio; the first stage production was given in Vienna on February 23, 1928.

Concerto in D for Violin and Orchestra (1931)

Stravinsky's classical period began with his Piano Concerto of 1924, which he himself played during his first American tour. There followed *Oedipus Rex*, the *Symphony of Psalms,* the *Capriccio*, and the Violin Concerto, all in various ways works of classical caliber. Stravinsky undertook the composition of the Violin Concerto as a commission from the Russian violinist Samuel Dushkin, who also advised him on technical matters. One day, at a lunch with Dushkin in a Paris restaurant, Stravinsky wrote a chord of three widely separated notes, D below the G-clef staff, E a ninth higher, and a high A an eleventh above the E, and asked Dushkin if it could be played on the violin. Dushkin looked at it in dismay and said, "No." "Quel dommage," remarked Stravinsky. What a shame. Returning home, Dushkin tried the chord on his instrument, and found that it was quite playable. He telephoned Stravinsky at once; the chord became a motto of the concerto, its "passport," as Stravinsky described it, opening each of the concerto's four movements.

In the Violin Concerto, the orchestration is "normal." The clarinet is the only supernumerary instrument in the score of the concerto; there is an English horn, which would stand in opposition to the practice of the nineteenth-century symphony, but not necessarily of the early eighteenth. The key of the concerto is that of D, major or minor, the most common (because the easiest for the strings) for all symphonies, concertos, and overtures up to about 1800. In this instance, Stravinsky is once more a conservative.

The mixture of styles that is immediately evident in the Concerto in D is really of no consequence. Some influences (we would call it deliberate admixtures) are quite unexpected, that of César Franck, for instance (the latter was a pioneer of remotely related suspensions and resolutions). Others are the familiar ghosts—Handel, Bach. Tchaikovsky is conspicuously absent, unless we attribute the episodic subject of the orchestra in the **Toccata** to his psychic voice. The very opening of the Toccata is in the general style of the early eighteenth century with corrections of the neoclassical movement. Again, the obvious dissonances, the wrong notes in the right place, are not the result of any newfangled systems of polytonal writing, but proceed from a higher sense of tonality.

The form of the concerto is that of an instrumental suite, austere, almost ascetic in its rejection of "**brio**." There is an element of virtuosity, but of a Baroque type devoid of any flourishes. The titles of the movements are descriptive of the formal structure: Toccata, **Aria** I, Aria II, and **Capriccio**; **Presto**. The Toccata, as the title suggests, presents a rapid current of even notes; the harmony is touched with nontoxic dissonances; the concluding chord contains the first five degrees of the D-major scale in spacious distribution.

The second and the third movement of the concerto bear the titles Aria I and Aria II. Here we have Stravinsky the Serene, revealed to us in Apollo. But we cannot pass by one technical device largely employed by Stravinsky that, for want of appro-

Toccata (It.). A composition for organ or harpsichord (piano), free and bold in style.

Con brio (It.). "With noise" and gusto; spiritedly.

Aria (It.). An air, song, tune, melody.

Capriccio (It.). An instrumental piece of free form, distinguished by originality in harmony and rhythm; a caprice.

Presto (It.). Fast, rapid; faster than "allegro."

priate terminology, may be described as "unfinished resolution," a sort of driving into a blind alley, making a dead stop when confluence is expected. Thus, in Aria I, the violin stops one degree short of the expected conclusion, in its scalelike passages, while the orchestral accompaniment, in a web of pure tonality, furnishes the implied resolution. This method is not new: in the Octet, Stravinsky showed several examples of similar "dead stops," and always against a background of perfect tonality.

Perhaps the most noble use of the "suspensions" of higher orders is made in the middle section of Aria II. The musical tension is ideally calculated to bring a perfect catharsis in the final resolution. It is in a movement like this that one begins to understand why it took Stravinsky a day to complete a measure. Every note seems to possess a directional force that likens it to a mathematical vector.

Aria I, after the presentation of the chordal "passport," turns to D minor; the melody is almost operatic in its **bel canto** expansiveness. Aria II, by contrast, abounds in **trills**, **ornaments**, and **arabesques**. The Capriccio reveals the persistence of eternal Stravinsky, with its splitting syncopations and tiny detonations of rhythmic energy at asymmetric time intervals; the concluding Presto brings up memories of the "Danse sacrale" in *The Rite of Spring*.

As far as the writing for the solo instrument is concerned, there is nothing particularly excruciating for a seasoned performer. The violin part of *The Soldier's Story* is without question the more complicated. Rhythmically, only the Violin Concerto's final Presto presents any serious difficulty. It took all the uncanny ingenuity of Stravinsky to graft it on to the Capriccio, to prepare it, as he did, with the dark gaps and falls of the immediately preceding music.

In another place and under other auspices it would not be difficult to prove a thesis that Stravinsky's melodies are always built within the walls of a tonic and its dominant, some-

Bel canto (It.). The art of "beautiful song," as exemplified by eighteenth and nineteenth century Italian scripts.
Trill. The even and rapid alternation of two tones which are a major or minor second apart.
Ornament. A grace, embellishment.
Arabesque. A type of fanciful pianoforte piece; ornamental passages accompanying or varying a theme.

times atonally (in "Petrushka's Cry" in the second scene of the ballet, in the mother's complaint in Scene 2 of *The Wedding*, etc.), sometimes tonally (as in the passage referred to above). In the Capriccio, there is a glimpse of the former Stravinsky in the ominous rests on the stronger parts of the measure. Finally, the crowning Presto bristles, as of old, with contrary rhythms set against the measured steps of the bass tones. What are these advancing and retreating chromatic tones of the cellos if not the familiar "bubbles" in "The "Kiss of the Earth" of *The Rite of Spring*? The relationship is much more than a more coincidence, or identity of procedure. In it is the spirit of *The Rite of Spring* that is with us again.

Every one of the four movements of the Violin Concerto opens with the identical chord of the violin, the D of the open string, the E, a ninth above it, and the high A, at two and a half octaves above the fundamental tone. Thus does Stravinsky establish the classical unity with an emphasis. In *The Wedding*, composed in 1917, the mysterious effect of a bell's clank at the end of the work is obtained by a similarly positioned chord, with the interval of a ninth at the root. This collation of harmonic textures alone will show how consistent Stravinsky's present idiom is with his past. In the first movement (the Toccata) we find a violin passage in **double stops** with the characteristic seesaw movement, in iambic prosody, which instantly recalls the parallel movements in *Petrushka*. Besides, in this passage Stravinsky's melody is characteristically confined within the interval of a fifth.

Double stop. In violin playing, to stop two strings together, thus obtaining two-part harmony.

What then was the ultimate purpose underlying the composition of this concerto? The answer may be simple: it was to write a Violin Concerto for Samuel Dushkin, the virtuoso. The work was commissioned and done according to the requirements of the commissioner. This honorable practice was responsible for many a masterpiece from Mozart and Beethoven; why should not Stravinsky do the like? In this he is only following a great tradition. A "notary's contract" here assumes a nonallegorical significance. What was the result of this contract? A masterpiece, which, in addition to its inherent qualities, is rich in demonstration of how a transient problem of style may be subordinated to a higher synthesis.

In the Violin Concerto, as in no other composition, Stravinsky fused his various styles, and also the styles of various other composers, so solidly that the mixture appears monolithic. This may be a tribute to the composer's technical mastery, but it also may be a revelation of unity in seemingly disparate elements, a revelation of Stravinsky in the true Platonic sense, as one face of many facets.

Perséphone *for Narrator, Tenor, Chorus, and Orchestra (1933; revised 1949)*

Stravinsky conducted the first performance of his ballet-melodrama *Perséphone* in Paris on April 30, 1934. The work is scored for tenor, chorus, and orchestra with a narrator, to the text by André Gide. Ida Rubinstein appeared in the title role as dancer and speaker. The myth of Persephone (in Roman usage, Proserpina) tells of the beautiful daughter of Zeus and Demeter abducted by Hades, or Pluto, the ruler of the netherworld, while gathering flowers in the fields of Sicily. Her mother's search for her is the subject of many legends and poems. She lit her torches by night from the fires of the volcano of Etna. When Zeus himself intervened, the lower world was forced to release Persephone for six months every year, a sojourn symbolic of the burying of the seed in the ground and the growth of the corn. After a period of barrenness, Demeter returns to her duties as the patroness of agriculture, and the fields are once more covered with corn. (The word "cereal" is derived from Ceres, the Roman form of Demeter.)

Stravinsky's language in *Perséphone* is marked by austerity of harmonic idiom and severe economy of sonorous means. In 1934, Stravinsky published a lengthy article in the Paris daily *Excelsior* on the eve of the performance of *Persé-*

phone, in which he resolutely renounced the practices that he had applied with such success in the ballet scores of his Russian period. "I abhor instrumental effects used solely for the sake of color," he wrote.

> In *Perséphone* the listener should not expect to be dazzled by seductive sonorities, for I have long ago abandoned the futility of brio. I abhor the necessity of wooing the public. It embarrasses me. Let those who make a profession of this honorable practice, in composing as well as in conducting, enjoy it to the point of complete satiety. The public expects the artist to disembowel himself and to exhibit his entrails. This action is regarded as the noblest expression of art, and is termed variously as Personality, Individuality, or Temperament. Things that are felt and things that are true are susceptible to projections on an enormous scale. I follow a very definite path. It cannot be the subject of a debate or criticism. One does not criticize somebody, or something, that functions. The nose is not manufactured. The nose is. So is my art.

Stravinsky's stern admonition to critics to watch their step aroused some consternation in the musical press. *Le Monde Musical* felt constrained to respond:

> M. Stravinsky warns us that his way in art is not to be debated or criticized. Such self-assurance is probably without precedent in music history. Bach, Mozart, Beethoven, Wagner, Debussy, Fauré, were all conscious of the validity of their art, but none of them presumed to guarantee the vitality and the durability of their works. Curiously, it is not as the composer of such works as *Petrushka*, *The Firebird*, *The Nightingale*, or *The Rite of Spring*, which have earned him world renown, that Stravinsky aspires to enter the Pantheon. No, it is his works which even his

most fervent admirers fail to acclaim, works written during the period of his "return to Bach," that he regards as "enormous projections." . . . At its first performance, *Perséphone* received scant appreciation from the audience. During the last scene, in which Persephone descends into Hell for the second time, someone was heard to whisper: "Let's hope she stays there."

Jeu de cartes: *Ballet in Three Deals* (1935–37)

Igor Stravinsky began his career as a ballet composer, and throughout his spectacular stylistic avatars, his first love for musical choreography never diminished. Despite the extraordinary harmonic and rhythmic complexity of his early masterpieces, such as *Petrushka* and *The Rite of Spring*, the sense of classical form is ever present in Stravinsky's ballet scores, so that the choreographer has a clearly drawn blueprint to follow. Owing to this classical structure, Stravinsky's ballets lend themselves naturally to concert performances in the form of a symphonic suite without stage action.

The genesis of *Jeu de cartes* (*Card Game*) was this: In 1935 Edward Warburg and Lincoln Kirstein asked Stravinsky to write a work for the recently organized American Ballet Company. George Balanchine, the Russian ballet master, long associated with Stravinsky, was to design the choreography. After consultation among all persons concerned, the choice was made, and the ballet was named *Jeu de cartes*, variously translated as *Card Game*, *A Game of Cards*, or *The Card Party*, the game itself being poker, of which Stravinsky was an aficionado.

Dramatically, the scenario unfolds as a morality play that might be entitled *Malice Punished*. The malefactor is the Joker, ideally suited for the role of a villain because of its chameleonic cunning in assuming the character of any other card in the pack and thus fitting into a winning hand. The scenario is in three deals. The cards are shuffled before each deal;

accordingly, the introductory measures illustrating the shuffling are identical in all three movements.

A moralistic motto is attached to the score, from La Fontaine's fable "The Wolves and the Sheep":

> Il faut faire aux méchants guerre continuelle.
> La paix est fort bonne de soi,
> J'en conviens; mais de quoi sert-elle
> Avec des ennemis sans foi?

> Continual war must be waged on evil men.
> Peace in itself is good, we know.
> I agree; but what will happen then
> If we deal with a faithless foe?

Stravinsky completed the score on December 6, 1936. He conducted its first performance presented by the American Ballet Company at the Metropolitan Opera House in New York on April 27, 1937. It had a cordial reception in the press.

The first deal opens in vigorous marchlike measures. A delicate *pas d'action* follows, introduced by a poetic flute solo, seconded by a grumpy bassoon. The duet undergoes metric contractions, creating a momentary nervous twitch. Then the Joker makes its arrogant entrance. "The Dance of the Joker" is marked by aggressive accents, terminating abruptly on an ascending scale of five notes, forming a straight, a promisingly strong hand. Then it stands pat. One of the players quits, but another remains to challenge the Joker. A waltz follows in tranquil motion.

The second deal, like the first, opens with a shuffling of the pack. The game proceeds with a march in hearts and spades, embellished with elegant **roulades** and interrupted by implosions of concentrated gambling energy. The Queens enter and coquettishly exhibit themselves in four handsome variations. The Queen of Hearts, making her pointes with ma-

Roulade (Fr.). A grace consisting of a move from one principal melody tone to another; a vocal or instrumental flourish.

tronly grace in allegretto, seems to have stepped out of the second movement of Beethoven's Eighth Symphony, **Allegretto scherzando**. The tonality, B-flat major, is the same, and the melody revolves around the same notes of the tonic triad. The coincidence is not unintentional. In one of his Delphic utterances, Stravinsky declared his right to delve into the treasury of old music for raw materials: "After studying many pages of a certain composer, I sense his musical personality and, like a detective, reconstruct his musical experience."

The second variation is a swift flight on gossamer wings, a dance in the finest tradition of the French Rococo. Its coruscating brilliance is peculiarly fitted to the suit of diamonds, which it represents in the scenario. There follows a stately variation for the Queen of Clubs, showing a fine panache. The fourth variation is a dance of the forbidding Queen of Spades, but a smile is painted on her face in gaudy colors. There is a resemblance in the violin countersubject in this variation to a theme from *Die Fledermaus* by Johann Strauss. The fifth variation is a *pas de quatre*, confident in the invincibility of the high hand of four of a kind. But its self-assurance soon vanishes in a precipitous coda in which the Joker joins the rival player and overwhelms the four Queens with four Aces. A triumphant march, with the victorious Joker strutting in the lead, concludes the second deal.

The cards are shuffled again in the introduction to the third deal, the most tense of the entire card game. All three players hold flushes, and they eye each other in a deceptively courteous waltz, in which an inquisitive listener may perceive echoes of Ravel's *La Valse*. Then a fierce contest between Spades and Hearts erupts in a presto. Here occurs one of the most direct quotations, from Rossini's *Barber of Seville*. The rhythms are identical; there are minor divergences in the degrees of the scale in the melody.

The Stravinsky-ized Rossini tune assumes a primary thematic significance in the Finale. The Joker, holding a straight

Allegro (It.). Lively, brisk, rapid.
Scherzando (It.). In a playful, sportive, toying manner; lightly, jestingly.

in Spades, parades his megalomania in brass. He ignores the diffident Hearts, not realizing that they are preparing a colossal bluff, concealing an all-conquering Royal Flush. The Joker is foiled, his malice punished, virtue triumphs, and the poker game ends with a diatonic ascent into the climactic chord of the minor seventh on the ground tone of E.

Symphony in Three Movements *(1942–45)*

Stravinsky entered the Pantheon as composer of immortal masterpieces of modern music, but his significance is enhanced by his extraordinary ability to anticipate, foresee and presage the vital changes in the nascent style of the time, and then to lead younger composers in the new directions by writing works that serve as models. This exercise in stylistic prolepsis has at various stages of his career confused and bewildered some of his admirers. The most drastic change occurred at the dawn of the neoclassical era, when Stravinsky gave up the luxuriance of fairy-tale music as revealed in dazzling color on the pages of The Firebird, Petrushka, and The Rite of Spring, and proclaimed the supremacy of music as fact, self-sufficient, economic, and unencumbered by illustrative representation. He made a declaration of principles in an article published in 1924: "I consider that music is only able to solve musical problems; and nothing else, neither the literary nor the picturesque can be in music of any real interest. The play of the musical elements is the thing." These views, it may be observed parenthetically, are similar in a remarkable degree to the postulates of musical aesthetics in Hanslick's famous book Vom Musikalisch-Schönen (On the Beautiful in Music) published in 1854.

Stravinsky's *Symphony in Three Movements* belongs to the period of "music as fact." It was written for and dedicated to the New York Philharmonic Society, which Stravinsky conducted in the work's first performance on January 24, 1946. In his program note he warns once more against speculative interpretation of the meaning of the work: "The Symphony has no program, nor is it a specific expression of any given occasion; it would be futile to seek these in my work." Then he retreats slightly, leaving the door ajar for intrusive seekers of hidden meanings: "During the process of creation in this our arduous time, of sharp and shifting events, of despair and hope, of continual torments, of tension and, at last, cessation and relief, it may be that all those repercussions have left traces in this symphony. It is not I [*sic*] to judge."

In a detailed and interesting analysis of the *Symphony in Three Movements*, published in the program book of the New York Philharmonic, Ingolf Dahl—himself a composer of eminence and knowledge, and an authoritative (and authorized) spokesman for Stravinsky for many years—emphasizes the "great seriousness" of the work and outlines its principal structural factors: additive construction of themes outside the framework of conventional **sonata form**, progress measured by succession of blocks, "unified by a steadily and logically evolved organic force." Dahl makes a prediction: "One day it will be universally recognized that the white house in the Hollywood Hills, in which this Symphony was written and which was regarded by some as an ivory tower, was just as close to the core of a world at war as the place where Picasso painted Guernica."

Sonata form. Usually the procedure used for first movements of classical symphonies, sonatas, and chamber works; may be used for other movements as well.

The revelation comes then that Stravinsky, an avid cinema buff, was inspired in the composition of the first movement of the *Symphony* by a documentary film of the scorched-earth policy in China during its desperate defense against Japanese invasion. Some sections, it appears from Stravinsky's own admission, actually represent in the form of an instrumental conversation the Chinese peasants digging the earth. The second movement also had its genesis in a film, its materials being part of the unrealized score for a motion picture of Franz Werfel's *Song of Bernadette*. As for the third movement, Stravinsky states that it was a musical reaction to watching the

Fugue. Contrapuntal imitation wherein a theme proposed by one part is taken up equally and successively by all participating parts.

Metronome. A double pendulum moved by clockwork and provided with a slider on a graduated scale marking beats per minute.

Fortissimo (It.). Extremely loud.

Counterpoint. Polyphonic composition; the combination of two or more simultaneous melodies.

Coda (It.). A "tail"; hence, a passage ending a movement.

goose-stepping Nazis in a newsreel, the final **fugue** reflecting the rise of the Allied powers, leading to victory. But these associations have, of course, nothing to do with the music of the symphony, which is to be judged by its intrinsic value. (Hanslick, who was as inimical to fanciful interpretations of music as Stravinsky, states plainly in his essay that it is a matter of utter indifference, aesthetically speaking, whether a composer did or did not associate his works with certain ideas, images or events.)

The three movements of the symphony are played without pause. In the New York Philharmonic program book, the first movement is entitled Symphony-Overture, but in the published edition there is no title, only a **metronome** mark, corresponding to a rapid tempo, of 160 beats to a minute, in 4/4 time. The opening is **fortissimo**, with a soaring motto rising powerfully. The regulated pulse of the rhythmic scheme suggests a toccata, an impression reinforced by the employment of the piano as a concertizing instrument in the orchestra. Baroque sequences and pandiatonically enriched triadic harmonies establish a classical mood. The common denominator of a quarter note is maintained rigorously, but there are subterranean eruptions of massive chords, causing the metrical bars to collapse asymmetrically.

This Stravinskian antinomy, in which absolute steadiness of the basic beat generates equally steady interference, may best be described by a term from rhetoric, *aposiopesis*, as if Stravinsky, with Virgil's Neptune, disciplines the rapid notes *Quos ego!* There is a remarkable episode for piano in terse **counterpoint** of single notes in the right and in the left hand, in multiple dialogues with other groups of the orchestra. The **coda** recalls the thematic materials of the opening; large chords of superincumbent harmonies herald the end, while the bass clarinet is left alone, alone, fluttering with instinctive wing motion. The concluding chord is a pandiatonic extension of the C-major triad, with the flute on the fifteenth overtone, B.

The second movement, **Andante**, opens with a tremor in the violins on the tonic of latent D major. It slides upward through a *Schleifer* ("slide") to the mediant of the key, but Stravinsky puts a noneuphonious F-natural against it. The ambivalence of the triadic third is of course Stravinsky's trademark, found in virtually all his works, beginning with the early cantata *Zvezdoliky* (*King of the Stars*) and used thematically in *The Rite of Spring*.

The bucolic dalliance of distilled tonality and the tantalizingly Rossinian melorhythmic devices are soon disrupted by the insertion of bars in asymmetrical time signatures, recalling the ambiance of *The Rite of Spring*. The resulting melodic accretion and apocopation create great tension, which is allowed to resolve in a moment of tranquilization in the form of a brief interlude.

Then, ***attacca!*** The last movement is a **Rondo**: Con moto, with the piano assuming the dominant role, in the double tonality of C major and C minor. The bassoons start a commotion underneath; there is considerable agitation elsewhere, but it subsides into a series of convulsive silences, with only a few pointed arrows shooting from a quick quiver of trombones in a dark exchange with sharp notes on the piano. Explosions—and implosions—follow. After a magistral figure, the symphony ends in fortissississimo, on a pandiatonic chord of D-flat major, with an added sixth and an added ninth.

Circus Polka *(1942; arranged for orchestra, 1944)*

Composers of all times and all ages liked to indulge in innocuous whimsicalities. Somehow, some of these light pastimes resulted in interesting musical discoveries. Mozart wrote a piece intended to make fun of village musicians, but in it he prophetically included passages in **whole-tone scales** and polytonal harmonies. Saint-Saëns classified pianists as animals in his suite *Carnival of the Animals*. Schoenberg inserted the song "Ach

Andante (It.). Going, moving; moderately slow tempo.

Attacca (It.). Begin what follows without pausing, or with a very short pause.
Rondo (It.). An instrumental piece in which the leading theme is repeated, alternating with the others.

Whole-tone scale. Scale consisting only of whole tones, lacking dominant and either major or minor triads; popularized by Debussy.

du lieber Augustin" in one of his string quartets. Erik Satie deliberately used nonsensical titles that somehow made sense.

As the well-known adage has it, humor is a very serious business. Stravinsky's humor invariably contains a grain of serious intent. For all the dashing nonchalance of his *Circus Polka*, the piece contains interesting contrapuntal and harmonic devices, stylistically related to Stravinsky's early ballets. Still, the music remains entirely functional, the kind that is commonly played by provincial bands. Stravinsky wrote his *Circus Polka* (for a young elephant) in Hollywood on February 15, 1942, on a commission from the Barnum & Bailey Circus, to be played at its regular shows. On January 14, 1944, Stravinsky conducted the piece in a fuller orchestral version with the Boston Symphony Orchestra.

The polka rhythm is but occasionally broken up by asymmetrical insertions of alien rhythms. Otherwise the piece proceeds without any pseudo-sophisticated notions. For the ending, Stravinsky regales his public with a magnificently cacophonous rendition of Schubert's Military March.

Coda

Long, long ago, I was hired by Serge Koussevitzky in Paris to play for him on the piano the scores he had to conduct. That was before the availability of long-playing records or any other mechanical aids to conducting, and Koussevitzky was accustomed to having a pianist hammer out his scores, while he practiced beating time. The immediate task for him was to master the changing meters in *The Rite of Spring*. We spent practically the entire summer in Biarritz in 1922 on *The Rite of Spring*, using the piano four-hand arrangement made by Stravinsky and published a few years before. I did my best to combine the main melodic and harmonic ingredients of the score, trying to get at least the meters and rhythms right. To me it was a great experience, a dream come true, with musical and other celebrities dropping in now and then—including Stravinsky, with whom we used to spend evenings playing poker at nominal stakes. (When Koussevitzky would raise the ante, Stravinsky would say "Into the bushes," a Russian phrase meaning "No contest," and would throw his cards on the table, even when he had a winning hand.)

It was not long before I realized that Koussevitzky was apt to add what he used to call a *Luftpause* (pause for breathing) to prime-number meters, such as 5 or 7, inevitably converting them to the more comfortable time signatures of 6 or 8. The crisis came in the final "Danse sacrale," which required a human metronome to get the minimal beats grouped into proper bar lines. Such sudden metrical changes as 2/8, 2/16 and 3/16 in rapid tempo simply did not work out, and Koussevitzky was becoming annoyed with himself and, by ricochet, with me. Having reached a rhythmic cul-de-sac, I experienced a sudden moment of plenary inspiration: I proposed to Koussevitzky to recombine the pesky bars so as to reduce them to the common denominator of an eighth note, with only an occasional intrusion of an intractable bar of 5/16 (e.g., 1/8 + 2/8 + 2/16 + 3/16 + 2/16 + 3/16 = 16/16 = 4/4, common march time). Koussevitzky rejected my plan out of hand on the ground that it would be tampering with Stravinsky's rhythmic structure. I assured him that the only change would be visual, in Koussevitzky's own beat, and that the original rhythmic sequences would remain unaltered, but he would not listen. We returned to Paris in the fall, and Koussevitzky had his first orchestral rehearsal of *The Rite of Spring*. It was a disaster. On his way back from the rehearsal he told me to try out my idea of rebarring the "Danse sacrale." I gladly complied. My version worked without a hitch. Koussevitzky was delighted, and told everybody that I was a great mathematician (he liked to boast about the excellence of his serfs). The mathematics involved in my arrangement required the knowledge of addition of simple fractions. The score with my realigned bars in blue pencil is still kept in the library at Symphony Hall, Boston, which was Koussevitzky's final preserve. In 1943, Stravinsky himself rearranged the meters of the "Danse sacrale" to facilitate performance; it was not in any way connected with my arrangement, but was motivated by Stravinsky's desire to simplify the notation.

SERGEI PROKOFIEV
(1891–1953)
His Signature—SRG PRKFV

SERGEI SERGEIEVICH PROKOFIEV did not believe in vowels: they were to him un-stable, subject to slurring, broadening, or clipping. He signed his name in consonants only: PRKFV. There was in this signature something of the man himself, a certain petu-lance, impatience, and a businesslike attitude of economy. There was also a spirit of independence, a refusal to conform, and perhaps a boyish defiance.

Prokofiev's imagination conjured up attractive monsters and humorous witches. He was nine years old when he completed an opera called *The Giant*, and it was duly performed at his uncle's estate in the country. The score was actually written out by Prokofiev himself, in piano arrangement, of course, in lieu of the orchestra. His cousin took the part of the orchestra at an upright piano; Prokofiev sang the role of the hero who overwhelms the giant with a toy pistol. A tall aunt was the giant. It was a costume performance, and every actor was attired in a most impressive garb.

After such a revelation of youthful ability, Prokofiev was taken to Moscow, where he was introduced to the greatest Russian **contrapuntist**, Sergei Taneyev, who treated him to a piece of chocolate and then listened to his playing of the overture to his second opera, called *Desert Islands*. After that, Taneyev told the boy's mother to take him to a conservatory student for harmony lessons. But even as a child, Prokofiev was full of his own notions about harmony, and was not happy to study with a student. Fortunately the famous Russian composer Reinhold Glière happened to be visiting Prokofiev's family and captivated the boy's imagination by explaining to him in simple, and yet learned, words the mysteries of **sonata form** and orchestration. Then the master and the pupil would play a game of croquet, and also chess, for Prokofiev was a prodigy not only in music but also in that intellectual game so beloved by Russians. He soon rose to the rank of first category, just a notch below that of chess master.

Even when Prokofiev became a famous composer, he still spent hours at the chessboard, in long arduous games with his musical colleagues. He played a public match with the violinist David Oistrakh. The terms were most curious: the winner was to receive a prize of the Club of the Masters of Art; the loser was to give a concert especially for professional musicians who were also chess players. For some reason, only seven out of the scheduled ten games were played, and no winner was announced. But both Prokofiev and Oistrakh gave their concerts as losers, and of course Oistrakh played Prokofiev's works, of which he was an ardent admirer.

Young Prokofiev knew so much about music when he entered the St. Petersburg Conservatory that he experienced difficulties in slowing himself down, even in the class of the great

Contrapuntist. One versed in the theory and practice of counterpoint.

Sonata form. Usually the procedure used for first movements of classical symphonies, sonatas, and chamber works; may be used for other movements as well.

Rimsky-Korsakov himself. Besides, he was risking his academic reputation by performing his utterly unorthodox piano pieces at concerts of modernistic societies in St. Petersburg. With great self-assurance, Prokofiev decided to play his own piano **concerto** for the commencement exercises at the conservatory. His pianism was of the highest caliber, and even though his concerto was **dissonant**, the conservatory jury felt compelled to give him the first prize, which was a grand piano.

Satire and grotesque are characteristic of Prokofiev's early music, but are not essential in his creative temperament, which is lyrical and poetic. Prokofiev, the composer of the piano suite *Sarcasms*, is also the author of the moving poem for voice and piano, "The Ugly Duckling," after the tale by Hans Christian Andersen, in which the beautiful cygnet is shunned and snubbed by the ducklings, whose idea of bird beauty is the opposite to swans. Maxim Gorky, the great Russian novelist, remarked, when he heard Prokofiev's "Ugly Duckling": "You know, he must have written this about himself." Indeed, Prokofiev was an ugly duckling of Russian music in the academic surroundings of the St. Petersburg Conservatory, where he was educated. At a time when dissonances were allowed in composition only when they were safely resolved into perfect concords, Prokofiev amused himself by writing piano pieces in which the right hand played in one key and the left in another. And he brought perturbation into the comfortable world of 1912 by composing a **Scherzo** for a quartet of bassoons. When the four players filed on the stage, armed with these forbidding-looking instruments, a sarcastic concertgoer observed to his companion: "Let's leave before they start shooting."

The secret of Prokofiev's strength is his directness of musical utterance. His style may be defined as romantic realism. As a realist, Prokofiev writes dynamic music full of motion, and strong contrasts of rhythm and accent. As a romanticist, he favors fantastic tales for subject matter, seasoned with fine humor or sharp grotesque.

Concerto (It.). An extended multi-movement composition for a solo instrument, usually with orchestra accompaniment and using (modified) sonata form.

Dissonance. A combination of two or more tones requiring resolution.

Scherzo (It.). A joke, jest; an instrumental piece of a light, piquant, humorous character. Also, a vivacious movement in the symphony, with strongly marked rhythm and sharp and unexpected contrasts in both rhythm and harmony; usually the third movement.

Chronologically Prokofiev's creative biography falls into three periods. The first, from childhood (Prokofiev began to compose very early) to his trip abroad in 1918, is characterized by abundant and aggressive energy. In 1914, he played his First Piano Concerto as a graduation piece at the St. Petersburg Conservatory. He was already known at that time as the author of piano pieces of semihumorous or fanciful inspiration. His first orchestral composition of importance was the *Scythian Suite*, composed in 1914–15. It was also his first work in the national Russian style. Like Stravinsky's *The Rite of Spring*, with which it has otherwise no points of contact, Prokofiev's *Scythian Suite* is inspired by the pagan era (Scythians were early inhabitants of the plain that is now European Russia). During the turbulent days of the Revolution, he wrote his most uncompromisingly dissonant score, the demoniac incantation, *Seven, They Are Seven*. And only shortly before that, he wrote the *Classical* Symphony (Symphony No. 1, Op. 25) ingeniously contrived in the style of a twentieth-century Mozart. The sketches of the First Violin Concerto were made at the same period.

Prokofiev's dual nature, stormy and impetuous on the one hand and lyrical and poetic on the other, is revealed in his **cantata**, *Seven, They Are Seven*, on an ancient Sumerian legend, and the *Classical* Symphony. They were both written in 1917, when Prokofiev was 26, but the contrast between the two could not be greater. The primitive force displayed in the cantata, with its raging dissonances and convulsive rhythms, is the very opposite of the *Classical* Symphony, gentle and easygoing. The witty **Gavotte** from the *Classical* Symphony is a series of deceptive cadences that lead into unexpected keys. No harmony laws are broken, but the effect of modernistic surprise is achieved with finesse.

Prokofiev began his career as the enfant terrible of Russian music, who shocked the sensibilities of his own professors at the St. Petersburg Conservatory and was the object of

Cantata (It.). A small-scaled multi-movement vocal work with instrumental accompaniment.

Gavotte (Fr.). A Gavot; an old French dance in strongly marked duple time (*alla breve*), beginning on the upbeat.

indignant reviews in Russian newspapers. When the Revolution came in 1917, Prokofiev was hailed by the artistic vanguard as a natural ally of the new society. But conditions for work in Russia, torn by civil war, were intolerable, and Prokofiev left St. Petersburg, went through Siberia to Japan, and from Japan to America. When he made his first American tour in 1918—he was twenty-seven years old then—his ability to shock was undiminished. "Every rule in the realm of traditional music writing was broken by Prokofiev," the *New York Sun* lamented in pain. "Dissonance followed dissonance in a fashion inconceivable to ears accustomed to melody and harmonic laws upon which their music comprehension has been reared."

His concerts in New York created a sensation. He was regarded as the very personification of Bolshevism in music. The American composer Reginald De Koven, author of the famous song "O Promise Me," could not contain himself in anger. "Mr. Prokofiev strikes me as a ribald Bolshevist innovator and musical agitator," he wrote in his capacity as music critic for the *New York Herald*. The respectable and knowledgeable critic of the *New York Tribune*, H. E. Krehbiel, declared that Prokofiev's compositions "invite their own damnation" and "die the death of abortions." His recital of his piano works prompted an American critic to describe his reaction in tumultuous prose: "Crashing Siberias, volcano hell, Krakatoa, sea-bottom crawlers! Incomprehensible? So is Prokofiev." But at the end of his review, he sounded an ironic note of caution, suggesting that the time might come when Prokofiev would be regarded as "the legitimate successor of Borodin, Mussorgsky and Rimsky-Korsakov." The warning was prophetic. Prokofiev is now acknowledged as a rightful heir of these great Russians, who in their time were also the targets of misguided obloquy. Perhaps the most amazing of these American reactions to Prokofiev was the report in *Musical America*:

Those who do not believe that genius is evident in superabundance of noise looked in vain for a new musical message in Mr. Prokofiev's work. Nor in the *Classical Symphony*, which the composer conducted, was there any cessation from the orgy of discordant sounds. As an exposition of the unhappy state of chaos from which Russia suffers, Mr. Prokofiev's music is interesting, but one hopes fervently that the future may hold better things both for Russia and listeners to Russian music.

It was in New York that Prokofiev produced his whimsical opera, *The Love for Three Oranges*, based on a comedy by the famous Italian eighteenth-century writer Carlo Gozzi. The opera was produced in Chicago on December 30, 1921. It leads with a prince who laughs at a witch, who, in retaliation, puts a curse on him that deprives him of all ability to laugh unless and until he finds three big oranges, which he does. A princess emerges from one of the oranges and asks for water. The prince cuts the second orange to get some orange juice to quench her thirst, but finds another princess there. He cuts the third and last orange, with a similar result. Fortunately, the third princess is not thirsty, and instead is full of romantic sentiments. There is an expected happy ending. Prokofiev's musical score is alive with rollicking melodies and exciting rhythms. The march from *The Love for Three Oranges* has become famous. Prokofiev started work on another opera in New York, *The Fiery Angel*, but completed it later in Europe.

In 1921, Prokofiev settled in Paris, the capital of modern music and modern art. There he found two champions of his music, the ballet impresario Sergei Diaghilev and the celebrated conductor Serge Koussevitzky. Prokofiev's association with Diaghilev was most fruitful, producing the ballets *Buffoon*, *Steel Step*, and *Prodigal Son*, of which the first was particularly popular. He also composed symphonies and concertos for Koussevitzky. This was a magnificent triumvirate of Sergeis. All three Sergeis were émigrés, but political estrangement from Russia was not to the youngest Sergei's liking.

In 1932, Prokofiev accepted an invitation from the Soviet government to give a few concerts of his music. In 1934, he returned permanently to Russia and settled in Moscow. He was received as a prodigal son, given a dacha to live in, an apartment in Moscow, and all the facilities for having his music performed. But in Stalin's Russia he had to tame his musical genius to meet the stipulations of "socialist realism," demanding that art be made accessible to the masses. Still, despite the annoying pressure, Prokofiev wrote some of his most felicitous scores after his return to Russia, notably the symphonic fairy tale *Peter and the Wolf*.

Prokofiev continued to compose tirelessly, for the stage, for the orchestra, for instruments, for voices. His style acquired a new nobility, and his music grew more intensely Russian in character. One of Prokofiev's most important works is the cantata *Alexander Nevsky*, based on his music for the Soviet film of the same name. Alexander Nevsky was the Russian prince who inflicted a decisive defeat on the Teutonic Knights in the battle of Lake Peipus, in Northern Russia, fought on April 5, 1242. The subject had obvious political implications. This rout of seven centuries ago would be repeated if the descendants of the Teutonic Knights would venture to attack Russia. Hitler failed to heed this musical warning, and indeed the Nazi legions suffered one of their greatest defeats near that same Lake Peipus.

Then trouble began. Prokofiev was accused of imitating the decadent ways of the West, of indulging in such cosmopolitan deviations as **atonality** and **polytonality**. He made a concession to the dominant Soviet policy of socialist realism by composing a Youth Symphony, quite conventional in its style. He even wrote an overture for Stalin's sixtieth birthday, an inferior work which received perfunctory notices

Atonality. The absence of tonality; music in which the traditional tonal structures are abandoned and there is no key signature.

Polytonality. Simultaneous use of two or more different tonalities found in modern music.

(none from Stalin himself) and was politely forgotten. There was no Russian soul in his music, his Soviet detractors proclaimed. Much more ominous was the attack on Prokofiev, Shostakovich, and other Soviet composers in a resolution of the Central Committee of the Communist Party of the Soviet Union in 1948, containing accusations of "formalism" and genuflection before the West. Prokofiev replied to it with dignity, protesting that he had never questioned the paramount importance of melody and tonality, the two mainstays of traditional music, but he admitted and mildly repented for the temptations he had undergone during his sojourn in Europe and America.

Libretto (It.). A "booklet"; the words of an opera, oratorio, etc.

At the end of his resources, and to prove that he could handle a Soviet theme, Prokofiev wrote an opera, *A Tale of a Real Man*, to an emotionally patriotic **libretto** dealing with a Soviet pilot who, despite the loss of both legs in combat, trained himself to use artificial limbs and was readmitted to active service. The opera was roundly condemned by Soviet officials after a private performance as lacking in melody and Russianism. Despite this rebuke, Prokofiev continued to compose productively. The hapless opera, not the best of Prokofiev's works, was premiered posthumously. The legless pilot, the hero of the opera, attended the production and expressed his admiration for Prokofiev's genius. His last symphony, the Seventh, was hailed as a true Soviet masterpiece. Predictably, it was deplored in the Western press as a sign of Prokofiev's decline.

Prokofiev died suddenly of a massive stroke in Moscow in the afternoon of March 5, 1953. By chronological irony, Stalin died in the same evening, a few hours after Prokofiev. Days passed before the composer's death was announced in the press, which was totally absorbed by the dictator's passing. Then the cult of Stalin was dispelled by his successor, Nikita Khrushchev. With the abrupt change of appreciation, Prokofiev was declared to be a great Russian composer and a postage stamp was issued in his honor, while Stalin's body was ignominiously removed from Lenin's mausoleum.

In large measure, Prokofiev helped to shape and organize the new musical language that is loosely called modern music. He began to speak it as a youth, and his contemporaries thought he was gibbering in an alien tongue. During his productive career, he gradually simplified, rather than complicated, this language, and suddenly the world began to understand it. The dissonance of Prokofiev's music has become the concord of musical children of today. Prokofiev's name has a secure place in the history of music. But to the very young among Prokofievites he is, above all, the author of *Peter and the Wolf*, a symphonic fairy tale for children, which he wrote in two weeks in April 1936 for a performance in the Children's Theater in Moscow. *Peter and the Wolf*, written for children, has enough musical spice in it to delight the professionals as well. And is not *Peter and the Wolf* a significant parable about the Nazi wolf who sets out to attack the peaceful neighbor? The bird's argument in favor of strong wings, capable of flying high, is justified by the untimely end of the unfortunate duck, a bird without air power.

ORCHESTRAL MUSIC

Sinfonietta, Op. 5/46 (1914; revised 1929)

Prokofiev wrote in his autobiography: "The first period of my creative work is classical, whose origin lies in my early childhood when I heard my mother play Beethoven's sonatas. It assumes a neoclassical aspect in the sonatas and the concertos, or imitates the classical style of the eighteenth century, as in the Gavottes, the *Classical* Symphony, and, in some respects, in the Sinfonietta."

Prokofiev's neoclassicism, however, is vastly different from the neoclassicism of other twentieth-century composers

Prokofiev Timeline

1891	Born in Sontsovka
1903-04	Studies with Reinhold Glière
1910	First published work, a piano sonata, premiered in Moscow
1913	Travels to Paris, London, Switzerland
1914	Graduates from St. Petersburg Conservatory; receives Anton Rubinstein Prize for Piano Concerto No. 1
1915	Composes *Scythian Suite* for orchestra
1916-17	Composes First ("Classical") Symphony
1918-19	Travels to Japan via Siberia, continues to United States
1920	Settles in Paris; ballets *Chout* (*Buffoon*), *Le Pas d'acier*, *L'Enfant prodigue* produced by Serge Diaghilev and Ballets Russes
1921	Returns to U.S. for premiere of *The Love for Three Oranges*, commissioned by Chicago Opera Company
1927	Returns to Russia to perform his piano works
1929	Following second visit to Russia, decides to stay
1935	Composes ballet *Romeo and Juliet* and symphonic fairy tale *Peter and the Wolf*
1938-39	Composes score (later made into a cantata) for Eisenstein's epic film *Alexander Nevsky*
1941-52	Composes opera *War and Peace*

(continued)

Prokofiev Timeline (cont.)

1948 ▶ Denounced by Communist Central Committee, along with Shostakovich, Khatchaturian, and others for "decadent, bourgeois formalism"; in unsuccessful attempt to appease authorities, composes opera, *A Tale about a Real Man*, depicting heroic WWII Soviet pilot

1953 ▶ Dies in Moscow, a few hours before the death of Stalin

who, having exhausted the resources of modern harmony, retreated into the safe harbors of the past. Prokofiev stylized the old forms with nostalgic irony, adding unexpected flourishes to their symmetrical arabesques, and interrupting the stately flow of quasi-classical melody with rude cadences, as if to say "Shut up!" He was the witty narrator of the old-fashioned tales, rather than a pious worshipper of the imperishable beauty of a venerated art. His best-known and most successful stylization of musical classicism was the *Classical* Symphony, written when he was twenty-six.

His Sinfonietta, composed much earlier, when he was only eighteen, is another example of neoclassicism à la Prokofiev. The original version was never performed and never published. Prokofiev rewrote the work for a performance by Alexander Siloti and his orchestra in St. Petersburg on October 24, 1915. He rewrote it again in Paris in 1929. The original score was marked Op. 5; the revision became Op. 48. The material for the second and the fourth movement was entirely new, and there is an inevitable discrepancy of style between this newly rewritten music and the virtually untouched harmonies of the first and third movements.

Symphony No. 1 in D Major, Op. 25 (Classical) (1916–17)

In wartime Petrograd (the city's name from 1914 to 1924), Prokofiev was the enfant terrible of Russian music. His piano pieces were the delight of the musical radicals, and the desperation of the pedagogues of the Petrograd Conservatory, of which Prokofiev was a product. It was not the ultramodern idiom that shocked the conservatory conservatives. Scriabin, in his last works, was much more destructive of tonality and time signature than Prokofiev ever was. But there was a certain impishness in Prokofiev that was offensive to the academic elders. The time signature, and even the tonality, were there, but the melody leaped from one octave to another, and the harmonies changed unexpectedly, in total disregard for the rules of **modulation**.

When Prokofiev decided to write a symphony, his first, he chose the classical idiom, partly to prove that he knew his métier, partly to tease his detractors, but mostly out of a desire to renovate, not to imitate, the classical form. Having shocked the Russian academicians with his dissonances, he set out, with exquisite irony, to write a piece of music in an entirely orthodox manner, with well-behaved harmonies, and in strict classical form—a "classical" symphony. Accordingly, he affixed the name *Classical* to his Symphony No. 1, Op. 25. He wrote it in 1916–17, fateful years for Russia, and conducted it for the first time at a concert in Petrograd—at that time a desolate, famine-stricken city—on April 21, 1918. Shortly afterward, he left Petrograd and Russia, arriving in America by the route of the Pacific Ocean, and then going to Europe.

The *Classical* Symphony in D major has an unmistakable something which is the essence of Prokofiev. There was no difficulty for Prokofiev to write in the classical style, if classicism means tonality, definite metrical structure and strong sense of form. Even the waggishness of Prokofiev's humor is classical, in the manner of Mozart and Haydn, rather than romantic à la Schumann. Prokofiev was a believer in architectonic construction, and was strongly anti-Impressionist. It would have been unnatural for Debussy to write a "classical" symphony, but for Prokofiev it was almost inevitable that he should have written one. It seems gratuitous, therefore, to suggest that he consciously tried to imitate Mozart, or any other model. For the *Classical* Symphony is not an imitation, but an augmentation, an enhancement of a style that is flexibly classical rather than stagnantly academic.

The first movement, **Allegro**, in 4/4, opens gaily, and follows the appointed course of all classical sonatas and symphonies. The trained ear will catch some very unusual turns and modulations. The contrasting theme, in the **dominant**

Modulation. Passage from one key into another.

Allegro (It.). Lively, brisk, rapid.

Dominant. The fifth tone in the major or minor scales; a chord based on that tone.

key, enters with a plunge of the violins two octaves down from a high note, with the bassoon accompanying in staccato figures. With the two themes having said their say, the official exposition of the classical form closes, and the unofficial part begins—the development section, where the themes are used in any or all keys, in various rhythmical forms. The return of the official business, or the recapitulation, comes without obvious preparation, but both themes are immediately recognizable. The movement ends gaily as it began.

This lyric second movement, **Larghetto**, in 3/4 time, is built on the model of a brief **rondo**. The principal melody begins on a high note of the violin (Prokofiev was fond of this device), and the mood is established forthwith. Episodes are introduced for contrast, and the pulse of the music is accelerated through the use of variations. The principal melody is heard for the third time, and the movement closes gently.

The third movement, **Gavotte**, is a tour de force of stylization. The form is perfect; the Gavotte starts with a half-bar **upbeat**, according to the customary formula, and the tonality is clear D major. A **musette** in G forms the middle section, giving the bagpipe effect, and the Gavotte returns, with slight modifications, ending gracefully without modern pretensions. But every bar brings a modulatory surprise. Prokofiev heads toward one key and lands in another, or so it seems. At strategic moments, however, there is always the expected tonic, and its appearance is timed according to the symmetry of the dance. A Russian poet of olden times used a happy figure for such welcome unexpectedness: "It is like cool lemonade in summertime."

The Finale is in 4/4, and again in sonata form. The orchestration is deft, and the woodwind instruments are treated with particular felicity. When the principal section returns in the form of a recapitulation, the orchestration is modified, a procedure that avoids the monotony of academic repetition. The ending is brilliant.

Larghetto (It.). The diminutive of largo, demanding a somewhat more rapid tempo.

Rondo (It.). An instrumental piece in which the leading theme is repeated, alternating with the others.

Gavotte (Fr.). A Gavot; an old French dance in strongly marked duple time (*alla breve*), beginning on the upbeat.

Upbeat. The raising of the hand in beating time; an unaccented part of a measure.

Musette (Fr.). 1. A small oboe. 2. A kind of bagpipe; also, a short piece imitating this bagpipe, with a drone bass. 3. A reed stop on the organ.

Concerto No. 1 in D Major for Violin and Orchestra, Op. 19 (1916–17)

Prokofiev began his career as an enfant terrible of Russian music. He horrified his professors at the St. Petersburg Conservatory by his musical inventions, including a piece written in two keys simultaneously. But he fascinated the moderns of his day by his intransigence, his daring, and his self-assurance. His percussive piano playing, in programs of his own works, with his strong fingers leaping in all directions at once, electrified sympathetic young audiences. Some called him a "white Negro," alluding to the unbridled syncopation of ragtime as performed by black Americans in vaudeville shows.

Despite his rebellious modernism (which he preferred to call *novatorstvo*, "innovationism"), Prokofiev kept faith with classical form and tonal harmony. His *Classical* Symphony demonstrates his ability to pull the *Zopf* ("pigtail") off the classical scalp, while retaining the viable elements of the old cranial structure. His famous fairy tale for children, *Peter and the Wolf*, written in a manner entirely free from elementary condescension, shows his natural affinity for the imaginative world of the very young.

Prokofiev's First Violin Concerto was written in 1917, when he was twenty-six, shortly before he left Russia for a lengthy sojourn in Western Europe. Its first performance did not take place until October 18, 1923, in Paris, with Marcel Darrieux as the soloist and Serge Koussevitzky conducting the orchestra. The concerto is in three movements, Andantino, **Vivacissimo**, and Moderato, in the key of D major, a tonality eminently suitable for the instrument. It is written in a virtuoso style, but its bravura is subordinated to the musical content.

Vivacissimo (It.). Very lively, *presto*.

The melodic, rhythmic, and harmonic elements of the score represent the four principal characteristics of Prokofiev's music, as he enumerated them himself in his autobiographical notes: classical, innovative, motoric, and lyrical.

In the opening movement, a general sense of tranquillity envelops the music. The second movement is a typical scherzo, and here he indulges his whimsy. There are special effects such as **glissandos** ending in harmonics, **pizzicatos** with the fingers of the left hand, etc. The finale returns to the contemplative mood of the opening movement, bringing the work to a close in a satisfyingly cyclical form.

Concerto No. 3 in C Major for Piano and Orchestra, Op. 26 (1917–21)

Glissando (It.). A slide; a rapid scale. On bowed instruments, a flowing, unaccented execution of a passage. On the piano, a rapid scale effect obtained by sliding the thumb, or thumb and one finger, over the keys.

Pizzicato (It.). Pinched; plucked with the finger; a direction to play notes by plucking the strings.

The career of Sergei Prokofiev is a tale of dramatic progress, from his early days as an enfant terrible in Old Russia who exasperated the bourgeoisie by his aggressively discordant music to his posthumous glorification as the true heir to the Russian national school of composition. Soviet musicologists made a convincing case in demonstrating that Prokofiev's most enduring works were written in Russia, and that his talent went into an eclipse during his peregrinations in Europe and America. Indeed, Prokofiev's most popular works—the *Classical* Symphony, *Peter and the Wolf*, *Romeo and Juliet*—were all composed in Russia. The sole exception seems to be the Third Piano Concerto, which Prokofiev played for the first time with the Chicago Symphony Orchestra on December 16, 1921. However, the concerto was sketched in almost complete detail before Prokofiev left Russia in 1918.

It has been a critical cliché to describe Prokofiev's music as being exclusively the product of rhythmic energy with little lyrical content. Prokofiev dispatched a wrathful letter to the author remonstrating with him for having stated in an article that there is an absolute preponderance of marching rhythms in Prokofiev's music, rebuking him for underestimating its inherent lyrical quality, and pointing out that 3/4 meters are encountered as frequently in his scores as marching 4/4 time.

The Third Piano Concerto tends to prove Prokofiev's contention. There is as much lyric sentiment in it as propulsive rhythmic energy. The introductory **andante** is music with a smile—**diatonic**, relaxed, humane. But immediately after that, an assault of virile bravura is launched on the white keys of the piano. Not a single sharp, not a flat, mars the whiteness of the precipitant **scales** and **arpeggios** in this Allegro for several pages of the score. Such displays of C-major power are hallmarks of Prokofiev's piano writing. The rhythmic momentum never slackens until an abrupt ending on C in unison.

The second movement, **Andantino**, is a theme with variations. The musical texture is limpid; the piano part is interlaced with the accommodating orchestral accompaniment in an untrammeled contrapuntal web. It is a poetic interlude of singular attractiveness.

The third and last movement, Allegro ma non troppo, in rondo form, opens with an ingratiatingly bland phrase in modally inflected A minor. Prokofiev's familiar tendency toward plagal cadences intensifies the modal impression. There are several extended **cadenzas** of fresh thematic content. In the **coda**, the orchestra is drawn into full participation. The concerto concludes pragmatically in a forceful succession of **pandiatonically** enriched C-major triads.

Divertimento, Op. 43 (1925, 1929)

The **Divertimento** is only nominally neoclassical. The title goes back to eighteenth-century practice, and so do the markings of the four movements. But the melodic and harmonic language is uncompromisingly modernistic. The Divertimento is compounded of materials from different periods. The first and third movements are taken from the ballet *Trapeze*, which Prokofiev wrote in 1925; the remaining movements were completed in 1929. The opus number was assigned later, and does not represent the exact chronology of his creative catalogue.

The first movement is marked Moderato, molto ritmato. There are harsh-sounding chords that might illustrate a determined action of scrubbing the floor clean, the relentless rhyth-

Andante (It.). Going, moving; moderately slow tempo.

Diatonic. Employing the tones of the standard major or minor scale.

Scale. The series of tones which form (a) any major or minor key (*diatonic* scale) or (b) the *chromatic* scale of successive semitonic steps. Also, the compass of a voice or instrument.

Arpeggio (It.). Playing the tones of a chord in rapid, even succession.

Andantino (It.). A little slower than andante, but often used as if meaning a little faster.

Cadenza (It.). An elaborate passage played or improvised by the solo instrument at the end of the first or last movements of a concerto.

Coda (It.). A "tail"; hence, a passage ending a movement.

Pandiatonicism. A modern term for a system of diatonic harmony making use of all seven degrees of the scale in dissonant combinations.

Divertimento (It.), **divertissement** (Fr.). A light and easy piece of instrumental music.

mic drive that is characteristic of the Russian ballet. But then there is suddenly heard a celestially tender chant, for the entry of gauze-clad ballerinas. The second movement, Larghetto, is not dependent on a ballet scene; it is a simple lyric invocation of the quality that Prokofiev himself regarded as of the greatest importance in his work. "My lyricism has for a long time been unappreciated, and it has for this reason, grown but slowly," he wrote in his autobiography. "But in later works, I devoted more and more attention to lyric expression."

The third movement, Allegro energico, is a spirited dance. In this movement, too, the stage action is vividly suggested by the music. This is a strongly rhythmed dance, with stamping and jumping. The last movement, Allegro non troppo e pesante, is, on the other hand, an exposition of purely musical, nonchoreographic elements. There are characteristic scale runs, beginning in one key and passing without benefit of modulatory transitions into another, a semitone higher as to the tonic. The mood changes from fast milling motion to songful meditation, in sudden contrasts, typical of Prokofiev's music.

Prokofiev conducted the first performance of the Divertimento in Paris on December 22, 1929. The reception was mixed; some critics found it a dazzling score, one of Prokofiev's best; others were not so sure. The critic of *Le Ménestrel* complained that the Divertimento was as little diverting as possible.

Concerto No. 5 in G Major for Piano and Orchestra, Op. 55 (1932)

Prokofiev wrote five piano concertos. The first was his graduation piece at the St. Petersburg Conservatory. The third became a standard work of the modern piano repertory. The Fourth Concerto, for left hand alone, was written for the one-armed Austrian pianist Paul Wittgenstein. The Fifth Piano Concerto, composed in Paris in 1932, represents the Western, neoclassical, and hedonistic period in Prokofiev's career. It originally bore a noncommittal title, Musique pour piano et orchestre, following the fashion of absolute music then prevalent in Europe. This derivation explains the fact that the work is in five movements rather than the usual three, thus assuming the structure of an instrumental suite with piano **concertante**. Prokofiev gave its first performance in Berlin on October 31, 1932, with Wilhelm Furtwängler conducting the Berlin Philharmonic.

The first movement, Allegro con brio, traverses the basic outline of sonata, in an abbreviated form, approximating that of a **sonatina**. There are two contrasting subjects, a vigorous fanfarelike projection, and a balladlike lyrical theme. The exposition is characteristically laconic, and the themes follow one another without gratuitous obliquity. Toward the end of the movement there is a lively **antiphonal** interchange between the soloist and the orchestra.

The second movement, **Moderato** ben accentuato, is a scherzo-march in rondo form. It is marked by the spirit of grotesquerie, reminiscent of Prokofiev's youthful *Sarcasms*. The third movement is **Toccata**: Allegro con fuoco. The toccata was always Prokofiev's favorite Baroque form, fitting perfectly into the scheme of his modern pianism. The element of mechanistic constructivism, fashionable at the time, finds its reflection in this toccata. The fourth movement is Larghetto. Here, Prokofiev is a true lyricist. A pastoral quietude breathes in the leisurely flow of this movement, permeated by the bucolic poetry of an eclogue.

The Finale: **Vivo**, is a study in digital dexterity. The music drives on with ruthless determination to a coda in a pyrotechnical display of G-major chords. It is interesting to note that virtually all the themes and motives in Prokofiev's Fifth Piano Concerto are in major keys, symbolic perhaps of the artificial optimism animating musicians and politicians alike in the era of unstable equilibrium between two world cataclysms.

Concertante (It.). 1. A concert piece. 2. A composition for two or more solo voices or instruments with accompaniment by orchestra or organ, in which each solo part is in turn brought into prominence. 3. A composition for two or more unaccompanied solo instruments in orchestral music.

Sonatina (It.), **sonatine** (Ger.). A short sonata in two or three (rarely four) movements, the first in the characteristic first-movement form, abbreviated.

Antiphonal. Responsive, alternating.

Moderato (It.). At a moderate tempo or rate of speed.

Toccata (It.). A composition for organ or harpsichord (piano), free and bold in style.

Vivo (It.). Lively, spiritedly, briskly.

Concerto No. 2 in G Minor for Violin and Orchestra, Op. 63 (1935)

As a professional pianist, Prokofiev naturally devoted much of his energies to the composition of piano music, but he also made a careful study of other instrumental techniques, and wrote concertos for violin and for the violoncello. His First Violin Concerto was composed in 1917 and presents a fine blend of Prokofiev's rhythmic propulsion and lyric poetry. He wrote his Second Violin Concerto in 1935, specially for the Belgian violinist Robert Soetens, with whom Prokofiev made a concert tour in Spain, Portugal, Morocco, Algeria, and Tunisia. The first performance took place in Madrid on December 1, 1935, with Prokofiev present in the audience. The soloist was Soetens, and the conductor was Fernández Arbós.

Prokofiev's Second Violin Concerto is, like the first, set in three movements, but stylistically the two concertos are different. The later work lacks the grotesquerie typical of young Prokofiev, and it is less cosmopolitan, more national than Prokofiev's previous instrumental compositions. Like the First Concerto, it is firmly tonal, but digressions from the fundamental key of G minor start immediately after the opening of the first movement, Allegro moderato. The form of sonata-allegro is clearly discernible, however. A lyrical second subject appears in fine contrast with the energetic first subject. Russian commentators find national melodic traits in Prokofiev's lyrical expansiveness here. Modulations are multitudinous; at least eight statements in eight different keys, major and minor, of both subjects can be found in the first movement.

The second movement, Andante assai, represents a set of variations, a technique in which Prokofiev was a master. The violin passages approach the Baroque usages in their elaboration, but the texture is light and the solo part is never obstructed.

The Finale: Allegro ben marcato, is full of kinetic energy, a modern bacchanal—brusque, aggressive, impetuous. The violin tosses its accented tones over its entire range. It is a typical display of Prokofiev's spirited manner, which led some friendly critics to describe his productions as "soccer music." And, for the first time in the concerto, there are identifiable modernites, such as polytonality. The rhythmic design is strongly accented, but there are sudden abscissions and apocopes, creating a stimulating asymmetry. There is an extraordinarily long coda, but the ending, with a plagal cadence often favored by Prokofiev, and with acridly dissonant harmonies, is decisive and curt.

Symphonie Concertante *in E Minor for Violoncello and Orchestra, Op. 125 (1952)*

Prokofiev was a pianist of unique powers, capable of maintaining an even percussive beat with his steely long fingers without deviating from a set tempo. It was a technique ideally suited for the performance of his own piano works. But he encountered difficulties in composing for other instruments in a virtuoso style. In technical matters he sought the advice of professionals, much as Brahms and Dvořák consulted with the violinist Joseph Joachim to help them along in the technical details of their violin concertos. In his violin music, Prokofiev had David Oistrakh for his Joachim. For his cello works, he had Mstislav Rostropovich.

Prokofiev's *Symphonie Concertante* is the doppelgänger of his First Concerto for cello and orchestra, written in 1938. He rewrote it radically, leaving intact only the designation of tempo of the movements and the principal tonality, E minor. What was to be a revision of his First Cello Concerto became practically a new piece. During the composition of this nonidentical musical twin, Prokofiev discussed technical details with Rostropovich in numerous sessions. The score was completed in 1952. Rostropovich played it for the first time in Moscow on February 18, 1952, a little more than a year before Prokofiev died.

It must be recalled that Prokofiev's last years of life were darkened by a series of personal and professional disasters. He had divorced his first wife, mother of his two sons, and married a younger woman, which alienated many of his friends. He was beset by circulatory ailments. Most ominous of all, he could not come to terms with the Soviet officialdom. He was made a target of the infamous decree of the Central Committee of the Communist Party of the USSR of February 10, 1948, for his modernistic aberrations and allegedly un-Soviet attitudes toward the official doctrine of socialist realism. He refused to go to Stalin's Canossa, and responded to the charges in a coldly factual letter, free of the expected protestations of loyalty or expressions of penitence.

In his instrumental music, Prokofiev was always a man of the theater, even though he never attached an explicit program to his symphonies and concertos. In his book on Prokofiev's symphonies, the Soviet composer Sergei Slonimsky (nephew of the author) speaks of the "cinematographic character" of Prokofiev's symphonic structures: "Just as in the cinema the artistic power of separate images is subordinated to the general creative concept and is infinitely expanded by its continuous succession, so in Prokofiev's symphonic production the juxtaposition and mutual relationship of numerous concrete episodes and incisive graphic details are parts of the purely symphonic thematic development and form."

The *Symphonie Concertante* justifies its title by its consistent symphonic development. There are three movements. The first, in E minor, in 2/4 time, is marked Andante. After a stormy but brief exordium in a series of divergent dissonant chords, the cello plays a gentle E-minor solo, built in swaying patterns with impulsive accents. The violins pick up the tune for a while; then the cello resumes its role as soloist. A dramatic change supervenes in a ponderous passage of accented beats, with the cello growling on the low C string. Rhythmic density increases; the orchestra roars; the cello solo travels from the lowest to the highest region of its range while maintaining a steady metric pace. The tonal fabric remains clear, but there are rapid modulations. The music comes to a boil in a succession of modal-sounding minor-seventh chords. After a lyric episode, followed by a review of the principal thematic materials, the tempo slackens to adagio, and the movement concludes in quiet E minor.

The second movement, Allegro giusto, in 4/4 time, in C major, is a kinetic toccata. The form of toccata is a favorite of Prokofiev, for it enables him to maintain a steady motion, creating a reservoir of cumulative energy. The pianistic key of C major holds Prokofiev in thrall even in writing for other instruments. When Prokofiev as a brash young man first assailed the academic ears of Russian audiences early in the century, he was called a soccer player of music. In his *Symphonie Concertante*, and particularly in the second movement, Prokofiev plays the game of soccer without allowing any interference on purely conventional grounds. But after a period of purposeful exertion, there is a dulcet episode in E major marked by a tranquilizing oscillating rhythm. The cello is given a long cadenza, and then the toccata movement resumes its course. The tonality is bland D minor, arrayed in triadic harmonies, but is ornamented by overhanging **semitones** which form atonal stalactites. Prokofiev's artful game then changes to antiphonal tennis, with softball chords tossed from the orchestra to the cello and back. The melodies, the harmonies, the rhythms are very Russian in the lyric interludes, such as a **cantabile** passage in the cello. Once more the sonorities swell up, and the cello sweeps the ground in large ambulating intervals. The toccata movement returns, Allegro assai, with an A-major ending.

The third and last movement, Andante con moto, in 3/2, is in the key of E major, in classical correspondence to the initial key of E minor. There is a recitative in the cello part, fol-

Semitone. A half tone; the smallest interval in the Western scale.

Cantabile (It.). "Singable"; in a singing or vocal style.

lowed by a harmonious chorale. The tempo changes decisively to vivace in 3/4 time. The rhythmic impetus is unfaltering in its steadfast succession of even eighth notes, and later in even quarter notes. The rondolike progress is free of circumlocution. The ending, on the tonic E, is pert, terse, and curt.

OTHER WORKS

The Fiery Angel *(1919)*

A subject that fascinated Russian composers was the realm of religious superstition magnified by the earnest belief in the power of witches. But rather than select a Russian tale of witchcraft, as did Glinka, Mussorgsky, and Rimsky-Korsakov, Prokofiev became interested in a historical drama after a novel by the Russian writer Valery Bryusov, *The Fiery Angel*, dealing with the tremendous upheaval during the Counter-Reformation in Germany in the sixteenth century.

A young woman, Renata, who suffers from hysteria, is accused of having carnal relations with Satan. She is protected by the heroic knight Ruprecht, who dares to deny the existence of witches. In this opera, Prokofiev adopts the unusual, for him, system of **leitmotivs**. Among secondary figures in the libretto are the terrifying image of the Grand Inquisitor and the almost comic attendants, Faust (who sings bass) and Mephistopheles (who is given the part of a tenor). *The Fiery Angel* of the title is Renata's treacherous lover, Count Heinrich, who abandons her after a brief encounter. The climax of the opera is Renata's trial as a witch (for she refuses to admit that the Fiery Angel is really the devil) and her immolation at the stake.

The score, composed in 1919, is perhaps the most effective of Prokofiev's stage works. Yet it had to wait many years before its first complete production, at the Venice Festival on

Leitmotiv (Ger.). Leading motive; any striking musical motive (theme, phrase) characterizing one of the actors in a drama or an idea, emotion, or situation.

September 14, 1955, more than two years after Prokofiev's death. Refusing to wait indefinitely for the production, Prokofiev used some thematic materials from *The Fiery Angel* in his Third Symphony.

String Quartet No. 1, Op. 50 (1931)

The **String Quartet** Op. 50, was a commissioned work, written for the Library of Congress and first performed by the Brosa Quartet at the Elizabeth Sprague Coolidge Festival in Washington, D.C., on April 25, 1931. It has an unusual construction: there are two slow Andante movements separated by a fast interlude. The material of the last movement of the quartet is used in one of the six piano pieces in Opus 52. Prokofiev frequently transplanted ideas and thematic material from one medium to another. This suggests that his musical thoughts had an absolute character, independent of the particular instrumental combination in which they originally appear. Yet Prokofiev was supremely adept in his use of instrumental techniques and his understanding of the nature of the instruments was complete. There was no idle experimenting, no splashes of impressionistic color, no **counterpoint** for counterpoint's sake only. Prokofiev used his medium economically and efficiently. His was the technique of classical music even though his harmony and rhythm were products of modern times.

String quartet. A composition for first and second violin, viola, and cello.

Counterpoint. Polyphonic composition; the combination of two or more simultaneous melodies.

Peter and the Wolf (1936)

There is a quality in all of Prokofiev's music that makes it peculiarly appealing. It is, perhaps, the underlying simplicity of the musical phrase, a strong feeling for a central tonality, the driving rhythmic pulse. Prokofiev's music is always marching on in 4/4 time, with dreamy lyrical interludes in 3/4 time for a contrast. In Soviet Russia, where Prokofiev made his home after years abroad, this marching quality was associated with optimism; and the lyrical strain was taken to reflect the universal humanism of emotion. Prokofiev was, therefore, accepted in Russia as a positive artistic force "consonant" with the times.

Prokofiev wrote much music based on fairy tales, but it is only in *Peter and the Wolf* that he succeeded in creating a masterpiece which, like the best in children's literature, appeals to sophisticated adults as well. The primary purpose in writing this "symphonic tale for children," as it is subtitled, was to teach the children to recognize the instruments of the orchestra. Each character is represented by an instrument, or a group of instruments: the bird by the flute, the duck by the oboe, the cat by the clarinet in the low register playing **staccato**, Grandfather by the bassoon, the wolf by the chord of three French horns, Peter by the strings, the shots of the hunters by the kettledrums and the bass drum.

Staccato (It.). Detached, separated; a style in which the notes played or sung are more or less abruptly disconnected.

Each character is also given a special leading motive. These leading motives are supposed to be played on the corresponding instruments before the performance so the children learn to associate them with the characters of the tale. The story, which is Prokofiev's own, is told by the narrator to the accompaniment of the music, or between the episodes, during the pauses. The tale has also an implied political significance, for in it the wolf, who during his career as a ruthless aggressor has gobbled up the defenseless duck and threatened the safety of the cat and the bird, is finally outwitted by the Soviet Boy Scout Peter, is caged by the hunters who come to Peter's aid, and is placed in the zoo for everyone to behold and marvel.

The original production of *Peter and the Wolf* took place at the Children's Theater in Moscow on May 2, 1936. Prokofiev sketched the music during the month of April 1936, and completed the scoring only a week before the performance. The text of the tale, with hints as to the orchestration, follows:

Early one morning Peter opened the gate and went out on a big green meadow. [Strings playing Peter's leading motive.] On a branch of a big tree sat a little bird, Peter's friend. "All is quiet," chirped the bird gaily. [The flute plays the bird's theme, later joined by violins pizzicato and the oboe. Peter's motive appears in the strings, while the flute plays roulades.]

Soon a duck came waddling around. She was glad that Peter had not closed the gate, and decided to take a nice swim in the deep pond in the meadow. [The duck's theme is played by the oboe, accompanied by other woodwinds and strings.] The flute-bird chirps in the high treble.

Seeing the duck, the little bird flew down upon the grass, settled next to the duck, and shrugged her shoulders: "What kind of bird are you if you can't fly?" said she. To this the duck replied: "What kind of bird are you if you can't swim?" and dived into the pond. [This dialogue is pictured in the orchestra by the **roulades** of the flute and the theme of the duck played by the oboe.]

They argued and argued, the duck swimming in the pond, the little bird hopping along the shore. Suddenly something caught Peter's attention. He noticed a cat crawling through the grass. [The cat's theme appears in the clarinet, playing staccato in the low register, and accompanied by the double-bass.] The cat thought: "The bird is busy arguing. I'll just grab her." Stealthily she crept toward her on her velvet paws. [The cat's theme is played a fourth higher by the clarinet.] "Look out," shouted Peter, and the bird immediately flew up into the tree [fluttering arpeggios in the flute against the pizzicatos of the strings], while the duck quacked angrily at the cat from the middle of the pond. The cat crawled around the tree and thought: "Is it worth climbing up so high? By the time I get there the bird will have flown away." [The cat's theme continues in the clarinet and there are gasping sounds in the flute.]

Roulade (Fr.). A grace consisting of a move from one principal melody tone to another; a vocal or instrumental flourish.

Grandfather came out. He was angry because Peter had gone to the meadow. It is a dangerous place. If a wolf should come out of the forest, then what would he do? [A grumbling phrase in the low register of the bassoon, against harp beats of the strings.] Peter paid no attention to Grandfather's words and declared that Boy Scouts are not afraid of wolves. [Peter's theme in the strings, doubled by the clarinet.] But grandfather took Peter by the hand, led him home, and locked the gate [Grandfather's theme in the bassoon].

No sooner had Peter gone than a big gray wolf came out of the forest. [Three horns in a sinister theme in a minor key.] The cat quickly scurried up the tree. [The cat's theme rising chromatically in the low register of the clarinet.] The duck quacked, and in her excitement jumped out of the pond. No matter how hard the duck tried to run, she couldn't escape the wolf. He was getting nearer, nearer, catching up with her, and then he's got her, and with one gulp swallowed her. (The muted trumpet trills on a high note. The cello harmonic is the duck's last sound, then the oboe "sadly and expressively" plays the duck's theme in **pianissimo**.)

Pianissimo (It.). Very soft.

And now, this is how things stood: the cat was sitting on one branch, the bird on another, not too close to the cat, and the wolf walked around the tree looking at them with greedy eyes. In the meantime, Peter stood without the slightest fear behind the closed gate watching all that was going on. He ran home, took a strong rope and climbed up the high stone wall. One of the branches of the tree around which the wolf was walking stretched out over the wall. Grabbing hold of the branch, Peter lightly climbed over onto the tree. Peter said to the bird: "Fly down and circle around the wolf's head, only take care that he doesn't catch you." [Each character is followed by his leading motive in the orchestra, but now the flute plays Peter's theme.]

The bird almost touched the wolf's head with her wings while the wolf snapped angrily at her from this side and that. How the bird did worry the wolf! How he wanted to catch her! But the bird was cleverer, and the wolf couldn't do anything about it [repeated chords in the orchestra].

Meanwhile, Peter made a lasso and, carefully letting it down, caught the wolf by the tail and pulled with all his might. [The lasso is represented by swirling passages in the violin.] Feeling himself caught, the wolf began to jump wildly, trying to get loose [muted trumpet with a loud chords in the orchestra]. But Peter tied the other end of the rope to the tree, and the wolf's jumping only made the rope around his tail tighter.

At that moment a group of hunters came out of the woods, following the wolf's trail and shooting as they went (a rollicking march in the orchestra). Peter, sitting in the tree, shouted: "Don't shoot! Birdie and I have already caught the wolf. Now help us take him to the zoo." (Peter's theme in waltz time.)

And now imagine the triumphant procession: Peter at the head, after him the hunters leading the wolf, and, winding up the procession, Grandfather and the cat. Grandfather tossed his head discontentedly: "Well, and if Peter hadn't caught the wolf? What then?" [The cat's clarinet theme and grandfather's bassoon theme in counterpoint. Then Peter's theme in the brass.] Above them flew the bird, chirping merrily: "My, what fine follows we are, Peter and I! Look, what we have caught!" [Flute playing variations on the hunters' march]. And if one would listen very carefully, he could hear the duck quacking in the wolf's belly, because the wolf in his hurry swallowed her alive. [The oboe plays the duck's theme, then the orchestra leads to a brief finale.]

Cinderella *(1946)*

Russian composers have always favored operas and ballets on the subject of virtue conquering evil; fairy tales are natural scenarios for such bittersweet productions. Prokofiev contributed to this genre in his ballet *Cinderella*; in it the repressed "cinder girl" wins the love of a prince, much to the annoyance of her envious stepsisters. The score is written in the classical manner, emulating the musical choreography of the European Rococo. "I want to make my Cinderella as danceable as possible," Prokofiev wrote in one of his pronouncements. And indeed, the music dances in numerous court entertainments, variations, gavottes, and interludes.

The overall style is typical of Prokofiev; there is a gentle irony in depicting Cinderella's gradual emancipation, and the orchestral sonority is subdued. In fact, Soviet critics complained that Prokofiev's tonal painting was "too tender" for the tradition of grand ballet, and even suggested a more robust and louder orchestration. In the end, Prokofiev's treatment of the fairy tale won out, and Cinderella, as a ballet and in the form of orchestral suites, became one of his most popular compositions. It was first produced in Moscow on November 21, 1945.

DMITRI SHOSTAKOVICH
(1906–75)
Besieged Nationalist

DMITRI DMITRIEVICH SHOSTAKOVICH's style and idiom of composition largely defined the nature of new Russian music. He was a member of a cultured Russian family: his father was an engineer employed in the government office of weights and measures, and his mother was a professional pianist. Shostakovich grew up during the most difficult period of Russian Revolutionary history, when famine and disease decimated the population of Petrograd (now St. Petersburg). Of frail physique, he suffered from malnutrition. Glazunov, the director of the Petrograd Conservatory, appealed personally to the commissar of education, Lunacharsky, to grant an increased food ration for Shostakovich, essential for his physical survival.

At the age of nine he commenced piano lessons with his mother, and in 1919 he entered the Petrograd Conservatory, where he studied piano with Leonid Nikolayev and composition with Maximilian Steinberg, graduating in piano in 1923, and in composition in 1925. As a graduation piece, he submitted his First Symphony, Op. 10, written at the age of eighteen. It was first performed by the Leningrad Philharmonic on May 12, 1926, under the direction of Nicolas Malko, and subsequently became one of Shostakovich's most popular works. His Second Symphony, Op. 14, composed for the tenth anniversary of the Russian Revolution in 1927, bearing the dedication "To October" and ending with a rousing choral **finale**, was less successful despite its Revolutionary sentiment. He then wrote a satirical opera, *The Nose*, Op. 15, after Gogol's whimsical story about the sudden disappearance of the nose from the face of a government functionary. Here, Shostakovich revealed his flair for musical satire; the score featured a variety of modernistic devices. *The Nose* was produced in Leningrad on January 12, 1930, to considerable popular acclaim, but was attacked by officious theater critics as a product of "bourgeois decadence," and was quickly withdrawn from the stage.

Somewhat in the same satirical style was the ballet *The Golden Age*, Op. 22 (1930), which included a celebrated dissonant **polka**, satirizing the current disarmament conference in Geneva. There followed the Symphony No. 3, Op. 20, with a choral finale saluting International Workers' Day. Despite its explicit Revolutionary content, it failed to earn the approbation of Soviet spokesmen, who dismissed the work as nothing more than a formal gesture of proletarian solidarity. Shostakovich's next work was to precipitate a crisis in his career, as well as in Soviet music in general: it was an opera to the **libretto** drawn from a short story by the nineteenth-century Russian writer Nikolai Leskov, entitled *Lady Macbeth of the District of Mtzensk*. It was produced in Leningrad on

Finale (It.). The last movement in a sonata or symphony.

Polka (Bohemian, *pulka*). A lively round dance in 2/4 time, originating about 1830 as a peasant dance in Bohemia.

Libretto (It.). A "booklet"; the words of an opera, oratorio, etc.

January 22, 1934, and was hailed by most Soviet musicians as a significant work comparable to the best productions of Western modern opera. But both the staging and the music ran counter to growing Soviet puritanism. A symphonic **interlude** portraying a scene of adultery behind the bedroom curtain, orchestrated with suggestive passages on the slide trombones, shocked the Soviet officials present at the performance by its bold naturalism. After the Moscow production of the opera, *Pravda*, the official organ of the Communist party, published an unsigned (and therefore all the more authoritative) article accusing Shostakovich of creating a "bedlam of noise." The brutality of this assault dismayed Shostakovich, who readily admitted his faults in both content and treatment of the subject, and declared his solemn determination to write music according to the then-emerging formula of "socialist realism."

Shostakovich's next stage production was a ballet, *The Limpid Brook*, Op. 39, portraying pastoral scenes on a Soviet collective farm. In this work, he tempered his dissonant idiom, and the subject seemed eminently fitting for the Soviet theater. But it, too, was condemned in *Pravda*, this time for an insufficiently dignified treatment of Soviet life. Having been rebuked twice for two radically different theater works, Shostakovich abandoned all attempts to write for the stage, and returned to purely instrumental composition. But, as though pursued by vengeful fate, he again suffered a painful reverse. His Symphony No. 4, Op. 43 (1935–36), was placed in rehearsal by the Leningrad Philharmonic, but withdrawn before the performance when representatives of musical officialdom and even the orchestra musicians themselves sharply criticized the piece. Shostakovich's rehabilitation finally came with the production of his Symphony No. 5, Op. 47 (first performance, Leningrad, November 21, 1937), a work of rhapsodic grandeur, culminating in a powerful climax. It was hailed, as though by spontaneous consensus, as a model of

Interlude. An intermezzo; an instrumental strain or passage connecting the lines or stanzas of a hymn, etc.

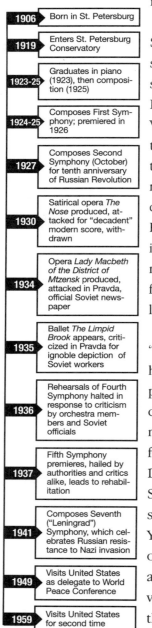

Shostakovich Timeline

1906	Born in St. Petersburg
1919	Enters St. Petersburg Conservatory
1923-25	Graduates in piano (1923), then composition (1925)
1924-25	Composes First Symphony; premiered in 1926
1927	Composes Second Symphony (October) for tenth anniversary of Russian Revolution
1930	Satirical opera *The Nose* produced, attacked for "decadent" modern score, withdrawn
1934	Opera *Lady Macbeth of the District of Mtzensk* produced, attacked in Pravda, official Soviet newspaper
1935	Ballet *The Limpid Brook* appears, criticized in Pravda for ignoble depiction of Soviet workers
1936	Rehearsals of Fourth Symphony halted in response to criticism by orchestra members and Soviet officials
1937	Fifth Symphony premieres, hailed by authorities and critics alike, leads to rehabilitation
1941	Composes Seventh ("Leningrad") Symphony, which celebrates Russian resistance to Nazi invasion
1949	Visits United States as delegate to World Peace Conference
1959	Visits United States for second time

(continued)

true Soviet art, classical in formal design, lucid in its harmonic idiom, and optimistic in its philosophical connotations.

The pinnacle of his rise to recognition was achieved in his Symphony No. 7, Op. 60. He began its composition during the siege of Leningrad by the Germans in the autumn of 1941. He served in the fire brigade during the air raids, then flew from Leningrad to the temporary Soviet capital in Kuibishev, on the Volga, where he completed the score, which was performed there on March 1, 1942. Its symphonic development is realistic in the extreme, with the theme of the Nazis, in mechanical march time, rising to monstrous loudness, only to be overcome and reduced to a pathetic drum dribble by a victorious Russian song. The work became a musical symbol of the Russian struggle against the overwhelmingly superior German war machine. It was given the nickname "Leningrad," and was performed during the war by virtually every orchestra in the Allied countries.

After the tremendous emotional appeal of the "Leningrad" Symphony, the Symphony No. 8, written in 1943, had a lesser impact. The Ninth, Tenth, and Eleventh Symphonies followed (1945, 1953, 1957) without attracting much comment; the Twelfth, Op. 112 (1960–61), dedicated to the memory of Lenin, aroused a little more interest. But it was left for his Symphony No. 13, Op. 113, premiered in Leningrad on December 18, 1962, to create a controversy that seemed to be Shostakovich's peculiar destiny. Its vocal first movement for solo bass and male chorus, to words by the Soviet poet Yevgeny Yevtushenko, expressing the horror of the massacre of Jews by the Nazis during their occupation of the city of Kiev and containing a warning against residual anti-Semitism in Soviet Russia, met with unexpected criticism by the chairman of the Communist party, Nikita Khrushchev, who complained about the exclusive attention in Yevtushenko's poem to Jewish victims, and his failure to mention the Ukrainians and other nationals who were also slaughtered. The text of the poem was altered to meet these objections, but the Symphony No. 13 never gained wide acceptance. There followed the remarkable Symphony No. 14, Op. 135 (1969), in eleven sections, scored for voices and orchestra, to words by Federico García Lorca, Apollinaire, Rilke, and the Russian poet Kuchelbecker.

Shostakovich's last symphony, No. 15, Op. 141, performed in Moscow under the direction of his son Maxim on January 8, 1972, demonstrated his undying spirit of innovation. The score is set in the key of C major, but it contains a dodecaphonic passage and literal allusions to motives from Rossini's *William Tell* Overture and the fate motive from Wagner's *The Valkyries*. Shostakovich's adoption, however limited, of themes built on twelve different notes, a procedure that he had himself condemned as antimusical, is interesting both from the psychological and sociological standpoint. He experimented with these techniques in several other works—his first explicit use of a twelve-tone subject occurred in his Twelfth **String Quartet** (1968). Equally illuminating is the use in some of his scores of a personal monogram DSCH (based on the German spelling of his name), standing for the notes D, Es, C, and H, German nomenclature for D, E-flat, C, and B.

One by one, his early works, originally condemned as unacceptable to Soviet reality, were returned to the stage and the concert hall. The objectionable Fourth and Thirteenth Symphonies were published and recorded. The operas *The Nose* and *Lady Macbeth of the District of Mtzensk* (renamed *Katerina Izmailova*, after the name of the heroine) had several successful revivals.

What is remarkable about Shostakovich is the unfailing consistency of his style of composition. His entire oeuvre, from his first work to the last (147 opus numbers in all), proclaims a personal article of faith. His idiom is unmistakably of the twentieth century, making free use of dissonant harmonies and intricate **contrapuntal** designs, yet never aban-

Shostakovich Timeline (cont.)

1962	Thirteenth Symphony, with Yevtushenko's Babi Yar as text, is criticized by Premier Khrushchev
1972	Fifteenth (last) Symphony premiered in Moscow under baton of composer's son Maxim
1975	Dies in Moscow

String quartet. A composition for first and second violin, viola, and cello.

Contrapuntal. Pertaining to composition with two or more simultaneous melodies.

doning inherent tonality. His music is teleological, leading invariably to a tonal climax, often in a triumphal triadic declaration. Most of his works carry key signatures and his metrical structure is governed by a unifying rhythmic pulse. Shostakovich is equally eloquent in dramatic and lyric utterance; he has no fear of prolonging his slow movements in relentless dynamic rise and fall, and the cumulative power of his kinetic drive in rapid movements is overwhelming.

Mode. Any scalar pattern of intervals, either traditional to a culture or invented.

Through all the peripeties of his career, he never changed his musical language in its fundamental **modalities**. When the flow of his music met obstacles, whether technical or external, he obviated them without changing the main direction. In a special announcement issued after Shostakovich's death, the government of the USSR summarized his work as a "remarkable example of fidelity to the traditions of musical classicism, and above all, to the Russian traditions, finding his inspiration in the reality of Soviet life, reasserting and developing in his creative innovations the art of socialist realism, and in so doing, contributing to universal progressive musical culture."

ORCHESTRAL MUSIC

Symphony No. 1, Op. 10 (1924–25)

Scherzo (It.). A joke, jest; an instrumental piece of a light, piquant, humorous character. Also, a vivacious movement in the symphony, with strongly marked rhythm and sharp and unexpected contrasts in both rhythm and harmony; usually the third movement.

Shostakovich's First Symphony, so popular in Russia and abroad, was a graduation piece, composed at the age of nineteen. It was performed by the Leningrad Philharmonic under the direction of Nicolas Malko, on May 12, 1926. There are four movements, and the symphony follows the standard form with this difference: not the third, but the second movement is a **scherzo** (as in Beethoven's Ninth).

Shostakovich remained faithful to this form in all his symphonies, and in the great majority of his other compositions. But within each movement there are deviations and striking individual touches that make for unmistakable originality. In the **recapitulation** he usually reverses the order of the first and second subjects of a sonata-**allegro**. The instrumentation is individualized, and Shostakovich likes to open a symphony with an instrumental solo. From the metric-rhythmic standpoint, there is a remarkable insistence on **duple time**. The rhythmic figure of an eighth note and two sixteenths is particularly frequent. When, as in the first movement of the First Symphony, there are episodes in 3/4 time, they often take the form of a caricature of a waltz.

This prevalence of duple time in Shostakovich's music is not peculiar to Shostakovich among Soviet composers, and it has something to do with a general, if unformulated, feeling that the marching duple time expresses healthy optimism, while the languid dactylic 3/4 time suggests laxity of spirit, out of keeping with the revolutionary times. It is also characteristic that in Shostakovich's music, as in the music of other Soviet composers, passages in 3/4 time are usually in minor modes. A notable exception to this is the Shostakovich type of rapid scherzo. But such scherzos are invariably *a quattro battute* (in four beats), and are simply masked bars of 12/4 or 12/8.

The following characteristics of Shostakovich's technique in the First Symphony became his trademarks, and are found in virtually the entire repertoire of his symphonic and **chamber music**:

1. A highly rhythmic opening subject, fundamentally **diatonic**, but embellished with **chromatics**. This theme is usually given to the clarinet or bassoon.
2. Individualized instrumentation with frequent division of the strings, and special effects, such as violin glissandos.
3. Exploitation of the lowest and highest registers, particularly the low reaches of the brass and high notes in the strings.
4. Independent role of the percussion. There is a kettledrum solo at the end of the First Symphony.
5. Inclusion of the piano in the orchestral score.
6. Inverted pedals in **tremolos** in the violins. In the second movement of the First Symphony, the high E in the second

Recapitulation. A return of the initial section of a movement in sonata form.

Allegro (It.). Lively, brisk, rapid.

Duple time. Double time; the number of beats to the measure is divisible by two.

Chamber music. Vocal or instrumental music suitable for performance in a room or small hall.

Diatonic. Employing the tones of the standard major or minor scale.

Chromatic. Relating to tones foreign to a given key (scale) or chord; opposed to diatonic.

Tremolo (It.). A quivering, fluttering, in singing; an unsteady tone.

violins is repeated 576 times at a stretch, for the total duration of one minute and thirty-eight seconds.
7. Extensive scale runs.
8. Sudden modulations, directly into the tonic.

Symphony No. 5, Op. 47 (1937)

On September 25, 1966, on the occasion of his sixtieth birthday, Dmitri Shostakovich was awarded the highest honor of
the Soviet Union, the Order of Hero of Socialist Labor. He was
the first Soviet musician to be given this distinction. A sentimental tribute was tendered him on the same day by the
Union of Soviet Composers, which organized a concert of his
works in Moscow with his son Maxim as conductor.
Shostakovich received an ovation at the end of the concert.

It was not always that Shostakovich was honored in his
native land. He knew bitter disappointments and was repeatedly attacked by the self-appointed legislators of Soviet dogma
according to the gospel of socialist realism. Particularly vicious
was a 1936 article in *Pravda* entitled "Bedlam Instead of
Music," which condemned Shostakovich for the signs of decadence and modernistic aberrations in his opera *Lady Macbeth
of the District of Mtzensk*, ominously pointing out that the
opera was suspiciously successful in Western Europe and
America. This was followed a short time later with a similar
blast in *Pravda* for Shostakovich's faulty representation of the
life on a Soviet collective farm in one of his ballets.

Discouraged and humiliated, Shostakovich abandoned
the musical theater and returned to his first love, symphonic
music. Shostakovich had every expectation to recoup his for-
tunes by writing a new symphony. His First Symphony, which
he wrote at the age of eighteen, scored an immediate success,
with repeated performances all over the world. His Second
and Third Symphonies, each with a choral ending to texts of
revolutionary content, failed to strike fire but obtained a suc-
cès d'estime. His Fourth Symphony met so much opposition
during rehearsals on account of its advanced harmonic idiom

that Shostakovich decided to withdraw it from performance. It was not performed until a quarter of a century later.

With grim determination, Shostakovich embarked on yet another symphony, his Fifth. It proved to be his winning piece. Its first performance on November 21, 1937, by the Leningrad Philharmonic Symphony Orchestra, under the direction of the modernistically minded conductor Eugene Mravinsky, earned instant acclaim. As if obeying a common impulse, novelists, aviators, actors, and plain Soviet citizens rushed into print to express their admiration for the new work. Shostakovich himself issued a statement announcing that the inner meaning of the symphony was the dignity of an individual, and that the finale represented the triumph of man over the doubts and the tragedies reflected in the first three movements.

Like most of Shostakovich's symphonies, the Fifth Symphony contains four movements: **Moderato**, **Allegretto**, **Largo**, and Allegro non troppo. The first movement opens with an eloquent exordium in D minor, Beethovenlike in its sweeping power. A lyrical subject is introduced in a brooding episode. The tension mounts; a characteristic rhythmic figure of two rapid beats followed by a note of double value, a motto of many of Shostakovich's scores, imparts an air of dramatic expectation. The initial Beethovenlike theme is brought back in amplified orchestral sonorities in the **recapitulation**. The movement ends softly.

The Allegretto is an optimistic scherzo. The formal structure is cyclic, with regular recurrences of principal themes. There follows a slow movement, Largo. Here the melodic presentation is spacious and solemn. Climaxes are built by the process of deliberate accumulation of dynamic power, with a détente leading to a quiet **coda**. The Finale: Allegro non troppo, is charged with kinetic energy. Lyrical interludes provide expressive contrasts. Then the initial theme of the movement reappears in proclamatory fanfares in D major. The peroration is one of the most protracted endings in sym-

Moderato (It.). At a moderate tempo or rate of speed.
Allegretto (It.). Quite lively; moderately fast.
Largo (It.). A slow and stately movement.

Recapitulation. A return of the initial section of a movement in sonata form.

Coda (It.). A "tail"; hence, a passage ending a movement.

Octave. A series of eight consecutive diatonic tones; the interval between the first and the eighth.

phonic literature; tension is built by a relentless reiteration of strategic notes. In the final measures, the strings, reinforced by the piano, play dominant A in multilevel **octaves** 253 times, with bulging sonorities reaching a bursting point before coming to a stop on the tonic D in unison.

Symphony No. 7, Op. 60 ("Leningrad") (1941)

It was during the epochal siege of Leningrad that Shostakovich composed his Seventh Symphony, commonly known as the "Leningrad" Symphony. The score bears no such title, but it is dedicated to the city of Leningrad. It is cast in the key of C major, associated with simple courage, unambiguous purpose, and victory.

In October 1941 Shostakovich flew out of Leningrad over the enemy lines to the wartime Soviet capital Kuibishev on the Volga River. There, on December 27, 1941, he completed the fourth and last movement of the symphony. By that time, the personnel of the Bolshoi Theater Orchestra of Moscow were also in Kuibishev, and the work was performed there for the first time on March 1, 1942.

It is typical of Shostakovich that he can draw a grand symphonic design, panoramic in its dimensions and admittedly representational in its source of inspiration, and yet preserve classical form in all its purity and orthodoxy. Each of his symphonies has an explicit or implicit program, but all can be interpreted as works of absolute music. In this respect he follows Mahler, who also liked to assign philosophical or psychological connotations to his symphonies. Mahler often repudiated the programmatic subtitles that he had originally sanctioned. Shostakovich, too, insisted that his symphonies should be judged solely on their musical merit and not according to their subject matter.

The "Leningrad" Symphony opens with an energetic Allegretto. The melodic structure of the main subject is wide-spaced, with emphatic rhythmic suspensions. (Some musical analysts see in this broad intervallic scheme a symbolic allusion to the immensity—and therefore invincibility—of Russia.) A contrasting second subject, of a lyric nature, is introduced and in turn generates a pastoral twin melody. The mood is gentle and pacific—a prelude to disaster, and it is not long in coming. The tonality shifts from serene C major to the somber key of E-flat major, which in the color scheme of Rimsky-Korsakov, the teacher of Shostakovich's teachers, is associated with fortified cities and camps. An ominous drumbeat introduces a mechanical march tune, the menacing **leitmotiv** of the Nazi machine; soon another drum joins the parade, and yet another. The monstrous beat grows by simple accretion and instrumental amplification. The tune is repeated eleven times without alteration, and soon takes possession of the entire orchestra.

Leitmotiv (Ger.). Leading motive; any striking musical motive (theme, phrase) characterizing one of the actors in a drama or an idea, emotion, or situation.

Unexpectedly, the Nazi machine runs into obstacles. A new song emerges powerfully from the depths; it is a Russian song, and it begins to undermine the Nazi tune, wrenching it out of shape and breaking it up. A fierce contrapuntal strife ensues; the drums still persevere in their mechanical beat, but the tide has turned. There is a tremendous accumulation of sounds, in which the **tonic**, the **dominant** and the **subdominant** are commingled in a **pandiatonic** complex. From this almost intolerable tension arises the main subject, but it is in a minor key. It grows and expels the musical enemy; at the end only broken fragments of the Nazi tune are audible among the debris.

Tonic. The keynote of a scale; the triad on the keynote (tonic chord).
Dominant. The fifth tone in the major or minor scales; a chord based on that tone.
Subdominant. The tone below the dominant in a diatonic scale; the fourth degree.
Pandiatonicism. A modern term for a system of diatonic harmony making use of all seven degrees of the scale in dissonant combinations.

Tchaikovsky's Overture "1812" comes to mind, for in that earlier patriotic piece, there was also a conflict between two warring melodies. It was unfortunate, from a musical standpoint, that Tchaikovsky was compelled to let the rather undistinguished czarist anthem conquer the inspiring "Marseillaise." In the Soviet version of the piece, the czarist hymn is replaced by the concluding chorus of Glinka's opera *A Life for the Czar* (which itself has been renamed *Ivan Susanin*, after its peasant hero).

It is interesting to note that the second half of the Nazi tune is nearly identical with the celebrated song "Then Go I to Maxim's," from Lehár's operetta *The Merry Widow*, very popular in Russia, and also beloved by Hitler, despite the non-Aryan extraction of its librettist. Could it be that Shostakovich unconsciously imitated this popular air? Bártok, who was slightly annoyed by the constant playing of Shostakovich's "Leningrad" Symphony on the radio as he lay ill in a New York hospital, incorporated the Lehár-Shostakovich fragment in the fourth movement of his Concerto for Orchestra, which he was composing at the time; he gave it to a cachinnating clarinet, and embellished it with sardonic **trills**.

Trill. The even and rapid alternation of two tones which are a major or minor second apart.

The second movement of the "Leningrad" Symphony, Moderato, is an elegiac scherzo. It bears no thematic or dramatic relationship to the war, but serves as a nostalgic reflection of happy youth. The form of a scherzo is a favorite of Shostakovich; it appears in virtually all his instrumental works, as a playful interlude between the dramatic first movement and the ensuing meditative section.

Strange and foreboding inaction pervades the third movement, Adagio. Shostakovich confided to friends that in it he intended to portray his native city, Leningrad, enveloped in misty twilight, when its vistas, its river, its granite embankments are immobile and poetical in their northern stillness. The sound of the flute floats fleetingly over the surfaces of the attenuated orchestral accompaniment. Three strokes of the soft **tam-tam** announce the end of the nocturnal dream, and

Tam-tam. A gong;. the Hindoo drum; also *tom-tom*.

the advent of the decisive last movement, Allegro non troppo. Its main subject appears with great force, and almost immediately sprouts new melodies and motives, with sharpened rhythms and restless accents.

In such varied developments Shostakovich is a true symphonist. And since his symphony is a Russian work, the concentration and accumulation of thematic material inevitably assumes the shape of a temperamental Russian dance. Both musical and psychological considerations compel the insertion of a wistful episode; in the "Leningrad" Symphony it becomes a threnody for the fallen. The principal key is that of C minor, and it takes a series of chromatic ascensions before the major tonic is reached. Shostakovich has never been reticent in his proclamatory finales, and the "Leningrad" Symphony, by its very nature, demanded a total mobilization of trumpets, horns, and trombones. Curiously, C minor perseveres almost to the end, alternating and even combining with C major. The dissonant sonorities created by this superposition heighten the dramatic tension and enhance the effect of the victorious C-major apotheosis. The symphony ends in glory.

In the United States, a lively competition developed for its first American performance. Serge Koussevitzky of the Boston Symphony Orchestra, forgetting his long-standing opposition to the Soviet regime, proclaimed that Shostakovich was for the twentieth century what Beethoven was for the nineteenth, a fighter for liberty. As a Russian, he tried hard to play the work first, but was frustrated in his desire because of the exigencies of schedules, and lost out to Arturo Toscanini, who gave the first performance of the "Leningrad" Symphony at one of his summer concerts with the NBC Symphony Orchestra in July 1942. The score was microfilmed in Russia, and the precious capsule was sent by air to Persia, by automobile from Teheran to Cairo, from there to Casablanca, to Brazil, and finally to New York. More than sixty performances of the "Leningrad" Symphony were given in America alone during the season 1942–43. Not all the music critics were enthusiastic, but they unanimously paid their respect to Shostakovich as a patriotic symphonist. *Life* magazine remarked, tongue in cheek, that criticism of the work might endanger the war effort and undermine the crucial Russian alliance.

Shostakovich was thirty-four years old when he wrote the

"Leningrad" Symphony. It was his *Eroica*. (Beethoven was not quite thirty-four when he completed the *Eroica*). Historically and aesthetically, the Leningrad Symphony is unique. No composer before Shostakovich had written a musical work depicting a still raging war, and no composer had ever attempted to describe a future victory in music with such power and conviction, at the time when his people were fighting for their very right to exist as a nation. No wonder then that the "Leningrad" Symphony became a symbol of the war effort, acquiring propaganda value in the most exalted sense of the word.

Music generated amid cataclysmic events seldom maintains its original impact. It was inevitable that the "Leningrad" Symphony should lose some of its overwhelming power, not because of the depreciation of its musical substance but because of the passage of historical time. What is remarkable is that it has endured, that it did not become a mere curiosity like Beethoven's *Wellington's Victory* and so many other ancient battle pieces. The "Leningrad" Symphony still remains a formidable accomplishment, a work of power and, to use Shostakovich's own favorite expression, spiritual beauty.

Symphony No. 10, Op. 93 (1953)

The Tenth Symphony follows the general lines of most of its predecessors. Shostakovich completed the score on October 27, 1953, and it had its first performances a few weeks later, on December 17, 1953, in Leningrad, and on December 28, 1953, in Moscow, both under the direction of Eugene Mravinsky.

The first movement, Moderato, establishes a contemplative mood at once in introspective wavelike figures in the lower strings. The tonality centers on E minor, and the principal time signature is 3/4, which is maintained almost without shifts. The entire movement represents the steady growth of the subject until a **fortissimo** climax is reached. Then the melodic arch curves on its downward slope. In conformity

Fortissimo (It.). Extremely loud.

with Shostakovich's concept of cyclic form, the movement comes to a close, returning to the original E-minor theme.

The second movement, Allegro, in 2/4, is set in the key of B-flat minor, polar to the initial key of the work. The melodious theme recalls Soviet marching songs as cultivated by youth organizations. The snare drum punctuates the symmetric rhythm. Joyful fanfares are heard, but they are strangely chromatic. Again the cyclic form compels the music to return to its source, after an episode in an alien key.

The third movement, Allegretto, is a scherzo, set in the vicinity of C minor. True to his musical credo, Shostakovich energetically reiterates the vigorous rhythmic beat. But there is something else in this movement that commands attention. The thematic four notes with which the scherzo begins are regrouped in the development, forming the configuration of the notes D, E-flat, C, B, which represents Shostakovich's monogram using the German spelling. This signature is an extraordinary projection for Shostakovich, whose extreme modesty rarely allowed him to inject personal references into his music.

In the scherzo, Shostakovich's monogram is so inconspicuous that it has to be searched for in order to be discovered. But in the finale, an andante followed by an Allegro, Shostakovich assigns it to the full brass section in fortissimo (*fff*). The Allegro has the familiar quality of the final movements in other symphonies by Shostakovich, a determined vital élan consonant with the Soviet ideas of youth and progress. His signature appears and reappears in the orchestra. In the end it forms a **stretto** in the kettledrums, a fantastically bold recourse. The coda is in flaming E major, the homonymous major key of the initial movement.

Stretto (It.). A division of a fugue in which subject and answer follow in such close succession as to overlap.

Symphony No. 11, Op. 103 ("The Year 1905") (1957)

The Eleventh Symphony is subtitled "The Year 1905." This was the year of the heroic but unsuccessful revolution against the czarist regime. Shostakovich wrote the symphony for the fortieth anniversary of the Bolshevik Revolution of 1917. It had its first performance in Moscow on October 30, 1957. Like most of his symphonies, the Eleventh Symphony is in four movements. Here, however, each movement is given a specific historical, topical, or symbolic title. The first movement, Adagio, is named "Palace Square." The music conveys the atmosphere of 1905 by interpolating chants from the ritual of the Russian Orthodox Church (Russia was a church state, and prayers were obligatory in schools and at official functions) and military bugle calls. In contrast to these czaristic sounds are heard strains from Revolutionary songs, particularly prison songs.

The second movement, called "January 9," is ominous in its associations. This was the day in 1905 when workers of St. Petersburg, then the capital of Russia, led by an unfrocked priest (who was later exposed as a double agent and executed by his former comrades), petitioned the czar for better living conditions but were met with rifle fire in front of the Winter Palace. The music derives from two contrasting subjects: that of the people, trustful, praying, demanding, and that of the brutal government authorities, unfeeling and automatic, somewhat akin to the Nazi theme in the "Leningrad" Symphony. A precipitous **fugato** leads to a dramatic denouement with trumpet calls and drumrolls illustrating the shooting down of the demonstrators. The melody of the revolutionary song "Boldly step forward!" appears momentarily, but is soon drowned in the intonations of horror and sorrow.

Fugato (It.). A passage or movement consisting of fugal imitations not worked out as a regular fugue.

The third movement, "Eternal Memory," is a revolutionary requiem. It opens with a complete quotation from the song popular in Russia early in the century: "You fell the victims of a fateful struggle, martyrs of unstinted love for the people." The spirit of passive lament exemplified by this song gives way to the proclamation of revolutionary action. Ringing bells arouse the people to take arms against the oppressive power of the autocratic government.

The last movement, "Alarm," contains melodies of many revolutionary songs, among them the old mournful Polish song "Warszawianka," which was very popular in Russian revolutionary circles in 1905. These songs become part of a complex polyphonic web, accompanied by dramatic sounds of distant bells. The Eleventh Symphony pictures the story of a revolutionary defeat in 1905, but it also foretells the triumph in 1917.

Concerto No. 1 for Piano, Trumpet, and Strings, Op. 35 (1933)

The aesthetics of popular appeal is not an exact science, but it is possible to state the reasons for Shostakovich's unquestionable gift of musical communication. It lies in his uncompromising sincerity of expression, his lucidity of musical statement, his adroitness in building powerful climaxes, his natural talent for melody, and his rhythmic drive. With all this, Shostakovich speaks a musical idiom which is his own, readily recognizable, and universally understandable. Shostakovich was a profoundly national composer, yet he never borrowed actual Russian songs for themes of his music. His Russianism lies in the characteristic inflection of his melodic line, in the intervallic turns, and in the pulsating rhythms. Shostakovich adopts large panoramic forms and yet manages to keep the details in sharp relief. His range of dynamics reaches from effective fortissimo to the faintest **pianissimo**, and he makes a point of utilizing the highest and the lowest instrumental register. He contrasts the slow, drawn-out tempo of his adagios with the rapid-fire movement of his **scherzos**.

Shostakovich's First Piano Concerto, first performed by the composer with the Leningrad Philharmonic on October 15, 1933, is a characteristic work, embodying the satirical and the lyrical side of his nature. It is scored for piano, trumpet, and string orchestra. The lyrical element is derived from Russian city ballads, while the satiric passages reveal a virtuoso

Pianissimo (It.). Very soft.

Scherzo (It.). A joke, jest; an instrumental piece of a light, piquant, humorous character. Also, a vivacious movement in the symphony, with strongly marked rhythm and sharp and unexpected contrasts in both rhythm and harmony; usually the third movement.

style, which in the piano part assumes at times a Czernylike aspect. The concerto ends in a remarkable succession of C-major chords in the extreme upper register of the piano keyboard, seconded by trumpet flourishes. The extraordinary effect produced by this ending on the audience is almost physiological in its impact. Shostakovich did not contrive such effects as a deliberate bid for applause, but neither did he recoil from applying a musical uppercut that may appear vulgar to the esoterically minded, but that is not alien to one who, like Shostakovich, had a healthy instinct for celebrating at the end of a good day's work.

Concerto for Violin and Orchestra, Op. 77 (1947–48)

In the world of contemporary music, Shostakovich occupied a position somewhat similar to that held by Sibelius at the turn of the century. Basically Shostakovich was a traditionalist. Most of his symphonies are cast in the classical four movements, and the construction of his musical phrases is remarkably uniform in its symmetry. The sense of **tonality** is strongly felt. What makes Shostakovich a distinctly twentieth-century figure is his freedom of handling these materials. Tonal melodies are apt to be diverted without the benefit of academic modulation. The stridently dissonant harmonies occasionally resulting from such usages seem natural. But Shostakovich does not pursue variety for variety's sake. He does not hesitate to resort to literal repetition when his sense of dramatic power demands it. The rhythmic pattern of an eighth note followed by two sixteenth notes is Shostakovich's musical monogram.

The Violin Concerto was first performed in Leningrad on October 29, 1955, with David Oistrakh, to whom the concerto is dedicated, as soloist. It is in four movements, each bearing a descriptive title: **Nocturne**, Scherzo, **Passacaglia**, and **Burlesque**. The Nocturne preserves the mood of tranquillity throughout. The basic key is A minor, but tonal digressions

Tonality. A cumulative concept that embraces all pertinent elements of tonal structure; a basic loyalty to tonal center.

Nocturne (Fr.). A piece of a dreamily romantic or sentimental character, without fixed form.

Passacaglia (It.). An old Italian dance in stately movement on a ground base of four measures.

Burlesque. A dramatic extravaganza, or farcical travesty of some serious subject, with more or less music.

into neighboring keys, typical of Shostakovich, impart a sense of mobility, enhanced also by increased rhythmic frequency. The ending, in which the solo violin is muted, travels into the highest treble. The Scherzo is in the key of B-flat minor. It is characteristically lively and light in substance. Playful **glissandos**, favorite with Shostakovich in his writing for strings, further enliven the music.

In the Passacaglia, set in F minor, Shostakovich follows the classical form of thematic variation. What is unique in this movement is a long introduction for orchestra, and an even longer cadenza for unaccompanied violin solo. Without a transition, the Passacaglia merges into the Finale: Burlesque. The rhythmic formula of Shostakovich's favorite pattern in eighth notes and sixteenth notes provides the final impetus. The violin solo repeats the highest available E fifty-six times in rapid movement, leading to an ending in A major, in a classical affirmation of the basic key of the concerto.

> **Glissando** (It.). A slide; a rapid scale. On bowed instruments, a flowing, unaccented execution of a passage. On the piano, a rapid scale effect obtained by sliding the thumb, or thumb and one finger, over the keys.

VOCAL WORKS

The Nose, *Op. 15 (1927–28)*

The Nose, an opera written in the same period as the Second Symphony, belongs to the constructivist type of composition. Shostakovich had absorbed the lessons of contemporary German opera, and the technique of writing of Arnold Schoenberg, Ernst Krenek, Paul Hindemith, and Alban Berg. Operas and orchestral works by these Western masters were widely performed in Leningrad in the late 1920s, and Shostakovich had the opportunity to study their effect. For his text, he selected Gogol's fantastic tale of the nose that became detached from a customer's face in a barber's chair, and began to live an independent life as a petty government official. Here, Shostakovich revealed his flair for musical satire; all sorts of absurdities occur, interspersed with satirical darts at czarist bureaucracy. In the end, the nose resumes its rightful place, much to its owner's relief.

The score is a brilliant exercise in modernistic grotesquerie. Shostakovich introduced such novel effects as an orchestral sneeze, the imitation of the sound of shaving in double-bass harmonics, hiccups on the harp, and an **octet** of eight janitors singing eight different advertisements. The orchestra of the opera is small, but the percussion instruments are greatly increased in numbers and are featured in an **interlude**. The part of the nose itself is to be sung with the nostrils closed, to produce a nasal effect.

When *The Nose* was presented for the first time in Leningrad on January 13, 1930, the direction of the theater thought it prudent to announce it as an "experimental spectacle." It was greeted with great exhilaration among Soviet musicians, but received a chilly blast from the Kremlin; officious theater critics attacked it as a product of "bourgeois decadence," accused Shostakovich of imitating decadent Western models, and silenced the work's advocates, leading to its being quickly withdrawn from the stage.

Lady Macbeth of the District of Mtzensk, *Op. 29 (1930–32)*

Both satirical and dramatic elements find their expression in Shostakovich's opera *Lady Macbeth of the District of Mtzensk*, which he himself described as a "tragic satire." It was written between 1930 and 1932 and first produced in Leningrad on January 22, 1934. The book, taken from a short story by the nineteenth-century Russian writer Nikolai Leskov, portrays a strong-willed woman who, stifled in her ambition and seeking an outlet for her energies, poisons her merchant husband at the instigation of her lover; later, czarist justice leads to a murder-suicide in prison.

In the introduction to the program book of the opera, Shostakovich states his intention to treat the Russian Lady

Octet. A composition for eight voices or instruments.

Interlude. An intermezzo; an instrumental strain or passage connecting the lines or stanzas of a hymn, etc.

D. SHOSTAKOVICH
op. 29/114

KATERINA IZMAILOVA

OPERA IN 4 ACTS, 9 SCENES
(REVISED EDITION, 1963)
LIBRETTO
BY A. PREISS AND D SHOSTAKOVICH
BASED ON N. LESKOV'S STORY
" LADY MACBETH
OF THE MTSENSK DISTRICT "
ENGLISH TRANSLATION BY E. DOWNES
SCORE
VOLUME I

ДЕЙСТВИЕ ПЕРВОЕ
Картина первая

ACT ONE
Scene One

Сад в доме Измайловых. В саду Катерина Львовна.
The garden of the Izmailovs' house. In the garden is Katerina Lvovna.

★ Контрабасы играют без сурдин на протяжении всей оперы
The doublebasses are never muted throughout the whole opera

2162

Macbeth as "a positive character, deserving the sympathy of the audience." Concerning the musical idiom of the opera, he writes:

> The musical development is projected on a symphonic plan, and in this respect my opera is not an imitation of old operas, built on separate numbers. The musical interludes between the scenes are continuations and developments of the preceding musical idea, and have an important bearing on the characterization of the events on the stage.

The opera was extremely successful with audiences and was hailed by the press as the greatest achievement of Soviet operatic art. It was produced in New York at the Metropolitan Opera House on February 5, 1935, by the Cleveland Orchestra, Artur Rodzinski conducting. The spectacle made a sensation, and the audience included ranking members of the capitalistic set of New York City. The production was more realistic than in Russia, and many were scandalized by the symphonic interlude, with suggestive trombone glissandos as the lovers retire behind the curtains of a bedroom on the stage.

But what seemed the peak of Shostakovich's popular achievement nearly proved his artistic undoing. On January 28, 1936, *Pravda*, the organ of the Communist party, published an article condemning the opera and its tendencies and raised the question, fatal to a Soviet composer, as to whether the success of *Lady Macbeth* among bourgeois audiences abroad was not due to its confused and politically neutral ideology, and to the fact that it "tickled the perverted tastes of the bourgeois audience by its jittery, noisy, and neurotic music." The opera was accused of vulgar naturalism and aesthetic snobbism. The writer was outraged by the attempt to "solve all problems on the merchant's bed," and by the author's expressed sympathy with the murderous heroine. The article had a profound effect on Soviet musicians, and opened a series of discussions in which not only Shostakovich himself but also his erstwhile exegetes were attacked.

Song of the Forests, *Oratorio for Children's Choir, Mixed Choir, Soloists, and Orchestra, Op. 81 (1949)*

Throughout his tempestuous career, Shostakovich was repeatedly urged by the Soviet policy makers to write music in the manner of socialist realism. His *Song of the Forests* came very close to that elusive ideal. To some admirers of Shostakovich, it may also represent a rather grim excursion to Canossa. When *Song of the Forests* was performed in Moscow on November 6, 1949, several musicians commented frankly that Shostakovich had betrayed his great gifts by writing this score. The unbelievers were promptly castigated by the critic of *Sovietskaya Musica* as "myopic retrogrades and camouflaged formalists." And the critic commended Shostakovich for his "boldness and honesty in repudiating his former means of self-expression which would obstruct the realistic treatment of a great contemporary subject."

It is characteristic of the duality of Shostakovich's nature that a year after the composition of *Song of the Forests*, he should have written a set of Twenty-four **Preludes** and **Fugues** for Piano, Op. 87 (inspired by his visit to Leipzig for the Bach bicentennial), which are totally different in style from the harmonic simplicity and folk-like quality of Song of the Forests. Shostakovich was promptly berated by the editorial writer of *Sovietskaya Musica* for this "reversion to a neoclassical stylization which strives to recreate on an elaborate modernistic plane some mournfully subjectivist pages of Bach which are farthest removed from our world outlook."

The text of *Song of the Forests*, by the Soviet poet Eugene Dolmatovsky, illustrates the extraordinary combination of intense nationalism with the glorification of communism, a fea-

Prelude. A musical introduction to a composition or drama.

Fugue (fewg). Contrapuntal imitation wherein a theme proposed by one part is taken up equally and successively by all participating parts.

ture of the Soviet arts in general. Most revealing in this respect are the lines in which the words "the dawn of communism" (*zaria communisma*) rhyme, by an assonance, with "sacred fatherland" (*suyataya otchizna*). The subject of the **oratorio** is the reforestation campaign undertaken in Russia to repair the devastation of the war. There are seven movements, arranged in a fine contrast of tempo and mood. A motto theme appears in every movement. This theme bears a remarkable similarity to that of "Of Youth" from Mahler's *Song of the Earth*. Whether this is a coincidence or a subconscious tribute to Mahler, of whom Shostakovich was fond, is a matter of conjecture. Of course, after it gets going, the theme branches out into traditional melorhythmic patterns of Russian folk music.

Oratorio (It.). An extended multi-movement composition for vocal solos and chorus accompanied by orchestra or organ.

The opening movement, descriptive of the end of the war and the advent of the "victorious spring," is the simplest in its melody and harmony. Yet even in this movement, Shostakovich allows himself a sudden modulation, from C major into E-flat major and back to C major, which smacks of essential modernism. The second movement is very Russian, with the typical melodic **cadences** effected by an upward leap from the subdominant to the tonic. The third movement, which evokes Old Russia, has an **aria** for bass solo that might have come from *Boris Godunov*. Despite this obvious derivation, the aria gives an impression of spontaneity and original inspiration. After all, Shostakovich is a talent of the first order, and even when he imitates others, he does honor to the source.

Cadence. Rhythm; also, the close or ending of a phrase, section, or movement.
Aria (It.). An air, song, tune, melody.

The fourth movement, descriptive of the planting of young trees by Soviet boys and girls, is musically the best of the entire oratorio. The muted trumpet theme, accompanied by a snare drum, that introduces the young planters is a first cousin of the second theme of the opening movement in Shostakovich's Seventh Symphony, even though the connotations of the two themes are diametrically opposite—young Soviet sprouts in *Song of the Forests* and the mechanized Nazi hordes in the Seventh Symphony. In this little fanfare, Shostakovich manages to create a mood of joyful work with remarkably simple means, by twisting the major third of the key into an **augmented** second. Then follows a gay children's chorus, with some acerbities that add spice to the simple folk-like melody.

Augmentation. Doubling (or increasing) the time value of the notes of a theme or motive, often in imitative counterpoint.

After this charming interlude, the music of the fifth movement, "Stalingraders Come Forward," relapses shockingly into unsophisticated vulgarity. The tune sounds very much like an incongruous replica of the march from *Aïda*. It is curious that the laudatory review of *Song of the Forests* in *Sovietskaya Musica* described this shabby tune as redolent of "the most characteristic intonations of the Soviet mass song." The sixth movement, "Tomorrow's Promenade," with its fine tenor aria, is lyric in mood. The motto theme reappears here in its original form, sung by the chorus without words. There follows an artful symphonic development.

The finale, in which all the combined musical forces take part, begins with a fugal introduction, and then proceeds according to the time-honored method of securing a rousing effect. Yet the music is not entirely undistinguished. Here and there are touches of the typical Shostakovich. The concluding chorus is a Soviet counterpart of the envoi of the biblical oratorio, "ad majorem Dei gloriam": "Glory be to the Leninist party! Glory to the people forever! To the wise Stalin—glory, glory!"

What is the moral to be drawn from this attempt of Shostakovich's to depart from his natural idiom in order to achieve a compromise with the temporal powers? *Song of the Forests* certainly cannot be dismissed as a worthless pastiche. This music, whatever its self-imposed limitations, is alive, and there are passages that are among the finest written by Shostakovich. Strangely enough, there are reminiscences in this work of such creations of Shostakovich's supposed formalistic past as the Cello Sonata of 1934 and the proscribed opera *Lady Macbeth of the District of Mtzensk*. Even when Shostakovich tries to repress his natural gift, he still comes out many notches higher than his orthodox Soviet contemporaries.

CHAMBER MUSIC

Quintet for Piano and String Quartet, Op. 57 (1940)

Shostakovich played the piano part in the first performance of the Quintet Op. 57 on November 23, 1940, at the Moscow Festival of Soviet Music. The reception was as favorable as that of his Fifth Symphony three years before, *Pravda* published an enthusiastic article:

> After the grandiose vistas of the tragically tense Fifth Symphony with its philosophical search, this Quintet, lyrically lucid, human and simple, may be an intermezzo before a new monumental work, in which the great talent of Shostakovich may depict heroic figures of our era. One thing is beyond doubt: Shostakovich's Quintet is not written as a recreation; it is not a step aside; it is music created in full measure of power, it is a work that propels the art of music, opening new broad horizons ahead. . . . Shostakovich's Quintet is not only the most significant of his attainments; it is undoubtedly the best musical composition of the year 1940.

This is the same *Pravda* that in 1936 had delivered a vitriolic attack on Shostakovich for his opera *Lady Macbeth of the District of Mtzensk* (the charge was erotic naturalism in the stage treatment and leftist aberration in the music) and the ballet *The Limpid Stream* (in which Soviet life was said to have received a frivolous and oversimplified treatment).

In a statement to the Soviet news agency TASS, Shostakovich expressed his gratification at the reception of the Quintet Op. 57 in these words:

> The year 1940 was a most significant year for me. In the summer of that year I composed my Quintet for **Pianoforte** and Strings. This work was very well received by the widest circles of Soviet audiences, and this means that my music is understood by the masses, that it satisfies their requirements. The knowledge of this gives me great joy, for there can be no greater satisfaction than to feel such close kinship with one's own people.

Pianoforte (It.). A stringed keyboard instrument with tones produced by hammers; a piano.

The quintet is in five movements. The first, entitled Prelude, opens with a slow introduction in the Beethoven manner, with a strong modal flavor redolent of the Russian folk song. The piano plays the opening measures, and is later joined by the string instruments. A scherzolike episode intervenes; then the original theme returns, in full sonority, ending on a G-major chord.

The second movement is a Fugue, almost school-like in its regular entries: the first violin, then the second, the cello, and the viola. But the melodic intervals are subtly changed, lending an unexpected modal quality to this most tonal of all musical forms. The movement is very slow, but there is an increase of tension when the theme, in double-quick time, is projected against itself at normal speed. After a short **recitative** in the piano, repeated in the cello, the themes are telescoped. The ending is peaceful and nostalgic in its aloofness from all motion.

Recitative. Declamatory singing, free in tempo and rhythm.

The third movement is a Scherzo, in quick 3/4 time, in a new key of B major. It is a typical perpetual motion in Shostakovich's favorite style, akin to a similar movement in the Cello Sonata. The dancing tune of the violin in the middle section has also had many relatives in other compositions of

Shostakovich. And the fanfares of the ending remind us of the finale of his First Piano Concerto.

The fourth movement is an Intermezzo. From a slow and expressive beginning, it progresses toward a passionate climax, receding again into the calm of open harmonies in the conclusion. The Finale opens with a piano solo, in pianissimo. The movement is animated with a marchlike rhythm, but lyrical interludes are many. The first violin plays a long passage in **staccato**, which leads to a poetic **coda** in G major, pianissimo. There is a hint of the Russian folk song, as in the choral ending of *Lady Macbeth of the District of Mtzensk*, and in a similar conclusion of the Cello Sonata.

The familiar earmarks of Shostakovich's style are all in evidence in this quintet: the boisterous scale passages running off to an alien tonic; the contrasting use of extreme registers with the gaping distances of three octaves in unison writing; the meditative lyricism of slow sections; the stubborn repetition of blocked chords and single notes; the emphatic rhythmic beat. The harmonic structure is a compromise between the sanctified classical models and the modernity of the present century. Shostakovich handles this hybrid idiom in a masterly fashion.

Staccato (It.). Detached, separated; a style in which the notes played or sung are more or less abruptly disconnected.

Coda (It.). A "tail"; hence, a passage ending a movement.

String Quartet No. 4, Op. 83 (1949), and String Quartet No. 8, Op. 110 (1960)

Since string quartets are symphonies in miniature, it is natural that they should reflect Shostakovich's symphonic conceptions. Most of his symphonies and most of his string quartets are in four movements of a classical design; a supernumerary fifth movement is apt to be a cyclic summation. A rondo type of sonata form is a favorite of Shostakovich for the opening and concluding movements. A rapid scherzo is invariably present. What is quite extraordinary is his predilection for long-drawn slow sections. Only a composer supremely confident of his capacity to maintain the inner logic of musical expression can risk the peril of monotony in such extensive prolongations. Sibelius and Mahler knew how to handle the problem of slow movements, but did not escape sharp criticism when they seemed to falter. Shostakovich met similar criticism stoically; he calmly explained that quiet contemplation was an integral part of his musical philosophy, as powerful in its expression as the triumphant spirit of his famous symphonic codas.

Was Shostakovich a true modernist? He was attacked by the conservatives as a purveyor of cacophony, and by the radicals as a masticator of old Russian tunes. By the evidence of his music, neither description is just. Perhaps he was an Unmodernistic Modern, an International Russian. No contradiction in terms is involved here. Shostakovich made use of the modern dissonant idiom within the framework of tonality, but he emphatically rejects modernistic experimentation, including the kind he practiced himself in his youthful works. His music is profoundly Russian, but this Russianism is of an international quality, like the Russianism of Mussorgsky. His music is of the modern age but is rooted in the melodic and harmonic traditions of the immediate past; his appeal is universal but the resources of his inspiration are national.

The Fourth String Quartet, Op. 83, was written in 1949 and belongs to the period of consolidation of Shostakovich's stylistic habits. Like most of his instrumental compositions, it is in four movements: Allegretto, **Andantino**, Allegretto, and still another Allegretto. All three Allegrettos are predominantly in 4/4 time, of four quarter notes to a bar; the slower movement, Andantino, is in 3/4 time. The principal tonality is D major, the most convenient key for string instruments. In the very opening we are confronted with a phenomenon not observed in modern music since Bruckner and Mahler: deliberate and conscious repetition! Such repetition, typical of Shostakovich in its literal application, can be stultifying, but it can also be mesmeric. As in Bruckner, as in Mahler, so in Shostakovich, the mesmeric quality prevails.

Andantino (It.). A little slower than andante, but often used as if meaning a little faster.

The first movement of this quartet is built on a series of **pedal points**; the tonic D in the bass is sustained for sixty-four bars before it yields to a modulatory development. The main theme is gay and simple, but somber moods supervene; the ending is effected in a gradual dynamic softening. The Andantino is a lyrical waltz in F minor alternating with major keys; as in the first movement, the ending is soft. The third movement displays considerable variety. The principal theme is given out by the muted cello; it is a broad Russian melody sung against the steady rhythms in the other instrumental parts. The opening is in C minor; the ending is in C major; syncopated rhythms in repeated patterns enliven the contrasting middle section of the movement. The final Allegretto opens in C major in a direct link with the preceding movement, but its character is totally different; the motion is swifter, the rhythms are broader, and the pedal points more binding. There are interesting technical effects in the slides toward natural harmonic tones. The pedal point is established on the tonic D, and the ending comes in the gentlest tonal transparencies.

Shostakovich wrote his Eighth String Quartet, Op. 110, in 1960. Although it is in five movements, the concluding Largo is in effect an epilogue and a recapitulation of the opening Largo. The fourth movement is also a Largo; thus we have three very slow movements in a single work. Not even Mahler essayed such a design! The second movement is an Allegro molto, and the third an Allegretto, performing the function of a scherzo. The Eighth Quartet is practically monothematic; what is even more remarkable is that Shostakovich does not attempt to present the main theme in varied forms. Quite to the contrary, it is introduced bleakly and determinedly, like a subject in a Bach fugue; it resembles, in fact, rhythmically and melodically the subject of the fourth fugue of the first volume of the *Well-Tempered Clavier*. It rarely modulates, but is heard time and again through the entire quartet in its original key of C minor. Why? The riddle is easily solved.

Pedal point. A tone sustained in one part to harmonies executed in the other parts.

The Eighth Quartet is an autobiographical work. Shostakovich's thematic signature D, Es, C, H, which appears here, is found also in the Tenth Symphony, written five years earlier than the quartet. Furthermore, the Eighth Quartet contains incidental melodic quotations from his First Symphony, written at the age of eighteen, and allusions to old Russian Revolutionary songs that he used in his programmatic Eleventh Symphony. The insistent repetition of these fragments, the slow cumulative rise of subsidiary contrapuntal voices, the systematic avoidance of contrasts, ought to create a feeling of musical frustration, even consternation, among the performers and the listeners. Instead, and contrary to all academic rules and admonitions, the total impression of this somber and solemn work is that of tragic consummation. Shostakovich has said that his Eighth Quartet is a personal dedication and a secular requiem for the victims of fascism. This explains the various thematic allusions. But no announced or implied programmatic intent, however noble, can elevate a composition above its intrinsic merit. It is the power of Shostakovich's music in this quartet that makes the listener accept the almost unacceptable persistence of thematic patterns, and only a master can exercise this power with such enormous effect.

Coda

When I met him in Leningrad in August 1935, Shostakovich was already a luminary of the first magnitude on the Russian horizon. The Intourist agency listed him among sightseeing attractions: "Come to the Soviet Union, see the Kremlin and hear Shostakovich." So I was eager to see Shostakovich.

One of the few remaining old-fashioned *izvostchiks* (buggy drivers) took me, for the sum of seven rubles, to Dmitrovsky Pereulok, No. 5, where Shostakovich lived with his widowed mother and his wife. I did not know which was his apartment, and there was no janitor of whom I could inquire. But suddenly I heard someone play the piano. It was an unusual sort of playing, and it was unusual music, rhythmic, simple in outline, but adorned with considerable dissonance. There could be no mistake; it was Shostakovich playing his own music. I ascended the stairs toward the source of that music, and soon found myself in front of a door on the third floor. I rang the bell. The door opened, and there was Shostakovich, a bespectacled young man, looking a little like a picture of Schubert. He led me to the studio, where a grand piano stood, and almost immediately plunged into a discussion of musical affairs in Russia and in America. On the piano I noticed the score of Stravinsky's *Symphony of Psalms*. Shostakovich told me that he admired the structural perfection of the work, and had even arranged it for four hands.

I observed that he was a very accurate sort of person. On the table there was a leather-bound book in which he noted the time of composition of each of his works, the year, month, and day, and sometimes the hour. There was nothing amateurish about the man. He was not given to temperamental outbursts, and was always glad to accept suggestions from his interlocutors, from his colleagues, from his correspondents.

After an hour or so of musical discussion, Shostakovich's mother announced that tea was served. We went to another room, not very spacious, but homelike, with flowerpots on the windowsill and a bird in a cage. Shostakovich introduced me to his wife. As I learned afterward, his mother was a musician, and a graduate of the St. Petersburg Conservatory in the piano department. She eagerly discussed her son's music, and wanted to know in detail what they thought of Shostakovich in America.

We returned to the studio. At the piano, I tried going over some of Shostakovich's preludes, which I was going to play in America. Then we went over the piano part of his Cello Sonata. There is one passage that sounds like exercises in scales, and I wanted to know how Shostakovich plays them, straightforwardly, or with humorous exaggeration. I was surprised to find that he was not a humorist by nature, and that the satirical strain in his music was not meant to be witty, but constructively critical of the subject. For instance, the scene at the police headquarters in *Lady Macbeth of the District of Mtzensk* was not intended to be grotesque, but served the purpose of exposing the rottenness of the regime of Czar Nicholas I. The celebrated polka from *The Golden Age* was originally a satire on the Disarmament Conference in Geneva. Shostakovich always considered himself a practical musician writing functional music, whether in satire or in glorification.

WEBSITES/BIBLIOGRAPHY/ DISCOGRAPHY

In compiling this list, it is impossible to be exhaustive or complete. All nineteen of these composers have generated mountains of literature and recordings; some pieces can be heard on fifty or more different CDs! It is also difficult if not impossible to recommend one recording as being "better" than all others. For this reason, the following lists give a selective sampling of books and CDs on each composer and composition covered in this book. The websites chosen give the reader an idea of what is available and indicate links to other sites that currently exist. Keep in mind that websites come and go; a good search engine will help you locate these and future sites quickly.

J. S. BACH

Websites

http://www.jsbach.org/

> J. S. Bach home page. An extensive biography, tour of Bach's life in Germany, catalog of his works, bibliography, recommended recordings, and other Bach resources on the Web.

http://www.basistech.com/bach/

> J. S. Bach newsgroup. The Frequently Asked Questions (FAQ) resource for the newsgroup is alt.music.j-s-bach.

http://www.jsbach.net/bcs/index.html

> Bach Central Station. Links to sites covering all aspects of Bach's life and work.

Books

Boyd, Malcolm. *Bach* (The Master Musicians). NY: Schirmer Books, 1997.

_____. *Bach: The Brandenburg Concertos*. NY: Cambridge, 1993.

_____, ed. *J. S. Bach, Oxford Companion of Music*. NY: Oxford, 1999.

Butt, John. *The Cambridge Companion to Bach*. NY: Cambridge, 1997.

_____. *Bach: Mass in B Minor*. NY: Cambridge, 1991.

David, Hans T., Arthur Mendel, and Christoph Wolff, eds. *The New Bach Reader: A Life of Johann Sebastian Bach in Letters and Documents*. NY: Norton, 1999.

Stauffer, George. *Bach, the Mass in B Minor: The Great Catholic Mass* (Monuments of Western Music). NY: Schirmer Books, 1996.

Wolff, Christoph, Eugene Helm, and Ernest Warburton. *The New Grove Bach Family* (The New Grove). NY: Norton 1997.

Recordings

INSTRUMENTAL WORKS

Chaconne in D Minor for Unaccompanied Violin; from Partita No. 2, BWV 1004 (1720)

> Julian Bream, guitar EMI Classics 55123
>
> C. Booth, harpsichord, Olympia 437

Orchestral Suite No. 3 in D Major, BWV 1068 (c. 1729–31)

> Berlin Academy of Early Music, Harmonia Mundi 901578
>
> Berlin Philharmonic (von Karajan, conductor), Deutsche Grammophon 453001-2
>
> Bach Festival Orchestra (Menuhin, conductor), Royal Classics 6481

Concerto No. 1 in C Minor for Two Harpsichords, BWV 1060 (1729)

> Hamburg Philharmonic; Frantz and Eschenbach, piano soloists, Detusche Grammophon 415665-2

ORGAN WORKS

Toccata, Adagio, and Fugue in C Major, BWV 564 (c. 1708–17)

> E. Power Biggs, Sony Masterworks 42644
>
> M. Murray, Telarc 80127

Passacaglia in C Minor, BWV 582 (c. 1708–17)

> Anthony Newman, Helicon Classics 1010
>
> Karl Richter, London Classic 455291-2

Ricercare à Six from *The Musical Offering*, BWV 1079 (1747) (orchestration by Anton Webern)

> Leipzig Bach Collegium, Capriccio 10 032

RELIGIOUS WORKS

Cantata No. 51 "Jauchzet Gott in Allen Landen" (date unknown)

> Stuttgart Bach Collegium, Novalis 150029
>
> American Bach Soloists, Koch International Classics 7138

Cantata No. 53, "Schlage Doch" (date unknown)

> Zagreb Solisti, Vanguard Classics 2-64

Cantata No. 158, "Der Friede Sei Mit Dir" (date unknown)

> Monteverdi Choir, Teldec 93687
>
> Leonhardt Consort, Teldec 2292-42633

The Passion of Our Lord According to St. Matthew, BWV 244 (1727)

English Baroque Soloists/Monteverdi Choir, Archiv 427648-2

Berlin Philharmonic (von Karajan, conductor), et al., Deutsche Grammophon 419789-2

Philharmonia Orchestra (Klemperer, conductor) EMI Classics 63058

Chicago Symphony (Solti, conductor), et al., London 42177-2

GEORGE FRIDERIC HANDEL

Websites

http://www.intr.net/bleissa/handel/home.html

Handel home page. Information and links on the composers.

http://www.intr.net/bleissa/ahs/

American Handel Society. Scholarly site with links.

Books

Burrows, Donald. *Handel*. NY: Schirmer Books, 1995.

_____. *Handel's Messiah*. NY: Cambridge, 1991.

_____, ed. *Cambridge Companion to Handel*. NY: Cambridge, 1998.

Dean, Winton. *Handel's Dramatic Oratorios and Masques*. NY: Oxford, 1959.

_____, and John Merrill Knapp. *Handel's Operas, 1704–1726* (revised edition). NY: Oxford, 1995.

_____, with Anthony Hicks. *The New Grove Handel*. NY: Norton, 1997.

LaRue, C. Steven. *Handel and His Singers: The Creation of the Royal Academy Operas, 1720–1728*. NY: Oxford, 1995.

Mann, Aflred. *Handel: The Orchestral Music*. NY: Schirmer Books, 1997.

Recordings

INSTRUMENTAL MUSIC

Overture to *Agrippina* (1709)

Academy of St. Martin in the Fields (Silito, conductor) Capriccio 10 420

The Faithful Shepherd (1712; rev. 1734)

London Philharmonic (Beecham, conductor) Dutton 8018

Water Music (1717)

New York Philharmonic (Boulez, conductor) Sony 38480

Academy of Ancient Music (Hogwood, conductor) L'Oiseau–Lyre 40059-2

Concerto Grosso No. 12 in G Major (1739)

Budapest Strings, Naxos 8.553028

Vienna Concentus Musicus, Teldec 95500-2

FRANZ JOSEPH HAYDN

Websites

http://home.wxs.nl/~cmr/haydn/index.htm

>   CMR Music Services Haydn home page.

http://w3.rz-berlin.mpg.de/cmp/haydnj.html

>   CMP Haydn home page. Biography, links, and bibliography.

Books

Larsen, Jens Peter. *The New Grove Haydn*. NY: Norton, 1997.

Rosen, Charles. *The Classical Style: Haydn, Mozart, Beethoven*. NY: Norton, 1997.

Sisman, Elaine, ed. *Haydn and His World* (Bard Music Festival Series). Princeton, NJ: Princeton U. Press, 1997.

Recordings

SYMPHONIES

Symphony No. 88 in G Major (1787)

>   Berlin Philharmonic (Furtwangler, conductor), Deutsche Grammophon 447439-2

>   Columbia Symphony (Walter, conductor), Sony Classical 66485

Symphony No. 92 in G Major ("Oxford") (1789)

>   Cleveland Orchestra (Szell, conductor), Sony Classical 46322

Symphony No. 95 in C Minor (1791)

>   New York Philharmonic (Bernstein, conductor), Sony Classical 47553

Symphony No. 99 in E-flat Major (1793)

>   Philharmonia Orchestra (Slatkin, conductor), RCA Red Seal 0902-68425-2

Symphony No. 104 in D Major ("London") (1795)

>   Royal Concertgebouw Orchestra (Harnoncourt, conductor), Teldec 2292-43526-2

>   Pittsburgh Symphony (Previn, conductor), EMI Classics 65178

CONCERTOS

Concerto for Violoncello in C Major (c. 1765)

>   English Chamber Orchestra (Barenboim, conductor), Jacqueline Du Pre (cello), EMI Classics 4780

>   Academy of St. Martin in the Fields (Brown, conductor), Mstislav Rostropovich (cello), EMI Classics 49305

Concerto for Violoncello in D Major (1783)

>   English Chamber Orchestra (Garcia, conductor), Yo-Yo Ma (cello), Sony 44562

Concerto for Trumpet in E-flat Major (1796)

English Chamber Orchestra (Leppard, conductor), Wynton Marsalis (trumpet), Sony Classical 57497

Academy of St. Martin in the Fields (Marriner, conductor), Alan Stringer (trumpet), London 430633-2

Symphonie Concertante in B-flat Major (1792)

Vienna Concentus Musicus (Harnoncourt, conductor), Teldec 2292-44196-2

OTHER WORKS

The Seven Last Words of Christ (1795–96)

Juilliard String Quartet, et al., Sony Classical 44914

The Seasons (1799–1801)

St. Paul Chamber Orchestra, Minnesota Chorale, Koch International 7065

Vienna Symphony, A. Schoenberg Choir, Teldec 2292-42699-2

WOLFGANG AMADEUS MOZART

Websites

http://www.frontiernet.net/~sboerner/mozart/

The Mozart Project website.

http://www.mhrcc.org/mozart/mozart.html

Links, bibliography, biography, and more.

Books

Clive, Peter. *Mozart and His Circle*. New Haven: Yale U. Press, 1993.

Dimond, Peter. *A Mozart Diary: A Chronological Reconstruction of the Composer's Life, 1761–1791*. Westport, CT: Greenwood, 1997.

Landon, H. C. Robbins. *Mozart: The Golden Years*. NY: Schirmer Books, 1989.

_____. *Mozart and Vienna*. NY: Schirmer Books, 1991.

Sadie, Stanley. *The New Grove Mozart*. NY: Norton, 1983.

Solomon, Maynard. *Mozart: A Life*. NY: HarperCollins, 1995.

Recordings

ORCHESTRAL MUSIC

Symphony No. 25 in G Minor, K. 183 (1773)

Vienna Philharmonic (Bernstein, conductor), Deutsche Grammophon 429221-2

Symphony No. 32 in G Major, K. 318 (1779)

Berlin Philharmonic (von Karajan, conductor), Deutsche Grammophon 429668-2

Symphony No. 36 in C Major, K. 425 ("Linz") (1783)

Berlin Philharmonic (Abbado, conductor), Sony Classical 66859

Symphony No. 38 in D Major, K. 504 ("Prague") (1787)

Vienna Philharmonic (Walter, conductor), Sony Classsical 64474

Symphony No. 39 in E-flat Major, K. 543 (1788)

Royal Concertgebouw Orchestra (Harnoncourt, conductor), Teldec 9031-77596-2

Symphony No. 40 in G Minor, K. 550 (1788)

Chicago Symphony (Levine, conductor) RCA 09026-61397-2

Overture to *Der Schauspieldirektor*, K. 486 (1786)

Calgary Philharmonic (Bernardi, conductor), CBC 5149

Overture to *The Marriage of Figaro*, K. 492 (1786)

New York Philharmonic (Bernstein, conductor), Sony Classical 47601

CONCERTOS

Concerto No. 5 for Violin in A Major, K. 219 (1775)

Jascha Heifetz (violin), Memories 3007/8

Concerto for Three Pianos in F Major, K. 242 (1776)

London Phlharmonic, Ashkenazy, Barenboim, and Ts'ong (piano), London 421577-2

Concerto for Flute and Harp in C Major, K. 299 (1778)

Chamber Orchestra of Europe, James Galway (flute), RCA Red Seal 7861-2

Concerto for Piano No. 24 in C Minor, K. 491 (1786)

RCA Victor Orchestra (Krips, conductor), Arthur Rubinstein (piano), RCA Gold Seal 7968-2

Concerto for Piano No. 25 in C Major, K. 503 (1786)

English Chamber Orchestra, Murray Perahia (piano and conductor), Sony 37267

Concerto for Piano No. 27 in B-flat Major, K. 595 (1791)

Philadelphia Orchestra (Ormandy, conductor), Rudolf Serkin (piano), Sony Odyssey 42533

Concerto for Clarinet in A Major, K. 622 (1791)

Academy of St. Martin in the Fields (Marriner, conductor), J. Brymer (clarinet), Philips 416483-2

Sinfonia Concertante for Violin and Viola in E-flat Major, K. 364/320d (1779)

Orpheus Chamber Orchestra, Deutsche Grammophon 429784-2

CHAMBER MUSIC

String Quartet No. 15 in D Minor, K. 421 (1783)

Guarneri String Quartet, Philips 426240-2

String Quartet No. 17 in B-flat Major ("Hunt"), K. 458 (1784)

Budapest String Quartet, Enterprise 99300

String Quartet No. 19 in C Major ("Dissonant"), K. 465 (1785)

Melos String Quartet, Deutsche Grammophon 429818-2

"Eine kleine Nachtmusik" (Serenade in G Major), K. 525 (1787)

Vienna Philharmonic (von Karajan, conductor), EMI Classics 66388

LUDWIG VAN BEETHOVEN

Websites

http://www.geocities.com/Vienna/Strasse/2914/beethoven/

Beethoven Experience. Biography, pictures, and compositions.

http://www.music.sjsu.edu/Beethoven/index/home_page.html

Beethoven Center. Course syllabi, journal, and general information from the American Beethoven Society.

Books

Grove, Sir George. *Beethoven's Nine Symphonies*. NY: Dover, 1962.

Kerman, Joseph, and Alan Tyson. *The New Grove Beethoven*. NY: Norton, 1997.

Levy, David. *The Ninth Symphony*. NY: Schirmer Books, 1995.

Sipe, Thomas. *"Eroica" Symphony*. NY: Cambridge, 1998.

Solomon, Maynard. *Beethoven*, 2nd revised ed. NY: Schirmer Books, 1998.

Recordings

SYMPHONIES

Symphony No. 3 in E-flat Major (*Eroica*), Op. 55 (1804)

New York Philharmonic (Bernstein, conductor), Sony Classical 47514

Philadelphia Orchestra (Muti, conductor), EMI Classics 69783

Symphony No. 5 in C Minor, Op. 67 (1807–8)

Berlin Philharmonic (von Karajan, conductor), Deutsche Grammophon 419051-4

Symphony No. 7 in A Major, Op. 92 (1811–12)

Vienna Philharmonic (Furtwangler, conductor), EMI Classics 68903

Symphony No. 8 in F Major, Op. 93 (1812)

Boston Symphony (Koussevitzky, conductor), Pearl 9185

Symphony No. 9 in D Minor ("Choral"), Op. 125 (1822–24)

Vienna Philharmonic (Abbado, conductor), Deutsche Grammophon 419598-2

OVERTURES

The Creatures of Prometheus, Op. 43 (1801)

Leonore Overture No. 3, Op. 72a, No. 3 (1806)

Coriolanus Overture, Op. 62 (1807)

Egmont Overture, Op. 84 (1810)

Overture to *King Stephen*, Op. 117 (1812)

Overture to *The Consecration of the House*, Op. 124 (1822)

> All six works: Vienna Philharmonic (Berstein, conductor), Deutsche Grammophon 423481-2

CONCERTOS

Piano Concerto No. 2 in B-flat Major, Op. 19 (1785; rev. 1794–95, 1798)

> Chicago Symphony (Levine, conductor), A. Brendel (piano), Philips 412787-2

Piano Concerto No. 3 in C Minor, Op. 37 (1800)

> Cleveland Orchestra (Ashkenazy, conductor and piano), London 433321-5

Romance in G for Violin and Orchestra, Op. 40 (1802)

> Scottish Chamber Orchestra (Laredo, conductor and violin), IMP Classics 977

Piano Concerto No. 4 in G Major, Op. 58 (1803–6)

> Royal Philharmonic (Previn, conductor), E. Ax (piano), RCA Silver Seal 60476-2

Piano Concerto No. 5 in E-flat Major ("Emperor"), Op. 73 (1809)

> Chicago Symphony (Reiner, conductor), Van Cliburn (piano), RCA Gold Seal 7943-2

Concerto in C Major for Violin, Cello, and Piano, Op. 56 (1804)

> Vienna Philharmonic, Camerata 25 CM 252

Violin Concerto in D Major, Op. 61 (1806)

> Isaac Stern, Sony Classical 66941

CHAMBER MUSIC

String Quartet No. 1 in F Major, Op. 18, No. 1 (1799–1800)

String Quartet No. 8 in E Minor ("Razumovsky" Quartets), Op. 59, No. 2 (1805–6)

String Quartet No.13 in B-flat Major, Op. 130 (1825–26)

String Quartet No. 14 in C-sharp Minor, Op. 131 (1825–26)

String Quartet No. 16 in F Major, Op. 135 (1826)

> Complete Recordings of the string quartets:
>
> Emerson String Quartet, Deutsche Grammophon 447075-2
>
> Guarneri String Quartet, RCA Red Seal 60456/57/58-2-RG

PIANO WORKS

Piano Sonata No. 14 in C-sharp Minor ("Moonlight"), Op. 27, No. 2 (1801)

> V. Horowitz, Sony Classical 53467
>
> A. Rubinstein, RCA Red Seal 5674-2

Piano Sonata No. 28 in A Major, Op. 101 (1816)

Vladimir Ashkenazy, London 452176-2

Piano Sonata No. 29 in B-flat Major ("Hammerklavier"), Op. 106 (1817–18)

A. Brendel, Philips 446093-2

G. Gould, Sony Classical 52645

FELIX MENDELSSOHN

Websites

http://utopia.knoware.nl/~jsmeets/m/mendelsb.htm

Links, biographical information, and more.

http://titan.iwu.edu/~mcooper/mendelssohns/

Mendelssohn at the millenium. Academic site.

Books

Todd, R. Larry. *Mendelssohn: The Hebrides and Other Overtures*. NY: Cambridge, 1993.

_____, ed. *Mendelssohn and His World*. Princeton, NJ: Princeton U. Press, 1991.

Vietrcik, Greg. *The Early Works of Felix Mendelssohn: A Study in the Romantic Sonata Style* (*Musicology*, Vol. 12). London: Gordon and Breach, 1993.

Recordings

Symphony No. 3 in A Minor, Op. 56 (*Scottish*) (1830–42)

Symphony No. 4, Op. 90 (*Italian*) (1833)

Both symphonies:

Lepizig Gewandhaus (Masur, conductor), Teldec 2292-43463-2

Berlin Philharmonic (Levine, conductor), Deutsche Grammophon 427670-2

Octet in E-flat Major, Op. 20 (1825)

Academy of St. Martin in the Fields Chamber Ensemble, Philips 420400-2

Overture to *A Midsummer Night's Dream* (1826, 1843)

Boston Symphony (Ozawa, conductor), Deutsche Grammophon 439897-2

Overture to *The Hebrides (Fingal's Cave)*, Op. 26 (1832)

Capriccio Brillant for Piano and Orchestra, Op. 22 (1832)

Philadelphia Orchestra (Ormandy, conductor), Ruold Serkin (piano), Sony Classical 48186

Overture to *Ruy Blas*, Op. 95 (1839)

Both overtures (and others by Mendelssohn):

Bamberg Symphony (Flor, conductor), RCA Red Seal 07863-57905-2

Concerto in E Minor for Violin and Orchestra, Op. 64 (1844)

Vienna State Opera Orchestra (Golschmann, conductor), M. Elman (violin), Vanguard Classics 8034

RICHARD WAGNER

Websites

http://www.geocities.com/Vienna/Strasse/2906/wagner.html

Wagner home page. "Beginner's guide" to the operas of Wagner.

http://www.zazz.com/wagner/index.shtml

Wagner on the Web. Links, FAQs, and bulletin board.

Books

Cord, William O. *An Introduction to Richard Wagner's* Der Ring des Nibelungen: *A Handbook*. Athens, OH: Ohio U. Press, 1995.

Deathridge, John, and Carl Dalhaus. *The New Grove Wagner*. NY: Norton, 1997.

Gutman, Robert W. Richard Wagner: *The Man, His Mind, and His Music*. NY: Harcourt, Brace, 1990.

Osborne, Charles. *The Complete Operas of Richard Wagner*. NY: Da Capo, 1993.

Spotts, Frederic. *Bayreuth: A History of the Wagner Festival*. New Haven: Yale U. Press, 1994.

Wagner, Richard. *Pilgrimage to Beethoven and Other Essays*. Lincoln: U. of Nebraska, 1994.

Recordings

Rienzi: Overture (1840)

Chicago Symphony (Reiner, conductor), Arlecchino 45

Cleveland Orchestra (Szell, conductor), Sony Classical 62403

Tannhäuser: Overture and Bacchanale (1842–45)

NBC Symphony (Toscanini, conductor), RCA Gold Seal 09026-60306-2

Twilight of the Gods (1848–52 and 1869–74): "Siegfried's Rhine Journey"

Both Selections:

Berlin Philharmonic (Maazel, conductor), Telarc 80154

The Ring of the Nibelung—The Valkyries (1851–56): Act I; Act III, "Ride of the Valkyries"

Tristan and Isolde: Prelude and Liebestod (1856–59)

Royal Opera House, Covent Garden, Orchestra (Elder, conductor), Jane Eaglen, (soprano), Sony Classical 62032

Parsifal: Prelude to Act I (1865 and 1877–82)

New York Philharmonic (Mehta, conductor), Sony Classical 45749

The Mastersingers of Nuremberg: Prelude (1868)

Berlin Philharmonic (von Karajan, conductor), Deutsche Grammophon 439022-2

Siegfried Idyll (1870)

London Classical Players (Norrington, conductor), EMI Classics 55479

JOHANNES BRAHMS

Websites

http://www.mjq.net/brahms/

> Brahms home page.

http://www.island-of-freedom.com/BRAHMS.HTM

> Biography, links, and other information.

Books

Avins, Styra. *Johannes Brahms: Life and Letters.* NY: Oxford University Press, 1997.

Botstein, Leon, ed. *The Complete Brahms.* NY: Norton, 1999.

Frisch, Walter. *Brahms: The Four Symphonies.* NY: Schirmer Books, 1996.

_____, ed. *Brahms and His World.* Princeton, NJ: Princeton U. Press, 1990.

MacDonald, Malcolm. *Brahms* (The Master Musicians). NY: Schirmer Books, 1993.

Musgrave, Michael. *The Cambridge Companion to Brahms.* NY: Cambridge, 1999.

Swafford, Jan. *Johannes Brahms: A Biography.* NY: Knopf, 1997.

Recordings

ORCHESTRAL MUSIC

Symphony No. 1 in C Minor, Op. 68 (1855–76)

Symphony No. 2 in D Major, Op. 73 (1877)

Symphony No. 3 in F Major, Op. 90 (1883)

Symphony No. 4 in E Minor, Op. 98 (1884–85)

> All four symphonies:
>
> Utah Sympohny (Abravanel, conductor), Vanguard Classics 1719
>
> Chicago Symphony (Barenboim, conductor), Erato 94817
>
> Houston Symphony (Eschenbach, conductor) Virgin Classics 61360

Concerto for Piano and Orchestra No. 1 in D Minor, Op. 15 (1854–58)

> Boston Symphony (Leinsdorf, conductor), Van Cliburn (piano), RCA Gold Seal 60357-2

Serenade No. 2 in A Major, Op. 16 (1858–59)

> New York Philharmonic (Bernstein, conductor), Sony Classical 47536

Variations on a Theme by Haydn, Op. 56A (1873)

> Philadelphia Orchestra (Ormandy, conductor), Sony Classical 63287

Concerto for Violin and Orchestra, in D Major, Op. 77 (1878)

> London Philharmonic (Tennstedt, conductor), Nigel Kennedy (violin), EMI Classics 54187

Academic Festival Overture, Op. 80 (1880)

> New York Philharmonic (Masur, conductor), Teldec 72291

OTHER WORKS

Intermezzos for Piano (1871–78)

Three Rhapsodies for Piano—Nos. 1 and 2, Op. 79 (1880); No. 3, Op. 119 (1892)

    Complete Piano Music:

    Martin Jones, Nimbus 1788

    Selections:

    Artur Rubinstein, RCA Gold Seal 09026-62592-2

Sonata for Piano and Clarinet (or Viola) No. 1 in F Minor, Op. 120 (1894)

    Pinchas Zuckerman, RCA Red Seal 09026-61276-2

PETER ILYICH TCHAIKOVSKY

Websites

http://www.geocities.com/Vienna/5648/

    The world of Tchaikovsky. Biography, links, picture gallery, and more.

Books

Kearney, Leslie. *Tchaikovsky and His World*. Princeton, NJ: Princeton U. Press, 1998.

Poznansky, Alexander. *Tchaikovsky: The Quest for the Inner Man*. NY: Schirmer Books, 1993.

_____. *Tchaikovsky's Last Days: A Documentary Study*. NY: Oxford, 1996.

Recordings

Symphony No. 4, Op. 36 (1877–78)

    Vienna Philharmonic (von Karajan, conductor), Deutsche Grammophon 439018-2

Symphony No. 5 in E Minor, Op. 64 (1888)

    Leipzig Gewandhaus (Masur, conductor), Teldec 18966 (also includes Symphonies 4 and 6)

Symphony No. 6 in B Minor, Op. 74 (*Pathétique*) (1893)

    London Symphony (Abbado, conductor), Deutgsche Grammophon 437401-2 (also includes Symphonies 4 and 5)

Manfred Symphony, Op. 58 (1885)

    Academy of St. Martin in the Fields (Marriner, conductor), Capriccio 10 433

Piano Concerto No. 1 in B-Flat Minor, Op. 23 (1875)

    New York Philharmonic (Bernstein, conductor), A. Watts (piano), Sony Classical 47630

Francesca da Rimini, Symphonic Fantasia, Op. 32 (1876)

    Chicago Symphony (Barrenboim, conductor), Deutsche Grammophon 44523-2

Variations on a Rococo Theme for Violoncello and Orchestra, Op. 33 (1877)

    Pittsburgh Symphony (Maazel, conductor), Yo-Yo Ma (cello), Sony Classical 48382

Violin Concerto in D Major, Op. 35 (1878)

> London Philharmonic (Barbirolli, conductor), J. Heifetz (violin), EMI Classics 64030

Overture "1812," Op. 49 (1880)

> Chicago Symphony (Abbado, conductor), Sony Classical 45939

NIKOLAI RIMSKY-KORSAKOV

Websites

http://www.geocities.com/Vienna/3606/

> Rimsky-Korsakov home page. Biography, works, and general information.

Books

Abraham, Gerald. *Rimsky-Korsakov: A Short Biography*. Ann Arbor, MI: AMS Press, 1975.

Rimsky-Korsakov, N. *My Musical Life*. Boston: Faber and Faber, [date??].

Seaman, Gerald R. *Nikolai Andreevich Rimsky-Korsakov, A Guide to Research*. NY: Garland, 1989.

Yastrebtsev, V. V. *Reminiscences of Rimsky-Korsakov*. Ed. and trans. Florence Jonas. NY: Columbia U. Press, 1985.

Recordings

Quintet for Piano, Flute, Clarinet, French Horn, and Bassoon (1876)

> Nash Ensemble, CRD 3409

The May Night (1829)

> Moscow Radio Orchestra & Radio Chorus (Golovanov, conductor), LYS 090/91

Capriccio espagnol, Op. 34 (1887)

> Berlin Philharmonic (Maazel, conductor), Deutsche Grammophon 449769-2

Symphonic Suite: *Scheherazade ("After 'A Thousand and One Nights'")*, Op. 35 (1888)

> New York Philharmonic (Bernstein, conductor), Sony Classical 47605

Le Coq d'Or (The Golden Cockerel): Introduction to the Wedding Procession) (1906–7)

> Philadelphia Orchestra (Ormandy, conductor), Sony Odyssey 39786

GUSTAV MAHLER

Websites

http://www.netaxs.com/~jgreshes/mahler/

> Mahler WWW site. Information, biography, and links.

http://www.visi.com/~mick/shrine.html

> Virtual shrine. Bulletin board for Mahler-philes.

Books

Carr, Jonathan. *Mahler: A Biography*. Woodstock, NY: Overlook Press, 1997.

Cooke, Deryck. *Gustav Mahler: An Introduction to His Music*, 2nd ed. NY: Cambridge, 1988.

de la Grange, Henry-Louis. *Gustav Mahler: Vienna: The Years of Challenge (1897–1904)*. NY: Oxford, 1995.

Mitchell, Donald. *Gustav Mahler: The Early Years*. Berkeley: U. of California Press, 1995.

_____, and Andrew Nicholson, eds. The Mahler Compendium. Clarendon: Oxford, 1999.

Recordings

SYMPHONIES

Symphony No. 1 in D Major (*Titan*) (1883–88)

    Berlin Philharmonic (Abbado, conductor), Deutsche Grammophon 431769-2

Symphony No. 4 in G Major (*Humoresque*) (1899–1901)

    Vienna Philharmonic (Walter, conductor), E. Schwarzkopf (soprano), Arkadia 767

Symphony No. 6 in A Minor ("Tragic") (1903–5)

    New York Philharmonic (Bernstein, conductor), Sony Classical 47581

VOCAL MUSIC

Songs of a Wayfarer (*Lieder eines fahrenden Gesellen*) (1883–85)

Songs on the Death of Children (*Kindertotenlieder*) (1901–4)

The Song of the Earth (*Das Lied von der Erde*) (1907–9)

    All three works:

    Halle Orchestra (Barbirolli, conductor), J. Baker (mezzo), EMI 62707

CLAUDE DEBUSSY

Websites

http://www.execpc.com/~mchadjin/debussy/

    Debussy page.

http://public.srce.hr/~fsupek/

    Musical impressions. In French and English; includes links, biography, and more.

Books

Nichols, Rogers. *The Life of Claude Debussy*. NY: Cambridge, 1998.

Parks, Richard S. *The Music of Claude Debussy*. New Haven: Yale U. Press, 1990.

Roberts, Paul. *Images: The Piano Music*. Seattle: Amadeus Press, 1996.

Recordings

Prelude à l'après-midi d'un faune (1892–94)

Pélléas et Mélisande (1893, 1898, 1901–2)

Lile National Orchestra (Deltour, conductor), Naxos 8.660047-9

Nocturnes (1892–99)

String Quartet, Op. 10 (1893)

Symphonic Suite: *La Mer* (1903–5)

Two Dances for Harp and String Orchestra (1903)

Los Angeles Chamber Orchestra (Schwarz, conductor), B. Allen (harp), EMI Classics 47520

Jeux (1912)

All three works:

Swiss Romande Orchestra (Ansermet, conductor), London 433711-2

Six epigraphes antiques (1914)

Katia and Marielle Labeque, Philips 289454771-2

RICHARD STRAUSS

Websites

http://people.unt.edu/~dmeek/rstrauss.html

Home page. Biography, links, and more.

Books

Boyden, Matthew. *Richard Strauss*. Boston: Northeastern U. Press, 1999.

Gilliam, Bryan. *Richard Strauss and His World*. Princeton, NJ: Princeton U. Press, 1992.

Kennedy, Michael. *Richard Strauss: Man, Music, Enigma*. NY: Cambridge, 1999.

_____. *Richard Strauss* (Master Musicians series). NY: Schirmer Books, 1996.

Williamson, John. *Strauss: Also Sprach Zarathustra*. NY: Cambridge, 1993.

Recordings

Don Juan, Op. 20 (1888–89)

Chicago Symphony (Barrenboim, conductor), Erato 2292-45625-2

Till Eulenspiegel's Merry Pranks, Op. 28 (1894–95)

New York Philharmonic (Bernstein, conductor), Sony Classical 47626

Thus Spake Zarathustra, Op. 30 (1895–96)

Berlin Philharmonic (von Karajan, conductor), Deutsche Grammophon 447441-2

Seattle Symphony (Schwarz, conductor), Delos 3052

Don Quixote, Op. 35 (1896–97)

Boston Symphony (Ozawa, conductor), Yo-Yo Ma (cello), Sony 39863

A Hero's Life, Op. 40 (1897–98)

Cleveland Orchestra (von Dohanyi, conductor), London 436444-2

Symphonia Domestica, Op. 53 (1902–3)

> Berlin Philharmonic (Furtwangler, conductor), Arabesque 6082

Salome (1903–5)

> Philadelphia Orchestra (Ormandy, conductor), Sony Classical 53511

Der Rosenkavalier (1909–10)

> Vienna Philharmonic/State Opera Chorus, London 425950-2

ARNOLD SCHOENBERG

Websites

http://www.primenet.com/~randols/schoenberg/schoenlinks.html

> Directory of information about Schoenberg, including links.

http://www.schoenberg.at/Default.htm

> Schoenberg Institute site (in English and German). Official site with general information.

Books

Bailey, Walter B. *Schoenberg Companion*. NY: Greenwood, 1998.

Frisch, Walter, ed. *Schoenberg and His World*. Princeton, NJ: Princeton U. Press, 1999.

Rosen, Charles. *Arnold Schoenberg*. Chicago: U. of Chicago Press, 1996.

Recordings

Transfigured Night, Op. 4 (1899)

> New York Philharmonic (Boulez, conductor), Sony Classical 48464

Gurre-Lieder (1900–1903 and 1910–11)

> Berlin Royal Symphony Orchestra, St. Hedwig's Cathedral Choir, Düsseldorf Municipal Choral Society, London 430321-2

Chamber Symphony No. 1, Op. 9 (1906)

> Chamber Orchestra of Europe (Holiger, conductor), Teldec 2292-46019-2

Pierrot lunaire, Op. 21 (1912)

> Contemporary Chamber Ensemble (Weisberg, conductor), Nonesuch 79237-2

Orchestration of Two Chorale Preludes by Bach (1922)

> Houston Symphony (Eschenbach, conductor), RCA Gold Seal 09026-68658-2

A Survivor from Warsaw, Op. 46 (1947)

> London Symphony Orchestra (Craft, conductor), Koch International Classics 7263

MAURICE RAVEL

Websites

http://www.paix.com/ravelpic.html

Biography of Ravel, plus the text of his essay "Recollections of My Lazy Childhood."

http://www.nycopera.com/education/ravel.html

NYC Opera biography. Short biographical sites.

Books

Burnett-James, David. *Ravel* (Illustrated Lives of the Composers). NY: Music Sales, 1988.

Larner, Gerald. *Maurice Ravel*. London: Phaidon, 1996.

Orenstein, Arbie. *Ravel: Man and Musician*. NY: Dover, 1991.

Recordings

ORCHESTRAL MUSIC

Alborada del gracioso (1908)

Valses nobles et sentimentales (1912)

Daphnis and Chloé: Suite #2 (1913)

Rapsodie espagnole (1919)

Le Tombeau de Couperin (1920)

La Valse (1920)

Orchestration of *Pictures at an Exhibition* by Modest Mussorgsky (1922)

New York Philharmonic (Bernstein, conductor), Sony Classical 47595

Boléro (1928)

All of these works:

Cleveland Orchestra (Boulez, conductor), Sony Classical 45842

Montreal Symphony (Dutoit, conductor), London 421458

French National Orchestra (Inbal, conductor), Denon 75001

WORKS FOR SOLO INSTRUMENT AND ORCHESTRA

Tzigane (1924)

Orchestra of Paris (Martinon, conductor) with I. Perlman (violin), EMI Clasics 47725

Concerto for the Left Hand (1931)

Baltimore Symphony (Comissiona, conductor), L. Fleisher (piano), Vanguard Classics 4002

Concerto for Piano and Orchestra in G Major (1932)

Columbia Symphony (Bernstein, conductor and piano), Sony Classical 47571

CHAMBER MUSIC

String Quartet in F Major (1903)

Cleveland String Quartet, Telarc 80011

Sonatine (1905)

St. Louis Symphony (Slatkin, conductor), A. de Larrocha (piano), RCA Red Seal 09026-60985-2

Introduction and Allegro (1907)

Academy of St. Martin in the Fields, Chandos 8261

BÉLA BARTÓK

Websites

http://www.futurenet.co.uk/classicalnet/reference/composers/bartok.html

Short biography, discography, and sound files.

http://www.ultranet.com/~cwholl/bartok/timeline.html

Timeline of Bartók's life.

Books

Chalmers, Kenneth. *Bartók* (20th Century Composers). London: Phaidon, 1995.

Cooper, David. *Concerto for Orchestra*. NY: Cambridge, 1998.

Laki, Peter, ed. *Bartók and His World*. Princeton, NJ: Princeton U. Press, 1995.

Milne, Hamish. *Bartók* (Illustrated Lives of the Great Composers). NY: Music Sales, 1987.

Suchoff, Benjamin. *Concerto for Orchestra*. NY: Schirmer Books, 1995.

_____, ed. *Bartók's Essays*. Lincoln: U. of Nebraska Press, 1992.

Wilson, Paul. *The Music of Béla Bartók*. New Haven: Yale U. Press, 1992.

Recordings

Duke Bluebeard's Castle (1911, rev. 1912, 1918)

Berlin Philharmonic (Hatink, conductor), EMI Classics 56162

The Miraculous Mandarin: Suite (1918–19)

Minnesota Orchestra (Skrowaczewski, conductor), Vox Box 3015

Concerto for Piano and Orchestra No. 1 (1926)

Hungarian State Orchestra (Fischer, conductor), G. Sandor (piano), Sony Classical 45835

Concerto for Piano and Orchestra No. 2 (1930–31)

Budapast Symphony (Ligeti, conductor), J. Jando (piano), Naxos 8.5501771

Music for String Instruments, Percussion, and Celesta (1936)

Chicago Symphony (Boulez, conductor), Deutsche Grammophon 447747-2

Concerto for Violin No. 2 (1937–38)

Minneapolis Symphony (Dorati, conductor), Y. Menuhin (violin), Mercury 434350-2

Contrasts for Violin, Clarinet, and Piano (1938)

Benny Goodman (clarinet), Joseph Szigeti (violin), Béla Bartók (piano), Hungaroton 12326/31; reissued on Magic Talent 48047

Concerto for Two Pianos and Orchestra (1940)

New York Philharmonic (Bernstein, conductor), P. Entremont (piano), Sony Classical 47511

Concerto for Orchestra (1943)

> Philadelphia Orchestra (Ormandy, conductor), Sony Classical 48263

IGOR STRAVINSKY

Websites

http://www.island-of-freedom.com/STRAV.HTM

> Island of Freedom. Links and MIDI files.

http://www.geocities.com/Vienna/1807/strav.html

> Stravinsky page. Biography, works, and essays.

Books

Craft, Robert. *Chronicle of a Friendship*. Nashville: Vanderbilt U. Press, 1994.

Cross, Jonathan. *The Stravinsky Legacy*. NY: Cambridge, 1998.

Oliver, Michael. *Igor Stravinsky*. London: Phaidon, 1995.

Stravinsky, I. *An Autobiography*. NY: Norton, 1998 (reissue).

_____. *Memories and Commentaries*. Berkeley: U. of California Press, 1981.

_____, and Robert Craft. *Expositions and Developments*. Berkeley: U. of California Press, 1983.

Taruskin, Richard. *Stravinsky and the Russian Traditions*. Berkeley: U. of California Press, 1996.

Walsh, Stephen and Patrick. *The Music of Igor Stravinsky*. Oxford: Clarendon Press, 1993.

Recordings

The Nightingale (*Le Rossignol*) (1908–14)

> London Symphony (Craft, conductor), MusicMasters 01612-67184-2

The Firebird: Suite (1910, rev. 1919, 1945)

> Houston Symphony (Stokowski, conductor), EMI Classics 65207

The Rite of Spring (*Le Sacre du printemps*) (1911–13)

> Boston Symphony (Monteux, conductor), RCA Gold Seal 09026-61898-2

Petrushka (1919)

> New York Philharmonic (Mehta, conductor), Sony 358223

The Wedding (*Les Noces*) (1921–23)

> Swiss Romande Orchstra (Ansermet, conductor), London 443467-2

Octet for Wind Instruments (1923)

> Netherlands Wind Ensemble, Chandos 9488

Oedipus Rex (1927, rev. 1948)

> Saito Kenon Orchestra (Ozawa, conductor), Philips 438865-2

Concerto in D for Violin and Orchestra (1931)

> Chicago Symphony (Barenboim, conductor), I. Perlman (violin), Teldec 4059 98255 2

Perséphone for Narrator, Tenor, Chorus, and Orchestra (1933, rev. 1949)

> Orchestra of St. Lukes (Craft, conductor), MusicMasters 01612-67103-2

Jeu de Cartes (Card Game): Ballet in Three Deals (1935–37)

> Chicago Symphony (Solti, conductor), London 443775

Symphony in Three Movements (1942–45)

> Israel Philharmonic (Bernstein, conductor), Deutsche Grammophon 445338-2

Circus Polka (1942; arr. for orchestra, 1944)

> London Symphony (Tilson Thomas, conductor), RCA Red Seal 09026-68865-2

SERGEI PROKOFIEV

Websites

http://musicinfo.gold.ac.uk/music/prokofiev.html

> Prokofiev archive. Collection of archival materials at the University of London, established by Prokofiev's widow.

http://web.mit.edu/eniale/www/music/prok.html

> Elaine's Prokofiev page. Essays on the composer, with links.

Books

Gutman, David. *Sergei Prokofiev* (Illustrated Lives of the Great Composers). NY: Music Sales, 1992.

Minturn, Neil. *The Music of Sergei Prokofiev*. New Haven: Yale U. Press, 1997.

Prokofiev, S. *Soviet Diary 1927 and Other Writings*. Boston: Northeastern U. Press, 1992.

Samuel, Claude. *Prokofiev*. NY: Marion Boyars, 1999.

Recordings

ORCHESTRAL MUSIC

Sinfonietta, Op. 5/46 (1914, rev. 1929)

> Royal Scottish National Orchestra (Jarvi, conductor), Chandos 8442

Symphony No. 1 in D Major, Op. 25 (*Classical*) (1916–17)

> Berlin Philharmonic (von Karajan, conductor), Deutsche Grammophon 437253-2

Concerto No. 1 in D for Violin and Orchestra, Op. 19 (1916–17)

Concerto No. 3 in C Major for Piano and Orchestra, Op. 26 (1917–21)

> Moscow Phlharmonic (Tchistiakov, conductor), E. Kissin (piano), RCA Red Seal 60051-2

Divertimento, Op. 43 (1925, 1929)

> Royal Scottish National Orchestra (Jarvi, conductor), Chandos 8728

Concerto No. 5 in G Major for Piano and Orchestra, Op. 55 (1932)

> Israel Philharmonic (Mehta, conductor), Y. Bronfman (piano), Sony Classical 52483

Concerto No. 2 in G Minor for Violin and Orchestra, Op. 63 (1935)

> Both Works:
>
> Los Angeles Philharmonic (Salonen, conductor), C-L Lin (violin), Sony Classical 53969
>
> BBC Symphony (Rozhdestvensky, conductor), I. Perlman (violin), EMI Classics 47025

Symphonie Concertante in E Minor for Violoncello and Orchestra, Op. 125 (1952)

> Pittsburgh Symphony (Maazel, conductor), Yo-Yo Ma (cello), Sony Classical 48382

OTHER WORKS

The Fiery Angel (1919)

> Paris National Opera, Ades 141572

String Quartet No. 1, Op. 50 (1931)

> Emerson String Quartet, Deutsche Grammophon 431772-2

Peter and the Wolf (1936)

> Vienna State Opera Orchestra (Goossens, conductor), J. Ferrer (narrator), MCA Classics 2-9820
>
> Atlanta Symphony (Levi, conductor), P. Schickele (narrator), Telarc 80350

Cinderella (1946)

> London Symphony (Previn, conductor), EMI Classics 68604

DMITRI SHOSTAKOVICH

Websites

http://www.siue.edu/~aho/musov/dmitri.html

> Shostakovichiana. Articles, reviews, and commentary.

Usenet - alt.fan.shostakovich

> Chat about the controversial book *Testimony* and other issues surrounding Shostakovich's life.

Books

Fay, Laurel E. *Shostakovich: A Life*. NY: Oxford, 1999.

Ho, Allan B., and Dmitry Feofanov. *Shostavoich Reconsidered*. London: Toccata Press, 1999.

Shostakovich, D. *Testimony: The Memoirs of Dmitri Shostakovich*. Ed. Solomon Volkov. NY: Proscenium, 1999.

Wilson, Elizabeth. *Shostakovich: A Life Remembered*. Princeton, NJ: Princeton U. Press, 1995.

Recordings

ORCHESTRAL MUSIC

Symphony No. 1, Op. 10 (1924–25)

> Royal Philharmonic (Ashkenazy, conductor), London 425609-2

Symphony No. 5, Op. 47 (1937)

> New York Philharmonic (Bernstein, conductor), Sony Classical 47615

Symphony No. 7, Op. 60 ("Leningrad") (1941)

> NBC Symphony (Toscanini, conductor), RCA Gold Seal 60293-2

Symphony No. 10, Op. 93 (1953)

> Cleveland Orchestra (von Dohnanyi, conductor), London 430844

Symphony No. 11, Op. 103 ("The Year 1905") (1957)

> Houston Symphony (Stokowski, conductor), EMI Classics 65206

Concerto No. 1 for Piano, Trumpet, and Strings, Op. 35 (1933)

> "Moscow Virtuosi," RCA Red Seal 60567-2

Concerto for Violin and Orchestra, Op. 77 (1947–48)

> Russian State Symphony (Vedernikov, conductor), M. Fedotov (violin), Triton 17006

VOCAL WORKS

The Nose, Op. 15 (1927–28)

> Not currently on disc.

Lady Macbeth of the District of Mtzensk, Op. 29 (1930–32)

> London Philharmonic (Rostropovich, conductor), Ambrosian Opera Chorus, EMI Classics 49955

Song of the Forests: Oratorio for Children's Choir, Mixed Choir, Soloists, and Orchestra, Op. 81 (1940)

> Moscow Philharmonic/State Boys' Choir/Yurlov Russian Choir, Russian Disc 11048

CHAMBER MUSIC

Quintet for Piano and String Quartet, Op. 57 (1940)

> Moscow String Quartet, C. Orbelian (piano), Russian Disc 10031

String Quartets Nos. 4 (Op. 83, 1949) and 8 (Op. 110, 1960)

> Kreutzer String Quartet, IMP 6600622

GLOSSARY

Absolute pitch. Ability to name instantly and without fail any note struck on the piano keyboard or played on an instrument. This is a rare, innate faculty, which appears in a musical child at a very early age, distinct from "relative pitch," common among all musicians, in which an interval is named in relation to a previously played note. Also known as "perfect pitch."

Accent. A stress.

Acciaccatura (It.) (äht-chäh-käh-toóräh). A note a second above, and struck with, the principal note and instantly released.

Adagio (It.) (ăh-däh′jŏh). Slow, leisurely; a slow movement.

Ad libitum (Lat.) (ähd li′bi-tŭm). A direction signifying that the performer's preferred tempo or expression may be employed; that a vocal or instrumental part may be left out.

Alla breve (It.). In modern music, two beats per measure with the half note carrying the beat; also called "cut time."

Allegretto (It.) (ăhl-lĕh-gret′tŏh). Quite lively; moderately fast.

Allegrissimo (It.) (ăhl-lĕh-gris′sē-mŏh). Very rapidly.

Allegro (It.) (ăh-lä′grŏh). Lively, brisk, rapid.

Alleluia. The Latin form of *Hallelujah!* (Praise the Lord!) as used in the Roman Catholic service.

Allemande (Fr.) (ăhl-l′mahn′d), **allemanda** (It.) (ăhl-lĕh-măhn′däh). A lively German dance in 3/4 time.

Andante (It.) (ăhn-dăhn′tĕh). Going, moving; moderately slow tempo.

Andantino (It.) (ăhn-dăhn-tē′nŏh). A little slower than andante, but often used as if meaning a little faster.

Antiphonal. Responsive, alternating.

Appoggiatura (It.) (ăhp-pŏhd-jäh-too′räh). "Leaning" note; a grace note that takes the accent and part of the time value of the following principal note.

Arabesque. A type of fanciful pianoforte piece; ornamental passages accompanying or varying a theme.

Arco (It.). Bow. *Arco in giù*, down-bow; *arco in su*, up-bow.

Aria (It.) (ah′rē-ăh). An air, song, tune, melody.

Aria da capo (It.). Three-part form of operatic aria: principal section with main theme; contrasting section with second theme and key change; elaborated repeat of principal section.

Arietta (It.) (ăhrē-et′täh), **ariette** (Fr.) (ah′rē-et′). A short air or song; a short aria.

Arpeggio (It.) (ar-ped′jŏh). Playing the tones of a chord in rapid, even succession.

Atonality. The absence of tonality; music in which the traditional tonal structures are abandoned and there is no key signature.

Attacca (It.). Begin what follows without pausing, or with a very short pause.

Augmentation. Doubling (or increasing) the time value of the notes of a theme or motive, often in imitative counterpoint.

Barcarole (Ger.). A vocal or instrumental piece imitating the song of the Venetian gondoliers.

Bel canto (It.) (bel kähn'töh). The art of "beautiful song," as exemplified by eighteenth and nineteenth century Italian singers.

Binary. Dual; two-part.

Binary form. Movement founded on two principal themes, or divided into two distinct or contrasted sections.

Bitonality. Harmony in two different tonalities, as C major and F sharp major played simultaneously.

Bolero (Sp.). A Spanish national dance in 3/4 time and lively tempo (*allegretto*), the dancer accompanying his steps with castanets.

Bourrée (Fr.) (boo-rä'). A dance of French or Spanish origin in rapid tempo in 2/4 or 4/4 time.

Burlesque. A dramatic extravaganza, or farcical travesty of some serious subject, with more or less music.

Cacophony. A raucous conglomeration of sound.

Cadence. Rhythm; also, the close or ending of a phrase, section, or movement.

Cadenza (It.) (käh-den'dzäh). An elaborate passage played or improvised by the solo instrument at the end of the first or last movement of a concerto.

Canon. Musical imitation in which two or more parts take up, in succession, the given subject note for note; the strictest form of musical imitation.

Cantabile (It.). "Singable"; in a singing or vocal style.

Cantata (It.) (kähn-tah'täh). A vocal work with instrumental accompaniment.

Canzonetta (It.), **canzonet.** A solo song or part-song; a brief instrumental piece.

Capriccio (It.). An instrumental piece of free form, distinguished by originality in harmony and rhythm; a caprice.

Castrato (It. (käh-strah'töh). A castrated adult male singer with soprano or alto voice.

Celesta. Percussion instrument consisting of tuned steel bars connected to a keyboard.

Cembalo (It.) (chĕm'bäh-löh). Harpsichord, pianoforte; in old times, a dulcimer.

Chaconne (Fr.) (shäh-köhn'). A Spanish dance; an instrumental set of variations over a ground bass, not over eight measures long and in slow 3/4 time.

Chamber music. Vocal or instrumental music suitable for performance in a room or small hall.

Chansonette (Fr.). A short song of a light nature.

Chorale (köh-rahl'). A hymn tune of the German Protestant Church, or one similar in style.

Chorus. A company of singers; a composition sung by several singers; also, the refrain of a song.

Chromatic. Relating to tones foreign to a given key (scale) or chord; opposed to diatonic.

Clavecin (Fr.). A harpsichord.

Coda (It.) (köh'däh). A "tail"; hence, a passage ending a movement.

Con brio (It.). "With noise" and gusto; spiritedly.

Concertante (It.). A concert piece; a composition for two or more solo voices or instruments with accompaniment by orchestra or organ, in which each solo part is in turn brought into prominence; a composition for two or more unaccompanied solo instruments in orchestral music.

Concertino (It.). A small concerto, scored for a small ensemble; the group of soloists in a concerto grosso.

Concerto (It.) (kŏhn-chär′tŏh). An extended multi-movement composition for a solo instrument, usually with orchestra accompaniment and using (modified) sonata form.

Concerto grosso (It.) (kŏhn-chär′tŏh grô′sŏh). An instrumental composition employing a small group of solo instruments against a larger group.

Con forza (It.). With force, forcibly.

Consonance. A combination of two or more tones, harmonious and pleasing, requiring no further progression.

Contralto (It.) (kŏhn-trähl′tŏh). The deeper of the two main divisions of women's or boys' voices, the soprano being the higher; also called alto.

Contrapuntal. Pertaining to the art or practice of counterpoint.

Contrapuntist. One versed in the theory and practice of counterpoint.

Counterpoint. Polyphonic composition; the combination of two or more simultaneous melodies.

Countertenor. A male singer with an alto range.

Courante (Fr.) (koo-rähn′t), **coranto** (It.). An old French dance in 3/2 time.

Crescendo (It.) (krĕh-shen′dŏh). Swelling, increasing in loudness.

Da capo (It.). From the beginning.

Development. The working out or evolution (elaboration) of a theme by presenting it in varied melodic, harmonic, or rhythmic treatment.

Diatonic. Employing the tones of the standard major or minor scale.

Diminished-seventh chord. A chord consisting of three conjunct minor thirds, outlining a diminished seventh between the top and bottom notes.

Diminuendo (It.) (dē-mē-noo-en′dŏh). Diminishing in loudness.

Diminution. The repetition or imitation of a theme in notes of smaller time value.

Dissonance. A combination of two or more tones requiring resolution.

Divertimento (It.) (dē-vâr-tē-men′tŏh), **divertissement** (Fr.) (dē-vâr-tēs-mahn′). A light and easy piece of instrumental music.

Dodecaphonic. Using the technique of modern composition in which the basic theme contains twelve different notes.

Dolce (It.). Sweet, soft, suave; a sweet-toned organ stop.

Dolcissimo (It.). Very sweetly, softly.

Dominant. The fifth tone in the major or minor scale; a chord based on that tone.

Double stop. In violin playing, to stop two strings together, thus obtaining two-part harmony.

Duple time. Double time; the number of beats to the measure is divisible by two.

Eighth note. A note equal to one-half of the duration of a quarter note.

Embellishment. Also called a grace; a vocal or instrumental ornament not essential to the melody or harmony of a composition.

Enharmonic. Differing in notation but alike in sound.

Entr'acte (Fr.). A light instrumental composition or short ballet for performance between acts.

Exposition. The opening of a sonata movement, in which the principal themes are presented for the first time.

Falsetto. The highest of the vocal registers.

Fandango (Sp.). A lively dance in triple time, for two dancers of opposite sex, who accompany themselves with castanets or tambourine.

Fantasia (It.) (făhn-täh-zē′äh), **Fantasie** (Ger.) (făhn-tä-zē′). An improvisation; an instrumental piece with free imitation in the seventeenth to eighteenth centuries; a piece free in form and more or less fantastic in character.

Finale (It.) (fē-nah′lĕh). The last movement in a sonata or symphony.

Fioritura (It.) (fē-ŏh-**r**e-too′răh). An ornamental turn, flourish, or phrase, introduced into a melody.

Flautando (It.). A direction in violin music to play near the fingerboard so as to produce a somewhat "fluty" tone.

Forlane (Fr.). A lively Italian dance in 6/8 or 6/4 time.

Forte (It.) (fôh**r**′tĕh). Loud, strong.

Fortissimo (It.) (fôh**r**-tis′sē-mŏh). Extremely loud.

Fugato (It.) (fŏŏ-gah′tŏh). "In fugue style"; a passage or movement consisting of fugal imitations not worked out as a regular fugue.

Fugue (fewg). Contrapuntal imitation wherein a theme proposed by one part is taken up equally and successively by all participating parts.

Gamelan. A typical Indonesian orchestra, variously comprised of tuned gongs, chimes, drums, flutes, chordophones, xylophones, and small cymbals.

Gavotte (Fr.). A Gavot; an old French dance in strongly marked duple time (*alla breve*), beginning on the upbeat.

Gigue (Fr.) (zhig), **giga** (It.) (jē′găh). A jig.

Glissando (It.). A slide; a rapid scale. On bowed instruments, a flowing, unaccented execution of a passage. On the piano, a rapid scale effect obtained by sliding the thumb, or thumb and one finger, over the keys.

Glockenspiel (Ger.). A set of bells or steel bars, tuned diatonically and struck with a small hammer. Also, an organ stop having bells instead of pipes.

Grace note. A note of embellishment, usually written small.

Grandioso (It.). With grandeur; majestically, pompously, loftily.

Gregorian chant. A system of liturgical plainchant in the Christian Church, revised by Pope Gregory I for the Roman Catholic ritual.

Gruppetto or **gruppo** (It.). Formerly, a trill; now, a turn. Also, any "group" of grace notes.

Habanera (Sp.). A Cuban dance, in duple meter, characterized by dotted or syncopated rhythms.

Half note. A note one-half the value of a whole note.

Harmony. A musical combination of tones or chords; a composition's texture, as two-part or three-part harmony.

Heckelphone. A double-reed instrument somewhat misleadingly called the baritone oboe; gives out a rich, somewhat hollow sound.

Hocket, hoquet. Texture in which one voice stops and another comes in, sometimes in the middle of a word; a hiccup.

Improvisation. Offhand musical performance, extemporizing.

Interlude. An intermezzo; an instrumental strain or passage connecting the lines or stanzas of a hymn, etc.

Intermezzo (It.) (-med′zŏh). A light musical entertainment alternating with the acts of the early Italian tragedies; incidental music; a short movement connecting the main divisions of a symphony.

Interval. The difference in pitch between two tones.

Inversion. The transposition of one of the notes of an interval by an octave; chord position with lowest note other than root.

Key. The series of tones forming any given major or minor scale.

Key signature. The sharps or flats at the head of the staff.

Konzertstück (Ger.). A concert piece, or a short concerto in one movement and free form.

Krebsgang (Ger.) (krĕps′gähng). Literally, "crab walk"; a retrograde motion of a given theme or passage.

Ländler (Ger.). A slow waltz of South Germany and the Tyrol (whence the French name "Tyrolienne") in 3/4 or 3/8 time.

Larghetto (It.) (lar-get′tŏh). The diminutive of largo, demanding a somewhat more rapid tempo.

Largo (It.) (lar′gŏh). Large, broad; a slow and stately movement.

Leitmotiv (Ger.) (līt′mŏh-tēf′). Leading motive; any striking musical motive (theme, phrase) characterizing one of the actors in a drama or an idea, emotion, or situation.

Lento (It.) (len′tŏh). Slow; calls for a tempo between andante and largo.

Libretto (It.) (lē-bret′tŏh). A "booklet"; the words of an opera, oratorio, etc.

Lydian mode. The church mode that corresponds to the scale from *F* to *F* on the white keys of the piano.

Madrigal. A vocal setting of a short lyric poem in three to eight parts.

Mediant. The third degree of the scale.

Melisma. A melodic ornament with more than one note to a syllable.

Melos (Gk.). The name bestowed by Wagner on the style of recitative employed in his later music dramas.

Meter, metre. In music, the symmetrical grouping of musical rhythms; in verse, the division into symmetrical lines.

Metronome. A double pendulum moved by clockwork and provided with a slider on a graduated scale marking beats per minute.

Minor. Latin word for "smaller," used in music in three different senses: 1. a *smaller* interval of a kind, as in minor second, minor third, minor sixth, minor seventh; 2. a key, as in *A* minor, or a scale, as in *A* minor scale; 3. a minor triad, consisting of a root, a minor third, and a perfect fifth above the root.

Minor ninth. A small interval between two notes.

Minor third. An interval of three half tones.

Minuetto (It.) (mē-noo-et′tŏh), **minuet**. An early French dance form.

Mode. A generic term applied to ancient Greek melodic progressions and to church scales established in the Middle Ages and codified in the system of Gregorian chant; any scalar pattern of intervals, either traditional to a culture or invented; the distinction between a major key (mode) and a minor key (mode).

Moderato (It.) (mŏh-dĕh-rah-tŏh). At a moderate tempo or rate of speed.

Modulation. Passage from one key into another.

Monodrama. A dramatic or musical presentation with a single performer.

Motive, motif (Fr.). A short phrase or figure used in development or imitation.

Musette (Fr.). A small oboe; a kind of bagpipe; also, a short piece imitating this bagpipe, with a drone bass; a reed stop on the organ.

Music drama. The original description of opera as it evolved in Florence early in the seventeenth century (*dramma per musica*).

Neoclassicism. A revival, in twentieth-century compositions, of eighteenth-century (or earlier) musical precepts, exemplified by many of the post-WWI works of both Stravinsky and Schoenberg.

Neumes. Signs used in the early Middle Ages to represent tones.

Nocturne (Fr.). A piece of a dreamily romantic or sentimental character, without fixed form.

Notation. The art of representing musical tones, and their modifications, by means of written characters.

Obbligato (It.) (ŏhb-blē-gah'tŏh). A concerted (and therefore essential) instrumental part.

Oboe (Ger.) (oh-boh'ĕ). An orchestral instrument with very reedy and penetrating though mild tone.

Oboe d'amore (It.). Literally, "oboe of love"; an oboe that sounds a minor third below the written notation; used in many old scores, and also in some modern revivals.

Octave. A series of eight consecutive diatonic tones; the interval between the first and the eighth.

Octet. A composition for eight voices or instruments.

Opéra bouffe (Fr.), **opera buffa** (It.). Light comic opera.

Operetta (It.), **opérette** (Fr.). A "little opera"; the poem is in anything but a serious vein; music is light and lively, often interrupted by dialogue.

Oratorio (It.) (ŏh-**răh**-tô'rē-ŏh). An extended multi-movement composition for vocal solos and chorus accompanied by orchestra or organ.

Orchestration. The art of writing music for performance by an orchestra; the science of combining, in an effective manner, the instruments constituting the orchestra.

Ornament. A grace, embellishment.

Ostinato (It.). Obstinate; in music, the incessant repetition of a theme with a varying contrapuntal accompaniment.

Overtone. Harmonic tone.

Overture. A musical introduction to an opera, oratorio, etc.

Pandiatonicism. A modern term for a system of diatonic harmony making use of all seven degrees of the scale in dissonant combinations.

Partita (It.) (par-tē'tăh). A suite.

Passacaglia (It.) (păhs-săh-cahl'yah). An old Italian dance in stately movement on a ground bass of four measures.

Pastoral. A scenic cantata representing pastoral life; an instrumental piece imitating in style and instrumentation rural and idyllic scenes.

Pedal point. A tone sustained in one part to harmonies executed in the other parts.

Pentatonic scale. A five-tone scale, usually that which avoids semitonic steps by skipping the fourth and seventh degrees in major and the second and sixth in minor.

Phrase. Half of an eight-measure period. Also, any short figure or passage complete in itself and unbroken in continuity.

Phrygian mode. A church mode corresponding to the scale from *E* to *E* on the white keys of the piano.

Pianissimo (It.) (pē-äh-nēs'sē-mŏh). Very soft.

Piano (It.) (pē-ah'nŏh). Soft, softly.

Pianoforte (It.) (pē-ah'nŏh-fôr'tĕh). A stringed keyboard instrument with tones produced by hammers; a piano.

Pitch. The position of a tone in the musical scale.

Pizzicato (It.) (pit-sē-kah'tŏh). Pinched; plucked with the finger; a direction to play notes by plucking the strings.

Plagal mode. A church mode in which the final keynote is a fourth above the lowest tone of the mode.

Polka (Bohemian, *pulka*). A lively round dance in 2/4 time, originating about 1830 as a peasant dance in Bohemia.

Polonaise (Fr.) (pŏh-lŏh-näz'). A dance of Polish origin, in 3/4 time and moderate tempo.

Polyphonic. Consisting of two or more independently treated melodies; contrapuntal; capable of producing two or more tones at the same time, as the piano, harp, violin, xylophone.

Polyrhythm. The simultaneous occurrence of several different rhythms.

Polytonality. Simultaneous use of two or more different tonalities or keys.

Prelude. A musical introduction to a composition or drama.

Prestissimo (It.) (prĕh-stis'sē-mŏh). Very rapidly.

Presto (It.) (prâ'stŏh). Fast, rapid; faster than "allegro."

Program music. A class of instrumental compositions intended to represent distinct moods or phases of emotion, or to depict actual scenes or events; sometimes called "descriptive music," as opposed to "absolute music."

Progression. The advance from one tone to another (melodic) or one chord to another (harmonic).

Quarter note. One quarter of a whole note; equal to one beat in any time signature with a denominator of 4.

Quintet(te). A concerted instrumental composition for five performers; a composition, movement, or number, vocal or instrumental, in five parts; also, the performers as a group.

Range. The scale of all the tones a voice or instrument can produce, from the lowest to the highest; also called "compass."

Recapitulation. A return of the initial section of a movement in sonata form.

Recitative (res'ĭta-tēv'). Declamatory singing, free in tempo and rhythm.

Reprise (Fr.) (rŭ-prēz). A repeat; reentrance of a part or theme after a rest or pause.

Retrograde. Performing a melody backwards; a crab movement. Also, one of three standard techniques in twelve-note composition (retrograde, inversion, transposition) wherein all notes of a set are played in reverse (i.e., backward).

Retrograde inversion. A standard technique in twelve-note composition wherein all notes of a set are played in a reverse succession, which also mirrors the original set.

Rhapsody, rapsodie (Fr.) (rähp-sŏh-dē'). An instrumental fantasia on folk songs or on motives taken from primitive national music.

Ricercare (It.) (rē-châr-käh'rĕh). Instrumental composition of the sixteenth and seventeenth centuries generally characterized by imitative treatment of the theme.

Rigaudon (Fr.), **rigadoon.** A lively French dance, generally in 4/4 time, that consists of three or four reprises.

Ripieno (It.) (rēp'yâ'nŏh). A part that reinforces the leading orchestral parts by doubling them or by filling in the harmony.

Ritornello (It.) (**r**ē-to**r**-nel'lŏh), **ritornelle** (Fr.) (**r**ē-too**r**-nel'). A repeat; in a concerto, the orchestral refrain.

Romanza (It.). A short romantic song or a solo instrumental piece.

Rondeau. A medieval French song with instrumental accompaniment, consisting of an aria and a choral refrain.

Rondo (It.) (**r**ohn'dŏh'). An instrumental piece in which the leading theme is repeated, alternating with the others.

Roulade (Fr.) (roo-lähd'). A grace consisting of a run from one principal melody tone to another; a vocal or instrumental flourish.

Rubato (It.) (**r**oo-bäh'tŏh). Prolonging prominent melody tones or chords.

Saltarella, -o (It.) (sähl-täh-**r**el'häh,-löh). A second division in many sixteenth-century dance tunes, in triple time; an Italian dance in 3/4 or 6/8 time.

Salto (It.) (sähl'tŏh). Leap; skip or cut.

Sarabande (Fr. (säh-**r**äh'bahn'd), Ger. (säh-**r**äh-bäh-n'dě). A dance of Spanish or Oriental origin; the slowest movement in the suite.

Scale. The series of tones that form (a) any major or minor key (*diatonic* scale) or (b) the *chromatic* scale of successive semitonic steps. Also, the compass of a voice or instrument.

Scherzando (It.) (skâr-tsähn'dŏh). In a playful, sportive, toying manner; lightly, jestingly.

Scherzo (It.) (skâr'tsŏh). A joke, jest; an instrumental piece of a light, piquant, humorous character. Also, a vivacious movement in the symphony, with strongly marked rhythm and sharp and unexpected contrasts in both rhythm and harmony; usually the third movement.

Score. A systematic arrangement of the vocal or instrumental parts of a composition on separate staves one above the other.

Semitone. A half tone; the smallest interval in the Western scale.

Serenade. An instrumental composition imitating in style an "evening song," sung by a lover before his lady's window.

Sforzando, sforzato (It.) (sfŏh**r**-tsähn'dŏh, sfŏh**r**-tsah'tŏh). A direction to perform the tone or chord with special stress, or marked and sudden emphasis.

Sinfonia (It.) (sin-fŏh-nē'äh). A symphony; an opera overture.

Singspiel (Ger.) (zing^ʰ'shpēl). A type of eighteenth century German opera; usually light, and characterized by spoken interludes.

Sonata (It.) (sŏh-nah'täh). An instrumental composition usually for a solo instrument or chamber ensemble, in three or four movements, contrasted in theme, tempo, meter, and mood.

Sonata form. Usually the procedure used for first movements of classical symphonies, sonatas, and chamber works; may be used for other movements as well.

Sonata-rondo form. A rondo-form movement in at least seven sections, where the central episode functions as a development section.

Sonatina (It.), **Sonatine** (Ger.). A short sonata in two or three (rarely four) movements, the first in the characteristic first-movement, i.e., sonata, form, abbreviated.

Soprano (It.). The highest class of the human voice; the female soprano, or treble, has a normal compass from c^1 to a^2.

Sostenuto (It.) (sŏh-stĕh-noo'tŏh). Sustained, prolonged; may also imply a tenuto, or a uniform rate of decreased speed.

Spinet (spin'et *or* spĭ-net'). An obsolete harpsichordlike instrument; a small modern piano.

Staccato (It.). Detached, separated; a style in which the notes played or sung are more or less abruptly disconnected.

Stop. That part of the organ mechanism that admits and "stops" the flow of wind into the pipes; on the violin, etc., the pressure of a finger on a string, to vary the latter's pitch; a *double stop* is when two or more strings are so pressed and sounded simultaneously; on the French horn, the partial closing of the bell by inserting the hand.

Stretto (It.) (stret'-tŏh, täh). A division of a fugue in which subject and answer follow in such close succession as to overlap; a musical climax when thematic and rhythmic elements reach the saturation point.

String quartet. A composition for four stringed instruments, usually first and second violin, viola, and cello.

Subdominant. The tone below the dominant in a diatonic scale; the fourth degree.

Submediant. The third scale tone below the tonic; the sixth degree.

Suite (Fr.). A set or series of pieces in various (idealized) dance forms. The earlier suites have four chief divisions: the Allemande, Courante, Sarabande, and Gigue.

Supertonic. The second degree of a diatonic scale.

Symphonic poem. An extended orchestral composition which follows in its development the thread of a story or the ideas of a poem, repeating and interweaving its themes appropriately; it has no fixed form, nor has it set divisions like those of a symphony.

Symphony. An orchestral composition in from three to five distinct movements or divisions, each with its own theme(s) and development.

Syncopation. The shifting of accents from strong beat to weak beat or between beats.

Tam-tam. A large Eastern unpitched suspended gong struck with a felt-covered stick.

Tarantella (It.) (täh-rähn-tel'läh). A southern Italian dance in 6/8 time, the rate of speed gradually increasing; also, an instrumental piece in a very rapid tempo and bold and brilliant style.

Tema con variazioni (It.). Composition in which the principal theme is clearly and explicitly stated at the beginning and is then followed by a number of variations.

Tempo (It.) (tem'pŏh). Rate of speed, movement; time, measure.

Tempo primo (It.). At the original pace.

Ternary. Composed of, or progressing by, threes.

Ternary form. Rondo form; ABA form, such as the minuet and trio.

Tessitura (It.) (tes-sē-too'räh). The range covered by the main body of the tones of a given part, not including infrequent high or low tones.

Tetrachord. The interval of a perfect fourth; the four scale-tones contained in a perfect fourth.

Timbre (Fr.) (tän'br). Tone color or quality.

Toccata (It.) (tŏhk-kah'täh). A composition for organ or harpsichord (piano), free and bold in style.

Tonality. A cumulative concept that embraces all pertinent elements of tonal structure; a basic loyalty to tonal center.

Tone-color. Quality of tone; timbre.

Tone poem. Also called "symphonic poem"; an extended orchestral composition that follows the thread of a story or the ideas of a poem.

Tone row. The fundamental subject in a twelve-tone composition.

Tonic. The keynote of a scale; the triad on the keynote (tonic chord).

Treble. Soprano. *Treble clef:* the *G* clef.

Tremolo (It.) (trâ′mŏh-lŏh). A quivering, fluttering; in singing, an unsteady tone.

Triad. A three-note chord composed of a given tone (the root), with its third and fifth in ascending order in the scale.

Trill. The even and rapid alternation of two tones a major or minor second apart.

Triplet. A group of three equal notes performed in the time of two of like value in the established rhythm.

Tritone. The interval of three whole tones.

Tutti (It.) (too′tē). The indication in a score that the entire orchestra or chorus is to enter.

Upbeat. The raising of the hand in beating time; an unaccented part of a measure.

Variations. Transformations of a theme by means of harmonic, rhythmic, and melodic changes and embellishments.

Violoncello (It.) (vē-ŏh-lŏhn-chel′-lŏh). A four-stringed bowed instrument familiarly called the cello.

Vivace (It.) (vē-vah′chěh). Lively, animated, brisk.

Vivacissimo (It.). Very lively, *presto*.

Vivo (It.). Lively, spiritedly, briskly.

Voice. The singing voice; used as synonym for "part."

Whole tone. A major second.

Whole-tone scale. Scale consisting only of whole tones, lacking dominant and either major or minor triads; popularized by Debussy.

Woodwind. Wind instruments that use reeds, and the flute.

INDEX

Page numbers in **boldface** indicate extensive treatments of the indexed entry (i.e., composer or composition).